Series: Of Islands and Women
Number 3

3011

Tasmania

Also by Susanna Hoe

Lady in the Chamber (Collins 1971)

God Save the Tsar (Michael Joseph/St Martin's Press 1978)

The Man Who Gave His Company Away: A Biography of Ernest Bader, Founder of the Scott Bader Commonwealth (Heinemann 1978)

The Private Life of Old Hong Kong: Western Women in the British Colony 1841–1941 (Oxford University Press 1991)

Chinese Footprints: Exploring Women's History in China, Hong Kong and Macau (Roundhouse Publications Asia 1996)

Stories for Eva: A Reader for Chinese Women Learning English (Hong Kong Language Fund 1997)

The Taking of Hong Kong: Charles and Clara Elliot in China Waters (with Derek Roebuck) (Curzon Press 1999; Hong Kong University Press 2009)

Women at the Siege, Peking 1900 (HOLO Books 2000)

At Home in Paradise: A House and Garden in Papua New Guinea (HOLO Books 2003)

Madeira: Women, History, Books and Places (HOLO Books 2004)

Crete: Women, History, Books and Places (HOLO Books 2005)

Watching the Flag Come Down: An Englishwoman in Hong Kong 1987–97 (HOLO Books 2007)

Tasmania

Women, History, Books and Places

Susanna Hoe

HOLO BOOKS
THE WOMEN'S HISTORY PRESS
OXFORD

Published in 2010 by The Women's History Press
A division of HOLO Books
Clarendon House
52 Cornmarket, Oxford OX1 3HJ
www.holobooks.co.uk

www.centralbooks.com

British Library Cataloguing in Publication Data
A catalogue record for this book is available from the British Library

ISBN 978-0-9544056-6-3

This book is printed on paper suitable for recycling and made from fully managed
and sustained forest sources. Logging, pulping and manufacturing processes are
expected to conform to the environmental regulations of the country of origin.

10   9   8   7   6   5   4   3   2   1

Designed and produced for HOLO Books by
Chase Publishing Services Ltd, 33 Livonia Road, Sidmouth EX10 9JB
Printed in the European Union

For Kath, Lucy and Anna

Contents

List of Illustrations

Preface

'Tasmania! Where's that?' cried Polly, a heroine of the writer Jessie Couvreur who so appreciated her childhood home that she adopted the penname Tasma. And there are still those today who confuse Tasmania with Tanzania. There are also those who, carelessly or deliberately, leave the smallish heart-shaped island off maps of the huge one of mainland Australia. This airbrushing is slightly less prevalent since one of Tasmania's daughters became Crown Princess Mary of Denmark.

Those outsiders more knowledgeable about Tasmania know mainly of its convict past or the nineteenth-century fate of its indigenous people. A visitor often comes to grips with the convict system by reading Marcus Clarke's *For the Term of His Natural Life* (1874). And that choice epitomises the purpose of my book because, before he wrote his novel based on wide reading and six weeks on journalistic assignment to Tasmania, Caroline Leakey, writing under the pseudonym Oliné Keese, published *The Broad Arrow* (1859). She had lived in Tasmania for five years and had access to many aspects of the convict system.

While it is generally acknowledged by the initiated that the earlier novel by a woman with a woman convict as heroine influenced Clarke's with its male hero, only they know and appreciate *The Broad Arrow*. The reason for its neglect is pithily summed up by the Australian feminist writer Dale Spender:

> Caroline Leakey [found] that her sex rather than her writing was used to determine the quality of her work. Whereas Marcus Clarke was praised for his powerful exposé of the horrors of the convict system, Caroline Leakey was censured for knowing too much about a subject so unseemly!

When my husband, Derek Roebuck, arrived to teach at the University of Tasmania in 1968 (he left to return to England in 1978), one's convict past was still a guilty secret. Indeed, an exhibition of convict documentation had to be bullet-proofed to protect it from purposeful vandalism. Those days are long gone: now, a convict ancestor provides an enviable pedigree of long-establishment, and there is a growth industry in finding one's roots. The outsider has to be careful when disentangling those roots to recreate a general history of women. As often as possible I have communicated with the families and properties I have included, of whatever ancestry, and apologise here for those which are omitted.

The growth in family and other areas of Tasmanian history brings into relief other pitfalls. The British administrators, settlers and convicts who began to arrive on the island in 1803/04 forcibly displaced the original inhabitants, and there the controversies really start – and the traps are pretty well unavoidable even by the most careful stranger. What is more, some of those who, since the early 1970s, have campaigned not only to have their Aboriginality accepted, but also to have Aboriginal land and other rights returned, are not always appreciative of attempts to recount their history. I have, though, presumed to do so as far as sources, nearly all non-Aboriginal, allow. I have taken advice where I have been able.

Unlike the islands about which I have earlier written – Madeira and Crete – much work has already been done on women's history in Tasmania. I hope I have drawn some strands together that fully acknowledge this, while peppering the mixture with the lively women's literature stretching back well over a century and what I have picked up on regular visits since 1980, the last few with this book in mind.

I devised the term 'livret' for those volumes I hoped would constitute the series 'Of Islands and Women'. I envisaged these little books would go in a pocket or bag so as easily to accompany the visitor to a particular place. Because of the richness of the available research into Tasmania's history and, indeed, the complexity of the island's past, this book has outgrown that concept, and that shape and size. But it still consists of half history, half itineraries, and it still seeks to explore and marry those elements of the subtitle, Women, History, Books and Places. The livret Tasmania has simply put on too much weight; it has grown into a tome.

Of Islands and Women

My proposition is that the most rewarding way for a woman to visit an island is to read books by women who have travelled there, or by or about women who have been part of its history, and to visit the places they describe or where they had their being. Each volume in the series suggests which books to read and gives a flavour of them. Itineraries are included, as well as historical background.

Oxford
July 2010

Author's Note

Tasmania was known to colonists as Van Diemen's Land until 1854. To avoid confusion, I have called it Tasmania from the start, except of course in quotations. Hobart, too, went by various earlier names, and Sydney was Port Jackson.

Women's names are in bold in the text where their fullest details occur, or where they are just mentioned once, and a bold page number in the index corresponds. As usual in my writing, I tend to be familiar and use first names. I am usually more formal with my contemporaries. As the acknowledgements suggest, however, many writers, researchers and informants have become friends. The page numbers in brackets in the text are cross-references to elsewhere in the history section or the itineraries, so that you can marry the two and complete the picture when visiting a site in reality or your imagination.

The itineraries include houses and properties that are privately owned. I hope I have made it clear if and from where and how these may be viewed. Sometimes it should be as an armchair traveller. You may deduce that once or twice in the course of my research I intruded; I should be mortified if I caused others to do the same.

Several places I had hoped to include have been omitted for reasons of length. Indeed, a couple of itineraries, those perhaps with less of a woman component, are missing. I am conscious that many visitors today head for the most unspoilt parts of the island, such as Cradle Mountain and the west coast. I hope to remedy the omission on the website www.holobooks.co.uk. To facilitate the use of the itineraries that are included in a book that has become less portable than intended, all itineraries can be downloaded separately from this website. Any other updates will also be put there, alongside those of Madeira and Crete. Anything you would like to add will be warmly received.

The bibliography is rather extensive, and may seem, at first sight, unduly complicated. It is split into several sections. If what you seek is not immediately obvious, persevere. I have drawn on all titles included. The internet has come into its own during the course of research and writing. I have tried in the bibliography to indicate websites from where I drew material but it is often easier just to enter the name of the subject of your search. There are websites from which even the most scholarly articles sometimes pop up and print out without reference or even date.

I have drawn on books of appeal to the general reader and articles by scholars indiscriminately in the text. To aid accessibility, I have omitted footnotes or endnotes, but for ease of identification, and for those who know more than I do, I have, where practical in the text, made it clear where quotations and information come from. To use the index, please read the introductory note.

I would have liked to include more illustrations, ideally in colour. The work of women artists is mentioned where appropriate but, where their work is not shown, it is always worth trying the internet by entering their name and the title of the work. That way, too, you may get a better impression of those included. The collection at the Tasmanian State Library is miraculous, with a website to match, www.images.statelibrary.tas.gov.au. I hope 'artists' in the index is helpful.

Only a map of Tasmania in relation to Australia and one of Tasmania which includes the places mentioned are provided here. Larger, general maps are usually available to visitors from abroad; these include street maps of the bigger towns. Town information centres provide up-to-date specific ones, often with sites marked. The text gives written directions.

Acknowledgements

The generosity of researchers into the history of Tasmania, particularly that of women, has been overwhelming and the list of those I would like to thank is long. But first and warmest thanks must be to Alison Alexander and Carmel Bird. They have given me constant support, answered countless questions and read and commented upon the manuscript. Lyndall Ryan is a later addition to those two whose kind words on the back cover are all the more precious for the depth of their own scholarship. Carmel also has skills all her own which are hinted at in my text.

Several others have read what I have done with their work and given their approval and their permission to quote; some have trusted me even without seeing the relevant text. Similarly, owners of properties, or those particularly knowledgeable about places or subjects, have added to my knowledge, usually through email exchanges, and then approved what I have written. They include: Sue Backhouse (Tasmanian Museum and Art Gallery), Max Bound, Rosemary Brown, Simon Cameron, Jill Cassidy, Helene Chung, Peter Conrad, Sue Dowling, Adrienne Eberhard, Arabella Edge, Lyn Flanagan, Pat Flanagan, Tim Flanagan, Lucy Frost, Tony Glyn (Batman Fawkner Inn), Fiona Hoskin (Fee and Me), Ted Lilley, Mark McDiarmid, Jennifer McKay, Thelma McKay, Clare McShane, Margaret Mason-Cox, Sheenah Pugh, Vivienne Rae-Ellis, Lynette Russell, Penny Russell, Joy Spence (Franklin House, National Trust), Keith Sykes (Scotch Oakburn College), Rebe Taylor, Vera Taylor, Kate Warner, Catherine Wolfhagen (Scotch Oakburn College), and John Young. Helen McDiarmid and I quickly became friends by email but she died on 30 December 2009 before she could read what I have written about Stanton, the Shones and her and Betty King. None of those who have read any part of this book are accountable for any errors that remain.

I thank the following for showing me round their place, as well as being generous with their time and knowledge: Louise Archer, Robert Bowen, Stephanie Burbury, Fiona Cardwell, Naomie Clark, David Cochrane, Susie Forbes Smith, Paddy Pearl, Paddy Prosser, Cassandra Pybus, Mary Ramsay, Tina Taylor and Bill Watkins. Several of them have read my drafts. Kath Alexander, Greg Hogg, Colette McAlpine, the late Bruce Poulson, Irene Schaffer and Elaine Stratford gave me the face to face benefit of their ideas and research, for which I am most grateful.

My thanks also to the following who have helped in any number of ways, sometimes many years ago: Yvonne Adkins (Queen Victoria Museum and Art Gallery), Lucy Alexander, Susan Alexander, Wally Alexander, John Askew, Marita Bardenhagen, Tim Bonyhady, Kate Bowden, Richard Bowden, Ronald Bristow, Tony Brown, Mrs Butler of Buckland, Debra Cadogan-Cowper (Tasmanian Wool Centre, Ross), Brian Clark, Rowena Clark, Patricianne Cochrane, Judith Cornish (Louisa's Walk), Rennie Cornock (Tasmanian Electoral Commission), Patsy Crawford, Leigh Dale, Kathy Davidson (Campbell Town Information Centre), John Davies, Samuel Dix (Narryna Heritage Museum), Doug Edmonds, Robyn Eastley (Tasmanian Archive and Heritage Office), Mae Edenborough (The Australian Merino Centre), Kathryn Evans, Wren Fraser, Shirley Freeman (Avoca Post Office), Jenny Gill, Patricia Grimshaw, Jim Hamell (Department of Africa, Oceania and the Americas, British Museum), Angus Hedlam, Meredith Hodgson, Elizabeth Hodson (Glamorgan and Spring Bay Historical Society Tasmania), Lyn Hurley (The Lodge on Elizabeth), Bill Jackson,

Maureen James (Batman Fawkner Inn), Sian Jenkins (Currency Press) John Kinsella, Hendrik Kolenberg, Don Lambourne, Lee (Bicheno Information Centre), Ray Lewis, (Glamorgan and Spring Bay Historical Society Tasmania), Lisa (Islington Hotel), Peter Macfie, Andrew McRobb, Gillian Marsden (Queen Victoria Museum and Art Gallery), Christopher Martin, Philip Mead, Peter Mehana, Nonie Midgley (Narryna Heritage Museum), Peter Mills, Miranda Morris, Ian Morrison (Tasmanian Archive and Heritage Office), Nicholas Parkinson-Bates, Kirsty Pancke (Batman Fawkner Inn), Jennifer Parrott, Chris Pearce (Hobart Bookshop), Susan Piddock, Nicole Piggott (Tasmanian Tourism Office), Laura Ponsonby, John Quigley, Bev Roberts (Entally), Annie Reynolds, Michael Roe, Paul Roebuck, Shirley Russell (Runnymede, National Trust), Alan Scott, David Scott (Heritage Tasmania), Lindy Scripps, Daisy Searls (Royal Historical Society of Victoria), Tim Shoobridge, Pierre Slicer, Debra Spohn (Tasmanian Wool Centre, Ross), Michael Sprod (Astrolabe), staff at the Bodleian Library and Rhodes House, Oxford, and the British Library, Susan Stratigos, David Taylor, Annick Thomas, John Upcher, Jacqui Ward (Tasmanian Museum and Art Gallery), Gemma Webberley (Runneymede, National Trust), Ted Woolford, Audrey Youl (Evandale Information Centre).

Not for the first time, Ray Addicott has taken an unwieldy manuscript and, with his usual patience and flair, transformed it.

As for my husband, Derek Roebuck, this is more of a shared book than any but the one we wrote together. It is no cliché to say that it could not, on any level, have been written without him.

Permissions

Picture locations and permissions are clear from the captions under the illustrations. Those who have helped me in securing images are thanked above. I have taken some from publications whose authors gained permission from private owners some time ago; I have named only my source. I apologise for any discourtesy.

Permissions to quote not only from publications but also from emails have nearly all been given directly by those who are acknowledged above, and who have often done more than that. Much information has been taken from the internet and the source acknowledged, where practicable, in the text or bibliography. In addition, I acknowledge the following:

James Calder, letter dated 27 March 1870, and following note, from Calder papers, Fbox 89/3, p300, State Library of Victoria.

Information from Lyn Flanagan, fifth-generation descendant of John Flanagan, living in Queensland, Australia.

'The Flanagans: Thomas and Mary', unpublished paper compiled by Arch Flanagan, February, 1991.

Diary of Eliza Marsh from 1 March 1851 to 15 April 1851 – a detailed account of their trip to Tasmania, 17pp typescript, MS000892, Box 191/3, Royal Historical Society of Victoria.

Meredith, Louisa Ann, text and illustrations from My Home in Tasmania, courtesy of Glamorgan and Spring Bay Historical Society Tasmania.

Map of Tasmania showing places mentioned

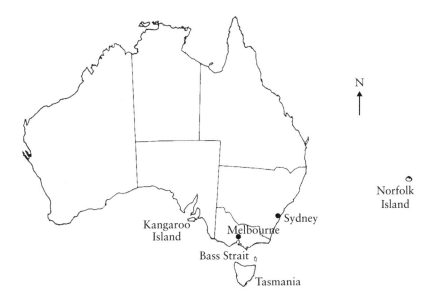

N

Norfolk
Island

Kangaroo
Island

Melbourne

Sydney

Bass Strait

Tasmania

Map of Tasmania in relation to Australia

Women's History

Part One – Early Days

1 – The South

The First White Woman – 1792–93

Deep under the sea off the coast of Tasmania, just south of Recherche Bay, a geophysics team deployed four recording magnetometers in 1996. The instruments, named Bruny, Huon, Rossel and Girardin, were to measure the earth's magnetic field in the tradition of measurements made 200 years earlier by a French scientific expedition to the South Seas.

When the four magnetometers were retrieved, those named after Admiral Bruny d'Entrecasteaux of the *Recherche* and Huon de Kermadec, captain of the *Espérance*, returned no data; that called after Rossel, in charge of the astronomical work, provided some that was usable. But the Girardin gave the best and received the most attention in the resulting scientific paper by Ted Lilley and others. Surprisingly, it was named after a rather minor, non-scientific member of the expedition – the youthful purser Louis Girardin, who only the leaders of the expedition knew for certain was a 38-year-old woman disguised as a man.

Louise Girardin (1754–1794) was undoubtedly the first white woman to set foot on the island we know as Tasmania, but until the 1990s she was a virtually unobserved footnote in exploration history. The magnetometer was named after her because of the romance and poignancy of her story then emerging, and she is now an integral part of Tasmania's history.

The d'Entrecasteaux expedition visited the Recherche Bay area – homeland of the Lyluequonny Aboriginal people – twice, in 1792 and again in 1793. Louise certainly went ashore during the second visit but there is some evidence that, unlike her fellows, she avoided interchange with the local people with whom the French quickly made friends. There is an explanation. Sub-lieutenant La Motte du Portail, one of those who kept a journal, notes that although the women went naked like the men, they made obvious efforts to conceal their femaleness in front of the strangers. But then he adds:

> Those feelings, no matter their origin and their purpose, did not prevent them from examining with the utmost attention the ones among us chosen by their husbands to be the object of some exploration from a bold and inquisitive hand, to learn the sex that our clothes concealed. The search was mainly addressed to the ones whose beardless faces seemed more promising, but they remained unavailing and this seemed to be a major cause for amazement. However, it was said that if they had explored, in the same way, the steward in charge of the supplies on the *Recherche*, they would have come across what they wished to find. The general opinion on board

that ship was that Mr Girardin was no more than a woman disguised as a man. We did not really have anything positive on which to ground our suspicion, and our suspicions were based only on the way this person was built. It is certain that if he had been with the others that day, his sex would not be a mystery any more!

And botanist Louis-August Deschamps writes of that same period:

> One thing intrigued them a great deal. Several of our men were bathing, and noticing that there were only men among them, they thought those who remained clothed must be women, and wished to make sure of this. Inspecting some young sailors and not finding what they were looking for, they gave evidence of their surprise and asked us where were the women. One of them who had boarded one of the ships began his researches again, not being able to imagine how men could live without companions.
>
> These ludicrous researches revealed in a measure a woman on board who was disguised. She was very careful in all kinds of innovation and had sometimes even gone with us for some distance in the hope of seeing the natives; but as soon as she heard us speak in an indecent manner as we reached the men, she would go no further. She even hid herself when one of them came on board.

Deschamps is known to have written up his account after events – Louise's disguise remained intact until her death at sea in 1794. However, many members of the crew were suspicious; indeed, the chief pilot was so offensive on the subject that Louise challenged him to an (illegal) duel. That, and how Louise came to be on board, as well as her end have more space in the itinerary 'Oyster Cove to Recherche Bay' pp295–7.

The main reason for Louise Girardin's emergence from obscurity is the campaign that was waged from 2002 to preserve the re-discovered French Garden, planted in 1792, from proposed logging – a campaign that involved all sorts of devices including a radio play by Paddy Prosser, a member of the campaign team, and a stage play by her, Bruce Poulson and Greg Hogg. In them Louise does meet Aboriginal women.

A male character says to Louise, 'What about when the native women set about looking for female members of our party? They were looking down the men's breeches. I can't recall you being there.'

Louise replies, 'Yes, I was sitting with one of the women playing with her baby. When she saw what was going on, she led me to one side, gently patted my breast and laid her fingers against her lips.'

The First Named Aborigine – 1802

The French accounts above (most accessible in *The General*, Brian Plomley and Josiane Piard-Bernier) are nicely unselfconscious about the Aborigines they describe but there are insurmountable problems with more generally using the accounts by European male seafarers to give even an impression of Aborigine women, not only because of their gender, ethnicity, lack of language and background but because they are describing, without differentiating, migrating peoples from different areas over a period.

Twentieth-century scholars deduced enough about pre-1803 Tasmania to provide some useful background. The island (the Aboriginal name for which is Trowunna) was part of the Australian mainland until 12,000 or so years ago and Aborigines had existed there for at least 40,000 years. Then the sea rose and cut off not only the land but also the people, animals and plant life. For the next twelve centuries they developed separately.

Before 1803 it is estimated that there were 4,000–9,000 Aborigines spread over 26,000 square miles. They were hunter gatherers divided first into family units, probably monogamous, of two to eight members, making bands of 40–50. There were at least 50 bands, of which 48 have been given a location. There may originally have been 70–85 of them and they were the 'landowning' group with foraging rights over a particular country as I am advised their territory should now be called. Five to fifteen of these bands would come together as nations (what were, until recently, called tribes) of between 250 and 700, and there were nine nations, their country defined in one of the invaluable maps in Lyndall Ryan's *The Aboriginal Tasmanians* (1981; 1996; update in preparation); a table identifies the bands.

The European 'discovery' of the island and writing about it started as early as 1642 with Abel Tasman who named it Van Diemen's Land, after the Governor General of the Dutch East Indies who had commissioned his expedition, and Maria Island off the east coast to honour Van Diemen's wife. The first glimpse of 'savages' is given by Frenchman Marion de Fresne sailing along the west coast a little north of today's Port Davey in 1772: 'They had with them their wives and children. Both men and women were of ordinary stature, in colour black, the hair woolly, and all were naked; some of the women carried their children on their back.' Captain Cook wrote a similar description in 1777 landing on today's Bruny Island in the east. They did not know then that Bruny was an island and I suspect that what Europeans had still to learn about the geography of the islands is indicative of the problems with trusting their ethnology.

Interestingly, the French did not make contact with any Aborigines on their first visit in 1792, though their accounts of 1793 are regarded as an important contribution. An example of the problems that arise in assessing the ethnography, even within an expedition's different accounts, is presented by that of d'Entrecasteaux himself (often drawing on the observations of his crew), in contrast to La Motte Portail's impression:

The posture of the women when they sit is quite remarkable; one of their heels is positioned to cover their natural parts; although their complete nudity on every other occasion does not permit one to believe that it is modesty that makes them hide what they are not bashful to display when they are not sitting down.

The reservations that such examples raise decided me not to include here disparate passages that might give some idea of women's life in Tasmania before 1803, but would be rather a hotchpotch. (A useful chronological compendium of voyagers' accounts is contained in RW Giblin's *The Early History of Tasmania, 1642–1804* (1928) though there are many more up-to-date individual accounts.) There is, however, something about a woman with a name that makes her more convincing, which is why I take us now to meet Ouray-Ouray (in French Ouré Ouré, sometimes written Oura Oura) through the eyes of a Frenchman.

In 1800 another French scientific expedition set out, under the leadership of Captain Baudin. It is from the account of 25-year-old zoologist François Péron, interested in anthropology (a science still in its infancy), that we meet **Ouray-Ouray** (bc1784) at today's Cygnet – the area on an inlet of the Huon River that d'Entrecasteaux named Port de Cigne because of the black swans. Péron writes about Ouray-Ouray and her family in some detail and she usefully represents at least the women of that area in 1802. She was of the Melukerdee band, one of the four groups of the South East people. Her death is mentioned in Chapter 8 (p116), and Cygnet is included in the itinerary 'Oyster Cove to Recherche Bay'.

When Péron, Henri de Freycinet and their companions ventured ashore at Cygnet, they first came across a young man and then an older man. Giblin's translation, modestly omitting female bodily details, without indicating the omissions, tells us that having satisfied himself that the intruders were harmless, the older man

> Signalled to two women who were some distance away to approach; they hesitated a little, when the leader of the pair came to us, the younger, more timid and agitated than the first, followed her. Like the old man the elder woman, who appeared to be about forty years old and was absolutely naked, seemed kind and well-disposed. The young woman, twenty-six to twenty-eight years of age, had a sturdy frame; like the other she was quite naked except for a kangaroo skin in which she carried a little unweaned baby girl. This young creature, like the old man and the elder woman, whom we supposed to be her father and mother, had an interesting countenance; her eyes had an expression and such a look of intelligence that surprised us, and that we have never found since then in any other female of that nation; she seemed moreover to idolize her child, and her care for it had that loving and sweet character that reappears amongst all peoples as a distinct attribute of maternal affection. M. Freycinet and I hastened to load this pleasing and interesting family with presents, but everything that we could offer was received with an indifference that astonished us, and that we have often since then had occasion to observe amongst others of the same race.

A little later, the younger woman took fright at the gloves of one of Péron's companions when he removed them to light a fire, thinking they were hands, or a layer of skin. When her father made off with a bottle of arrack and took exception to being made to return it, the family disappeared. But they were soon to meet again. Walking further, the Frenchmen came across a hut, the remains of shellfish, a recently extinguished fire, and a canoe which they deduced belonged to the family; indeed, they soon bumped into them on the beach. 'As soon as they saw us', Péron wrote, 'they gave vent to great shouts of joy and doubled their speed to rejoin us.'

There were now nine members of the family – three generations: the older couple were obviously the parents of the younger woman they had already met. The younger man was either her brother or husband. A girl of 16, who turns out to be Ouray-Ouray, Péron deduces is her sister. Then, in addition to the baby on the older sister's back, she has three other children, two boys of four or five, and a daughter of three or so. Péron continues:

> The family was then returning from fishing, in which they had certainly been successful, for most of them were loaded with shell-fish belonging to the large species of sea-ears [abalone, *Haliotis Gigantea*] peculiar to those coasts. The old man, taking M. Freycinet by the hand, signed to us to follow him, and conducted us to the poor hut we had lately quitted. A fire had been lighted in a second, and after having repeated several times 'may-dee' (sit down, sit down), which we did, the savages squatted on their heels and each one set out to eat the produce of his fishing. The cooking was neither long nor difficult to perform; those great shells were placed on the fire and there, as in a dish, the animal was baked and then eaten without any other kind of seasoning or preparation.

What this account does not suggest, but others do, is that it was the women who did the diving into the sea – sometimes staying under for as long as five minutes – to collect the shellfish. In a later account of a meeting on Bruny Island, Péron noted that the women (later known to be of the Nuenone band) carried loads of shellfish in 'rush-bags'. 'These bags were fastened round the forehead by cord loops, and hung down their backs. Some of these bags were quite heavy, and we sincerely pitied the females for having to bear such burdens.'

The Frenchmen in Cygnet then sang to their hosts 'that hymn so unhappily misused in the revolution', presumably the 'Marseillaise', and some lighter arias which had a mixed reception. Ouray-Ouray now took centre stage, and I mix two translations of Péron to describe her:

> Like the rest of her family, Ouray-Ouray was completely naked and seemed to have no idea that this might seem somewhat immodest or indecent. Much slenderer than her sister and brother, she was also livelier and more passionate. M. Freycinet, sitting beside her, appeared to be the particular object of her attention and anyone could detect in the glances of this innocent child of Nature that subtle difference which lends a more serious and deliberate edge to simple banter. Coquetry was called upon to add to natural allure.

Ouray-Ouray showed us for the first time the nature of the paint of those regions and the method of using it. Taking some charcoal in her hands she crushed it into a very fine powder; keeping this dust in her left hand she then rubbed some of it with her right hand first on her forehead and then on her cheeks, thereby making herself fearfully black. What appeared to us most singular was the air of satisfaction with which the young creature regarded us after this operation and the look of confidence that this novel decoration had given to her countenance. Thus it is that a feeling for coquetry, a taste for ornament, form a natural craving, so to speak, in the hearts of womankind ...

... Ouray-Ouray alone carried a bag made of rushes, of a neat and unusual construction, which I much wished to obtain. As the young girl had been very friendly with me, I risked making a request for her little bag; immediately, without hesitation, she put it in my hand, accompanying her present by a pleasing smile and some affectionate words that I was sorry I could not understand. In return, I gave her a handkerchief and a hammer-axe. The manner of using this, which I showed to her brother was the cause of astonishment and clamour amongst the whole family.

As it grew dark, the Frenchmen prepared to leave, and several members of the family, including Ouray-Ouray, accompanied them. Though the bushes that lined the path lashed out at them, the 'poor natives' seemed oblivious of the cuts and scratches they received; they particularly pitied Ouray-Ouray. 'But,' continues Péron, 'she did not seem to notice the many scratches that covered her thighs and abdomen, walking fearlessly through the dense brush, chattering – without any chance of being understood – to M. Freycinet. She talked with such provocative gestures and gracious smiles that the art of flirtation could not have been more obvious.'

Then gun shots alarmed Ouray-Ouray and she had to be reassured by Henri de Freycinet. The shots came from other companions, including his brother Louis and M. Breton who had been looking for water. The newcomers vied in presenting gifts to the Aborigines; but

... nothing pleased them so much as a long red feather which M. Breton gave to Ouray-Ouray. She jumped for joy, she called her father and her brothers, she shouted, she laughed, in a word she seemed intoxicated with delight and happiness. At length we got back to the beach and embarked. Our good Diemenese did not leave us for an instant, and when we put off from the shore their distress showed itself in a most affecting manner, and they made signs for us to come back and see them.

Later in the expedition, Péron visited Bruny Island and detailed his impressions of women which were quite different from those he had received at Port Cygnet though, once again, he met an outstanding woman, later identified as Arra Maïda. That meeting is included in the itinerary in 'Oyster Cove to Recherche Bay' (p288–9).

Giblin, writing in 1928, sees the French accounts from Baudin's expedition as among the 'best' in describing the Aborigines pre-1803 in 'their natural state'. Tim Flannery in *The Future Eaters* (1994) suggests that Péron 'loved' the Tasmanian people he met. But Lyndall Ryan in her seminal work is less impressed and suggests that he did them a disservice:

> Péron's unscientific conclusion that the Aborigines of Van Diemen's Land were the most removed from European civilisation had considerable scientific impact in Europe and formed the basis of the later Social Darwinist belief that they were the missing link between ape and man. More recently this conclusion has formed the basis for the view that the Tasmanian Aborigines were incapable of progressing further along the road of their own civilization because their isolation had caused them to suffer from a slow strangulation of the mind.

An analysis and comparison of French and Aboriginal sex and sensuality, based on Péron's writing, is to be found in Patty O'Brien's *The Pacific Muse: Exotic Femininity and the Colonial Pacific* (2006).

The First White Woman in Australia? – 1788

Louise Girardin may have been the first white woman to set foot in Tasmania, but not in mainland Australia. In a churchyard in New Norfolk, Tasmania, is a gravestone that reads 'Near this spot was laid to rest Betty King, the first white woman to set foot in Australia'. And this is Betty King's claim to fame. Although she did not arrive in Tasmania until 1808, she was typical of those convicts transported from Britain known as the 'First Fleeters' – the first to arrive in Botany Bay, near today's Sydney.

The fleet set out in 1787 to sail virtually into the unknown. Captain Cook had paused briefly at Botany Bay in 1770 but there had been no further exploration of the potential new colony – one that was to be the new gaol for Britain's 'criminal class' now that the American Revolutionary War had brought an end to transportation there. During the years of transportation, 160,000 men, women and children were to be shipped to Australia, 24,960 of them women. Until the early 1820s, almost all went to New South Wales. Tasmania eventually took over as the final destination. Sixty-seven thousand convicts arrived in Tasmania from British and Irish ports between 1803 and 1853. By 1820, 500 women had arrived in Tasmania indirectly; thereafter, they came direct.

On 26 January 1788, the fleet of eleven vessels carrying 1,030 people, including 188 women convicts, entered Port Jackson (Sydney). Among them, on board the *Lady Penrhyn*, was **Elizabeth Thackery** (c1775–1856) who had been convicted at Manchester in May 1786 of stealing a handkerchief, or two. Because of the claim on her gravestone, research has been done to test its validity. To be the first in anything in this story of the new colony had an allure and a cachet that will become further evident. This works well for me trying to tell the story, for it is impossible to tell that of every Tasmanian woman; the 'firsts' act as their representatives.

The voyage from England for Betty, as she became known, had been typical of that for women convicts, then and in the future: dark, damp ships, ill-health, male and female convicts segregated inadequately, drink, prostitution – the women also prey to the crew and marines. The male convicts were gradually landed. On 28 January, 17 women, marine wives, and their children went ashore. Betty Thackery (spelt in records variously, Thackary, Thacey, Hackery and Hackley, later King), convict, was not among them. In February she was still on board. On 5 February, five of the best-behaved from the *Lady Penrhyn* were allowed ashore to serve officers. Because of Betty's record during the voyage, she would not have been one of them. She appears finally to have set foot on shore on 6 February. As the women arrived, scenes of debauchery ensued. Her further story is in the 'New Norfolk' itinerary (p307).

Betty King was certainly among the first white women ashore in Australia, and it may well be that she was the last known surviving woman of the First Fleet.

The First White Woman at Risdon Cove – 1803

Captain Baudin and Philip Gidley King (no relation of Betty), Governor of New South Wales, had struck up such good relations during the five-month French stay in Sydney in 1802 that King allowed Mary Beckwith, an English convict stowed away in men's clothes on Baudin's departing ship, to leave with her protector. Nevertheless, the French expeditions had caused anxiety in the infant colony. To pre-empt any French expansionist designs in the area, it was resolved to increase British settlement.

The first expedition with the brief to settle the island to the south and thus to 'establish His Majesty's right to Van Diemen's Land' – was in the charge of a 23-year-old naval lieutenant, John Bowen. It is difficult to better Alison Alexander's start to *Obliged to Submit: Wives and Mistresses of Colonial Governors* (1987):

> Martha Hayes always remembered the eleventh of September 1803, for on that day she became the first white woman to set foot in Van Diemen's Land. This respectable and quite commendable title is usually mentioned when the name Martha Hayes arises; that she was the commandant's mistress, and pregnant as well, does not.

That is what was thought at the time and, indeed, until the discovery of Louise Girardin's place in history. Seventeen-year-old **Martha Hayes** (1786–1871) was not a convict, but her mother was. **Mary Hayes** (née Denight, c1761–1843), licensee of the Bell Inn at Red Lion Market, White Cross Street in London, was sentenced in 1801 to 14 years' transportation for receiving. (There were 5,000 public houses in London, many of them scenes of crime.) Young Martha was implicated but not charged, and her carpenter father, Henry, was acquitted. In September 1802, Mary joined a vessel taking women convicts to Sydney; it is assumed that Martha accompanied her – as many children did their convict mothers. On board ship was Lieutenant John Bowen, son of an admiral. Again it is assumed that Martha and Bowen met then. In 1803, upon arrival in Sydney, Mary set herself up as a milliner; Martha resided with John Bowen which probably accounted for her mother's freedom to engage in her craft which would not normally be possible for a convict. Mary advertised that 'Such commands that [ladies] may be pleased to honour her with … shall be executed in a Style of fashionable taste and neatness, with the utmost punctuality.' She was obviously multi-talented, and her convict record notes that she could read and write. Whether or not it was Martha's wish to live with Bowen is not known, but it was commonplace for officers to keep mistresses, and natural for women convicts to make the best of their situation.

Bowen was commissioned in March 1803 to settle at the mouth of the Derwent River, but it was not until August that two ships headed south bearing Bowen, a two-month pregnant Martha and 47 others: convicts, soldiers and a few settlers, including, as far as can be ascertained from incomplete lists, three women convicts, three marine wives and several settler wives, some with children. I have not listed their names here because sources disagree.

Following a difficult and delayed journey, Martha was eventually carried ashore – 'Racing with another white woman,' Alison Alexander writes, 'she made her celebrated landing.' There is even a suggestion elsewhere that sailors, with women perhaps riding piggy-back, raced through the shallows to be first ashore at Risdon Cove. Thereafter, Martha was, apparently, to trade on her claim to have been first.

If, as seems clear, the convict **Mary Lawler** (c1782–1814) was there from the start, one account suggests that she may have acted as servant to the commandant's mistress. She had been convicted in Dublin in 1799 and arrived in Sydney in 1801. I have not seen her claimed as the first Irish woman in Tasmania, so I shall do it for her now! She later joined her convict husband, Michael, in Hobart and they farmed in Rokeby.

Martha was installed in Bowen's tent, probably a ship's mainsail. Their home soon became a small wooden hut with a garden. Bowen had chosen the highest point with the best view over the Derwent River. The convict women were set to cutting grass, not only to clear the ground but also to provide roof thatching and the material to create wattle and daub walls. Provisions and livestock had been brought as government supplies to be rationed out; these were supplemented with kangaroo, emu, swans and other water fowl.

The ships when unloaded returned to Sydney with dispatches – datelined 'Hobart' – and two black swans as a present for Mrs King.

At this stage, there is barely a mention of the indigenous people of the Risdon Cove area; that is yet to come. But this landing and settlement are also known as the 'invasion'.

The First White Woman at Sullivans Cove (Hobart) – 1804

In one of his dispatches, Bowen noted to King that 'opposite Risdon Cove is a fine inlet and Deep Waters the largest I have seen in the Derwent and had but little noticed in the chart'. This was Sullivans Cove to the west. As for Risdon Cove on the east bank, when Bowen and his party arrived towards the end of the southern winter in 1803, grassy woodland stretched beyond the cove; four months later drought had created a parched landscape limiting attempts to grow food. Bowen's diverse flock soon began to prove unmanageable; stores were robbed; escapes were engineered. Bowen returned to Sydney to report, and possibly even to resign.

Meanwhile, Lieutenant Colonel David Collins of the Royal Marines, appointed Lieutenant Governor for the task, had left England with a party of civil officers, Royal Marines, settlers and convicts on the large frigate HMS *Calcutta* and the transporter *Ocean* to establish a settlement on the south coast of the mainland, at Port Phillip. Not long after arrival there, he dismissed its possibilities and was eventually authorised to sail south towards the Derwent. At Risdon Cove he decided even more quickly that Bowen had made a mistake in his choice of site and, receiving advice about Sullivans Cove at the foot of Mount Table (Mount Wellington), transferred his attention there – to what is now Hobart.

Collins has had his critics for not persevering with Port Phillip – after all, Melbourne was later founded not so far away – but not for moving from Risdon to Sullivans Cove. The only account by a woman I have been able to find for this period comes in a letter home on 23 May 1805, written by settler wife **Hezekiah Hartley** who, with her husband John, had sailed from England with Collins. She writes first of Port Phillip:

> We arrived in October, 1803: my pen is not able to describe half the beauties of that delightful spot: we were four months there. Much to my mortification, as well as loss, we were obliged to abandon the settlement through the whim and caprice of the Lieutenant-Governor ... additional expense to government, and additional loss to individuals, were incurred by removing to Van Diemen's Land, which there is little hope ever can be made to answer ... Port Phillip is my favorite, and has my warmest wishes. During the time we were there, I never felt one ache or pain, and parted from it with more regret than I did from my native land.

It is hard to accept that Mrs Hartley's first name was Hezekiah – invariably a male name; but I have been unable to gainsay Marjorie Tipping. Could she have been called Keziah – a more common, similar, female name? (This confusion has a precedent in memory slippage in my husband's family.)

In Port Phillip, the Hartleys, accompanied by their son Joshua, the son of Sir Charles Hamilton under their protection, and their servant, John Joachim Gravy, a German free settler, cutler and armourer, had tried to make themselves at home. They built a 'house' and Hartley became 'the first trader' there; he had brought a large supply of goods with him and he complained that Collins did not do enough to help the settlers establish themselves.

When the party from Port Phillip arrived at Risdon, most remained on board, but the Hartleys immediately went ashore and set up a tent and then built a house. And Mrs Hartley obviously thought little of Risdon, burnt by the summer sun and soon moving into autumn.

Also among Collins' party was the former labourer George Kearley (sometimes Kearly, Cearley, Curley, Kerley, Karley), sergeant in the Royal Marines and servant to Lieutenant Edward Lord. With Kearley was his wife of a year who allows us another charming vignette, for some claimed that **Mary Kearley** (née Cook, 1779–1859) was the first white woman, on 18 February 1804, to land on Tasmanian soil. This ignores Martha Hayes (who was not listed in Bowen's party, perhaps for obvious reasons) and the other women of the Risdon Cove settlement, let alone Louise Girardin, for Sullivans Cove was to be the real Hobart. The story is told in 'The Kearley Family' by Jayne Balmer and John Horton which I was pleased to find on the internet (and less vividly in a history of New Norfolk), of how when the *Ocean* and Lieutenant Governor Collins arrived, Collins wished his 'housekeeper' Mrs Power to have that honour,

> But some of the crew lowered another boat, and laughingly called out, 'Come on Mother Kearley, and see if you can't be first.' They hurried her into the boat, and reached the shore before Collins' party. The Lieutenant Governor was disappointed at being forestalled, but good humouredly remarked: 'You cannot beat the devil and a woman to get the better of a man!'

Hannah Power (also called Powers, bc1780) was rather more than Collins' housekeeper: it is recorded how, on the voyage out, Collins had engaged a convict's wife 'to attend on him as his mistress'. The informant was John Pascoe Fawkner, a lad of eleven at the time, travelling out with his convict father and accompanying mother and sister. His anecdotal, gossipy and scanty *Reminiscences* written many years later, in 1856, (they were published only in 2009) and drawing on others' memories and accounts, are not necessarily reliable. He also tells how 'This madam, coming off to the ship in a hurry, had left her fancy pet dog ashore, and the two ships were detained nearly two days, to gratify this country woman, and mistress of the Lieutenant Governor.' Collins' biographer calls this story 'apocryphal'. But Fawkner may have had well-remembered inside knowledge.

His Cornish mother, **Hannah Fawkner** (née Pascoe, c1773–1825), had determined to keep the family together when her husband was sentenced to transportation. Finding out that the *Calcutta* was to sail on 10 February, and having received permission, after an interview at the Home Office, to go out as a free settler, she raced with her two children (two others died in infancy) over 7 hours, to catch it; but the ship was delayed in reaching Spithead until mid-February. Hannah Power and her husband, Matthew, had both been accused of forging and uttering; when she was acquitted but her husband sentenced to 14 years' transportation, she, too, chose to accompany him. The two Hannahs would have known each other on board, for Mrs Fawkner had money in her own right and paid 20 guineas for a cabin in the forecastle, though she was not best pleased to be compelled to swap the feather beds she had brought with flock ones.

Twenty-three-year-old Hannah Power was not 46-year-old Collins' first mistress, and he had left his wife Maria behind as she was too fragile to withstand the rigours of Australia. He already had two children by Yorkshire milliner **Nan** (Ann or Nancy) **Yeates** (bc1768) with whom he had consorted for six years during an earlier posting in Sydney. It was not simply the frontier society of the new colony and family separation that prompted liaisons outside marriage; this was the Georgian period of loose morals brought to life in Amanda Foreman's *Georgiana, Duchess of Devonshire* (1998) and Hallie Rubehold's *Lady Worsley's Whim: An Eighteenth Century Tale of Sex, Scandal and Divorce* (2008). It had yet to be replaced by the family values encouraged by Queen Victoria's marriage to Prince Albert in 1840.

Nan Yeates, too, had come out on the *Lady Penrhyn* of the First Fleet. Arrested aged 17 in 1785 for breaking and entering and stealing 36 yards of printed cotton, she was sentenced to be hanged, but reprieved and sentenced instead to be transported. On board ship, Lieutenant David Collins was one of the officers in charge of her guards, but it was another man, a seaman, who fathered her first child before the First Fleet left England, and she gave birth just before the Fleet reached Botany Bay. With David Collins she had two children, in 1790 and 1793, Marianne and George Collins. While Nan remained in Sydney on Collins' return to England and did not accompany him to Tasmania, nor apparently visit him, their two children were openly acknowledged, stayed with him in Hobart, and were received in the best society. By 1820, **Marianne Collins Chace** (1790–1860), who, aged 15, had married a hard-bitten seaman, roamer of the Bass Strait for several years, was living in Hobart with six children. By 1826 she was a widow; Captain Chace and his ship were lost off Maria Island.

And Hannah Power, with the collusion of her husband whom it benefited to share her with the Lieutenant Governor, was not to be his last mistress.

The First White Child Born in Tasmania – 1804

It is rather easy to confuse Sullivans Cove with Sullivan Bay, especially when, in Marjorie Tipping's impressive and invaluable, but expensive to come by, *Convicts Unbound: The Story of the Calcutta Convicts and their Settlement in Australia* (1988) there is a baptismal sketch with a caption that reads:

I publickly baptised Sargent Thorn's child. The Governor, Lieutenant Johnson, Mrs Powers and Mrs Whitehead stood for the child, the first birth in the colony. (Knopwood, Diaries, Christmas Day 1803) ... impressions of one of the highlights at Sullivan Bay in [November]1803.

Ann Thorne (née Luckwell, m1796, d1820) and Sergeant Samuel Thorne arrived in Tasmania with Collins and became such respected settlers that there is a Samuel Thorne Reserve (p280) and the remains of their house at Lewisham, near where I often stay in Tasmania. (Samuel was district constable at nearby Sorell.) But Sullivan Bay is the abandoned settlement at Port Phillip (near today's Melbourne; not the same as Sullivans Cove – Hobart) and little William Thorne was not the first European child born in Tasmania. It is said that he was first christened William James Port Phillip Thorne but later changed his name to William James Hobart Thorne. The Reverend Robert Knopwood's baptismal records do not confirm that nice conceit – he was Hobart (the name of the Secretary for the Colonies) from the start.

That first birth claim is more reasonably, though rather liberally, made for little Catherine Potaski. Her father was a refugee from the troubles in Poland, but he was convicted and sentenced to transportation in 1802 at Horsham in Sussex for stealing a woman's shawl from Mrs Pollard's shop at Newhaven. When he married Catherine O'Sullivan from Connaught, Ireland, is not clear, but they already had a son by the time she accompanied him to serve his sentence in Australia. Young Catherine was conceived on the high seas and born on board Collins' ship *Ocean* anchored off Risdon Cove on 17 February 1804. As with Ann Thorne's experience in the six-week-old settlement at Port Phillip, it hardly seems necessary to suggest the conditions under which the two women gave birth.

Fawkner describes John Potaski as an 'incorrigibly bad man' and his wife **Catherine Potaski** (c1759–1855) as a 'lowbred, dirty, idle Connaught woman', adding that they 'reared their children in filth and ignorance' and 'evil practices'. In 'John Potaski, Australia's First Polish Settler' (2004) Desmond Cahill gives these details and adds, 'Marjorie Tipping … notes wryly, "Other records neither confirm nor deny this less than flattering description."' And it is true that one of their children came to a sticky end: young John was found guilty of rape and hanged in Hobart in 1821. Young Catherine had an illegitimate son at the age of 16, and there are allegations of prostitution, though she later married and settled down.

Catherine senior was granted a plot of land at Clarence Plains (now Rokeby, just outside Hobart) and her husband John was freed in 1810. By 1816 he rented farms at Risdon and Kangaroo Point (now Bellerive, home of Hobart's cricket ground). There the Potaskis had a comfortable home. On Catherine's land they grew wheat which they provided to the Commissariat and additional pasture for John's cattle and sheep.

Marjorie Tipping suggests that young Master Hopley (Richard William York) 'was the first European born in Hobart' but she does not, unfortunately give a precise date in 1804, nor has my further searching been able to produce one. His mother **Judith Hopley** (née Hobbs, c1781–1813) was part of an interesting family group to arrive with Collins' 200-strong first contingent. Her mother, **Jane Hobbs** (c1761–1813) was the American widow of a British Royal Navy officer. Judith, also born in America, was the wife of Dr William Hopley – officer and assistant surgeon on the *Calcutta*. Other members of the

Hobbs/Hopley family included 16-year-old Rebecca, 15-year-old Anne Jane, and Charity Hobbs, aged 13.

Marjorie Tipping suggests that Jane Hobbs 'provided the settlement with its most desirable commodity – four daughters without a "convict stain" to "taint" the next generation'.

Judith Hobbs Hopley, pregnant with her second child at sea, and with a daughter, Julia, in tow, was described by Fawkner as 'an attentive kind wife, a tender mother and a thorough English matron: her conduct was exemplary and had some weight in counteracting the gross immorality in high places'. He was referring to Collins, of course, but I am afraid that Judith's sister **Rebecca Hobbs** was not entirely virtuous: she became pregnant en voyage by John Ingle, overseer of convicts. Her baby was born at Port Phillip and they were married by the Reverend Robert Knopwood on 1 July, soon after their arrival in Hobart. Ingle was to become a prosperous merchant and shipowner and leave his name on the house in Macquarie Street that features in the itinerary 'Around and About Macquarie Street'. Their daughter Elizabeth was among the first to be baptised in Hobart, on 28 July 1804. They had seven children in all.

In 1805, Judith and Rebecca's sister **Anne Jane Hobbs** (1784–1862) was to marry George Prideaux Harris, surveyor, whose letters, edited by Barbara Hamilton-Arnold, provide useful information about this early period of Hobart. Their shipboard romance had been less productive than Rebecca's. Harris, pining over a recent failed love affair, wrote home of that time: 'We soon became inseperable [sic] and used to sit or walk together by hours of a moonlight on the Quarter Deck. But I sought no more than a friend ...' After their marriage he described Anne Jane to his mother: 'My sweet little girl is one of the most amenable disposition I ever met with and her affectionate attachment to me is such as must render my life devoted to her happiness.'

Once on shore, married and badly housed, he, too, contrasted the behaviour of some with that of others: 'Only one Officer has yet had a House built for him ... tho God knows he has had time enough since he has built *elegant houses* for *convicts* where the *Wife* was a *favourite*.' From the beginning, Hannah Power's tent had been immediately behind her lover's. And it was not only Collins and Hannah and Matthew Power that Harris was getting at, for he added in that letter which must have somewhat disturbed his mother: 'I cannot visit *with* my wife most of my brother Officers because they have female companions.' He does not appear to have told his family about his sister-in-law Rebecca's premature pregnancy and hasty marriage.

If Catherine Potaski was born on board ship, even if just off shore (or, as Marjorie Tipping has it, 'shortly before arrival'), and we do not know the date of Master Hopley's birth at Hobart, then it must be Martha Hayes' daughter, Henrietta, who should claim the accolade of first-born European on Tasmanian soil, on or about 29 March 1804. To make the occasion happier for her, Martha's convict mother, Mary, and father, Henry (who had come out with Collins as far as Port Phillip to join his family in Sydney) arrived on 10 March from Sydney just in time for the birth. It is assumed that convict

Mary was 'assigned' to her free-settler husband as a servant on the 100-acre allotment in New Town to which they moved in due course – named Henrietta Farm after their granddaughter.

Henry's millwright brother, Thomas, with his wife **Elizabeth Hayes** (née Fellows) and children, had also travelled out with Collins, gone on to Sydney, and now arrived in Tasmania. The family's names become interchangeable in the records because of regulations that not only allowed Thomas and Elizabeth to travel but also gave them government rations. Elizabeth Hayes is said to have received rations at Risdon Cove, but it was probably Mary, or even Martha. It is clear that united families, even when convicts were involved, were encouraged for the stability they provided.

John Bowen returned from Sydney on the same ship as the Hayes; at least one source suggests that one of his reasons for going to Sydney was to try and get Martha's mother to her and that he was aware that his career prospects might be blighted by his absence from the renewed Napoleonic Wars. Before he left Risdon Cove in January, his relationship with Martha had begun to show strain; indeed, he may well have sought to desert both her and his post. Now, however, he and his settlement vied with Collins and his: there was a Governor of Sullivans Cove and one of Risdon Cove. But at least Bowen acknowledged his daughter who was known as Miss Bowen.

I have seen Mary Kearley's son George claimed as the first white child born in Tasmania although he was, in fact, born after Miss Bowen. He is also claimed as the first white *male* child. His gravestone says that he was born on 9 July; Knopwood's records show he was baptised on 14 July; he died the following day and was buried in the new cemetery – now St David's Park (itinerary 'Around and About Macquarie Street'). Little George was not, however, the first child to be buried there: that was Elizabeth who died on 27 April 1804, daughter of free woman **Elizabeth Edwards** and her husband, convict Joseph Edwards.

Until the arrival of a second contingent from Port Phillip on 25 June, Mary Kearley had been the only wife among the marines at Hobart (though, of course, not the only woman). At Port Phillip, Mary had been one of the laundresses for the marines and she probably continued this task, as well as other domestic chores. Cooking was done in iron pots, of which one was provided to each hut, and it was the task of the women to keep the fire, over which the pots hung, going at all times.

Mary must have felt isolated and put upon, especially as she was pregnant in one of the cold, damp huts that housed the marines. It was mid-winter when she gave birth. Among the items listed in Collins' first order were blankets and rugs for 396 people. Scurvy, of which several died, diarrhoea and catarrh were prevalent. The new arrivals brought the total in Hobart to 433, including 39 women and 36 children. Even then, the ratio of men to women was ten to one, creating sexual tensions to add to others.

Mary was soon pregnant again; their second child, Joseph, was born on 30 May 1805 and died on 5 August. His birth and death are included on the headstone of his older brother. Another son, William, was born in 1807,

John in 1809, and Charlotte, their first daughter, in 1811. They continued to have children but only five of them survived to adulthood. All three of their daughters married convicts assigned as servants to the family or who had worked in the neighbourhood with a ticket-of-leave (part of the process that led to eventual freedom). From 1812, married marines were allowed to leave the service and remain in Tasmania, and that is what George Kearley chose to do. The family became settlers in 1813 in the Pontville-Brighton area. Mary Kearley should not be confused, as is sometimes the case, with Catherine Kearney who features in due course.

The Risdon Cove Massacre – 1804

What happened at Risdon Cove on 3 May 1804 was not only the first documented clash between Aborigines and British incomers but heralded, too, a process leading to the near annihilation of Tasmania's Aborigines. Today it is not just the place where, for some, Aborigines were gunned down on their ancestral land, and for others the place of first British settlement, but it also epitomises differences in perception (often seen as fact) regarding events, and thus the difficulties of recreating Tasmania's history.

In 'Dirty Domestics and Worse Cooks: Aboriginal Women's Agency and Domestic Frontiers, Southern Australia 1800–1850' (2007), Lynette Russell introduced me to the term 'history wars': 'The disputes most commonly consist of conservative commentators and apologists denying wholesale massacre, disease and death, and trained historians producing what has been disparagingly labelled "black arm-band history".'

For an outsider like me, the situation is even more fraught – but what happened at Risdon Cove is not an incident that can be ignored or skated over, though I do not presume to offer any original clarification. The status of the area today will be raised again in the itinerary 'Risdon Cove to Port Arthur'. Lyndall Ryan sets the 1804 scene in *The Aboriginal Tasmanians*:

> Risdon lay in the territory of the Oyster Bay tribe and was the home of the Moomairremener band. It was part of the corridor that gave the Leenowwenne and Pangerninghe bands of the Big River tribe access to the rich shellfish and lagoon areas of the Coal River and Pittwater and to the kangaroo grounds of the east bank of the Derwent. The parkland aspect that attracted Bowen to Risdon had been created by the constant firing of the area by the Moomairremener to flush out game.

On 28 November 1992 an article on page 19 of the Weekend Review of the *Mercury* was entitled 'Hobart history written in the blood of Risdon Cove'. Its first paragraph reads: 'According to "Our Story of Risdon Cove" a Tasmanian Aboriginal Centre leaflet "close to a hundred Aboriginals were killed" by British soldiers.'

A commission set up by Governor Arthur to look into such incidents reported in 1830. It found it 'indisputable that a most lamentable encounter did at that time ensue, in which the numbers of slain, of men, women and children, had been estimated as high as 50'. It hoped that the numbers had been inflated. The author of the *Mercury* article, John Thompson, then goes through accounts of the incident in histories of Tasmania and Australia. A more detailed and scholarly version, 'Risdon Cove and the Massacre of 3 May 1804' (2004) by Lyndall Ryan, marked the 200th anniversary of the event. There is still no agreement over what happened and how many were killed.

When you are trying to get to the truth through several conflicting accounts – in this case both of the time and of today's reconstructions and interpretations, sometimes you have to close your eyes, open your mind, and form your own picture. I see several hundred (probably 300) Aborigines coming over the hill, out of the trees, on a traditional and noisy kangaroo hunt and creating panic in the settlement of 80 or so Europeans, including soldiers with muskets and at least two carronades (twelve-pounder naval guns firing balls comparable to those from a cannon).

If there were hundreds of Aborigines, they must have been more than the Moomairremener band, as that unit usually consisted of 40–50 members; nations numbered from 250–700. The Aborigines probably knew that the incomers were encamped on traditional hunting ground and eating their game – even if they were passing through, information would surely have been shared. There had been non-violent tussles over kangaroos with the Moomairremener, and there was another earlier that day. The Aborigines may well have been consciously seeking to make a point. But they did not know about the power of firearms, the reaction that panic might cause, and the fact that the incomers regarded the place as British by settlement.

That women and children were among the Aborigines is confirmed by the fact that a toddler at the scene was orphaned, taken into European care and, as Knopwood noted in his diary, christened Robert Hobart May (after himself, the place, and the month). Some accounts – then and more recently – suggest that a handful or fewer of Aborigines were killed, but for two parents to die out of a crowd of hundreds suggests a larger number. And figures normally given do not discuss the lightly or severely wounded who would presumably have been taken by their people as they dispersed. And the dead? It is said that the surgeon Jacob Mountgarrett proudly proclaimed to have dissected at least one corpse, and he took two boxes of bones to Sydney.

It seems that part of the panic was caused by the surrounding of a settler family's hut, and fear for the safety of the wife; Knopwood was told and recorded that the house was to be set on fire and the wife 'ill-treated'. The name given in accounts is Burke, corrected to Birt. **Mrs Aaron** (or William) **Birt** was one of the settler wives who had originally arrived with Bowen and had three young children with her. Her husband was a carpenter and they had a half-acre allotment at Risdon Cove and a goat and three swine from the government's livestock.

Alison Alexander tells a slightly different story, one involving Martha Hayes. John Bowen, still in charge there, was away exploring. Fawkner, whose reliability has been questioned, relates that it was Martha Hayes who, terrified of the blacks, begged Dr Mountgarret to take measures to protect her 'in the condition in which she was'. It was only a month since Henrietta's birth, and possibly the young mother felt delicate.

Once again, Fawkner may have known something others did not, for Martha's mother, Mary, and his father had been sentenced to transportation for their part in the same offence. Some support is also given for Martha's involvement by WF Refshauge's article that reconsiders the facts through the topography of the area and ballistics, 'An Analytical Approach to the Events at Risdon Cove on 3 May 1804' (2007): 'Allowing a little latitude, the Aborigines descended upon the settlement between White's Creek [the 'creek' mentioned by the witness convict White] and the soldiers' encampment, perhaps even spilling over towards Bowen's hut.' That hut was about a quarter of a mile from the Birts'.

Lyndall Ryan suggests a possible further part played by Martha: since she was still alive in the historian James Bonwick's day, the claim that Lieutenant William Moore, the marine in charge that day, was drunk – which Bonwick was told by a settler – came from her.

As for little 'Robert', he was apparently cared for in the Risdon settlement, presumably by one of the settler women. In November 1805, he was vaccinated against smallpox at the Sullivans Cove hospital (actually two tents on the site of today's Royal Hobart Hospital), though Collins had ordered at the time that the child be returned 'to any Party of Natives that might be seen in the Neighbourhood of Risdon Cove', as an act of reconciliation. He rejected Mountgarrett's plan to take the child to England. Thereafter 'Robert' seems to have disappeared from history.

It is worth noting here that in the early days Collins wrote to King that he intended to 'inform everybody that the Aborigines of this country are as much under the protection of the Laws of Great Britain as they themselves are'.

The First Homes and Farms in Hobart

The European inhabitants of Risdon Cove began to move across the Derwent to Sullivans Cove as early as June 1804. Some families stayed, including the newly-arrived Hartleys. But soon realising that it was impractical to do so, John Hartley told Collins that he wanted a town allotment, servants, provisions, permission to build a boat, and £500 compensation for the two houses, and their vegetable gardens, he had built at Port Phillip and Risdon. Collins did not oblige, though he did pay him over the odds, £50, for an English sow and her offspring and a boar, and the Hartleys resolved to leave Tasmania, with its 'barren mountains,' as she wrote. This they did on 9 August. Marjorie Tipping writes of Mrs Hartley, who had so many physical aches and pains at Risdon, 'One can only wonder how she survived the psychological pain if her husband was really as cantankerous as others depicted him.' From Sydney, they left for England in 1805, but returned to Sydney as immigrants in 1809 'to cause more trouble'. They returned to England in 1814.

Also still at Risdon were Martha, Henrietta and Bowen. In July, knowing he was instructed to leave his post (apparently against his wishes), Bowen ensured that Martha was declared a free settler, allowing her formally to receive government rations and be given a grant of land, convict servants, some seed and livestock – eight sheep and two goats. The land – 50 acres, half the usual allocation to male settlers, but the first of two grants to women – was in Prince of Wales Bay, New Town, near that of the rest of her family. Alison Alexander starts the chapter on farming in her as yet unpublished doctoral thesis, 'The Public Role of Women in Tasmania, 1803–1914' (1989), 'Martha Hayes was Tasmania's first woman farmer.'

Bowen slept at the house, probably the first habitation in what was to become Glenorchy, he had built for Martha before he left for Sydney on 9 August 1804, and some time in that last month she became pregnant. **Charlotte Bowen** was born on 3 April 1805, but Bowen was not there, nor was he ever to see her – he left for England from Sydney in 1805 to pursue his career as a naval captain – though he did send her a wedding present when she got married in 1823 (to the assistant surgeon Dr Robert Garrett). Nor was he to see again Martha or Henrietta (who died in 1823, aged 19). From Sydney, he made arrangements for Martha to receive pigs, wheat and maize – rather insecure arrangements, suggests Alison Alexander who, in *Obliged to Submit*, provides most of the information about Martha.

Martha was renowned for her looks – an Irish visitor of 1805 describes her as 'the prettiest violet that I saw growing at the Derwent'; but she was not a suitable marriage partner for a man of Bowen's status. In the rather different society of Hobart, she, her children and her parents were to prosper; indeed, Collins was godfather to both girls and the Reverend Robert Knopwood was a close friend of the family: he makes frequent references to visiting them in his diary.

But then, not only Governor Collins was leading a free and easy life: Knopwood himself seems not to have valued sexual morality too highly. On board the *Calcutta* the newly-married marine wife, Maria Sergeant, was noticed often going in and out of his cabin, until she took up with someone else. She features in more detail in Chapter 9.

Fawkner, who despised Knopwood, described him, in his role as magistrate, as 'a cruel and vindictive man' (he had once sentenced Fawkner to 500 lashes); he also gossiped about his morals. In Hobart, the parson's housekeeper was **Mary McAuley** (c1780–1865), wife of the senior sergeant of the detachment, James McAuley. In later years, according to Fawkner, she would walk each day from Knopwood's house in Battery Point to the nearby grog shop in Macquarie Street and have half a gallon of rum poured into a lime-juice bottle; this the two of them shared during the day. Fawkner commented, 'There were no other people living in this house but the parson and this woman.' It is difficult to see half a gallon in one of today's lime-juice bottles, or even the consumption by two people of that amount of rum in a day, day after day, but it makes a good story.

Mary McAuley was also said (by Mabel Hookey in *The Chaplain* (1970)) to be the first white woman to land in Tasmania – she arrived from Port Phillip in 1804. In due course, she was widowed and married the convict son of a gentleman farmer in England who had been assigned as the servant of the McAuleys, Edward Busby, 19 years her junior. He left her widowed again in 1856. She died, aged 85, nine years later and was buried at St Mathews, Rokeby.

Knopwood kept a record in 1805 of which children he christened born within marriage (eight) and without (six), so he was obviously alert to the sexual morals of the society in which he was the spiritual leader. One philosopher at Port Phillip wondered at women's dilemma created by the novelty of their situation there in a way that can apply equally to Hobart's early days: 'What once seemed more valuable than life itself, even female virtue, grows weaker by degrees and at last falls sacrifice to present circumstances.' Fawkner, however, extolled the virtue of most early women – 'Good wives, tender mothers and guides to the rising generation.'

The sort of house that Martha lived in then probably resembled that of Hannah Fawkner who came ashore with her family on 16 February. Instead of sharing a tent (each family given a third of it), as families such as the Hopleys did, she used her funds to hire convict labour to build a dwelling. She and her husband were granted 50 acres each and young John 90 acres. He later described their first 'house':

> The frame of our hut consisted of natural timber, four inches in diameter, sunk two feet into the ground. These posts were set two feet apart and joined with laths or wattles, the interstices being filled with mud, dry grass acting as a binder. The roof was round, with posts for rafters and wattled with branches and thatched with swamp grass and reeds. The door was at first a canvas blind, and the window spaces were left uncovered except for shutters used at night to keep out the cold. Eventually a large chimney of timber and turf was erected with a sandstone hearth.

This house was soon burnt down, perhaps because of the intemperance of Hannah's husband, and most of their possessions were lost. Hannah went back to England for two or so years in 1806 and her twelve-year-old daughter, Betsy, took her place. **Betsy Fawkner** (Elizabeth, 1795–1851) was married in 1809, aged 14, to former *Calcutta* convict Thomas Green, aged 23, and given her own grant of land – 50 acres. But, by 1812, she was a widow with two children, one of whom died the following year. By 1816, she had remarried, Constable Richard Lucas, a Norfolk Islander, after giving birth to his daughter four months earlier. They were to have nine children by 1835.

From the description of the Fawkners' first house, we can begin to imagine Martha, Hannah and Betsy's immediate surroundings in 1804. The setting of those dwellings is best conveyed by Jorgen Jorgensen who was briefly there then but was to return some years later, and to marry a rather rumbustious convict woman to be met in Chapter 5 and more than one itinerary. There are not at this stage, unfortunately, any first-hand accounts by women (except the letter from Mrs Hartley). Jorgen wrote in 1835:

> As I walk up and down the streets of this now crowded and large town, I cannot always divest myself of the remembrance of what it was at that time – 32 years ago. The spot where the Bank of Van Diemen's Land, the Hope and Anchor and the late Mrs Kearney's habitation now are, was then an impervious grove of the thickest brushwood, surmounted with some of the largest gum trees that this island can produce, and all along the rivulet as far up as where the Old or Upper mill is now, was impassable from the denseness of the shrubs and underwood, and the huge collections of prostrate trees and dead timber which had been washed down by the stream and was strewed all around. These had in parts blocked up the channel, and many places which are now dry and built upon or cultivated in fruitful gardens were covered with rushes and water.

By October 1806, Martha Hayes had planted two acres with wheat and she now had two cows, 14 goats and 35 sheep. By then food supplies had begun to be short in the colony; Edward Lord, whose wife Maria soon appears, described the early period: 'During eight or nine years we entirely depended on the woods. We had 2 lbs of biscuit weekly for thirteen months. I have often myself been glad to go to bed for want of bread.' Salome Pitt (p40) describes how 'Provisions becoming scarce, the people often cooked maritime plants collected on the sea shore … Sometimes they collected for food the crap or refuse of the blubber whales, out of which the oil had been taken by whaling vessels and which was washed up on the shores.' But Martha and her family were able to cope. And by 1807 she had doubled her crop planting and increased her livestock; and she managed, when government rations discontinued, to support the family.

Later, in 1811, in her mid-twenties, Martha married a 42-year-old Scot, Andrew Whitehead, a neighbouring farmer. Formerly a clerk convicted of embezzlement, he had been on the *Calcutta* with Collins who, appreciating his ability, appointed him manager of the government farm at Cornelian Bay and he was given a free pardon in 1807. In the quotation concerning the 1803 baptism in Port Phillip of Ann Thorne's son, a Mrs Whitehead, along with Hannah Power, is noted as godmother. They shared quarters in the gunroom of the *Calcutta* from England. But on the voyage **Mary Whitehead** became the mistress of Deputy Commissioner Leonard Fosbrook. In 1805, Andrew Whitehead was in trouble, described as 'ill-conduct to Fosbrook'. When it turned out that the Whiteheads were not married, Collins packed her off to Sydney, in spite of the fact that she had acted as his mistress' chaperone.

In *Gender, Crime and Empire: Convicts, Settlers and the State in Early Colonial Australia* (2007), Kirsty Reid reasonably accuses Collins of hypocrisy over Mary Whitehead's banishment. Mary's problem seems to have been that the home government had paid for her to travel as Whitehead's wife; then, not only had she two-timed him but neither could she marry him as Collins required, because she already had a husband in England. But then neither could Hannah Power, the Governor's mistress, regularise her situation.

Fosbrook later lived with free woman **Fanny Anchor** (Frances Ankers), wife of the convict butcher Daniel Anchor – an example of a free woman married to a convict trading up. Fanny also shared those quarters on the *Calcutta* – near those of Collins and Fosbrook. So a lovely friendship between shipboard sisters may have faltered. Hannah and Fanny, whose husbands had been gaoled and sentenced together at Maidstone for a similar crime, remained friends. No doubt as a result of their special services, Fanny and Hannah had accumulated livestock. Matthew Power, initially Hannah's 'servant', was given a free pardon in 1805. The Powers stayed together and, having done very well for themselves in Hobart, left for England in 1809. Fanny and Fosbrook, who became well known as corrupt, left for England together in 1814.

Martha and Whitehead had a daughter, Mary, in 1813 (their son died in infancy), and that same year he was granted the government farm outright. At the time of their marriage, Martha had secured a prenuptial agreement whereby all her livestock – then 964 sheep and about 80 cattle – was to be held in trust, with her father as trustee, for her daughters by Bowen.

Another woman granted land – 40 acres – at the same time as Martha Hayes, and in the same area, was free woman **Mary Ann Peters** (née Hughes or Hews, c1780–1819). Her husband Thomas, convicted for his part in stealing ten valuable old silver pint pots, was assigned to her as a servant. And you have to wonder how such marriages worked, however much of a formality the assignment might be in practice, particularly as wives of convicts were recognised as settlers. The Peters already had a two-year-old daughter when they set out from England; a second, Martha, was conceived at Port Phillip and born in Hobart in September 1804, and six more girls and one boy were born in Tasmania.

By 1807, Mary Ann, who had even purchased fowl on board the *Calcutta* before landing at Port Phillip, had increased her stock to two cows, two bull calves, two ewes and a female goat, and was growing wheat and barley. For some reason, the family was victimised by other convicts: one of their convict servants, **Anne Allen,** was sent to Sydney to be tried for committing arson in their house, and three convict men for stealing Mary Ann's bullock. One reason might have been that a ship laden with rum had just arrived and much of Hobart went on a spree. The Peters later expanded to a larger farm in the Brighton area, and had a house in Elizabeth Street in town where Thomas plied his craft as a blacksmith and had a small stud. It was there that Mary Ann died of a throat infection in 1819, aged only 39. An obituary in the *Hobart Town Gazette* described her as 'an inhabitant much respected' leaving her younger children 'at a time when they most needed their mother's care'. In 1830, two of her daughters, Sophia and Ann, were speared by Aborigines. Anne died, but Sophia, aged ten, whose stays deflected the spear, recovered (p335).

2 – The North

The Firsts in Launceston – 1804

Not long after Lieutenant Colonel William Paterson produced evidence that a French officer had shown him a map marking a possible French settlement in the north of Tasmania, King, with instructions from London, appointed him Lieutenant Governor of the British settlement to be founded there.

After a stormy passage of three weeks during which most of the livestock died, the *Buffalo* arrived at Port Dalrymple (p382) at the mouth of the Tamar in November 1804 with 67 rank and file of the New South Wales Corps (Paterson's regiment), 74 convicts and two convict wives, and some public servants and free settlers including 20 women and 14 children.

Among the convicts were the wife and husband **Ann Middlebrook Keating** (c1755–1841) and James Keating and immediately on arrival, on the same day, 11 November, she gave birth to a son – William Dalrymple. She was 49 years old and they had married in Sydney, whither they were first transported, shortly before leaving. I suspect the birth must have taken place on board. One historical account describes the location as 'windswept'; I hesitate to suggest the weather that day, but you get the picture.

Both Ann and James had been transported for stealing; she in England, he in Ireland. Their story did not have a happy ending. Assigned as a cooper in the convict settlement Paterson set up, James was accused of stealing from government stores in January 1806, sent to Sydney, convicted, and sent to Hobart to be hanged – on 14 April.

Ann remarried in 1811 and died in Longford many years later. Her tombstone reads: 'Sacred to the memory of Annie Edmonds who departed this life Oct 25, 1841 aged 86 years who was the mother of the first child of British descent born on the Northern side of Van Diemen's Land'.

By the end of November, Paterson had started to explore and, on the 28th, he and his party had their first sighting of 'natives' near the western arm of the Tamar – presumably a band of the North Midlands nation; he reported to London:

> This day saw about forty natives, including men, women and children. They were very shy at first. After endeavouring to convince them that we were friendly, one of them threw some stones at a soldier who I sent with a handkerchief. Observing he would not allow the soldier to approach, I desired him to leave the handkerchief and a tomahawk, which they afterwards picked up, much pleased with the present.

The Aborigines then followed them, and the man with the handkerchief

> Gave the soldier a necklace of small shells, which had a white metal button strung on it, and had the appearance of being worn for a length of time.

Observing them so very friendly, I sent the boat on shore ... with some fish, and also some trinkets; but on their seeing the boat they went into the woods, which ended our interview. But from the fires we observed in that neighbourhood since, it is probable they live chiefly in this quarter.

A couple of things are striking about that report: the family units seem to have gathered, perhaps to reconnoitre the new arrivals; it was women who made the shell necklaces, but where had the metal button come from? Later encounters had less fortunate outcomes – an Aborigine was killed over a misunderstanding concerning a trinket.

Elizabeth Paterson (née Driver, c1760–1825) arrived on the *Buffalo* to join her husband in April 1805. She disembarked to live in a 'portable cottage' at York Town (p382) to where Paterson had moved the settlement.

The Patersons had been married since about 1787 and she was used to overseas assignments. They had arrived for a posting in Sydney in 1791, travelling in the same ship as Anna King. Anna had married Philip Gidley King four days before their ship sailed from England; he was returning as Lieutenant Governor to Norfolk Island, the subordinate convict settlement, which he had earlier been appointed to set up. Paterson was immediately posted to join King on Norfolk Island, and during their two-year stay Elizabeth and Anna, the only 'ladies' there, formed a lifelong friendship, cemented by the fact that Anna gave birth six weeks after her arrival there and while King had been absent in England his deputy had allowed the settlement to become difficult to manage.

Later, when King became Governor of New South Wales in 1802 and Paterson Lieutenant Governor, the two women founded an orphan school and Elizabeth was a daily visitor during 1803–04. According to Patricia Clarke and Dale Spender in *Lifelines: Australian Women's Letters and Diaries 1788–1840* (1992), 'They were the first women in Australian history to undertake charitable work in an organised way.' The Patersons had no children but 'adopted' from the orphanage, as their ward, **Elizabeth Mackellar** (1793–1859), the first of five children born in Sydney to convict Sarah Cooley and Captain Neil Mackellar, King's aide-de-camp, lost at sea in 1802. The twelve-year-old accompanied Elizabeth to Tasmania.

Also in the party were **Sophia Riley** (née Hardwick) recently married to Alexander Riley, storekeeper and magistrate at Port Dalrymple, and **Elizabeth Kemp** (c1786–1865), sister of Alexander and recently married to Anthony Fenn Kemp, second in command to Paterson.

Elizabeth Kemp is notable not only as one of the first 'ladies' in Launceston; she was to spend most of her younger life producing and caring for eleven daughters and seven sons. One of her daughters was to become the 'notorious' Elizabeth Kemp Sorell, daughter-in-law of the third Governor of Tasmania; and her granddaughter was the much-gossiped-about Julia Sorell Arnold, mother of the writer Mrs Humphrey Ward. Julia's life is touched on briefly in Chapter 11, and she and her daughter feature in the 'New Town' itinerary (p266).

Elizabeth Paterson's maid was convict **Hannah Williams**, transported to New South Wales in 1801. She later married the soldier Michael Murphy and they had four daughters. Murphy's regimental duties took him back to Sydney in 1817, but he died in 1822. Hannah continued to run their small north Tasmanian farm.

In 1806, Paterson formed the new settlement of Patersonia at the junction of the North Esk, South Esk and Tamar Rivers – what became Launceston – though he and Elizabeth continued often to live in York Town where they started a garden, went on botanical expeditions and collected plants and seeds for friends, including the botanist Joseph Banks. An archaeological attempt to reconstruct the lives of that settlement features in the itinerary 'North West Coast – Launceston to Cape Grim' (p382). There and in Launceston Elizabeth acted as Governor's wife, described by an early colonial diarist as 'a good cosy Scottish lass well fitted for a soldier's wife', and she entertained visitors; surveyor George Prideaux Harris spent five weeks with Colonel and Mrs Paterson 'in the most delightful manner possible'. We also have a glimpse of her riding on her horse to Clarence Point to meet a ship. In later days, she nursed her husband who was increasingly ill.

Paterson was appointed governor of New South Wales in 1809. Riley, whom he had promoted to Deputy Commissary in York Town in 1805, went with him as Secretary to the colony, parting the two Riley women. In Sydney Elizabeth Paterson was noted for trying to restore peace after the upheavals of the Bligh governorship which spilled over into Hobart, as we shall see. As first and last Governor's wife of northern Tasmania, she was granted 2,000 acres there in 1808; she called the property 'Spring Grove'. But when her husband died at sea on the way home to England in 1810, she was, apparently impoverished, refused a pension and ordered to repay some £200 he had paid in public salaries without authority. I have been unable to find out what happened to her 2,000 acres in Tasmania. In March 1814 she remarried, but was widowed again in May.

What became of Elizabeth Mackellar remains a mystery, but a younger sister, **Isabella Mackellar** (1798–1883), of whom there is an 1851 portrait by Thomas Bock, arrived in Tasmania in 1816 to marry Edward Lord's clerk, Richard Lewis, later a prosperous merchant.

Separate from Elizabeth Paterson's party leaving Sydney in March 1805 for Port Dalrymple on the *Buffalo* was 40-year-old **Mary Bowater** (c1765–1849). She had been sentenced to transportation for stealing in 1802, and arrived in Sydney, leaving a husband and son behind, two years later. Also on board the *Buffalo* was Thomas Smith. He and Mary may have met in Sydney, according to Irene Schaffer in her research paper 'A Remarkable Woman: Mary Bowater, Convict and Landholder' (2005), and been allowed to travel to Tasmania together. They married in Launceston in 1811, the first marriage in the north when Knopwood was able to travel there from Hobart. By 1823, Mary was a prosperous widow, very much her own woman. We catch up with her in the itinerary 'Around Longford' (p382).

Charlotte Badger and Catherine Hagerty's arrival at Port Dalrymple in 1806 was a little different from Ann Keating's in 1804 or Mary Bowater's a year later. Captain of the *Venus*, Marianne Collins' husband, Samuel Chace, was asked in Sydney to take on board two male and two female convicts, one with a child. The woman about whom we know most was **Charlotte Badger** (c1778–c1816) who was convicted at the Bromsgrove Assizes in 1796 of housebreaking, aged 18. Following her arrival in Sydney in 1801, she served five years of her sentence at the Paramatta Female Factory, there giving birth to a daughter, and making friends with Catherine.

The two were then assigned to settlers in Hobart and set sail; the voyage ended dramatically. At one stage Chace found his crew drunk and the two women dancing half-naked, Catherine by then co-habiting with one of the male convicts. On 17 June, Chace went ashore at Port Dalrymple. While he was absent, the ship was taken over, assisted by the women, and sailed off towards New Zealand, stopping at the Bay of Islands where the women, at least, disembarked.

Myth surrounds the women's part in the hijacking. One source claims that they incited the men to mutiny, another that Charlotte, dressed as a man, flogged the captain, armed herself with a pistol and raided another vessel for supplies and weapons. She was later described in the 'Wanted for Piracy' notice as 'very corpulent, with thick lips'. Catherine had fair hair and was described by Chace as a slut.

Catherine appears to have died in 1807, but Charlotte survived, and is known as one of the first white women to live in New Zealand, probably with a lesser Maori chief. The last sighting of her was in Tonga in 1816. Badger Head, to the west of the mouth of the Tamar in northern Tasmania, is said to be named after her – Australia's first woman pirate (p383).

Aborigines and Sealers

Over 100,000 seal skins were collected between 1800 and 1806 from the Bass Strait that separates northern Tasmania from the south coast of the mainland. Lyndall Ryan explains, in *The Aboriginal Tasmanians*, how at first, at the end of the eighteenth century, ships stopped and collected as many skins as possible; later, a dozen or so European and American men were left on the islands, until gradually there were hundreds of them. From 1804, sealers began to visit the north coast for repairs and sustenance, their visits coinciding with the Aborigines' summer pilgrimages to the coast for shellfish, seals, muttonbirds and other birds and their eggs. After about 1808, when sealing on a large scale became less economic to the entrepreneurs who sent out the sealers, a different type of straitsman became more prevalent; those who, in the Pacific Islands, were termed beachcombers, together with ships' deserters, some renegades, a few absconders, took over the reduced trade.

In 'Mannalargenna's Daughters' (2000), Cassandra Pybus, visiting that coast and describing what was to follow, wrote lyrically of early Aboriginal life,

Behind me in the sand dunes the evidence of those first people is everywhere. Any disturbance to the soft surface exposes a shell scatter from ancient middens, the accumulated detritus of Aboriginal summer feasts, when tribal groups would converge along the coast to consume yolla [muttonbird] eggs, abalone and scallops. Over many millennia they came – at least twenty thousand years – the same seasonal migration; the same ritual feasts.

Not any more.

Soon the Aborigines overcame their caution and began to trade, exchanging seal and kangaroo skins for tobacco, flour and tea. In 'Going Out and Coming In: Co-operation between Aborigines and Europeans in Early Tasmania' (1995–96), Maria Moneypenny suggests:

It would be a mistake to assume that, because Aborigines were prepared to accommodate Europeans, they saw themselves becoming part of the European world. It is possible that, initially, they saw Europeans as becoming part of *their* world, and that it was on that basis that they were willing to co-operate with the newcomers.

Agreeing with this, Lyndall Ryan explains what was to become increasingly a bone of contention between Aborigines and Whites, as well as making people today with any sensitivity squirm: 'This contact intensified when the Aborigines offered women in an attempt to incorporate the visitors into their own society. When the sealers reciprocated by offering dogs, the means were provided for mutually advantageous interaction.'

This exchange became formalised by 1810: members of the North East nation would gather in anticipation of trade. Some women would accompany sealers for a season, but the Aborigines might also abduct women from other nations to exchange. The function of the women was twofold: to catch seals, at which they were expert, and to provide sex.

Patsy Adam-Smith, an authority on the people of the islands, describes, in *Islands of Bass Strait* (1976), their seal-catching expertise:

An early chronicle has told how the girls divested themselves of their kangaroo hide frocks and smeared their body with oil from the blubber of the seals. They then slithered along the rocks and lay among the seals. They used their arms as flippers, imitating the seals' movements, at times even feigning sleep. When the animals were no longer suspicious, the women rose at a signal and clubbed to death as many seals as they could before the remainder escaped into the sea.

'It was the Aboriginal women', writes Stephen Murray-Smith in 1973, 'who, in giving up whatever freedom they possessed, made it possible for the sealers to find a form of freedom for themselves among the islands.'

Typical of the Aboriginal men involved in the trade between Aborigines and sealers was Mannalargenna from Cape Portland, leader of the Trawlwoolway band of the North East people. He oversaw negotiations and cemented deals by the marriage in 1810 of his 13-year-old daughter **Woretermoeteyenner** (also known as Watamutina, Pung, Bung and Margaret, 1797–1847) to a man he deemed to have similar status, George Briggs. Maggie Walter in her entry for Woretermoeteyenner in *The Companion to Tasmanian History* (2005, ed. Alison Alexander) describes her as the 'matriarch of many contemporary Tasmanian Aborigines'. She had five children by Briggs, one of whom was **Dolly Dalrymple Briggs** (c1810–1864) from whom many descend. Dolly is said to be the first child born to Aboriginal women by Bass Strait sealers but, as Lynette Russell points out, it is more likely that she was the first officially recorded, living child. Dolly's life and house are included in the itinerary 'North West Coast – Launceston to Cape Grim' (p384).

Diana Wyllie in *Dolly Dalrymple* (2004) suggests that Briggs 'abducted' Woretermoeteyenner and that she lived and worked with him for 17 years. Cassandra Pybus tells us that when sealing had begun to run its course, Briggs sold her to a fellow sealer for a guinea and disappeared. Diana Wyllie suggests it may have been a form of divorce.

With sealing less profitable, the men turned to muttonbirding, the trade in women became raiding parties by white men on Aboriginal groups and the theft of their women. The descriptions of how the women were abused and humiliated were recorded later, many of them by George Robinson, known with a certain irony as the 'Conciliator of Aborigines'. This is a typical account, included by Patsy Adam-Smith:

> 'Jumbo' told Robinson how she was taken from her people. 'She said Munro and others rushed them at their fires and took six, that she was a little girl and could just crawl, that she had been with Munro ever since. She said the white men tie the black women to trees and stretch out their arms (at this she showed Robinson how the men had tied them). And then they flog them "very much; plenty much blood; plenty much cry – this they do if the girl take biscuit or sugar."'

Jumbo's Cape Portland name was **Drummernerlooner** (Rumernalu, perhaps Bulyer, later, Louisa, c1811–1847–51). James Munro, a time-expired convict from Sydney, had four women living with and working for him in 1819; at one time he had six 'wives' by whom he had several children. He tended to be a leader among the sealers.

Similar accounts are used in articles such as 'Tasmanian Aboriginal Women as Slaves' (1976) by Anne McMahon and 'The Cross-Cultural Relationships Between the Sealers and the Tasmanian Aboriginal Women at Bass Strait and Kangaroo Island in the Early 19th Century' (2003) by Kay Merry.

The abuse is summed up coolly in an official report of 1815 paraphrased in *The History of Tasmania* (John West, first published 1852): 'The sealers customarily obtained such women "by force" and kept them "as slaves" to hunt and forage for them. "Several have from two to six women" whom they punished brutally if they did not "comply with their desires or orders".'

1. Louisa ('Jumbo') by John Skinner Prout, 1845,
courtesy of the Trustees of the British Library

Rebe Taylor, English-born author of *Unearthed: The Aboriginal Tasmanians of Kangaroo Island* (2002; 2008), tells of regular childhood holidays on Kangaroo Island when the family had settled in nearby Adelaide, and how she came to overlay childhood memories with later scholarly research. She writes with feeling of 'Lubra Creek',

> It was said that an Aboriginal woman had tried to escape by swimming across the Backstairs Passage from the mouth of the creek. On realising she couldn't make it, she turned back. There she was caught by Nat Thomas and beaten 'for her troubles'. These words have echoed through the generations of telling. Their shocking brutality could turn the serenity at Lubra Creek into an eerie silence.

It was one of many such stories she learned of sealing days.

Not surprisingly, the brutality was not confined to the sealers. One of Woretermoeteyenner's daughters by Briggs died in 1811 'after being thrown into a camp fire by Aborigines near Launceston', according to the encyclopaedia. This story is told in detail by an 1822 surveyor in Tasmania and quoted in full by Diana Wyllie in her biography of a surviving daughter, only to question its authenticity. There is some evidence, though, that infanticide of children with white fathers took place, often by their mothers. Jumbo is said by Robinson to have beaten her belly to abort, her sister to have burnt her baby. Dolly Dalrymple herself received the protection, from when she was a toddler, of Jacob and Bridget Mountgarrett in Launceston.

It should not be thought that all Aboriginal women, exchanged or abducted, indefinitely accepted the role assigned to them or forced upon them. **Tarenorerer** (Tarenore, Tarereenore, **Walyer**, Mary Anne c1800–1831), from either the Tomeginere (Tommeginne) or Plairherehillerplue (Plairleke-lillerplue) band of the North people, was abducted in her teens from the Port Sorell district and exchanged with a sealer for dogs and flour or, in another version, she went of her own free will after falling out with her people. By 1828, as Chapter 8 shows, she had changed her own life, and attempted to change that of her people (p113).

Lynette Russell introduces another element, explaining, 'I seek to find ways of understanding historical relationships with an appreciation for subtlety, complexity and uncertainty.' And there is more to it than a meticulous and experienced anthropologist/archaeologist/historian at work, for her father and his cousins were of Aboriginal and European descent and she describes the implications of that (I have elided three separated ideas that seemed to me best to sum up her point):

> Their maternal great-grandmother was a Pallawah (Aboriginal Tasmanian) woman who lived on the Bass Strait Islands and undertook sealing activities with her European 'husband'. I naively characterized her as a victim of the colonial encounter and, as I recall, even used the term 'slave'. This was seen as insulting by her descendants, who pointed out that such a characteriza-tion disempowered her and ascribed the status of 'slave owner' to their great-grandfather ...
>
> ... My analysis reveals that the domestic arrangements that emerged between Aboriginal women and newcomer men working in the sealing industry destabilized the colonial process and enabled the women to maintain their culture ...
>
> ... However, I must emphasize that simply because I choose to focus on the negotiated aspects of European-Aboriginal contact, I do not wish to trivialize or underestimate the degree to which these interactions were sometimes violent.

When pursuing the cruelty meted out by white men to Aboriginal women, we should not ignore, either, how many sealers themselves came to be brutalised, well described by Rebe Taylor, or what Joan Goodrick writes of Hobart in *Life in Old Van Diemen's Land* (1977): 'It was reported [in 1816] that the practice of beating wives had become so general that the assistance of the police was often needed.' Tasmanian society was, in the early days, pretty brutal and the sealers were without even the social sanctions that prevailed in Hobart. And this is an appropriate place to add Marjorie Tipping's view of the underpinning of that society: 'The transportation system, conceived in the minds of those who governed, and born of evil like the spirit that always denies, was still slavery of some magnitude. It could only have been invented by a nation of shopkeepers expecting good recompense for their investment.'

3 – 1805–10

The First Businesswomen

Maria Risley (1780–1859) arrived in New South Wales on 24 June 1804. Aged 22, she had been convicted at the Surrey Assizes in August 1802 of stealing from a dwelling house and sentenced to transportation. By early 1805 she was pregnant and living at the Paramatta 'Female Factory' in Sydney. Women convicts assigned to settlers were, formally, servants but they were often expected to provide sexual services as well. Pregnant convicts were housed in the factory until they gave birth. Since details of Maria's earlier life are scarce, you have to draw your own conclusions. The name of the father on the birth certificate of Maria's daughter Caroline, born later that year, was John Thompson.

By December 1805, Maria was living in Hobart assigned to Lieutenant Edward Lord. The almost mythical story, the only one we have to go on, provided once again by John Pascoe Fawkner, is that in April 1805, Edward Lord, 24 years old, ambitious nephew and then brother of a baronet and MP, travelled to Sydney from Hobart where he had been stationed since arriving with Collins, determined to return with a woman. He chose Maria from a line up at the Female Factory. 'She was at once let out, and he took possession of her,' wrote Fawkner, 'as truly for a slave to do his behests, or suffer for neglect or refusal.'

The story seems at first hard to square with another that Alison Alexander tells in *Obliged to Submit*. Early in 1805, Lord met the Lieutenant Governor walking arm in arm with Hannah Power and refused to bow to his superior officer. When called upon to explain himself, Lord replied that it was because Collins had his 'leman' on his arm. But this apparent hypocrisy needs to be seen in the light of Marjorie Tipping's suggestion that before Hannah became Collins' mistress on the *Calcutta* – which did not leave England for some time after its human cargo was loaded – she was Lord's. Did Collins play the senior and nudge Lord aside? What is more, Lord and Matthew Power were continually in dispute in Hobart and Collins tended to take Power's side.

In 1806, Maria opened a shop with the goods she and Lord had brought from Sydney in a building on what is now Queen's Domain owned by the harbour master, 48-year-old William Collins. (He was perhaps a relative of the Lieutenant Governor and was to marry 18-year-old **Charity Hobbs** in 1808.) Maria's shop was almost the first in the infant colony, certainly the first run by a woman, though, in the same year, widowed settler **Sarah Piroelle** (née Riebary, c1772–1828; 1827 m. Francis Cobb) was one of four licensed bakers – her husband, who died in 1804, was a confectioner. Maria's shop prospered, not only because it filled a need but because she knew how to charge in times of shortage. And its success was in spite of Maria's continual pregnancies. Elizabeth, born in August 1806, died within a few days. In 1808, another Elizabeth was baptised by Knopwood who, in his diary, called Maria Lord's 'friend'. Caroline was inoculated in December 1805 in the name of Caroline Maria Risaley, but thereafter, apart from on her marriage certificate, she was known as Miss Lord and treated as his child.

While Maria ran her shop, Lord, as an officer prohibited from trading, made sure that she was well supplied, particularly with rum; Knopwood discreetly suggests that Lord engaged in smuggling. Marjorie Tipping tells a slightly different story about Knopwood's drinking from the one I allude to earlier concerning his 'housekeeper' Mary McAuley. She writes that it was Maria Lord who sent to the pastor 'the gallons of porter that he demanded in the grubby little notes his messengers brought to her'.

By 1806, Lord was considered the 'largest stockholder in Van Diemen's Land'. By 1807, aged 26, he was second in command to Collins and he and Maria moved into a bigger house, Cottage Farm in Sandy Bay – 'the best house in Hobart', according to Collins' biographer. Lord and Collins were now friends with interests in common. And Lord and Maria were 'established leaders in the small business world of Hobart Town'. At the same time, Fawkner, who obviously looked askance at Lord, wrote of the couple:

> She was a worldly wise woman and set herself to make a home, and to provide means for herself, her children and her master. She foresaw that much money was to be made and how. She by the credit of her master, and her own tact and shrewdness obtained a quantity of goods and proceeded with these under her own control to Hobart Town set up a shop almost the first there, and continued for years trading successfully. He, rambling about and fooling away the money she made for the family.

It is worth remembering the size of Hobart between 1805 and 1807: the European population was 487, of which 327 were convicts, six emancipists, 49 free settlers and 99 civil servants and military personnel.

In 1808, Lord obtained a pardon for Maria (after six years of her seven-year sentence) and married her on 8 October. They were to have seven children, including Caroline, by 1819, all to be partly educated, or to spend time, in England, though Maria was never to return there. A portrait of **Emma Lord** (b1819) in the Tasmanian Museum and Art Gallery may give some idea of how her mother looked.

A month after their wedding, Maria briefly became First Lady of Tasmania when Collins went to New Norfolk – a developing area west of Hobart where an unexpected influx of convicts, former convicts and settlers from the subsidiary penal settlement of Norfolk Island was taking up residence. And now followed an awkward time for Maria as she became involved in two upheavals.

One of the Lords' assigned convict servants was **Mary Granger**. On 2 December, Mary was accused of stealing a tumbler. Edward Lord, acting Lieutenant Governor, had her put in the stocks on the parade ground. This arbitrary act was watched by a group of Mary's convict friends, including **Martha Hudson** (c1789–1830). Martha, who had come out from England with Maria Risley Lord on the *Experiment* four years earlier, approached Maria, asking her, as a former convict, to intercede with her husband. When Maria demurred, Martha laid into her, using 'language reflecting on Mrs Lord's former character'.

The Norfolk Islander James Belbin relates that Martha's contretemps with Maria arose when she called at Maria's shop. Belbin continued:

> Mrs R had a devilish nasty practice of ripping up old stories and telling more unpalatable truths than an ordinary woman could be expected to bear and kept up such a fusillade over the counter that the shop-keeping lady was at last fain to take cover in some distant Recess.

'Mrs R' could be Maria Risley Lord or Martha Hudson Roberts, which is what Martha later became; but it must be the latter, since the 'shop-keeping lady' is surely Maria.

As a result of this incident, Lord had Martha tied to a cart's tail, Belbin adds, 'stripped to the waist', and flogged the length of the parade ground, without a surgeon in attendance, until she was hanging in a faint. Where exactly Maria fitted into all that followed Martha's appeal to her and, indeed, what went before, we cannot know.

At that time of the day, George Prideaux Harris was leaving his mother-in-law's nearby house to return to his pregnant wife, Anne Jane. Harris was later to point out (for the main account of the incident is his) that it was only the second time in the colony's history that a woman had been subjected to such public punishment and, in the previous case, she had appeared first before a magistrate. As a magistrate and humanitarian, he approached Lord at the parade ground to 'learn what was going forward'. He asked if it 'was a civil or military punishment'. Lord, with his 'born to rule' disposition, reinforced by the military's predominance in the colony, took exception to his apparent interference and, after a fierce row, Harris was put under house arrest, accused of mutiny. Lord may well have continued to act with a heavy hand because, as Harris recorded, 'Some of the women who were spectators of the punishment rather loudly expressed their disapproval and threatened revenge.'

The row, now a scandal, ran on for some months; the last extant letter from Harris on the subject is dated July 1809. Collins took the side of Lord to maintain the authority of Lieutenant Governor which Lord had briefly been, refusing to intervene to smooth things over. Anne Jane, of course, took her husband's side and gave birth, after a difficult pregnancy, to a daughter, **Elizabeth Mary Anne Harris** (Eliza, 1809–1892), in early 1809, while he was still under arrest. The matter was then overtaken by events, though the family was permanently scarred: Harris was to die in October 1810. Anne Jane's sister Judith Hopley, and their mother, were dead by 1813. Anne Jane's remarriage appears in the itinerary 'Risdon Cove to Port Arthur' (p277).

The incident that provoked this long drawn out case provides a necessary corrective for what may, until now, have seemed like a relatively easy life for women convicts. Certainly there does seem to have been more latitude granted them, particularly in Tasmania where their number was initially few – by 1810 there were only 23 – than in later years when their number increased. Charlotte Badger shows, too, how convict women could become brutalised, while Maria Lord is an example of a young woman rising above her circumstances but perhaps careless of those whose past she shared.

It doubtless seemed important to Maria to dissociate herself from her former shipmates who were prone to land themselves in trouble. Rebecca Hobbs Ingle and her husband, John, had two former *Experiment* convicts assigned to them over the years. In 1805 **Jane Wilmot** (convicted at Hampshire Quarter Session in 1802) was accused of abusing Ingle and striking Rebecca. Any sentence passed was not recorded. In 1816, **Anne Ward**, who did not arrive in Tasmania from Sydney until 1813, was accused of stealing property of her master John Ingle and sentenced to wear an iron collar for a week and 'kept to hard labour in the gaol'. These collars could weigh as much as five and a half pounds.

As for Martha Hudson, in 1818, aged 29, she married William Roberts (a *Calcutta* convict) and, in 1830, by an awful irony, considering her brutal punishment in 1808, she died when the cart in which the family was returning from church overturned.

That 1808 row involving Maria Lord was now superseded by another in which her tangential role was even less of her making. On 29 March 1809, William Bligh arrived in the mouth of the Derwent on HMS *Porpoise*. Until a year previously, Bligh, known best for Mutiny on the Bounty, had been Governor of New South Wales, but he had managed to provoke another mutiny – known as the Rum Rebellion – one that led to him being deposed.

Bligh's first lady during his governorship – in the absence of his wife who could not face another move abroad – was his daughter, Mary, married to his aide-de-camp, John Putland. **Mary Bligh Putland** (1783–1864), is not generally given much space in the story of her father, but Shirley Seale in 'The Life of Mary Putland' (to be found on the internet) describes an interesting young woman: 'The sauciest, daintiest and most determined spitfire ever to preside at government house.' When the soldiers, with fixed bayonets, came on 26 January 1808 to depose her father, it was she – widowed two weeks previously – who physically attempted to detain them; as they pushed past her, trampling over her husband's grave, she set about them with her parasol, screaming the while. When after a year of house arrest Bligh refused to leave quietly for England, they came to detain him; Mary ran, in the midday heat, after the carriage taking him away, and insisted on sharing his detention.

Bligh eventually agreed to leave for England, but instead sailed for Tasmania. Mary arrived at Hobart very seasick and, according to her father, 'in a very weak state'; Collins immediately vacated his house for them, though Bligh only used it as his daytime headquarters. Bligh described it as a 'poor miserable shell, with three rooms, the walls a brick thick and neither wind nor water proof, lately built and without conveniences'. And, for a while, Collins and Bligh got on well enough, helped by the fact that Collins had some sympathy for the Governor in his predicament – though he refused in so many words to condemn the mutineers – and that Bligh, as the de jure superior, promised not to interfere with Collins' governing of Tasmania. But over the weeks and months, the relationship deteriorated, not only because Bligh did start to interfere and encourage the grumbling new arrivals from Norfolk Island to support him.

Among those arrivals was **Elizabeth Eddington,** a widowed settler who, with her late convict husband, had farmed a smallholding on Norfolk Island. She brought with her a 13-year-old son and a 15-year-old daughter, Margaret, who had already given birth to a son, now a year old. Since it was widely believed that the father was the governor of Norfolk Island, Captain John Piper, it was not surprising that when the Eddington family set off for Tasmania, Piper consigned them to Collins' care. (Piper is known to have fathered at least five children born to teenage girls – look out for Elizabeth Nichols Gibson, p138.)

Young **Margaret Eddington** (c1792–1822) went to live at Government House not long before the Blighs' arrival, but not apparently as a ward; she must have conceived at that time because she was pregnant during their stay and little **Eliza Eddington Collins** was born in December 1809 (d1869). Collins did nothing to conceal his pregnant mistress whom he described as 'most beautiful', Fawkner as 'good-looking', and some in Hobart as 'a common prostitute'. The term 'prostitute' was bandied about rather loosely in the early days of Australia; the Reverend William Henry of the London Missionary Society, for example, observed in 1799, 'It is as common, and in fact more thought of here for a man to keep a prostitute and have a number of children by her than it is for a man to have a wife and children in England.' This is one of the aspects that Kay Daniels explored in 'Prostitution in Tasmania during the Transition from Penal Settlement to "Civilized" Society' (1984); she noted that 'what has been called prostitution, was, in fact, co-habitation'.

When the relationship between Collins and Bligh ran aground and Bligh suspected something was afoot because the sentry outside his house was removed, he wrote to the Foreign Secretary with his various complaints, including:

> The sentinel being taken away, and the General Order … are two reasons for my quitting Government House, but a very principal private reason exists also, and that was – walking with his kept woman (a poor, low creature) arm-in-arm about the town, and bringing her almost daily to his office adjoining the house, directly in view of my daughter. As a military offence this was very great; but it was in a moral and civil point of view as great an insult as could be offered. He should not be surprised, therefore, at my avoiding it.

Bligh conveyed his daughter back to live on the *Porpoise*, though she was 'very little restored in strength from the effects of what she had long suffered'. Mary was doubtless in poor spirits after all she had been through in the previous year, but she may not have needed to be protected from the indelicacy of the moral situation, given the description of her as 'saucy'; she seems to have been quite tough. Bligh also gave orders that Nan Yeates' son by Collins, a midshipman on the *Porpoise*, be punished with 24 lashes.

Margaret Eddington was not Bligh's only moral target. Early on, Edward Lord was deputed to show him round the colony. Bligh objected not only because Lord had sided with those who deposed him. Bligh described Maria Lord as 'a convict woman of infamous character' and obviously not an effective front for her husband's forbidden business activities, nor those of her landlord William Collins. Bligh wrote to the Foreign Secretary:

> I found this place to be Sydney in miniature. All the indulgencies were put into the hands of a few to accumulate wealth, and the poor the sufferers.
>
> Upon what principle Colonel Collins has done it I know not; but a Mr Collins has been appointed Naval Officer at fifteen shillings a day, who in partnership with Lieutenant Lord, professedly keeps a shop, and engrosses the advantage of trade to the great injury of the settlement.

Kay Daniels, who started *Convict Women* (1989) with the story of Maria Lord, wrote of Bligh's antipathy to Lord and attack on his wife, 'his words need to be read in the context of his relationship with Lord rather than as an accurate account of Maria's virtue.' But Kay Daniels omits the corollary to Bligh's words: Philip Tardif suggests in the meticulously gathered records contained in *Notorious Strumpets and Dangerous Girls: Convict Women in Van Diemen's Land* (1990; CD 2004) that Bligh tried to countermand Maria's pardon.

During the stand-off with Collins – who was acting under the instructions of Governor Paterson of New South Wales, hurriedly transferred from northern Tasmania when Bligh was deposed – Bligh hove to further down the river, first off Sandy Bay, and then off Bruny Island, victualled by Norfolk Islander supporters, and tried to block the colony's shipping. Given Bligh's views on morality and his concern for his daughter's well-being, it is interesting to note that during that period, according to the historian KR von Stieglitz, 'Women from the Bruny Island tribes of natives were seduced by Bligh's men and in consequence a constant look-out had to be maintained against the vengeful attacks of their menfolk.'

The impasse came to an end when Lachlan Macquarie arrived as the new governor of New South Wales; at the end of December, Bligh sailed off to Sydney to put his case to him. While there, Mary Bligh Putland, then twenty seven, formed an attachment with 42-year-old bachelor Maurice O'Connell, commander of the regiment accompanying Macquarie and the Lieutenant Governor. Before her father left for England, she had accepted O'Connell's proposal – a marriage that was to give her a position from which to snipe at her father's opponents. O'Connell, influenced by his wife, was so disruptive that he and his regiment were eventually transferred to Ceylon.

Not all the newcomers to Tasmania from Norfolk Island were intransigent, uprooted as many of them were from land they had been farming there when it was decided to close the uneconomic settlement and not given what they regarded as their due in Tasmania. (Norfolk Island reopened as a harsh penal settlement in later years.) **Catherine Kearney** (c1769–1830) was well-received and was greatly to prosper. Her details have in the past been confused with those of Mary Kearley who came out with her marine husband on the *Calcutta* with Collins – a case of forcing jigsaw pieces to fit, even by such well-regarded writers as John Rowland Skemp in *Letters to Anne* (1956). Such confusion has been finally scotched by the assiduous researcher Irene Schaffer in her slender publication *Catherine Kearney: Dairy Farmer Hobart Rivulet 1808–1830* (2007).

Catherine was convicted in Ireland in 1791, aged 22, under the name Catherine Kearnon, and arrived at Port Jackson (Sydney) named McKearnan in 1796 with 232 other convicts, 70 of them women. She became pregnant on the voyage by Mathew Wilson who may have been a sailor on the *Marquis of Cornwallis*. He does not feature again, and the daughter baptised in Sydney died, possibly on Norfolk Island where Catherine was sent later in 1796. She lived there with Thomas Smith and had two sons. Then she lived with the convict Roger Gavin with whom she remained close over the years to come, and had another son in 1803. She gained her freedom by servitude in 1802, and most of the others originally sent to Norfolk Island as convicts had also completed their sentences.

She arrived in Hobart as Catherine Kearney, with two sons, nine-year-old William, and seven-year-old Thomas (both with her surname), on 1 March 1808 and, although recorded as being a 'seditious and troublesome character', was allotted a town lease of 1,677 square feet. This grant and her sons' name might, I surmise, tie in with the description of her in some sources as a widow who had been married to a man named Kearney. There, on the Hobart Rivulet, she began her dairy farm. Since it was difficult for Hobart to absorb and feed the 554 newcomers from Norfolk Island who had arrived in 1807 and 1808 (doubling the town's population to nearly 1,000) it is no wonder that Catherine Kearney, an indomitable sort of woman, was to prosper over the next 23 years. She features in the itinerary 'Around and About Macquarie Street' (p238) and she and her progeny in 'Risdon Cove to Port Arthur' (p275). She also has a vignette devoted to her in Chapter 4.

In 1810, Mary Hayes, Martha's mother, received a free pardon; she had served nine years of her 14-year sentence. During that time she helped the family finances by plaiting straw from local grasses and breeding dogs which were in great demand. Her puppies cost £10 each! Taking advantage of her new position – from assigned servant to her husband on his farm – Mary opened the Derwent Hotel in Central Hobart, at Number 1 Elizabeth Street; it soon became the best, sought after for inquests, auctions, raffles and weddings.

In 1813, Henry Hayes died and, in 1816, 54-year-old Mary, whom Marjorie Tipping describes as 'a nimble-tongued businesswoman' and 'intimidating', married widower William Stocker, 42, a former convict who had made good. (His wife Ann had died on board the *Calcutta* from England in an advanced stage of pregnancy.) The *Hobart Town Gazette* reported that the wedding was 'after a tedious courtship of *two* years'. Mary retained Henry's farm, though Stocker had it transferred to his name and in 1817 opened a much-frequented butcher's in Collins Street, presumably on the strength of it, as well as several other business interests. And although he was to build onto the Derwent, he was later to write that Mary had 'always managed the Derwent Hotel in Macquarie Street, from its first erection and for several years while [still] Mrs Hayes without interference since marriage'.

It is not surprising that Mary should have opened the Derwent; she had, we should remember, been the licensee of the Bell Inn in London before transportation. It is worth considering the difference between the teeming streets of London and the early years of Hobart experienced by the Hayes women and others from the same milieu.

The Derwent thrived in the Stockers' hands until 1838. The couple were so respectable that they had their own pew in St David's Church (later Cathedral), as did Mary's daughter, Martha Whitehead, and her husband. When Martha died in 1871, the *Mercury* headlined her obituary *The Last of the First*. That would undoubtedly have pleased her.

Mount Wellington and the First White Woman – 1810

Salome Pitt (Salona, 1792–1872) arrived in Tasmania in 1804, aged twelve. Her father, Richard, a settler member of Collins' expedition, had, rather adventurously, brought his three children, a daughter and two sons, with him, while his wife, Jane Tanner, remained in England with their eldest son. There is no evidence that Pitt brought anyone to help him look after the children; and Phillip was only five.

From what little we know of Pitt, he was knowledgeable about agricultural land. When Collins realised that the settlement must grow fresh vegetables, and that a government farm should be established, it was Pitt who suggested that the site chosen was a mistake and that the river flats alongside the New Town Creek offered much better soil and a larger area suitable for paddocks. His recommendation was followed, and the farm flourished, as well as providing a refreshing place to visit; Collins would take Hannah Power there with a picnic hamper. The Cornelian Bay Cemetery is now where once were government wheat fields.

Pitt's own farm was in the same area; indeed, the first in what was initially known as Stainforth's Cove. The family had at first camped at Sullivans Cove but for perhaps less time than many others. James Backhouse, who arrived in Hobart in 1832, wrote, it is assumed of the Pitts:

> I had some conversation with a person who was brought to the colony in 1804 ... At that period she was but a child. On landing [they] were lodged with some others under a blanket supported by sticks, near the place where the Commissariat-office now stands in Hobart Town, which at that time was covered with wood. After spending a night there, they were removed to the spot where the village of New Town now stands, and lodged in a hollow tree.

Salome's distinction in Hobart's early history is marked, at first prompting, by a couple of lines on the websites of both Mount Wellington and Tasmanian Women of Distinction: '1810 Salome Pitt (the first European woman) and an Aboriginal girl known as Miss Story climb the Mountain.' Salome Pitt becomes clearer the harder one looks – but Miss Story is totally elusive.

Because of what was to happen later to the Aborigines of Tasmania, to those of Aboriginal descent today it is almost inconceivable that there should ever have been good relations between the communities. My informant, and her informants, are highly sceptical that 'Miss Story' was Aboriginal. She may well have been black but, if so, from elsewhere. There were certainly blacks in Tasmania's colonist history who were not Tasmanian Aborigines. But it is worth another look at early relations.

The potential after-effects of the Risdon Cove Massacre cannot lightly be dismissed; and there was increasing ill-feeling on the part of the Aborigines as the colonists vied with them over game on their traditional hunting grounds. Food for the colonists was so scarce that they depended largely on game. The first white settler was killed by Aborigines in 1807. But the encroaching onto Aboriginal territory by permanent settlement, except in the environs of Hobart, was yet to come. The tit for tat killing was in the future, as were the horrors of the 'Black War', Flinders Island, and Oyster Cove. Sealers were already exchanging dogs and flour for Aboriginal women, but that was on the north coast.

That quotation from Backhouse about the Pitts ends 'Here [in New Town] they were first visited by the Aborigines, with whom the children were often left, and who treated them kindly.' The substantial Pitt farmstead – which still stands (see 'New Town' itinerary) – was to be built on the New Town Rivulet which leads directly to the base of Mount Wellington.

There is some evidence that relations between colonists and Aborigines were relatively friendly in the early years covered by this chapter. According to 'The Kearley Family', 'The Kearleys and other farmers left flour, bread and blankets out for the use of passing Aborigines', once they had their property after 1813.

Robert Knopwood becomes almost endearing from two entries in his diary about life at Cottage Green in today's Battery Point:

At 8 am a native girl about 17 was in my garden, the first I ever see near me. She ran away some small distance and then stopd. I went to her, she wanted some fire which I got for her, and some fish and bread, but returning to get some more fire she ran off.

And again, as late as 1815:

At 7 a party of natives came to my house. They went into the kitchen; two women, 3 girls and two boys. I ordered them some bread and meat and gave them potatoes; they roasted them. In the eve I took them a doll which my little orphan girl Mary Mack had dressed and shewd them it.

They thought it was one of our children that was dead, and the poor old woman took it in her arms and kept it. (When their young children die they carry it about with them.)

Elizabeth de Quincey, in *The History of Mount Wellington: A Tasmanian Sketchbook* (1987) tells the story of the climb of Mount Wellington taken by Salome Pitt and 'Miss Story' in a little more detail than the bald internet statement: 'It was during this year [1810] that Salome, with her brother Philip and Miss Story, climbed to the top of the Mountain by following the New Town Rivulet and probably going by the same route taken earlier by Dr Bass and later by Humphrey and Brown.'

The hollow tree in which Backhouse mentions Salome lodging may well have had something to do with her Mount Wellington adventure for the mineralogist Adolarius Humphrey (whose wife Harriet Sutton features in the 'New Norfolk' itinerary, p308) describes the 'largest trees in the world' on the side of the mountain when he climbed it in 1804. He added of the night he spent there,

We slept in the hollow of one, which hollow measured eleven feet in diameter. This is but a small tree; one near the Camp measures 44 feet [13.4 metres] round at breast height. Mr Brown told me that he had seen a Tree lying on the Earth, large enough for a Coach and Six to be driven along it; it measured upward of 70 feet [23.5 metres] in circumference.

I thought I had tracked down the original source for the story of the women's climb – at least the one that Elizabeth de Quincey used. In the State Library of Victoria is a rather insubstantial note to the surveyor and recorder of his life and times in Tasmania, James Calder. I have detailed my search because it has been a bit like chasing a Will-o'-the-wisp, particularly where Miss Story is concerned. The note reads, with Calder's inserted * and added information:

In reply to your note, Mrs Bateman says it is fifty years* as nearly as she can recollect since she with her Brother Phillip Pitt and a Miss Story a native ascended the mountain by way of New Town[.] [T]here was no track at that time[.] Mrs B was then Miss Pitt first white Female who ascended the mountain. Yours truly Geo Bateman

* The above note was received 27 March 1870. Mr G Bateman called on me next day and said that when he asked his sister in law about her trip up Mt Wellington, she was too ill to recall her recollections of it, but that she afterwards remembered it was in 1810.

For all its lack of substance, and that 'native' could mean white woman born in New South Wales, the letter from Salome's husband to Calder establishes that Miss Story was not white – Salome was the first, and therefore the only, white female then to climb Mount Wellington.

Earlier I had come across what seemed like a puzzling version of the story – without the source being clear – in David Davies' *The Last of the Tasmanians* (1973). But I have since tracked it down, almost word for word, in the more personally researched *The Last of the Tasmanians* (1870; 1969) by the nineteenth-century historian of the Aborigines, James Bonwick. He writes of 'a venerable old lady who came to Hobart in 1804, with her parents' and says that she 'gave me much information of her early days'. She told him how

She had heard people express their fears of the wild Blacks, and her mother gave her a caution about venturing far into the bush, because she might be killed and eaten by cannibals. ... A bold and enterprising child, she had long wished to have a nearer gaze at the magnificent Mount Wellington ... Prevailing on her little brother to accompany her, she set off one day when her parents were absent and trudged through the bush till she was lost amidst the dense foliage of the mountain gullies. There she fell in with some Aborigines. The spirited lassie exhibited no alarm, and found herself kindly treated by the sable throng. She furthermore told me that when a girl she had often met them in the Camp, as Hobart Town was then called, and that they were always quiet and well conducted.

The main factual problem with this account is that Salome's mother apparently never went to Tasmania; perhaps the warning was by letter. The language is of its day, and no doubt hyperbole was used to scare children into obedience, but sources do not suggest that cannibalism was a feature of Tasmanian Aboriginal culture. And surely Salome, aged 17 or 18 in 1810, would not be thought of as a 'child', even in Victorian days. What is more, she had lived for six years in the rough-hewn early days of Tasmania, undoubtedly in charge of the household and her younger brothers. Though I rely on Bonwick as a source here and there, his account of Salome and Mount Wellington does suggest the need for caution. (Bonwick was hired to Tasmania as a teacher, arriving in 1841 with his (nameless) wife, also a teacher, and stayed, having set up their own school, until 1850. Some of his sources were contemporary, though he wrote after they had left the colony.)

What a different account there is of when Salome was friends with **Sally Nash** (1800–1879). Sally, who features in more detail in the itinerary 'Risdon Cove to Port Arthur' p278), was born on Norfolk Island. Her grandson, the family's biographer, wrote in *That Yesterday Was Home* (Roy Bridges, 1948):

I fear Miss Sally and her bosom friend Salome (pronounced Slome) Pitt, had set bright young eyes on young Mr Wood at his shipyard near the mouth of the rivulet. I like to picture them so – the pretty girls, the handsome lad, the flutter of muslins and ribbons and the little sunshades in the breeze off Frederick Henry Bay.

That imagined day was before 1818, when Miss Sally and John Wood married. Salome Pitt, Elizabeth de Quincey tells us, became a school teacher and was 'kindhearted and firm; she fed her young pupils bread and honey, but was not above despatching a smart box over the ear if a reprimand was required'. In 1830, aged 38, she married John Redman Bateman who became the Harbour Master at Launceston and they had two sons.

To learn of Salome's marriage is then to encounter a rather delightful description of her, and how society was to change over the years. In 1834, when the Cowie family – more detailed in Avoca in the 'Midland Highway' itinerary (p344) – had just disembarked in Hobart, 21-year-old **Georgiana Cowie** (later Oakden, b1813) wrote in her diary following a tea party with the Grants and the Batemans,

> Mrs B tho' not a refined woman is very chatty and amusing and having left England when quite a child knows nothing of many things, which to us are familiar objects as the sun and the sky. For instance, it is rather strange to hear a person asking the definition of a damask rose.

Four years after Georgiana's slightly mocking impression of Salome, Jane Franklin, Governor's wife, visited the north, assisted by Salome's harbour master husband; she gives us a harsher opinion: 'Another individual was Mrs Bateman ... a common & cross-looking person.'

The de Quincey account ends: 'Salome was the first white woman to climb Mount Wellington, and remembered the event until the day she died in 1872, when nearly eighty years of age.' Sadly for us, the ascent of Mount Wellington by the first white woman was the essence of the accounts, whichever is nearer the reality, and not the identity of Miss Story. She is still an enigma waiting to be unravelled. I have another inconclusive go at that in Chapter 8 (p100).

The End of the Beginning – 1810

Lieutenant Governor David Collins died suddenly on 24 March 1810; he was 54. His death was unforeseen and, although he had a cold, it became a subject of speculation then and later. One story has it that Macquarie, briefed by Bligh about Margaret Eddington, sent him 'a very severe letter' and that it 'dropd out of his Hand and he fell on the Floor and expired a short time after'. There is also a suggestion that Macquarie was to recommend Collins' recall. But, according to Collins biographer, John Currey, that letter had arrived a few days earlier, and Collins was recovering well from his cold. His doctor, Matthew Bowden, was visiting him almost socially when he appeared to have a fit and died almost instantly.

Edward Lord, second in command, was summoned and, later that day, or that night, Lord, Bowden and Knopwood went through the dead man's papers, ostensibly searching for a will. Gossip had it that they burned some papers and that Lord took charge of others. William Maum, an assistant to the commissariat who had arrived with Bligh, informed the Land Commissioners years later that 'Mr ____ and Mrs ____ went over to Government House, and in the Governor's office, for purposes best known to themselves, destroyed by fire all the official documents.' That report is assumed quite reasonably by Marjorie Tipping, who has written in detail about Collins' death, to refer to the Lords, and she makes something of it – 'Some documents were said to have been unfavourable regarding land they hoped to acquire.' But Maria Lord's part is not substantiated by historians who have written extensively about her – such as Kay Daniels and Alison Alexander; indeed, Alison tells us that Maria gave birth to a son in Sydney early in 1810, by implication at around the time of Collins' death. And, although the story of burnt or removed papers (without Maria's part) gained credence – Bonwick writes, 'I was so unfortunate as to discover no papers relative to the first six years of settlement' – and conclusions were drawn, Currey suggests that some burning of papers on such an occasion was not uncommon and that no significant body of Collins' documents went missing. Edward Lord may well have been capable of anything underhand, but Maum can be assumed to be *parti pris*. In Knopwood's diary, however, there is a gap from 1808 to 1814, termed 'suspicious' – though it is easy enough for volumes of diary to go missing without an ulterior motive.

Edward Lord now became acting Lieutenant Governor and remained so between March and July; and Maria was, therefore, in theory, First Lady, though she apparently remained in Sydney for those months. Lord applied to London to be appointed to the vacant post, without success – Macquarie did not care for him. But this was by no means the end of Maria Lord's story. She has appeared here as the first Tasmanian businesswoman but, because Lord was officially prohibited from trade, and her enterprise has been seen as his, her ventures officially begin in 1813. And, while her entrepreneurial progress went from strength to strength, their relationship was, in the early 1820s, to founder in a public and unpleasant manner. Both these strands, and her death, are developed in the next chapter and touched on in three itineraries: 'Around and About Macquarie Street' (Ingle Hall, p239), 'Bothwell' (Priory Lodge, p334) and 'New Norfolk' (Stephen Street Cemetery, p304).

But what of Margaret Eddington? Currey suggests that she was not in the house at the time of Collins' death. Alison Alexander, in *Obliged to Submit*, quotes another version with some scepticism:

Directly after the Governor fell back in his chair his relative ran out of the apartment for assistance, but in the hurry and excitement of the moment he entered by mistake a room that was used as a nursery, where a beautiful female was discovered in the maternal office of nursing an infant. It was not a moment for ceremonious observances, so hastily acquainting her with what had just happened, he entreated her assistance. But the suddenness of the disclosure was too much for her, and an outburst of sorrowful feeling far too poignant for a mere attendant or domestic revealed the secret of her connection with the domiciliation at Government House, and a single inquiry from the lieutenant elicited the fact that the child was the offspring of her intimacy with the Governor.

Lord arranged an elaborate and costly funeral for Collins, attended by much of Hobart, including eleven marine wives and their four servants arrayed in new black gowns, petticoats, stockings, European shoes, silk and leather gloves, bonnets and even handkerchiefs. Normally, as the Kearley family account suggests, marine wives 'probably wore working clothes very similar to those issued to convict women – a brown serge jacket and petticoat (skirt) over a shift (loose fitting undergarment dress/petticoat) and a hat or cap to cover their head'. The mourners also included 600 settlers, their wives and families, and numerous female and male convicts. But Fawkner, who managed to profit financially from clothing the mourners, commented that 'Not much appearance of grief was shown for the Governor except it was by his young mistress who lost her position as Governor's Lady.'

Financially, Collins was found to have nothing to leave his wife, Maria, in England, let alone his young mistress and her two children, one of them his. Margaret found herself destitute, back in 'a mean hut' with her mother and brother. Edward Lord and William Collins did raise a small sum for her.

Whatever Margaret's feelings for Collins, she now had only her looks to depend on. Knopwood was a frequent visitor to her – and there was gossip about it – but by 1811 she had married handsome and prospering George Watts, a former convict who became a sheep stealer and bushranger; but he died in 1817. Margaret meanwhile supplied meat to the commissariat, perhaps as a result of her husband's activities. In 1819, now the owner of 900 sheep, she married another former convict, Charles Connelly, publican and farmer. She died three years later, aged 29, and there were 300 mourners at her funeral. Alison Alexander describes those years in more detail, but I am still puzzled by the number of mourners, which was a large proportion of Hobart's population.

By each of her lovers and husbands Margaret had a child. **Mary Watts** (Maria) was baptised in 1812 but probably born in 1810 or 1811 (d1884); **Ann Connelly** (Annie, 1819–1888) was baptised nine months after her parents' marriage and probably born earlier. Margaret's four children were left orphaned in 1825 when Connelly died during a visit to England, but her three daughters continued to manage and went at some stage to the select Ellinthorp school ('Midland Highway' itinerary, p336). Knopwood writes about them mixing in Hobart society – Eliza Eddington Collins attended a party with Maria Lord's daughter, and was delivered to school by Maria. All three girls married well. Eliza was granted land, and owned cattle before her marriage which is described in the itinerary 'Around Longford' (p353).

Martha Hayes, Maria Lord, and Margaret Eddington were all, in their unconventional ways, the First Ladies of Tasmania – Martha and Margaret so very young at the time. They may not have been from the top drawer – indeed, all three had convict backgrounds – and they may not have contributed to creating a moral climate, but they were determined survivors who played a part in the economic growth of the raw and struggling colony. And the early years illustrate how, in spite of the negative aspects of transportation, for some women it was a way out or, as Marjorie Tipping expressed it, 'Their

2. Mary Watts Lord, from Alexander, *Obliged to Submit*

standard of living was much superior to the pauperism and poverty that most had known.' And even those who left no story to be told here created families, many of which continued to develop not only Tasmania but also respectable descendants of which live there today. It was not until the late twentieth century, though, that they were able to feel proud of that heritage.

In a personal address in Hobart in 1995, Marjorie Tipping told of her second visit there from her home in Melbourne in 1940: 'At that time few Tasmanians would talk openly about the early days. I could not understand their diffidence, because, whatever might have been the past for some they were beautiful people who were enjoying then what seemed to be paradise.'

Alison Alexander published *Tasmania's Convicts: How Felons Built a Free Society* (2010) just as my book was completed. In it she explores, through interviews with many descendants of convicts, the past and the present. Those bits personal to her are the best. She starts the chapter 'Out in the Open': 'As I was growing up, our family had no idea that any of our ancestors had been convicts.'

Part Two – 1810–37

4 – Governors' Consorts

Mrs Murray, wife of the Lieutenant Governor of Tasmania, is not mentioned in the diary that Governor Lachlan Macquarie kept when he and his wife Elizabeth visited Tasmania from Sydney in November 1811. And it had all started so well. In August 1810, a couple of months before he died, George Prideaux Harris wrote home to his mother about the new man, Captain John Murray (thought to be a better bet than Edward Lord), and Mrs Murray (her first name remains apparently unknown):

> Captain M has brought his Wife with him which makes it very pleasant to the Married Officers of the Colony, whose Ladies in Govr Collins's time never went to entertainments at Government House – Several splendid ones have been given by the new Commandant – He is a very pleasant Gentlemanlike Man and Mrs M a most accomplish'd Woman – they are indeed an acquisition in these remote parts.

But Robert Bayles, who stayed around longer, wrote of the couple in his 'Secret Diary':

> The man I am speaking of has long been launched into the Vortex of Dissipation and a contemptible ambition of excelling his Companions in ostentatious and licentious Practices & he brought a kept Miss with him whose taste was congenial to his own for every fashionable folly & the most profuse extravagances.

It would be easy to think that Bayles, apparently a convict though I have found nothing more about him, had an axe to grind, but the situation, described in *Obliged to Submit* in the sort of detail that makes the reader put exclamation marks in the margin, went from bad to worse. Murray was spendthrift with the colony's limited funds, not to mention dishonest, harsh with its citizens, and drank to excess. Mrs Murray, if such she was, eventually took a lover. The Lieutenant Governor, catching them *in flagrante*, fought a duel with Lieutenant Wright, Inspector of Public Works (in which neither was hurt). As a result, the Murrays separated.

Next Mrs Murray went to live with Judge Samuel Bate whom Murray had once imprisoned, and whom Macquarie described as 'much addicted to Drunkenness and low company, totally ignorant of the Law and a very troublesome, ill-tempered Man'. Or that is how Mrs Murray's move generally appears. But Bate's biographer puts a different complexion on it, suggesting that she took refuge in his household. There is some backing for the lack of a sexual liaison: on 19 September 1810, Samuel Bate, widower, had married by special licence **Matilda King** (d1867), single woman; a daughter had been born to the couple the previous year. Whatever Mrs Murray's motive, the situation was bound to exacerbate the tension between Murray and Bate, and provide Hobart with yet more gossip.

It was at this point that Governor Macquarie decided to visit Tasmania to judge for himself what was going on. But not only does he not mention Mrs Murray – who was presumably not then acting as First Lady – but neither does he even hint at his disappointment regarding her husband's stewardship. The visit was apparently all sweetness and light.

I read Macquarie's diary (which you can download from the internet) before I knew anything about Mrs Murray, so it is aspects of his wife, **Elizabeth Macquarie** (née Campbell, 1778–1835), that intrigued me then. Imagine this gently nurtured woman arriving in the Hobart of 1811, however different Sydney itself may have been from her brother's estate in Scotland where she lived until she married Lachlan Macquarie in 1807. She was 29, he 46. Two years later, he was appointed Governor of New South Wales. There they found a colony torn apart by the Bligh years which demanded much sensitiveness on Elizabeth's part. She also concerned herself with the welfare of Aborigines and women convicts.

3. Elizabeth Macquarie, by Richard Read,
1819, courtesy of the Tasmanian Museum
and Art Gallery

Elizabeth's first Tasmanian test came on the customary rough voyage to Hobart, after which her husband wrote that she was 'a most excellent brave sailor'. Once on the island, she travelled widely with him, on horseback; her reward was to have a myriad places named after her (in 1811 and on a later visit in 1821). What is now the town of New Norfolk was for many years Elizabeth Town; Macquarie wrote: 'The situation appeared to me so eligible and so remarkably well adapted for a Township, being Twenty miles only from Hobart Town, that I have determined to erect one here for the District of New Norfolk, naming it "Elizabeth-Town", in honor of my dear good wife.' The town itself was part of Macquarie's policy of setting up a network of small, stable communities.

He named today's Hobart suburb of Glenorchy after Elizabeth's home in Scotland. In the midlands he named a river after her in 1811 and then, in 1821, he wrote: 'Having determined on establishing a Township on the North Bank of the Elizabeth River, I have named it "Campbell-Town" in honor of Mrs Macquarie's maiden name.' Then there was Elizabeth Street in Hobart, Elizabeth Creek in the midlands, and Elizabeth Valley. Perhaps he feared there were too many Elizabeths, for he now turned to her second name, writing: 'About half a mile further on [from Anill's Ponds], and to the right of our Track is a very beautiful and singular round Hill, with the top perfectly flat – hitherto called Donn's Battery – but which I have now named "Mount-Henrietta" in honor of Mrs M.' And then, 'Travelling for Ten miles through Epping Forest, which is all very poor bad soil, to the open Plains; which I have named Henrietta Plains ... These Plains are by far the richest and most beautiful we have yet seen in Van Diemen's Land.' (The plains are now Powranna, see Midland Highway (p351).) Henrietta Valley followed. To top it off, he recorded in 1821: 'The fine Tract of Land on the West side of the Jordan, I have named (after Mrs Macquarie's mother's Family Estate) "Stonefield Plains".'

Perhaps the most beguiling of all these namings was Tin Dish Rivulet which came about when a man sent by Elizabeth to get a dish of water accidentally let it slip. On their second visit, perhaps feeling that was a bit of an in-joke, Macquarie changed it to Sorell Springs (in honour of the latest Lieutenant Governor) – which is a pity!

It is worth noting that Elizabeth Macquarie was not necessarily a passive monument in all this naming. She had taken to Australia a collection of architectural books which were used in the designing of Sydney buildings, and it was she who planned the road named after her which ran round the Government Domain there.

Then there is the delightful vignette which reflects equally well on both Elizabeth Macquarie and the dairy entrepreneur Catherine Kearney, though I fear it may be apocryphal – unless it should have referred to the 1821 visit. The story is much repeated but seems to originate in John West's *The History of Tasmania* (1852; 1971):

> It is said that Mrs Kate Kearney, when the high price of her butter was complained of by the governor, stopped the supply. Mrs Macquarie, curious to see this independent milk-seller, paid her a visit: when she entered, the old lady received her very graciously, and asked after the health of the

Governor, and added, 'how is the young Prince?'. The story goes, that she received a valuable grant of land for this well-timed compliment.

Unfortunately, young Lachlan was not born until 1814. Although Catherine was only 42 in 1811, it was not uncommon to be called old at 40 and she had had a hard life, even by early nineteenth-century colonial standards. However, she continued to do business profitably for many years, and did not die until 1830, aged 61.

On their arrival in Hobart, Macquarie had written: 'Capt. Murray conducted us to a very pretty little Cottage of his own to take up our residence in, the Government House being much out of repair.' He does not mention that Murray had bought it with government funds, nor was he to know until later what happened to the cottage. He did, however, resolve to replace Murray, but kindly, by finding him another job. Then Mrs Murray moved back in with her husband and Macquarie wrote to him:

> The late very extraordinary and highly unjustifiable Step you have adopted, of taking back and living with your wife, after being yourself the Publisher to the World of her shameful and abandoned conduct justly forfeits the good opinion, respect, and friendship of not only myself, but also of all your Brother officers and other Persons here …

Mrs Murray was sent away again. When Knopwood's diary reopens in 1814, they are both in the colony, but living apart. Soon Mrs Murray is living with merchant and speculator Thomas Kent, fairly new in Hobart. The best moment for the gossips must have been when Kent bought 'the pretty little cottage' from Murray and the vendor pocketed the money, which belonged to the government. Eventually Kent and Mrs Murray left for England; there, learning of her husband's death, she is assumed to have married her lover. A few years later, the couple brazenly returned to Hobart, dining with Knopwood. Kent died in Sydney in 1832; the erstwhile Mrs Murray appears to have been dead by 1846.

All Mrs Murray seems to have contributed to the development of Hobart through her antics over the years is a little light relief. Alison Alexander is rather kindly disposed towards her, as a representative of women who could not survive in that society without the protection of a man; she writes: 'She certainly took up with a succession of unsavoury men, although it must have been difficult to find any savoury men in Van Diemen's Land at this time.'

Meanwhile, **Mary Geils** (née Noble) had arrived with the new, but acting, Lieutenant Governor – Andrew Geils - in February 1812. 'Not a breath of scandal has ever been recorded about Mary Geils', observes Alison Alexander. 'She was respectable and well-behaved, the first governor's wife about whom this can be said.' Governor's wives had yet to create a role for themselves, but Mary did have seven children to bring up and probably educate. Geils himself was, however, another disappointment to Macquarie. By February 1814, the family had gone – Geils' regiment ordered to Ceylon. The most lasting impression Mary Geils leaves us is of a grieving mother, for when four of her sons were sent home from Ceylon to school in England, the ship sank and they were drowned.

The new Lieutenant Governor – Thomas Davey – his wife, 46-year-old Margaret, and daughter Lucy had arrived a year earlier, in February 1813. Davey was an eccentric, not always lovable. **Margaret Davey** (1867–1827) was rather badly treated by her husband. This is best illustrated by the fact that he set off for his post in Tasmania without telling her. But, learning of it by chance, she and Lucy reached the ship before it sailed. Margaret had little luggage; Davey's was in another ship which was taken by American privateers. It would have been hard for her to cut a dash in Sydney where they first spent three months and where Macquarie found that Davey was a 'frivolous buffoon'.

Margaret and Lucy settled down in Hobart in a Government House that Davey described as a barn. Davey was not only eccentric and thoughtless but also drank even more than Murray; he was constantly falling down and injuring himself, presumably nursed back to health by Margaret. In spite of his failures, Davey was liked and the couple started to hold balls at Government House, at the first of which, in 1814, Lucy Davey, and the Misses Geils were almost the only single women present. At this time, Knopwood drew up a list of 'ladies' in the colony – these included Martha Hayes Whitehead (erstwhile mistress of John Bowen) and Maria Risley Lord (former convict).

Davey was often away from home on his duties, so the life of mother and daughter would have been quite constrained, though there was a country property at Coal River (part of Davey's compensation for his lost luggage) they could repair to, and Knopwood notes pleasant outings. Carrington is included in the itinerary 'Risdon Cove to Port Arthur' (p275).

Davey reported that 'During the time myself and family were representatives at Van Diemen's Land, Religion, Virtue, Morality and Example was the order of every Succeeding Day.' Macquarie, describing Davey's shortcomings, commented: 'What renders this Debasement the more gross and offensive is that He is a Married Man, and his Wife and Daughter, who live with him, are both very amiable and respectable.'

Late in 1816, Macquarie told Davey he was to be replaced. The Daveys retired to Carrington but, by 1820, the farm had to be mortgaged and, the following year, it was sold. Davey sailed for England leaving his wife and daughter without financial provision. Happily, Lucy had met Dr James Scott and, when they were married in 1821, the Macquaries were once more in Tasmania. Macquarie wrote: 'I attended the Marriage of Miss Davey and Dr Scott this day – and gave her a grant of 1000 acres of Land for her own exclusive use.' One source says that he gave her away. Davey died in England in 1823, without returning to his wife. But she had her daughter comfortably married and living at Boa Vista, though she herself died just after the house was completed. Lucy's life, and that of the women, including convict servants, who followed her, feature in that house in the itinerary 'New Town' (p264). Lucy named her second child Elizabeth Lachlina in honour of her benefactor.

Once again, Alison Alexander gently probes the reasons for a governor's wife's actions, or lack of them: the difficulties for such a woman to leave such a husband. Margaret Davey was obviously not a Mrs Murray; neither was she a Martha Whitehead, a Maria Lord, nor a Margaret Eddington – they met their vicissitudes head-on.

You really would have thought that, by the time Lieutenant Colonel and Mrs Sorell arrived at Government House in March 1817, Tasmania was due a family there to set an all round good example. And William Sorell was a good and much liked governor and obviously loved charming and very pretty Louisa and their children (another was on the way). Unfortunately, she was not his wife, and that only too soon became common knowledge. Louisa is now known not as Mrs Sorell, but as Mrs Kent, for she was still married to her husband of seven years, Lieutenant William Kent (nothing to do with Mrs Murray's Thomas Kent).

Louisa Matilda Cox (bc1787), daughter of a general, married William Kent of the 21st Light Dragoons in 1804; by 1807 he was stationed at the Cape of Good Hope and there the couple became friends with Lieutenant Colonel William Sorell, Deputy Adjutant General of the Forces. He even became godfather to one of their children. The Macquaries met him when they stopped at the Cape on their way to New South Wales, but would have known nothing about his private life. Leonie Mickleborough suggests they would also have met Louisa Kent and would have known who she was when they welcomed Sorell in Sydney on his way to Hobart.

Just before he left for South Africa, Sorell had married Harriet Coleman, an apparently illiterate woman, by whom he already had seven children, the oldest of whom was seven. By the marriage of their parents, they became recognised as his and, while he was in South Africa, Harriet received half his pay and letters of introduction to eminent men who could protect her in case of need.

In 1811, Kent was either ordered back to England, or returned for personal reasons. Within weeks Sorell followed, and very soon he and Louisa were living together. Funds to Harriet were cut off and she found herself in the workhouse until one of her protectors intervened. This pattern was to be repeated over the years. Sorell's treatment of Harriet makes you wonder about his character, as much as about their odd marriage – though, as in all such matters, there are two sides to the story, and their different wishes for their children's future may have contributed to the estrangement and its repercussions.

On losing his wife, Kent had initiated proceedings against Sorell – 'for criminal conversation with the plaintiff's wife' – but these did not bear fruit until 1816 when Sorell resigned his commission. But his abilities were respected and he and Louisa still had friends and family in high places – which is how he came to be appointed to Tasmania – a post well away from England.

To begin with, Louisa was accepted as Mrs Sorell and the family was installed in Birch Castle on Macquarie Street, the castellated home of Sarah and Thomas Birch, much to be preferred to the unsuitable barn of government house. Birch Castle was to become the Macquarie Hotel and features in the itinerary 'Around and About Macquarie Street' (p245). In due course, the Sorells moved into the newly renovated Government House on the site of today's Franklin Square; it was demolished in 1859 and also features in that itinerary (p242).

On 5 July 1817, Lieutenant Kent was awarded £3,000 compensation (Sorell's salary was £800 per annum). It did not take long for the London newspapers to arrive in Hobart. Settler Janet Ranken wrote to a cousin in Ireland: 'Governor Mr Sorell is married, but he left his own wife in England and brought another man's wife with him in her stead.'

Anthony Fenn Kemp, whom we first met with his wife Elizabeth Riley in the first days of Launceston, and who had followed Paterson when he left to become Governor of New South Wales, was involved against Bligh in the Rum Rebellion. Having returned to Tasmania as a merchant in 1816, he leapt at the chance to do down Sorell with whom he was in continuing dispute. Circulating the law report from *The Times*, he poured venom. By 1818, he was writing to Macquarie: 'Lieutenant-Governor Sorell is publicly parading Mrs Kent about in the Government carriage, and introducing her to the military and civil officers as Mrs Sorell ...'

Jane Sorell, writing an account of three generations of her family in *Governor, William and Julia Sorell* (c1994) suggests that Elizabeth Kemp – mother of 16 children – may have 'helped to fan her husband's indignation'. His second letter to Macquarie asked: '... as a family man and father, whether you would not feel indignant to see a woman living in adultery, paraded about the garrison by the highest authority, in an equipage purchased at Government expense, to the confusion and shame of all married women and to the evil example of the rising generation'.

Hobart society was, of course, in a quandary: the men tended quite happily to visit the popular Governor and his beautiful partner; Knopwood even referred to Mrs Sorell in his diary – not something he did for every non-wife – and the judge advocate escorted Louisa into dinner. And Louisa certainly continued to travel with Sorell round the colony. But 'respectable' women did feel obliged to stay away from Government House.

Macquarie was used to Kemp's attacks on authority and pleased at the way Sorell governed Tasmania, so took little notice, but Kemp continued his campaign, writing to the authorities in London. When a commissioner was appointed to look into the system of transportation, it was asked to include Sorell's private life. In 1823, when Sorell was relieved of his post, the citizens of Hobart rallied round him and tried to get the decision rescinded. Their leader was Anthony Fenn Kemp.

On the arrival of Sorell's successor in May 1824, Sorell and his family moved to the government cottage in New Norfolk – Turriff Lodge features in the 'New Norfolk' itinerary (p302). A month later, Sorell, Louisa and seven children sailed for England after seven years in the colony. One child was Kent's daughter. Louisa and Sorell had had nine children by this time, the youngest three of whom died in Hobart – one of the three, born and died in 1822, was named Lachlan Macquarie Sorell, which suggests the two men's regard for each other. Macquarie and Elizabeth had visited Tasmania again the previous year before leaving New South Wales in 1822, after twelve years.

When Sorell died in 1848, after a peripatetic 25 years or so, Louisa was granted administration of his estate in the name of Louise Matilda Sorell, widow. So they married at a date unknown when their spouses died. Sorell may have suffered professionally from their relationship, but it is fair to assume that both were sustained by their long relationship which happily survived such buffeting.

Sorell's eldest son by Harriet, also William, arrived in Tasmania before his father left and was warmly greeted and found a suitable post. In 1825, he married the Kemps' beautiful, if tempestuous, daughter Elizabeth. By 1838, **Elizabeth Kemp Sorell** (1808–1900) had abandoned her husband. In what must have seemed somewhat of an irony to Hobart society, as well as her father, she took her children to Brussels, apparently to further their education, dumped them on her father-in-law and Louisa Kent who were living there, and ran off to India with Colonel George Deare, who had commanded a regiment in Hobart from 1835. Deare and Elizabeth married in 1861 when they learnt that young William Sorell was dead. They had meanwhile had three daughters and a son. Elizabeth and William Sorell's daughter, Julia, and her daughter, Mary, feature in the 'New Town' itinerary (p266).

'Very proper, a devoted wife and mother,' writes Alison Alexander of Eliza Arthur, 'a supporter of charities to help unfortunate women, with no criticism possible of her except that she was a little dull, she was a model governor's wife.'

Eliza Orde Ussher Arthur (née Smith, 1796–1855) was born into a senior army family stationed in Jamaica and, upon marriage to Lieutenant Colonel George Arthur in 1814, accompanied her husband to his eight-year posting as Lieutenant Governor of Honduras where she had five surviving children. In Tasmania from 1824, she was to create a pattern for Governors' wives who were to come after her – excluding her successor, Jane Franklin, who was to try and take the post to a much superior plane. George Arthur, a Calvinist Evangelical, with his wife faithfully at his side, was, during his 14-year governorship, to lick the colony into a rather different shape from that which he found. Tasmania – made a separate colony from New South Wales the year after the Arthurs' arrival – was to be seen by the Home government primarily as a gaol; with this Arthur fully agreed. He was something of a martinet, not to say autocrat and, under his governorship, convicts and Aborigines were to suffer, the latter fatally. During the most notorious of his actions, the so-called 'Black Line' of 1830, he set off to direct operations, leaving Eliza not only in labour but also ill. She did not recover well, but four more children were born in Tasmania – a total of 13 births in under 20 years. Eliza Arthur and the four Governors' First Consorts who preceded her following Collins' death, with their Governors, create a chronological framework for the rest of Part II.

5 – Women Convicts

When Mary Lawler arrived as a convict from Ireland in 1803, Tasmania would have seemed like the end of the world, and there were many vicissitudes to be overcome, not necessarily to do with her convict status. But, by 1805, when Maria Risley came over from Sydney assigned to Edward Lord, whom she was to marry three years later, it was already a land of opportunity for a woman convict with determination.

By 1810, there were only 23 women convicts in Tasmania. The flogging incident of Martha Hudson of 1808 has shown that it was not all a bed of roses, but the years 1803–13 have been termed an 'open prison'. Lyndall Ryan, in 'From Stridency to Silence: The Policing of Convict Women 1803–1853' (1995), tellingly describes it as a period of 'exile' and explains that it was a response to the industrialisation of Britain that began in 1750 and reached a critical point in 1815.

When 200 women convicts arrived from Britain via Sydney on the *Kangaroo* in 1813, and 60 more from Ireland in 1814, an inevitable change took place with the increase in numbers. Now there began a systematic transportation of convict women from Britain (still via Sydney) and Lyndall Ryan describes the period 1815–43 as 'a coherent system of forced domestic labour'. The end of the Napoleonic Wars had brought their own problems of labour and poverty. This was the time of assignment of convicts as servants, often straight off the ship – though, even then, there was a certain flexibility: for some men, servants and wives were interchangeable. West, writing in 1852, described that first arrival:

> Proclamation was made and the settlers were invited to receive them. There was little delicacy of choice: they landed, and vanished; and some carried into the bush, changed their destination before they reached their homes. Yet such is the power of social affections, that several of these unions yielded all the ordinary consolations of domestic life.

The arrivals of the *Kangaroo* took place under the governorship of Davey who rather enjoyed the company of convicts. The later historian James Fenton, in *History of Tasmania* (1884), paints a cruder picture; he claims that when Sorell arrived in 1817 he found:

> The convict women were supplied with food and clothing, but no place of shelter was afforded them for the night. This led to a degree of depravity almost unparalleled in the annals of British colonialisation. Government officials were living in open concubinage with the convict women. The rite of matrimony was seldom observed; and it is said sales of wives were common. One wife was sold for 50 ewes; another for £5 and a gallon of rum; a third for 20 ewes and a gallon of rum.

Sorell made an effort to tackle such disorder but, as Kirsty Reid points out, 'The impact of his measures was limited necessarily by the example he himself set.' Under Arthur from 1824 moral laxity was firmly clamped down on and assignment, and punishment, became formalised.

The later years, 1844–53, were a darker period, described by Lyndall Ryan as 'probation/incarceration'. Many of the 12,806 women convicts who arrived in Tasmania during the 50 years of transportation there came in that later period, after 1840, when transportation to New South Wales had ceased; that was just over half the total number transported to Australia. The probation system, Lyndall Ryan explains, was an answer to the political and social unrest in Britain and Ireland, and to new ideas about female penal reform. Mrs Bowden, whom we meet in Chapter 11, was particularly experienced in that field.

Lyndall Ryan's terms were taken up by Kay Daniels in her comprehensive study *Convict Women* (1998) which followed Philip Tardif's magisterial *Notorious Strumpets and Dangerous Girls* (1990) – the title of which encapsulates much of historical attitudes towards women convicts. Tardif attempted to record the details of the 1,675 women transported to Tasmania before 1830 (Chapter 11 shows that many more arrived after that date) and these were later issued on CD which I have not found very easy to use, but which is easier and cheaper to get hold of than the original tome.

Kirsty Reid's more recent *Gender, Crime and Empire* (2007) provides an extension of the social and political context. For those wishing to follow particular women, there is also a slew of books, often taking the women from one particular ship and giving details, usually brief, of their lives before and after arrival in Tasmania. (On the internet, too, you can download lists of the women who travelled on a particular ship.) Or the book may concentrate on a group such as the women from Ireland. Perhaps the most arresting account, told in 'Convict Women of the *Amphitrite*' (EM Finlay, 1991), is of a shipload of 102 convict women and twelve children who did not reach Tasmania. The *Amphitrite* foundered in a storm off Boulogne in August 1833 and all were left to drown by those responsible for them. Although the women were buried in a common grave in Boulogne, the author has meticulously resurrected them all – and there is a more concrete monument erected and inscribed to them too by the British residents of the French town. This was by no means the only foundering of a convict ship and loss of life over the years. In 1835, the *Neva*, on its way to New South Wales, went down in the Bass Strait with the loss of 144 women convicts, nine free women and 55 children. (The same year, 127 male convicts on the *George III* were drowned in the d'Entrecasteaux channel – again, avoidable deaths.)

Here I shall only give a broad sweep of the years 1810–37 and introduce you to a few illustrative women convicts about whom we know more than the bare facts. It is worth noting that, from the convict records, we know more about particular working class women who could not, or did not, record their own lives through letters and diaries than we do about those in Britain who did not run foul of the law, and thus about life more generally on the margins of Georgian and Victorian society.

History does not relate what Hannah Fawkner made of her daughter-in-law Eliza Cobb. At first sight she may well have been taken aback, but her son, 26-year-old John Pascoe Fawkner, had been in considerable trouble since we last met the family, and Hannah may well have been glad to see him settle down.

Fawkner tells how, in November 1818, he went down to the Hobart dock armed with a marriage certificate, and having made wedding arrangements with Knopwood, to choose himself a wife from the 30 women due to arrive on the government brig *Elizabeth Henrietta* (named after Mrs Macquarie who had been on an adventurous journey in it). Fawkner suggested that his future wife was an immigrant, whereas in fact he was meeting a convict ship and women convicts in the early days had to wait a year before they could marry (this time was later extended to three years, and permission had to be given).

Having squared the master of the brig, Fawkner took off with the prettiest of the women but, either meeting a friend who inveigled her away, or a burly man who knocked him down and relieved him of his prize, he was left bereft. He returned to the dock to find the last woman disembarking. Eighteen-year-old **Eliza Cobb** (1800–1879) had been convicted the year before at Middlesex for child stealing. Employed as a maid in a grand house in Kensington, she had persuaded a little girl to hand over her four-month-old baby brother. She was illiterate, badly pock-marked and with a cast in her left eye, but she and Fawkner, to whom she was assigned, went off happily together and, by 1819, were in Launceston where, in the itinerary, we shall catch up with them at the Cornwall Hotel and marrying (p368). Eliza was to have as successful and apparently fulfilling a life as any woman convict in the Antipodes – except that she never gave birth to her own child.

The first female convicts to travel direct from Britain to Tasmania arrived on the *Providence* in December 1821. Of the 103 women on board, only one died, which was regarded as a good voyage. Among those women was **Eliza Callaghan** (also Thompson, later Batman, 1802 or 1804–1852). She was Irish, with brown hair and eyes and five feet two and a half inches tall. In London in 1820, described as a servant, she was convicted for passing a £1 counterfeit banknote and sentenced to death, commuted to 14 years' transportation. It may not have been her first such offence; she had got in with a bad lot.

The paperback cover of the novel *Eliza Callaghan* (Robert Close, 1957) shows Eliza as a bit of a bombshell. The lurid details of her life awaiting trial and transportation and on board ship, as well as thereafter, encourage that image. It is the sort of novel that you are ashamed to rather enjoy – get it second-hand on the internet and keep it for reading on the beach. A newspaper headline on publication called it 'scurrilous' and a descendant was 'horrified by its inaccuracy'. Quite a lot of serious research has been done on Eliza because of whom she married but there are still gaps for the novelist, and this one does convey rather well the life of women convicts and Hobart of the period; Eliza even nips into Maria Lord's shop.

On landing in Hobart, Eliza was assigned to John Petchey, a former convict, by then keeper of the Town Gaol with a reputation for cruelty. His wife since 1814 was **Mary Skelhorn** (also Skelthorn or Skelton, 1796–1843) who, aged seven, arrived with her mother, Anne, a free settler, as part of the Collins expedition – her father, a cutler, died on the voyage, and her mother's remarriage, to Corporal William Gangell, was the first marriage ceremony in Hobart. Anne died in 1816. The novel's details about Mary Petchey are inaccurate.

The last official record of Eliza as Petchey's assigned servant is of a third offence. For the first, in March 1822, being drunk and disorderly, she was sentenced to gaol for a week, made to wear an iron collar for that period, and twice sit in the stocks for two hours. Three months later, she was sentenced to the stocks for three hours for absconding and remaining absent all night. She did the same in 1823, and was on a bread and water diet for a week with daily stints in the stocks.

'The Rise and Fall of Eliza Batman' (Max Cameron, 1985), a sober and scholarly account of Eliza's life, notes that when Petchey died in 1850 he was supposed to have left a widow, 'Elizabeth née Callaghan'. But there is no record of such a marriage, Eliza's later marriage takes no account of it, and Mary Petchey did not die until 1843, when the widower married Elizabeth Ayton.

Petchey's position as keeper of the gaol, and Eliza's punishment therein, illustrate not only the power possibilities in that particular family but show that Eliza, by her acts of rebellion, was not easily cowed. Her acts, though, were typical of women in her situation, as was the punishment they provoked. She appears to have been with the Petcheys for just over a year and probably helped look after their two small daughters, **Ann Petchey** (b1816) and **Sarah Ann Petchey** (b1819, later Russell). Eliza was assigned to a couple more families, then she absconded for good. The rest of her rather romantic story, with its tragic ending, is found in the 'Midland Highway' itinerary (Kingston, p345) and 'Launceston' (St John's Church p376). She (as Eliza Batman) and Eliza Cobb (as Eliza Fawkner) were, by chance, to become united in a quite other venture than transportation – the founding of Melbourne.

The same year that Eliza Callaghan arrived in Tasmania, 1821, and started on her path of kicking against authority, an institution was set up to punish convicts who would not knuckle under. The first penal settlement was established at Macquarie Harbour on the remote and inhospitable west coast of the island. Its reputation, until it was closed in 1833, was of the most brutal – the narrow passage into the harbour was known as 'the gates of hell' – and, while it was mostly recalcitrant men (re-sentenced absconders) who were sent there, among the first batch of convicts who were landed in January 1822, after a long and arduous journey, were eight women.

Irene Schaffer, in one of her many invaluable research papers, 'The Forgotten Women Convicts, Macquarie Harbour 1821–1826' has not been able to fathom why these particular women should have been sent there: 'Their crimes when they arrived in Hobart were not worse than many under sentence at the time.' And she writes of Grummet Island where the women were first landed, 'It could almost be compared with being shipwrecked on a desert island' – for those first arrivals there was not even proper shelter to begin with. Later they were moved to Sarah Island, the main penal settlement.

Rather than tell the sorry stories of all the women, I am choosing the two youngest. **Margaret Morgan** (c1801–1832) was given seven years at Antrim in 1817, aged 16, for picking pockets. She arrived in New South Wales in 1818 and Hobart in 1820. Irene Schaffer describes her life of crime in Tasmania:

> From her conduct record she was to sit in the stocks for 6 hours for neglect of duty at the hospital in February 1821. In May 1822 she was sentenced to wear an iron collar for 7 days for raising a scandalous false report prejudicial to the character of John Anderson, Overseer at Macquarie Harbour. By 1823 she was back in Hobart and continued to commit all sorts of crimes, even breaching the Dog Licensing Act by having a dog without a license. Poor Margaret died at the Female House of Correction in 1832, aged 31 Years.

Mary O'Hara (bc1802) was a year younger than Margaret when she was sentenced in the same place, at the same time, for the same crime, though Irene Schaffer presents no evidence that they were part of the same 'gang'. They travelled on the same ship to New South Wales, when Mary was only 16, with all the privation that meant over 13,000 miles, and then in the same ship to Hobart, another 1,000 miles. There is nothing to explain Mary's arrival at Macquarie Harbour. By 1823 she had left and was a servant near Hobart; in 1826, a felony case against her was dismissed. The only other information available is that she had a child in Launceston in 1844.

At Macquarie Harbour, when the women's conduct was deemed good, three of them lived as housekeepers to the commandant, pilot and superintendent of convicts; one as a nurse in the hospital, and three to wash shirts for all. But minor infringements resulted in the stocks; for more serious ones, they were sent to Grummet Island (initially called Small Island, for obvious reasons), or to the mainland to cut grass. As they waded ashore from the launch, the icy water in winter would be up to their hips. The men convicts, it is said, were too weak to carry them – under the circumstances, a surprising detail of expected gallantry. For more severe misdemeanours, such as the occasion, told in more than one version, when some marines were seen near their accommodation ('exhibiting unsoldierlike conduct') five of the women were sent off in a whaleboat to an ocean beach beyond the Heads, 35 miles from the settlement. Supplied only with an old musket, rations for a week and a cooking pot and blankets, they were marooned there to collect oyster shells for lime burning. As Margaret Morgan's details show, the convict women had problems with the overseer which may, I suspect, have led to false accusations against them.

Thomas Lempriere, who, with his wife Charlotte and family, arrived at the settlement, as Commissariat Officer in 1827, and stayed until it closed, wrote in *Penal Settlements in Van Diemen's Land* (1839): 'The grossest immorality could not fail to reign in a place where there were no means of keeping the sexes apart ... Numerous were the cases of immorality, but we will pass them over with the silent disgust they merit.' Charlotte Lempriere appears again in the itinerary 'Risdon Cove to Port Arthur' (p281).

Eliza Cobb Fawkner and Eliza Callaghan Batman have survived the anonymity of history-telling common to so many women because of whom they married, though they deserve to be remembered in their own right. The same is true of **Norah Corbett** (or Cobbett, 1800–1840).

Poor Norah, described by one secondary source as 'an insane convict harridan', never managed to get her life together as did the two Elizas. As an assigned servant to Lucy Davey Scott at Boa Vista, New Town, in April 1828, Norah was twice found intoxicated, and Miranda Morris, in *Placing Women* (1997), once to be found on the internet, describes her as suffering from 'suicidal depressions'.

The story of Norah's continuing descent is told in most detail in Sarah Bakewell's *The English Dane: A Story of Empire and Adventure from Iceland to Tasmania* (2005) – a biography of Jorgen Jorgenson, briefly met in Chapter 1. There he was witness, as a seafarer, to the very early days of Hobart. Thereafter, he had a fantastical interlude in Iceland, ended up in London and in 1826 was transported to Tasmania where, granted his ticket-of-leave the following year, he became an explorer, journalist and capturer of bushrangers.

On 1 December 1828 near Campbell Town, he captured part of a gang – William Axford and his girlfriend Norah Corbett, who had absconded from where she was assigned 'disguised in male attire'. Norah, an illiterate milkmaid from County Cork, had been in Tasmania since the previous August, transported for theft. The five foot four inch 28-year old, with dark brown hair, brown eyes, and a scar on her right arm, was placed, as a government witness, in Jorgenson's charge, to protect her from revenge and deliver her to court. With him, she was installed in an inn as a decoy. The *Hobart Town Courier* noted in March 1829:

> Serious fears have been entertained here during the last two days that Jorgan [sic] Jorgenson, and a most important witness, named Norah Corbett, under his charge, will be put to death by some murderous wretches denounced by this woman. Her important disclosures render her life of immense value to the community.

Not surprisingly, Norah and Jorgenson became intimate – Sarah Bakewell suggests that Jorgenson, then nearly 50, fell in love with Norah at first sight and asked her to marry him within weeks. During the lead up to the trial and beyond; indeed, for the rest of their life together, he tried to protect her from drink, usually unsuccessfully. When drunk she became violent. One source describes her rather nicely as 'genial yet eruptive'.

Just before the trial, Norah was got at and plied with gin; Jorgenson lost his temper with her and nearly ruined the case. In the end, the trial was successful and there were several convictions, though the sentences were not long. Norah was then assigned to a series of households in country areas, to keep her out of mischief, while Jorgenson continued to apply to marry her. She was given her ticket-of-leave at the end of 1829. The rest of her story is told in three itineraries: 'New Town' (Boa Vista, p264), 'New Norfolk' (St Matthew's Church, p304) and 'Midland Highway' (Ross, p337).

In 1828, Female Factories (otherwise known as Female Houses of Correction), not only as places prior to assignment or reassignment but also of punishment for women convicts, became a substantial feature of the system when the Cascades brewery was bought by the government for that purpose. Previously, there was a makeshift house in George Town in the north and a few rooms attached to Hobart Gaol on the corner of Macquarie and Murray Streets in Hobart (where Eliza Callaghan was confined) (p244).

By 1853, there were five major court yards accommodating 1,000 women and 175 children at Cascades 'in a bog at the bottom of a deep sunless valley'. In those days, the Factory was not part of Hobart, as the area is today, not only to remove women from temptation but also to protect Hobart's men.

The Factory held several classes of convict: assignable, petty crime/probation, serious crime, and hospital and nursery. It was often overcrowded until it was expanded, holding as many as 500 women at a time. Pregnant convicts were sentenced to six months in the crime class following the weaning of their babies. Infant mortality was, not surprisingly, high, caused by too-early weaning, overcrowding and lack of hygiene. In 1833, 44 out of 103 children died. Those who survived were sent to the orphan school, one side for girls, the other for boys, set up in 1828 and called at first the King's Orphanage and, after 1837, and Victoria's ascent to the throne, the Queen's Orphanage. The girls' half is described in more detail in the 'New Town' itinerary (p262). The women then deprived of their children became reassignable. New arrivals to Hobart with children were similarly separated.

In spite of the earlier prevalence of co-habitation and apparent acceptance of it, women convicts were punished for perceived immorality, such as pregnancy outside marriage. The women, generally, were seen as little more than 'common prostitutes'. Kay Daniel's chapter in *So Much Hard Work: Women and Prostitution in Australian History* (1984) explores all the complexities of the subject, including the work of other, particularly feminist, historians. Aspects and examples of exploitation and necessity arouse anger, pity and sympathy in today's reader but one of them is almost heart-warming:

> Brothels and disorderly houses (often cheap lodging houses) seem to have played an important part in convict sub-culture providing shelter for absconding prisoners and a place for social as well as sexual activities … Among the information given by prisoners to all newcomers at the Female Factory was a list of those disorderly houses which would receive absconders; as one convict woman said 'Women hear in the Factory at what houses they can obtain liquor on the sly and those houses at which shelter can be obtained when they abscond.' … It seems that places referred to as

brothels had ... a less specialized function than the term now conveys – they were an integral part of convict/poor working-class culture.

Often women were punished for being found in brothels and, therefore, 'on the town' when, in fact, they may have been using the establishment as a refuge or community centre. In *Richmond Gaol* (1997) Geoff Lennox suggests that while women 'on the town' might be selling sex, the term could also mean 'living on your wits'.

Other brothels were less homely. In 1831, Launceston Hospital was found to be little more than a 'Bawdy-house' where women convicts were concerned, not run by them but by male hospital doctors and administrators. This came to light, as Kay Daniels recounts, when 21-year-old former milliner and dressmaker **Jane Torr** (1811–1852), a convict patient, was found outside looking decidedly dishevelled. Kay Daniels sums up her case: 'Jane Torr, for whom a stolen gown meant transportation for seven years, earnt money and spent it on clothes. There was no other way but through prostitution that an assigned female convict could achieve such affluence.' It is worth noting that prostitutes were often accomplished pickpockets. Ellen Reece told a court in Salford in 1837, 'I have lived entirely by prostitution and plunder – seven times as much by robbery as by the hire of prostitution.' Jane Torr married William Garner in Launceston in 1841. She was 30, he was seven years her junior; they had three children.

There are countless stories to be told about the inmates of the Hobart Female Factory. Ann Solomon was one of the first to be sent there and I choose her to represent the many, not only because you can read about her life in some detail in Judith Sackville-O'Donnell's *The First Fagin: The True Life of Ikey Solomon* (2002), but also because her case illustrates the vagaries of the assignment system, and confinement not just as punishment but as social control as well.

Dressmaker Ann (Hannah) Julian, daughter of an Aldgate coachmaker, married Isaac (Ikey) Solomon in 1807. He owned a jewellery shop that was a front for receiving stolen goods, and in 1810 he was arrested for pickpocketing and sentenced to transportation. Before that could happen, and after four years in the hulks, he escaped and returned to London, setting up as a fence and pawnbroker. In 1827, he was arrested again for theft and receiving, escaped again, and fled to the United States.

Ann Solomon (c1787 or 1790–1877) was arrested, it can reasonably be suggested, in his stead, and sentenced to 14 years' transportation for receiving stolen goods. She arrived in Hobart in 1828, aged about 40, only five feet tall, and illiterate, with the four youngest of her six children. Three of them were sent to the King's Orphanage so that she could be assigned to Richard Newman, a police officer, and his wife, **Sarah Newman**, a woman who had followed her soldier husband throughout much of the Peninsular War and lost two children in the process.

Phillip Tardif tells a rather different story from Judith Sackville-O'Donnell, under the heading 'Lives Less Typical' in *Notorious Strumpets and Dangerous*

Girls, which, again, concentrates on Ikey, as does his source (*Prince of Fences*). He says that Ann was a barmaid at the Blue Anchor Inn, Petticoat Lane, London, when she and Ikey met and married and that they then 'formed a formidable partnership and by 1825 controlled a chain of London brothels and clearing houses for the laundering of stolen property'. Perhaps 'brothel' here has the wider meaning that Kay Daniels suggests for those in Hobart. This version does not see Ann as the fall-guy.

Whatever the provenance of her funds, and her past, Ann, together with her unweaned son, seems to have been able to live with the Newmans more as a lodger than a servant. Ann's record in Tardif notes that 'according to another servant she was not required to work, Mrs Newsman doing "all the drudgery of the house"'. (Presumably the servant belonged to another household, or she would have been doing the drudgery.) Meanwhile, Ann's two adult sons arrived in Hobart and opened a shop with goods they had brought from London. All seemed to be well until Ikey, learning of Ann's situation, also turned up in Hobart. He was recognised by a woman convict who reported him – but he had committed no crime in Tasmania and Governor Arthur had to send to London for instructions. The Newmans took advantage of Ikey's ambiguous situation and demanded a more substantial sum from the family than five Solomons and their effects in their household warranted. Not surprisingly, there was a falling out. Ann's version of events tells part of the story:

> It was after some money transactions took place between Mr Newman and my Son John that Mrs Newman struck me – she quarrelled with me about the money affairs – Mr Newman never struck, or quarrelled with me or ill treated me in any way whatever – all my differences were with Mrs Newman – Mr Newman was never present on any occasion but the last, nor was he even then present when I was *struck* by Mrs Newman – he was in another room – my Son John saw it – I was not comfortable at all at Mrs Newman's which was wholly owing to her Temper and Habits as I believe.

Ikey complained to the magistrate about Mrs Newman's behaviour; Newman retaliated with a letter of criticism of Ann since Ikey's arrival that enabled Arthur, unable to move against Ikey, to have Ann removed from the Newmans and, on 13 November 1828, imprisoned in the women's prison on Murray Street (p244). There, far too many women slept in two unventilated rooms. A few weeks later that closed down and she was transferred to the new one at Cascades, together with 99 other women and 33 children. Ikey, with his eldest son as his front, campaigned for Ann's release, initially without success, though the three younger children were freed from the orphanage.

It is notable that the biography gives us no details of what Ann underwent in the Factory – though Ikey did call it a 'place of oblivion' when he explained to the authorities that his wife's absence was 'to the utter discomfort and bereavement of your unhappy Memorialist and his six children'. Did she have her hair cut, or her head shaved? Did she work in isolation, and exercise in silence? Did she sleep on a hammock in a locked dormitory without windows, to prevent escape or, as another description of the Factory has it, was the dormitory 'extremely damp and unwholesome ... the beds [mattresses?] being placed on the floors ... in the water which oozes beneath the walls of the building'? Occupation consisted of picking and spinning wool and laundering.

Given her financial resources outside the Factory, Ann may have been able to supplement the inadequate prison diet even, at a price, with luxuries such as tea and sugar, tobacco and liquor. If she was punished, it would have been bread and water. There was a long gap between meals and that and lack of essential vitamins and minerals led to increased tension. This spilled over into riot in February 1829 when inmates called out to soldiers outside who began throwing parcels of food to them. These were confiscated, leading to confrontation and finally the use of burning materials, spreading fire and smoke. Women not involved feared for their lives and, afterwards, all the women, guilty or innocent, were punished.

Details of a sub-culture in the Female Factories, sometimes called the 'Flash Mob', suggest that some women convicts were hard-core; and you can imagine the sort of hierarchies and bullying that would prevail. The question of whether or not Ann Solomon might, in such a climate, suffer from being Jewish, can only be left hanging; on the other hand, Ikey's London reputation, or even her own, might have protected her.

Arthur remained unmoved by Ikey's appeal, and it was only after the intervention of important people who guaranteed a bond offered by Ikey that, on 17 March 1829, after four months' confinement, Ann was released and assigned as servant to her husband.

That was by no means the end of the story – one too involved to detail here. Briefly, while Ann worked in a shop Ikey had meanwhile set up, and was assigned to her son, Ikey was sent to England to be tried, returned to Hobart as a convict and was incarcerated in Richmond Gaol and Port Arthur (where, ironically, I note that Newman had been posted as Chief Constable). On his release, Ikey accused Ann of being unfaithful and they quarrelled violently. Tardif's version has Ann actually living with George Madden. Ann was sent once more to the Female Factory, for 'disorderly conduct', in July 1835. A visit her daughter Nancy made to Governor Arthur had no effect; nothing daunted, she wrote to the authorities: 'I am in the most constant and anxious suspense on my unfortunate mother's account, she is very ill and unless something is *immediately* done for her [her] present pitiable situation will I fear destroy her.' The colonial secretary minuted on the back of the letter: 'This certainly seems to be a hard case because Mrs Solomon cannot agree with her husband ... she is to be kept in the factory ' – and Ann was released in September.

In November she was granted her ticket-of-leave, a conditional pardon in 1840, and her Certificate of Freedom in 1841 – though this did nothing to quell the domestic ructions. In 1850, when Ikey died, Ann moved to Melbourne, where she died aged 87.

Ann's circumstances were mostly unenviable, but they do not compare with those of **Mary McLauchlan** (c1801–1830) – perhaps the most notable inmate of the new Female Factory – and not only because she is an example of a sexually exploited convict woman.

Mary had married a weaver, William Sutherland, in Scotland and had two daughters by him. Her daughters (three and five years old) probably did not accompany her when, in April 1828, she was convicted in Glasgow of theft by housebreaking, sentenced to 14 years and transported.

Following her arrival in Hobart in January 1829, she was assigned to Charles Ross Nairne and his wife, **Katherine Nairne** (née Sirling, m1825). Mary, who was literate, described herself as servant of all work and a plain cook. In August, Nairne charged her with leaving the house without permission and, when Mary counter-charged that she had not received the 'proper quantity of clothing', she was remanded to the House of Correction until Mrs Nairne could give evidence (Katherine Nairne had her third child in 1829, which may have caused the delay). When Mary's complaint was dismissed, she was sentenced to six days on bread and water in the cells and six months in the crime class – there she may have had her head shaved, though it was rare after 1829. She would then be reassigned out of Hobart.

Before her imprisonment, however, Mary had formed a sexual attachment, or someone had seduced, perhaps even raped, her. It was said to be a gentleman whose name she, apparently, never divulged and, in April 1830, in the Factory, she gave birth to a boy. She strangled him and attempted to dispose of his body in a lavatory. The historian Richard Davis suggests that this act was 'an hysterical post-parturient attempt to hide the evidence of her shame from her legitimate family'. But the *Hobart Town Courier* of 24 April 1830 reported: 'While pregnant she was often heard to wish that the infant she bore might not be born alive, and there appeared no other perceptible motive to incite her to the dreadful murder, on the little innocent offspring of her own bosom, than that of malice towards the father.'

Today Mary's action might be viewed differently but, then, she was charged with infanticide or, as the record has it, 'the wilful murder of her male bastard child', and sentenced to death. Governor Arthur and his council debated her fate but, as Lindy Scripps suggests in *Women's Sites and Lives in Hobart* (2000), 'Arthur was a puritanical man who hated sexual immorality and, although he possessed the ultimate power and responsibility, he did not grant a reprieve.' In England at the time, though she may have been sentenced to death for the crime, she would not have been executed but, ironically, transported. She was executed at the gaol in Murray Street on 19 April 1830 ('Around and About Macquarie Street', p244). She was the first, but not the last, woman to be hanged in Tasmania.

The lives of the women convicts at the Female Factories were pretty grim, and we have already seen that Margaret Morgan died there in 1832, of what there are no details, but those of the female staff were not exactly carefree. The best-known matron at Cascades, **Mary Hutchinson** (1810–1880) was only 21 when her husband was invited by Arthur in January 1832 to accept the post of Superintendent. As RC Hutchinson writes in 'Mrs Hutchinson and the Female Factories of Early Australia' (1962), the regulations suggest that Mrs Hutchinson 'was under almost as much restraint as the women prisoners in her charge'.

More of her earlier life and more feminist insight is shown in Lucy Frost's as-yet unpublished '"At Home" on a Mission Station and in a Female Factory: Imagining Mary Hutchinson'. As Lucy Frost puts it, 'Mary was certainly institutionalised within a prison environment over a period rarely endured by prisoners or staff.' She already had four children when she arrived, and was to have eight more there – half of whom suffered the same fate as those of many convict women's children – death. From 1832 to 1851, Mary was matron at the Cascades Female Factory. In 1838, the Female Factory was subjected to a three-week newspaper crusade against mismanagement during which 29-year-old Mary was singled out for a sustained and personal attack. When she left Hobart, and until 1854, she was in charge of the Female Factory in Launceston which, in 1834, had replaced the institution in George Town. As the longest surviving matron of female factories, Mary's contribution has been recognised by the 2006 naming after her of the new women's section at Risdon Prison, Hobart.

Today, a visit to the archaeological remains established as a memorial to those women who passed through the Cascades Female Factory can break your heart but also let you, in your imagination, into their world. As well as the many books available about women convicts, a more specific one is *Female Factory, Female Convicts* (Tony Rayner, 2005). There is also a booklet, available at the shop: *Footsteps and Voices: A Historical Look into the Cascades Female Factory* with a text by Lucy Frost and, as I write, she and Alison Alexander, among others, are involved in a long-term project – part of the work of the Female Factory Research Group. They have started to put the results of this research on the internet, including a database, continuing to be worked on, of the names of women who passed through the gates of the various female factories – 4,412 at Cascades. The site is the last in the itinerary 'Around and About Macquarie Street'. The remains of the Female Factory at Ross, set up in 1848, features in the 'Midland Highway' itinerary.

The creation of the Assignment Board in 1830 was, as Kirsty Reid explains, 'not merely to distribute convict labour but to review all cases where settlers were accused of contravening regulations or committing other offences'. And regulations for the assignment of women were 'particularly tight'. For any falling down of required standards, settlers might be deprived of their assigned servants. One of those to suffer was Mary McAuley (Knopwood's 'housekeeper').

Mary seems to have had problems with her servants from the start. Lyndall Ryan recounts that on 9 May 1807, **Ann Byrne**, who was sentenced in Dublin in 1795 to seven years' transportation and arrived in Hobart in 1805, was charged with selling 'a petticoat which had been stolen from Mrs McCawley, which she could not give satisfactory account of how she came possessed of'. Ann was sentenced to six months' hard labour on the Government Farm. (She had obviously committed some offence in New South Wales or she would have completed her original sentence before she arrived in Hobart on the *Sophia* in 1805 with women convicts such as Martha Hudson.) Sometime after 1830, Mary McAuley had her servants withdrawn for some breach which, as she testified, 'seriously' affected 'my interests'. As Kirsty Reid explains, the withdrawal of your servants also affected your reputation.

The relationship between settlers and their assigned servants was bound to be somewhat nuanced. Absconding, for any number of motives, including poor or cruel treatment, or a wish to change assignment, was commonplace, as was drinking, which was also done for many reasons; but, in addition, few of the convicts were trained servants to start with. The settlers' point of view is put by **Elizabeth Leake** (née Bell, 1786–1852) in a letter to a friend in England in 1833:

> One of our greatest drawbacks is the want of respectable female servants. It is almost impossible for those families who study the quiet and morality of their children to endure the female convicts and it makes many people only employ men about their household work. I have only had one woman 4 months with the exception of a free woman brought out with us, who, as is usual, left us after a few months.

It is difficult reading that in our times to be totally sympathetic towards Elizabeth. Jessie Couvreur, better known as the Tasmanian writer Tasma, shows how this relationship could be dealt with in fiction in her short story 'An Old-time Episode in Tasmania' (1891). Mr Paton and his daughter are cared for by his distinctly unpleasant sister; they need a new servant and Mr Paton knows what he must do:

> It was not the first time he had been sent upon the delicate mission of choosing a maid for his sister from the female prison, politely called the Factory, at the foot of Mount Wellington. For some reason it would be difficult to explain, his selections were generally rather more successful than hers. Besides which, it was a satisfaction to have some one upon whom to throw the responsibility of the inevitable catastrophe that terminated the career of every successive ticket-of-leave in turn.

Mr Paton develops a passion for the newcomer; unfortunately, her affections seem to rest, instead, with another servant. Mr Paton will have his revenge; a demon whispers in his ear:

> 'Richard Cole is in love with No. 27. The time for him to regain his freedom is at hand. The first use he will make of it will be to leave you, and the next to marry Amelia Clare. You will thus be deprived of everything at one blow. You will lose the best man-servant you have ever known, and your sister, the best maid.' ... To this demon Mr Paton would reply energetically, 'I won't give the fellow the chance of marrying No. 27. As soon as he has

his freedom, I will give him the sack, and forbid him the premises. As for Amelia, she is my prisoner, and I would send her back to gaol to-morrow if I thought there were any nonsense up between her and him.'

Happily, there is a nice twist to this tale, and Tasma herself has more to say in the 'Around Hobart' itinerary, first about Mount Wellington (p251) and then when we visit what was Highfield, her family home (p256), where much of her novel *Not Counting the Cost* (1895) is set. Other stories find their place in the itineraries 'Risdon Cove to Port Arthur' (p272) and 'New Norfolk' (p299).

Catherine Shepherd's play *Daybreak*, first produced at the Theatre Royal, Hobart, in 1938 to critical acclaim, but set in 1830, also explores relations between settlers and convicts. Simon Martel's daughters Caroline and Jeanne are warned off friendship or, indeed, any sort of engagement, by their aunt, Mrs Carmichael: 'My dears, your papa's wishes are that you avoid all unnecessary speech with the assigned servants. They are men and women of bad character, with whom he wishes you to have no intercourse.' Jeanne, I'm afraid, ignores these strictures, gets involved with a young man of 'seditious opinions' who talks in polite company of 'slave labour', and all ends in tears. The convicts also have their say. The play's first production appears in the itinerary 'Around and About Macquarie Street' (Theatre Royal, p237).

The negative views about assigned servants, and the treatment of them, were not the only ones to prevail. **Ellen Viveash** (née Tanner, 1803–1842) had a different experience in 1834. She arrived as a settler with her husband Charles in 1831, and lived in the same area as the Leakes, who had arrived in 1823, within striking distance of Campbell Town; she wrote in a letter home:

> The woman servant is come, she is respectable looking and her behaviour is so likewise. I am agreeably surprised with what I have seen. She goes about her work very willingly and does things better than is usual here. She is an excellent washer and not slow. Her washing will earn her keep and cloathes. She tries much to oblige, not officiously, but by doing things well and instantly doing something useful without waiting to be told. I have remarked many things which augur well, such as useful cloathes which many get rid of when sent into the factory for punishment as she was. She lived 15 months at one place a long time for Hobart Town. She says she can cook in a plain way, sew in a plain way and does not dislike working on the whole. I hope to keep her some time as she can scarcely hope to get an easier place nor I a better servant.

By January 1835, Ellen's nameless convict servant had formed an attachment with the family's 'freed by servitude' shepherd (about whom Ellen is also complimentary) and Ellen wrote: 'He is going to marry our convict servant when she has been with us for a year and behaves well.' Although I'm not always that keen on Ellen, she is good for gossip; we know what she and her husband thought of Elizabeth Leake's husband:

We are going to get rid of our worse than useless acting Police Magistrate (Mr Leake) on the first of next month ... Leake has offended all the magistrates. He has behaved very ill to Charles a long time past. Mr Crear, we think, has at last ousted Leake ... he is very sincere and honest and the exact reverse of Leake.

Perhaps, therefore, we have to reassess any lack of sympathy for Elizabeth Leake who felt so isolated, particularly when her husband was working as an accountant in Hobart, that she told him in 1828: 'I never felt more lonely in my life. I am at times almost melancholy.' So, who were Elizabeth Leake, Ellen Viveash and their fellow women settlers?

6 – Women Settlers and Land Grants

Free settlers were not new before 1810 – several travelled out from England with Collins; spouses, mainly wives, accompanied convicts as free settlers and, soon, other settlers started to drift in. After about 1815, the pace of emigration, often well-to-do-families, expecting free land grants commensurate with the capital they had brought to develop it, and assigned servants and labourers, gathered some momentum, though most arrived in the 'twenties. They were immigrants, but usually called settlers. Immigrants were those who came without funds seeking work and new opportunities and are described in Chapter 9. An exception to those two categories were those who came in the second wave from Norfolk Island – they had farmed there and expected land grants in Tasmania; eventually many were settled just south of Launceston.

In the early years, as we have seen with Martha Hayes, Mary Anne Peters and Catherine Kearney, women were given land grants, though not as large as those of men. But, in 1813, when Macquarie discovered that Davey had granted land to Mrs Jemott, he intervened: 'I cannot on any account,' he wrote, 'authorise Mrs Jemott to receive lands in her own right.' Adding, 'It being against the rules I have laid down.' The solution was to allow Mary Jemott's husband, and men like him, the right to cultivate a smallholding 'till they are emancipated'.

William Knight Jemott was not the usual sort of convict: he had been court martialled by the Admiralty and tried at the old Bailey for piracy in 1812; sentenced to death, this had, after more than one date set for his execution, been commuted to a life sentence. **Mary Jemott** (née Mack, c1778–1851) accompanied him to Tasmania as a free settler. She was obviously a woman of some character for it appears that she tried to intercede on his behalf during the proceedings against him. He was pardoned in 1816 and they seem for some years to have had a property near Richmond; when he died in 1847, Mary, aged 69, moved to New South Wales and died there four years later.

Marjorie Tipping comments tellingly on the fate of free wives granted land who were married to convict husbands:

> Those stalwart wives who in earlier times had received land grants and stock in their own right became bound when their husbands became unbound, so that after a few years both wives and children were no more than extra property, namelessly recorded among the returns of the landholder, after the acreage under cultivation and the amount of stock held had been taken into account.

That may account for why Catherine Kearney did not marry her long-time friend.

It should also be noted what life was like for the early farming settlers. Macquarie, during his 1811 visit, wrote of New Norfolk, in spite of the good quality of the land, '... the houses of settlers are mean and badly built and themselves miserably clothed'. And he saw noticeably worse south of Launceston, in the South Esk River area and wrote, '... the Habitations of the settlers are wretchedly mean and themselves *dirty* and miserably clothed'.

In spite of Macquarie's strictures on land grants to women, Mary Geils, wife of the temporary Lieutenant Governor, was granted 860 acres in 1813/14 – although it was clear that it was intended for her husband whose position barred him from receiving it; the same was true of Elizabeth Paterson. One is left to wonder how he justified granting, in person, land to Lucy Davey Scott on her marriage in 1821; her father, Davey, may have been a lieutenant governor but not only had he left for England but also Lucy's property, as in the case of all wives, would belong to her husband.

Macquarie's reason for not granting land to women was not so much because he did not have the relevant instructions from London but 'on the ground that such persons are incapable of cultivating Land, and thereby not adding to the resources of the colony'. That this was patently untrue is confirmed in the Land Commission's report of 1826 when they wrote of Adolarius Humphrey's farm:

> Mr Humphrey being occupied as Superintendent of Police, Member of the Executive Council, devoted little or none of his time to his Estate, but under Mrs Humphrey's management, everything is carried on in superior Style, the first object that attracts your attention, is, a Hedge row of beautiful white Thorn, protected by an admirable Hurdle Fence, and reaching from the creek to the River Styx ... the land itself is not of excellent quality, but the Crops are superior from good culture. A large Flock of highly improved Sheep, some fine Merino Rams, a beautiful Suffolk Bull and some Cows of Mr Marsden's breed, a large well cropped Garden, Poultry yard & excellent Pig Yard, render Humphreyville one of the most gratifying sights in the Colony.

We meet **Harriett Humphrey** (née Sutton), daughter of a convict storekeeper, and her romantic 1812 marriage, again in the 'New Norfolk' itinerary (Hawthorn Lodge, p308). And, of course, Martha Hayes, Mary Anne Peters and Catherine Kearney, among others, had already proved the case for women landholders and managers. Elizabeth Leake, incidentally, and according to Miranda Morris, managed the family's property, Rosedale, while her husband was about his business in Hobart. Similar wife-managers of this period included Mary Meredith, who appears in the 'East Coast' itinerary (Cambria, p317), and Eliza Forlong whose place is in the 'Midland Highway' itinerary (Kenilworth, p340) – and who played an acknowledged part in Tasmania's economic history.

Not all unattached women were prepared to accept land-granting discrimination. Sharon Morgan tells the story in *Land Settlements in Early Tasmania: Creating an Antipodean England* (1992):

Only the persistence of two determined women led to the case being clearly stated in 1826 and 1827. In 1823 Eliza Walsh appealed to Earl Bathurst to change the policy. She argued that it did not 'appear altogether ... just ... to exclude Ladies from making use of their money for the benefit of the Colony in consequence of their Sex'; nor, she argued, could it 'be deemed a great objection that a Lady should not be able to conduct a Farm ... without a Gentleman'.

I can find no more details of the intrepid **Eliza Walsh**.

The other woman, details about whom I have garnered from other sources, appears to have been **Anne Turnbull,** the unmarried sister of **Mary Anstey** (1777–1862), both members of an extended settler family typical of those then arriving in Tasmania. This 1823 party included not only Mary's husband Thomas, whom she had married in 1811, and three of their five children, but also Mary and Anne's sister **Lucy** (Mrs James Cubbiston **Sutherland**) who was on her honeymoon, Sutherland's sister **Anne Sutherland, Miss McBain,** aged 19, niece of Mary Anstey and **Miss Agnes Galloway** (1791–1870) from Edinburgh and 'famous for her beauty'.

Anne Turnbull brought with her, independently, property valued at over £600, the sort of capital required for a free land grant. Sorell, working to Macquarie's rules, refused her, as a single woman, even though her brother-in-law, Sutherland, would manage for her. He did, however, advise her what steps to take, so she wrote to Lord Bathurst, 'I was greatly disappointed to find from his Honour that he cannot give Land to Ladies, without a letter from your Lordship, which he recommended me to procure ...' She was given 500 acres.

Miss Galloway, who had initially lived with Miss Sutherland and Miss Turnbull, had brought with her £1,000 and, in due course, was also granted 500 acres ('Blackadder'). She must have been more than a reasonable catch – what with money, land and looks - when she married Walter Davidson in 1825. Though simply being a single woman would have been enough!

I fear that Ellen Viveash did not care for all members of the Anstey family. She wrote of Sutherland, 'Poor man I am sorry for him with all his loads of faults ... Only think of such a disagreeable man being in the hands of his friends – Mr Anstie his rich brother-in-law cannot bear him but he would doubtless aid him.' When Ellen was having a difficult pregnancy and her usual neighbours could not be with her, Sutherland intervened; Ellen wrote: 'He had proposed Miss Turnbulls coming up before I became ill and I was obliged to give almost a rude negative to prevent a thing I so dreaded.' Goodness knows what Ellen's mother made of these unpleasant characters whom she did not know dancing across the pages of the letters taking months to cross thousands of miles.

Fortunately, we do not have to rely just on this one source, for Sharon Morgan, drawing partly on Sutherland's diary, paints a picture of a man who was forever helping his neighbours in the Isis River area, and being helped in return, particularly when Lucy was giving birth to their child in 1825. When 'dear baby' would not suckle, Mrs Cox, 'who has lots of milk', stepped in.

For some reason, Governor Arthur gave a little island – an acre in size – in Lake Dulverton, just east of Oatlands, to Mary Anstey for a picnic ground – a suitable occupation for a lady, no doubt. It was, therefore, called Mary's Isle.

Elizabeth Badley, mother-in-law of John Eddie, who arrived with his wife in 1825, bypassed Bathurst and wrote direct to Downing Street. She was not going to be fobbed off by the 'little colonel', as the disrespectful called Arthur. She wrote:

> I have ordered goods to be purchased for this market in London to the extent of £1,000 cash. I have an annuity of £300 and an unencumbered and most valuable coffee plantation in Jamaica [her old home], valued at £3,000. Also jewellery, etc., to the value of £300.

She got her land, near Jericho, next door to that of her son-in-law (who sold his and moved away).

By 1826, Ralph Darling was Governor of New South Wales. Bathurst, Colonial Secretary, informed Macquarie that he was unaware

> of any reason why females, who are unmarried, should be secluded [sic] from holding Lands in the Colony, provided they possess sufficient funds for the purpose, intend *bona fide* to reside on their Lands, and to fulfil any other stipulations which may be required of them in common with all other Grantees.

A year later, this was confirmed to Arthur in Tasmania who strongly supported Macquarie's policy not to grant land to women. Kirsty Reid offers a useful angle on Arthur's reluctance which marries with his responsibility for managing a colony not only that had become separate from New South Wales in 1825 – with its own judicial establishment and legislative council – but was also, in many respects, a gaol. 'It is to be regretted,' he commented, that 'Ladies should ever attempt the management of a Farm with servants whom they cannot control.' And, commenting on Arthur's land policy, she adds that what Arthur required was 'a particular type of masculine authority: middling-class men, resident upon their land, personally active in its improvement, and willing and able to intervene in the lives of their convict workers'.

The least rebuffed woman landseeker of this period was widowed **Jacobina Burn** (née Hunter, 1763–1851); she was either canny or lucky, or both. She had married the architect David Burn in Edinburgh in 1797. Following his death, she set off for Tasmania in 1821, aged nearly 60, accompanied only by a 17-year-old nephew. Apparently she dined more than once with the Macquaries during their last visit to Tasmania and got on very well with them; it probably helped that they were all Scots. She obviously mentioned her desire for land. Perhaps Macquarie thought her sons would farm it; perhaps she intimated that they would – though they did not accompany her. He granted her 2,000 acres near Hamilton which became 'Ellangowan' and by 1829 she had another 1,000 (she wanted to make her farm as square as possible) and 2,000 sheep and 150 cattle. Quakers who visited Jacobina in 1832, when she was nearly 70, give us an insight both into her and settler life; Walker wrote:

We walked over to dine with our hospitable friend Jacobina Burn. After tea, according to custom the servants, men and women and a few soldiers who have for some time been on the estate to protect them from the aborigines, were called in to have the Scriptures read to them ... Mrs Burn is a serious as well as a sensible and energetic woman, and has induced a considerable number of her relatives to emigrate from Scotland. They seem one and all to have been prosperous, and are for the most part persons of piety.

I wonder which relative was not a person of piety! Jacobina later lived in Bothwell, near her sister Katharina Hunter Patterson, and appears in that itinerary (p332); (Ellangowan no longer exists to visit).

The advantage of women settlers to the recreation of Tasmania's history is that several of them, like Ellen Viveash, left accounts – diaries or letters. Some, such as Elizabeth Leake's, are still unpublished papers in libraries. Ellen's appear in *The Tanner Letters: A Pioneer Saga of Swan River & Tasmania 1831–45* (1981), compiled and researched by Pamela Statham who usefully sums up the background and motivation of many of the settler families of this period:

The new colony offered the opportunity to prove that new methods and new ways worked; to redress the declining incomes experienced by so many English landed families in the depressed period following the Napoleonic Wars, to make a fortune and 'prove' oneself to one's kin.

Ellen and her husband Charles left England in 1830 with Ellen's brother William who was married to Charles's sister Hester. By a complicated process, the Tanners ended up in New South Wales, while the Viveashs settled in Tasmania in 1831 at a property they called Baskerville; there they concentrated on sheep and wheat. Paying off debts, including to family members, and accumulating capital was their preoccupation; Ellen talks constantly of money. Snippets from her letters, which only date from 1834 and 1835 have already illuminated relations with convict servants, and her neighbours, most of whom she got on with. She was a nice gossipy writer for this purpose and her views – usually sharp – will further appear. She seemed settled in Tasmania, apart from a stillborn child and her husband's ill-health (of which there is much detail). She wrote in January 1835, 'I expect this country will always be our home or that we shall always have land here.' But a year later, they left for England and did not return.

A settler family which lasted much longer on their land grant was the Reids. **Mary Reid** (née Muirhead, 1789–1867) and her husband Alexander arrived in 1822 with their seven-year-old daughter Jane and infant son Alex, 'a respectable person well acquainted with farming', and 'a *sheep dog* completed our number of live stock', we are told. **Jane Reid** (1815–1897), the author of those words, is also known as Jane Williams because in 1829, aged only 14, she married the army officer William Williams and went with him to his posting in India. She was widowed by 19 when she returned to the family property Ratho, Bothwell. Her mother's letters to her in India, together with a draft reminiscence, which Jane probably wrote in 1840, as well as her letters written on her return, and a well-informed interlinking text are contained in *The Clyde Company Papers*, mainly in the *Prologue 1821–35* (edited by PL Brown, 1941). It is to Jane's draft reminiscence that we owe how such a venture was viewed by those at home:

> It was not, as now, an event of everyday occurrence for a family to relinquish the attachments and comforts of their home in the old world to seek their fortunes in those far off islands of the South Sea ... it was consequently viewed as no small undertaking by all [my father's] friends. By some it was looked upon as a species of madness, by others as a rash and unwise act of which the cost had not been counted: all united in considering it a most dreadful description of banishment, and my mother a heroine to encounter the prospect of all things strange and horrible.

It is to Jane, too, that we owe an impression of Hobart in 1822:

> We soon arrived before the little straggling village of Hobarton. What might have been the feelings of the other passengers I do not remember, but in my own disappointment certainly predominated. There were but three objects which fixed my attention and stood out as landmarks amid the little varandahed cottages around them. These were Government House, a large irregular-looking pile of buildings formed of wood and having much the appearance of a large bungala; St David's, or the English Church, of stone; and the Macquarie Hotel, a handsome brick building consisting of three storeys – all standing in the principal street of the town, Macquarie Street.

There is something comforting in knowing that Macquarie Street is still the main street. As for Bothwell, whither the family proceeded, Jane's impressions inform that part of the 'Midland Highway' itinerary.

The arrival of **Elizabeth Fenton** (1804–1875) was a little different from that of the Reids seven years earlier, though there is a link. Widowed in India, Elizabeth Campbell, née Knox, had married her late husband's fellow officer Michael Fenton. When the Fentons sailed for Tasmania, she was already pregnant and stopped in Mauritius to have her daughter, Flora, and recover from indisposition, while he continued the journey. She arrived in Hobart to find him absent: he had set out on the ocean to meet her. Eventually they retrieved each other and, though some of Elizabeth's impressions, from *Mrs Fenton's Journal: A Narrative of her Life in India, the Isle of France –Mauritius*

– *and Tasman during the Years 1826–1830* (1901), are sprinkled elsewhere, most of their life together is in the 'New Norfolk' itinerary (Fenton Forest, p310, and Plenty, p312) where they settled, and where they died. She wrote as she approached Hobart in 1830 – and we are almost on the ship with her as it moves slowly forward:

> As we sail up this beautiful Derwent, every mile most distinctly marks the progress of civilisation. We *now* are in sight of Hobarton, a small irregularly built town, viewing it at this distance, but with an indefinable 'English air'. Mount Wellington, yonder table mountain, rising abruptly over the town, is topped with snow …
>
> There seems no lack of wood here, the hills – and the whole country appears a succession of hills, and gentle undulations – are clothed to the very summit, the foliage at this distance is very sombre. Not tropical – there are no graceful bamboos or feathery cocas. Still, from the uniformity of the colouring, not altogether English.
>
> As we advance, pretty cottage residences are visible in what appeared impervious jungle. I wonder if these are 'farm houses.' There are streaks of lovely yellow sand, fringing each diminutive bay or inlet of the waters among the hills; there are wide fields freshly ploughed and ploughmen and sowers all busy at their labour with English smock-frocks.

Elizabeth Ackworth Prinsep (née Ommaney, 1804–1885) had a similar background to Mrs Fenton; indeed, their husbands had business dealings in Tasmania. Elizabeth married Augustus Prinsep of the Bengal civil service in Calcutta in 1828 and arrived in Hobart in 1829 to help him recover his health, unsuccessfully. Unfortunately, too, *The Journal of a Voyage from Calcutta to Van Diemen's Land … From Original Letters* (1833) is not by her, as is often assumed. KR von Stieglitz, for example, writes in *A History of New Norfolk*, 'A visitor, Mrs Augustus Princep [sic], published a little book about her six months' stay in Tasmania …' But not only does the title continue '*selected* [my italics] by Mrs Prinsep', but in the editor's preface she observes, 'The letters from which the following pages were compiled, afforded mere passing notices of the places visited, which the abler hand of the lamented writer, had he lived, might have embodied in a shape more fit.' (And she continues in this vein, common to self-deprecating women of her day publishing their late husband's writing.)

You will sometimes see quotations in historical reconstructions as if from Mrs Prinsep, and even Eliza Arthur saw it as Mrs Prinsep's book – perhaps she knew something. Often Elizabeth Prinsep was with her husband and shared the experiences he described – though she would have been constrained by the presence of their newborn daughter – and she may well have made some judicious amendments to the final version, but the body of the letters is his. Nevertheless, should you see an original (not later versions) of the rather slight book, some of the illustrations are by Elizabeth (p303), for she was an accomplished artist, and some of his observations are entirely relevant to her;

this one, written from their rented house in New Town, is particularly lively: 'Even in our small ménage, our cook has committed murder, our footman burglary, and the housemaid bigamy! But these formidable truths are hushed up, or tried to be so.' Another derogatory description of women convict servants is more conventional; and the more one comes across them, the more one has to accept that this was the received wisdom.

By 1830, free land grants were no longer to be had for waving your capital about; indeed, little land was to be had at all between Hobart and Launceston. Grants were officially replaced by sale on 31 January 1831. Augustus Prinsep appears to have negotiated to buy – he hoped to spend £100 and that in five years the land would be worth £750 – but they seem to have left that year empty handed. Augustus died during a sea voyage taken later that year for him to recuperate. He was 28, Elizabeth was 27, and pregnant. She lived for another 55 years, remarrying in 1840.

'I had fully anticipated, when I left this country that my voyage would have ended at Van Diemen's Land', wrote **Jane Roberts** in *Two Years at Sea: Being the Narrative of a Voyage to the Swan River and Van Diemen's Land during the Years 1829, 30, 31* (1834). And she explained: 'But a severe affliction obliged my immediate return.' She was there in the winter months, May and June 1830, and her observations are slight, but a couple are worth quoting; this one shows how Hobart seems to have improved since the Reids arrived eight years earlier:

> Hobart Town is straggling, and looks more so than it really is, from the great variety of its buildings; the interior houses of some of the first settlers still remaining by the side of the smart shops of later residents. The principal streets, Macquarie and Elizabeth, are straight and good, and the shops contain everything you can wish, for at nearly the same price as in England: indeed, it is quite astonishing that goods can be conveyed so great a distance at so cheap a rate.
>
> The Government-house is not large, nor the grounds extensive. The road leading from it to the Barracks is beautiful, adorned with detached white houses with green verandahs, situated in the midst of gardens, which, in their clear atmosphere look very cheerful and inviting.

The editor of Jane Reid Williams' papers supplements this impression when, after listing the occupations to cater to male needs, he adds those required by women that had mushroomed by 1831: 'The greengrocer, the gardener, the broom-maker, the hosier and glover, the haberdasher, the bonnet-maker, the milliner, the needlewoman, the mantua-maker, the confectioner, the jeweller and goldsmith, the painter and engraver, the professional musician – and Mrs McTavish, an accoucheuse of Elizabeth Street.'

I cannot skip on without elaborating a little on **Janet McTavish** (1774–1858) who, as a trained midwife with a glowing testimonial, arrived steerage from Edinburgh in 1824 with her daughter **Janet Young** (1799–1871), son-in-law Thomas, a solicitor, and their children. Janet immediately advertised her

4. Janet McTavish, by Thomas Bock, 1848,
from Dunbar, *Thomas Bock*

services in the *Hobart Town Gazette* and practised at first at 117 Elizabeth Street. In 1831, she managed to secure her land grant and built Rosebank (where she had her own practice) in what is now the Mt Stuart district of North Hobart; indeed, McTavish Avenue, leading into Elizabeth Street, acknowledges her contribution to the community. Rosebank was at numbers 8–9 there. In 1837, she had two women convict servants, **Sophia Moses** and **Jane McCarty** (as well as two men). Of convicts in 1830, Jane Roberts wrote, contradicting other accounts:

> Those sent into private families are without any mark of disgrace, but are apparently the same as hired servants in England; they are fed and clothed, but receive no wages. It is said they never forgive a person who accidentally calls them 'convicts'; they denominate themselves 'servants of the crown', and settlers invariably do the same.

Whatever the attitude to convict servants, that towards former women convicts who had made good is surely exemplified by **Janet Ranken** (c1796–1887). Janet Hutchinson of Dumfriesshire married her cousin George Ranken in 1821 and sailed soon thereafter in a ship chartered by Colonel Campbell and carrying his wife, 13 children, the eldest daughter's husband and their three children, together with servants. On arrival in Tasmania, George Ranken set off for New South Wales to see the lie of the land, leaving pregnant Janet in Hobart. She wrote to her sister in 1821, after Maria Lord had been a recognised entrepreneur for 15 years, and a respectable married woman for 13; when she was described by Knopwood as one of the colony's 'Ladies':

The society here is abominable. Mr Lord a man worth half a million money, is married to a convict woman … Mrs Lord sent her daughter Miss Lord and her sister Mrs Simpson to call upon me when I came here but I have never returned the call yet nor shall I although wile Governor McWharie [Macquarie] and his lady were here paying there [sic] last visit Mrs Lord was Mrs McWharies most intimate friend and I have been advised to visit her but they say 'evil communication corrupts good manners' so I shall rather be without the kindnesses that Mrs Lord has in her power to show me than visit her.

You have to wonder how prevalent Janet Ranken's attitude was among the new women settlers, in spite of Elizabeth Macquarie's lack of side. Maria Lord may, indeed, provide a clue, for it was at this time that Edward Lord began to distance himself from his wife and a recent publication (James Boyce, 2008) suggests that it was because of her convict background. Certainly there is evidence in contemporary women's letters to support Kirsty Reid's conclusion that 'a cultural shift had occurred in the domestic order of the colony with the arrival of free emigrants of reputedly higher social and moral status'.

Since 1810, Maria Lord and her family had continued to prosper, largely thanks to her as her husband's agent because he was often away, for any number of reasons – including taking their children (which Maria continued to produce) to England to be educated and visiting a second family there.

The Lords had moved into the fine house, known now as Ingle Hall, in Macquarie Street, and there they led Hobart society. In 1814, for example, they held a ball which Knopwood described as 'the greatest dinner given in the colony'. And in 1816 they gave a 'splendid and most hospitable entertainment of Dinner, Ball and Supper'. By 1819, they owned 6,974 acres, much of it supporting crops but also 3,400 cattle and 4,500 sheep – and Maria supplied meat to the Commissariat, as well as other goods to the government. They had 41 horses, 50 convict servants, and 25 free workers.

By 1820, they had a new property at Lawrenny, near what became Hamilton. But, as Alison Alexander suggests, during Lord's stay in Hobart that year relations between the couple were less cordial than previously. And near them at Lawrenny a new settler, 26-year-old Old Etonian magistrate Charles Rowcroft, had arrived; he seemed to become part of the Lord family, both when Edward Lord was in the colony, and when he was not.

Business and family now began to fall apart. In August 1823 a notice appeared in the *Hobart Town Gazette* withdrawing Mrs Lord's authority over the Lord enterprises; that October, Knopwood noted that Maria left Ingle Hall. Exactly a year later, Lord took Rowcroft to court charging him with criminal conversation with his 40-year-old wife. Lord won, and left for England where he stayed, and most of the children never saw their mother again. Found guilty of adultery, Maria had no claim on her husband's property. Kay Daniels summed up the result of the trial:

[It] not only confirmed that Maria had committed adultery but demonstrated that her civil status was now such that her sexual behaviour was a matter of legal consequence in a way it was not before her marriage to Edward. She had moved from being a convict whore to a mistress to a lawful wife, but the trial which branded her again 'a whore' took place not only because of sexual morality and marital status but because of property.

Lord did not, however, divorce Maria, though pressure was put on him to do so. Newly-arrived solicitor William Parramore supported the idea of a divorce. He wrote to his own fiancée on 20 December 1824 of the trial that it

Lasted 11 days and there was as much nauseous detail as in the other notorious trial [Caroline of Brunswick, Queen of George IV]. The same object as was attributed to the king, was said to be the aim of Lord – a divorce from a wife whom he is now ashamed of, because she can't read and *can* put herself into the most *original* passions and curse and swear.

The suggestion that Maria was illiterate is not new but seems unlikely, given the business empire she ran, the social position she had risen to, her husband's background, and the years that had elapsed since her transportation. RL Murray, former convict (transported for bigamy) and journalist, wrote of Lord: 'I heartily hope that he may yet enjoy the Society of an honourable and virtuous woman, who may know how to appreciate his value and be deserving of his affection.'

The final irony of this case comes from Charles Rowcroft who soon sailed for England – a pauper but married en route in Rio de Janeiro to a recent widow with eight children whom he had met on board. He later published an account of the colony which included the altogether perfect observation:

I have been a witness, in Van Diemen's Land, of the evil effects of a contrary course of conduct on the part of the wives of emigrants. To my knowledge, more than one failure has happened from the fancies, and fine-lady affectations, and frettings, and sulkiness of settlers' helpmates; forgetting how much of a man's comfort and happiness, and, in a colony, of his success, depends on the cheerful humour, the kindly good temper, and the hearty co-operation of his wife.

As for Maria, she may well not have been seen as a society lady after this – because there were now so many of those who aspired to the real thing; but she did not retire from her previous life, nor had her relations with her husband completely ended. She opened two shops, and advertised in the *Hobart Town Courier* on 10 February 1826:

Maria Lord begs to return her grateful thanks to her Friends and the Public, for the liberal Support she has received since she opened her Stores in Eliza-beth-Street, and takes the liberty of acquainting them, that in addition to her usual Assortment of Teas, Sugar, Preserves, Pickles, Spices, Butter, Cheese, Hams, and other Articles of Grocery and Provisions, she has supplied herself from the recent English arrivals, with a large and elegant Stock of coloured Prints, Muslins, Gowns of the newest fashions, Fancy Flowers and Feather, Ladies' Shoes, Carpeting, etc. together with a great variety of other Articles in general use; Spirits and Wines, of superior flavour, in Quantities not less than 5 Gallons. – She takes this opportunity also of announcing, that she has lately added the Business of a Butcher to her Stores, and that her Friends may at all times be sure of a Supply of Meat of the very best Quality, and which she will be happy to furnish them for Monthly Payments.

In another advertisement, 'she trusts that the experience of the whole Colony, of her integrity and assiduity in Business for the last 16 years, will be sufficient guarantee for her future Exertions'. As for Edward Lord, he visited Tasmania from time to time, and in 1828 Knopwood noted that he was 'very ill at Maria Lds'. By his nurse, probably on that occasion, he had a son, and that on top of his second family in England – the nanny of his children by Maria – with whom he had another five children. These convoluted ménages put into perspective Maria's relations with Rowcroft, whether or not they had been intimate. You would have to suggest that Lord was a bit of a hypocrite, though, of course, typical of his day. He was in England, Maria in Hobart, when in 1829 their elder son, John, was drowned in the Derwent at Lawrenny. Alison Alexander ends her chapter on Maria:

> Edward Lord died in 1859. His will was a lengthy, involved document in which he tried to divide his diminished estate between his first illegitimate family, his legal children, and his English illegitimate offspring. He kindly left his wife an annuity, but she died, aged seventy-nine, two months after he did.

Before her death, Maria had moved to Bothwell where we meet her again (The Priory, p334); it was in the Lord vault in New Norfolk that she was buried (Stephen Street Cemetery, p304).

It is hardly surprising that Janet Ranken looked down upon Maria Lord as she did: she continued that same 1821 letter,

> There are a great many settlers come out here this season all of them the grandest people I ever saw they are surely come to spend and not to make money as for their wives and daughters they are so much of fine things that they cannot put on there [sic] own clothes they must all have maids to do that for them and there papas are all Major Colonel and for Captains they are like to knock one another down that is never *hard* if you may find *clarks* to some of the great store keepers here ... We are all come here to make money and money we will have by hook or by crook so to talk of friendship would be a sad prostitution of the word *trust no one* but for your own *interest* appear to trust everyone.

Whether or not Lord's case against Maria and the sundering of their business and personal relations were really indicative of his embarrassment at her convict origins, Janet Ranken was not the only one to note and act upon the differences in social status in the colony that had earlier hardly been an issue. Elizabeth Fenton was also a bit of a snob: she wrote in her first days,

> I … saw a very dashing person, a Mrs Roper, quite the rage here, and also just arrived; but though handsome and dressed from top to toe in the exuberance of French fashion, I could never like or admire. She had the indefinable air of a second-rate actress. Her husband, too, did not look aristocratic, or anything bordering on it.

I cannot clarify Mrs Roper's background, but she may have been married to the magistrate Frederick Roper.

Octavia Dawson wrote to the guardian of her son in Belfast in August 1829, soon after her arrival with her husband Samuel Robinson Dawson, with the gay abandon of punctuation displayed by Janet Ranken:

> In the first place I was to tell you how I like the place, I do not like it at all the country I must say is beautiful no person can find fault with it but then it is a new colony and there is a great deal for a settler to encounter particularly a female, next the people, they are either very *high* or very *low* the upper class are all military or naval men such as cols Majors and Capns. that you have no chance with them and the lower class are convicts. There is such a party spirit amongst them that if you are at all noticed you must be either one side or other so that it makes you quite uncomfortable, as for us we know very few.

But worse was to come. Patricia Clarke and Dale Spender, who include Octavia's letter (as well as Janet Ranken's and Anne Horden's) in *Lifelines: Australian Women's Letters and Diaries 1788–1840* (1992), assume that, in the following extract, George is her brother:

> I suppose you have heard of Georges marriage poor fellow he has done for himself forever I have only seen him at a distance since our arrival if she had been any kind of woman that I could have been on terms with how comfortable it wd have been for me but it seems as if I was to be disappointed in everything – it seems that she was well known on the Commercial Road as Betty Duff god knows how true it is but this I know that she is one of the greatest drinkers and one of the worst tempered women I have ever met with.

I have not been able to get to the bottom of 'Commercial Road' to satisfy myself that Betty Duff – who is not among Philip Tardif's convict women by that name – was a prostitute as the editors imply.

The Dawsons established themselves at what is now Bellerive where, in 1860, he was elected a councillor, and Octavia's granddaughter married well, so presumably she eventually overcame her reservations about Tasmanian society. And Sharon Morgan mentions a fact about landholders that is worth bearing in mind: 'At least one-fifth, but probably more than half, of people granted land before 1824 were ex-convicts.'

In her letter, Octavia mentions one couple who lead me neatly to the professional writer who published the ultimate condemnation of life in the colony: 'We know ... a Mr and Mrs Aidey he is a banker and she is a very clever woman ...'

Lucy Leman Adey (née Rede) had been in Tasmania since 1826; she was a member of another of those extended families whose arrival in Tasmania in the 1820s was so common. Her husband Stephen was one of the first commissioners of the Van Diemen's Land Company; her sister **Louisa Leman Rede** was to marry Alexander Goldie, also of the Company.

Because of Lucy's refusal to leave Hobart for the wild unknown, her husband, initially involved in surveying the north, where the Company was to have its extensive lands, was obliged to stay in the capital and act as the Hobart agent. Lucy was obviously a determined woman who had also obliged her husband to involve himself in several lawsuits against the captain of their ship from England, and she and Louisa also had literary aspirations. This is undoubtedly why, when 'Letter from a Lady' was published in the London *Morning Herald* on 24 September 1827, it was assumed to be by her – an error that was perpetuated for some time and caused her problems, including having attitudes as a new settler ascribed to her that were not necessarily true; and it looks as if Octavia Dawson, too, believed that she wrote it. But it is now accepted that it was by **Mary Leman Grimstone** (née Rede, c1796–1869), the third sister, who was already an established writer.

Mary Grimstone, probably a widow, though no one knows anything about Mr Grimstone, had travelled out with the Adeys and spent the years 1826–29 with them in Macquarie Street. She had been writing a novel on the journey out, later published as *Louise Egerton* (1830). In Hobart, she published some poetry anonymously, including, in 1826, 'On Visiting the Cemetery in Hobart Town' (which can be found in *Effects of Light: The Poetry of Tasmania* (1985), edited by Margaret Scott). She also wrote most of her feminist novel *Women's Love* (1832) – underpinned by a plea for the recognition of women's intellectual qualities as qualifications for public life. It is also an indicator of the changes taking place in English society in the 1820s.

In spite of its English setting, it may well have been the first novel written in Australia. An 1832 review in *La Belle Assemblee* (edited by Caroline Norton) describes it as written in Van Diemen's Land, adding: 'It has something of the warmth and freshness of the scenes amidst which it was composed.' Tasmania appears only in the last lines of volume 3: 'Guy Burroughs and some others of the accomplices of Saville cross the South Pacific to redeem or renew in another sphere the crimes they had committed in this.' Mary Grimstone explains why Tasmania did not feature more:

5.   Mary Grimstone, from Roe,
'Mary Grimstone'

It may be asked, why did I not look around me for the materials for my story? First, because to use the language of the eloquent LEL [Letitia Elizabeth Landon], I am 'intensely English' and during my absence from home, found one of my greatest enjoyments in giving to it my imagination. Secondly, in the small circle of colonial community, I could scarcely have escaped, however unreal might be the characters I drew, the charge of designed personality. But I have not come away without recollections of one of the most beautiful islands in the world, endeared to me by the ties of affection and friendship, and I may yet return to it, at least in fancy.

She did return to it in fancy, in at least three short stories which appeared in 1846 in the literary magazine *The People's Journal*. These can only be tracked down in, say, the British Library, and are not really worth it. Mary meant well but her heroines are a bit too angelic for my taste. But it is to 'Letter from a Lady' which found its way from London to Hobart's *Colonial Advocate* in May 1828 that she owes a certain infamy in Tasmania, for, whatever she was to say later about her feelings for the place, she was not impressed by it when she had been there a few months. The complete text of this letter can be found as an appendix to the historical paper 'Mary Leman Grimstone ... For Women's Rights and Tasmanian Patriotism' (Michael Roe, 1989). Here is a taste:

I remember you wished me to give you a sketch of the society in this place, and that I can now do, as we are acquainted with almost every body, that is any body here. In the first place, you could hardly imagine that a country like England could produce such an illiterate cub as this Colony. Who would not have expected to find by this time a Library at least. They had one at South Carolina before it was established twelve months. Saturn is not more remote from the Sun, than Hobart Town from all Science and Literature. Variety is a word unknown in its vocabulary, and the light that surrounds you must be all from within. The mercantile classes are animated by an avaricious (or I should rather say *voracious*) spirit of money-getting, which engenders jealousy and ill-will when there is the least collision of interest or chance of rivalry. They are the democracy of the Colony, and proscribed at Government House, and hostile to all the measures than [that?] emanate thence; and looking to Murray, the Editor of the *Colonial Times*, as their political leader. The Government and Law Officers, etc. form, and are, completely the Aristocracy. They are dull, reserved, punctiliously jealous of compromising their rank, all etiquette and caution. One reason for all this is, that there are a great many mushrooms amongst them; and there is no pride so stiff and ungraceful as upstarts. Entertainments are occasionally given; but, as Madame de Stael says of the Germans, they are rather ceremonies than parties of pleasure; and this remark applies to the first house [Government House] in this place.

We are left to speculate why, in May 1834, Ellen Viveash, who arrived in 1831, after Mary Grimstone had left in 1829, dubbed her as she did: 'We have just received ... some "Examiners". The nun Grimstone, authoress of "Character" etc. has been out here and has a brother here. I forget who but must enquire as I see her work named above praise by the "Examiner".' (She is referring to *Character: or Jew and Gentile* (1835) in which Mary Grimstone, as Michael Roe suggests, 'further attacked brute punishment as a response to social problems'.)

I wish Mary, when describing the government and legal officers as the aristocracy, had used the rather delightful term 'pure merinos' which I have seen used elsewhere at this time to describe them, and, indeed, anyone in Australia conscious of their status. Still, 'mushrooms' does pretty well in describing social climbers. The *Colonial Times* called its competitor the *Courier* 'that merino journal' because of its propensity to appeal to 'the elite of Hobart'.

By 1829, Stephen Adey was, as Octavia Dawson knew him, a prosperous banker. As for the settlers who farmed, however grand their background or self-regarding their attitudes, life was not easy, particularly at the beginning and when there were economic downturns. Jane Reid Williams' editor puts it succinctly, 'Until they could produce, comparatively cheaply, an article in wide and constant demand, they must remain subordinate – a handful of persons at subsistence level, under military rule, existing to feed and employ a greater number of felons.'

The felons and economic situation are highlighted by **Anne Hordern** (née Woodhead, b1794, m1817) who, with her husband, a London wheelwright and coachmaker, and three small sons, passed through Hobart from England (travelling steerage) in 1825. They were on their way to Sydney where they would do well in the retail trade. The *Phoenix* remained docked for a month in Hobart where Ann, a stay and bonnet maker's daughter, picked up a mass of information and adverse impressions. I cannot resist the rather long Hobart extract of her letter home of March that year, contained in the family biography *Children of One Family* (Lesley Hordern, 1985):

> There have been such dreadful murders and robberies continually. There were eight hanged the same day we got there – there were robberies every night too. They robbed the governor's house while we were there. There were a great many under sentance of death, and the prison was quite full of others waiting to be tried. Indeed the Judges are sitting every day the whole year round to try them – Sundays excepted. Therefore I will leave you to Judge the awful stage of Van Dieman's land. Therefore neither person nor property is ever safe. When first we took a view of the town it gave me a kind of disgust. There was none of the stately buildings we have been accustomed to in England. The Houses in general being on the ground floor, except the few that have lately been built of brick that are one storey high; the others weather boarded. The one that Mather (who kept a hosier's shop in Sun Street, who married Mr Benson's daughter – the editor of the Wesleyan Society) lives in is weather boarded and all on the ground floor. He gives one pound a week in rent on a lease for a short time. House rent is very dear indeed.
>
> You cannot at Hobart town get an empty room under seven or eight shillings a week – a house with three rooms and a wash-house £1. Then such little places and theaves frequently get in at the top. Trade in general is very dead, owing to farmers' crops failing for want of rain. They have had little or no rain for this eighteen months past so badly were they off that they were put on allowance until they went to Sydney, for wheat at that time was £1 to £1.5s a bushel; now 10s a bushel and a two-pound loaf 9d at this time potatoes were 12s a cwt. Butter 3s 6d Eggs 2s a dozen Milk 1s a quart, mutton and beef 6d a pound, draught porter 1s 6d a quart, bottled 2s and 2s 6d a bottle. Colonial beer 1s a quart – no better than your London table beer. The money here is very bad, being paper even so low as threepence and most every man a banker. Any man can issue out his [promissory] notes that likes, so that the colony is overrun with rubbishy money. We landed most of the passengers at Van Dieman's Land but they would most of them have been glad to have gone back again to London if they had enough to have gone back with. The flies here are large and flyblow the meat before it is half cold; it is enough to turn one against it. There are a great many fleas and bugs; and many mosquitoes that bite worse than bugs. They sting one and leave a large bump and it is very tormenting in the hot weather.

Ann mentions the Mather and Benson families. **Anne Benson Mather** (m1811, d1831) and her husband had arrived in 1822 when he set up in business; the shop, by 1825, being attached to their house at the corner of Elizabeth and

Liverpool Streets. The family, Wesleyan then, became Quaker, perhaps as a result of meeting the humanitarian George Washington Walker whom the Mathers' daughter, Sarah, married. The Walkers were to live in Narryna, the historic house in Battery Point, and Sarah features in the itinerary 'Around Hobart'(p249).

For a broader picture of colonial life, particularly that of settlers, you cannot do better than GB Lancaster's novel *Pageant* (1933). **Edith Lyttleton** (1873–1945), who published under that pseudonym, was the great-grand-daughter of Frenchwoman **Marie Hyacinth Geneviève de Gouges Wood** (1794–1854) who settled with her husband Captain William Wood at Hawkridge, Powranna, just to the east of today's Midland Highway, in 1830.

6.   Mrs William Wood (Marie de Gouge Wood)
by Henry Mundy, courtesy of the Queen Victoria
Museum and Art Gallery, Launceston,
Groom family bequest

Mme Comyn, the most beguiling of the nicely-drawn characters, is based upon Mme Wood, and Clent Hall upon Hawkridge. We meet them again in the 'Midland Highway' itinerary (p351). The story starts in the 1840s, reverts to 1826, and then takes us forward – a perfectly-contrived and engrossing study of settler life and attitudes over the years. Madame's decidedly French take on Tasmania sums up arrestingly:

Forty years back the French *tri-couleur* would have flown where Hobart Town now stood if the English had not suddenly flung on the shore a handful of convicts, settlers, what-nots grabbed out of Botany Bay, while the French were still systematically marking out the channel as they passed up it.

And what had the English done with the country since? Stuffed it with redcoats and yellow convict jackets. Bribed with convenable grants of land such of the gentlemen adventurers as were on their beam-ends at close of the wars (plenty of these, thought Madam, grimly) and then put – what was it? – spokes in their carriages by causing the name of Van Diemen's Land to stink in the nose of the world.

A little later in that passage, Madame Comyn has thoughts that lead comfortably into the next chapter, for the settlers had plenty to fear as well as crop failure, bankruptcy and their children marrying beneath them:

She moved about, touching the flowers in their tall vases, glancing in the long mirrors, and hating the heavy velvet curtains veiling the shuttered windows. Bush-rangers made shutters needful, but many times Madam desired to fling them wide and scream into the night scented of box and trodden gum leaves and distant sheep-trampled grass: 'Come then, devils! We have no fear of you.'
She had fear though.

7 – Bushrangers and Women

Many male convicts had cause to be even more brutalised than were women because of more severe physical punishment. The result was sometimes disastrous for settlers, particularly women, and for Aboriginal women and, ultimately, their people. Some of the worst types, persistent or vicious offenders, were sent to places such as Macquarie Harbour and Port Arthur, the terrible new penal settlement established in 1830. (Although only men were inmates, wives accompanied those who controlled them and will appear in the itinerary 'Risdon Cove to Port Arthur', p280.)

In the early days, convicts had been sent into the bush to hunt for meat for the community; then some men – assigned servants or penal settlement inmates – escaped from convict life into the bush and became bushrangers – a euphemism for those who absconded and raided settler homesteads. Some men committed acts of violence as assigned servants or labourers.

Perhaps the most notable of these latter incidents took place in 1830 at Anstey Barton, near Oatlands, the home of Mary and Thomas Anstey. Their daughter **Julia Capper Anstey** (1824–1850) had been born in Tasmania the year after the family's arrival (their sixth child) and was only six when she was gang-raped by convicts assigned to the family. In spite of Ellen Viveash's poor opinion of James Sutherland, the Ansteys' brother-in-law, it was he who comforted them and was responsible for committing the perpetrators to Launceston Gaol. Julia went to stay for a while at nearby Bowsden with **Mary Hudspeth** (née Lowry, c1793–1853) and her doctor husband. The Ansteys had to give evidence at the trial and the three men, found guilty, were hanged. It is clear from the correspondence between Mary Reid and her daughter in India, Jane Williams, that the Anstey tragedy was common knowledge and that it terrified mothers with daughters.

I have not seen raised the motive for the attack on Julia, which was surely not just sexual, but perhaps connected to Anstey's position as police magistrate with overall responsibility for tracking down cattle and sheep thieves, bushrangers and absconding convicts – though KR von Stieglitz credits him with 'common sense and [a] kindly nature'. The attack is said to have seriously undermined the father's health. Although Julia married John Doughty, a surgeon in Oatlands, in 1842 and they had three children, she was only 25 when she died.

Bushrangers – absconding convicts, usually male but occasionally female – were to be a perennial problem, with incidents affecting women from at least 1814 to the late 1860s. Some bushrangers, such as Matthew Brady, Martin Cash and Michael Howe, achieved legendary status, their modus operandi well-known. Matthew Brady, regarded by the military as dangerous, considered himself a gentleman, who never robbed or insulted a woman. One internet account goes so far as to say that he 'endeared himself to the female population and so became Australia's first sex symbol'.

Michael Howe, the most notorious early bushranger, had turned from soldier to highwayman in England. Transported in 1812, by 1814 he had not only absconded but also built up what resembled an army of 28 fellows. Macquarie proclaimed an amnesty for absconders which achieved little; Davey proclaimed martial law and a strict curfew. Society was in a panic. It was then, in October 1814, that Howe and his gang swooped upon the McCarty homestead in New Norfolk – the first house to be built there.

Dennis McCarty, who had come out as a convict with Collins, had done well – he was pardoned in 1810 and appointed constable – but he remained a bit of a rascal and was in prison in Sydney at the time of the raid for smuggling 2,400 gallons of arrack. **Mary Ann McCarty** (sometimes McCarthy, or Carty, 1795–1865) was sitting in the parlour with a 'gentleman friend' when a sudden scream from the kitchen, from servant **Ann Jones**, gave the alarm.

Mary Ann was the daughter of **Ellen Wainwright** (or Winwright, 1769?–1839) a First Fleeter, transported for stealing a scarlet woollen cloak, a blue stuff quilted petticoat and a black silk hat. Sent from Sydney to Norfolk Island, she appears to have had children by different fathers, including two Mary Anns, the first of whom died. She arrived in Tasmania in 1808 with a Thomas Guy who was 'located' in New Norfolk, rather than granted land, and whom she married in 1812. Her daughter Mary Ann had, meanwhile, married McCarty in 1811, aged 16.

When the bushrangers attacked in October 1814, Mary Ann must have been fairly obviously pregnant, for her daughter Sophia was born on 27 January 1815. In this condition she dived under the parlour table hidden by a heavy cloth. Her companion, Mr Holsgrove, tells the story of how a bushranger discovered her there and put a hand on her but was persuaded not to 'violate' her. This was presumably in response to the comment that they had not come to hurt anyone 'except that damned whore Mrs M and she they would f___'. This quotation, unearthed by Nicholas Shakespeare (unfortunately without a source), replaces von Stieglitz's version, 'They had all spoken of Mrs McCarty as an (unprintable) fallen woman.' I have found no evidence about Mary Ann's past that justifies their opinion of her. Given an assurance that she would not be harmed, she emerged and directed the raiders towards the arms they knew from a convict servant were in the house.

Mary Ann was tied up, as was her sister, and her neighbour **Ann Hibbins** (née Clark 1767 or 1777–1851, m1803), when they were discovered. Mary Ann was instructed to make the intruders tea. Among themselves, as well as bad-mouthing Mary Ann (whom another source describes as 'elegant'), they laughed at Macquarie's proclamation. They allowed Mary Ann to keep a treasured box but escaped with £550 worth of booty in McCarty's boat. Mary Ann appears briefly in the 'New Norfolk' itinerary (p304), and Michael Howe in the chapter on Aborigines that follows, as does Ellen Wainwright Guy. (The story of Ann Hibbins, whose husband and father were Norfolk Island officials, would be too much of a diversion to tell here, but you could google Thomas Hibbins and he will emerge from the online *Australian Dictionary of Biography*.)

For Jane Reid Williams of Ratho, her first distinct memory of Tasmania is of a raid by bushrangers in 1822. She was seven, her brother was an infant, and the family had arrived in Tasmania that year, trekked to Bothwell with all their worldly goods and settled temporarily in a door and windowless turf cottage which Captain Patrick Wood had already erected at Dennistoun, near what was to be their home at Ratho (p329).

Jane's mother, Mary Reid, was hearing her repeat the shorter catechism, her father was in Hobart, 48 miles away, her brother was asleep in his crib, and Patrick Wood and another neighbour were working nearby,

> When an armed man looked into the hut, saying he was a constable looking for bushrangers. My mother told him he could see there was no one there, but he took up his station at the door, or where a door should have been, with his loaded gun ready to fire if any of us had attempted to escape. In the mean time others of the party went out and told the gentlemen that Mrs Reid and the women were terrified by some bushrangers, whereupon Captain Wood came running to the hut, on which he and Mr Russell were seized and handcuffed, as were all the men, and brought into the kitchen hut and seated round the fire, while two of the men watched them. The others took axes and began to break open the chests of drawers, boxes, etc., when my mother with her usual admirable composure told them it was a pity to destroy the furniture, and if they were determined to help themselves she would open the drawers, and getting her bunch of keys threw everything open, while they turned out the stores of clothing and other comforts my father had provided, thinking to give us all the necessaries of life which could not then be obtained in the bush.

The bushrangers worked through the night, making the servants drunk on Reid's wine bought en route at the Cape, while keeping sober themselves, ransacking the place, including around the crib. Little Alick awoke and begged them not to take his father's telescope – which they handed to him. Jane continues the story:

> Captain Wood urged my mother to put laudanum in their drink, or cut the cords that tied his hands; but patient submission she thought better, and lest there might be bloodshed would not agree. Eventually they went away, in the morning, taking as much as fourteen men could carry in sheets, and comforting us by saying they would soon come back and take the rest.
>
> My father arrived from town that day, and vowed he would not stay another day in such a place, but go and try Sydney. But my mother said, 'I've come so far with you, and I can go no further'.

Some of the bushrangers were caught in Hobart wearing Alexander Reid's shirts, with his name in them. Jane concludes the story: 'My mother always spoke of the great mercy it was that they were quite civil to her and the women servants.'

7   Mary Muirhead Reid, c1810, from Brown,
Clyde Company Papers, Prologue

Faced with a raid by bushrangers, women settlers almost without exception seem to have been brave and commonsensical. In *Pageant*, GB Lancaster noted, 'Fainting and megrims were all the fashion when all went well, but no pioneer woman gave way in times of stress.' In 1836, Henry Hunt attacked the dwelling of James Kerr and his wife. She was in the kitchen preparing the evening meal when she heard her husband shouting for help. KR von Stieglitz takes up the story in *A History of Evandale* (1967):

> She could see the two men rolling over and over on the ground, both covered from head to foot with the filthy slush of a primitive stable yard. Seizing the loaded musket that was always kept in a handy place for such an emergency, she sallied forth and ran to the place where they were struggling. But with the fading light and the thick coating of mud she could not distinguish one man from the other.
>
> 'Which is you, Jim? Which is you?' she begged, as gun in hand she prepared to give battle. Jim lost no time in making it quite plain which he was, and must have been relieved to feel the bushranger suddenly collapse in his arms, as Mrs Kerr brought down the butt of the gun with all her might on the unfortunate creature's head.

Hunt's skull was fractured, the stock of the gun 'shivered beyond repair'. James Kerr was given a £300 reward for the part he and his wife had played in Hunt's capture.

Von Stieglitz tells an 1840s story of a woman's presence of mind in *A Short History of Campbell Town* (1965) when

> Two bushrangers forced their way into the house ... while Connell and his wife and a maid were having breakfast. Looking up and thinking quickly, old Mrs Connell screamed, 'Oh, me hundred pounds!' and rushed upstairs closely followed by one of the bandits. There she waited for him behind the door of her bedroom and while he hesitated for a moment in the darkness, she whipped out of the door, slapping and locking it behind her. She was a tall long-armed Irish woman and not one to be easily outwitted. Creeping downstairs on tiptoe, she came to the kitchen door where she saw the other bushranger with his back to her, menacing her husband and the girl with a blunderbuss. Throwing her strong arms round his neck she dragged him to the floor while her husband snatched the blunderbuss from him and the maid beat him on the head with a pot stick.

There is another version of the story which has Mrs Connell tricking the bushranger upstairs, where, while scooping flour, he was tipped head first into the bin – showing that myths tended to grow up around these incidents. But **Margaret Connell** of Glen Connell was very much a real person for, in trying to find out more about her (and still failing to be sure of her dates), I discovered the Irish couple and their son John were very much involved in the well-being and escape of the Irish political prisoners who arrived in the early 1850s; indeed, there is an entry in John Mitchel's diary for 17 October 1851 that not only tells us more about Margaret but also about the vicissitudes of settler life from 1819:

> This morning we took a conveyance ... and drove sixteen miles through the valley of the Macquarie River to the Sugar-loaf; where dwells a worthy Irish family, emigrants of thirty two years ago from the county Cork ... Mr Connell and his wife have had severe hardships in their early days of settlement – a wild forest to tame and convert into green fields – wilder black natives to keep watch and ward against – and wildest convict bushrangers to fight sometimes in their own house. Mrs Connell is a thorough Celtic Irishwoman – has the Munster accent as fresh as if she had left Cork last year and is, in short, as genuine an Irish *Vanithee*, or 'Woman of the House', as you will find in Ireland at this day ... Most of their laborious toil and struggle is over; their farm smiles with green cornfields and their sheep whiten the pastures; their banks are well furnished with bees, and Mrs Connell's *mead* is seductive; the black Tasmanians have all disappeared before convict civilisation; and even the bushrangers are not 'out' so often these late years. Still it is needful that every lonely house should be well supplied with arms: and not many years have gone by since Mrs Connell performed, against these marauders, an achievement memorable in colonial story.

Mitchel then tells another version about the bushranger being locked in the closet and the second being pinioned by her from behind, then continues:

> Then, with the help of the children, [she] disarmed and tied him, and immediately securing the doors, began firing out upon the two rascals in the yard: they returned two or three shots, and decamped, leaving their comrades in the hands of Mrs Connell; *they* were hanged of course; and the family of Sugar-loaf ... had an additional grant of land allowed them for the exploit.

The Mitchel version suggests that Mr Connell was absent when the bushrangers attacked and von Stieglitz says the land was given to her. Another source says that she became a popular hero, which would account for the different versions of her story. She named the new property Black Snake Marsh. (Jenny and John Mitchel have space of their own in the 'Bothwell' itinerary, which also includes a Bothwell bushranger story, as experienced and told by Mary Brown Nicholas (Cluny, p330).)

Elizabeth (?) Tibbs (1807–1828) was not so lucky. In 1826 she was living with her husband of two years, their five-month-old infant and an elderly stockman at Lagan Falls near Evandale, five miles south of Launceston, when they were attacked by the absconder Thomas Jeffries, notorious as a cannibal. Again, there is more than one version of what happened next but one has the stockman shot dead, Mr Tibbs badly injured (one version has him killed) and Elizabeth Tibbs and her son taken off. At some stage, the child was grabbed from her arms and murdered. One version has him swung by his legs and dashed against a tree in front of his mother. But other facts suggest that she did not know where his body was; she begged Jeffries to tell her. It was discovered a week later attacked by a wild animal and decomposed. Jeffries was eventually caught and Elizabeth had to face him in court; not surprisingly she was in a state of collapse. If I have found the right Mrs Tibbs in the online archives, she died two years after the murder of her son, aged only 21.

At much the same time as Jeffries was on trial, Matthew Brady, the so-called gentleman, had also been captured. It is said that he was so disgusted by Jeffries' behaviour towards baby Tibbs that he wanted to lead his gang to where he was imprisoned and flog him to death.

Brady himself had, in 1825, attacked the Meredith house, Cambria, on the East Coast (p317) while George Meredith was in Hobart, but he assured Mary and her stepdaughters that they would not be harmed as he and his gang emptied the house of supplies and silver, in the meantime getting the women to cook a meal. They drank well from the Meredith wines.

At Mrs Ransom's public house, the Royal Oak, at Kempton, near another Brady raid, he asked only for a glass of wine, with which he drank her health, as his first assigned post had been with her before he was sent to Macquarie Harbour and escaped. Mrs Ransom and her well known pub appear in the 'Midland Highway' itinerary (p327).

The Brady gang arrived at Valleyfield near Campbell Town, the home of the Taylors, a branch of which is still known as breeders of fine Saxon Merino sheep (p340), in July 1824. Fifty-nine-year old **Mary Taylor** (née Low, c1765–1850; m1791) and her husband had arrived from Scotland the previous year with their eight grown-up children. Warned by a son who rushed ahead of the gang, the family took up defensive positions, forcing the bushrangers away with a storm of musket fire, 'the ladies of the household loading the firearms with unshakeable bravery'. Most of the gang fled, leaving behind stores and ammunition, but two of them were captured and the Taylor son who had warned the family, young George, lost the use of an arm. (He was speared to death by Aborigines two years later, in spite of previously having good relations with those who knew him.)

Brady was hanged in 1826, after many appeals for clemency from the public, and it is said that at his execution (at the same time as Jeffries') women wept and threw flowers. He was not the only gentleman. Ellen Viveash, telling in 1834 how there was a bushranger raid not far from them, concludes, perhaps to allay the fears of her family at home:

> They have been most polite and in some instances kind … returning watches if requested to do so by ladies and, in one instance, on hearing from the master of the house that his wife had just been confined, and his sister-in-law gone to bed fatigued, they passed the rooms on tip toe so that the ladies did not know of the robbery until the next morning and then the four armed men's leader said if they had known the case they would have waited a few days!

Martin Cash arrived in Tasmania in 1837 from New South Wales where, as a ticket-of-leave man, he had become suspected of sheep-stealing. With him came his companion of two years, **Bessie Clifford**, who had left her husband to live with him – he was, like Brady, a dashing fellow. Bessie and Cash worked together on various farms in Tasmania until he was accused of a theft he may not have committed, and he was given another seven years. Soon he absconded, was recaptured, escaped, and met up with Bessie. The two were on the run. But Cash was caught again, and twice attempted to escape from Port Arthur; the second time, in 1842, successfully. He was now in a bushranger gang of fellow escapees known for short as 'Cash and Co.'.

On 22 February 1843, **Susannah Shone** (née Westlake, 1799–1882), her husband Thomas, and a friend were dining at Stanton, Back River, New Norfolk, when their neighbour James Bradshaw knocked and Susannah opened the door. He was propelled into the room by Cash and Co. who made them all sit on the floor and then brought in seven servants tied up. At that moment, a carriage drew up and the Shones' son Frederick, their 22-year-old daughter **Mary Anne Shone** (later, 1824, Jillett), and her friend **Margaret Carter** were helped to alight by a polite gentleman, Martin Cash. The Shones lost not only possessions, including dresses and jewellery, but their assigned servants as well: they were withdrawn by the authorities because Shone had given in to the bushrangers. Meanwhile, Bessie Clifford was arrested and charged with receiving stolen goods, for the finery had been stolen for her. Cash wrote to Shone:

> In consequence of my observing in the public journals that my wife is in custody charged with having property in her possession belonging to you, I hereby caution you not to prosecute her, or, if you do, we will visit you and burn you and all that belongs to you. Signed Cash, Cavanagh, Jones.

And he sent this note to the governor:

> Messrs Cash & Co beg to notify His Excellency Sir John Franklin that a very respectable person named Mrs Cash is now falsely imprisoned in Hobart Town, and if the said Mrs Cash is not released forthwith and properly remunerated we will, in the first instance, visit Government House and beginning with Sir John, administer a wholesome lesson in the shape of a sound flogging; after which we will pay the same currency to all his followers.

Bessie was released, but not as a result of the threats; the authorities hoped she would lead them to Cash and Co. But it seemed, instead of doing that, she had taken up with another man. (Cash's entry in *The Companion to Tasmanian History* suggests that at some stage Bessie worked as a prostitute, but that is the only hint in all that I have perused.) On hearing of her betrayal, Cash rampaged into town to confront her, but was arrested in a gun fight in which he shot dead a policeman. For some reason, he was not hanged, but sent to the reopened penal settlement on Norfolk Island where he eventually married a ticket-of-leave-woman **Mary Bennett**, returned to Tasmania with her, became respectable, and died in his bed. As for Bessie Clifford, who knows what happened to her? The Shones appear again in the 'New Norfolk' itinerary (p307).

The novelist Isabel Dick, who spent time in a family home in New Norfolk, and whom we also meet in that itinerary, took advantage of the time that Martin Cash spent holed up in the area near the Shones to include him making a visit to her heroine Harriat Halifax, a new settler, in her best known novel *Wild Orchard* (1946). It is not as powerful a novel of settler life as GB Lancaster's *Pageant* – it is about a young couple at a moment in time, rather than extended family over the decades – but definitely worth a read, and Martin Cash's visit is neatly done; it starts:

> Coming through the hall to cross into her bedroom with the baby, Harry was surprised to come suddenly upon a man in riding breeches with his foot on the doorstep, about to enter. There was no sign of a horse and she was opening her mouth to ask what brought him when he questioned briskly:
> 'Is Mr Halifax at home, Ma'am? Not? Too bad. I have come a long way to see him too.' His manner conveyed that he was an old acquaintance. Still, Harry felt it best to be on her guard.

Harriat keeps her cool as she entertains the stranger, which impresses him, and, when he disappears, she finds a note pinned to the arm of the chair by her knitting needle signed by the notorious bushranger.

It is important not to be romantic about bushrangers. George Jones of Cash and Co., left alone when his companions were arrested, turned, with new comrades, to robbing the poor and is said to have tortured **Harriet Devereaux** when he believed she had more money than she had already handed over.

You will remember that in John Mitchel's description of Margaret Connell's difficult early days as a settler, he observed: 'wilder black natives to keep watch and ward against ... the black Tasmanians have all disappeared before convict civilisation'. What had been happening? And what was the relationship between settlers and Aborigines and bushrangers and Aborigines? And how had black Tasmanians 'disappeared'?

8 – Aborigines, Settlers, Bushrangers, Sealers and Wybalenna

From almost the beginning of British settlement in 1803, the game which had been seasonally hunted by the Aborigines since time immemorial as they moved between their traditional hunting grounds became a bone of contention. Because of the shortage of food in the settlement, convicts were sent off to hunt for the same prey in the same places, not realising, or caring about, the significance of their actions on the ecology or the Aborigines. But hunting indiscriminately created scarcity and thus exerted pressure on resources and led to tension.

The free settlers, arriving in increasing numbers in the 1820s, were granted acres on this same traditional Aboriginal land.

Bushrangers living permanently off the land, as well as raiding settlers' properties for their wherewithal, also came into conflict with Aborigines. Just like sealers in the early days, bushrangers and settler men living in remote places, or labourers without access to women, sought out Aboriginal women, often brutally. James Bonwick, who talked to people involved at the time for his study *The Last of the Tasmanians*, wrote:

> If perchance a woman was decoyed to the shepherd's hut, no gentleness of usage was employed to win her regard, and secure her stay; threatening language, the lash, and the chain were the harsher expedients of his savage love. … We hear of another who, having caught an unhappy girl, sought to relieve her fears, or subdue her sulks, as it was termed, by first giving her a morning's flogging with a bullock-whip, and then fastening her to a tree near his hut until he returned in the evening. The same fellow was afterwards found speared to death at a water hole.

Aborigines, naturally enough, began to exact vengeance, and to intrude on settlers' lands which were often, after all, their own. Colonists also borrowed or took, 'stole' is the word commonly used, children for their labour force – household servants and farmhands. The nineteenth-century historian West calls them 'juvenile slaves'. In 1814, Governor Davey issued a proclamation containing the remark: 'It is not without the most extreme concern that he has learnt that the resentment of these poor uncultivated beings has been justly excited by a most barbarous and inhuman mode of proceeding towards them, viz the robbery of their children.' Sorell commented on the practice in 1819. (It was not until the 1833 Factory Act that it was against the law in Britain to employ children under the age of nine in a factory, and the hours of those aged 9–13 years were limited to nine hours a day.) According to Lyndall Ryan, by 1817 there were at least 50 Aboriginal children in settlers' homes. Plomley gives a list of 49 – roughly the same number of girls and boys – who were baptised between 1810 and 1836.

By 1818, the Aboriginal population, which had been about 4,000 in 1803, had dwindled to less than 2,000; there were 3,114 colonists. By 1823, the colonists had risen to 10,000, by 1824 to 12,643 and by 1830 to 23,500, of whom 6,000 were free settlers. Between 1816 and 1823, the number of their sheep had grown from 54,600 to 200,000 and by 1826, to 553,698. In 1830, there were 1 million sheep.

As the pressure on land grew and tension mounted, colonist men would deliberately kill Aborigines, ostensibly for protection – 'The settlers and stock-keepers are determined to annihilate every Black who may act hostilely' – but often for sport. 'One man boasted he had thrown an old woman upon the fire, and burnt her to death.' The 1817 proclamation outlawing 'The habit of maliciously firing at, and destroying, the defenceless NATIVES or ABORIGINES of this island' followed already-established policy but seems to have been fairly ineffective. Bonwick records an undated story but typical of attitudes and actions of the time of the well-known bushranger Howe:

> Another worthy, who had left his country for his country's good, about fifty years ago, declared to me that he heard from a friend of Michael Howe, that the celebrated ruffian would lay down his musket to induce Blacks to come toward him, but that on their approach he would fire at them from his retreat, pulling the trigger with his toes. The Bushranger Dunn carried off Native women to his lair, and cruelly abused them.

Such depredations were known sometimes to lead to the murder by Aborigines of innocent settlers. But Howe was to get his comeuppance. (It should be noted, however, that West, in a footnote, maintains that Howe punished any of his fellows who wantonly mistreated an Aborigine – a fight was a different matter.)

Aboriginal women were known to colonists generically as 'gins' or, derogatorily, 'lubra' but, in a relationship, they might be given a name; Howe's companion was known as **Black Mary** – a name that crops up in connection with other black women, but also refers specifically to Howe's companion. She is known, too, as **Mary Cockerell** (d1819) or Cockerill. A family (**Anne Elizabeth Cockerell,** her husband William, and their three children,) also spelt both ways in the sources, came over with Collins as free settlers in 1804, and he was granted 100 acres at Stainforth Cove (now Moonah, New Town) at the same time as, and near to, Richard Pitt whose daughter Salome climbed Mount Wellington with the mystery Aborigine Miss Story.

I mention this slight diversion here because the internet correspondent, Carol Brill (whom I tried unsuccessfully to contact), writes of her settler ancestors and Black Mary, 'I do believe that Mary Cockerell was one of the local Aborigines who attached herself to the Cockerell family.' Could Mary have been a 'borrowed' child? Not all were stolen, some were apparently lent by Aborigines to cement reciprocal relations. And could Miss Story have a similar provenance? Neither name is on the baptismal list. The most likely explanation is that Mary Cockerell was orphaned in an affray with her parents and was thus taken into a colonist home. This ties in with one Howe source that says she was kidnapped during a raid on her people

Whatever Mary's background, she had been living with Howe as his 'wife', and as the gang's eyes and ears, since 1814 when, in April 1817, a party of soldiers in search of the bushranger caught up with him near Jericho. Mary was with him, perhaps pregnant, and finding it difficult to keep up as they fled. Did he shoot her to stop her talking, as one story has it, and as she seems afterwards to have been told? Or did he, aiming at their pursuers, hit her by mistake, as he later claimed? Whatever the truth, he left her lying there injured and, as Mary Pownall puts it, 'Then and there he exchanged devotion for retribution.' Questioned about the gang's activities and whereabouts, Mary led the soldiers to a hideout where they found some stolen sheep.

Mary was taken back to Hobart, and when she had recovered from her wound and given birth to her child (if she was pregnant), was set to track Howe and his gang and, with another woman, other bushrangers too. Howe was not to meet his grisly end in 1818 at her hand but she was responsible for the pressure put upon him which led to it, and for other members of his gang being captured. Later in 1817, she was sent to Sydney as a witness in their trial. I have found no mention of any child she may have had. When she died, the following appeared in the *Hobart Town Gazette* of 3 July 1819 (taken from Lindy Scripps *Women's Sites and Lives in Hobart*, which provides a useful version of Mary's story):

> On Tuesday died in the Colonial Hospital, the native woman usually called Black Mary, particularly known as having been at one time the partner of Michael Howe, and subsequently as a guide to the parties of troops which were employed successfully in subduing the gang of bushrangers; in which her knowledge of the country and of their haunts, and especially her instinctive quickness in tracking footsteps, rendered her a main instrument of the success which attended their exertions. She had been victualled from His Majesty's store, and had received other indulgences in clothing, etc; but a complication of disorders, which had long been gaining ground upon her, terminating last year in pulmonic affection, put an end to her life.

Even colonist men who did not establish relationships with Aboriginal women, brutal or otherwise, might be conscious of them as women. George Meredith, whose treatment of his wife Mary features in the 'East Coast' itinerary (Cambria, p317), wrote strangely to her in March 1823:

> We were honoured by the visit of six black *ladies* to breakfast the next morning who caught us craw fish and Mutton Fish [abalone] in abundance in return for bread we gave them – you would be much amused to see them Swim and Dive. Although I do not think you would easily reconcile yourself to the open display they make of their charms. Poor things, they are innocent and unconscious of any impropriety or indelicacy. They were chiefly young

and two or three well proportioned and comparatively well looking. So you see had I fancied a Black wife I had both opportunity and choice.

Was there any chance of friendly relations between Aboriginal and white women, apart from that hinted at between Salome Pitt and Miss Story and Anne Elizabeth Cockerell and Mary Cockerell? Miranda Morris makes a comment in *Placing Women* that suggests much:

> European women, frequently left unarmed and alone in isolated areas, lived in fear of their lives during the late 1820s. Unlike Aboriginal women they had little or no knowledge of the bush and no spiritual connection with it, nor had there been much attempt by the European population as a whole to learn from the Aborigines. Aboriginal Tasmanians on the other hand, had observed European behaviour in great detail, and many could understand English. Although European women had some cause to fear being killed, there were no reports of them being raped by Aboriginal men, nor were they kidnapped or forced into labour by them.

I have found only one example of a direct sisterly act. Again, Bonwick tells the story, and it relates to Ellen Wainwright Guy (mother of Mary Ann McCarty), the First Fleeter who had come over from Norfolk Island and who one might have expected to have had much of the milk of human kindness drained from her:

> Mrs Guy, of New Norfolk, gave me proof of attempted ruffianism in her day. Once when standing by her door she saw a native woman, pursued by three Englishmen, run to the high bank, leap into the Derwent, and swim across the broad stream. The benevolent lady hastened down to the poor creature, and found her much agitated with fear, and trembling violently. Taking her home, she gave her some warm tea, and bound a blanket around her. The husband came afterwards to thank the lady, and voluntarily cut up a lot of firewood in her yard as a return of gratitude.

Jacobina Burn's granddaughter, best known as the artist and conchologist **Jemima Frances Irvine** (née Burn, 1822–1919), told the historian KR von Stieglitz in her old age: 'I remember seeing the blacks when I was a child, coming to "Ellangowan" quite quietly, and my grandmother giving them handfuls of sugar and flour. They were very fond of flour and would dip their hands into it and lick it off or rub it all over their faces.' But she also remembered how 'A man came running up excitedly and gave the alarm that a mob of murderous blacks had gathered just over the hill.' He then ran off, and Jemima remembered how 'My poor grandmother walked up and down the room wringing her hands in her distress and saying over and over again, "Oh, I have brought this poor bairn here to be murdered before my very eyes."' Later, soldiers arrived to protect them.

That white women were increasingly frightened is illustrated, too, by Ellen in Harriet Martineau's 'novel' *Homes Abroad* (1834), discussed in more detail in the next chapter. It is Ellen's wedding morning when she is subject to attack – and there follows an image that someone must have conveyed from Tasmania to England:

> Immediately the black form she dreaded to see began to appear. A crouching, grovelling, savage, lean and coarse as an ape, showing his teeth among his painted beard and fixing his snake like eyes upon her, came creeping on his knees ... if it had been a wild beast she would have snatched up the musket ... but this was a man; among all his deformities, still a man, and she was kept motionless by a more enervating horror than she would have believed any human could inspire her with.

Whatever one makes of that description, Aborigines did descend on settlers. In the early days it was for food but, increasingly, they were fighting against a takeover of their hunting land, way of life, women and children – the depleting of a people of its women would have obvious repercussions for future generations. They would terrify settlers and quite often kill them, including women; indeed, there was the sort of horrifying tit for tat brutality that the world still sees in conflict between ethnic groups. The period from the mid 1820s to 1831 has been described as a guerrilla war or the Black War which, in 1830, following the declaration of martial law in 1828, became the Black Line – of settlers against Aborigines, ending with the relocation of Aborigines to Flinders Island and, finally, to Oyster Cove. The conflict and its outcome have been termed genocide of Tasmania's Aborigines.

According to Lyndall Ryan's paper 'Abduction and Multiple Killings of Aborigines in Tasmania 1804–1835' (nd), between July and October 1828, 'Aborigines appear to have killed 15 colonists in 11 incidents'. Between November 1828 and October 1830, 'there is evidence to estimate ... [that] at least 141 Aborigines were killed in 30 incidents, in which 116 died in at least 11 multiple killings. In the same period it is estimated that 75 colonists were killed by Aborigines in 53 incidents.'

Although women were less involved in most aspects than men, the treatment of Aboriginal women by white men has already been illustrated, and the fact that such treatment was one of the causes of Aboriginal violence. And Aboriginal women were often behind the scenes when retribution took place; it was they who reconnoitred and kept watch.

John Leake discovered four women by his fence in 1824 and after discussion with them returned with bread, Elizabeth Leake and some of their children, but he remained suspicious and added to his account:

> I am of the opinion these women come about as spies for the men, who ... deal very treacherously, and take every opportunity to spear a white man when it is in their power. I even saw one of the women, at a time when she thought herself unobserved, using violent gestures, and, as I thought,

cursing the ground, but it might all be imagination. No doubt, however, they look upon us as intruders.

But Charles Meredith, writing up notes about the past for his wife Louisa Anne Meredith (whose life and work dominate the 'East Coast' itinerary), gave another version: 'In several instances, the lives of white people were saved by the native women, who would often steal away from the tribe, and give notice of an intended attack.'

But the Jones family experienced a more concerted attempt at attack in 1826 and, again, Aboriginal women played their part on the *qui vive*. Robert Jones was one of those in charge of the Lords' livestock between the Clyde and Ouse Rivers, and had just arrived home from seeing to some sheep when his little boy came running in to **Mrs Jones** to say that there were Aborigines about. While Jones went to investigate, his wife stood at the door with a loaded pistol. On Jones' return to the house, the Aborigines came closer. Mrs Jones waved her pistol at them and one of them responded in English, ending with threatening gestures, 'As for you ma-am – as for you ma-am – I will put you in the bloody river, ma-am.' Jones described their saviour rather ambiguously: 'We had with us a courageous and faithful little girl'; she set off to get help from neighbours. When they arrived, 'the native women upon the tier gave out a signal and the blacks all fled'. It is difficult to interpret the status or even the ethnic origin of the 'little girl'.

While Mrs Jones waved her pistol menacingly, a woman, who may have been a **Mrs Parker**, caught in a similar situation, put her broom to her shoulder, pointed it at the attackers, and ordered them away. They went.

There were several versions of Margaret Connell's defence of the homestead against bushrangers in later years; you may remember that there was also a hint in John Mitchel's account of her past of an attack by Aborigines (p94). John West provides the only possible confirmation I can find when he writes, without giving a date, 'Mrs Connel defended her house with a musket; a little child, of four years, bringing one to her as she fired off another; she was within a few days of her confinement.' Bonwick elaborates on this account, without even giving a name. But there was a little girl involved, too, who ladled pannikins of water onto the fire started by the attackers. And, in this version, the brave little boy had been wounded by a spear. It ends: 'Governor Arthur was so pleased with the heroism of the woman that he presented her with a grant of three hundred acres of land, and undertook to provide for the future of the brave boy and girl.' Since Arthur was Governor, it was after 1824. It may be that Margaret Connell's dates are 1798–1890, and that she had a daughter called Margaret in 1817. (There are several Margaret Connells in the records, without any useful elaboration).

Successful defence by the woman, sometimes alone, was not always the fortunate outcome when Aborigines came to a settler homestead. Again, the accounts are given in most detail in the notes which Louisa Anne Meredith used wholesale in *My Home in Tasmania* (1852; 2003) – though these accounts do not always tally with those from other sources such as the historian von Stieglitz.

In 1827, a small farmer named Hooper lived with his wife and seven children near Jericho. It appears that for several days a group of Aborigines watched as Hooper set out for the fields. On the day that he did so without his gun, they struck, felling him with their *waddies* (clubs). They then proceeded to the house, either setting it on fire and killing all within or, as Meredith has it, setting about **Mrs Hooper** and her children with spears, not only murdering them, but mutilating them too. The Meredith account ends with the claim that 'A Black woman some time after told the whole of their plans and schemes to achieve this terrible murder.' Louisa Anne was so upset by this history that she wrote an epic poem 'A Tasmanian Memory of 1834' about the murder of the Hooper family. She gave a public reading of it in 1869.

In October 1828, the Meredith stock-keeper Josiah or John Gough was in his hut with the family servant **Anne Geary** when their neighbour **Nancy Mortimer** ('Mother Mortimer') came panting in, begging Gough to come quickly to save possessions from her hut which the Aborigines had set on fire – her husband was away. Gough set off, leaving Nancy, his wife and daughters at home. The Mortimers' hut was beyond saving, but Gough instinctively turned round and raced for his own. Meredith records:

> The first object that met his sight was the body of his young wife, pierced with many spears, and her brains knocked out. A little beyond lay the old woman Mortimer, her head cloven in two with an axe. Near to the hut he found his eldest girl, her head beaten to pieces; and near her the youngest, stunned with blows on the head, and otherwise dreadfully hurt, but still alive and moaning.

The wounded daughter told what had happened, how the women had barricaded themselves in but the spears rained upon the windows and then the attackers came down the chimney, as Nancy Mortimer tried to stop them.

The von Stieglitz version differs: he tells how two small daughters, Esther and Alicia, were killed and Gough, his other two daughters, and Anne Geary were severely wounded and that a few days later the killers returned and murdered **Mrs Gough**, her husband arriving back in time for her to die in his arms. Von Stieglitz ends that it was believed that the attacks were in reprisal for the mutilation and killing of two Aboriginal women by stock-keepers employed by Gough.

Since the attack was on a Meredith employee, perhaps that version is more factual – though he may have wished to be discreet about the Aboriginal women killed. When another man employed by the Merediths was also killed, George Meredith told an 1830 inquiry, 'In neither case was provocation given by the whites.' This is interesting, given how Louisa Anne ends her accounts of the killing of the Hooper and Gough families:

But enough of these harrowing details! Surely I need transcribe no more; nor would I have particularised even these, but in the hope of making known something of the real state of affairs as formerly existing between the aborigines and the colonists, which is so greatly misunderstood in England; where, as I well know, the white people are most erroneously believed to have been the aggressors.

The same month as the Gough murders, settler **Mrs Langford** and her two children were attacked; her 14-year-old daughter was killed. The Langford attack in October was widely reported in the press and led to demands for military protection; martial law was proclaimed in November. Does the higher social profile of free settler Mrs Langford over that of former convict Mrs Gough suggest that the attack on the former led to action, or was the violence against colonist women and reaction to it cumulative?

During this time, colonist men and Aborigines, including women, but without recorded names, continued to be murdered. The most notorious event occurred in February 1828 at Cape Grim, in the north west, the lands of the Van Diemen's Land Company – it is still known as the Cape Grim Massacre, but is not always mentioned in mainstream histories of Tasmania; where it is, controversy has followed.

The massacre had its beginnings, as Lyndall Ryan recounts in *The Aboriginal Tasmanians*, in November the previous year when some Peerapper people, visiting the area as they customarily did in search of muttonbird eggs and seals, found instead shepherds' huts and a large flock of sheep. When the shepherds tried to entice some Peerapper women into their huts, the Aboriginal men objected and a skirmish ensued during which a shepherd was wounded and a Peerapper man shot. In retaliation, the Peerapper drove a flock of 118 sheep by spear and *waddy* over the cliff into the sea.

Six weeks later, the shepherds crept up on some Pennemukeer, Aborigines from a different band, while they were muttonbirding on Company land. They shot 30 and threw their bodies onto the rocks below. In her separate paper, Lyndall Ryan tells how the Company Superintendent reported the incident to Governor Arthur. An Aboriginal woman at the inquiry set up said that many women had been shot; the four perpetrators said that only one woman was among the murdered. Edward Curr, the Company manager, in his dispatch to London, reported six dead in total, revised down to three. (A useful exploration of the facts is contained in 'The Van Diemen's Land Company and the Tasmanian Aborigines: A Reappraisal', G Lennox, 1990.) According to the entry in the *Encyclopaedia of Aboriginal Australia* (1994), 'a whole band was wiped out' in that single event. (The encyclopaedia is, however, disappointing in the number of its Tasmanian entries.)

Rosalie Hare (1809–1880), whose new husband was captain of the *Caroline*, stayed with Mrs Curr for some weeks from January 1828 while their husbands went off on business, and wrote in her journal edited as *The Voyage of the Caroline* (1927, edited by Ida Lee), 'While we remained at Circular Head there were several accounts of considerable numbers of natives having been shot by them (the Company's men), they wishing to extirpate them entirely, if possible.' (More of what she wrote appears in the 'North West Coast' itinerary, p389.)

Whatever the true figure, and the incident and reports of it can be seen in the same light as the Risdon Massacre of 1804, writers such as Cassandra Pybus and Carmel Bird, with their acute historical sensitivity, find ways of keeping it in public consciousness. In *Community of Thieves* (1991), Cassandra Pybus follows up the contemporary witness statements – from Aboriginal women and one of the shepherds – given to George Robinson. The shepherd confirmed the figure 30, and the women that the incidents had arisen over women, and the intention of the shepherds to rape them. Cassandra writes:

On enquiry I am told that busybodies like myself, sharing Robinson's credulity, have caused the company any amount of trouble by repeating patent mistruths about scores of bodies heaved over the cliff. Didn't happen. Couldn't have happened.

Carmel Bird underpins her novel *Cape Grimm* (2004) with the ghosts of the past. From the journal of her character Virginia, she quotes:

Historians and others continue to do battle over the lost truths of the conflicts between black and white in the remote little corner of Van Diemen's Land at Cape Grimm. I entertain a fanciful notion that the cataclysmic grisly violence of the nineteenth century infects the air and the land and the sea around Cape Grimm.

Virginia is deeply affected by what happened and communicates with the ghost of one of the women victims – Mannaginna. Finally we have a name, even if it comes from Carmel's imagination. More of the novel appears in the 'North West Coast' itinerary (p390).

Once martial law was declared, the authorities had to take action. This culminated in September 1830 in what was called the Black Line. The idea was to drive the Aborigines before a steadily advancing line of combined forces – military, civil, and ticket-of-leave men – into unsettled areas. The manoeuvre itself was an expensive failure – two Aborigines were captured, the rest slipped the net – but it did clear them from settled areas. Mary Reid wrote to her daughter Jane Williams in India on 20 December 1830: 'The war in which the whole country was engaged against the Natives ... has proved completely unsuccessful; they have eluded the strictest search.'

At the same time as the military attempt to solve the Aborigine problem, there was another proposed solution – one of 'pacification' or, the more usual term, 'conciliation'. To carry it out, the authorities employed George Augustus Robinson, a builder and lay preacher, who had arrived from London in 1824. His wife, **Maria Robinson** (née Evens, c1788–1848, m1814) and five children had joined him in 1826. Maria was obviously not thrilled about his appointment, for Robinson remarked, 'I reasoned the matter over with Mrs Robinson and with difficulty obtained her consent.'

Robinson started to prepare for the job as conciliator by going (without his growing family) to Bruny Island in March 1829 and getting to know Aborigines there. He planned to establish a settlement where they could be 'civilised' and 'Christianised'. Tiring of the problems that venture created, on 28 January 1830, he set out, mostly on foot, around Tasmania with several Aborigines from Bruny Island who were to help him in his conciliation mission. Among them was a young woman called **Trukanini** (also, Trugernanner and, most commonly, Truganini or Truganinni, c1812–1876). (The transliteration of the original sound of her name into English is somewhere between a 'g' and a 'k'; I have taken advice about which most appropriate spelling to use). She was the daughter of Mangana, leader of the Lyluequonny of the South East nation which moved between Bruny Island and Recherche Bay where she was born.

Cassandra Pybus, descendant of early settlers, wears her heart on her sleeve, as she often does in her writing, when she notes in 'Mannalargenna's Daughters':

My ancestor was Robinson's good friend and neighbour. Our family inherited what was Truganinni's birthright, a massive tract of land which was handed over to my great-great-great grandfather as a free grant in 1829, even as Truganinni and her family still lived on it. This is a grim historical legacy and there are times that I would wish to shift the burden. How much more pleasing would it be if my attachment to this temperate paradise was not the result of false promises and outright theft, but based rather on an unbroken connection to the land spanning millennia.

By the time Trukanini was 17, the invaders of her land (not Cassandra's ancestors!) had stabbed her mother to death, when Trukanini was small, murdered her fiancé in a terrible manner in her presence as she was abducted by boat and then raped, kidnapped her stepmother, and abducted her birth sister **Moorina** (Murreninghe, Kit, d?1830) and her tribal sisters **Lowhenunhue** (Lorewenunhe, d1829) and **Maggerleede** (Makelede, Sal). I have not found a record of the name of her mother or stepmother. The absence of their names may have a cultural significance. Her sisters were taken to Kangaroo Island just off today's Adelaide. Moorina was later shot by a sealer.

Trukanini is usually said to have been childless, but the ghosted autobiography of Banjo Clarke, *Wisdom Man* (2003, Camilla Chance) claims that he is descended from her daughter **Louisa Esme** (1827–1925) who must have been conceived at about this time; indeed, that is apparently why she kept quiet about the conception and birth. Louisa is said to have married John Briggs, son of the sealer George Briggs and Woretermoeteyenner, in 1844 and was thus sister-in-law of Dolly Dalrymple Briggs. Banjo Clarke knew Louisa as Granny Briggs, and she was quite clear about her parentage. Ida West, in her Trukanini entry in the *Encyclopedia of Aboriginal Australia*, wrote: 'Truganini, had no known descendant but had been heard to speak of a child she had borne.' Ida noted that Esme Briggs claimed her as a mother, and the Clarkes, saying they were descendants, attended Trukanini's final ceremony in 1976. Other sources give a different birth date, place and parentage for Louisa Esme Briggs. There are details from the Clarke book about Trukanini taking Louisa over to the mainland in Chapter 12.

8.   Truggernana (Trukanini), by Thomas Bock, 1832, courtesy of the Tasmanian Museum and Art Gallery

In 1829, Trukanini married Wooraddy of the Nuenone of Bruny Island – a man 20 years older than her and with two sons from a former relationship. By 1830, Trukanini, four feet five inches tall, was about 18 and an orphan. There are numerous attempt to convey an image of her, mostly in old age. But Bonwick, while going for the overblown, did at least know her then and had first-hand information of her when younger from a European woman; he wrote:

When I saw her, thirty years after her wonderful career with Mr Robinson, I understood the stories told of her vivacity and intelligence. Her eyes were still beautiful, and full of mischievous fun. Thirty years before, she would have been captivating to men of her colour, and not by any means an uninteresting object to those of whiter skins. Her mind was of no ordinary kind. Fertile in expedient, sagacious in council, courageous in difficulty, she had the wisdom and the fascination of the serpent, the intrepidity and nobility of the royal ruler of the desert. Would that we could say that her purity of morals equalled the brilliancy of her thoughts, and that her love of virtue was akin to her love of adventure! She was but a savage maiden, trained in the wilderness. A lady described to me her appearance in 1832. She declared her exquisitely formed, with small and beautifully-rounded breasts. The little dress she wore was thrown loosely around her person, but always with a grace and a coquettish love of display.

Trukanini labours under various historical burdens. First, because of the vicissitudes of her life, and the part she played in the near-elimination of her people, and the fact that she herself survived into gracious old age, she is used as the Aboriginal woman of Tasmania, almost to the exclusion of all others, thus skewing the story of those about whom comparatively little is known. Apart from written accounts, it is she who is commemorated as no other is, on Mount Nelson above Sandy Bay (p251) and on Bruny Island (p288).

Second, her motivation has been constantly picked over. Vivienne Rae-Ellis, who has written most about her, uses the provocative title for her biography *Trucanini: Queen or Traitor* (1981), which gives a flavour of the controversy surrounding her. (With Nancy Cato, she also earlier wrote the novel *Queen Trucanini* (1976).)

Among the unresolved issues is Trukanini and Robinson's relationship. As it set out on the arduous journey that was to last from 1830 to 1835, Robinson's band also included Wooraddy, and Trukanini's girlfriends **Pagerly** (bc1811) and **Dray** (Drayduric, c1799–1861). With them it is said that she used to go with the convict woodcutters and European whalers who increasingly frequented those waters and that from them they all contracted sexually transmitted diseases. Vivienne Rae-Ellis has decided that, in due course, Trukanini and Robinson became lovers, and gives as evidence for this interpretation of codes in Robinson's diary and correspondence. Cassandra Pybus thinks differently; she writes in *Community of Thieves*:

> Truganini ... displayed an intense loyalty and attachment to Robinson that has fascinated generations of Tasmanians ... Some say that the attraction was sexual and that she and Robinson had a long liaison ... many men found her desirable, while she had no aversion to sexual relationships with white men. Still, I can find no evidence to suggest a sexual relationship. It is an obvious deduction to make, but it is quite out of character for Robinson and the good father role he chose for himself. Truganini had been subjected to some horrendous violence from white men in her nineteen years, and must have been traumatised by the disaster that enveloped her people. She appears to have fixed on Robinson with a fierce determination that he would be the agent of her survival.

Whatever their relationship, Trukanini was to remain intensely loyal, saving Robinson's life at least once, and he could not have managed in the task he set himself without her and his other Aboriginal companions. Dray, for example, as a member of the Port Davey nation in the west, acted as go-between when they reached there. Robinson later claimed that 20 members of her nation agreed to be resettled. According to Trukanini, recounted by James Calder, surveyor and historian between 1829 and 1882, Dray had been stolen from her people and getting home was her main reason for accompanying Robinson. Robinson later rewarded Dray 'with a print gown sewn by a soldier's wife'.

Bulyer (Bullrer, Leemuenerkallerwanner) joined the mission later, from the north east where she had lived with sealers on the Bass Strait islands; she told Robinson about the brutality she and women like her had experienced. (Brian Plomley suggests in more than one of his publications that Bulyer was the same woman as Jumbo, mentioned in Chapter 1 – but Lyndall Ryan's later comprehensive appendix of names does not confirm that. Bulyer was the daughter of **Poolrerrener** (Bullrub), born before her mother was kidnapped many years earlier.) By 1830, there were 74 Aboriginal women living with sealers, or straitsmen, on the islands.

Everywhere Robinson travelled, with convict porters and his Aboriginal team, the women sometimes wearing gaudy ribbons to attract the eye, he first sought to establish friendly relations; then on a second visit – some time, perhaps years, later – he persuaded the Aborigines, partly through force of personality (though he was overweight and bewigged), partly through dissembling, that it was in their interests, for their safety and well-being, to move elsewhere. Later he resorted to threats. Every Aborigine he rounded up brought him a financial reward. The violence implicit in the Black Line, and the violence that had preceded it, made his task easier. On one of his visits to Cape Grim, Robinson interviewed one of the shepherds involved in the 1828 massacre and the women in the sealers' camp on nearby Robbins Island who knew all about it.

Other Aborigines helped Robinson for months and years at a time, without being aware of the implications of his mission. Most notable was Mannalargenna (also called Limina Bungana) who had earlier resisted settler incursion. Now, as Cassandra Pybus tells us, he 'was desperate to negotiate a deal'. That is, in addition to the one he had made years before with the sealers regarding women of his family. 'He formed a compact with Robinson', Cassandra recounts, 'to repatriate his four daughters, his sister, his wife, and her two sisters who had been taken by sealers.' One source suggests that he only appeared to help, while another suggests that Robinson was unsuccessful in his part of the bargain, to retrieve the women.

Certainly Mannalargenna's daughter **Nimmeranna** (Teekoolterme) continued living with the sealer John Thomas on Cape Barren Island; not all the women wished to leave what had become home and Robinson, who tried every means of persuasion, commented in his journal on the difficulties caused by such women's intransigence. The fact that the sealers themselves protested at the removal of their women was not totally self-serving, and one case, at least, is rendered poignant by the letter Thomas Beedon (Beeton, convicted in 1817 as James Baden) wrote to Governor Arthur in about 1831, part of which is quoted here from Lynette Russell's article (with her editing):

About 5 and a half years since I fell in with an aboriginal female ... on Woody Is. [Bass Strait] who had been for some time previous been living with one of the sealers named Harrington who had then been dead about 1 ½ years before I had any knowledge of the said woman. From a feeling of humanity towards the woman owing to her apparent desire to make herself useful and from her own particular requests, ... I beg now to state to your Excellency that I have had by the same woman two children, one of which is now living, aged 2 years[,] and that she is now far advanced in a state of pregnancy when she was made acquainted with the intentions of Mr Robinson to separate her from me she expressed a strong feeling against leaving me … [W]hen I took her to Mr Robinson [and] asked her in his presence if she would like to stay [with Robinson] she most indignantly refused. Under the above circumstances I humbly hope your Excellency will be graciously pleased to allow the woman again to be restored to my protection for the sake of her infant child.

Such letters and other approaches by straitsmen to the authorities were, on the whole, successful. Although the woman mentioned by Beedon is not named, a couple of years earlier, **Emmerenna** (Woreterneemmerunner, Bet Smith, b1790) from Cape Portland was the mother of Lucy Beedon, and Thomas Beedon the father. Emmerenna had been abducted as a child by another sealer. Vivienne Rae-Ellis suggests that she was another of the women who were forced, or chose, not to have the children conceived from these unions – in Bet Smith's case, by stuffing grass into the mouths of two sons. Lucy was later to become a pillar of her community, elaborated on in Chapter 12 (p193).

Another woman who stood by her man or, rather, swam, was **Wauba Debar** (1792–1832). She was abducted by sealers as a teenager near Oyster Bay but, when her de facto sealer husband and a mate were shipwrecked in a storm a kilometre from shore, she rescued them and their cargo of sealskins, and then nursed her husband back to health (p321).

By supreme irony, it was the women who had gone willingly or unwillingly with the sealers, and stayed, who were to survive the fate of their fellows, and it is their descendants who survive to this day.

As for Mannalargenner's wife, Benjamin Duterreau, portraitist of both the Great Portland chief and **Tanlebonyer** (sometimes Tanleboueyer, Sall, Sarah, d1863) from Swanport, told Bonwick that she and her sister 'Were originally stolen from their country, when children, and held in bondage until emancipated by Mr Robinson (in 1830).' When, then, one has to ask, if she was stolen as a child, and rescued as his wife in 1830, did they marry? I have done my best to check and double-check details, but this shows how women were confused one with another; they were often passed from one sealer to another and several women had the same European name; there were at least eight Salls. Duterreau also says of Tanlebonyer:

This woman laboured incessantly to promote the objects of the Mission … She was superior to the other Natives both in person and intelligence, and possessed much dignity of manners, seldom participating in those frivolities the others indulged in. She was exceedingly attached to her husband. The feeling was mutual, for during the period of six years they were with Mr Robinson they never quarrelled.

Not everyone was cooperative. In 1828, Walyer (p32) escaped from the sealers who had abducted her in her younger days. Returning to the north coast,

9.   Tanleboueyer (Tanlebonyer) by Benjamin
Duterrau, 1835, courtesy of the Allport Library
and Museum of Fine Arts, Tasmanian Archive
and Heritage Office

she gathered around her a group of women and men from the Lairmairrener
people of Emu Bay to fight the invaders. She taught them the use of firearms
– the skill she had learned from the sealers – and ordered them to strike the
luta tawin (whiteman) when they were at their most vulnerable, between the
time that their guns were discharged and before they were able to reload. She
felt about the *luta tawin* as she did the black snake. As Lyndall Ryan puts it:
'Walyer was known to stand on a hill and give orders to her men to attack
the whites, taunting them to come out of their huts to be speared.'
     Robinson came across Walyer's band in September 1830. They were stalking
him, probably to kill him, so he moved on. Challenged by other Aborigines
whom she seems also to have attacked for being on the wrong side, Walyer
escaped to Port Sorell, her original home, with two of her sisters – perhaps
Trildoborrer and **Noendapper** (d1821) – and two brothers, but was taken
by sealers; with them she passed under the name Mary Anne. Then she was
taken to Forsyth Island. In December she was plotting to kill one of the
sealers but was, instead, taken by one of Robinson's agents to the temporary
settlement on Swan Island where her identity as the woman Robinson called
'the Amazon' was revealed when she called out to her dog Whiskey by name.

(Dogs, introduced to Aborigines by colonists as a form of currency, quickly became part of Aboriginal culture.)

Robinson felt it was a real coup – 'A matter of considerable importance to the peace and tranquillity of those districts where she and her formidable coadjutors had made themselves so conspicuous in their wanton and barbarous aggression.' On Swan Island, Walyer was isolated to stop her conniving. In February 1831, she was moved to Gun Carriage (Vansittart) Island where, on 5 June, she died of influenza. History has dealt more kindly with Walyer: she is now seen as a resistance fighter, and a material manifestation of that appears in the 'North West Coast' itinerary (Burnie, p387).

How common fighting women were is open to question. But Bonwick mentions how one fierce chief, Montpeliata (Big River), when face to face with Robinson and his mission, and surrounded by his own men, walked 'slowly to the rear to confer with the old women – the real arbiters of war'. The rump of the Eastern nations consisted then of 16 men, nine women and one child but, brandishing their spears, they were a terrifying sight to those who accompanied Robinson.

Between 1824 and 1831, those Aborigines had killed at least 60 colonists. A second chief in the party, Tongerlongter, told Robinson, Lyndall Ryan reports, 'that the reason for their outrages upon the white inhabitants [was] that they and their forefathers had been cruelly abused, that their country had been taken from them, their wives and daughters had been violated and taken away, and that they had experienced a multitude of wrongs from a variety of sources'. They were exhausted, and though calling for compensation, agreed to accompany Robinson.

In one letter, quoted in Vivienne Rae-Ellis' biography of Robinson – *Black Robinson: Protector of Aborigines* (1988) – he wrote: 'I have promised them an interview with the Lieutenant-Governor, and told them that the government will be sure to re-dress their grievances.' The first part was true, but not the second. Vivienne Rae-Ellis, who clearly does not like her subject, suggests that Robinson manipulated the truth, not only to the Aborigines but to the government as well.

In *Fate of a Free People* (1995; 2000), the Tasmanian historian Henry Reynolds builds on the incident with the Big River people, adding strands from elsewhere, to suggest an important role for Aboriginal women in tribal life, one that makes Robinson's deviousness more of a betrayal. There was more involved than consultation with the old women as arbiters; on the same occasion, Robinson notes how 'Some of [his] courageous female guides had glided round, and were holding quiet, earnest converse with their wilder sisters.' Then the women threw up their arms three times – 'the inviolable sign of peace'. In her discussions with James Calder, Trukanini explained how she had recognised that there was no holding back the influx of colonists, and how, through trusting and working with Robinson, 'I hoped we would save all my people that were left.' She became, Reynolds suggests, 'a major promoter of the peace settlement'. Then there is Dray, acting as an invaluable go-between with the west coast people. Reynolds concludes that 'It is quite possible that women had a major customary role in diplomacy and inter-tribal relations.'

If that offers clarification of the women's hopes and understanding, historians still discuss Robinson's motives and intentions. Having gathered Aborigines together from various areas over the years of his mission, some, like the Big River people, were taken in triumph to Hobart where they were well-received.

It is probable that the 'Lines – Written on the recent visit of the Aborigines to Hobart Town' and published in the *Hobart Town Magazine* in 1834 under the name 'Frances', marks that visit. The poet is assumed to be **Frances Hannah Gunn** (1808–1887) who was born in Sydney to Elizabeth Burleigh, former convict wife of Dr Thomas Arndell, surgeon to the First Fleet. She went to Tasmania in 1814 to live with her sister **Elizabeth Gordon** (b1792) of Forcett (p279), who that year married the magistrate James Gordon (Elizabeth Island in Macquarie Harbour was named after her). In 1829, Frances married Lieutenant William Gunn (who had lost his right arm in an attack at Sorell by the bushranger Matthew Brady); they were to have six daughters and three sons. But Frances found time for further occupation. Morris Miller describes her as 'the first native-born woman to write and publish verse in Australia'. The 'Lines' start:

> They are come in their pride, but no helmet is gleaming,
> On the dark brow'd race of their native land;
> No lances are glittering, nor bright banners streaming –
> O'er the warriors brave, of that gallant band.

And the 'Song of the Aborigines' ends:

> Then shall each mountain, vale and river,
> Our glorious hopes proclaim,
> Our winds shall breathe, and our waters roll –
> Blessing the Christian's name.

> And when to the judgment bar of Heav'n,
> Ye shall lead our ransom'd band –
> Ye Shall mercy find, for ye brought us
> When lost, to this promised land.

I would not presume to suggest what Aborigines would have thought of her sentiments on their behalf. Some Aborigines taken to Hobart lived for a while in a building attached to the Robinsons' house in Elizabeth Street. Maria Robinson did not see her husband for a year after he first set out. She was left in charge of his building business and his financial affairs in spite of her large family, and the death of their youngest son soon after Robinson left. He was not a good husband or father – confirmed by his eldest daughter **Maria Amelia Robinson** (bc1818, later Allen) – and Maria suffered social ostracism as his reputation was increasingly attacked. He did, however, negotiate with the government that she and each of their six remaining children should receive a pension in the event of his death. He was, meanwhile, accumulating considerable material reward from his mission.

Most of the 'conciliated' Aborigines were sent to holding centres such as that on Swan Island in the Bass Strait; finally all were transported to the newly established settlement at Wybalenna on Flinders Island. Those gathered there were from many nations, not necessarily reconciled to each other, or speaking each other's language (there were between eight and ten different languages or dialects spoken in 1834), and conditions were so dissimilar to their traditional life that the population began to decline through illness and unhappiness. Many simply pined away. By 1835, there were only 150 Aborigines left alive there. Typical of the deaths was that of Ouray-Ouray, the first woman to be named (by Péron) in European sources (pp6–8), described by David Davies without, unfortunately, giving a source or a date.

I can find no record among the many deaths year after year at Wybalenna of a name anything like hers, or, indeed, her name among the living. Bonwick, from whom Davies draws material, mentions her in connection with Wybalenna only after reading a rosy account of life there in 1832: 'Really, after reading this romantic account of the Flinders' residents, especially of the musical agriculturalists, we quite fancy we are listening to the entranced Frenchman, and expect to behold the rosy cheeks of the innocent and modest Oura-Oura.' Strangely, the end of the Davies passage includes a direct short quotation contained in Bonwick, but the latter gives no name to the woman who uttered it, nor suggests even by implication that it was Ouray-Ouray – she was simply a 'dying gin'. Davies writes:

> In the end the greatest beauty of their race, Oura-Oura, though now old, was also brought to Flinders Island, 'to die as they all die'. As the surgeon put it: 'It is a strange sickness of the stomach – in other words, home-sickness.' She was fortunate, her end was swift. She asked the surgeon to take her to the shutters and open them. In the foreground was the bleak and barren wastes of the island, but as the dawn light strengthened, clear beyond were the white slopes of Ben Lomond, on the mainland, its snows sparkling in the gleaming sunshine, and Oura-Oura with a shaking finger and arm pointed it out to him, in a trembling voice, in the pidgin English so patronizingly taught her by her nation's conquerors. Her last words were, 'That-Me-Country.' Ben Lomond still sparkled but she was dead.

It may be that you can see Ben Lomond from a hut in Wybalenna – there is evidence that you can from a ship at sea a bit further south, particularly when it is snow-capped and caught by the sun – but Ouray-Ouray did not come from there but from Port Cygnet some way to the southeast. Tanleboneyer (also known as Evannah at Wybalenna, and elsewhere as Sall) died in 1836, less than a year after her husband, Mannalargenna. She was familiar with Ben Lomond. It is also assumed that Pagerly died on Flinders Island; Dray, known there as Sophia, survived it. Lyndall Ryan confirms in correspondence that there is no evidence of Ouray-Ouray's presence at Wybalenna.

In *Wild Orchard*, Isabel Dick chooses assigned servant Maggie to explain to fearful newcomer settler Harriat her opinion of what was happening at Wybalenna:

> To my astonishment Maggie argued that it was a cruel shame; that they had been gathered together across over there on Flinders Island by hard men who couldn't understand, that no matter what colour their skins, folks' hearts must beat the same, and she'd heard tales of the way the poor things were dying one after another of some queer catching complaint, but others said it was just homesickness for their own land.

Trukanini, who arrived at Wybalenna with Robinson in 1835 when he took up the post of commandant, was not impressed with either the place or her status. Robinson, so keen formerly to learn about and adapt to Aboriginal custom, now set about reinforcing an alien 'civilisation' on his flock. His reports of improvements were, according to his biographer, 'deliberately misleading if not downright dishonest'. I should add that Claudia Sagona, in a detailed 1988 review of Vivienne Rae-Ellis' biography, refutes such judgements.

It is easy to criticise Robinson's habit of renaming the Aborigines at Wybalenna, but he says in his diary that they begged him to give them new names. Lyndall Ryan has given this matter much thought and wrote to me:

> It was not uncommon for Aboriginal people to have different names that related to each of the different places they were associated with. [Those] at Flinders Island wanted new names bestowed by Robinson to reflect their relationship to him at Flinders Island. They expected the names to be European. Many of the Aborigines were pleased with their new names but saw them as an addition to the names they already had, rather than as substitutes. Robinson bestowed upon them names drawn from famous people in history and literature and indicated their status in Flinders Island Aboriginal society.

Robinson renamed Trukanini Lalla Rookh, it is said after the princess who was the last of her people in a popular poem by the Irish poet Thomas Moore – Trukanini's father was called a chief by colonists and she was apparently the last of the Aborigines from Recherche Bay and Bruny Island. (But Lalla Rookh was also the name of a ship that regularly visited Tasmania). After a few months, Trukanini returned to the mainland to search for other Aborigines. The rest of her story is told in Chapter 12, 'Oyster Cove to Recherche Bay' (pp290, 297) and 'Around and About Macquarie Street' (p246).

Another attempt to come to terms with the Aborigines – one criticised by Robinson – was made by John Batman, living with his wife Eliza Callaghan and their daughters at Kingston. The accounts include both Eliza and Aboriginal women helpers and fit well in the 'Midland Highway' itinerary (p345).

Maria Robinson and their family, including a newborn daughter, with a governess, **Miss Mood,** joined him at Wybalenna in 1836, as did a nurse, **Ellen Brown.** (It is not clear if she was a nursemaid for the new baby or a medical nurse.) They also had convict servants. One was **Anne Bibbey** who was sentenced to seven days' imprisonment for insolence; on another occasion seven days in solitary confinement for staying out late and, in due course, she was incarcerated for six months in the Launceston Female Factory.

Another servant, though only for some months in 1837, was **Catherine Henrys** (1807–1855), a shipmate of Anne Bibbey's. She has been chosen as a representative of convicts in '200 Australian Women', available online, and meriting a chapter by Fiona MacFarlane in *Convict Lives: Women at Cascades Female Factories* (Female Factory Research Group, 2009). By 1837, following her arrival from England to where the previous year she had migrated from Ireland, she had already had several 'masters' and, in 1838, was to have another six. Her behaviour before and after transportation was unrestrained. At Wybalenna she was, for example, accused of 'having [sexual] connection' with four men at the stockyard; she stole and destroyed three ducks; she even attempted to strike Robinson. She absconded from a later assignment and, dressed in men's clothes, lived the live of a bushranger – one of a handful of women bushrangers. Not for nothing did Catherine – tall, tattooed, smallpox-scarred, with black hair and eyebrows – become known as 'Jemmy the Rover'. She was punished often at Wybalenna, perhaps not always without cause; treatment more generally of convicts there was rather less humane than that of Aborigines – though they did not die.

While there was a disproportionate number of deaths of Aborigines at Wybalenna, there were births too; two baby girls, both born in about 1834, also continue the Aboriginal story. Mathinna's mother was **Wongerneep** (Eveline, d1837 or 1840) and her father Towterrer (Romeo), both of the Toogee people from Port Davey, Dray's homeland. Nan Chauncy, the English-born Tasmanian writer whose work and home is discussed more fully in the 'Midland Highway' itinerary (Bagdad, p325), introduces the reader to Wongerneep and Towterrer, leader of his people, in her young person's novella *Mathinna's People* (1967). She conjures up west coast Aboriginal life pre-Robinson that rings touchingly true – at least to those who don't know better. And then Robinson and his team, including Dray and Trukanini, arrive; Trukanini's husband, Woorady, or, as the Toogee people see him, 'the fat one with some arrogance', addresses them, but

> The Tribe scarcely heard; all were staring at the woman behind him. *Ki! – she was Dray, the sister of Neenevuther!* She had left the Poynduc people when she married, going to walk in a far country. She seemed uneasy under their eyes, and looked away from her brother. The men's eyes accused her of betraying their race, of becoming a *num* [white person].

That was in 1830; in 1833, when Robinson and his team returned and pursued the Togee people, Wongerneep and Towterrer fled, somehow leaving behind their baby daughter. To retrieve her, they gave themselves up and Robinson learned that the child had been named Mr Robinson Duke in his honour. The parents ended up on Wybalenna, but the child was sent to the Orphan School where, two years later, she died. At much the same time, the parents, grieving their exile, had a new daughter. Following Mathinna's birth, 'Wongerneep, carrying the little girl in her arms, hitched up the awkward 'skirt' and climbed the rocks with the rest. It was something to do at last – something to take them all away from the cold, unhappy huts.'

Then came the renaming by Robinson, and Wongerneep makes clear her feelings, not just of her new name:

'I am Wongerneep of the Niblin' – she lifted her chin proudly – 'I am not glad he calls me Queen Eveline!' ...

'Trugernanna, too! I will show how she looks when she hears Meester Robeenson give her fine name, "Lalla Rookh"!' Wongerneep strutted a few steps like an emu, her long 'skirt' hitched up, and made talk like the small woman. 'I have a fine name! I am Lalla Rookh!' she squealed.

Mathinna (Mittimer, Mithinner, Methinna, Arwennia, Mary, 1834 or 1835–1852) was to be orphaned, to spend time at Government House, and to end her days in a ditch (Chapter 12).

The second girl born is best known as **Fanny Cochrane Smith** (1834–1905). Her mother was **Tarenootairrer** (Tanganutura, Ploorernelle, Tib, Sarah, 1806–1858), a Cape Portland woman who, as Tib, had been rescued, together with Bulyer, at the end of 1830 from sealers such as Cotrell Cochrane, father of her daughter **Mary Ann Cochrane** (c1819–1871). (Cochrane may have been a corruption of coxswain John Smith. Tarenootairrer was originally abducted by James Parish, who may, instead, have been Mary Anne's father). Tib, too, had joined Robinson's team. Fanny's father is said by several reliable sources to have been Nicermenic (Eugene) – and elsewhere to have been part of Walyer's guerrilla band. But the identity of her father was later to become a bone of contention. Her end was very different from Mathinna's. The Cochrane sisters appear further in Chapter 12; there Mary Ann comes into her own. Her death is in the itinerary 'Around and About Macquarie Street' (p238). Fanny's later life is in 'Oyster Cove to Recherche Bay' (p290).

At Wybalenna, Fanny was fostered by **Bessy Clark** (d1849) and her husband, the catechist Robert Clark, who arrived that year with their children. Bessy was also in charge of 50 women whom, the way Lyndall Ryan describes it, she regimented as if they were girls in a very old-fashioned boarding school or, indeed, a women's prison. It was Bessy, too, who taught Trukanini to keep house for her husband, which did not please her, though West suggests that the women generally 'had seen the wives of the soldiers washing [the garments of their husbands] and inferred that this exercise was the special privilege of women'.

Trukanini was not the only woman who refused to conform at Wybalenna; the other members of Robinson's team too, seeing the conditions and deaths, as Lyndall Ryan puts it, 'Openly defied Robinson's authority, wore ochre, incised their bodies with bottle glass and performed ceremonial rites.' Then there were the 14 sealing women he had so heroically 'rescued'; as Lyndall Ryan describes them:

> Their better health, familiarity with European customs, and readiness to dispense with some of the more 'distasteful' traditional ceremonial dances had led him to believe that they could form the vanguard of his new society. But he soon discovered that they performed the equally distasteful dances they had developed in cohabitation with the sealers, that their knowledge of English was liberally strewn with epithets, the lingua franca they introduced to the establishment was a powerful weapon of ridicule, and their religious view of the world was controlled not by God but by the devil. In the second half of 1837 they emerged as a significant dissident group, critical of the establishment and resisting both Robinson's authority and that of the Aboriginal men.

The fact that they rebelled, exercised their autonomy at Wybalenna, supports Lynette Russell's thesis that the lives of the women with the sealers was not all violence and victimhood:

> For some of the women the domestic arrangements and sexual relationships also afforded the opportunity to maintain their Aboriginal traditions by teaching their children language, customs, stories, and skills as they themselves had been taught. They could also conduct a number of traditional activities including hunting and gathering 'bush foods', often spending many hours away from the men. In these instances the women clearly sought the opportunity to negotiate these encounters and exercise control over their lives.

Rebe Taylor, writing of Kangaroo Island, not only tells of the violence with which many of the 22 or so women were both taken and treated, but also describes those traditional activities and newly acquired ones:

> Young women who could crew on the sealing boats, catch fish, dive for shellfish, trap wallabies, find mutton-bird eggs, and stitch jackets out of skins and shoes from the hides of seals ... Aboriginal women from Van Diemen's Land who could pull mutton-birds out of holes, pluck their feathers and squeeze out their oil.

By the 1830s, the nomadic phase of the straitsmen's lives was changing to a more settled one on the islands of the Furneaux Group, more particularly those around Cape Barren Island, where they grew vegetables and other crops and kept livestock, as well as still relying on the women gathering wild plants and roots and retrieving mutton birds and their eggs. Muttonbirds meant not only food but also fertiliser and power for light and trade.

According to Rebe Taylor, six Tasmanian women still lived free on Kangaroo Island after the removal of so many to Flinders Island. The Tasmanian women 'regarded themselves as much superior in every respect' to Aboriginal women from the mainland. Sal, one of Trukanini's tribal sisters kidnapped from Bruny Island was, Rebe Taylor suggests, still on Kangaroo Island in 1836; at one stage, until he was murdered, she lived with George Meredith, son of the settler family of Cambria. Sal, according to another source, seems still to have been there in 1862, old, infirm and 'abandoned', but continuing a traditional way of life and 'fiercely independent'. There is a suggestion that she died in 1894, though more likely it was 1874, and her Tasmanian companion Suke in 1880. Tasmanian Betty, the main subject of Rebe's study, probably died a little before, but her descendants live on.

One of Mannalargenna's daughters, **Wottecowidyer** (Wot, Wotty, Harriet, 1808–1851/54) who remained with her straitsman husband, James Everett, is the ancestor of **Molly Mallett** (Née Maynard, 1926–2005) whose *My Past – Their Future: Stories from Cape Barren Island* (2001) epitomises the continuing story of the Bass Strait women who stayed with their straitsmen.

Another surviving strand from the islands includes Ida West whose *Pride Against Prejudice: Reminiscences of a Tasmanian Aborigine* (1987) is highly regarded, as she was in her lifetime of service to her community. **Ida West** (née Armstrong, 1919–2003) talks of her 'Great Grand-Aunt Lucy Beeton', and her mother was an Everett, but she does not give a family tree like Molly; you have to read her text carefully to deduce her precise sealer ancestry, and the revelation comes in a bittersweet anecdote that adds a dimension to Thomas Beedon's 1831 letter to Governor Arthur about his pregnant wife:

> Great-great-grandfather Beeton might have been a viscount for it has been said that he received money from England or through a merchant in Launceston. His wife, Emmerenna, used to have dresses sent to her from England but when great-great-grandfather died a relation of his wrote from England asking for her photograph. After she sent it she received no more clothes.

And to be able to make that deduction is almost like listening at the keyhole, for she writes earlier: 'Such a lot of people like police, the councillors, the wardens, all stand up and ask for our history but if they stopped to think, they have one too. Perhaps they don't want that put in a book either.'

Patsy Cameron, who grew up on Flinders Island, and her co-author, also of Aboriginal descent, Vicki Matson-Green, is even more fierce in 'Pallawah Women: Their Historical Contribution to Our Survival' (1994):

> Historians, authors, teachers, lecturers, curriculum developers and the general public must recognise our right to be the owners, interpreters and recorders of our own history. For too long now, with the exception of a few, those professionals ... have portrayed our history through the eyes, values and interpretations of luta tawin.

Thus, they suggest, 'It becomes and remains the property of the dominant white society.' And I have received an even more excoriating letter from elsewhere in response to questions. But how would it be if I ignored their women ancestors in this overview of women's history? And, as I, a complete outsider, try and get things right, I cannot help but empathise with Rebe Taylor's admission on questioning an Aboriginal descendant on Kangaroo Island that 'I was insensitive with curiosity'.

However much the women refused to toe the line at Wybalenna, there was an inevitability to what transpired. In the three years and four months that Robinson was Commandant there, 59 Aborigines died; 29 of them in 1837. With the establishment of the settlement, confining the rounded-up Aboriginal population to an offshore island, the colonists of Tasmania could begin to relax and return to creating prosperity.

9 – Immigrants, Status and Society

Most of the settlers of the 1820s and 'thirties hoped to prosper from agricultural produce derived from their land grants. And trade in goods, exports and imports, were part of the plan to make money and expand. But in a colony where, as Joan Goodrick has it, there were ten European men to one woman, there was another factor to be considered, put pithily by a man's letter home in 1824: 'The best articles of traffic in this settlement would be respectable females.' (Henry Melville, presumably writing of a later date, when the remedy had begun to take effect, put the population discrepancy at three to one; and Bonwick suggests an 1834 population of 40,283, of which 11,482 were females.)

The British government's response was not entirely altruistic. Britain, following the end of the Napoleonic Wars in 1815, had problems of its own: unemployment, high prices, particularly of bread, movement from country to town and increasingly bad living and work conditions there. Those left in the villages were badly hit, and parishes, obliged to support parishioners fallen on hard times, were required to encourage emigration to the colonies.

Looked at from the perspective of Tasmanian history, John West writes of the response to that colony's needs of the 1820s that the British government determined 'to promote the emigration of mechanics and females'. There is something about that juxtaposition! (It is more understandable when you know that John West was not only a historian but arrived in Tasmania in 1839 as a Congregational minister and, as part of his ministry in Launceston, set up the Mechanics Institute there.)

In 1831, the Secretary of State established a scheme to assist female emigration to Tasmania, the implementation of which was to have a few hiccups. The two shiploads of immigrants that have been most written about are the *Princess Royal* which arrived in Hobart in September 1832, and the *Strathfieldsay* in August 1834. On 14 August 1832, this advertisement appeared in the *Tasmanian Gazette*:

> We are informed that the Female Emigrants, who are daily expected, have been selected in England by a committee, on whose discretion entire reliance may be placed: and that they will most probably be willing to engage as house and farm servants. They will have their own choice of service. Settlers and others wishing to secure their services to intimate the same to the Colonial Secretary immediately.

But before it docked in Hobart, after a four month voyage, the ship grounded at today's Dodges Ferry (p279), and 50 of its 200 women passengers were taken to hospital. A news report described them as 'women of the worst character'. It transpired that most of the passengers were from institutions. You can, without difficulty, download the passenger list which details exactly where each woman – most of them in their teens and twenties – was from, ranging from 'workhouse' to 'the London Female Penitentiary, Pentonville', from 'the National Guardian Servants' Institution' to 'the Refuge for the Destitute'.

That list is only a hint of the research that went into Thelma McKay's *The Princess Royal Girls: The First Free Female Immigration ship to Van Diemen's Land – 1832* (2007, most readily available from Thelma McKay herself or Tasmanian libraries). In the introduction to this meticulous labour of love, Thelma categorises and explains the groups of women – and a few children and male relatives – but her most noteworthy conclusion is that most of the women considered 'bad' by the authorities 'did in fact lead a respectable life'. Thelma explains that no listing has been found giving details of each of the migrant women's employment following arrival in Tasmania and the Australian mainland; she has, however, dug some up, together with a mass of information about their personal life, and sometimes that of their children born in Tasmania and the mainland, where many of them settled. Lindy Scripps gives an overview of employment prospects:

> Initially, less than half of the women were able to gain employment as dress-makers or milliners, or in respectable service, the remainder being considered the dregs of the workhouses and more depraved than the convicts. Arthur was unable to bring himself to write about their gross behaviour on the voyage out.

Millinery was an obvious venture for women – **Anne Rachel Lovell** (née Ousten d1834), wife of a general merchant, had opened such a business in Melville Street in 1823. (In 1825, Anne Lovell became the predecessor of Mary Hutchinson (Chapter 5) as matron of the women's factory at Cascades when her husband Esh Lovell was appointed superintendent. She was accused of using convicts as needleworkers for her family of six children. When Anne died, he remarried (p276).)

Thelma McKay has been able to piece together confirmation of the attraction of millinery through the respectable Neistrip family – **Naomi Neistrip** (d1860), her husband Thomas, 21-year-old **Amelia** (b1813), **Elizabeth** (1815–1905), **Naomi** (b1820) and twelve-year-old **Sarah** (1821–1876). The Neistrips had emigrated because clothier Thomas was unsuccessful in business; he acted as a captain's clerk on the *Princess Royal* and advertised similar services on arrival in Hobart. The Neistrip women wasted no time either: also on 28 September, they advertised in the *Colonial Times* that they intended to 'carry on the business of millinery and dress-making and the dressing of ladies' hair, which they had previous experience in at one of the first houses in London'. Thomas Neistrip died in 1837 and, thereafter, the family migrated to the mainland.

The more personal fate of one immigrant appears in a court report in *The Hobart Town Magazine* (1834): 'Another case of breach of promise of marriage will also be brought on – the fair plaintiff is a Princess Royal, and a highly respectable young woman – and who the defendant is will appear in due course.' 'Princess Royal' or 'Royal' became terms commonly used to describe the women, often derogatorily. The term '"Royal" language' was in use in the press by 1835 to denote bad language. 'Very steady Methodist' **Harriett Shaw** (also Caroline, b1803) had become Mrs William Shoobridge and was in altercation with a neighbour. She justified herself: '… true it was, that she had come to this Colony under peculiar circumstances and might be called a "Princess Royal" but …'

10. Anne Ousten Lovell, from Skemp,
Letters to Anne

As for the jilted woman, Thelma McKay reveals her as dressmaker **Jane Stone** (1807–1844) described in court by the ship's surgeon as 'extremely well behaved during the whole passage; that she was very quiet, modest and industrious in her conduct and manners'. The blackguard was Charles MacArthur who had promised to marry her but, when she became pregnant by him, rejected her. The chief justice returned a verdict of £15 to be paid to the plaintiff and when baby Emily was born the father was named as carpenter James Westwood whom Jane married in 1835 when he received his conditional pardon.

The 'Princess Royals' had, before arrival, been called ladies; this was soon downgraded to 'female'. But, in her unpublished thesis, Alison Alexander suggests that of the 48 immigrants whose lives in the colony were recorded (she was writing before Thelma McKay published), only six became prostitutes. Two of these may have been 16-year-old **Frances Britton** (1816–1853) and **Sarah Harrington** (1808–1896). The two, described as 'Royals', were found drunk in New Town in November 1832; the constable making the report said that 'He could no longer suffer the intoxicated habits of the two "Queens" who live near him.'

Frances went on to have four daughters by different men outside marriage, but she married in 1850. The following year, the family moved to the mainland where she died in childbirth two years later. Sarah married a former convict the year after being described as a 'queen' and, in the mid 1840s, that family, too, moved to the mainland.

More than 80 of the Royals had married by December 1835, often acting as witness at each other's wedding, and later several children, and even grandchildren, married into each other's families. It was possible to fall between being respectable or ending up 'on the town': 30 Royals were expelled for 'improper conduct' from the King's Orphanage where they had been taken and looked after by the Ladies Committee; only three entered the convict system.

Louisa Arpin (1813–1912), classed in Arthur's dispatch as one of the 30 who were 'abandoned', gives a clue to problems encountered. Remembering many details of her earlier life with extraordinary clarity, she recounted in a 1905 interview in Melbourne: 'We had been promised positions at 8/- to 10/- per week, which was regarded as good wages in those days. We soon found that there were too many of us, and it was extremely difficult to get good places.' Thelma McKay suggests that Louisa, who died aged 98, was possibly the last Royal alive. The fact that so many of them moved to the mainland does suggest that the experiment to bring poor women en masse to Tasmania was flawed.

But what was the story behind the voyage itself? As so often with the Island's most distinctive history, the *Princess Royal* has inspired artistic creativity. In 2003, Tasdance, the Launceston-based dance company founded in 1981, performed 'Fair Game' under its artistic director Annie Greig. The imagination of the choreographers was fed by a narrative provided for them by the novelist Carmel Bird. Some years earlier, she had received from a friend the lithograph by Ducote of St Martin's Lane: 'E-Migration or a Flight of Fair Game', published on 17 June 1832. It depicts the women as butterflies moving from the Old Country to Tasmania, with the men in Hobart awaiting their arrival there with butterfly nets.

The narrative Carmel created for Tasdance, as well as being found in their printed programme, is included in *Best Stories Under the Sun* (Michael Wilding and David Myers, 2004). Tasdance performs in the Princess Theatre, Launceston (p372), and the Theatre Royal, Hobart (p335).

Carmel's poetic and moving text was based on careful research into which she wove imaginary characters and their diaries, including that of the daughter of one of the ladies bountiful who interviewed the prospective emigrants, and the thoughts of a young girl sexually exploited on the journey out. One of Carmel's women diarists was real – 26-year-old **Catherine Price** (née Brogden, 1806–1893), the newly-ordained Congregational chaplain's wife, married a week before the ship sailed.

Catherine's diary (to be found as an appendix to Thelma McKay's book), though short, contains some useful entries. She observed that the poop deck was allowed to 'cabin passengers' only; the immigrant women were forbidden to walk there. The Neistrip family is captured as they cross the equator; the high jinks that still accompany that moment did not amuse everyone: 'I saw a mother and four daughters in distress', Catherine wrote, 'on account of their father who was forced into the dirty water by the sailors.'

Then there is the detailed entry that may provide a clue to the reported unseemly behaviour on board:

> Some of the worst females on board offended the Surgeon but not without a just cause for so doing, he was frequently intoxicated and very unguarded in his manner of speaking to the women, he gave them so much calomel [purgative] that he salivated more than twenty. Last evening just at the time for Mr P to go below deck to pray and read with the females the Surgeon said he was going down to the women. Mr P reminded him of the consequences if he did go below. He was in a fine rage, said he would go down and they should see if he feared any of them. He went below and Mr P followed close behind him. One of the women began to exclaim against the Dr and he took a pistol out of his pocket but he took care not to hurt anyone. He feared the women much more than they feared him. I saw the Dr take the pistol and put it into his pocket. I felt very much agitated until Mr P returned to the cuddy. I did not know what they were doing below. I could only hear the noise below deck, could not sleep much last night.

As Price's biographer tells us, the hearts of both Prices 'were already fixed on the principles of temperance' and Charles Price was to found the Temperance Movement in Launceston, so I am amused to note from Catherine's diary that when she and her husband were seasick off the Isle of Wight, 'brandy was our only comfort'.

The surgeon with the strange behaviour was Thomas Richards and, with him, were his wife, **Hannah Elsemere Richards** (née Adams) and their infant son. Richards, it seems, was to shoulder some of the blame for what happened on board – whatever the specifics of it were. *The Hobart Town Magazine* talks of 'evils … which have arisen from the associations of a number of sailors and females, who had just broken loose from restraint'. A biographical entry says that Richards was to 'encounter criticism about the control exercised over the free female migrants'. Governor Arthur wrote criticising him, and the Secretary of State regretted that Richards 'should have proved so unworthy of the confidence reposed in him'.

A week after the ship's arrival in Hobart, Richards placed this advertisement in the *Hobart Town Courier*: 'I pledge myself to embody a candid, correct and faithful account of this most extraordinary expedition in the fervent hope that the home government will never again inflict upon this colony so grievous a visitation as this, their first experimental cargo of free female immigrants.' As Carmel wrote when she sent me the advertisement, 'So he seems to have had a wish to clear his own name of some slur.' Who knows where his account is, and what exactly the slur was?

In August 1833, Richards also wrote semi-anonymously in the *Hobart Town Magazine* that he

> ... recollects the very interesting cargo of which I had the medical charge, as well as the strange mode in which the charge was confided to me by the government. Several 'incidents' occurred on board. The Captain quarrelled with the surgeon and the surgeon quarrelled with the Captain ... one month on board ship will enable you to acquire a more correct notion of a person's character than one year on shore.

What is not clear either is what duties and authority Richards had. The captain of the ship was only responsible for his vessel. In later years, a surgeon superintendent, incorporating two functions, was to be appointed. There does not seem to have been a superintendent on board the *Princess Royal*, but there was a matron in charge of domestic arrangements; she surely had some responsibility.

Emma Mathews (Matthews) was accompanied by her daughter Emma. Catherine Price does not mention either of them nor, indeed, does Richards, but Thelma McKay tells us that when young Emma became ill before leaving England, Richards, discovering this when coming on board, 'said he thought she should leave the ship. Miss Mathews declined to leave saying she felt better and would not go back.' It is unlikely, therefore, that matron and surgeon were able happily to cooperate either. The Hobart ladies committee which received the new arrivals spoke highly of Mrs Mathews, and Arthur wrote to London to that effect. But Mrs Mathews herself was obviously unhappy, because another document recounts that

> Mrs Mathews undertook the office of Matron upon the distinct understanding that the females placed under her care were to be of respectable character, but, the result having proved the reverse, she has not only been subjected with her daughter who acted as her assistant, to the greatest insults during the voyage, but has been robbed of wearing apparel to a considerable amount and the sum of £40 in sovereigns, the only means she possessed of establishing a little school, which was her object in emigrating.

Mrs Mathews was recompensed, and mother and daughter left Tasmania for the mainland soon afterwards.

Catherine Price noted, as her final diary entry, 'Have clean linen to go ashore in. We have had no washing done on board.' Water was always rationed on board. After the ship ran aground, the Prices remained near Dodges Ferry for over a week with Elizabeth and James Gordon (p115, p279) and then proceeded to Hobart by bullock-dray and boat. The other women were also stuck there, presumably under less pleasant conditions. A plaque honouring Ralph Dodge at the site of his ferry service (started in 1830), erected in 2003, mentions the *Princess Royal* which he spotted in distress and signalled an alert, and I do see **Charlotte Morris Dodge** (c1804–1866) trying to help the stranded Royals; she had the fourth of her eleven children that year (p280).

After a career diversion until 1836, the Prices settled in Launceston where the grammar school he set up to support his family of Catherine and, eventually, four children, was on the same plot of land as the chapel he built and their home. His ministry, with Catherine at his side – his biographer suggests that they were very much a team – lasted 55 years.

Catherine Price's diary does not mention Hannah Richards. How she coped on board the *Princess Royal*, and not only with her husband's behaviour, neither the ballet nor Thelma McKay suggest, and nor can I. But we do have some idea of Hannah's life in Tasmania. Her husband set up as a surgeon in Elizabeth Town (New Norfolk), edited and contributed to Henry Melville's short-lived *The Hobart Town Magazine*, and was then editor of the *Tasmanian*. He became better known as a writer and newspaper editor than a doctor – he had mixed in literary circles in England – indeed, one biographical source calls him 'The Father of the Tasmanian Press'. He was but one of several pressmen to receive that epithet and seems to have been contentious in his literary relations.

Although neither Richards' official account of the *Princess Royal* voyage nor the diary he says he kept appear to be extant, he did write about the voyage, as I have already quoted, under initials in *The Hobart Town Magazine*. In June 1833, in 'An Emigration Voyage' the *Tom Thumb* is thinly disguised. He even writes: 'One of the passengers had a wife and four daughters ... and when Neptune hailed, the "fooling commenced", the husband was shaved, his wife and family became very upset.' And then he describes the storm and the grounding of the ship. Hearing from friends in England that his behaviour on board was questioned, Richards wrote to the Colonial Office that if he had 'behaved ill to my unhappy charges on board ship, would they now seek my professional assistance and every advice I could afford them'. Certainly, as we have seen, he appeared in court for Jane Stone.

Hannah Richards, too, as well as having four daughters and a son in Tasmania between 1834 and 1846, contributed her own writing under the initials 'HER' or 'H' to the magazine. Morris Miller, in *Pressmen and Governors* (1952; 1973) suggests that she also helped Thomas with his literary work. Her 1833 poem 'Home' is described by Miller as 'A specimen of early verse, composed in Australia, it is worthy of recognition in an anthology, historically arranged.' It is not really to my taste, but if you apply yourself, perhaps the poem has something to do with her life; can one read unhappiness in Hobart into these lines?

> In all its wanderings still the heart is true
> To that lov'd scene where its young feelings grew:
> E'en when its wither'd hopes around it fall,
> Like faded wreaths in some forsaken hall,
> Still o'er the waste of sorrow unforgot,
> Green and unfading blooms that hallow'd spot;
> Its memory steals along life's sullen stream,
> As breaks o'er clouded seas the setting beam.

But then there are the lines 'But, oh! sad his fate whom early crimes / Have doom'd to die in far and friendless climes.' These must refer to convicts, and perhaps the poem also speaks of the nostalgia for home felt by Hannah's fellow passengers on the *Princess Royal*.

The full, and long, poem can be found in *The Hobart Town Magazine* (1834), the first monthly magazine with real literary pretensions published in Australia, a reprint of 1834 can now be bought 'print on demand' (watch out for missed pages).

Following the scandal of the first batch of female immigrants, rumours must have abounded: *The Hobart Town Magazine* alerted its readers that the *Leyton* (sic) had left London and that 'It appears that this batch will not be so good as that of the Princess Royal … Street walkers, it is said, will constitute the greater part of the live cargo.' There was obviously something else amiss: because of an unfortunate difference between the superintendent and the surgeon of the *Layton*, some of the women arrived 'in an unsatisfactory state'. That is all I have found out about the *Layton* and its passengers or those in authority. The *Shipping Arrivals and Departures Tasmania* does not record an arrival of the *Layton* in 1834; indeed, the ship's only recorded arrivals in any year were of male convicts.

Undaunted by the saga of the *Princess Royal*, the Committee for Promoting the Emigration of Single Women advertised in 1834 for

> Single women and widows of good character, from 15 to 50 years of age, desirous of bettering their condition by emigrating to that healthy and highly prosperous colony, where the number of females compared with the entire population is greatly deficient and subsequently from the great demand for servants, and other female employments, the wages are comparatively high.

The cost to the immigrant was initially £5 (some sources say £8); later travel was covered by the British government from the sale of land in Tasmania. When the *Strathfieldsay* arrived to disembark 286 passengers in August 1834, this time with many 'respectable' (but poor) women, the situation was worse than before. The fullest description is given in a very long footnote in Melville's *The History of Van Diemen's Land* (1835; 1965) which described and criticised Arthur's administration and had to be smuggled abroad to be published. Lindy Scripps provides a taste of the footnote:

> Of all the disgusting, abominable sights we have ever witnessed, nothing ever equalled the scene which took place on that occasion … At this time the mob waiting to witness the landing of these women, could not be less in number than a couple of thousand. As soon as the first boat reached the shore, there was a regular rush towards the spot, and the half dozen constables present, could scarcely open a passage sufficient to allow the females to pass from the boats; and now the most, unheard of, disgusting scenes ensued – the avenue opened through the crowd was of considerable length and as each female passed, she was jeered by the blackguards who

stationed themselves, as it were, purposely to insult. The most vile and brutal language was addressed to every woman as she passed along.

The women were devastated, which only acted as a provocation to what seems to have been a rent-a-mob of convicts. When the exhausted women arrived at the accommodation arranged for them, little improved: 'Mrs Arthur and one or two more ladies, assisted all in their power, but so soon as the ladies left, so soon did the scenes of infamy re-commence.'

Was Melville's American wife of three years, **Eliza Romney Fisher Melville**, among the 'ladies'? She obviously had something about her because she told Bonwick how she carried food to her husband when, in 1835, he was imprisoned for contempt of court for an article he wrote in the *Colonial Times* (not about women immigrants), and she brought away fresh articles 'to maintain the press struggle'. This was in the tradition of newspaper wives running the press when their husbands were imprisoned.

Mary Bent (née Kirk, b1797; m1816) did the same when Governor Arthur imprisoned Andrew Bent in 1825 and 1828. Bent had, indeed, sold the *Colonial Times* to Melville. Coincidentally, when a later owner of the *Colonial Times*, John Campbell McDougall, died in 1848, his second wife, **Mary Ann McDougall** (née Butler, 1817–1857; m1834) continued to manage it until she sold it in 1855 (and remarried, a Melbourne man).

When you think you have constructed a coherent narrative about an incident, a source pops up to throw it askew. James Bonwick, who is supposed to be reliable, includes, without references or the name of the ship, a passage in *Curious Facts of Old Colonial Days* (1870) that does just that. Because of the number of passengers quoted, it seems to refer to the *Strathfieldsay* but, I suppose, by coincidence, it could refer to the *Layton* – it would suit other known facts better if it did! He writes:

One of the female immigrants wrote thus to a friend in England, 'Out of the two hundred and sixty eight that came out with me, I verily believe that there were not more than twenty who have any claim to a good name, being driven to the most wretched and loathsome debauchery.'

The *Sarah*, which arrived in 1835, was it is said altogether better organised than the *Strathfieldsay*, though women had been put off from applying because of newspaper articles about previous voyages. We know about a later one from the careful research underpinning 'A Proper Class of Female Immigrants: The Boadicea Women 1834–36' (Hugh Campbell, 1988). Unlike Thomas Richards' account of the *Princess Royal*, that of the surgeon superintendent John Vaughan Thomson throws much light on every aspect. Not only were he and his wife to superintend the well-being of the 190 or so emigrants, but he was also to appoint four matrons. (I have to interpose that the only wife he had, according to records, died in 1832, so perhaps the woman travelling with him as his wife was not legally so.)

In spite of the improvements to those in charge, there were problems on board, for not all the women and other passengers were solid citizens; there were nine women 'of very light character'. What is more, the *Hobart Town Courier* of 12 February 1836 regretfully reported: 'We find that the heads of these young females are filled with such notions as that "Van Diemen's Land is a splendid little spot, filled with pretty cottages each with single men of all ranks and callings waiting for wives".' Nevertheless, most of the *Boadicea*'s female emigrants apparently went into situations 'of one kind or another'.

But an eye-opening eye-witness view of the *Boadicea* immigrants is provided by George Lovelace, leader of the Tolpuddle Martyrs who, while most of his trade union confrères, including his brother, were transported to the mainland, was sent alone to Tasmania. In the pamphlet written on his return home in 1837, 'The Victims of Whiggery', detailing his life in Tasmania, the more general treatment of convicts (mostly male) and his call to arms to his fellow labourers in England, he also notes:

Nor is Van Diemen's Land the garden of Eden for emigrants that the deluded people of England imagine. I would just mention a few words in reference to the young females that are sent to this part of the world. About two ships arrived yearly, with young women while I was staying in the country. I speak more particularly in reference to those that arrived by the ship 'Boadicia' in the month of February, 1836, as I had opportunities of talking with several of them: but what is said of them, may, with propriety, be said of others also. In their passage out, I was told, they had not the best usage given them.

When they arrived they were put into a house provided by the government; advertisements were circulated throughout the colony, giving notice of their arrival, and requesting all who were in want of servants to make early application for them. Applications being made, a number of them were soon scattered over the colony; others for a long time could not get situations, and about fifty were found to be under fifteen years of age. The principal inhabitants of Hobart town were talking, when I left for the interior, of making a subscription to send them home again; but whether they succeeded or not I do not know. Soon, however, many of those who had situations lost them; for a number of the young women that emigrate to that country have not been bred to hard work; others who have been accustomed to it find something worse there. Dissatisfaction arises between them and their employers – they talk of leaving. 'You may go' is the reply; 'we can get plenty of government servants without paying them wages.' They leave and try for new situations, but few of them can obtain any for want of recommendations from their last employers. They are destitute, and none are found to pity them. They wander without friends and without home, until they are driven, by dire necessity (a greater part of them) upon the town. I have conversed with several of them, who have wept and lamented over their folly, in having listened to the flattering and enticing offers of the emigration agents; and decoyed from home and all that was dear to them, to be rendered miserable in a distant land. I have heard some of them offering gentlemen of Hobart Town, or rather their ladies, to come into their house and do anything required for their food, rather than follow the general example; and wishing they could enter the service of some gentleman's family going to England, and serve them for only a little food on the voyage.

In all, five boatloads of immigrants arrived between 1832 and 1835, a total of 1,186 women (that excludes those on the *Boadicea* of 1836) and, as West so sweetly puts it, 'The women of decent habits, found that destiny for which nature designed them.'

That destiny undoubtedly included childbearing, which accounts for the setting up in 1835 of the Dorcas Society – 'to provide material assistance to poor respectable women during childbirth' – with Eliza Arthur as its patron. She certainly knew about childbirth and, as a result of her constant pregnancies, did nothing but provide her name. It was the first philanthropic society to be run by women who held monthly meetings, sewing layettes while they discussed their cases. They also made home visits to deliver the Dorcas Box, or Bag. The deserving cases did not include those whose morals did not reach the required standards; 'they might be unwedded, or drunkards or untrustworthy'.

The only comment I can find from women settlers on women immigrants comes in 1834 from Ellen Viveash: 'Babbington our surveyor is going to be married to a girl who cannot read or write. Mr Gregory our Treasurer (appointed when Charles applied) to a lady after a courtship of 21 days – a lady lately arrived from England.'

Harriet Martineau interestingly depicts what was happening in England, and the life that awaited the poverty stricken from there in Tasmania, in *Homes Abroad* (1832). I use the word 'interestingly' because, although it purports to be a novel, it is more a treatise dressed up as one. Indeed, a biographical entry describes the series she devised as 'a scheme to illustrate political economy for the ordinary reader by making use of fictional illustrations'.

The series consists of nine volumes, published between 1832 and 1834, and they were an instant success, not only bringing Harriet Martineau financial independence, but making her famous as well. In *Homes Abroad* she shows the complexity of the situation in both England and Tasmania through a large family – the Castles – part of which emigrates through poverty sponsored by parish and government and becomes bond servants, epitomised by Ellen Castle; the other, such as Ellen's half-brother Jerry, transported for stealing – but he stole on purpose in order to be transported to a new life of opportunity.

On the farm where she works, Ellen is billeted with a spiteful convict. Jerry absconds, becomes a bushranger, and takes up with an Aboriginal woman. Ellen becomes a dairymaid in the Norfolk Plains south of Launceston and meets a good man. Ellen's brother, Frank, working free of his indenture, writes to the clergyman in England who helped them emigrate, persuading him to come out as a teacher cleric gentleman settler, extolling the virtues of

England/Tasmania economic relations and the rewarding life, even for the cleric's growing daughters.

In the end, though, it is the convict Bob who does best, allowing the author to write against convict colonisation, showing how the offenders benefit, because of their vice, to the detriment of honest migrants – by implication, Bob over his honest siblings.

This novel is almost impossible to get hold of – sending off for what you think is a print-on-demand copy may leave you as short-changed as I was: it did not contain that novella. As so often, the only recourse was the British Library. Australian libraries may be better served.

The confusion of the status of convict and poor migrant could lead to trouble. One case, at least, is recorded and, although it dates from a later period, 1854, it fits in well here. **Eliza Maguire**, an Irish domestic, was marched 30 miles to Hobart Gaol, accompanied by a single police constable with no control over how he treated her, because she had been impertinent to her mistress. She was sentenced under the Master and Servant Act to three months' imprisonment and loss of two months' wages. She also had her waist-length hair cropped. But it transpired that she was a free immigrant (another source calls her an indentured servant) who had arrived three months earlier on a passenger ship. A special government bill set her free. But it could not obliterate the experience, nor the shame of her shorn locks.

As more women arrived, society became more differentiated, more class conscious. Janet Ranken and her settler attitude to Maria Lord, former convict, has already made that clear as early as 1821, and Jane Roberts, the passer-through, shows how it was manifest at the highest level by 1830 when she attended a function at Government House: 'All were kindly received, with only just as much form and ceremony as was necessary to keep up a certain distinction of rank. The ball-room was crowded with genteel, well-dressed, people; and the supper was nicely arranged.' The Dorcas Society makes it even clearer. But it was not quite so simple.

There were poor 'respectable' women, and 'disreputable' women making good. Maria Lord is the most obvious example of the latter, but there were a string of others who started off with less determined status. Typical of them was **Maria Sergeant** (Sargeant, Sargent, Sarjent, Serjeant, 1782–1855). Knopwood married Maria Stanfield, camp follower from Gosport, to a sergeant in the marines, Richard Sergeant, the day the *Calcutta* sailed from Portsmouth in 1803. Marjorie Tipping describes Maria as 'obviously intent on a life of adventure'. On the *Calcutta,* Fawkner noticed that she was often in Knopwood's cabin. During the period in Port Phillip, she became intimate with the expedition's surgeon, Matthew Bowden, who had sailed on the *Ocean,* and from then on was his de facto wife. Her legal husband was arrested during that stay for drunkenness and misconduct and court-martialled, but treated leniently due to some 'alleviating circumstances'.

Landed in Hobart, Bowden was granted 100 acres at Humphrey's Rivulet where he and Maria planted a vegetable garden and started to grow crops. Knopwood baptised their first child in October 1806 – and had lunch with them, so he fully accepted their relationship, in spite of having married Maria to Richard Sergeant. The child was among the first to be inoculated with the new and controversial smallpox vaccine. They were to have three children.

During his 1811 tour of inspection, Macquarie interfered with the status quo: 'The commandant is not to permit Assistant Surgeon Bowden to presume to molest Richard Sargeant of the Detachment of Marines, on account of his having had his lawful Wife this day restored to him by my Orders.' But Maria was soon back with Bowden and, when he died in 1814, she had inscribed on his tomb in St David's Park, how their children were left 'with a disconsolate mother to lament the loss of their dear protector who fulfilled the duties of an affectionate father, a tender husband and a faithful friend'.

Not surprisingly, she was his executrix and beneficiary, inheriting the farm at Glenorchy, a property at Coal River, and one in town on the corner of Campbell and Liverpool Street of which Lindy Scripps has a picture, taken before it was demolished in the 1890s.

Maria was supplying meat and wheat to the Commissariat by 1817; in 1818, she opened a public house, nostalgically named the *Calcutta*; and, by 1830, she was operating a bakery from her house. In 1842, she was appointed postmistress at Glenorchy, the first woman to be thus appointed on her own merits, described as 'a person of good character and worthy of trust'. She resigned because she was expected to work on Sundays – a seven-day week.

Running a public house or hotel was a business venture open to women, as Mary Hayes Stocker has illustrated with the earlier Derwent. Sarah Birch turned Birch's Castle into the Macquarie Hotel after her husband's death in 1821, and everyone stayed there (p245). Mrs Ransom (Catherine McNally) – another woman with a complicated private life – and the Royal Oak at Green Ponds (Kempton) were equally famous from about 1822 (p327). Ann Bridger opened the Bush Inn at New Norfolk (still there) from about 1825 (p300). Eliza Cobb Fawkner opened the Cornwall Hotel in Launceston with her husband in 1822 (p368) and widowed Mary Ann Cox ran it between 1837 and 1849, as well as taking over her husband's coach service from Launceston to Hobart.

Some public houses were bracketed with brothels, though there is no evidence that any of the above were. The first theatrical venue – another perceived link with prostitution – was the Freemason's Arms where productions were organised by **Cordelia Cameron** and her husband Samson, a respectable couple who had arrived in 1833. Theatrical performances became increasingly well-attended and, although they were not deemed respectable by all, a proper theatre was mooted. The foundation stone of what is now the Theatre Royal (p235) was laid in 1834 attended by 1,000 spectators amid much ceremony. The theatre opened in 1837 and became the venue not only for respectable patrons but also for prostitutes. As the *Hobart Town Courier* put it: 'The equality of the nymph of the pave to the virtuous female, was recognised by the close proximity of their seats.' Although in fact prostitutes sat in the slips, they could mingle during the interval.

Theatrical life and gossip became part of Hobart; companies from mainland Australia visited, as did individual actors from abroad, some of whom stayed for a while and then moved on to the mainland. There was no lack of home-grown performers, nor, indeed, of playwrights – Catherine Shepherd, with her play highlighting the evils of the convict system, though later, was typical of the best (p237). And the impresario Anne Clarke, who, with her husband, took over the lease of the theatre in 1842, was to play an important part in improving theatrical standards (p235).

With the influx of so many new people, education became increasingly important. The first school teacher was Jane Noel who, in 1806, apparently came down from Sydney and opened her 'hut' – just off Collins Street – as a school; I have found no mention of her original status. In 1815, Macquarie sent the 37-year-old former convict and widow of a surgeon in the Royal Navy, Mary Martin, from Sydney with orders that she be employed as a school mistress. Thomas Fitzgerald who, as a clerk, had been transported for receiving and arrived in Tasmania with Collins in 1804, was already a teacher in Hobart; he snapped her up and married her in August that year – 'a remarkably fine day', wrote Knopwood which makes more of an impact when a reader from the northern hemisphere remembers that it was mid-winter in Tasmania.

Mary Martin Fizgerald (1778–1831) already had a six-year-old son, and the couple were to have at least four children which, given that Mary was 37 when she married and the last child was born in 1825, after the death of his father, is worth noting.

Meanwhile, the Fitzgeralds set up a school in their house. By 1820, Mary had 24 girl pupils, and Thomas 35 boys. The newly-appointed Superintendent of Schools discovered that, of the 236 Hobart children aged between four and 17, the Fizgeralds were educating, or had educated, 200 of them. Bonwick wrote of Mary that it was 'highly honourable to the gentle sex that a woman was the earliest teacher of the young … in Hobart Town'. And, in 1817, Mary received financial recognition from Governor Sorell because 'She pays much attention to the female scholars.'

Following Thomas' death, Mary announced – explaining that she was the widow of a respectable schoolmaster left to maintain a large family – that she was opening a new day school. The term 'respectable' was obviously important, since in at least one instance, she was subjected to sexual harassment from a man I deduce was a parent, and had to state in her letter of complaint to a magistrate that her own 'conduct will allow complete scrutiny'. How Mary originally became a convict, Marjorie Tipping, to whom I owe the Tasmanian details of her life, did not unearth. Mary married widower William Nicholls in 1829 and died in 1831.

Hannah Maria Davice opened a school in Hobart with her friend **Elinor Binfield** (1802–1876) in 1823 the year of their arrival. Elinor married landowner Joseph Archer of Panshanger (p358) the following year, but Hannah, marrying later that same year, did not give up teaching. Instead, in 1825 she moved the school to larger premises, Carr Field House. There, that year, Hannah gave birth to a still-born child. Then, she and her husband George Carr Clark, with adjoining land grants near Ross, built Ellinthorp

Hall there and opened it as a school in 1827. This establishment for young ladies and, indeed, its head teacher, were to make a considerable impact on Tasmanian society from then until 1840. **Hannah Maria Clark** (née Davice, c1794–1847) and Ellinthorp (later Ellenthorpe) Hall – together with an attack by bushrangers – feature in the 'Midland Highway' itinerary (p336).

11. Hannah Maria Clark, from Stillwell, 'Mr and Mrs George Carr Clarke of "Ellinthorp" Hall'

What is notable about this select academy, as an ending to this chapter which has shown how Tasmanian society changed from Collins' day to 1837, is that it was attended by the daughters and then the granddaughters of women who had not been considered so respectable when they arrived in Tasmania, as well as those who considered themselves settlers of substance.

Typical of the first kind were Eliza Collins, daughter of the Governor's youngest and last mistress, Margaret Eddington; Mary, Margaret's daughter by George Watts; and Annie, her daughter by Charles Connelly. And when Eliza made a very good marriage, her daughters were to go there too. Alison Alexander describes Eliza and Mary as 'one illegitimate and the other the daughter of an illiterate convict bushranger'. Von Stieglitz writes: 'All the really nice girls used to go to Mrs Clarke's school.'

Where did Maria Robinson, the 'Conciliator's' eldest daughter, fit in socially? She attended Ellinthorp for three years from 1833. And the same could be asked of **Ann Maria Blackler** (Anna, c1814–1898). She had arrived on the ill-fated *Princess Royal* in 1832, aged 16, without an institution or, indeed, any designation against her name on the list. But Thelma McKay notes that she had been a housemaid in England and seems to have travelled out with her employers, Mr and Mrs Tyrrell. She shared a cabin with 15-year-old Susannah Tyrrell, their older daughter. The father, Robert Tyrrell, was a cook on board. We learn from 'Mr and Mrs George Carr Clark of "Ellinthorp Hall"' (1962, GT Stilwell) that Anna Maria became George Clark's ward. The Quakers Walker and Backhouse talk of 'Several young women who have been brought up in the school, and are apprentices.' It emerges that there was a Devon/Tasmanian Dowling family connection with Miss Blackler and, therefore, one with Mrs Clark too.

In 1836, at Ellinthorp Hall, Anna Maria Blackler married John, eldest son (of ten children) of the Gibson family of Pleasant Banks, Evandale. John's father, David, had arrived as a convict on the *Calcutta* and his maternal grandmother, **Elizabeth Hayward** (1773–1836) was, at 13, probably the youngest female First Fleeter. But, by 1828, the Gibsons owned 7,300 acres. Eliza Hayward's daughter, **Elizabeth Nichols Gibson** (1794–1872), another of those girls to give birth, aged 15, to a child by the Governor of Norfolk Island, John Piper, was also quite an accumulator of land and livestock there – a facility she obviously brought to Tasmania when she took up with David Gibson on the neighbouring land grant. (They lived together from 1815, and married in 1819.) Did she and Collins' mistress Margaret Eddington know that their first-born were half-siblings (p37)?

Anna Maria Blackler Gibson had eight surviving children and eventually became mistress of Pleasant Banks. **Mary Ann Blackler,** assumed to have been, confusingly, Anna Maria's sister, arrived in Tasmania in 1841 and married William, John Gibson's brother, two years later; she, too, had eight children.

Among the really nice girls was probably Jane Reid Williams; her editor remarks: 'One fancies upon her the mark of Ellinthorpe Hall.' Other settler pupils include **Sarah Elizabeth Leake** (1816–1880), daughter of lonely Elizabeth Leake and her husband John of Rosedale, two Grey daughters of the extended family of Avoca (pp269, 340); Elizabeth Crowther, later of New Norfolk (pp288, 308); Mary Allen Reibey of Entally (p364), and the rich and beautiful Agnes Galloway Davidson's two daughters, **Marion Davidson** (1826–1898) and **Euphemia Jane Davidson** (1831–1899).

Ellen Viveash introduces us to another former pupil, Miss Allison, who seems to have been a neighbour and companion to her when Charles was ill in 1834. She must have been one of the daughters of **Susannah Race Allison** (1794–1872; m1811) and her husband Francis, a master mariner who had fought with Nelson and who arrived in 1822 with Susannah and their five children. Miss Allison was presumably the oldest daughter, **Hannah Bedlington Allison** (1817–1897, later King).

By 1834, the Allisons had ten children and were to have two more, a girl a year later, seemingly named after Ellen Viveash, and a boy in 1838 (when Susannah was 44) with the third name Baskerville – the name of the Viveash property, as well as Charles' second name. The Allison family had also had several setbacks so it is not surprising that Ellen Viveash wrote of Miss Allison, 'She is very fond of being here as they live in a poor way at home and we have books.' But she also writes of the young woman: 'She has spirit and would not be tiranized over by Mrs Clarke, her school mistress.'

So, if Ellinthorp Hall can be seen as the melting pot that contributed to what Tasmanian society is today, Miss Allison is a good example of its spirited women of the past – whatever their social status.

Part Three – 1837–58

10 – Jane Franklin

Queen Victoria ascended the throne in 1837 and Jane Franklin arrived as Governor's wife the same year. The people of Britain were to get used to a woman in a commanding position over 64 years. Tasmania, in the seven years that Jane Franklin was there, was never to come to terms with the 'celebrated blue stocking' nor the 'man in petticoats', as the chaplain to the Hobart Female House of Correction was to dub her. But there was no way he, nor anyone else, could correct the clever woman who had descended upon the colony determined to leave it a better place, especially intellectually, than she found it.

Jane Franklin (neé Griffin, 1891–1875), 36 when she married the distinguished sailor and explorer Sir John Franklin, and 45 when she arrived in Hobart, was not only highly intelligent, but also forceful and adventurous. Everything she did – and she did much in Tasmania – offended someone and it was constantly brought to public attention by what she came to call 'the contemptible felon press'. And she meant so well, and it started so well.

After 13 years of Governor Arthur, John Franklin was seen as a new and benign broom. Although as a midshipman he had been part of the voyage of discovery to Australia made by his uncle Matthew Flinders – the region was not new to him – he was inexperienced as a colonial Governor; he felt it right, therefore, to stick with the Arthurite clique (two of them nephews by marriage of the former Governor) who were administering the colony. But, when Franklin failed to follow the whims of those he had inherited, particularly John Montagu, the Colonial Secretary, they turned against him. By that time, those who had opposed Arthur had given up on Franklin. As her husband struggled against the growing tide of colonial intransigence and criticism, so Jane Franklin, with her brain, determination and devotion, came to his aid, bringing increasing publicity and odium upon herself; the Franklins were much briefed against in Tasmania and within the government in Britain where Montagu had contacts.

That, in summary, is the Franklins' time in Tasmania, and yet Jane was not without achievement there and, although they went home in 1843 when he was recalled under a cloud, she left distinct and distinctive traces of herself that endure.

Much has been written about Jane Franklin. The several sources upon which I have drawn are in the bibliography, as well as sprinkled in this and the next two chapters, and in several itineraries, but some, such as the 1951 biography *Portrait of Jane* by Frances Woodward, and Kathleen Fitzpatrick's *Sir John Franklin in Tasmania* (1949), are difficult or expensive to get hold of, and analytical articles are in journals available only in specialist libraries. For the general reader who wants to read about Jane, and in context, you cannot do better than the chapter in Alison Alexander's *Obliged to Submit* – that title, apposite for several Governors' wives, is an ironic comment upon Jane Franklin. Alison sums her up:

> What [she] did show were the limitations of the role of governor's wife, and indeed of all colonial women. No one expected them to build temples, eradicate snakes, climb mountains, have Aborigines in their houses and definitely not interfere in male domains like politics. Womanly activities such as balls and dancing were fine, but many colonists, men and women, just could not cope with a woman doing anything outside what they considered her sphere.

12. Jane Franklin, from a sketch by
Thomas Bock, c1840, courtesy of the
WL Crowther Library, Tasmanian
Archives and Heritage Office

And perhaps Alison adds an important element when, as a Tasmanian (and an intellectual) herself, she writes:

> If Lady Franklin was installed in Government House today, one senses that many people would disapprove of her gallivanting around and dislike her attempts to raise the cultural level, with all the condescension that implies. Only a minority could really appreciate Lady Franklin.

'Condescension' is the word an Englishwoman today particularly notices. Tasmania, as has already been implied and as will become clearer, was trying to stand on its own feet and find a voice of its own. That, in spite of the words Isabel Dick put into the mouth of an 1841 character in *Wild Orchard*:

> If folks at home could realize how we crave to out-British the British! Think how we read and re-read the illustrated papers, think how minutely we watch out for any and every detail of the Royal Family, see how we shape our homes and gardens in the pattern, so far as we are able, of our old homes.

There seems little doubt that Jane Franklin was imperial as well as progressive, and was not without a touch of imperiousness, particularly to people en masse. This is illustrated in a quirky way by her suggestion that there should be an annual aquatic carnival, starting in December 1838, to commemorate the Dutchman Tasman's sighting of Van Diemen's Land in 1642. There were, however, to be 'higher objects than mere boating and sailing'; these were to be the results of honest toil: homecrafts, agricultural produce, fishing and whaling displays. It turned into a holiday when people got drunk. Jane's response was 'With a different class of people to deal with, it might have been so innocent as well as beautiful.' From somewhere emerged the non-scanning jingle:

> The British Tars both high and low will make a joyous chatter
> Sir John's fair lady will show her smiles at the regatta.

Mary Morton Allport (née Chapman, 1806–1895), the first professional woman artist in Tasmania, who had arrived in 1831 and was advertising her portraiture six months later, painted a lively watercolour of the Sandy Bay Regatta held on 1 December 1842, and composed a poem to go with it:

> And see, our tall ships crowd the circling main;
> E'en British sailors chase our boats in vain;
> Long live our Whalers – the bravest in the world;
> May no Regatta find their canvas furled.
> Hail Tasmania! The gem of southern seas;
> 'Tis Franklin gives the white sails to the breeze.

Jane Franklin's diaries and letters have been much mined by scholars, though, as yet, there is no published diary of the Tasmanian years. Some of her letters to her sister, Mary Simpkinson, and some extracts from her diaries, were edited in 1947 (George Mackaness) and they are available in two pamphlet-sized volumes second-hand. I bought mine, and many other books, from Astrolabe; the Hobart Bookshop round the corner is also first-rate for books on Tasmania.

13. Regatta, Sandy Bay, December 1842, by Mary Morton Allport, courtesy of the
Allport Library and Museum of Fine Arts, Tasmanian Archive and Heritage Office

In her letters Jane lets her hair down about her hopes, plans, and hurt.
What she wrote and did about convict women features in Chapter 11, and
her Aboriginal contacts in Chapter 12. Another of her main preoccupations
was education, in both the broad and narrow sense. Jane herself, the daughter
of a prosperous London silk merchant, had received scant formal education
at 21 Bedford Row (which you can visit if you stay at the Penn Club) but
she was determinedly and exhaustively self-taught – a process that continued
throughout her life. Between 1837 and 1839, for example, and as she listed
in a notebook, she read 295 books, and she often copied passages that had
appealed to her into her diary.

The college the Franklins planned for boys appears in the 'New Norfolk'
itinerary (Turriff Lodge, p302). But on 28 April 1840, Jane wrote to Mary
about her plans for girls' education in much more detail than I am going to
quote; and her views on Tasmanians suggest why both they and scholars have
such an ambivalent attitude towards her, as well as illustrating her wish to
ameliorate and the force of her personality; her comment about Ellinthorp
Hall which, as it happens, closed in 1840, is telling:

I have told you of my plan for establishing a lady's school of the highest
order in this country. It is greatly needed, there is no provision whatever for
the education of girls – a few miserable schools at Hobarton and one in the
interior (noted for its balls and concerts and match making) not deserving
scarcely the name. I am no admirer of a school education for girls, and if

fifty governesses, very sensible and good women, could be found as easily as one or two, I should prefer importing them, in order to distribute them through the country in private families, to any other mode of encouraging female education. But not only are such people not to be found, but if they came, they could not be happy, and would not remain ...

The colony is even more in want of education for girls than for boys, for boys can go home to England and the girls cannot and do not ...

Their frivolity, emptiness and ignorance, and boldness of manner are deplorable – at least in this town. However naturally shy and reserved, they lose it all as soon as they go into society, and yet they are sharp witted, and pretty, and no doubt have as much moral aptitude for good things as the generations from which they sprang ...

I would have the older girls continually with me by turns, or together, so as to introduce them gradually into Society and give them a taste for better things than they are accustomed to, and I should wish to be on the most friendly terms of fellowship and sympathy with the heads of the house. Such an institution if it contained only twelve or twenty girls would gradually leaven the whole mass.

Jane's girls' school came to nothing, but she started several other 'educational' initiatives. The sort of ground into which they fell is described by Louisa Anne Meredith who arrived in Tasmania in October 1840 and admired and sympathised with Jane Franklin. She wrote nine years later in *My Home in Tasmania*:

Among the young ladies, both married and single, in Tasmania, as in Sydney, a very 'general one-ness' prevails as to the taste for dancing, from the love of which but a small share of regard can be spared for any other accomplishment or study, save a little singing and music; and Lady Franklin's attempts to introduce evening parties in the 'conversazione' style were highly unpopular with the pretty Tasmanians, who declared that they 'had no idea of being asked to an evening party, and then stuck up in rooms full of pictures and books, and shells and stones, and other rubbish, with nothing to do but to hear people talk lectures, or else sit as mute as mice listening to what was called good music. Why could not Lady Franklin have the military band in, and the carpets out, and give dances, instead of such stupid preaching about philosophy and science, and a parcel of stuff that nobody could understand?

It is noticeable that both Jane and Louisa Anne talk of the good looks of Tasmanian girls. Almost the first comment on Jane Franklin, in February 1837, comes from the 22-year-old widow Jane Reid Williams of Ratho, made when the Governor and his party visited Bothwell. A dinner and ball was arranged for them and Jane Williams was compelled by her father to go; she wrote: '... we were all formally introduced to Sir John and Lady F., who was dressed like the pictures of two centuries back, &, as well as her two nieces, is very plain'.

Jane Franklin's women companions would have been her husband's nieces, both in their early twenties: **Mary Franklin** (c1811–1891) who was, less than a year later, to marry John Price, a recently arrived settler in the Huon Valley and later a harsh penal administrator on Norfolk Island (he is said to be the inspiration for Maurice Frere in Marcus Clarke's *For the Term of His Natural Life* (1874)); and **Sophia Cracroft** who, in spite of several minor flirtations in Tasmania, was to stay with Jane Franklin for the rest of her long life. They were part of the large gubernatorial party that had come with the Franklins from England and included Eleanor, the Governor's twelve-year-old daughter by his deceased first wife; Eleanor's governess **Miss Williamson**; Jane's two maids, one of them called Stewart, and the other who spoke only French; and Franklin's private secretary, naval officer and geographer (and later prison reformer) Alexander Maconochie, his wife **Mary Maconochie** (née Hutton-Brown, m1822) and their six children.

Jane Williams' opinion of her dress sense, even if she had been aware of it, would have left Jane Franklin unmoved. And disapproval was no deterrent to her projects and adventures. Together she and her husband founded the Natural History Society with its regular meetings, and a quarterly journal, that soon became widely respected though in some circles in Tasmania it was dubbed 'the Scientific Humbug Society' and 'the Blue Stocking Association'. A copy of the first volume of the *Tasmanian Journal of Natural Science* was presented to Queen Victoria and another earmarked for Harriet Martineau who had lost much of her hearing when she was eighteen. Jane wrote to her sister – and one can assume that she had read *Home Abroad*:

> I should like to present her from me in testimony both of my admiration of her talent and my sympathy of her suffering with the four numbers now out of the Tasmanian Journal – not because it is interesting or entertaining or clever, but simply because it is written and published in this 'paradoxical' corner of the Globe & as a tribute from the Antipodes of the pride we feel in our distinguished countrywoman.

Every opportunity was taken to welcome natural scientists, explorers and geographers to the colony and, although the society faltered after the Franklins' departure, its modern manifestation is the Royal Society of Tasmania. Mary Allport was a founder member.

Jane bought land in today's Lenah Valley for a botanical garden and had built there a Greek temple (completed in 1842) named Ancanthe to be a library and museum to which she started to contribute books and objects. There is more detail about it in the 'New Town' itinerary (p270). Jane's personal fortune, which enabled her to make this and other such purchases, no doubt contributed towards her independent spirit.

The 640 acres she bought in the Huon Valley in 1838 had a quite different purpose: to provide smallholdings on easy terms to less affluent families. And she had built the *Huon Pine* at a cost of £300 to carry their produce to market. Today's flourishing town of Franklin and its memories and appreciation of

Jane are described in the itinerary 'Oyster Cove to Recherche Bay' (p293). She bought Betsey Island, just off Hobart, and some years later gave it to the colony. It was, thereafter, for a while, called Franklin Island. Jane's proposal to London that Van Diemen's Land be renamed Tasmania bore fruit, though not in her time. You may have noted Mary Allport's use of the name Tasmania in her poem, when the formal change from Van Diemen's Land was still a decade or so away. Hobart, instead of Hobarton or Hobart Town, was also Jane's preference.

Jane Franklin was by no means just cerebral. On the five month voyage to Tasmania, she had not only organised shipboard life, she had also climbed Table Mountain when they stopped in Cape Town, so one of her first Tasmanian adventures was to take a party up Mount Wellington. She was not, as is sometimes claimed, the first woman to make her way up, not even in her own day, but she did make it respectable for women to venture there. This expedition is more detailed in that itinerary as, appropriately, are her various other travels in Tasmania, typical of which was her attempt in December 1838 to find the garden the French under d'Entrecasteaux had planted at Recherche Bay – now a major environmental project (pp4, 253, 298).

Jane always explored exhaustively and noted in detail everything she saw. Alison Alexander sums up her trip to the penitentiary at Port Arthur:

> Saturday was very wet, but Lady Franklin went all through the workshops and dockyard. On Easter Sunday she missed church and visited the semaphore station. By Wednesday she had seen everything, met the ladies, tasted the prisoners' soup, tried on handcuffs, seen men at work, found out how to make 'steamer' out of pork and kangaroo, inspected a canoe made by convicts of a hollowed gum tree, and a 'curious raft' and counterfeit dollars also produced by convicts. She visited the boys' establishment at Point Puer and was impressed when one boy asked her for a Bible; but Captain Booth said the boy was a hypocrite.

Jane also travelled without her husband from the newly established Melbourne to Sydney, the first white woman to do so, and to and within New Zealand – her diaries of the former journey have been edited by Penny Russell, today's main Jane scholar, as *This Errant Lady* (2002). Travel was nothing new to her: she had travelled before meeting John Franklin; she did so when, as a naval officer, he was posted to the Mediterranean (see the web update of *Crete: Women, History, Books and Places* in this series); and she would do so in later life to the United States, India, Japan and Hawaii.

Her Tasmanian expeditions with Franklin, particularly that to Macquarie Harbour which kept them away for two months, instead of the expected several days, and led to fears for the gubernatorial party's safety, were certainly not what was expected of a first lady, nor did any aspect of them meet with approval. The following tirade against Jane, and panegyric of Eliza Arthur, appeared in the *Van Diemen's Land Chronicle* on 15 October 1842; (the square bracket is an insertion by the historian KR von Stieglitz who chose Jane as one of his *Six Pioneer Women of Tasmania*):

> The truth is that Lady Arthur was a gentlewoman and did not go out on a gypsy expedition traipsing all over the wilds of New South Wales in a bullock dray in the company of men. She had no sawing establishments at the Huon, and no botanical garden. She undertook no expedition to Macquarie Harbour in company with a lot of prisoners of the very worst description, to whom tickets of leave and pardons, etc., etc., were afterwards given, thus letting loose a lot of ruffians on Society.
>
> Lady Arthur never invited the gentry of the land to a ball at Government House and then left their company and went to bed [As a matter of fact, Lady Franklin had suddenly taken ill.] ... These are only a few of the monstrosities of this most despicable dynasty who now rule over us.

The campaign waged by Montagu against the Franklins and, particularly, Jane was reaching its climax. Not for nothing had Mary Maconochie written to a friend in England:

> You will probably meet our deadly enemy Capt. Montagu – that snake in the grass, sleek, smooth, & slippery, a specimen of our Genus homo well worthy of the attention of the naturalist ... – like many noxious animals he has the power of soothing & fanning his victims to sleep, never attacking openly or boldly ... But from close & repeated examination, it is found he possesses *invisible* tentacula, which come from many quarters, puncturing, & injuring the victim, gradually destroying & undermining its character.

Jane may have encouraged a campaign against snakes in Tasmania, offering a shilling for each head brought to a police station, to the relief of many women and profit of convicts, but ridiculed by the press (she was £600 poorer as a result), but she did not appreciate the effectiveness of Montagu's venom. When John Franklin, pushed to the limit by Montagu, resolved to dispense with his services, Jane succumbed to Montagu's approach to her and, although John refused to back down, her pressure caused him to be less forceful in his letter of explanation to the Colonial Office than he might have been. John Franklin's own recall reached all Hobart before it reached Government House. From the Colonial Office came the mealy-mouthed response to his letter about the dismissal:

> Reluctant as I am to employ a single expression which is likely to be unwelcome to you, I am compelled to add that your proceedings in this case of Mr Montagu do not appear to me to have been well-judged, and that your suspension of him from office is not, in my opinion, sufficiently vindicated.

Everyone learned, too, that 'Mr Montagu revealed that his line of defence with Lord Stanley had been this, – he was the victim of Lady Franklin's hatred, and she alone was the cause of his suspension.' Elsewhere, Montagu accused Franklin of 'imbecility' and his wife of 'intrigue'.

Although Hobart loved the scandal, Franklin had been a good and fair Governor, and Jane was admired and respected by many. The first Bishop of Tasmania arrived in 1843 with his wife **Anna Maria Nixon** (née Woodcock, c1802–1868, m1836) whose story is best told in the 'New Town' itinerary (Runnymede, p260). Anna Maria wrote of Jane, whom she found in poor health when she and her large family were guests at Government House before their own home was ready,

> Lady Franklin is a very superior woman, but retiring and shy in her manner, and too unworldly to be popular in the very second-rate society there is here. Her whole mind seems bent on doing good to the Colony, and future generations will bless her memory. But, oh, she has been fearfully traduced … I remember your hearing in Downing Street that Lady Franklin was Governor here. Now, this is one among many falsehoods disseminated by the Montague party. Though a very superior woman, she has taken no part in public measures. But alas, I might fill pages with this sad topic … you could not believe how shamefully [Montagu and his clique] have behaved, nor how much mischief he contrived to do while in England.

And Bishop Nixon, by no means a pushover, added his opinion of Jane: 'The most amiable, simple unassuming person he ever met with, and that if her stockings are blue, her petticoats are so long that he never found it out.' (With the Bishop's arrival, St David's Church became a cathedral and Hobart a city; a Roman Catholic bishop arrived two years later.) But John Franklin's protective September 1843 comment to a friend is the most touching: 'She cannot help being clever, but that is what the party cannot bear.' From his first wife, Eleanor Porden, Franklin had, as Katherine Fitzpatrick has it, learnt 'to respect the independence of an intelligent woman'.

Penny Russell wrote of Jane in 'Displaced Loyalties: Vice-Regal Women in Colonial Australia' (1999): 'She became a focus of the jealousies of women, the anxieties of men, and the rancour of all.' Exploring that anxiety of men, Penny Russell suggests that Jane 'Embodied female power, represented as illegitimate, irresponsible, and based on a whim and a caprice.' As for Jane herself, she had written to her sister in February 1839:

> [Y]ou must not suppose that I think myself in a very extraordinary position & even a very wonderful person. I think quite the contrary – I suppose every woman whose husband is in public life helps him if she can & he gives her the opportunity which he will not fail to do if he can trust in her ability & discretion.

But Penny Russell sees it not through the Franklins' nor the Nixons' eyes:

> What the colonists saw, with some justification, was not a woman who submerged her talents in her husband's interests, but a woman whose

extreme energy, ability and enthusiasm constantly obtruded upon, exceeded, and overshadowed Sir John's administration.

In another article, '"Her Excellency": Lady Franklin, Female Convicts and the Problem of Authority in Van Diemen's Land' (1997), Penny Russell caps her own analysis when she writes: 'The dual threat of imperial power and female power was constantly evoked. Both threats were united in frequent newspaper references to Lady Franklin as "Her Excellency".'

Anne McMahon, in 'The Lady in Early Tasmanian Society: A Psychological Portrait' (1979), has a more pragmatic take:

> Little wonder ... that among the colonists she became a kind of Amazon striding across their world, while the scarce females of the society were held captive to the males, enabling them to develop and keep a tenuous hold on their new lands, which could be made viable only with the use of the family as a labour force. In these circumstances the spectre of an independent woman viewing their struggles and achievements with detachment, making forthright judgements of their competence, and exposing their intrigues, was a dangerous presence.

One of the most sympathetic views of Jane Franklin is that of Catherine Shepherd in her 1951 play *Jane, My Love*, first performed, like the earlier *Daybreak*, at the Theatre Royal, Hobart. It is included in Susan Pfisterer's *Tremendous Worlds: Australian Women's Drama 1890–* (1999) and described by the editor as 'a significant document in Australian history which shows how feminist cultural memory has an important role to play in the formation of our historical consciousness'. The play, touching on the period of Franklin's governorship, 1838–43, and many aspects of Jane Franklin's involvement in Tasmania, attempts to show her at her best. This speech, made at that time of the first regatta, ends Act 1 and sums up her love of the place and her aspirations:

> My head is full of plans for it. I thought perhaps the wattle flower could be a kind of national emblem to be worn on that day ... Oh, there is so much to do. As we came across the dark water tonight, it seemed as if great spaces of mountains and bushland stretched behind us – with dangers and loneliness. And ahead you could see the lights of the town – such a small sprinkling of lanterns about the wharf and lighted windows above. And I thought how those lights would spread out over the hills one day ... in a larger town ... a greater nation. There is so much I should like to give them ... and so little we can do. The difficulties are so great ... But one day, perhaps, there will be a harvest ... if we can plant good seed.

The play ends with Franklin's recall. Sir John Eardley-Wilmot, the new Governor, arrived 30 hours before formal notice of it by another ship. The Franklins' departing weeks are explored in the 'Oyster Cove to Recherche

Bay' itinerary (p294). They arrived back in England in June 1844. By May the following year, John Franklin had been appointed to command an Arctic expedition to find the North West Passage. He had tried once before and, although 59, was driven by the need to wipe out the shame of his Tasmanian recall.

Jane waited two years for his return, travelling herself, with Eleanor and Sophia Cracroft, in the meantime. But he never came back. She devoted the next twelve years to finding him, badgering the Admiralty to send out search vessels and even approaching the President of the United States for help. The *Fox*, which she financed herself, eventually, in 1859, brought news of relics of the expedition. John Franklin had fulfilled his dream but died, in 1847, in the process.

The ballad 'Lady Franklin's Lament' (sung to the tune of 'The Croppy Boy') is said to date from 1855, and even to have been written by Jane herself. But it is more likely that the words were put into her mouth since there are several versions on the internet. Only that quoted in *Lady Franklin's Revenge: A True Story of Ambition, Obsession and the Remaking of Arctic History* (Ken McGoogan, 2006) seems personal to Jane. The most appealing version is sung and discussed by Sinéad O'Connor on YouTube.

Linking this period with the Franklins' Tasmanian life are the first lines of the Welsh poet Sheenagh Pugh's 'Lady Franklin Begins to be Concerned 1847' (*The Beautiful Lie*, 2002):

> When first you sailed, all my pictures of you
> were bright. I could fancy all your lines
> smoothing away in the wind, the northern light
> you love so well.
>
> That stiffness in your shoulder would start to ease
> with action; even the headaches would fade,
> as the hate-filled faces of Hobart
> fell back in your wake.

A nice image starts *Lady Franklin's Revenge*:

> On November 15, 1866, three weeks before she turned seventy-five, an elegantly dressed, petite woman sat in a comfortable, high-backed chair on the second floor of the Athenaeum Club in Central London, looking out a window at a ceremonial unveiling in Waterloo Place.

If you sit there yourself, at the far end of the drawing room on the first floor, looking towards Parliament and Westminster Abbey, you can see, as Jane Franklin did that day, the statue of her husband she had commissioned, identifying him as the discoverer of the North West Passage; indeed, Jane not only hired the best sculptor but stipulated the pose, telescope in hand, and the exact placing of the statue to be seen to best advantage. His achievement – which has since been questioned – vindicated John Franklin's Tasmanian career, but the colony had not forgotten its former Governor and his wife: its inhabitants happily contributed £1,700 (worth over £100,000 today) towards Jane's searches. A copy of the statue stands in Hobart's Franklin Square which replaced the old Government House in which Jane had worked on her projects and from where she had sallied forth on her adventures.

However ambivalent the feelings towards the Franklins were in Tasmania during his governorship, and the same ambivalence in historical reconstruction, Alison Alexander quotes an 1873 visitor to Hobart that allows a positive conclusion:

> We are very much struck by the way in which everyone seems to look back to Sir John Franklin's days here, as *the* golden days of Tasmania ... *the* Governor who did nearly everything that ever was done for the colony. Both he and Lady Franklin are spoken of with the greatest veneration.

An up-to-date view of Jane Franklin came to me by email from Paddy Prosser, expert on Louise Girardin (p4); she wrote:

> I'm sure you have read Lady Franklin's revenge by Ken McGoogan. He is a Canadian writer. I love the way nations take ownership of famous people. As far as he is concerned she is theirs because Sir John died there. Well, excuse me she is ours!

11 – From Probation to the End of Transportation

Jane Franklin arrived in Tasmania in 1837 at a time when a reassessment of the convict system was pending. By the time she left in 1843, the assignment of new convicts was giving way to their probation. Although the assignment system was criticised by many, John Franklin had, in the meantime, to administer it. By 1840, transportation to New South Wales had ceased and Tasmania became the main dumping ground, resources allocated were insufficient and the colony was on the cusp of a severe economic downturn.

Alexander Maconochie, Franklin's friend and private secretary had, before leaving England with the Franklins, been commissioned to investigate the convict system. But when his condemnatory 'Report on the State of Prison Discipline in Van Diemen's Land', with its more human and liberal approach towards convicts, was published in London as a parliamentary paper in 1838, it created such a stink in Tasmania that Franklin had no option but to dismiss him. Maconochie had also reported that 'The selfish feelings everywhere predominate; their expression everywhere runs riot; and as everyone, from highest to lowest, appeals directly to the governor, the turmoil in which he lives is incessant.' Now only Jane was left with her husband's professional interests at heart. And though Maconochie and his wife, Mary – who so much better than Jane appreciated the extent of Montagu's perfidy – remained living at Government House for a while before his posting to Norfolk Island, relations were very awkward; friendship faltered. From the letters of Charles Dickens, we learn that Mary Maconochie was intensely loyal to her husband and supported his reforms.

Before they set out, Jane Franklin had been briefed by the prison reformer Elizabeth Fry whose aim was to provide proper facilities for the reception and management of female convicts in the Antipodes. But to make any changes was not as easy to do as Jane had anticipated. She was to write to her sister early in 1843: 'It has been the one object I have thought most about, and cared for most, since I have been in this colony, – yet what have I done – what have I been allowed to do?'

That is very much two questions. About the first, what, in her judgement, could be done for the women, as determined by the nature of the women themselves, she answered in a letter to her sister of 1838:

I have never written to Mrs Fry and am afraid I must be very low in her estimation on that account. As for doing anything with the women here, in the factory, it seems next to impossible, huddled as they all are together, and such impudent creatures almost all of them.

But there was more to it: Jane thought 'the whole system of transportation, and particularly female assignment in service, so faulty and vicious, that to attempt to deal with the women who are the subjects of it seems a waste of time and labour'.

As with so many of Jane's aspirations and projects, attitudes of others towards them were ambivalent then, and little has changed. Alison Alexander writes of Jane's efforts on behalf of women convicts that 'It does not seem that she tried very hard.' Penny Russell, in 'Her Excellency' – her article on Jane and the convict system – is at her harshest for, as she writes,

> Contemplation of Jane Franklin's views on social relations in general and social reform in particular is a somewhat distressing activity for her biographer. In no way does she resemble a feminist heroine. Self-centred, self-absorbed and blindly prejudiced in favour of all things English and middle class, she divided her world into two categories: a small elite capable of self-regulation and self-discipline and a large incapable mass in need of external regulation.

While Jane believed the transport system inherently bad for women, given its existence she was in favour of punishment, corrective discipline and moral and religious instruction. She was, thus, faced with a quandary when trying to fulfil the mission entrusted to her by Elizabeth Fry and on which she had set her heart. And in any case, whatever she proposed, as she soon discovered, would be opposed, for it was none of her business. She wrote to her sister on 10 January 1843:

> I could wish to be Governor of Van Diemen's Land for that alone, but with anything short of his power, I mean such power as must silence objections, and bear down opposition, and override prejudice, and establish faith, there will be nothing done.

In spite of her reservations, Jane did eventually, in September 1841, set up the Tasmanian Ladies' Society for the Reformation of Female Prisoners with its aim to provide 'the religious and general instruction of female convicts' and, if feasible, to suggest improvements. Its secretary was 23-year-old **Kezia Hayter** (c1818–1885) who, at the instigation of Elizabeth Fry, and with a brief to report back, had come out as an independent matron – from her previous post at the Millbank Penitentiary – with 180 women convicts on the *Rajah*.

One of Elizabeth Fry's innovations was to make the character of the voyage itself more humane; to that end, each woman was provided with a bag of haberdashery and fabric pieces – known as 'the bag of useful things'. By the time the *Rajah* docked in July 1841, the women, under the supervision of Kezia, had produced what is known as the Rajah Quilt. It was presented to Jane Franklin as tangible evidence of the cooperative work that could be achieved under such circumstances. Although 15 of the women's occupations were listed as tailoring or needlework, some of them were obviously inexperienced if the pinpricks of blood on the quilt, with its 2,815 pieces, are anything to go by. A detail of the quilt, which was at first sent to England to be presented to Elizabeth Fry, reads:

TO THE LADIES
of the Convict Ship Committee
This quilt was worked by the Convicts of the Ship Rajah during the voyage to van Diemans Land is presented as a testimony of the gratitude with which they remember their exertions for their welfare while in England and during their passage and also as a proof that they have not neglected the ladies kind admonitions of being industrious.
June 1841

The quilt went to ground for some time but, since 1989, has been a treasure in the National Gallery of Australia, Canberra, where, because of its fragility, it is apparently only available for viewing once a year. The voyage of the *Rajah* is the subject of work in progress by Dianne Snowden and Trudy Cowley. They are also contributors to the latest work to come out of the Female Factory Research Group – *Convict Lives: Women at Cascades Female Factory* (2009), about to be published as I write.

Unfortunately, Kezia Hayter was too young, inexperienced and thin-skinned to take the punishment meted out by the opposing forces – especially to her as an unmarried woman visiting prisons. And Kezia herself had reservations about the level of Jane Franklin's spirituality: 'How very amiable Lady F is,' she wrote, 'how fascinating – what a grievous thing it is her heart is not under correct influences – may the time come when it will be so.' Jane, while continuing to visit prisons with Kezia, wrote that she was 'a very sanguine young person, but somewhat deficient in stability'. As Penny Russell observes of Jane Franklin, 'The problem ... lay with both the strength of male opposition to her efforts and the weakness of the women to whom she looked for support.'

After some particularly hurtful remarks about the ladies' committee in the *Review*, Kezia resigned and retired to Brickendon to work as governess to the Archer family (p361) while she waited for Captain Charles Ferguson of the *Rajah*, with whom she had fallen in love, to come back and claim her. They married in 1843 and, thereafter, Kezia, giving birth to seven children, led a peripatetic sea life away from the travails of Tasmania and convicts.

With Kezia's resignation, the committee folded. The problem for Jane Franklin was not only that she herself was involved in the committee's work and that it was regarded as silly women's affairs, but that the male powers-that-be were satisfied with the system as it was. As Penny Russell expresses it:

While [Jane Franklin] openly deplored the lack of either punishment or inducements to reform inherent in [the] system, it is likely that her references to corrupting influences to which female convicts were exposed represented a veiled critique of the system of sexual slavery.

Of all the opprobrium heaped on Jane, the *Colonial Times* did, at least, praise her for organising the Factory women into making clothes for children in the Orphan School. And Catherine Shepherd's play, *Jane, My Love*, gives a sympathetic flavour of her motivation towards convict women. This extract from Act 2, Scene 2, takes place in 1841 at a gathering of the ladies' committee at Government House after adverse press reports of their activities:

> JANE: ... But we must consider the conditions to which these women have been subjected. Many of them were simple country girls, found guilty of some small misdemeanour and sentenced to transportation. On the transport ships they were thrown together with city drabs and thieves and worse. Then, in a strange land, they were assigned as domestic servants to settlers and often most evilly used ...
>
> MRS DOWBIGGIN: ... Pray, Lady Franklin, do not mention such things!
>
> JANE: But they have existed, Mrs Dowbiggin. When the women became unmanageable through drink, or had unwanted babies, they were packed back to the Factory – a place of horror and wickedness and disease.
>
> MRS DOWBIGGIN: ... Oh, dear!
>
> JANE: We cannot be content to say 'Oh, dear!' and cast a pitying glance as we pass in our carriages. At our meeting we agreed to inspect the establishment, to visit the unhappy inmates and see what could be done to help them.
>
> MISS HAYTER: You were so eloquent, Lady Franklin. And we did not know ... what it would be like.
>
> JANE: Well, you know now. Surely you agree that it is work which needs doing?
>
> MRS BARTON: I cannot think that it is women's work.
>
> JANE: Not women's work – to minister to women?

Jane Franklin's reservations about the regime in the Female Factories is confirmed from an interesting source. In 1841, her husband appointed a committee to enquire into female prison discipline. Its report was never published, but has been made use of by Lucy Frost who reveals that five women convicts gave evidence to the committee and, in 'Eliza Churchill Tells', contained in *Chain Letters: Narrating Convict Lives* (2001), we finally have traces of the woman convict's point of view, not written by **Eliza Churchill** – she could not write – but spoken by her as narrative, uninterrupted by questioning, and transcribed. Eliza was 19 when, in 1840, she was convicted in Plymouth for stealing a cloak and a silk umbrella (which she pawned) and sentenced to 14 years' transportation. Described as a shoebinder, a skilled job, as Lucy Frost points out, she was assigned as a servant soon after she disembarked. Eliza comments on assignment: because she was in Launceston, she was more open to temptation and was punished twice for being absent without leave. It was, she suggested, easier for women assigned in the countryside. Eliza was finally consigned to the Female Factory for three weeks when she was ill.

Opened in 1834, the Launceston factory building was designed to house 80–100; by 1842, there were 198 women and 29 children. This is a sample of what Eliza had to say, which Lucy Frost sets in a wider context, exploring, too, the reasons for the more general silence of convict women:

> During the day time the women in the factory amuse themselves the best way they can, dancing & singing etc. in fact if it were not for being separated from some friends outside it would be no punishment to be in the factory as the women can get any thing they please if they have money & generally bring in some concealed where it is almost impossible to find it.

These details were relatively anodyne, but Eliza also revealed information about relations between women – 'unnatural connexions' – and gave fuel to antagonisms between the limited staff: **Mrs Pearson**, matron, and her husband, the superintendent, and **Anne Littler** (?née Summers, mc1840), sub-matron, and her husband, the gatekeeper. It was never clear if Eliza was being used, or naïve in what she reported; she certainly stirred up an internal hornets' nest. In exchange for her narrative, Eliza was granted her freedom and was married in 1842 at St John's, Launceston, to William Weeks.

Eliza was well out of the factory. One of the fellow convicts she had implicated, **Catharine Owens** – whom Lucy Frost calls 'a formidable character to take on' – was the cause of a riot that October. Catharine was visited by Anne Littler when she pleaded illness in solitary confinement. Her fellows rushed her cell, released her, took the sub-matron hostage and, armed with anything to hand, barricaded them all into the messroom. For some hours they beat off the police. When eventually the incident was brought under control, the ringleaders were sent to Hobart for trial and sentenced to hard labour at the Cascades Factory. In court, the women 'exhibited the most outrageous Conduct abusing and threatening the magistrates to their face'.

Kay Daniels suggests that the riot was 'striking for the solidarity between the convict women, the numbers involved and the boldness of its execution'. It is clear, too, that there were some very hardened women in the Launceston factory and, while today's reader may favour the idea of solidarity, I suspect there was also a fair degree of intimidation and fear.

Anne Bartlett, in her article 'The Launceston Female Factory' (1994), covering some of the same ground as Lucy Frost and Kay Daniels, writes: 'It is now known that some of the women's unruly behaviour can be attributed to their nutritionally unbalanced diet.'

The other woman of the 'formidable' couple involved in lesbian relationships mentioned by Eliza Churchill was **Ellen Scott** – doyenne of the so-called 'Flash Mob' which operated in both the Hobart and Launceston Factories. Lucy Frost develops her activities in *Chain Letters*, but Ellen also has a chapter of her own by Trudy Cowley in the more recent *Convict Lives*. Ellen was transported for life in 1829 for stealing a watch chain from the person. Assigned in Hobart, she was 'out of bed at an unreasonable hour on Sunday last' and also disobeyed orders. This was the first of 48 offences during her sentence.

One of the reasons for including Ellen here is that a myth has grown up about an incident in which members of the Flash Mob bared their bottoms during a visit to the Cascade Factory by Jane Franklin, her husband and the chaplain. Scholars of women convicts have found no evidence that such an incident, as passed down, took place. But it does emerge that in October 1833 Ellen Scott was serving a three-month sentence for being absent without leave and, while in Cascades, was charged with 'indecent behaviour during the performance of divine service by the Revd Wm Bedford Junr at the Female House of Correction'. This, as Trudy Cowley suggests, may have given rise to the elaboration – but Jane Franklin had not then arrived in Tasmania.

Ellen Scott's final offences were in 1843 when she was charged with being in 'the same bedroom as her master' and then 'introducing tobacco into the factory'. She received her conditional pardon in 1847 – and no more is known of her.

Lucy Frost ends her chapter about the evidence given to the 1841 enquiry, 'Perhaps some day the autobiography of a convict woman will come to light: meanwhile, we look for their words in unexpected places like the evidence of a committee whose report never went to the printers.'

In 1843, with Jane Franklin then on her way back to England, Mrs Cotton with fellow Quakers revived the ladies' committee. The most obvious Mrs Cotton was **Anna Maria Cotton** (née Tilney, 1800–1882) who had arrived with her husband and five children in 1828. In due course, the family had built up their property Kelvedon, near Swansea on the east coast, regarded as a centre for the growing Quaker community. Anna Maria's involvement with convict women, other than her own servants, is not mentioned, though, in either *Kettle on the Hob* (1886), an account of the family by a descendant, Frances Cotton, nor in Lois Nyman's *The East Coasters* (1990.) Perhaps the resurrection of the committee was rather short-lived; not surprising since Anna Maria's 14 pregnancies undermined her health, so that she often ran her affairs from her bed. Mostly she stayed at Kelvedon while her husband travelled regularly to Hobart 90 miles away on farming and Quaker business.

In 1844, the *Woodbridge* (carrying male prisoners) arrived with **Philippa Bowden**, her husband and his daughter **Amelia Bowden** by his first marriage on board, and now the probation system, particularly as it affected women, was to get into full swing. Jennifer Parrot writes in 'Elizabeth Fry and Female Transportation' (1995):

> It is not difficult to see the results of the reports from Miss Hayter and Lady Franklin and the representations made to the Colonial Secretary by Mrs Fry and the Society in the organisation of the female convict ship *Woodbridge* and the establishment of the *Anson* as a probation hulk for female convicts.

Whatever charges may be levelled at the probation system and the *Anson* moored in the River Derwent off Risdon Cove, no one could have been more qualified to look after the women held there on probation than Philippa Bowden. Louisa Anne Meredith sets the assignment scene before her arrival:

Prisoner women servants are generally of a far lower grade than the men, and at the time of which I now write, Mrs Bowden had not begun her admirable reformatory work among them. My first prisoner nurse-girl was taken at random by our agent in Hobarton, from among the herd of incorrigibles in the female house of correction, or 'Factory', as it is termed; and was indeed a notable example:- *dirty*, beyond imagining! She drank rum, smoked tobacco, swore awfully, and was in all respects the lowest specimen of woman-kind I ever had the sorrow to behold. Before I had time to procure another, she drank herself into violent fits, so that four men could not hold her from knocking herself against the walls and floor, then went to the hospital, and, finally, got married!

Following the revelations of conditions and behaviour in the female factories unearthed by the Franklin-commissioned report, his successor from August 1843, John Eardley-Wilmot, confronted with the situation, wrote: 'I shall hail the arrival of Dr and Mrs Boden [sic] and the new system of female convict discipline with the greatest satisfaction.' Anna Maria Nixon wrote on 2 January 1844, of the previous month: 'I watched the "Woodbridge" as she sailed into harbour with her unhappy crew; though, thanks to Dr and Mrs Bowden, a more orderly and better set of convicts has never arrived.'

When she married Edmund Bowden in April 1841, Philippa Bull Powell was matron of Hanwell Asylum (St Bernard's Hospital) – a post she seems to have held from 1839, though records of her training and previous employment do not seem to have been disinterred. With its 1,000 inmates, Hanwell was one of the largest of the British pauper asylums. She was the daughter of a surgeon at Hanwell, and the principal assistant of Dr John Conolly who, from 1839, instituted a regime of humane treatment there; every form of mechanical restraint, such as whips and chains, was considered cruel and dehumanising, and discontinued. Conolly himself attributed much of the success of his pioneer work in the treatment of the insane to Philippa Bowden. Hanwell's 'humane and enlightened management' impressed Harriet Martineau, among others, when she visited it.

Philippa Bowden, to be described by West as 'a lady of majestic presence and enlightened mind', was appointed matron and her husband superintendent of HMS *Anson*, the temporary floating female prison to initiate the new probation system; the plan was eventually to build a new women's penitentiary at Oyster Cove – what was built was never used, but the station, as the next chapter shows, was used for other purposes. The couple were to receive £500 per annum, with a further £300 for Dr Bowden as medical inspector. Philippa was to be responsible for the organisation and discipline of the women, to be the driving force of the new regime. To help her, she had a carefully chosen staff of six women who travelled out with her on the *Woodbridge*. Five who were her nurses at Hanwell included three sisters: **Susannah Holdich** (b1818) (assistant matron), **Martha Holdich** (b1816) (principal warder) and **Jane Holdich** (school mistress) – daughters of a yeoman farmer of Lincolnshire who seems to have accompanied them.

Instead of being assigned straight from the ship on which they were transported, with all the problems they might expect to encounter from lack of supervision or guidance, female convicts were, in future, to spend six months on the *Anson* learning self-discipline and skills, and receiving moral guidance. (Male convicts under the probation system spent their initial period of two years in public works gangs on stations outside the main settlements.)

The *Anson* had only arrived in February and not undergone the necessary conversion; in addition to living quarters, it needed laundry, mangling room, kitchen, provision store, offices, library, hospital, infirmary and shoemaking areas. Before the ship was ready, the newly-arrived convict women were detained at New Town Farm Station where, in January, a fracas ensued and **Eliza Carr** and **Mary Wills Stroud**, assistants under Bowden, were hard pressed to regain control.

The Bowdens took possession of the *Anson* on 25 April 1844. One of the early women to come under Philippa's wing was short, sandy-haired **Anne Battersby** (b1822), a Lancashire weaver's daughter. Out of work in 1841, Ann began to steal. She appeared several times in court before, in October 1843, she was sentenced to ten years' transportation. In April 1844 she boarded the *Angelina* with 170 other women convicts, and eight of their children, and arrived in Hobart in August. Her story, and the parallel story of that of convict William Lyall, is told in Judith O'Neil's *Transported to Van Diemen's Land* (1977). By September, after the women from the *Angelina* had joined the *Anson*, there were 519 women on board.

In October 1844, a reporter from the *Hobart Town Courier* visited the *Anson* and wrote a mostly glowing report, part of which reads:

We found besides the necessary duties of the establishment in washing and cooking, the women were employed in various descriptions of needlework, in the manufacture of shoes, straw-hats, door mats, etc, as far as the very limited means at Mrs Bowden's command will allow. Every part of the ship exhibited remarkable cleanliness, and we could not have expected to witness such general health, and to find the ventilation so good, where so large a number are collected together in a limited space. But these physical appearances constitute the least recommendation of those who superintend the arrangements on board the Anson. We remarked with great satisfaction the subdued, respectful, and throughout proper deportment of the women, exhibiting a very striking contrast with what we have been too long accustomed to in similar establishments in this country.

But, unfortunately for Philippa Bowden, her good work was not followed up; after six months, the women who had been in her care were relocated to the Brickfields Hiring Depot (established 1842) where affairs were not so well planned. The *Courier* journalist remarks: 'We only lament that one so well fitted for her sphere of duty, and actuated by principles so high, and distinguished by energy so great, should not find everything favourable to her permanent success.'

A report by magistrates in 1844 noted that Brickfields was filthy; the floors, for example, 'covered with expectoration' because the women smoked incessantly. In addition, they 'have no employment, a state of absolute Idleness'. The visiting magistrates conceived 'the whole system is one of great mismanagement dangerous to the community & destructive of any hope that might otherwise be entertained of the moral reformation of any of the class'.

Anna Maria Nixon is more forthright in a letter of 30 September 1844, just before the first *Anson* women would be ready to proceed to the hiring depot where 400 women were already detained. Most of them had come from the 'House of Correction' where, as Anna Maria wrote, 'I am thankful to hear, they have pretty hard work and plenty of it, besides instruction and strict supervision.' She continued:

> Captain Forster [director of the probation system] says the Government have no right to coerce these women, so they are allowed full licence; they are left in total idleness; they dance, play, dress up for acting, and spend all that they have on tobacco and spirits. In vain Mr Wilson [Brickfields' superintendent] represents all this to the Bishop [Anna Maria's husband]; the answer is, 'We have no right to control them, the money they have is their own.' So now the common scheme is for an idle woman to go into service on a month's trial (the mistress is obliged to sign an agreement to keep her for a month or pay), and often the first week she proves herself totally inefficient, the mistress is thankful to be rid of her and the whole of her month's wages is spent in the Brickfields. Just before leaving Hobart Town, Mr Wilson told us that Captain Forster proposes, as a further improvement upon this system, to let these 400 women loose upon the town every Sunday afternoon, that they may enjoy the same indulgence as a certain class of men probationers who wander about the town on a Saturday afternoon, professedly to seek a job of work; but I can assure you that I have, with many others, made a rule never to go into the streets on a Saturday, nor to allow any of the servants to do so unless upon necessity, such is the disorder and drunkenness that prevail; and, alas, now Sunday is to be desecrated by a like horde of wandering women ... It is very wretched and disheartening to reflect that after thousands of pounds of public money has been squandered upon the 'Anson' establishment, let a woman but be inefficient in service, and the atom of good she may have had instilled by the 'Bowdler' [Bowden?] system will and must be all swept away in that sink of iniquity the Brickfields Factory, from which in a very short time no decent family will hire a servant; so there they remain till they get their 'ticket' and go forth to add to this hideous population.

By 1847, however, hiring at the end of probation was advertised direct from the *Anson*. And Anne Battersby seems to have been lucky. After a year on the *Anson*, she was declared a passholder and appointed to the household of **Agnes Power** (née Brooke) and her husband Robert, who had arrived in Tasmania in 1841 with four children and two servants. Two daughters had been left in Paris with Robert's notorious sister Lady Blessington to be educated. Power was surveyor general and the family lived at Derwent Water, a fine house in Sandy Bay, a property which, from a painting of 1834, and a photograph of 1881, appears to have taken up much of today's Red Chapel Avenue (p250). Seventeen months after Ann began to work for the Powers, William Lyall applied for permission to marry her, and did so in February 1847. In August 1848, she was granted her ticket-of-leave and, in 1851, her conditional pardon.

Eardley-Wilmot may have been pleased at the prospect of the Bowdens' arrival, but it was not long before he turned against the probation system, partly for reasons of economy. Intrigues against the Bowdens became a feature. But Philippa had support in high places and Geoffrey Lennox, in 'A Private and Confidential Dispatch of Eardley-Wilmot' (1982), suggests that she may have been one of the influences behind his April 1846 dismissal. A Colonial Office minute records: 'Mrs Bowden entertains the opinions so commonly entertained respecting the Lt.-Governor's habits of life and ascribes to them the feelings of indifference or distrust with which he regards her and her labours.' (Lady Eardley-Wilmot had not accompanied her husband to Tasmania and he had gained a reputation, in her absence, for being a bit of a ladies' man, particularly in respect of 18-year-old Julia Sorell ('New Town' itinerary, p266). There were rumours, too, that women convicts from the Female Factory were dressed up to attend his parties. He was dismissed mainly as a result but died, it is said of grief, before leaving Tasmania. Times had changed.)

Caroline Denison (née Hornby, c1815–1899; m1838) arrived, barely in her thirties, with her husband Sir William Denison, the new Governor, five children under eight and a staff in January 1847, and was to stay exactly eight years. By March, she was already accompanying him on a visit to the *Anson*. Thanks to the publication of *Varieties of Vice-Regal Life* (edited by Richard Davis and Stefan Petrow, 2004), the diaries and letters of the Denisons, we know what she thought:

> It was a melancholy sight; there were 486 prisoners on board, some of them young girls of twelve, thirteen, and fourteen years old. One of them, to whom I spoke, told me, in answer to my questions, that she came from Blackburn in Lancashire, where she had been employed in a factory; and Mrs Bowden, the superintendent, who reigns with pretty despotic authority on board the 'Anson', told me that a great number of the poor factory girls from our large towns come out here as prisoners, some of them, as we see, at a very early age. All those to whom I spoke were quiet and respectful in their manner, and I was really touched with one, a poor Irishwoman, one of a large party who arrived only a few days ago, in a convict ship from Dublin. I made some enquiry from her respecting the children, a great number of whom, I knew, had come out in the ship with their mothers. The tears started into her eyes the moment I began to speak of them, and she told me she had two of her own amongst them, a boy and a girl; 'and indeed,' she added, 'I am breaking my heart after them!' Mrs H_____, who

14.   Caroline Denison, Beattie's Studio, courtesy of
the Allport Library and Museum of Fine Arts,
Tasmanian Archive and Heritage Office

was with us, told her they would be very well taken care of at the Orphan
School whither they had gone; and I said that if she conducted herself well,
she would be allowed to see them, as soon as her period of probation on
board the 'Anson' was out; and all this seemed a comfort to her.

'Mrs H' was, the editors conclude, **Mary Hampton** (née Essex), wife of the
Comptroller General of convicts, a man suspected of being both cruel and
corrupt where convicts were concerned, but who, following eight years in
Tasmania, was, in 1862, appointed Governor of Western Australia. The
Hamptons had arrived in Hobart only a few months before the Denisons
and the visit to the *Anson*.

It was Caroline Denison's meeting with the woman parted from her children, and then with another in similar circumstances, that made the greatest impact on her. After her visit, she suggested to her husband that the mothers be allowed to see their children more often – though it is not known what became of that suggestion – and, when she was more settled, she visited the Orphan School regularly and was anxious about the well-being of the children: 'all so unnaturally quiet and orderly'.

Caroline's opinion of Philippa Bowden and her work seems ambiguous, and her husband, influenced or not by her, was also to push, together with Hampton, for changes to the system, against continuation of the *Anson*. Denison strongly believed in 'real and efficient punishment' rather than 'reformation'.

Caroline Denison called Philippa 'superintendent' but she was then matron. In September that year, however, her husband died aged only 46 and she did indeed become superintendent. How he died is not noted but the dampness of the river did cause health problems. Philippa carried on, but with difficulty. Grieving and in bad health herself, and her brother dying in England, she applied for twelve months' leave and sailed in February 1848. Her stepdaughter Amelia had 'eloped' to Sydney a few months before her father's death. Philippa did not return to Hobart. In England, she continued to defend the *Anson* project but the decision was taken to empty the hulk and break it up. What happened to Philippa following her arrival in England, and during the rest of her life, does not appear to be recorded, nor have I been able to find the dates of her birth or death.

Eighteen months after Philippa Bowden's departure, **Ellen Lydon** (b1826), her cousin **Mary Lydon** (b1820) and Mary's 21-month-old son, arrived in Hobart on board the *Australasia*. The young peasant women had been sentenced for killing a sheep during the Great Famine in Ireland. Ellen's story and that of her future husband is told by their great grandson in *To Hell or Hobart* (Patrick Howard, 1993). By the time the cousins were received on board the *Anson*, among the last to be so, Susannah Holdich was acting matron and assistant superintendent under a Church of England pastor. The Roman Catholic catechist on board, **Sarah Troy** (b1822), who had been there since 1846, not only shepherded the women of that faith but also acted as interpreter for those, like the Lydon cousins, who spoke only Gaelic. Little Bartholomew seems to have been on the *Anson* with his mother.

By February 1850, the two women were ready to go to the Brickfields Hiring Depot where the matron was **Mrs Williams** and her husband the superintendent. Ellen spent 21 months there, as there were more women convicts than demand for their labour. In June 1850, there were 556 women in depots in Hobart, Launceston and Ross awaiting hire. Irish women were apparently unwelcome since they were unversed in domestic service. Irish convicts were particularly prevalent; over 14,000 were sent to Tasmania between 1803 and 1853, of which 4,637 were women. Not all were criminals: several were political, typical being John Mitchel who arrived in 1851 and whose wife Jenny joined him; her story is told in the 'Bothwell' itinerary (p331). His comrade Thomas Meagher married Tasmanian Catherine Bennett who appears in 'Risdon Cove to Port Arthur' (p275) and 'Midland Highway' (p338).

Ellen Lydon was hired by **Elizabeth Hogg**, a blacksmith's wife, on 19 January 1852, but only lasted there 16 days, for reasons that are not spelt out – she should have been taught skills on the *Anson* but Brickfields was not conducive to maintaining skills. Her next employment was even shorter, but her third attempt lasted until she received her ticket-of-leave in August and, in 1854, she married former convict Stephen Howard; they had nine children. Mary Lydon married James Toole in 1850 and had one more child.

Susan E Johnson's 'The Irish Convict Women of the *Phoebe*: A Follow-up to their Arrival in 1845' (1998) analyses the convictions and life after sentence of 127 Irishwomen who arrived during that period and is thus less dependent on sifting nuggets of relevance from the broad historical picture than the story of Ellen Lydon. This is among the interesting statistics and conclusions it contains:

> Considering that 30 women were noted on their records as having been 'on the town', it is surprising that only one woman was later convicted for prostitution. ... the evidence supports the view ... that many of the women's original crimes were the result of poverty rather than criminal tendencies.

A much earlier study was 'A Statistical Study of Female Convicts in Tasmania 1843–53' (HS Payne, 1961) which looked closely at 150 personal histories of the 7,024 women transported in that period. The study notes that many Irish women had already tried to escape the poverty at home; they were arrested in the industrial north of England and the Midlands. But England itself was undergoing a ferment of labour unrest, put in context by Friedrich Engels' *The Condition of the Working Class in England* (1844), a work brought closer to us by the fact that Engels was introduced to conditions by his common-law wife Mary Burns, an Irish-born millworker with Chartist sympathies.

Following the decision in January 1849 to close the *Anson*, Martha Holdich married the army officer Thomas Abbott that year and had two children, but was widowed in 1857. In mid July 1849, the *Anson*, with its female cargo reduced to 136, was brought down river to Hobart Town Harbour. In 1850, it was broken up and some of the timber redistributed to various buildings in Hobart. The same year, Susannah Holdich married Robert Harcourt and also had two children. They left for Victoria in 1856 and she died in England in the 1880s. Jane married Joe Allen Learmouth and died in England aged 95. Sarah Troy married James McGowan. These weddings suggest that responsible women felt released from their obligations and ready to have a private life. It also suggests that, while unmarried in England, they were, as single women, in demand in Tasmania.

For the next couple of years, the probation period was served in Britain – 2,000 women passed through this system before being transported to Tasmania, granted their ticket-of-leave, and put into employment. If they transgressed, they were, as previously, sent to one of the female factories.

During the twelve months ending June 1852, 100 children died in the Cascades Factory.

The publications from which I have drawn all have their points of interest, but to gain both an overview of the probation system in its broader colonial context and to be able to identify with a particular woman passing through the system, the unmissable account comes in the form of a novel, Oliné Keese's *The Broad Arrow: Being Passages from the History of Maida Gwynnham* (1859; 1988), originally published in two volumes, but an abridged paperback version is more readily available.

The *Broad Arrow* tells the story of motherless Maida, sent to London by her country gentleman father to complete her education. She falls in love with Captain Norwell, gets pregnant, is abandoned, and gives birth in such poverty that the child soon dies. Meanwhile, Norwell has returned, only to use her to falsify a cheque. When the police come to arrest her, they find her burying her child. She is arrested, instead, for infanticide, which she does not deny, to protect Norwell, and is found guilty and transported under the name Martha Grylls.

The author, publishing under a pseudonym based on her name, was **Caroline Leakey** (1827–1881). Aged 20, she arrived in Hobart in January 1848 to help her married sister, **Eliza Medland** (d1880), who was expecting her second child. Anna Maria Nixon wrote of Eliza during her earlier pregnancy, about to move to an isolated posting outside Hobart: '… she, poor thing, is not likely to have a single female companion, and in six weeks she expects her confinement'.

Back in Hobart, Eliza and her husband, the Reverend Joseph Medland, moved in circles knowledgeable about the convict system – indeed, Medland was chaplain to Brickfields – and involved in charitable works: Eliza, for example, collected for the Maternal Dorcas Society of which Anna Maria Nixon was President, and Caroline Denison patron.

During the five years that Caroline Leakey lived in Hobart she was mostly ill, but she not only got out and about enough – including some months spent recuperating with a clerical family attached to the Port Arthur Penal Settlement – but she was already experienced, through her religious upbringing, in philanthropy herself. And, after she left Tasmania, following the publication of *The Broad Arrow*, she raised funds to establish a refuge for 'fallen women' in Exeter which, over the 20 years from 1861, helped 345 women. When all was said and done, Maida was such a one.

Caroline knew what she was writing about which meant that, because by the 1859 date of publication Tasmanians were trying to leave convict times behind them, her novel was not warmly received. Added to that, she included known characters, often with their names little changed; that was not regarded as the done thing. Gillian Winter brings the modern reader up to date with who was who in '"We Speak That We Do Know, and Testify That We Have Seen": Caroline Leakey's Tasmanian Experiences and Her Novel *The Broad Arrow*' (1993). She notes: 'The more closely I read her novel and checked her Hobart against other records of the town at that time, the more it seemed that

Leakey was a very close and accurate observer and recorder of her setting.'
Caroline's heroine Maida/Martha is partly herself.

On her arrival in Hobart, Maida is held in probation on the *Anson*. On the
voyage out she had protected Lucy, a young convict who had got into trouble.
When Lucy is assigned to the Evelyn family and they need another servant,
she persuades George Evelyn, in the temporary absence of his Tasmanian-born
wife, to hire Maida. Evelyn visits the *Anson* with his niece Bridget, newly
arrived from England. She sees Tasmania, like Maida, through new eyes,
though what they see is rather different.

The visit, which takes place when Philippa Bowden has already left for
England, is so detailed that it is fair to assume that Caroline Leakey must
have visited the *Anson*, or known someone who did. The 'Mrs Deputy' must
be Susannah Holdich. George Evelyn makes some remarks about probation
and reformation causing her to become defensive:

> Mrs Deputy looked much hurt, and exclaimed, '*Here* on the *Anson*, surely,
> Mr Evelyn, you do not call it indiscriminate association: we have distinct
> classes – bad, better, and best. Surely nothing can be superior to Mrs
> Bowden's excellent system?'
> 'Than Mrs Bowden I know no more gifted and prudent Lady-Superin-
> tendent; were all officers selected with the discernment, it would be well for
> the prisoner. Mrs Deputy, may I take my niece through the wards?' asked
> Mr Evelyn, anxious to avoid a discussion.

As Maida leaves the *Anson*:

> All the women tried to give her a nod on the sly; and many anxious eyes
> followed the party as the grated door closed, and an audible sigh was
> simultaneously heaved by those whom it imprisoned. Each prisoner envied
> Martha, and wished it had been her lot to fall to so sweet a looking lady
> as that bright-eyed girl who smiles on her in passing.

And then Maida steps into the unknown:

> She started as from a dream when the boat jerked against the jetty. A
> ghastly pallor struck her every feature as she stept ashore. For an instant
> she covered her face; then, gradually withdrawing her hands, the Maida
> Gwynnham of olden days discovered herself in the unabated dignity of that
> upraised hand, and in the strength of purpose outshining from the purple
> depths of those undimmed eyes.

Maida has not yet been crushed by the system. But she has further trials to
face, not least her fellow convicts in the household and her mistress Mrs
Evelyn. Then there are spells in Brickfields and the Cascades Female Factory,
then another unsympathetic mistress. How she copes, and how Caroline
Leakey reveals the two warring sides of the author herself – passionate

and religious – through both Maida and the Evelyns' angelic invalid niece, Emmeline, with her Christian resignation, underpin this novel that also lays bare Hobart society and the convict system of the 1840s. I agree with the opinion expressed in Shirley Walker's chapter '"Wild and Wilful" Women: Caroline Leakey and The Broad Arrow' in *A Bright and Fiery Troop* (Debra Adelaide, 1988):

> Its fall from favour is probably due to a publisher's notion that modern readers are out of tune with its melodramatic plot and passages of religious preaching. Yet to come for the first time to *The Broad Arrow* is, because of the experience it deals with, and because of the power of the writing, a stunning experience. The reader can discern beyond the melodrama and preaching, a powerful novel of female experience under extreme conditions ... The hero, Maida Gwynnham, is undoubtedly the most powerful female creation in Australian Colonial literature ... Above all, *The Broad Arrow* is compelling as a feminist text; a novel written for women by a woman and dealing with the experience of a proud and passionate female hero who is tested to extremity by the patriarchal structures of a moralistic and punitive society.

Like Jane Franklin, Caroline Leakey was regarded, even at 20, as a 'blue stocking'; indeed, on the voyage out, an officer labelled her thus. Her lines of response reveal a Caroline Leakey worth knowing as one reads *The Broad Arrow* and her sister Emily's memoir of her after her death aged 54, *Clear Shining Light* (1882), which concentrates on those virtues that would raise funds for her fallen women's refuge in Exeter:

> If I am a blue stocking, sir,
> I was not knit for you;
> Not one inch of wool
> From your thin fleece I drew.

That riposte was recorded in the diary of Mary Cameron, newly married into the settler dynasty of Forden, Nile, whom we meet in the 'Midland Highway' itinerary (Kingson p349). She described Caroline, who she thought was 25: 'Miss L looks a perfect child ... not pretty, certainly not pretty, very much marked with the smallpox ... I think Miss L is rather too unsophisticated.' However young Caroline was, and in whatever ways, when she left England, five years in Tasmania provided her with intellectual and creative muscle. *The Broad Arrow* was the result. Other aspects of the novel and Caroline Leakey's life emerge in the itineraries that include Boa Vista (p264) and Port Arthur (p283).

GB Lancaster's convict in *Pageant* is a man; the slant she brings is to have one of her settler women, Ellen Merrick, a sister-in-law of the Comyn family, fall in love with him and set her heart on marrying him. Mme Comyn's son

Mab finds out – 'How you ... how any lady could do such a thing' – and takes steps to have him detained for years at Port Arthur, thus ruining both lives.

Meanwhile, moves were afoot to stop transportation to Tasmania. Looked at from today's perspective, and in the light of what we know of the convict system, to come across information that Mary Ann Cox, licensee of the Cornwall Hotel, Launceston (p369), since the death of her husband in 1837, was 'famous for her efforts to abolish the transport of convicts' is to rejoice. The Anti-Transportation Society of Launceston was, indeed, formed at a meeting in the assembly rooms of the hotel in 1849. (The Anti-Transportation League, Hobart, came into being in 1850, and the Australasian league in February 1851.) What is more, this seems to be the first time a woman, leaving aside Jane Franklin, was actively involving herself in politics.

Undoubtedly there were some concerned about the convicts themselves, who were against transportation for humanitarian reasons. And that may have been the case with Mary Ann Cox. But some lines from Mary Grimstone's poem 'Van Diemen's Land' give a clue to what was on the mind of many, if not most, abolitionists:

> Why was the fettered felon sent
> Thy balmy breath to taste?
> *Thou* should receive the good, the free,
> From lands of woe and vice.

It was the well-being of non-convicts in Tasmania that mattered – the stain on their reputation caused by the convict system, and the evils (crime and bad influences) that they had to put up with. And the fact that a convict-dominated, inferior servant-providing society discouraged both free servants from immigrating and investment. Captain Comyn in GB Lancaster's *Pageant* encapsulates some of the issues at the heart of abolition in a rant to his son when 'Denison's damned circular' arrives:

> 'England had no right to grant land to gentlemen if she meant the colony to continue penal once those gentlemen were established. It's a personal insult to us. Until we get an influx of free settlers, who'll put money into the country? – who'll buy and sell and manufacture with us? – how the unnameable deuce d'you imagine it's possible for us to go ahead? And we'll never get free settlers until the convict element is scotched. They're afraid, and, gad! I don't blame 'em.'
>
> 'Many convicts are very decent fellows, sir. And they make good servants.'
>
> 'Servants? How long d'you think they'll be content to remain servants? Have you the foggiest notion of their number in the colony now?'
>
> 'No, sir. But –'
>
> 'Of course you haven't,' triumphed the Captain, who happened to have heard that morning in Trienna. 'Well, I have. Our present population is about forty-four thousand free people and twenty-four thousand convicts. And about thirteen thousand out of the forty-four are time-expired, which

makes the criminal quantum outnumber us. To control them in a country almost as large as Scotland – twice the size of Belgium, anyway, and that was big enough to give Napoleon his Waterloo – what troops have we? About two thousand military and constabulary all told. The thing's a farce. Why, sir, if England directs upon us the whole of her convict importations, as she is always threatening to do, are you so utterly imbecile that you can't see what will happen? They'll take charge. One bloody day we'll all be murdered in our beds and our women outraged. Don't talk to me!'

Denison, in his dispatches, was in favour of continuation. In a letter to his brother of January 1847, he had written: 'The people who complained of the convicts being sent here, will be clamouring in short time, for labour.' Certain echelons in the colony became split between pro- and anti-abolition. Harriat Halifax's husband, in Isabel Dick's *Wild Orchard* confirms that. He has gone to Hobart to try and sort out their future, leaving her in New Norfolk; in a long letter, he writes:

> I tell you, the town is full of gossip and intrigue. A certain honest faction there is, of course, and their argument is that the colony can never be rid of this undercurrent of insidious cunning until the British Government ceases throwing the refuse from gaol and houses of correction into our midst. Already there are many who are working for cessation and many again who are ready to say it will be the ruin of us. From the settlers' point of view, who will provide cheap labour, they say? Cessation is a thing in which you at any rate can see eye to eye with me! God be thanked that we have our land far enough away from the capital to be completely out of reach of the eternal entanglement of politics, and also that we have honest fellows at Parklands who have never seen the inside of a gaol.

Caroline Denison saw the intrigue not as an issue of transportation but as the antis against her husband; at its most petty, it was setting up a rival regatta in January 1853. 'No sooner did Messrs G[regson] and co find that [my husband] was to patronise [that at Kangaroo point],' she wrote, 'than they set to work to make it fail; … they endeavoured at the last moment, to get an opposition regatta for the same day at Sandy Bay.' She does not, even in her journal/letter, enter into the politics behind the incident.

Thomas Gregson, who had arrived with his wife, **Elizabeth Gregson** (c1797–1879), in 1821, and lived at Risdon Cove, had caused trouble to every Governor since. He was a member of the legislative council and, in elections of 1851, in which 16 out of 24 seats were eligible for election, the anti-transportationists were victorious. His constant opposition was not conducive to his wife being welcomed at Government House over the years; in 1857 he was Premier for two months – a time she may, or may not have enjoyed – but he did not have the right temperament to last longer.

Denison was by no means the only one in favour of continuation. In 'Against the League: Fighting the "Hated Stain"' (1995–96) Anne McLaughlin, seeking to redress the balance of historical reconstruction towards anti-abolitionists, quoted Louisa Ann Meredith who seems to have changed her mind about assigned servants when she writes: 'I feel no more, perhaps even less fear of attack or molestation' than in England. The old assignment system, though labelled 'white slavery', successfully converted 'five cases out of six, of idle unprincipled outcasts into industrious trustworthy servants'.

Then there were the 'anti anti-transportationists'; typical of these were the Baileys. **Mary Bailey** (née Walker, 1792–1873) had married the Reverend William Bailey in 1832 in England. In 1843, as private chaplain to her family in Westminster, London, he was convicted of uttering a forged promissory note to his sister and sentenced to transportation. Mary, already an established writer, followed him to Tasmania the following year with their son, bringing with her an introduction to then Governor Eardley-Wilmot.

In 1846, Mary advertised for private pupils at her home in Fitzroy Place, Hobart. From her arrival, she had regularly contributed verse to the *Colonial Times* and she was to continue to do so until 1850. As Morris Miller explains, she tended to 'supplement her poems with long etymological comments and extensive quotations from classical authors', to the despair of the printers. The editor of the *Colonial Times*, however, regarded her poetical talent as 'certainly superior to any in the colony', and added, giving us echoes of the reception of Mary Grimstone, Jane Franklin and Caroline Leakey: 'Learned ladies are not often considered very valuable either in public or private life, but the spirit breathed into the verses of "M.B." is such as to entitle her to every consideration.'

One of Mary's poems was the elegy 'Monody on the death of Sir John Eardley-Wilmot'; the colony had been rather stricken with guilt at the gossip that had contributed to his dismissal. On top of his philandering, he was not a good Governor, but her penultimate verse reads:

> Warm was thy heart – thy friendship true –
> Thy bosom bled for others' grief;
> The prisoner well thy kindness knew,
> When oft thy hand hath brought relief.

The Governor may have been particularly kind to the Baileys. Miller adds: 'It is without doubt that Mary Bailey's creative writing and scholarship have left traces in the literary heritage of the island.'

Bailey was granted a ticket-of-leave in 1847 and wife and husband opened girls' and boys' schools. He also became editor of the *Hobarton Guardian*, the proprietor of which advocated the continuation of a modified system of transportation on economic and social grounds. Although, according to the sources, Bailey quarrelled with the proprietor, the cause is not clear and he did not resign. The emancipists (time-expired convicts) whom the *Guardian* supported formed the Prisoners' Protection Society – over 300 attended its first meeting in October 1850. Turned into the more neutrally named Tasmanian Union, it was active, though unsuccessful, in the first Assembly elections of

1851. In this cause, Mary composed an ode, 'Poem: Address to the Tasmanian Union' (*Guardian*, 16 November, 1850) which starts:

> Ye who so long in helplessness have borne
> Your vaunting fellow-man's unpitying scorn;
> Whose tears – whose blood have water'd oft the soil
> Where deserts, changed to gardens, own your toil;
> Lift from the dust, once more, your sorrowing eyes –
> The auspicious hour is come – arise, arise!

And it ends:

> Arise – united – in fraternal band!
> Let those, who cry 'contamination', see,
> In YOU – a course of strict integrity.
> An honourable life will put to shame
> Those, who would brand you, with opprobrious name.
> Beware divisions – UNITY is might.
> Dissentions will your fairest prospect blight.

There is something more touching than ironic that a couple so affected by transportation themselves, who had had their lives turned upside down by it, should have apparently supported its continuation. They knew what it was like, and that convicts needed to be protected rather than excoriated. That was the drive behind the 'anti anti-transportationists', as they were called. It was not that they favoured transportation but that they strongly objected to the smear tactics of the abolitionists – members of the various abolition leagues – against all convicts and emancipists. Mary Bailey suggested that no one was guilt-free when she wrote:

> Are they quite pure, who cast the deadly stone? –
> It may RECOIL – the missile they have thrown!
> Since ALL HAVE SINNED – not only bond but FREE.

What is more, there was more than a touch of hypocrisy: Captain Comyn, and real abolitionists whom Mary McLaughlin names, were only too happy to have assigned convict servants and labourers when it benefited them, but wanted no more influx of the dregs of society when it no longer did.

As for the Baileys' personal situation, perhaps leaving England, where they had been tied to her family, had given them the freedom to blossom. They left, though, for Sydney in 1855 when he received a pardon conditional on his residence in the colonies; there, unhappily, his past was exposed.

The campaign in Tasmania and Britain – where the moral case for abolition tended to be put – reached its climax in 1852. In a dispatch dated 14 December, the Secretary of State for the Colonies advised Denison that his government would abolish transportation to Van Diemen's Land at 'no distant future'. The last load of women to be delivered, 216 of them and 27 of their children, arrived on the *Duchess of Northumberland* on 21 April the following year. Three women and seven children had died during the very rough five-month voyage.

Details of their cases, and their records in Tasmania, are contained in Christine Woods' *The Last Ladies* (2004). To peruse the entries is to note that, while transportation may have ceased soon after they arrived, life for the women once assigned as servants in Tasmania still consisted of such heinous crimes as being out after hours. Punishment was seven days in the cells. I highlight two women in particular because they were assigned to Matilda Dandridge who appears at the end of Chapter 12 and in the itinerary 'Around and About Macquarie Street' (p246) and who seems to have been a good woman. In the light of that, I would expect her to have been a decent mistress of servants.

Absent from the Dandridges' service on 18 September 1853, **Elizabeth Davies** (c1827–1902), transported for stealing a handkerchief, with previous convictions for stealing, was sentenced to four months' imprisonment with hard labour, and the recommendation that she thereafter be hired in the interior. She was a widow who had brought a four-year-old daughter with her – two others presumably left in Wales. She was literate and a milliner/dressmaker. She continued for the next 25 years or so to appear in court – latterly for being drunk and disorderly.

The Dandridges already had another servant from the *Duchess of Northumberland*, **Christie Ewing** (c1837–1863), aged 16, sentenced for housebreaking and stealing in Glasgow, also with previous convictions – which was the norm for being transported in this era. She was a 'nursegirl' but, in October 1853, 'she was sentenced to seven days solitary confinement for insolence to Mrs Dandridge by refusing to pick up a baby when she was asked'. The baby was presumably Catherine Dandridge, born the previous year. Matilda Dandridge told the court that Christie's conduct had been good over the previous six months. In 1856, Christie married a Tasmanian-born farmer but, by 1863, having had four children, she was dead, aged 26.

In May 1853, the month after the *Duchess of Northumberland* arrived, the newly-elected British government implemented the decision of its predecessor to abolish transportation. When the news reached Tasmania, it was greeted with jubilation, and 10 August was declared a public holiday. Typical of the celebrations was that captured in the watercolour 'Cessation of Transportation Celebrations, Launceston, VDL' by **Susan Fereday** (1810–1878), artist and botanist wife of the Reverend John Fereday of George Town who had arrived in Tasmania in 1846. A medal was also struck to commemorate the occasion.

In 1853, the Cascades Female Factory consisted of five major courtyards accommodating 1,000 women and 175 children; now, with no new arrivals, staff and inmates in the Female Factories began to be shed. The Ross Factory closed in 1854; in 1855 the Launceston Factory was officially proclaimed a gaol. Mary Hutchinson had been matron of Cascades from 1832 and latterly, when her superintendent husband's health declined, borne the full burden of the institution, but she had not been considered suitable to take his place officially when he retired in 1851 (even though Denison himself called her 'virtually the superintendent'). She had, instead, been sent as matron-in-charge to the Launceston Factory. In August 1854 she retired on a pension of £60. The Cascades Factory closed in 1856 and it and Launceston, as gaols, were transferred to local control.

15.   Cessation of Transportation Celebrations, Launceston, 1853, by Susan Fereday,
courtesy of the Allport Library and Museum of Fine Arts,
Tasmanian Archive and Heritage Office

The irony of the end of transportation came with the acute shortage of labour that had been building up since the discovery of gold at Port Phillip, south of the newly-created Melbourne, and the stampede of everyone who could get there. Caroline Denison wrote home several times of the inconvenience at Government House, of not being able to get the least thing attended to – her children, by this time greatly increased in number – even lost their singing teacher. Another example of these complaints was written on 25 February 1853 following a visit to Launceston: '... the principal hotel there, in these *golden* days is so destitute of servants that I doubt if they could have received us ...' But her best piece of writing on the subject of gold and its effect on Tasmania came on 8 October 1852 just as transportation was about to end:

The State of things here is really most curious. I am not sorry to have seen it, though certainly residence in or near a gold country cannot be said to be agreeable. This place has been sadly spoiled by it. It is painful to see the successful gold-diggers rioting through the streets, and spending their money in the way they do; for those who come back in this way never think of settling to work again, but drink and throw away their money while it lasts, and when all is gone, go off to the diggings again. There would be something absurd, were it not too painful, in the sight of the cabs full of noisy men and women, dressed out in the most extravagant style, driving about, and, alas! Stopping at the doors of all the public houses. The dress is the most comical part of the business. I saw a woman the other day, walking through the streets in dirty weather, dressed in a beautiful silver grey satin gown, the sort of gown that I should never think of wearing, except at some large evening party, but which she did not even take the trouble to hold up out of the mud. Another woman is said to have been seen walking on the wharf arrayed in bright pink velvet or plush! But to my mind all these 'signs of the times' are really too sad to laugh at.

The Governor himself calculated that, in the four months from September 1851, 2,139 people left Hobart for Port Phillip, and 2,188 from Launceston. Caroline Denison was not the only settler-class woman to complain of the shortage of servants, in contrast to the life apparently led by those benefiting from the gold rush. Mary Morton Allport lamented in her journal in 1853:

I often feel that my life is wasted. I would willingly teach my children, and believe myself quite able to do it, up to a certain point, but I am compelled to send them to school, because my time is broken up by the necessities of housekeeping, for which I have no vocation.

Mary's life is touched upon in the itineraries that include the Allport Library and Museum of Fine Arts (p244) and Jane Franklin Hall, Elboden Street (p255).
    George Washington Walker, husband of **Sarah Benson Walker** (née Mather, 1812–1893), wrote of her to their eldest son on 24 October 1853, when they were living at Narryna between 1852 and 1854:

Thy dear mother gave birth to a little girl on the 15 of last month … I had hoped [she] would have written to thee, but thou has no idea of the difficulties she has to encounter with regard to servants. For months we have been without a kitchen maid, and for some time we were also without a housemaid, and could only now and then procure a charwoman as a favour at four shillings a day! This state of things renders thy poor mother a perfect slave.

The booklet *Narryna: Heritage Museum* (2002, Peter Mercer) is also of use in the itinerary 'Around Hobart' (p249). Earlier in her life, Sarah Benson Walker had found time to be a member of Jane Franklin's prison visiting committee; indeed, Jane Franklin had recognised Sarah's father from an occasion in England when she had visited the Sunday school where he was superintendent – the place where he met Sarah's mother, Ann Benson, a young woman rather superior to him in social standing. That titbit comes from 'Reminiscences of the Life of Sarah Benson Mather', apparently only available in one university library in Britain under the title *All That We Inherit*

(Peter Benson Walker, 1968) but, miraculously, a handwritten copy can be downloaded from the internet.

On 1 January 1854, to remove the stain of its convict past, Van Diemen's Land became Tasmania. The best means for Tasmanians to forget that past was to be in denial of what it had meant, both in Britain and their penal colony. In *Pageant* GB Lancaster captures the mood of 1856 when Cascades must have been on the verge of closing. The Comyn granddaughter, Jenny, has been to Hobart and now sits at Madame's knee to recount her adventures:

> '... we came home past the Cascades, Grandma, and went into the brewery. Mr Degrasse gave us an impromptu *régal* of cakes and wine, with ale for the gentlemen, and picked such a bouquet of roses. But I left that at the female House of Correction.'
>
> 'Did Julia take you there? She should have known better.'
>
> 'The females seem very content. And they have a musical box to dance to, and lots of babies to play with. What gown shall I wear to-night, do you think?'

The nursery for women with children, after having been earlier temporarily relocated to the New Town Farm, returned to Cascades in 1854, though it appears to have moved again to the Infirmary, Liverpool Street, in 1855. GB Lancaster may not have been aware of these finer chronological details. If I had to choose two books to read on holiday in Tasmania that would let me into its history of settlers and convicts, they would both be novels: *Pageant* and *The Broad Arrow*.

In 1855, the British government passed the Constitutional Act, whereby, in 1856, Tasmania became self-governing, with its own fully elected bicameral legislature. Lieutenant Governors became Governors representing the British monarch. Women, of course, had no vote. That is a struggle for Chapter 13 to explore.

Meanwhile, there had been one further matter to deal with, one creating a stain that was less easily wiped out – that of the indigenous people of Tasmania.

12 – From Wybalenna to Oyster Cove

One of the places to which Jane Franklin accompanied her husband on a formal visit, in January 1838, was Flinders Island – not only to visit Wybalenna but also to stray into the bush, what she called 'a horse and tent excursion'. George Robinson was able to convince the gubernatorial couple that all was well at the Aboriginal settlement. Some months later, he attended a dinner at Government House and obviously discussed with Jane Franklin sending a boy and a girl to her.

Adolphus (Tymenidic), apparently the last of his west coast people, in due course arrived in Hobart. His mother was **Larratong** (Queen Adelaide, 1792–1837), his father Wymurric, chief of the West Point people, who had 'surrendered' to Robinson in July 1832.

In October 1839, Eleanor Franklin described the eleven-year-old boy as 'anxious to be able to read and write well'. And continued: 'He waits at table and does other little things. But unfortunately he is very idle and obstinate, so that it is difficult to keep him to his duty, unless he is constantly watched.' And in June 1840 Jane Franklin wrote to her sister: 'You have heard of my unsuccessful experiment to civilize a native boy from Flinders, whither he has returned; if my servants had helped me better in the matter, I might perhaps have been more lucky.' Adolphus seems to have died between 1845 and 1847.

In February 1839, Robinson left Wybalenna for newly-opened-up Port Phillip (Victoria) to take up the post of Protector of Aborigines in South Australia – a post he was to hold for eleven years. Jane Franklin arrived in Melbourne in April for her solo visit to the mainland and bumped into him. But neither he nor Maria, who had arrived from Wybalenna the day before, took up Jane's invitation to her soirée. Maria knew that the mess her husband had left had been discovered, that John Franklin had set up an enquiry. She was extremely stressed and going through the menopause. It is hardly surprising that the couple now avoided Jane Franklin.

That is the background to the arrival at Government House from Wybalenna of Mary, renamed Mathinna, at an unrecorded date in 1840 or 1841. The mystery of Mathinna's arrival on Jane Franklin's doorstep, after both Robinsons had left Wybalenna, and when an enquiry into affairs there was in progress, is compounded by other lacunae. According to Lyndall Ryan's careful list of Aborigines and the dates she was able to establish from Robinson's journal, both Mathinna's parents, Wongerneep and Towterrer of the Port Davey nation, died in 1837 when she was about four. But some sources say that Wongerneep died in 1840 after remarrying. Nicholas Cree suggests in *Oyster Cove* (1979), his little book about the area where his ancestors settled, that Aboriginal custom dictated that Wongerneep renounce parentage on remarrying. Robinson's journal also shows that Jane Franklin first saw Mathinna at Wybalenna during her 1838 visit.

Whatever Wongerneep's situation or, indeed, her wishes, five- or six-year-old Mathinna, wearing a kangaroo skin and shell necklace and clutching a pet opossum, settled in at Government House. 'Mathinna' is said to mean 'necklace', and to have inspired her new name, but Plomley suggests that 'Mairreener' is the word for necklace and may be another name by which Mathinna was originally known. It more resembles her first Western name, Mary.

In her new home, Mathinna was said to be treated as a member of the family and educated by Eleanor's governess Miss Williamson, though at least one source suggests that she was educated by a servant. Mathinna was taught to read and write, to dance and sing, and to converse politely even, though only a small child, and according to a later article excoriating Jane Franklin, in the ballroom. To suggest, as I have read, that the two girls were to be companions is to forget that Eleanor Franklin would by then have been 15. On the other hand, Eleanor's future husband, John Gell, a frequent visitor, in an 1841 letter to his father, wrote that Mathinna was a 'great favourite' and 'lives with Miss Franklin and her governess'.

Little Mathinna and her fate have caught the imagination of many, initially inspired by a captivating portrait of her in a red dress commissioned by Jane Franklin from Thomas Bock. Carmel Bird, in the pen portrait of Mathinna to be found on her website, quotes the 'letter' contained in Eleanor's diary that Mathinna wrote on 14 November 1841 to her 'father':

Mathinna is six years old. Her mother Eveline, father, modern name Hannibal, Cape Sorell tribe. I am a good little girl. I have pen and ink cause I am a good little girl. I do love my father. I have got a doll and a shift and a petticoat. I read. My father I thank thee for sleep. I have got a red frock. Like my father. Come here to see my father. I have got sore feet and shoes and stockings and I am very glad. All great ships. Tell my father two rooms.

Mathinna's mention of Hannibal (Parley) as her father does seem to confirm that Wongerneep outlived Towterrer (Romeo) and married again, though the child also seems to include God and John Franklin in 'father'.

Eleanor Franklin wrote of Aborigines and Mathinna: 'The last Aborigines were caught about a fortnight ago, and sent to Flinders Island, so that our little native girl is the only one remaining here. She is improving I think, though it will be a long time before she becomes quite civilised.' The 'last Aborigines' were a family – mother, father and five sons – from Cape Grim who 'gave themselves up' in December 1842.

The Bock watercolour in the Tasmanian Museum and Art Gallery, Hobart, is not in fact the one commissioned by Jane Franklin which she took to England with her (and the whereabouts of which are unknown), but a copy made by Bock and given to the Museum by his granddaughter. Of the original, Jane wrote to her sister on 14 February 1843, in a letter seemingly quoted only in Plomley's 'Notes on Some of the Tasmanian Aborigines and on Portraits of Them' (1978):

Mathinna's portrait is extremely like, but the figure is too large and tall – she looks there like a girl of 12, but is only 7 – the attitude is exactly hers, and she always wears the dress you see her in – when she goes out, she wears red stockings and black shoes …

16.   Mathinna by Thomas Bock, 1842, courtesy of
the Tasmanian Museum and Art Gallery

As the copy was originally framed, Mathinna's feet seem to have been omitted; had she perhaps kicked off her confining shoes, and that was disapproved of? But it was the oval frame that did this to the rectangular portrait; removed from it, as one often sees in reproduction, her feet are there, distinctly unshod.

In a recent portrait by Christina Henri, inspired by Mathinna's 'letter', and hung in the foyer of the Stanley Burbury Theatre at the University of Tasmania, the delicately arched feet are unmistakably revealed, as the artist explains, 'free from the encumbrance of European footwear'. Christina Henri is offended by Jane Franklin's description of her 'adopted' child as she describes the portrait in another, more often quoted, letter to her sister; what strikes me more is how Jane's perception differs from what Bock captured:

Mathinna's [portrait] will show the influence of some degree of civilization upon a child of as pure a race as they [Aborigines], and who in spite of every endeavour, and though entirely apart from her own people, retains much of the unconquerable nature of the savage; extreme uncertainty of will and temper, great want of perseverance and attention, little if any self-control, and great acuteness of the senses and facility of imitation.

Looking at the Bock portrait as we see it today and reading Jane's remarks, you wonder if Mathinna was not just a wilful little girl, as no doubt Jane had been herself, or was strong enough, even against Jane, to retain memories of her original culture, about which one might rejoice. Jane, it should be said, subjected herself when young to great self-discipline where education was concerned.

The baton is also picked up in Cassandra Pybus' review of the Bangarra Dance Theatre's 2008 ballet 'Mathinna', performed at the Sydney Opera House and created by the indigenous Australian choreographer Stephen Page who depicts Mathinna as the archetypal 'stolen child'. For Cassandra, Mathinna 'encapsulates the catastrophe that befell her people'. Carmel Bird, who also wrote a BBC radio play – 'In her Father's House' – wrote to me: 'Personally Mathinna's story always brings tears to my eyes – and I have a strange wish that I could reach her and comfort her and tell her how sorry I am.' For Mathinna's life was to change dramatically when the Franklins left unexpectedly in 1843.

Should Jane Franklin have taken eight-year-old Mathinna with her to England? That is the most obvious question. She certainly appears to have considered doing so. The story is that Jane consulted medical opinion and was advised that the child had a weak chest which would not stand up to the cold and fog of London. And it is certainly true that chest infections were proving fatal to Aborigines. It is worth noting, too, that Jane herself had been in poor health for much of the previous year. But could she find no Hobart family who would look after Mathinna? Instead, a month before the Franklins left Government House, she was consigned to the Queen's Orphan School (where 56 children died of scarlet fever that year).

In 1856, the hostile *Hobart Town Mercury* article described Mathinna's situation in 1843: '[She was] transferred sobbing and broken-hearted from the tender care of one who had always proved far more than a mother to her and the luxury and grandeur of Government House to a cold stretcher in the dormitory of the Queen's Asylum.'

It is hard at this remove to fathom Jane Franklin's motivation concerning Mathinna and her plans for her future, plans which were obviously skewed by her husband's unexpected and humiliating recall. The Tasmanian poet Adrienne Eberhard is much taken by Jane Franklin, putting herself in her place and publishing *Jane, Lady Franklin* (2004). Of Mathinna's arrival, she exalts:

> She's here! She's here!
> Her small face dark with delight.
> My own daughter.
> Her small hands clasping mine,
> Her bare feet grasping the cool floor.
> Oh, to cuddle her,
> Clothe her,
> Rock her to sleep.
> I want my arms to articulate her world.
> Mathinna,
> My darling.

But towards the end Jane is thinking:

> Somehow you escape me
> It seems you're not really here
> Your essence is gone
>
> You are all spirit
> Dispersed in the wind
> Your heart is wild.
>
> You were never really mine.

That is one way of looking at it. But was Mathinna perhaps, like Adolphus, simply a social experiment? If so, Jane Franklin would have had a more pragmatic approach. Mathinna's late sister, Duke, had been sent to the Orphan School, and so, in 1842, had her contemporary born at Wybalenna Fanny Cochrane (better known by her later name Fanny Cochrane Smith). Fanny was being taught domestic skills there and perhaps Jane Franklin thought that the two girls would support each other in what, for Aborigines, had been made an alien and hostile world. There were other Aborigine girls there as well. Lyndall Ryan tells us that the women at Wybalenna 'lamented the loss of their children to the Orphan School, where they could not learn the traditions of their parents'. So it was not only Mathinna who was being intentionally decultured.

To 'civilise' Aboriginal children was a widespread Australian experiment well into the twentieth century – a process which continued to devastate Aborigines long after it was recognised as unethical, if not downright cruel and unacceptable, and dropped. A 1988 caption against the portrait of Mathinna in an exhibition even went so far as to say: 'This girl was trained or attempted to be trained by Lady Franklin as a servant.' This certainly puts a different complexion on relations between Mathinna and Jane Franklin, but any conclusion all these years later and without evidence can only be speculative.

Mathinna was apparently sent back to Wybalenna in 1844. It was there, in 1845, that the artist John Skinner Prout painted the portrait of Methinna (as he called her), in graphite and water colour, that is rather less well known than the Bock one, but equally touching. This time her dress is white rather than red, rather religious in effect and perhaps even in fact. This portrait – shown on the back cover – is in the British Museum and seems to be mentioned only by Plomley.

Although Fanny Cochrane's's biographical details give no date for her own return to Wybalenna, it is fair to assume that she went at the same time as Mathinna. Before her departure for the Orphan School, Fanny lived, from the age of five, with the catechist Robert Clark and his wife Bessy; on her return, aged probably no more than ten, she is said to have become a servant, paid a pittance, in the Clarks' household. Mathinna, too, was housed with them, though her status is unclear.

It was common for children at Wybalenna to be taken from their parents by the Clarks, so it may well be that it was they who sent Mathinna to Jane Franklin in 1840 on the instruction of Robinson from Port Phillip. Although the Europeans at Wybalenna were a nest of vipers, Clark and Robinson had established a modus vivendi based on common interest. The historian Bonwick tells us that in 1841 Clark 'brought to my house ... four Tasmanian youths' who were 'clean, cheerful and intelligent'. He does not specify if they were visitors or left to be educated by him in his role as teacher.

Fanny Cochrane is said, either before or after her sojourn at the Orphan School, to have lived at the Clarks 'in conditions of appalling squalor, neglect and brutality' and, in other biographical details, to have been 'often chained and flogged by Clark as punishment for rebelling against her treatment'. As a result, Fanny attempted to burn down the Clarks' house.

When, some years later, Clark was accused of 'cruel treatment and neglect of children under his care', he did not deny it but 'declared he had done it in religious anger at their moral offences. One in particular had been seduced into improper society and was long kept in rigid seclusion.' The child is not named.

By the time Fanny Cochrane and Mathinna returned to Wybalenna, Trukanini and Mary Ann Cochrane Arthur, Fanny's half-sister, were back there too. When Robinson left for Port Phillip, he took with him Trukanini, her husband Woorraddy and several other of 'his' Aborigines. It is at this time that Trukanini's daughter Louisa, born in 1827, is said to have been taken from Tasmania to the mainland where, as her descendant Banjo Clark told Camilla Chance, she was left with an Aboriginal family. From there she was kidnapped by a white sealer and carried off to Preservation Island in Bass Strait. In 1844, she married John Briggs, son of Woretermoeteyenner, also known as Pung and Bung, and the sealer George Briggs, and became known later as 'Granny Briggs'. A different, though related, story is told, and dates given, of Louisa Briggs in '200 Australian Women' (available online). Trukanini is not given as her mother in that version, though both say she became a respected midwife and then matron.

Robinson's Aborigines, including Trukanini, got involved in the murder of two whalers in Port Phillip, but Trukanini managed to extricate herself and was deported. She arrived back at Wybalenna in 1842 a widow – Woorraddy having died on the return voyage. She was perhaps deliberately sidelined in the events that followed by being married off, later that year, to the steady widower Alphonso from the Big River people. He died in 1847.

When Maria Robinson followed her husband to Port Phillip in April 1839, she was accompanied by other Aborigines, including Mary Ann Cochrane and her husband Walter Arthur. The nearest I have been able to get to Mary Ann's life before her marriage comes from Bonwick who was later to write of her Aboriginal mother and white sealer father:

> My half-caste friend Maryann gave a pleasing account of her father and mother in their island homestead. Before removal to Flinders Island she had resided at Launceston, being conveyed there by her father to the care of a friend. Although she was of superior ability to most white children, and would, if more happily situated, have become a truly distinguished woman, she was thrown by officials among the degraded Blacks of the island, to her own serious moral and intellectual loss. Repelled in cold disdain by her father's blood, she clung to her mother's kind, and ultimately contracted a childless marriage with Walter George Arthur, the most intelligent and educated of the Native race.

Walter George Arthur, at one time named Friday but renamed in honour of Governor Arthur, was a senior man of the Ben Lomond nation. He had also lived for some time in Launceston. In 1832, aged about twelve, he, too, had been sent from Flinders to the Orphan School (Boys') where he had become literate. On Flinders Island again, a young man of obvious intelligence, he was designated a teacher, as was Mary Ann – thus, in 1837, when she was about 18 and Walter a year younger, they began a relationship. When they were discovered in bed together by one of Robinson's daughters, Walter Arthur was sentenced, by an 'Aboriginal jury' to four days in prison. Then a marriage was arranged for them by officers of the settlement. Robinson described the ceremony, with its mixture of Aboriginal and European custom, in his journal – I quote only part of it:

> This morning early preparation making for the marriage of Mary Ann and Walter G Arthur. At 2 pm a large party of the native women who had previously assembled at my quarters and who had their heads decorated with chaplets or garlands of flowers and dressed in their best habiliments, formed in procession two and two. Myself and clergyman walked first, then the bride with a headdress of ribbons and ostrich feather and a gilt chain round her neck and other garish ornaments …The bride and bridegroom was introduced within the circle and the ceremony was performed by the Revd T Dove after the manner of the Scottish church, when after the conclusion the natives were regaled with a good dinner of mutton, vegetables and rice. Four bottles of port wine was given to them to drink the health of the happy couple.

In drinking the toast, did the Aborigines really say 'go to hell', instead of 'good health'? Thereafter, for nine months, the couple were sent off to shepherd the settlement flock on small islands off Flinders. Since what I have juxtaposed comes from different sources, it would be false to suggest that one was punishment for the other!

In 1842, when the Arthurs returned to Wybalenna from Port Phillip, Dr Henry Jeanneret had just been appointed by John Franklin as 'Protector of Aborigines, Surgeon and Commandant and Justice of the Peace'. He brought with him his wife **Harriet Jeanneret** (née Merrit, d1874), a Sydney woman whom he had married in 1832 during his five-year posting there. She has been described as a 'benevolent and learned lady ... ever interested in blacks'. Before Wybalenna, Jeanneret had practised in Hobart and later been in 'Medical and Spiritual charge' of the boy convicts (aged between eight and 20) at Port Puer, Port Arthur, where he had run up against the commandant.

By this time, there were only 52 Aborigines surviving at Wybalenna – twelve married couples, six single women, eleven single men, and eleven children, all of them in various stages of ill-health. Jeanneret was much shocked at what he found and soon started causing trouble, so much so that, in November 1843, he was dismissed. By then Franklin was no longer Governor, but he and Jane did stop briefly at Flinders in November on their way from Tasmania to England; indeed, a letter reads:

> Dear Mrs Jeanneret,
> We shall remember our visit to you with much interest and pleasure and I beg you to accept my earnest wishes for your improved health and strength and for your future welfare. With kind compliments to Dr Jeanneret. Believe me dear Mrs Jeanneret.
> Very truly yours,
> Jane Franklin.

On his return to Hobart, Jeanneret harassed the government concerning his dismissal and, when that proved unsuccessful, he appealed to London. Joseph Milligan, appointed to Wybalenna, suggested to Walter Arthur that if the Aborigines did not want Jeanneret to return they should write to the Quaker George Washington Walker saying, as Lyndall Ryan expresses it, 'His people did not want another commandant, for they could grow their wheat and potatoes and use muttonbirds and their eggs for provisions.' They also had sheep. Above all, they wanted land so they could be entirely independent.

Cassandra Pybus quotes, from an undated letter from Walker to Harriet Jeanneret, words that were hardly likely to appeal to Mary Ann and Walter Arthur. He asked that Jeanneret use more kindness; 'convince them, in short by the eloquent language of conduct that you are their friends, and I believe you might still mould them to every right purpose you desire ... deal with them as with uninformed and undisciplined children'.

What Milligan's motives were in this support are not clear. He had been appointed to replace Jeanneret but he suffered a severe loss at Wybalenna. In

March 1843, he had married **Elizabeth Lawrence** (c1825–1844) of Launceston. In July the following year she gave birth to a son on Flinders Island. Ten days later she was dead. She was barely nineteen years old. Elizabeth's youth, and her short time at Wybalenna, make even stranger the letter that Harriet Jeanneret wrote sometime between 1843 and 1844 to the Chief Secretary:

> Then there is Mathinna, a black girl whom Lady Franklin brought up some time back and in whose welfare I take an interest. My complaints are that Mrs Milligan ordered Mathinna away from my care, and that there is now no opportunity of speaking to her. But I have seen her twice with Aboriginals, very wretched, dirty and miserable in appearance.

It is the following year that Prout painted Mathinna – not resembling that description. Cree suggests that she was used as a weapon between the Milligans and Jeannerets.

Elizabeth Milligan was buried next to the 100 or so Aboriginal graves at Wybalenna. Among them, too, is that of the eleven-year-old son of Bessy and Robert Clark, and of 24-year-old **Margaret Monaghan** (c1816–1840) and her two children. In December 1840 she had come to join her husband, a private in the King's Own Light Infantry who was garrisoned at Wybalenna. But, as the longboat to take them ashore was lowered, Margaret's crinoline was caught by a gust of wind and got tangled in the rigging of the brig in which they had travelled. The boat capsized. How many other military wives there were at Wybalenna history does not relate, but Margaret's death, and that of Elizabeth Milligan and young master Clark, add a depth to the strange settlement that had been thrown up there.

Jeanneret was reinstated and in March 1846 the family returned to Wybalenna – a delay being caused by Harriet's ill-health. Robert Clark had long been a thorn in Jeanneret's side and there is evidence to suggest that he stirred up the Aborigines against him. That is not to say that they did not have legitimate grievances nor that they were incapable of expressing these themselves but, as NJB Plomley, the twentieth-century father of Aboriginal studies, suggests, 'The natives would not have known how to proceed except by instruction.'

The true situation is not easy to determine. On the one hand Bonwick quotes Bishop Nixon as writing, '... of all men I know [there were] few with more real kindness of nature, or more profound regard for his duty to God. For his pious and gentle Lady the Natives cherished tender feelings.' On the other hand there is the petition to Queen Victoria which the Aborigines drew up, dated 17 February 1846, when they learnt of Jeanneret's reinstatement, calling for his dismissal. Although women were not included in the eight signatories, Henry Reynolds is quite clear that Mary Ann was as much in the vanguard of the complainants as her husband. **Matilda** (Pyterruner, c1819 to 1851–54) of the Port Davey people was also involved.

The petition, from the 'free Aboriginal people of Van Diemen's Land' complained of Jeanneret's behaviour and his arbitrary use of power; more specifically, and among other complaints, he was said to carry pistols in his pockets and 'threatened very often to shoot us and make us run away in fright'. The people were poorly housed, poorly clothed and his pigs rampaged through their vegetable gardens and destroyed and ate their food.

Some claim that the petition used deliberately simple language but was in fact drawn up by Clark. Plomley, who writes about the whole saga in detail, and printed the petition in full in *Weep in Silence* (1987), suggests that 'What is so very evident is the extent to which the Aborigines were used in this war, which was really one between Clark and Jeanneret, with the government a willing recipient of anything to Jeanneret's disadvantage.' Plomley lays much blame for problems at Clark's door, but Henry Reynolds looks at the underlying tensions and the assumptions made by the Aborigines articulated by Mary Ann Cochrane Arthur and her husband who both wrote subsequent letters to the Governor soliciting support for their rights.

The Aborigines did not regard themselves as detained – 'we were not taken prisoner, but freely gave up our country', they declared. And 'Mr Robinson made for us and with Colonel Arthur an agreement which we have not lost from our minds since and we have our part of it good.' They still remembered the agreement and expected the authorities to do the same. Lyndall Ryan quotes more fully from Mary Ann's letter of 10 June 1846:

> Dr Jeanneret wants to make out my husband and myself very bad wicked people and talks plenty about putting us into Jail and that he will hang us for helping to write this petition to the Queen from our countrypeople … Dr Jeanneret does not like us for we do not like to be his slaves nor wish our poor countrypeople to be treated badly or made slaves.

In an effort to make him renounce the petition, later in the year Jeanneret imprisoned Walter Arthur for 17 days. Arthur's letter of complaint, coupled with all that had gone before, prompted the setting up of an enquiry which, in turn, led to the removal of the Aborigines from Flinders Island to Oyster Cove, a few miles south of Hobart and, though to a large extent exonerating Jeanneret, led to his replacement by Milligan. As the Under-secretary at the Colonial Office noted: 'Why we should persevere with a policy at once so costly to the author, and so fatal to the objects of it, I cannot imagine.' Milligan effected the transition in October 1847.

There were only 47 Aborigines left alive to make the journey: 22 women, 15 men, and ten children – five girls and five boys. Most suffered from chest complaints; four were obese. Between March 1839 and October 1847, 30 Aborigines had died. And one man died shortly after arriving at Oyster Cove.

Oyster Cove had, in 1843, been planned as a women convicts' settlement; instead, they went on the *Anson*. Later it had been used for male convicts; now it was made ready, though not renovated, for its new inhabitants – the couples on one side of the square, the single people on the other. The children were to be sent to the Orphan School. But, before that, Caroline Denison's husband instructed her that the Aborigines were to be entertained at the New

Norfolk Government House Christmas party – her first in Tasmania, and she was in the early stages of pregnancy. Her journal gives her account of the occasion and we see some of the characters with whom we are familiar through her eyes:

> ... you will want to know something of the names, appearances, &c. of our guests. There were four men; their names Walter (who calls himself a chief, but is not as great, evidently, in the eyes of his companions as in his own) ... Of the women, the most remarkable character was Marianne, the chieftainess, Walter's wife: an immense, stout, masculine-looking creature, apparently a person of far more influence than her husband. I could not catch all the women's names: there was one called 'old Sarah,' Marianne's mother; two called Martha and Nanny, whom I did not learn to distinguish from one another, and two girls called Methinna [sic] and Hannah. They spoke a very comical sort of broken English: one very favourite expression of theirs is 'gammon,' a word whose meaning they are quite aware of; and they have not the least hesitation in applying it to anything you tell them, which seems to them at all surprising, or difficult to believe. They were inclined to think it was 'gammon' when they were told that William was the Governor, whom they had come to see, because, as they remarked, he had not got a *cocked hat on* ... when I asked Marianne the age of one of the girls, she at first shook her head, intimating that she did not know, then assured me in general terms, that the girl was 'old fellow,' and afterwards answered my question through the medium of Dr Milligan ... by naming to him certain events which had happened about the time of the birth of this girl, from which he deduced for me that the said 'old fellow' must be about thirteen or fourteen years old.

One would give anything to have Mary Ann's impression of Caroline Denison who, in spite of her condescension, was being liberal for her day by entertaining them. And her husband, who evidence shows cared about the well-being of the Aborigines, had to work hard to get the move from faraway Flinders Island tolerated by colonists. Louisa Anne Meredith, for example, wrote what she felt was the view of those who had previously suffered from Aboriginal actions, that 'Every adult man among [the Aborigines] had been actively engaged in ... the most brutal and unprovoked murders, and that in all probability a return to their old haunts would lead to a renewal of horrors.'

Was Mary Ann playing the role expected of her at the Christmas party? She was to ask a visitor to Oyster Cove for books and had apparently read Harriet Beecher Stowe's *Uncle Tom's Cabin*, an indication of both her literacy and her political development. Bonwick talks of both her 'vigour and intellect' and a 'strength and independence of will stamped upon her expansive features'.'

Mary and Walter continued to agitate, without success, for improvement in the conditions at Oyster Cove. They complained, for example, of the cold. Visiting the Aborigines in the summer of 1849, the Governor found them 'sitting over large fires; the room very close, and themselves wrapped up in the thickest blanket wrappers you can imagine'. They had no incentive to be active – which might have helped – since everything, however basic or unsatisfactory, was provided for them. The women had embroidered, among other activities, at Wybalenna – sent the fabric, it would seem, by the Dorcas Society – but wherewithal provided for them at Oyster Cove remained unused.

The cold and damp affected not only the Aborigines there: the Clarks had accompanied them from Wybalenna but, later in 1849, Bessy died: her health, as Bonwick explains, 'affected by the ill-conditioned quarters allotted to her family'. She had been briefly removed to Hobart, but it failed to save her. Her husband returned to Oyster Cove a changed man, depressed, too, by the condition of the Aborigines, and died soon after her, in March 1850. Although there is some evidence that Clark caused dissension between the Aborigines and their neighbours at Oyster Cove, to Mary Ann Cochrane Arthur, at least, the Clarks were seen as 'Mother' and 'Father'.

Mary Ann had helped Clark's 17-year-old daughter, **Fanny Jane Clark** (bc1833) nurse him in his last days. Now the young family, including a four-year-old boy and 18-month-old Ebenezer who had learning difficulties (Plomley calls him an 'idiot') were left destitute. Fanny Clark wrote to the government on 3 April and some assistance was provided and the boys sent to the Orphan School. I can find no other sighting of Fanny. We can only speculate on her life growing up in a household full of harshly-disciplined Aboriginal children at Wybalenna. Were she and Mathinna and Fanny Cochrane in any sense playmates? After all, they were only a couple of years apart. And what about Fanny Clark's mother, Bessy, when her husband was in a constant state of war with Jeanneret? How did she relate to Harriet Jeanneret in those suffocating confines?

Bonwick, who had moved to the mainland, returned to Tasmania in 1859 and visited the Arthurs at Oyster Cove. Four years earlier, they had left the station to live on a 15-acre grant nearby which they tried to cultivate. Bonwick writes of the visit:

> Arrived at the door of a near three-roomed bush cottage, I was received with many smiles by the buxom Mary Ann ... The room into which I was brought had many tokens of civilization and gentility wanting in most of the country cottages of England. The furniture, though homely, was suitable and comfortable. A carpet covered the floor. Not a particle of dust could be seen. A few prints adorned the walls, and books lay on a side-table. The Bible occupied a conspicuous position. The daily newspaper was there, as Walter was a regular subscriber to the press. The table was laid with quite a tempting appearance, and a thorough good cup of tea was handed round by the jovial-looking hostess. It was about the last evidence of civilization to be witnessed in connexion with the interesting race of Tasmanians.

At Wybalenna, under Jeanneret, Mary Ann had refused to clean her house, unless given better clothes. As Bonwick left, she gave him a necklace of 'brilliantly-polished shells' for his daughter.

Caroline Denison might scoff at Walter calling himself chief, but Reynolds points out that animating his 'political activity was his demand to be treated like a "white free man", like a European who was not a convict'. What Bonwick does not mention is that Walter had started drinking heavily. It is clear that most of the Aborigines drank and that this habit was encouraged and exploited by those selling them grog.

It may well be that Mary Ann also drank; in any case, as Plomley narrates, a report reached the Colonial Secretary of 'continued misconduct of Walter and his wife'. And when an effort was made to sober them up through ultimatums, they were said to 'Shew a sort of sulky resentment at having been interfered with, and are evidently meditating some kind of revenge.' But Davies has, from somewhere, and undated, found Mary Ann's response; it reads well:

We had soul in Flinders but we have none here. There, we were looked after, and the bad whites were kept from annoying us. But here we are thrown upon the scum of society. They have brought us among the offscouring of the earth. Here are bad of all sorts. We would be a great deal better off if someone would read and pray for us. We are tempted to drink and all bad practices, but there is neither reading nor prayer. While they give us food for the body, they might give us food for the soul. They might think of the remnant of us poor creatures, and make us happy, nobody cares for us.

After that Denison Christmas party when the age Caroline asked about is probably that of Mathinna, she was sent back to the Orphan School; she was now properly an orphan, her stepfather having died before the transfer from Flinders Island. In 1851, aged 17, she was returned to Oyster Cove. The dates for what happened next are not consistent and that is probably because of a letter dated 1855 from a magistrate to the Colonial Secretary.

Plomley tells of the visit of James Woodhouse Kirwan in April. The magistrate reported on the 'filthy state' of the station and how 'The first place to which [the natives] resort is the public house', near which occurred 'scenes of disgusting immorality on the part of the native women and white men in open day'. A month later, Kirwan wrote a letter about four Aboriginal men and three women who had visited an inn at Kingston, had been drunk and 'exposing the person', and had to be removed by the police. As Plomley then says, Kirwan went on to remind the Colonial Secretary of 'the case of a native woman named ARWENIA – this was MATHINNA – who, having become drunk at an inn at North West Bay had fallen on her face [in a puddle on the road] on her way home and was found dead the next morning'.

Although recent sources give 1855 or 1856 as the date of Mathinna's wretched death, Kirwan's 1855 letter apparently refers to 1 September 1852, when Mathinna was about 18. What I have earlier called an anti-Jane Franklin article, and quoted from, also misleads with its date of 1856. Bonwick describes the article: '... a friend has sent me his own sketch of the girl. It appeared in the *Hobart Town Mercury* last June', and he quotes from his version of the article (I have seen other versions and, in my extracts, I have changed the order of Bonwick's version); here, having extolled her appearance, he describes her death:

> She stood when I saw her last, about five feet eight inches high, was very erect, with a quick, thoughtless, or perhaps thinking, if you please, toss about her head now and then. Her hair still curled short as before, but seemed to struggle into length, and was blacker than black, bright, glossy, and oh! So beautiful! Her features were well chiselled, and singularly regular, while her voice was light, quick, yet sighed like, and somewhat plaintive ...
>
> ... Too soon alas! She fell into the habits of the rest; and, as they were permitted to wander about in the bush in all directions, among sawyers, splitters, and characters of the deepest depravity, the reader may guess for himself what my pen refuses to write. One night, however, Mathinna was missing; and, although *cooey* after *cooey* resounded from mountain to mountain, and from gully to gully, no tidings were heard of the lost girl. In the morning the search was continued, till at length the wanderer was found. The little wild girl, with the shell necklace, and the pet opossum – the scarlet-coated, bare-headed beauty in the carriage – the *protégé* of the noblewoman – the reclaimed daughter of the native chief, had *died*, abandoned by every virtue and – *drunk* – in the river!

Bonwick does not name the friend; earlier in the paragraph he discussed Mathinna at Oyster Cove with the Superintendent, who is likely to have been Milligan who stayed until 1854, though he did not live on the premises and only visited from time to time. It is not very satisfactory that almost all we know of Mathinna's life comes from that anti-Jane Franklin article. If only Caroline Denison had told a version of it. Did she know at the New Norfolk Christmas party that the girl she called Methinna had once apparently been 'one of the family' at Government House? Although she does not hint at it in her description of the party, Harriet Jeanneret had written to her from Wybalenna on 9 June 1847 asking her to intervene in the case of Methinna (sic) who was living in the Clarks' house. Harriet also wrote to Anna Maria Nixon, the Bishop's wife, more generally about the children living with the Clarks.

On 11 January Caroline Denison recorded in her journal a visit to the Orphan School a week or so after the Christmas party, when the Aboriginal children had been sent there; and one other visit, on 31 January, is recorded. But that is all; and Mathinna is not mentioned, though she is probably lumped in 'four black girls [were] very much pleased to see us again'. On the first visit, the girls danced and sang for the gubernatorial couple and Caroline noted that, 'These natives now living together, were all, to begin with, of different tribes; and it is a curious thing that each tribe had a language, which did not seem to have even a single root in common with that of the other tribes.' Thus, English was, to a large extent, their common language, and, though they could sing a song in their own language, taught by their elders, 'they had not an idea what it meant'. Read today, Caroline's well-intentioned pontificating might not be so well-received, though she does highlight language problems obvious at Wybalenna but, apparently, taken little account of. Certainly, apart from Mathinna, the four girls do not appear to have had tribal names.

Caroline Denison observed, too, that the girls 'are treated, apparently, with great indulgence, not bound down strictly to the ordinary rules of the school, but at present allowed to follow their own devices to a greater extent than any of the other children; because, of course, it is only by gentle degrees that one can expect to bring them into regular and civilised habits'.

While Mathinna makes no impact, Caroline does name 'half-caste' **Hannah** who, on her second visit, was 'very tidily' knitting a stocking. Hannah, assumed by Lyndall Ryan to have died later that year, according to Plomley went back to Flinders Island in 1850. **Nannie**, according to him, and the records, died at the Orphan school in 1849. **Martha** (b1835), I deduce the fourth girl, about the same age as Mathinna and Fanny Cochrane, died on 2 February 1851, aged 16, probably at Oyster Cove. So much for their 'education'!

Fanny Cochrane is not listed among those women and girls at the 1847 Christmas party; she was probably already in domestic service in Hobart. By coincidence it was with the Dandridges, a couple who were later to play a major role in the life (and death) of the remaining Aborigines. But Plomley writes of Fanny, 'By the end of 1848 she had so misconducted herself that the Dandridges sent her back to Oyster Cove.' There she lived with her mother, Sarah (Tarenootairer, Tanganootera, Tib) and sister Mary Ann. It is fair to assume that she moved between the two homes as her father, Eugene (Nicermenic) did not die until November 1850.

In April 1851, George Robinson, en route between his post in Victoria and England, visited Oyster Cove where he was supplied with a list of Aborigines still alive. He had not seen his flock for twelve years. Fanny had already moved there. He noted in his journal:

> At Oyster Cove, Read prayer spoke to the people. Got necklace from Mary Ann and Fanny and went to Little Oyster Cove. The natives want to return to Flinders Island. The Brune Islands occupied. All agree that the place is unhealthy too cold. Damp. Like a funnel all wind out of mountains. Natives fat: Mary Ann, Walter, Jack Allen, Hamish …

It is noticeable that Robinson does not mention Trukanini or Mathinna.

In 1854, in Hobart, Fanny Cochrane married William Smith, an English sawyer and ex-convict originally transported for stealing a donkey. Upon her marriage, she received a £24 annuity, presumably from the government. She and William ran a boarding house in Hobart. When her younger brother died in 1857, they moved to land near Oyster Cove, at Nicholls Rivulet, where the government granted her 100 acres. Between 1855 and 1880, the couple had five girls and six boys. Meanwhile, they grew their own produce, but timber gave them their income; both worked at fencing and shingle splitting. Fanny, too, lugged them out of the bush. She also walked the 31 miles (50 kilometres) to Hobart for supplies.

In 1889, Fanny was granted a further 600 acres and she was 'recognised by parliament'. This is said to acknowledge that her father was an Aborigine, Nicermenic, although it was also claimed then, and still claimed by some today, that her father was white. Plomley, who one turns to for much detailed twentieth-century scholarship, may well be responsible for that, particularly in his paper about portraits where he lays out the case for her possible parentage. The controversy has generated much heat. The identity of the white father of her half-sister, Mary Ann, is unclear, but Fanny was born some years later, and at Wybalenna rather than on one of the sealer islands. Sarah arrived at Wybalenna in 1832; Nicermenic was captured by Robinson and taken there in 1829.

In later life, Fanny became a Methodist and donated land to build a church (itinerary 'Oyster Cove to Recherche Bay', p290). She was proud of her Aboriginal heritage, and passed on the stories of her people, as well as practising traditional medicine, collecting bush food, weaving baskets and creating shell necklaces. Most of those details come from several biographical entries for Fanny; she has become increasingly important as an Aboriginal matriarch.

Another who was not, apparently, at the New Norfolk Christmas party was Trukanini. In a way, she came into her own following the transfer from Flinders Island in the north to Oyster Cove on the d'Entrecasteaux Channel. From the settlement, she could see the home of her people, Bruny Island and, indeed, would swim or boat there, in spite of the settlers, such as Cassandra Pybus' ancestors, who had taken over the Aboriginal lands.

Some of the most touching images of both Fanny and Trukanini come from information that Fanny's daughter, **Sarah Laurel Smith** (later Miller, bc1862) gave the Quaker amateur anthropologist and geologist Ernest Westlake between 1908 and 1910 (edited by NJB Plomley):

Truc was mostly right handed, as far as remember. Her hair was always short. Went bare footed in hunting; showed us how climbed a tree and make ropes out of the stringy bark, how would pull it, wind it and twist it till knowed it was strong enough. Liked to lie on the floor, curled up and lying on the side. Very fond of squatting on floor and on ground out of doors ...

...Trucaninni one day thought she would take us out to hunt, and we were all excitement to see how she would hunt. She had a waddy about two feet long. The poor old thing cautioned us to be very quiet before she shook the bushes otherwise the WEROWA would hunt the ringtail [opossum] away. My sister Flora forgot what poor old Truc had told her – we always called Truc Lallah – and the minute she shook a ringtail on to the ground from a bush, when my sister saw the animal she sang out 'here Lally, here Lally', and the ringtail ran up a trunk and escaped. Truc was so disgusted she took us back to mother at once and would never take out 'blob-mouth' Flora no more, and told mother that WEROWA had hunted the ringtail away. This the only time I've heard the word, and I've always felt it was an evil spirit of some kind.

Another informant, a Mrs Pybus, told Westlake that Trukanini was 'awfully fond of cricket and of watching the game'. Of Fanny, an inspector of police told Westlake in 1909:

> Fanny Smith was certainly very intelligent and what she said may be taken as reliable. She travelled with the tribes, could speak the languages and sing the songs. Could keep a whole room entertained. Bright sparkling eyes, was a most intellectual woman.

A JP at Huonville informed Westlake: 'I reckon Fanny Smith was a full-blooded native, from looks, manner and the way she walked.' Fanny's daughter Sarah described her thus to Westlake:

> Mother was a beautiful cook and a good dressmaker, had a good voice and was a sweet singer. She was really one of nature's ladies, refined and gentle. Wouldn't allow us to sing out; if we did we used to get hauled over the coals for being what she called rowdy; but had a very forgiving spirit. Yet mother was very pleasant company; there was nothing dull about her.

There is a recording of her, made in 1903, singing a tribal song, in the Tasmanian Museum and Art Gallery (p241).

By 1854, only 16 Aborigines were alive at Oyster Cove, Sarah Smith's grandmother, after whose European name she was named, died in 1858; her granddaughter told Westlake what happened:

> On the evening my grandmother (TANGANOOTERA=Sarah) was taken bad at Oyster Cove, my mother said, 'Bill I can hear the natives calling me'. Shortly after a native came with the news. My mother then went to my grandmother's, and when she got there my grandmother said, 'Didn't you hear me call you'. And mother said 'yes.'

Of other women mentioned in earlier chapters, Jumbo (Bulyer?, Louisa) died between 1847 and 1851 (that is after the removal from Flinders but before Robinson's visit), and Mannalargenna's daughter Wottecowidyer (Wot, Harriet), between 1851 and 1854, as did Matilda, one of the campaigners of Wybalenna. Dray (Sophia), a crucial member of Robinson's mission team, died in 1861, and another of the daughters of the Portland chief who had helped Robinson, **Wapperty** (Wobberretee), died in 1867. Bonwick wrote of Sophia during his visit eight years earlier: 'A troop of mangy dogs accompanied their aged mistress, who held forth long harangues to the curs, that answered in snapping barks of recognition. Two of them lay in her wretched bed with her, to keep her back warm, as she told me' (p110).

In 1855, Milligan was dismissed as a result of Kirwan's report, and was replaced by John Strange Dandridge, accompanied by his wife who was said to have been influential in his career advancement. **Matilda Dandridge** (b1830) was the daughter of the harpist **Maria Prout** (née Marsh) and her husband

John, the artist who painted the 1845 portrait of Mathinna and tutored several of Hobart's aspiring women artists. The Dandridges married in 1847 and they had a daughter and four sons between 1848 and 1854. It is not clear if the children, three of whom were born after their move to Oyster Cove, went with them. It seems unlikely, given the conditions there. And they already had a house in Hobart, as their hiring of convict servants in Chapter 11 suggests. Matilda's part in the deaths of both Mary Ann Cochrane Arthur in 1871 and Trukanini in 1876 is described in the itinerary 'Around and About Macquarie Street'. Walter Arthur fell overboard from a fishing boat in 1861 and drowned. Earlier he had left a public house and was unfit to put to sea.

17.   Mrs Dandridge with Mary Ann and Walter Arthur, by Annie Benbow, c1900, courtesy of the WL Crowther Library, Tasmanian Archive and Heritage Office

The sketch by Annie Benbow of Mary Ann and Walter Arthur with Matilda Dandridge may give little idea of how any of them looked – though Walter is rather nattily dressed – but it does suggest a comfortable relationship. **Annie Benbow** (née McDowell, 1841–1917) was the daughter of the sergeant in charge at Oyster Cove. She married Sarsfield Benbow in 1869, had four children, and is buried at Kettering, near Oyster Cove. She made several rather crude drawings of Aborigines at Oyster Cove from memory in about 1900.

Though the Aborigines from the settlement at Wybalenna had been moved to Oyster Cove, Aboriginal women, sealers and their progeny remained on other Bass Strait islands. The most notable and best known woman was **Lucy Beedon** (Beeton, Beadon, 1829–1886), daughter of Emmerenna and Thomas Beedon. Lucy grew up on Gun Carriage Island and was educated by private tutors in Launceston while staying in a doctor's family. Patsy Adam-Smith records in *Moonbird People* (1965) that her father belonged to a London family of jewellers and goldsmiths which sent him funds via a solicitor in Launceston. Lucy was taught business skills and sailing by her father.

18.   Lucy Beedon, from West, *Pride Against Prejudice*

By 1848 a policy had been developed towards the islanders giving them certain rights in return for a peppercorn rent, but in 1850 the government rejected a petition to appoint a catechist-teacher on Gun Carriage, so Lucy took on the task herself. An 1854 view of Lucy comes from the journal kept by Anna Maria Nixon's husband, the Bishop, during his tour of the islands; he wrote in *The Cruise of the Beacon* (1857):

We came at last to the residence of the 'greatest lady' it has been my good fortune to encounter. Lucy Beadon, a noble-looking half-caste of some twenty five years of age, bears the burden of twenty three stone. Good-humoured and kind-hearted, she is everyone's friend upon the island. High-minded, and earnest in her Christian profession, she has set herself to work to do good in her generation. From the pure love of those around her, she daily gathers together the children of the sealers, and does her best to import to them the rudiments both of secular and religious knowledge.

By 1860, the extended Beedon family had moved to Badger Island. When Lucy's father died in 1862, she took over the family business and soon controlled the islanders' trading operations with Launceston; indeed, she became known as 'Queen of the Isles' and 'the Commodore'. Her trading operations often involved sailing to Launceston with a fleet of boats bearing muttonbirds and their eggs, feathers, fat and oil. She made every effort, too, to gain land for the islanders, especially muttonbird rookeries, to compensate Tasmanian Aborigines for their dispossession. She was herself awarded a lifetime lease on Badger Island at a yearly rent of £24.

She continued to oversee education, pressing the government for a school and teachers, eventually hiring two teachers from Melbourne herself and setting up a school in a tent until the government relented.

When Canon Marcus Brownrigg of Launceston visited the islands, as he did on 13 occasions between 1872 and 1885, he would always receive hospitality from Lucy Beedon and hold prayers in her house. Ida West, Lucy's great-great-niece, gives an impression of it: 'The old home on Badger Island had a verandah with a grape vine growing around it. Inside there were many beautiful ornaments and pieces of furniture, including a piano.' Brownrigg wrote in *The Cruise of the Freak* in 1872:

> I spent the evening at Miss Beedon's. I cannot here forbear mentioning a matter which shows that there is, at least, one tender heart that feels a true sympathy for poor Lalla Rookh ... In the course of the conversation, Miss Beedon mentioned how much and how often she had longed to offer to Lalla Rookh a home where she might spend her remaining days among the descendants of her own race. I at once undertook to enquire at head quarters whether such an arrangement might be effected, should it also meet the wishes, as I expected it would, of Lalla Rookh herself. To this matter I gave immediate attention on my return to Launceston, forwarding to the Governor's Private Secretary the written invitation Miss Beedon had addressed to Lalla Rookh, accompanying it with a few lines of explanation myself, but I fear the kindly wish of Miss Beedon is not likely to be gratified.

Trukanini did, indeed, prefer to remain near her own land. But Lucy Beedon's offer gives an inkling of the ties that bound those remaining Aboriginal women: Trukanini, the Aboriginal partners and offspring of white sealers on the islands, and the two matriarchs on the mainland of Tasmania, Dolly Dalrymple Briggs and Fanny Cochrane Smith. Though Lucy Beedon never married and had children, she, too, for her campaigning on behalf of her dispossessed people, was and is known as 'Matriarch of the Straits'. In the early 1970s the descendants of the matriarchs were to begin to reclaim their inheritance, as the chronology at the end of Chapter 13 shows. And, as Plomley notes, 'the aboriginal elements transmitted ... concerned only aspects of [the] culture that were accessible to women'.

Part IV – 1847–2010

13 – From Philanthropy to Politics

With the last convicts and the end of any threat from Aborigines, Tasmania, as it was now officially named, became a different place. Carmel Bird, in an account of her birthplace to a meeting in Barcelona in 2001, explains rather powerfully what happened in 'an attempt to cleanse the past, to obliterate from memory the horrors and the tragedy and the violent grotesquerie of recent life, to go forward with a false confidence based on some kind of fictional innocence':

> Many written records of the convict and Aboriginal past were officially destroyed, and families with blood ties to convicts and Aborigines re-wrote the family history to exclude the shameful ancestors. If your grandfather was a horse-thief from Ireland, and a bushranger in Van Diemen's Land, and your grandmother was an Aborigine, then chances were your grandfather raped your grandmother and was not joined to her in holy wedlock. Your family history was stained with shame but you were now a respectable farmer who read the lesson in church every Sunday and so you certainly didn't need those ancestors. You were constructing your dream of paradise in a little paradise island far far from the real centres of power and civilisation and as far as possible from some sort of recorded truth.

In her novels, presentations and website historical explorations, Tasmanian-born but Victoria resident Carmel Bird evokes a troubled spirit of place in spite of or perhaps because of her respectable ancestry. For the more factual reconstruction of women's lives covering more extended periods, I have often turned to proudly convict-descended Alison Alexander, mostly in *Obliged to Submit* or her as-yet unpublished doctoral thesis 'The Public Role of Women in Tasmania 1803–1914' (1989). It is the latter that has given me many leads for this chapter. In it, women's public involvement suggests, not surprisingly, a chronological development best indicated by subheadings.

Philanthropy

Jane Franklin, ahead of her day, had mixed philanthropy and politics, to her cost. Caroline Denison, who arrived in 1847, four years after Jane's departure, visited the convict hulk *Anson*, children in the Orphan School, including Aborigines, and was, like her predecessors Eliza Arthur and Jane Franklin, patroness of the Maternal and Dorcas Society, the first women's philanthropic venture. Unlike the earlier two, she went regularly to its meetings, which made attendance by others all the keener. But, as Alison Alexander recounts, as *Obliged to Submit* draws to an end, that society's concern was for poor but worthy married women. In 1848, Caroline Denison, prompted by Anna Maria Nixon, attempted to branch out, to help prostitutes, by establishing a refuge for them, the Van Diemen's Land Asylum for the Protection of Destitute and Unfortunate Females. At first there was some enthusiasm, including from Dorcas committee members, 'to provide a refuge for those who, from adverse circumstances, may be exposed to more than ordinary temptation to sin'.

Caroline involved herself fully, visiting the matron and seeing to the running of the asylum. Then the matron resigned and the inmates misbehaved. In September 1850, the committee closed the institution and sold its contents to pay its debts. Alison Alexander sums up the failure of Caroline Denison to extend her first lady role:

> One possible reason is that public opinion did not expect this sort of activity from the Governor's wife. Such a lady was not meant to be interested in riff-raff like natives, fallen women, convicts' children or female convicts. The Dorcas Society, helping respectable women, was acceptable, but as for the others, it wasn't fitting. A social circle so involved with precedence and etiquette was not likely to look kindly on its leading lady mixing with the worst elements in society.

After the failure of the refuge, until she left in 1855, Caroline Denison concentrated on her growing family and what was expected of her socially, trying to ignore the increasing unpopularity of her husband. Alison Alexander sums up those years: 'She had turned into just the sort of governor's wife the middle classes hoped for: a polite, charming figurehead, all individuality squashed.' From Tasmania, the Denisons moved to Sydney where, for six years, he was Governor General of the Australian colonies.

To separate the strands of philanthropy that were to follow from the 1860s, is like unravelling a tangled skein of wool, not only because many of the women were involved in several charities, often established over time, but also because it is sometimes hard to distinguish between wives and their husbands. The Hobart Benevolent Society to help the poor was founded in 1859, prompted by the recession and floods of that year to 'relieve the poor, the distressed and afflicted'. It is said to have been supported by the Mather, Kennerley and Salier families. The chair at its first annual meeting was Salome Pitt Bateman's husband, credited with playing an important part in the Society. But what part, and did mountain-climbing Salome concern herself? Bateman had also 'brought in' Aborigines for George Robinson, a strange link with Salome's early life (p40).

As for any involvement by Mather women, the strands I have tried to follow are too speculative and dry to detail. By family, the source may have meant brothers: Robert Andrew Mather became Chair in 1865, and his brother, Joseph Benson Mather, was a well-known philanthropist – both had wives, and a still living stepmother. The involvement of their sister, Sarah Benson Mather Walker, is specifically mentioned in another source though, in the

1850s, we have already met her overwhelmed by the cares of the household and childbearing; in earlier years, she was a member of Jane Franklin's prison visiting committee.

The role of **Jane Rouse Kennerley** (1809–1877) in the Society is not specified but, when Alfred, her husband of 35 years, magistrate, Legislative Councillor and later Premier, founded the Boys' Home and Industrial School in 1869, she seems to have helped plan and run it, according to the fulsome tribute paid after her death. She was a constant visitor 'ever cheering the Master and Matron by her presence, and aiding them with friendly counsel and advice'. Alison Alexander, in one of her lively asides, remarks: 'Whether the professionals wanted amateur advice was not considered.' The boys – the well-conducted ones – would visit her every Saturday to work in the garden and 'enjoy a comfortable meal'. Their clothing was made in her house 'under her direction'. In 1906, the *Mercury* suggested that those such as the Kennerleys liked being 'Lady Bountiful or Lord of the Manor'.

The Salier wives' involvement in charitable work is less clear, particularly since there were two of them. **Harriet Mary Salier** (neé Willis, d1902) is the more likely. She had married widower and merchant George Salier in 1846 and, according to Miranda Morris who has written most about the Dorcas Society, she joined it in 1854 and was to become one of its longest-serving members – indeed, she was an active member until she died. More than that, as Alison Alexander suggests, she did not condescend like some but was genuinely fond of her cases and received affection in return. Minutes record that 'Mrs Salier has always purchased the material for the mother and children's clothing and cut them out this has been rather too much for her lately but she refused to give up.'

In 1851 merchant James Salier married **Emily Mary Salier** (née Allen, c1818–1894). Both brothers were on several philanthropic committees. James became Chair of the Benevolent Society and joined George on the committee of the Girls' Industrial School. This charity, established in 1862, is interesting because, instead of attempting to rescue prostitutes, it provided live-in accommodation for 'needy or criminal girls whose own homes had failed them'. They were to be saved in advance from a life on the town. Training them for domestic work would create both much-needed servants, now that the convict supply had dried up, and good wives. In addition, the home took in laundry, both inducting the girls in that task and raising funds for the institution.

Harriet Salier was Secretary of both the Girls Industrial School Committee and that of the Van Diemen's Land Asylum. She also made the younger girls of the Industrial School 'cosy red hoods' which might have seemed odd if we did not know about her other sewing activities; this was on top of having given birth to 13 children, five of whom did not live longer than four years. She was either pregnant, or had just given birth to Kate Sarah, who died when she was four, when she joined the Dorcas Society. She also looked after the three children of her husband's first wife. The family lived on Elizabeth Street in a Georgian house built in 1829 which now, designated a heritage site, provides accommodation (the Lodge, no. 249). Harriet's sister-in-law Emily Salier had four children; it may be that sometimes a record of a Mrs Salier refers to her.

From 1862 to 1914, 113 women served on the committee of the Girls' Industrial School. In 1905, it merged with the Hobart Girls' Training School, or Reformatory, established in 1881 for children 'found to be begging, vagrant, in the company of reputed thieves, deserted or declared uncontrollable'. In the old gaol building of the Anglesea Barracks, these girls, aged 15–18, were locked in their cells each night. The Salvation Army took over the establishment, by then in New Town, in 1945, and it was renamed Marylands Girls' Home; it closed in 1981.

The Launceston Girls' Industrial School lasted from 1863–1867, restarted in 1877 and ran until 1914. Although one of its purposes was said to be to make the girls 'really comfortable and happy', in 1913 the committee refused to allow them a Christmas holiday for which a benefactor had raised money; they were, as Alison Alexander explains, being 'brought up as servants and it was not good for them to have too much pleasure'. The *Daily Post* labelled this depriving the girls of 'the ordinary pleasures of childhood' and the lady committee members' attitude as 'insolent superiority'.

Into the early days of the new wave of philanthropy came, in 1861, Governor's wife **Harriet Gore Browne** (née Campbell, 1829–1906; m1851). Aged 26, she had accompanied her husband, Thomas, 20 years her senior, to New Zealand when he became Governor in 1855. According to her entry in the *Dictionary of New Zealand Biography*, she was described as 'a woman out of a Book of Beauty ... ample white muslin flounces and fine long dark tresses'. She was to make Government House in Auckland the centre of cultural and political life. There are traces of Jane Franklin in her activities in New Zealand. A woman contemporary wrote of her in 1860, 'She is remarkably energetic and clever ... she really governs the country as much as the Governor, for he does nothing and writes nothing without consulting her first.' This remark was perhaps intended to cause trouble.

Harriet had three children in New Zealand and was to have three more in Tasmania, but information about her contribution there during her seven-year stay is sociological rather than political. Perhaps she had learned a lesson in her husband's previous posting, or had heard rumours of Jane Franklin's Tasmanian fate. She is said to have helped establish 'the Industrial Reform School', though Tasmanian accounts do not mention her in that connection, the same applies to her teaching at one of the Ragged Schools, and her reading to the dying in hospital. She also supported the staging of theatricals at Government House (p258).

She wrote to a friend that she was 'patroness of a female refuge, an orphan asylum, a ragged school and the Dorcas Society' but, she added, 'I am not up to working with committees and do not understand my duty as president.' Nevertheless, when she left in 1868, she was presented with an embossed certificate from the Ladies' Committee of the Girls Reformatory and Industrial School. It stated that 'the origin of the Reformatory is almost due to yourself'. In 1898, eleven years a widow, Harriet visited Tasmania again.

The four Hobart Ragged Schools, the first of which was established in 1854, served the 'perishing and dangerous classes' and were to keep neglected children, whose destitution prevented them from attending other schools, off the streets. The Benevolent Society reported that the first – which looked after 69 girls and 66 boys – was in 'a low neighbourhood'. St Luke's Ragged School, Anglesea Street, was opened in 1868 by the Catholic Sisters of Charity. From their arrival in 1847, they had aided transportees, particularly women at the Cascades Women's Factory, and the destitute children at the Queen's Orphan School. In 1879, they opened their own orphanage. The Ragged School Association was dissolved in 1911.

It may have been the Dorcas Society which sent embroidery materials to Wybalenna before the move to Oyster Cove in 1847 – though it was outside their remit. But of all the formal philanthropy that was to blossom, none appears to have been directed towards the last few Aborigines at the cove, nor to the Bass Strait islands community – descendants of Aboriginal mothers and sealers. Alison Alexander suggests that part of the reason was that Tasmanian charities tended to be based on their British counterparts and that Tasmanian women required strong encouragement to form and join them.

In the 1870s, those families settled on several islands were 'relocated' to Cape Barren Island and, in 1881, a formal 'reserve' was established there in which basic social services were provided. By 1908, there was a population of 250 and, in 1912, the Cape Barren Act was passed to encourage self-sufficiency through incentives and disincentives.

In the 1930s, under general child welfare legislation, there was a policy of forcible removal from Cape Barren Island – and indeed of Aboriginal children all over Australia – to orphanages or foster parents away from their home place. This policy gathered momentum in the 1950s. The children were to become known as 'Stolen Children' or the 'Stolen Generations'. It was not until the early 1970s, as the chronology at the end of this chapter shows, that Tasmanian Aborigines, through their own impetus, began to impinge again on white Tasmanian consciousness.

What later came to general public consciousness was the forcible transfer, between 1929 and 1967, of British children in care to Australia, including Tasmania – through a policy of convenience for Britain and white repopulation for Australia – and the ill-treatment they received. There is a certain irony in the fact that much of women's philanthropic activity in the last two decades of the nineteenth century was to concentrate on children.

The Women's Sanitary Association

In many ways, **Teresa Hamilton** (née Reynolds, c1840–1932; m1877), with her Australian background and Tasmanian family connections was to succeed as First Lady in areas where Jane Franklin and Caroline Denison had failed, and where Harriet Gore Browne had felt spare. She started well: soon after her arrival in 1887, accompanying her husband, Robert, the new Governor, a newspaper report of a reception described her thus:

[She] looked very handsome in a pale tan armure frock, with tints of white moiré softening it in a marvellous way, and a tiny fawn bonnet, while her face is so good, so true, one cannot help instinctively admiring the nobility of character speaking through it.

(Armure is 'a fabric made of wool, silk, or both, with a twilled or ribbed surface' –*OED*.) Even Teresa's surroundings were different from those put up with by Jane Franklin and Caroline Denison. Governors and their families had occupied a new Government House since 1858. Teresa's stepdaughter wrote:

Slowly we threaded our way into the beautiful town of Hobart till the town opened up on our left lying at the foot of its famous Mount Wellington. Right in front of us, on a promontory of its own, stood our new home, a large and dignified house of more or less gothic design, looking straight down the wide river.

Actually, it is more like a storybook castle and still very much in use by the Governor. Lady Hamilton is best known, or only known, for establishing the *Nil Desperandum* Literary Society at Government House which, although longer lasting than any society, showed her to be slightly less angelic than reports suggest. But, however useful the spreading of literature among a few middle-class women was, her contribution to Tasmania's physical well-being during her five years there was undoubtedly more helpful.

Typhoid, earlier endemic, became an epidemic in Tasmania in the 1880s. There was a sequence of hot, dry summers, not only affecting water quality but street cleaning. This was coupled with changes in the disposal of excrement which led to sewage disposal in gutters, and an increase in population after years of stagnation caused overcrowding. Maisie Fulton wrote of Hobart then in a piece to mark the centenary of Lady Hamilton's Literary Society, 'Many people lived in cramped miserable houses, in pitiable poverty. It was still in the era of a hard life after tragic beginnings.' And Vera Read wrote in 'A Letter Lady Hamilton Might Have Written to a Friend if She Had Had Time':

The very word, *typhoid*, has cast its shadow over my soul – not only because our own dear boy was stricken – but it was while nursing him, that I resolved to speak about the disease that has caused 39 – or was it 49? – deaths. It was one or the other – too many.

In the old country, faulty drainage and lack of proper sanitary arrangements would most certainly have been blamed for the onset of such a disease, but in this health resort of the Australian colonies, so highly endowed by nature, such a state of affairs cries aloud for reform. So, I have appealed to the Corporation, as an individual, to set the drainage work to rights. And I have asked all mothers and housewives to burn all refuse, to ventilate their rooms and to flush out the abominations of stagnant gutters as best they can.

19. Teresa Hamilton, by Philip Tennyson Cole,
courtesy of the Tasmanian Museum
and Art Gallery

In 1887, the St John's Ambulance Association was established in Launceston and branches soon spread. From 1887, Teresa lectured on health to groups such as the Young Women's Christian Association (YWCA), though any past experience she may have had in public speaking or health is not recorded in Tasmanian accounts. In 1892, she formed a Nursing Band from YWCA members, to nurse the sick in their homes. In one year, members paid 700 visits to 80 cases. In 1896, it became the Hobart District Nursing Association. Women doctors, trained elsewhere, did not start to practise in Tasmania until 1907–08, and it was a bumpy ride.

In 1889, Teresa Hamilton instigated first aid classes in Hobart, introduced by her, given by doctors. Examinations and certificates encouraged women to nurse their families, as well as allowing them to earn a living. There is more detail in Alison Alexander's 'Teresa Hamilton in Tasmania: First Wave Feminism in Action' (1997). The double meaning of 'action' is nice.

These initiatives helped the sick and gave the women involved confidence but, in 1891, she chaired a meeting of what became the Women's Sanitary Association (WSA) which not only drew more women into the public sphere but, eventually, into politics too. At that packed first meeting in the Town Hall (p242), Teresa told her audience of women that their highest duty was to guard the health of their husbands, for man's life and income plus 'all those gentle souls who depend on him' relied on it. We might not respond to such sentiments today, but they were ideal for the homebodies of nineteenth-century Tasmania. The sting in the tail, of which Teresa may well have been aware, was that Council inertia and that of the all-male Sanitary Association were behind the colony's health problems.

A committee of influential women was formed which included Maud Montgomery, the Bishop's wife, and Emily Dobson, wife of a leading politician. 'We have to protest', exhorted Emily, 'Let us cast off our proverbial lethargy.' Unprecedented activity, or action, followed: Hobart was divided into districts, learning from the Dorcas Society and, as a matter of urgency, 5,740 signatures were collected and the petition was presented to the Council and the House of Assembly pressing for the passing of the Deep Drainage Bill before it. Thereafter, the 80-strong membership of the Association set out to visit every house proselytising the virtues of hygiene. In due course, Teresa Hamilton wrote a series of articles on 'Sanitation and Public Health'; she was anxious that the WSA concentrate on education and avoid confrontation.

Maud Montgomery (née Farrar, bc1865) is best-known for being the mother of Field Marshal Viscount Montgomery of Alamein. She was a woman you might not have expected to go down well in the Tasmania of her day, 1889–1901. In 1881, aged not yet 17, when her father was Canon of Westminster, she married his former curate, Henry Montgomery. He was 18 years her senior and they had been engaged since she was 14. Dean Stanley, to whom Montgomery had been private secretary, and almost a son, insisted on the wedding taking place in Henry VII's chapel in Westminster Abbey because a Henry and a Maud had not been married there since King Henry and Queen Maud.

Maud Montgomery proceeded to have nine children. The Field Marshal, born when his mother was 22, two years before the family arrived in Tasmania, was the fourth. A 1976 review of a biography of the Field Marshal gives us some idea, however slanted through her son's eyes, of Maud Montgomery:

> Son of an Anglican clergyman and a strong, determined young woman, Montgomery was, in his own words, 'a dreadful boy'. In frontier Tasmania, young Bernard was reared by his mother, Maud, firmly committed to keeping control of the family while her husband travelled throughout the island on church business. The boy's inherent rebelliousness caused running civil war with his mother, a war without an armistice and the source of many of his mature attitudes and eccentricities ... Montgomery's peers and especially his siblings agree that the apparent lack of affection between mother and son was the key to his personality. His determination to strike at his mother probably led to a military career. His obsession with winning – possibly to make up for the early battles lost to her – led to his disagreeing with senior officers and personalizing conflict, even to the point of putting pictures of Rommel and von Rundstedt ... on the walls of his command vehicle.

A biographical entry for Montgomery suggests that Maud subjected her children to constant beatings and ignored them the rest of the time as she performed the public duties of a Bishop's wife; they were educated by tutors brought from England. This may not be so different to parenting methods of the times less analysed by later recollections and biographies, and you have to wonder how impossible young Bernard was in his own right and how he could have been constantly fighting his mother if she ignored her children. And the analysis does not suggest how Maud took the death of her seven-year-old daughter Sibyl from acute peritonitis a month after her arrival in Tasmania; she had at least two more children there, in 1894 and 1895. The often-absent Bishop was recalled by his illustrious son as a 'hen-pecked saint'. Whatever the truth of this picture, Maud brought enthusiasm for hard work, business acumen (gained from a penny-pinching early marriage) and talent as a public speaker, no doubt acquired from the milieu of her upbringing, to her public role in Tasmania.

Maud also brought with her from England, Alison Alexander tells us, 'new ideas of social purity and a new role for women'. Under the auspices of the Anglican church, she organised children into a Children's Home Mission, and women into a Ladies' Home Mission Union, whose members donated money. The Union's aim was limited and its existence short-lived. She also urged women to work actively for the Home of Mercy which helped prostitutes.

Before Maud's arrival in 1887, **Grace Soltau** (née Tapson), had set up the Rescue Home of Hope in Launceston with the same purpose. She was the wife of a Christian Brethren missionary and mother of seven children, in Launceston since earlier in the 1880s; she had twins in 1890. The Home was run by volunteers until 1892 when it was taken over by the Church of England which did not 'dare' to remain inactive longer in the 'difficult work of seeking out fallen women'. When the Hobart Home of Mercy opened in 1890, Maud 'repeatedly visited' prostitutes in gaol or in their 'evil haunts' subjecting them to 'all entreaties' and making 'the most strenuous efforts' to reform them.

Using her persuasive talents, Maud spoke to women about others who, 'overcoming their first shrinking, had found their work of helping to guide their unhappy sisters well repays their efforts'. The Home also needed more women prepared to employ reformed prostitutes as servants. Alison Alexander hints that Maud did not set a good example.

After Maud left in 1901, the work of the Home was done by paid staff, while the Ladies' Committee fund-raised. The emphasis shifted from dealing with prostitutes to helping girls in danger of taking to the streets. The Catholic Magdalen Home which received and reformed the 'unfortunate class' was established in 1893, and the Salvation Army Elim Maternity Home in 1897.

In 1893, the non-denominational Anchor Refuge Home was set up by Teresa Hamilton. Run by a voluntary committee, but with a paid matron, it cared for pregnant women and their babies for a year, and then found the women positions as servants. It lasted until 1911 and was, as Alison Alexander says, the 'only example of volunteer women running such an institution successfully'. She adds: 'The reason for its success is not clear, though it was probably easier to assist pregnant women for a year than to reform prostitutes for ever.'

The third top woman on that initial committee of the Women's Sanitary Association, **Emily Dobson** (née Lempriere, 1842–1934), was as strong a character as Teresa Hamilton and Maud Montgomery. Where philanthropy was concerned, Emily was to become the Queen Bee of Tasmania, and she was to be the one to make the feminine link to conservative politics.

We have already briefly met Emily's parents, Thomas and **Charlotte Lempriere** (née Smith, c1803–1890) when he was posted, with his wife and three children, to the penal settlement at Macquarie Harbour in 1827 and reported on the shocking conditions there. Emily was born in 1842 during his posting to Port Arthur. She was the penultimate of twelve children, and was only ten when her father died at sea. In spite of her later life being quite well documented, her childhood and girlhood are not but, in 1868, aged 26, she married the lawyer Henry Dobson at Bothwell, probably because her older sister Lucy had married into the Reid family there; she was the sister-in-law of our informant Jane Reid Williams.

Emily had half the number of children produced by her mother and the youngest was nine, and she was 49, the year she started her philanthropical activities with the Women's Sanitary Association. It was the same year, 1891, that her husband entered politics and, by the following year he was premier and she was on the way to dominating women's activities for the next decades. I suspect that her dominant, if not domineering personality, was given encouragement in the extended Dobson family. Henry's half-brother, Sir (William) Lambert Dobson, was Attorney General at the time of Emily's marriage and was soon to become a judge. When the Hamiltons arrived he was Administrator and handed over to the new Governor.

Emily and Henry wasted no time in catching up in prominence, and the term 'Dobsonia' was coined by the socialist newspaper the *Clipper* to describe their joint aspirations. The term 'Dobsony' also came into existence. The best way to define it is how it was used to describe **Ethel Dobson** (b1868), daughter of Lambert Dobson, by then Chief Justice, and for that we need to move to Lady Hamilton's Literary Society – in her day, *Nil Desperandum*.

Lady Hamilton's Literary Society

In 1891, at the time of the Women's Sanitary Association's birth, a few women found it more fun to attend parties for naval officers visiting Hobart than to attend the twice monthly literary gatherings at Government House hosted by Teresa Hamilton and for which she chose the subjects and the speakers; each member was expected to give a paper which the others then discussed – for 'mutual pleasure and intellectual profit'.

Ethel, 23 years old, the main culprit, wrote a letter of so-called apology for her absence. What she said is not recorded, but **Sarah Thompson Walker** (1849–1905, daughter of Quaker Sarah Benson Mather Walker, takes up the story; she is not on Teresa's side, the Walkers, sister and brother, having come up against her bossiness when she served on the Council of the Hobart Ladies' College in which they were involved. Sarah was a teacher there before she set up her own school in 1892. She had been asked to join the literary group and commented 'I suppose I'd better'; she had presented a paper on trade unions. The Miss Patty she mentions is **Patty Mault**, to be known as a fine lacemaker. And Maud Montgomery we already know. Sarah wrote to her sister:

> There is a grand quarrel between Lady H and the Dobsons ... Ethel wrote a note to the secretary of the Literary which her Excellency considered insulting but which Miss Patty says was an ordinary note of apology. Her Ladyship wrote demanding her resignation. Ethel replied saying if it was as her guest of course she would but if as a member of the Club she did not see that she had done anything to require it of her. The whole matter is to come up at the next meeting. Miss Patty and some others are going to resign if Lady H persists in her present course. Miss P is vice president and her main stay. Lady H read the note at the previous meeting and wanted the members to expel her. She has been very foolish and undignified I think. The reason I think is first the never friendly feeling between the two families [Dobsons and Hamiltons], secondly that only three members appeared at the previous meeting which made her furious, the members generally wanted to put off the meeting for a time but she said if she could find time to come surely they could. I fancy it was to discourage the rush after officers ... Mrs Montgomery went out and tried to bring about a peace but Lady H does not love Mrs M – she is too independent I think, & she did no good.

Sarah Walker's second letter is even more detailed; although it is rather long, I cannot resist quoting it, too, as did Alison Alexander's mother-in-law, Cynthia Alexander, in 'The Itinerants – a Ladies' Literary Society' (1985) about a society of which she has been a long-time member. The detail does throw an interesting light on the women who attempted to work together in various associations. Sarah continues the saga on 21 February:

> I think I told you that Ethel Dobson had written a letter to the secretary Amy Chapman which Lady H was so angry at that she read it to the meeting & asked them to expel her – the meeting seems to have given a somewhat uncertain sound, at least some of them – others specially Miss Patty and Mrs Montgomery who begged her not to demand her resignation but Her Excellency was obstinate – then followed several letters, Ethel's being evidently the judges [her father's], the general feeling was that Ethel's letter was in bad taste to Lady H. Very *Dobsony* [my italics], you know the manner but that Lady H's course was altogether out of proportion to the offence. Miss Patty had determined to resign in the first meeting but the next meeting was such a scene. Miss Patty, Emily Mac [Maxwell] and Maude M were prepared to resign, the others were all uncertain as to what they should do. The whole afternoon was spent in discussing the affair – they voted on it first. I don't know exactly how the question was put but there were only two out of the whole 17 there for Lady H. Then she told them that she wished all those who thought Ethel had been treated harshly

would resign – that there was pen and paper there and they could do it at once, whereupon ten resigned. Emily Maxwell said she never was present at such a scene, the tension was so extreme – she said the poor young ones went up white & trembling like martyrs to the stake. You know they stand in great awe of Lady H and she has been very kind to some of them – Milly Stephens and May Belstead especially. I did not think either of them could have had the pluck to stand Lady H out to her face, but they went up white & crying. Lucy Hudspeth was trembling all over too – in fact Emily said that she wondered taking mind on these white and anxious faces that Lady H had the heart to hold out but she was furious. Miss Patty said to her Would not her own daughter have gone to her father in a case of the kind, & she said If she had done such a thing 'big as she is I would have her whipped', & Mrs Montgomery said afterwards that she really thought she would have struck Miss Patty in the face she looked so furious. It was rather dreadful was it not?

An interesting aspect of this row is the light it throws, too, on relations between Teresa Hamilton and her stepdaughter. In Anne Weigall's autobiography *My Little World* (1934) she writes, and it is the only mention of Teresa in the book:

In the winter there were informal dances and dinners, and long walks for those who were strong enough to undertake them. My stepmother started a literary club, and a sketching club, and with one thing and another, the years slid pleasantly by.

Eventually the literary storm blew itself out. The Hamiltons left in December 1892 and *Nil Desperandum*, renamed after Teresa as its founder continued and, indeed, flourished. **Amy Chapman** (1862–1942) remained its Secretary and attended every meeting for 50 years, until her death, and the Governors' wives who followed Teresa Hamilton were its patron. Records of the continuing society survive, apart from a gap between 1907 and 1935 when Amy left the minute books on a tram. It continues still.

Amy's mother, **Catherine Chapman** (née Swan) was, as Agnes Morris quotes in *Lady Hamilton's Tasmania* (1966), 'In spite of her imperious manner ... a leader of the women's movements which were a feature of the life of the period.' In another quotation, Mr and Mrs Chapman are described as 'probably the most important political couple in Tasmania in the early years of responsible government'. Thomas Chapman's biographical details tell of his life as a merchant and politician – he was, for example President of the Hobart Branch of the Anti-Transportation League, possibly for humanitarian reasons, was elected to the first House of Assembly, having played a prominent part in its establishment, and was Premier when Amy was born. But all it says of Catherine Chapman, who married him in 1843, is that she had four daughters and six sons, and survived him. She does not appear in accounts of women's activities. Amy Chapman, as Alison Alexander suggests, was the 'Alix' who, following the first meeting of the WSA wrote in her newspaper column that it was bound to succeed, led as it was by 'two such earnest, hardworking, good and clever women as the wives of our Governor and Bishop'. By the third meeting, Teresa was President and Emily Dobson Secretary. When Teresa left, Alix wrote,

> It can never be forgotten ... what time and pains Lady Hamilton has expended in her endeavours to make the women of Tasmania interested in matters relating to the health and comfort of themselves, their families, their dependents and their houses, as well as the research she has initiated into standard works on hygiene.

Women's arrival in the public sphere may not have been appreciated by everyone – there were some snide comments – but, with the setting up of the WSA and its activities, the position of women had changed.

In 1894, the literary rebels formed the Itinerants Ladies' Literary Society, a move that may well have been led by the third member of the WSA triumvirate, Maud Montgomery. **May Dobson** (b1859), Ethel's sister, was a member, but not apparently Ethel herself nor, indeed, another sister, Edith, who had tried to join the Dorcas Society but was deemed too young and unmarried for such work. Other literary members in earlier years included Ida McAulay, whom we shall come across, and Patty Mault, who resigned in 1898 for unspecified reasons. The name came from meetings being held in different members' houses.

A male visitor to Tasmania blogging in 2005 was told that Maud had founded this breakaway Ladies' Literary Society 'in opposition to a similar society run by the governor's wife'. But it was founded some years after Teresa Hamilton's departure, though her successor was probably patron of her original. The blogger continues: 'I'm told that the society still exists but that it is not widely known of because membership can only be inherited by women through their mothers-in-law.' Behind the myth-making, Maud's disciplined approach bore on the standard of papers produced by the Itinerants.

The literary diversion was partly to explain the meaning of 'Dobsony', although Emily Dobson does not appear to have had anything to do with either society, leaving it to her nieces. She was far too busy, and had other fish to fry. It could be said that Emily, Tasmanian born, bred and married, took over where Teresa Hamilton, departing Governor's wife, left off, though obviously with her own agenda.

As Alison Alexander, who does not care for her, sums her up: 'Emily Dobson is the prime example of a confident middle-class woman who had no hesitation in encouraging or even pushing the poor to acquire middle-class virtues like thrift, hard work and sobriety.' And, elsewhere, she suggests that women like Emily 'enjoyed instructing the poor for their own good'.

Emily's granddaughter, rather more impressed by her, tells us that 'It was a family joke that she was president of nearly everything.' The list of all the associations with which she was involved from 1891 until the end of her life, most of which she started, would make impressive, though perhaps tedious, reading here; it was so long that she had a full-time secretary to help her. She was perfectly capable, too, of putting the visiting Prince of Wales in his place during his 1920 visit to Tasmania, and doing the same to Kaiser Wilhelm II when she visited Potsdam. Of course, she was fluent in German, and spoke several other languages, and travelled the world on behalf of her many associations.

The Women's Christian Temperance Union

From 1892, and for the next few years, the WSA was to vie for influence with a new organisation, the Women's Christian Temperance Union (WCTU). This was by no means the first attempt to curb excess drinking, the bane of the new colony. **Sarah Crouch** (née Rothwell, c1805–1876) had been there before. Sarah, from Limehouse, London, had met her husband Thomas Crouch when passing through Hobart as a governess. They married in 1832 and she became involved with the Quakers and various charities. She was active with the Dorcas Society and Caroline Denison's Van Diemen's Land Asylum for prostitutes, as well as visiting female paupers at New Town, Cascades and Brickfields. This may have been, as Miranda Morris suggests, Jane Franklin's committee. The Crouches also founded, in 1833, the first temperance society and Sarah organised a women's petition for a Maine-style liquor law, and another to forestall Sunday licensing. She set up the Gore House Home for Servants which attempted to keep women between jobs from the streets and taverns by providing cheap rooms and respectable company. She also had at least eight children, most of whom died in childhood. She became paralysed in the late 1860s and died in 1876.

In the 1850s, further temperance attempts were made. At that time, there were 180 public houses in Hobart – it is said, one for every 127 inhabitants, men, women and children. In 1885, women were in the forefront of another effort but it faltered. It was not until 1892 and a visit by American **Jessie A Ackermann** (c1857–1951), roving missionary for the United States-based WCTU, and by then inaugural President of the Australasian organisation, that it really took off. Jessie toured Tasmania for four months, lecturing to women-only meetings dressed in Chinese costume. Typical of her views was that of 1894: 'The true dignity of labor is being taught to girls and the world is beginning to look with discredit upon women who hang helplessly on men, instead of doing their own work, and, if necessary, earning their own living.'

The first Tasmanian annual convention of the WCTU was held in 1893, attended by 16 local unions. From then, under its first President, Grace Soltau, the WCTU decided on a campaign to gain women's suffrage as a means to an end – liquor prohibition. It was not pressing for women's rights per se, but political influence was intended to bring about a more compassionate and moral society that would protect helpless women and children. None had the right to be a 'modest violet'. **Ethel Searle**, having already read a paper on women's suffrage in a private house, repeated it at the convention and was elected suffrage superintendent.

Grace Soltau travelled the country talking at branch meetings; she wrote that 'I get many confessions of ignorance and inability [but] I believe our Union is a great education for women with a niche for everyone.' She was only too aware of how campaigning by women had the power to cause upset in the community: 'We will be sure to receive many rebuffs, sneers and incredulity that women will have the courage to continue. Do not be discouraged ... I know some of you are feeling downhearted just now, and wonder if it is worthwhile to go on.'

When Grace left for Sydney in 1894, **Annie Blair** (née Woodhead, b1849; m1872) of Launceston, mother of eight, was surprised to be asked to stand as president, feeling she had no brilliant gifts or educational advantage. Nevertheless, she proved an energetic leader: in 1895, for example, she attended 98 meetings and dealt with a large correspondence. Branches increased to 21 and membership to thousands; coffee booths were set up at shows and regattas, as an alternative to liquor, and petitions were signed. When she resigned in 1898, she claimed there was less prejudice against the Union, and drunkenness had decreased. She felt, however, that more women needed to get involved, criticising those 'satisfied to go to their graves without having made a single creature better or happier outside the narrow circle they called "home" but which is really "self"'. Whatever ups and downs there were in Tasmania, the WCTU was the first national women's organisation.

Women's Suffrage

New political influences were more generally coming to bear in Tasmania in the 1880s and 1890s. Vicky Pearce in '"A Few Viragos on a Stump": The Womanhood suffrage campaign in Tasmania 1880–1920' (1985) explains that 'the laissez-faire liberalism of the oligarchy of land and commerce was coming into conflict with the "new liberalism" of the urban professional class'.

The Better Protection of and Prevention of Cruelty to Children Act came into the political equation in 1895 and, the following year, the Youthful Offenders, Destitute and Neglected Children's Act which established the Neglected Children's Department. In 'State Girls: Their Lives as Apprentices 1896–1935' (1994), Caroline Evans writes from the point of view of the girls caught up in the system devised by the 1896 Act. At the age of 13, most girls at risk were apprenticed by the state as domestic servants, which could include childminding and dairying. Many of them rebelled, and employers often grumbled about their behaviour – almost a re-run of the earlier convict assigned servants.

Caroline Evans tells the story of the child welfare policy in 'Landmarks in Mothering: Tasmanian Child Welfare Legislation 1895–1918' (2006). The WCTU 'campaigned for these laws to bring motherly values to the public sphere'.

Annie Blair deplored 'the wretched homes from which these poor waifs come [where] drunkenness and impurity reign, instead of these poor children being shielded by their parents, they are in many cases driven to sin'. Caroline

Evans explains that the WCTU wanted the vote to deal with issues like these and to end what they considered was the corrupt masculine management of political life.

Into the fray came **Sara Inez Gill** (née Jacobs, b1850), in charge of the *Tasmanian News* since about 1886, the year her sixth and last child was born. Her husband since 1870, Henry Gill, had launched the newspaper in 1883 but when he became more interested in entering parliament himself – he was successful in 1887 – Sara took his place as editor.

Alison Alexander records how Sara 'fought a hard fight against vested interests, and roused public opinion among the working class. She was in favour of female suffrage and sympathetic to the unemployed.' The paper published a series of articles by a 'special reporter' sent on 'a sort of special commission' to find out about juvenile street-vending. Caroline Evans explains how it was discovered often to be a front for prostitution. Alcoholism and laxity of the parents, especially the mothers, were most to blame. The left-leaning *Clipper* argued, however, that the causes were economic.

The WCTU called a meeting to discuss the articles. It was decided that the proposed bill did not go far enough and that representation should be made to the Attorney General. A week later the WCTU held a second meeting but it was upstaged by one called by Sara Gill and dominated by the Women's Sanitary Association. The WCTU meeting adjourned to join it. Emily Dobson was in the chair and Maud Montgomery gave the address. Further cooperation was not helped by Emily Dobson who was supportive neither of women's franchise nor of temperance. That clash of meeting times is as indicative as anything else of underlying tensions. Certainly Sara Gill had supported the WCTU, as had the monthly Temperance paper *People's Friend*, whose editor's wife, **Mrs L Lodge**, was an executive member of the WCTU.

Members of the WCTU had spent months reading up on the suffrage issue to prepare themselves for a bill introduced in 1895, and organised a number of meetings to support it. But it lapsed. The following year, opposition to granting votes to women was voiced in both parliament and the press. A campaign of petitioning for and against was waged in 1896 and 1897. The columnist Alix thought, as Alison Alexander paraphrases, that 'most women were indifferent to suffrage, federation, and most of the questions of the day, despite societies trying to interest them. Why? Was it the fault of family, education, or the enervating climate? Tasmanian women were more eager to be emancipated by the bicycle than by voting.' Alix had been against suffrage but later changed her mind; she did think, though, that it was a pity it was allied to temperance.

By 1896, **Jessie Spink Rooke** (née Walker, 1845–1906), born in London, in Melbourne by 1867, in Tasmania with her second husband by the early 'nineties, was president of the Burnie WCTU, in northern Tasmania. Though fragile in health, she travelled widely in the winter of that year, a journey of 200 miles by draughty train and rickety coach. She was accompanied by the suffrage superintendent (from 1895), member of the Campbell Town WCTU, **Georgiana Kermode** (née Fawns, m1885; d1923), wife of a wealthy landowner, whose family and friends opposed her activities. Large gatherings of women, and some men, greeted them to learn that 'the Franchise should be extended to women as an act of common justice'. At one lecture, challenged by a doctor that women were not as intelligent as men because their brains were smaller, Jessie retorted that it was the quality of the brain that counted, not the quantity. By the end of their tour, thousands had signed their petition and campaign funds had swelled. Jessie became President of Tasmania's WCTU in 1898; by then she was known as 'a lady of enormous debating power', and the best-known Tasmanian suffragist.

20.   Jessie Rooke, from *White Ribbon Signal*, journal of the
Women's Christian Temperance Union of New South Wales,
February 1906, courtesy of the Tasmanian Archive and
Heritage Office

The influence of individual women's groups such as the WCTU was both weakened and strengthened by the formation in 1899 of the Tasmanian branch of the National Council of Women (NCW). Beguiled by the Countess of Aberdeen, international President, **Emma Dodds** (née Norman, m1867), wife of Tasmania's Administrator in between Governors, organised an inaugural meeting in May. Emily finger-in-every-pie Dobson, who did not support women's suffrage, was on the committee. As she put it: 'such a meeting, composed of earnest, thoughtful women ... must result in good'.

Emily became Vice President in 1900, and President in 1904, a position she held for the next 30 years, until her death. In 1906, she became President of the Australian NCW, also till her death – enabling her to travel the world networking (at her own expense). How she became national President was described as 'a bit of a scramble' for it, including crossing-out of minutes, 'foolish bickering' and a public accusation that she exercised autocratic power. In 1906, she was accused of tampering with reports. She was also an international Vice President.

The NCW flourished, becoming an umbrella for 33 women's organisations in Tasmania. **Caroline Morton** (née Mills, 1857–1933; m1884) who, instead of Amy Chapman, may have been the columnist Alix, encapsulated its purpose in 1904: 'Wherever there is a little child neglected, a home comfortless, a girl astray, a man inebriated, a city insanitary, a mind left uncultivated, a willing hand left idle for the want of hiring, there is need for the National Council of Women.' The Labor press criticised it for its 'ignorant and harmful twaddle ... vapid and malicious foolishness'. When in 1910 Emily Dobson appealed for a crusade to stop immorality, she was accused of 'impertinence' and 'the cool assumption that immorality only exists in the ranks of the workers and artisans'. Though it may have been Emily's energy that kept the NCW going, she was President of many of the affiliated societies which made it difficult for them to withdraw. In 1919 The Tasmanian NCW established the Emily Dobson Philanthropic Prize for welfare organisations.

The WCTU was only one of many under the NCW umbrella – its pre-eminence among women's groups declined, though initially Mrs L Lodge was on the NCW executive committee, and it never did succeed in its temperance aim. Nevertheless, as Wendy Rimon puts it on the useful Tasmanian government website devoted to women's affairs, 'It had demonstrated that women could speak in public, run an organisation efficiently, maintain international links and put forward views that challenged authority.'

There was a certain irony in an attempt by the WCTU to re-arouse interest in women's suffrage in 1903. Few attended the public lecture given to the National Council of Women by Jessie Rooke and **Josephine Mercer** (née Archdall, 1852–1907), wife of the Anglican Bishop who took over from Montgomery in 1902.

Not long after the lecture, in spite of the 'giddy old roosters' in the Legislative Council, the Electoral Act of 1903 was passed, granting women the vote by changing the eligibility criterion in the 1900 Electoral Act from man to person. Women became eligible to vote in 1904. It would be nice to think that the Act was the result of the suffrage campaign but, after the Australian federal franchise was granted in 1902 (following the federation of six self-governing British colonies in 1901), it was necessary to avoid an electoral anomaly.

The intricacies of the campaign over the years of extending the vote, not just to women but also to formerly disenfranchised men, are accessible in a chapter on Tasmania in Audrey Oldfield's *Women's Suffrage in Australia: A Gift or a Struggle* (1992). One problem that emerged in the proposal to extend the property qualification, for example, was the enfranchisement of propertied prostitutes, while upper-class women who respectably looked after their families would lose out.

Jessie Rooke, still President of the WCTU in 1903, formed the Women's Suffrage Association (WSA) to mobilise women for the coming federal election. When the state vote was conceded, its name was changed to the Women's Political Association (WPA) and it looked forward as well to the Tasmanian House of Assembly elections in 1906. Voting in Legislative Council elections came much later, as did women standing for election. The aim of the WPA was to educate women in their electoral duties and encourage registration by holding meetings, at which candidates could put forward policies, and mock elections. That same year, Jessie became President of the Australian WCTU, though the WPA, with a new, mainly middle-class membership, was entirely separate in its aims. It is not clear if Jessie was involved with the association until her death in 1906.

From Suffrage to Politics

Apparently taking over early as President from Jessie, or President of the WPA from the start, was **Ida McAulay** (née Butler, 1858–1949), prominent in the Itinerants' Literary Society. She was also prominent in Hobart society as the daughter of a solicitor and wife, since 1895, of a mathematician and physicist at the newly-established University of Tasmania, though she must, as a self-confessed feminist, be considered on her own merits, which were many.

Ida had represented the Itinerants at a meeting of three literary groups on women's suffrage in 1899. She noted that she was the only one of her group in favour and was surprised that 'so intelligent a group of women should ... help to block one of the paths to upward mobility of themselves and their sisters'. For her, 'a woman's sphere is just what she chooses to make it'. She was also concerned that necessary social reform be achieved through women's suffrage, should include divorce and custody of children. Her handwritten 1899 paper on suffrage is preserved in the archives.

Another paper on education asserted the intellectual ability of women and extolled the study of science and mathematics. She rejected the argument of intrinsic differences in 'the mind-stuff of the sexes'. She also supported sex education and the need for women to restrict the size of their families; she had only three children, two of them probably twins. She was by no means against motherhood but believed that girls should be trained for it; she outlined an extensive curriculum, including physiology, hygiene, first aid, nursing, cookery and domestic economy.

Ironically, when the New Educationalists introduced the extension of state schooling beyond primary years in 1913, and 113 girls enrolled in the two high schools, only two of them elected to take the domestic science course offering studies in chemistry, cookery, laundry work, dressmaking, sanitary science and hygiene; and in the first seven years, only 31 girls chose that preparation for their later life. The commercial course was the most popular that first year. In due course, domestic science became compulsory. Ida McAulay's opinion of whether or not the course incorporated sufficient of her proposal does not seem to have been recorded. Ida was not all intellect: she was also a good shot with a rifle and formed a women's rifle club.

Ida resigned from the WPA on an issue of principle in 1905. Although the organisation was deliberately non-party, in due course it was taken over by Emily Dobson; she then used it to support her husband's right-wing, Liberal political career. Even before then, as soon as women were enfranchised, she canvassed shops and workrooms on his behalf. She was assisted by Amy Chapman and Georgiana Kermode. Henry Dobson was elected to the Federal Senate in 1901 and retired from politics when he was defeated in 1910. Women's issues were, however, central to the WPA, as they were to Emily throughout her activist life and, by the time she died, aged 92, 16 years after Henry, she was known as the 'Grand Old Lady'.

Alicia O'Shea Petersen (1862–1923) joined the WCTU and WSA/WPA in about 1903, at the same time as joining the Workers' Political League (forerunner of Tasmania's Labor party) founded that year by her cousin John Earle. Three years younger than her, they were brought up in an extended Catholic farming family in Bridgewater, north of Hobart. Her father, Hugh McShane, was the brother of John's mother, **Ann Teresa McShane** (b1834).

John Earle went into mining and then into union politics; Alicia, as a young woman, became a machinist in the notorious sweated-labour clothing industry. That seems only to have lasted until her marriage, aged 22, to draper and widower Patrick O'Shea. She was left widowed, with a stepson, in 1886, and remarried in 1891 Hjalma Petersen, a mining investor from Sweden. She was widowed again in 1912. But before that, obviously not forgetting her youthful employment and, it is suggested, influenced by her cousin, later the first Labor Premier (1909, 1914), she began her political activities.

In 1903, she wrote an open letter to the press offering herself as a senate candidate in the federal election, the first in which all Australian women, except Aborigines in some states, were able to vote and stand, and in which there were four women from other states standing. Alicia set out her policies: she favoured old age pensions, equal pay for equal work and arbitration to prevent strikes. She added that 'I will ask no favour for a woman that I am not prepared to give to a man.' What persuaded Alicia to change her mind is not recorded but, within a week of her announcement, she had withdrawn her candidacy. Nevertheless, she remained active throughout the election campaign.

By 1906, an issue of which she had personal experience had come to the fore. Former convicts and women immigrants had gained employment as seamstresses – an activity made somewhat easier and faster when the first sewing machines appeared in the 1860s. By the 1880s, clothing factories were common and factory owners preferred women employees; they could be paid less than men and the machines did not require undue strength. The 1881 census lists 1,273 women working in industry and the 1911 one, 2,548;

90 per cent were in clothing. The regulations for improvement of conditions in the 1884 Factory Act were not enforced. In 1894, the *Clipper* reported that dressmaking was 'the most wretchedly paid of all', with long hours and hard work.

In 1902, the WCTU asked for women factory inspectors to enforce legislation. The proposal was adopted to the extent that Nurse **Ethel Keach** (b1864) was appointed in 1903, resulting in a few improvements. But in 1906, the case of **Olive Coulson** (1889–1906) surfaced. The 16-year-old was employed as a cashier handling large sums of money, 300 times her weekly salary of only £20 a year. She stole money from her employer, confessed, was dismissed and, from shame, committed suicide. A jury said her salary was scandalously low. Olive's case was the spur to the infant Labor party, led by John Earle, campaigning for a royal commission into the working conditions and wages of workers, including what was known as 'sweating' or 'sweated labour'.

During that 1906 campaign, Alicia O'Shea Petersen spoke on behalf of the Citizens' Social and Moral Reform League established by Josephine Mercer's husband, the Bishop by then becoming notorious as a Christian Socialist. He described conditions for women as 'little less than slow murder'. A royal commission was set up in 1907 and the evidence it collected, particularly about prominent Hobart citizens, was so damning that the report was suppressed. Alison Alexander tells how, in spite of the cover-up, a Wages Board Act of 1910 established boards for individual crafts to fix minimum rates of pay and maximum hours. A new Factories Act was enacted the same year requiring a complete registration and inspection of factories, but, as the entry for 'sweating' in the *Companion to Tasmanian History* has it, 'Despite this legislation, sweating took some time to eradicate.'

That is given some support by Jessie A Ackermann in *Australia from a Woman's Point of View* (1913). She visited Australia again in 1910 and worked tirelessly in organisations on the mainland to urge women to exercise their vote until she left for the last time in December 1911. The book, written as a result of her stay, was published two years later, at the same time as *What Women Have Done with the Vote* (1913), which I have not been able to see. She introduces her only comment on Tasmania – a damning one – with a more general conclusion:

> Thousands of women in Australia have been forced into factory work and other toilsome occupations in order to cope with human needs. In some of the States their condition is awful in the extreme. They are being sweated to the very verge of the grave ...
>
> ... In Tasmania, the women engaged in the manufacture of clothing work ten hours a day, and women operators of from three to five years' service, up to twenty-six years of age, receive 12s. a week. The women over there at the present moment are utterly consumed in their 'anti' attitude towards [electoral] candidates, and are spending energy enough in trying to keep the other side out to right every wrong and relieve the shocking

oppression from which they and their families reap the benefit of cheap labour. Women citizens who could right such wrongs, who refuse to rescue helpless women from the bondage of slavery and outrage, are unworthy of the power which has been placed in their hands, and should be relegated to the ranks from which they were elevated by the franchise. It is nothing but the unspeakable and criminal selfishness of well-to-do women that makes such a state of affairs possible.

Jessie's 1913 comments may, of course, have been slightly out of date by then, but you cannot help but surmise that she was referring to Emily Dobson and her kind.

I have been unable to establish a link between Marie Pitt and Alicia O'Shea Petersen and her cousin John Earle, in spite of the fact that Marie's husband was a miner in the eastern mining town of Mathinna, as was John Earle, and Marie herself was involved in mining union politics, and both Alicia and Marie were later to be involved in anti-war activities. I feel there is still one to be found, though sources are unclear about dates.

Marie Pitt (née McKeown, 1869–1948), poet, socialist, feminist, was the daughter of a goldminer in Victoria where, as a small child, she laboured in her parents' smallholding. In 1893, aged 24, she met and married a Tasmanian man from Longford and, for the next twelve years, he mined in various sites to the east and west of the island. In Mathinna, Marie was elected Vice President of the Workers' Political League (p324). Since Earle was a founder of that organisation in Zeehan in 1901, it must have been thereafter. But the Pitts were also involved in the Amalgamated Miners' Association after a branch was set up in Zeehan in the 1890s. Marie was active, too, on behalf of George Burns in Queenstown in the 1903 election when three Labor candidates from mining areas, including him, were elected. Marie's husband, William, was to contract the mining lung-disease phthisis and, as a result, the couple left Tasmania for the mainland in 1905 with their three surviving children. But Marie's experience in Tasmania continued to colour much of her writing, both poetry and prose.

Marie's feminism, too, infused her writing; she believed that miners' wives had it even harder than their husbands. In a newspaper article in 1912 she wrote:

> To those who have always lived outside the 'vicious circle' of a mining town or centre it would be well nigh impossible, humanly speaking, to convey any conception of the sleepless terror of impending evil – the grisly obsession of 'who next' – that tugs at the heart of every woman whose husband, son, brother or lover goes 'below'. Particularly is this so when the body or bodies of someone's breadwinner or winners lies at the changing-house waiting for the packed inquest that formality demands – while the grinding gear moans its incessant dirge, and the siren shrieks at the change of shifts 'more blood!' – 'more blood!'. To the sensitive spectator the whole thing conjures up a vision of the drafting pens of the slaughter yard.

21.   Marie McKeown Pitt (before her marriage),
from Burke, *Doherty's Corner*

Marie's political involvement in Tasmania ended when they left, but she lived with the consequences of their stay and continued to write about it long afterwards. When her husband became ill, she found herself in the same position as many other miners' wives. In Melbourne she struggled by her writing to keep the family's head above water. She finally brought herself to write to the Chairman and Board of Directors of the New Golden Gate Mine, Mathinna, asking for compensation:

> My husband sold to you during the four years that he worked for you, not his time, nor his labour, but his life, his usefulness, his wife and children's future bread and shelter. I appeal to you as men and in the name of justice, remember this when you consider my appeal.

The reply was courteous, but unyielding: 'We have no funds out of which such help could be given ...' It was then that Marie wrote the poem 'The Keening' which first appeared in *Horses of the Hills* (1911); it starts:

> We are the women and children
> Of the men that mined for gold:
> Heavy are we with sorrow,
> Heavy as heart can hold;
> Galled are we with injustice,
> Sick to the soul of loss –
> Husbands and sons and brothers
> Slain for the yellow dross!

William died in 1912. During 17 years, 80 miners who had worked in the Golden Gate Mine died of phthisis. Many of Marie's poems, including 'The Keening', are to be found in Colleen Burke's *Doherty's Corner: The Life and Work of Marie J Pitt* (1985). 'Doherty's Corner' is a poem in which Marie expressed her concern for the environment.

1913 was a key year for Alicia O'Shea Petersen. In the intervening years, she was involved in the formation of the Housewives' Union (1912) as a Labor counterweight to the Ladies' Liberal Association, though committed herself to a non-party stance. The inaugural President of the Housewives' Union was **Alicia Katz** (Alice, née Watkins, 1876–1964) whose militant unionist husband Frederick Katz had been sent to Tasmania to organise the Carters' and Drivers' Union.

For Alicia Katz, the object of the Housewives' Union was to defend Labor principles and fight for the solidarity of the Labor movement, as well as defending women's interests. The Union began with 226 members, but Alison Alexander suggests that, 'For whatever reason once in the union they did little, and there was never any mention ... of defending women's interests or Labor ideals.' However, at the beginning of a strike of the Carters' and Drivers' Union in 1911, Alicia Katz addressed an open air meeting and during the strike organised 300 wives of strikers to march through Hobart under the banner 'Help Us Fight for Our Little Ones'. The strike ended successfully. It is worth noting that working-class women were not yet used to political associating, and they did take advantage of the social side of the union which was a start. The Katzes had to return to Melbourne in 1914 for the sake of their daughter Olive's health, though that was by no means the end of Alicia's political involvement.

Although childless herself, Alicia O'Shea Petersen involved herself in the concerns of mothers and children. In 1908 she and **Frances Edwards** served on a committee to investigate ways of widening the definition of neglect which resulted in the Children's Charter. She also supported the establishment of the Bush Nursing and Child Welfare Association between 1910 and 1914 by the pianist **Sarah Alice Keating** (Lallie, née Monks, 1885–1939). As well as taking the lead in several other organisations, Alicia continued writing to the press and became known for her caustic and witty comments. At some stage, she subscribed to the British Hansard and regularly attended Tasmanian parliamentary sittings.

By 1913 she obviously felt herself more qualified to seek election. She became the first woman to stand for parliament in Tasmania when she contested the federal seat of Denison as an independent. Though her main concern was for women and children, the policies she proposed were much broader; she also revealed that she was a member of the Peace Society, about which I can find no details but which is significant in the light of developments. The press ignored her wider platform and trivialised her candidacy. She was accused of taking funds from both the Labor and National parties who, in turn, brought women organisers from the mainland to campaign against her. There is some evidence, too, that Alicia Katz of the Labor party and Emily Dobson of the Liberal party felt that women's interests could be best served by supporting mainstream parties. Alicia, the candidate, received only 261 of the 17,043 votes polled. I like to imagine the confusion in any organisation in which they were both involved of having two Alicias.

Anti-Conscription and Feminism

The First World War was declared soon afterwards and Alicia O'Shea Petersen was in the forefront of the women's anti-conscription campaign. At that time she may well have fallen out with her cousin and his second wife, **Susanna Jane Earle** (née Blackmore, b1880; m1914), an ardent Labor party supporter but also, like him, committed to conscription. Susanna probably influenced him to espouse the principle of 'equality of sacrifice' – 'In a fight like this,' she declared, 'it should be "one out all out"' – a stand that led him to being expelled from the Labor party, though it was not the end of his political life.

The women's anti-conscription campaign was waged through the Women's Peace Army (1915–1919) established in the offices of the Women's Political Association in Melbourne which **Vida Goldstein** (1869–1949) had formed in 1903, the year when she had, unlike Alicia O'Shea Petersen, gone ahead with her candidature for the Federal Senate elections. She, too, had had her candidacy ridiculed, but polled 51,497 votes. The poem 'Vida Goldstein's Problem', written to explain her defeat and to illustrate that Australians were not ready to vote for a woman, let alone a pretty, well-dressed and highly intelligent one like Vida, starts:

> She was pretty,
> She was fair;
> Tailor-made and
> Debonair
>
> She was clever
> She was bright;
> And her politics
> Were right

And ends:

> For the great Australian nation,
> Though it loves to woo and flirt,
> Will never bend its noodle
> To unmitigated skirt.

Vida's mother was a confirmed suffragist and worker for social reform, and Vida's political career began in about 1890 when she helped her mother collect signatures for a women's suffrage petition. In the 1890s she became involved in the National Anti-Sweating League. Vida stood again for the senate as an independent in 1910 and 1917 when she lost her deposit partly because of her uncompromising position on pacifism.

Two referendums were held in Australia during the war to introduce compulsory conscription, the first in October 1916. Among those most fervently against was, of course, the Women's Peace Army. The poem 'The Blood Vote' was written for an anti-conscription campaign leaflet (banned in some states and handed out by women illegally). The first verse reads:

> Why is your face so white, Mother?
> Why do you choke for breath?
> O, I dreamt in the night, my son,
> That I doomed a man to death.

And two other verses:

> They gave me the ballot paper,
> The grim death-warrant of doom,
> And I smugly sentenced the man to death
> In that dreadful little room.
>
> I put it inside the Box of Blood
> Nor thought of the man I'd slain,
> Till at midnight came like a 'whelming flood
> God's word – and the Brand of Cain.

The referendum was defeated, though both Victoria and Tasmania voted in favour. Tasmania sent 14,025 men to fight in Europe.

In 1917, Vida Goldstein travelled to Tasmania and appeared on an anti-conscription platform with Alicia O'Shea Petersen. The flags there would have been in the feminist colours of purple, green and white and, although it had been banned in 1915 because of its effectiveness, it is hard to imagine that they did not sing 'I Didn't Raise my Son to be a Soldier', made popular on such occasions by the fine contralto voice of the co-founder of the Women's Peace Army, Tasmanian-born **Cecilia John** (1877–1955).

In her early teens, Cecilia had gone from Hobart to Melbourne to study music. In due course she became an early member of Vida Goldstein's Women's Political Association and supported her bid for the Federal Parliament in 1913. The Women's Peace Army, of which Cecilia was Financial Secretary, attracted the more radical of Melbourne's feminists. It called for the abolition of conscription and militarism, for equal rights for women and for the control of production by the people. There is more than one version of the anthem that Cecilia made famous but this is the first verse of that found most easily on the internet.

> I didn't raise my son to be a soldier
> I raised him up to be my pride and joy
> Why should he put a musket to his shoulder
> To kill another mother's darling boy
> Why should he fight in someone else's quarrels
> It's time to throw the sword and gun away.
> There would be no war today
> If the nations all would say
> No I didn't raise my son to be a soldier

Alicia Katz, back in Melbourne, was also a member of the Women's Peace Army. At its September 1915 meeting, she had moved a resolution that governments of the world put an end to bloodshed; women be granted equal political rights with men; and Australian women be given direct representation in the council appointed to consider the terms of peace. It took moral courage for pacifist women like Alicia to air their views, particularly when her husband had been tarred and feathered for his. Post-war, in 1924, she was the first woman candidate to stand for election in the parliament of Victoria; she was unsuccessful and there was no woman in that parliament until 1967.

In Melbourne, too, Marie Pitt had joined the Victoria Socialist party and used her pen for the cause, as well as editing their journal. When war came, her strongest weapon was, once again, her pen; sources do not suggest that she was a member of the Women's Peace Army, though. Her poem, 'Confiteor' (I confess) (1918), is also to be most easily found in Colleen Burke's biography. In it Marie explores the idea that war is caused by the 'piteous greed of men'. A less well-known poem, published in her 1925 collection, is 'The Mercy', in which she questioned the glory of war and attacked what have been called 'the hallowed icons of both Gallipoli and the Anzac'; Sari Baira was the site of a Gallipoli engagement:

> Oh, was it dream or was it trance,
> Or was it I was there
> And saw Hell's host of devils dance
> On bloody Sari Bair?

The 1917 conscription referendum was also defeated. There is said to have been a branch of another pacifist women's organisation in Tasmania – the Sisterhood of International Peace; but I can find no details of membership or activities. It became the Women's International League for Peace and Freedom (WILPF) in 1920 in Tasmania and the rest of Australia following the creation of the international organisation the previous year; Vida Goldstein and Cecilia John travelled for ten weeks to the congress in Zurich that set it up. In 'The Women's International League for Peace and Freedom' (2003), Alison Alexander regrets that she could find no information about WILPF in Tasmania in those early days, except that it was 'active' and that a meeting between it and the National Council of Women and others in 1924 discussed the prevention of the causes of war and the speakers were 'splendidly supported'. But the Tasmanian branch of WILPF was disbanded in 1943; strong opposition to fascism was probably the cause. Quakers, as elsewhere, continued pacifist. WILPF re-emerged in the 1960s, as the chronology at the end of this chapter shows, and played an active part in the Anti-Vietnam War Moratorium of the 1970s, as well as later peace initiatives.

Standing for Election

In 1920, Tasmanian women who had served as nurses in the First World War became eligible to vote in Legislative Council elections. Women became eligible to stand for the House of Assembly and the Legislative Council in February 1922, and three of them did so in elections that year. Alicia O'Shea Petersen stood in June as the candidate for Denison in the House of Assembly but, by then, she was already ill with cancer. She was unable to campaign so placed a notice in the press asking voters to judge her on her 20 years of work. She gained only 0.6 per cent of the vote and died on 22 January the following year. For many years she was forgotten, but is now recognised as a leading feminist activist of her day.

Annette Youl (née Wiggan, 1865–1937; m1891), a farmer's daughter and second wife of the farmer and politician Alfred Youl, stood unsuccessfully for Wilmot. I have yet to find out more about her.

Edith Waterworth (née Hawker, 1873–1957) was the endorsed candidate of the Women's Non-Party League which she had established in 1920, and of which she became President in 1929. The party has been described by Marilyn Lake in *Getting Equal: The History of Australian Feminism* (1999) as one of the post-suffrage organisations 'more consciously concerned to realise the promise of equal citizenship'.

Edith, born in Lancashire, educated in Brisbane whither her family had emigrated, taught in a state school there for 14 years before she married John Newham Waterworth in 1903. Though born in Yorkshire, he had been a tailor in Queenstown, Tasmania, before arriving in Brisbane and becoming a Methodist lay-preacher. The couple moved to Sydney and then Launceston before arriving in Hobart in about 1909. There he unsuccessfully contested the seat of Wilmot in 1909, and Denison in 1912 and 1913 as a Labor candidate. He then withdrew from public life to support Edith in her welfare activities.

From 1911, as a mother of three sons, Edith's only public work appears to have been a column in the *Daily Post* written under the byline 'Hypatia' – an interesting pseudonym which did not suggest much modesty! In her columns, Edith appeared a well-informed Labor sympathiser believing that women had a right to take part in public affairs and work with men. As Alison Alexander puts it, 'More than any other journalist [she] encouraged her readers to expand women's role.'

Caroline Evans notes that Edith was a 'confirmed eugenicist' – fashionable at the time – telling the Chief Secretary in 1914 that it was pointless to spend money on state children while 'outside a perfect army of degenerates is being bred'.

In the 1922 election, standing in Denison, which covered all Hobart, Edith campaigned on rights for deserted wives, and for widows and their children. As a member of the Women's Criminal Law Reform Association, she called for the admission of women to juries, the appointment of women justices, and new procedures to ensure that women had the support of a female companion when they were cross examined. She received 6.5 per cent of the vote. She stood again in 1925, stressing health issues. She also likened the state to a large home which needed both sexes to manage it, and argued that women had a special place in public affairs as guardians of the human race.

Edith is best-known for her work in improving the welfare of women and children. She merits an entry in the *Australian Dictionary of Biography* (by Jill Waters) which notes that she toured Tasmania in 1935, fund-raising for the King George V and Queen Mary maternal and infant welfare appeal on the slogan 'Make Motherhood Worthwhile'. Concerned with the falling birthrate, she appreciated that, to raise the status of motherhood, the position of women in the home had to be improved. In 1937 she convened a state-wide conference aimed at co-ordinating welfare work for women and children; it led to the formation of the Tasmania Council for Mother and Child which she chaired for 18 years. She was also founder and Secretary of the Child Welfare Association (1917). Emily Dobson, not surprisingly, was its first Vice President.

A 2003 review (obtained online from the History Cooperative website) by Naomi Parry of Marilyn Lake's *Getting Equal* is less sanguine about the outcome of the ideology that underpinned these activities; she writes:

I question Lake's notion that the achievement of the post-suffrage feminists was to develop a 'maternalist welfare state'. Lake does not explain how 'maternalism' differs from paternalism. Neither does she consider the dark side of the 'mother-hearted' post-suffrage feminists, who frequently insisted that the state should control the activities and modes of living of lower-class women and their children. In Tasmania crusaders such as Edith Waterworth (whom Lake mentions) saved lives with campaigns for pure milk and baby clinics. However, Waterworth also asked that clinics have the power to force inspections of mothers' homes if babies failed to thrive. When confronted by women and children suffering venereal disease she could be vicious, and her target was *not* the men who had infected them, but the women and children themselves. Waterworth and women's organisations on the left and right of politics also supported Tasmania's Mental Deficiency Act 1920, which segregated certain 'mental' and 'moral' defectives to prevent their reproduction, including promiscuous young girls who were permanently institutionalised.

As a former columnist, Edith Waterworth had good relations with the *Mercury* to which she sent frequent outspoken letters to the editor, earning herself the sobriquet 'Mrs Hot Waterworth'. She was again unsuccessful when, in 1943, she stood for the Legislative Council seat of Hobart. She died aged 84.

There were two other women candidates in the 1925 election: **Enid Lyons** (née Burnell, 1897–1981) and her mother **Eliza Burnell** (née Taggett, 1869–1941, m.1888). What is more, Enid stood against Edith Waterhouse; indeed, Enid's husband, Joseph Lyons, by then Labor Premier of Tasmania, felt the party needed a woman candidate in Denison to draw votes away from Edith, a women's non-party candidate who had polled strongly in the previous election.

Enid was born in a remote timber camp where her father was a sawyer. Eliza Burnell ran a store in Cooee, a small town, now more of a suburb, just to the west of Burnie on the north west coast. When Eliza left for New South Wales for her health , 13-year-old Enid was left to manage the store, the post office and the housework.

Eliza was also a member of the local Workers' Political League, with its debating society and Labor discussion group, probably the one – the Duck River Branch – started by Joe Lyons when he was a school teacher there in 1905. She was certainly friendly with Joe's dressmaker sister **Adeline Lyons** (b1873) and, through her, met Joe; eleven-year-old Enid, who had been made to take elocution lessons, was even brought in to recite in front of the guests at tea. In 1912, while Enid, aged 15, was attending teachers' training college in Hobart, her mother took her to a parliamentary session, and among those who clustered round the Burnell mother and daughters was the 33-year-old parliamentarian Joe Lyons.

During 1913, Enid and her teacher sister **Nell Burnell** (b1894) often went to hear the evening debates. Enid and Joe had immediately become friends and, before her 18th birthday in 1915, they married, in spite of Joe, by then Deputy Leader of the Labor party and Minister for Education in John Earle's government, being accused publicly of cradle-snatching, and Enid feeling the need to convert from Methodism to Catholicism. The couple entered not just into an enduring marriage, but into a political partnership as well, described in Enid's autobiography *So We Take Comfort* (1965). But some details, such as how old Enid was when they met and were attracted to each other, are corrected by Kate White in *A Political Love Story: Joe and Edith Lyons* (1987). Enid admitted in an interview in 1972 that Joe was embarrassed about her age.

22.   Enid Lyons, from Lyons, *Among the Carrion Crows*

In the years that followed, Enid would accompany Joe to Labor conferences. During the war, he was against conscription, and took over from Earle when the Labor party split on the issue in 1916. Sources say that Enid made her first political speech in 1920, but Kate White tells how she made an anti-war motion stronger at a Labor party conference in May 1918. She grew used to addressing political rallies in Joe's place and did his electoral paperwork when he became Premier of Tasmania in 1923.

By the time she stood for election, she was the mother of seven children. Enid, prompted by Joe to stand, protested: 'Can you see me sitting in the House with all the babies? Don't be a lunatic.' He replied: 'But you can't win, you know that. People won't vote for a woman for ages yet. In Denison you can do the campaign and be home every night.'

Enid was number 5 on the Labor ticket, so had, indeed, no hope of winning, but she launched into an active campaign. During it, the children came down with measles, chickenpox, whooping cough and mumps. She was helped at home by **Ada** and a woman with nursing experience. When she was at home, Enid would send her helpers to bed and take over mothering and nursing duties.

But in the north she also had her mother and sisters to rely on, and later one of Joe's sisters. And her mother, as well as Joe, guided her political development and aspiration to be a parliamentarian as well as a mother; Eliza was one of the first women appointed Justice of the Peace – ironically, a campaign demand of Edith Waterworth in 1922. By her appointment in 1924 Eliza seems to have been head teacher of Burnie High School, though it is not clear how she made the transition from shopkeeper.

Giving a speech on a platform of Labor candidates in the Prince of Wales Theatre, Hobart, in June 1925, Enid asserted, as the *Mercury* reported, that she was not there as a woman, 'but as a Labor candidate with the men'. The report continued: 'She had been asked whether she thought it a fair thing that she, a woman whose husband was premier of the state and getting a good "screw", should try and get into Parliament and keep a man out of a job.' She retorted that,

> If being a member of Parliament had developed in that sort of way no wonder they witnessed the disgraceful things they did in Parliament. If people got into Parliament because they were at a loose end, it was indeed bad for the state ... no one asked Mr McPhee (the opposition leader) and other Parliamentarians why they wanted 300 pounds a year, and why they should ask her she could not understand. She was afraid that was the introduction of the sex issue in politics, and she scorned that.

Enid also mentioned a letter to the *Mercury* that criticised Joe for permitting his wife to stand for parliament. 'Permitted his wife to stand', she repeated sarcastically. 'I am in the proud position of having a husband who realizes that his wife and other women in the community have equal civil rights with himself and other men.' Although Enid was eliminated after the primaries, her votes went to the other Labor candidates and enabled Labor to win four out of six seats in Denison. Any joy in the family fled with the death from pneumonia of ten-month-old Garnett, their sixth child, a few months later. An anonymous letter accused Enid of 'killing my baby with neglect'.

Between entry into parliament in 1909 and 1922, Joe had described himself as a Socialist. Now, he and Enid started to move towards the right in acknowledgement of a conservative electorate. Or, as Enid put it, 'The wild Irishman I had married had mellowed with the years.' Joe's minority government of 1923 had Nationalist support; and it was returned in 1925 and 1928. He won a federal seat in 1929 and, in 1931, formally changed political sides – to the Australia United Party (AUP) of which he became parliamentary leader and, following the election in which the AUP defeated the Labor government of which he had been a member, formed an AUP government. A man wrote to Enid of the switch that it was 'just about the lowest thing anyone could do'.

Joe wrote to Enid of his success: 'Whatever honours or distinctions come are ours, not mine.' He was Prime Minister of Australia from 1932, with Enid very much at his side in Canberra and travelling the world. They attended the coronation of George VI in 1937 and Enid was made a Dame. The following year was the 150th anniversary of British settlement of Australia, known as the sesquicentennial. A women's conference, with the theme 'This Changing

World', was held to mark it and, among other women from the Australian women's movement, Dame Enid Lyons addressed it on 'The Mother and the Modern World'. Edith Waterworth moved the vote of thanks.

Neither the general colonial grovelling around the sesquicentennial celebrations nor the 'suffocating suburban respectability' of the feminist movement went down well with **Miles Franklin** (1879–1954), whose auto-biographical novel *My Brilliant Career* had brought her to public attention in 1901, and whose major literary success, *All That Swagger*, had been published in 1936. Enid Lyons at the conference seems to have epitomised everything she abhorred. Quoted by Marilyn Lake, Miles Franklin described Enid thus:

> A neat face spoiled by fat. She has no depth or originality but is a smart politician – just that ... She talked and talked for an hour or more, on and on, and blew over it a vast wheeze from the bellows of motherhood ... Other women condemned as freaks and perverts have gone before and made it possible for her thus to air herself on the public platform.

As for the fat face, Faye Gardem tells us in 'Dame Enid Lyons – A Lady with Style' (1996) that Enid, by her own admission, 'regretted her matronly figure, and dressed to please her husband, who preferred a dress style which did not emphasise the difference in their ages'. And her ability to take exercise was reduced by the continuing effects of a pelvis broken at the time of her first confinement.

Ground down by the dissension around him in government, Joe died in office in 1939. Enid was left a widow, aged 41, with eleven children ranging in age from five to 23. She appeared to retire from the political scene to the family property, Home Hill in Devonport in north west Tasmania, which she bequeathed to the state and which is now a National Trust public museum ('North West Coast' itinerary, p386). But in 1943 one of her daughters persuaded her to stand as a candidate for election to the Federal House of Representatives and, as her husband's widow, the AUP gave her preference. She won the seat of Darwin for them, becoming not just the first Tasmanian woman to enter parliament, but the first woman to enter any Australian lower house; Dorothy Tangye entered the Australian Senate at the same time.

In her maiden speech Enid acknowledged the moment: 'This is the first occasion on which a woman has addressed this house. For that reason, it's an occasion which for every woman in the Commonwealth marks in some degree a turning point in history.' A former Prime Minister described her as 'a bird of paradise among the carrion crows', and she told the story of the eight years of her parliamentary life in *Among the Carrion Crows* (1972).

The fairly detailed overview of Tasmanian women's history contained in these chapters comes to a natural end with the inter-war work of Edith Waterworth and her contemporaries and the election of Enid Lyons in 1943. What I hope is a useful addition is the chronological list that follows of milestones that include a new cause for pacifist activism in the 1960s, the second wave of feminism in the early 1970s at the same time as the

230 Women's History Part Four – 1847–2010

re-emergence of Tasmanian Aborigines, and the leading role of women in the environmental movement. The first Green party in the world was in Tasmania.

Chronology 1948–2010

1948   **Margaret McIntyre** (1886–1948) – first woman Member of Parliament in Tasmania; elected as independent for the seat of Cornwall in the Legislative Council in May, by male voters and female nurses; killed in a car accident in September.

1949   **Dorothy Edwards** (1907–) – first woman elected to Launceston City Council.

1949   **Enid Lyons** – first woman to hold cabinet rank in Federal Parliament. Cape Barren Island Reserve closed; some islanders forcibly removed; welfare authorities took children into care = 'Stolen Children'.

1952   **Mabel Miller** (1906–1978) – first woman member of Hobart City Council.

1954   Spouses of property owners eligible to vote in Legislative Council elections.

1955   **Amelia Best** (Millie, 1900–1979) – one of first two women elected, as Liberal for Wilmot, to Tasmanian House of Assembly; with Mabel Miller (Liberal, Franklin).

1959   **Enid Campbell** – first woman lecturer in Law School, University of Tasmania (the first woman to graduate from Law School was **Helen Ida Dunbar** in 1931).

1962   **Lynda Heaven** (1902–1987) – first Labor woman member of House of Assembly; she was also the first woman to sit on a jury, in 1939. All Aborigines entitled to vote in Commonwealth elections.

1963   **Dr Mildred Thynne** (1888–1978) organised a meeting that led to the re-emergence of the Women's International League for Peace and Freedom (WILPF); **Dr Edith Emery** became first President; Lynda Heaven was also a founder member.

1964–66   Tasmanian women start to campaign against the Vietnam War: 1964, **Marie Lamp** (née Kaiser, 1927–1995) organised an open meeting in Launceston; 1966, **Barbara Bound** (née Dawson, 1936–2006) as Secretary of the Tasmanian Union of Australian Women, organised Hobart's first demonstration; **Bronwen Meredith** (1919–) played a major role in organising the WILPF's first vigil against Australian involvement in Vietnam War and conscription.

1967   Disastrous fire which killed 62 in the Hobart area.

1968   **Phyllis Benjamin** (1907–1996) – first woman in Australia to lead an upper house (she became a Labor member of the Legislative Council for Hobart in 1952 and was the longest-serving woman politician in Australian political history).

1969   **Kath Venn** (1926–) – first woman State Secretary of a major Australian political party (Labor); (she took over Phyllis Benjamin's Legislative Council seat in 1976).

1970   Vietnam War Moratorium demonstration, leading to continuing Moratorium against the war; the WILPF and other women active – Bronwen Meredith (WILPF Secretary) Barbara Bound (member of the Communist Party of Australia), Marie Lamp (President of Labor Women's Group), **Margot Roe** (1932–) (later President of the WILPF), **Lesley Alcorso**, **Jean Perkins** (1911–2004), **Austra Maddox** (1945–) (in 1993, first woman President of the Tasmanian Trades and Labour Council), and **Bertha Rolls** of Amnesty International.

1970   Tasmanian University Union Women's Liberation (student group); beginning of second-wave feminist movement in Tasmania.

1972   Hobart Women's Action Group (HWAG) – academics, University of Tasmania.

1972   Women's Electoral Lobby (WEL) established.

1972   Lake Pedder became Serpentine (hydro-electric) Dam, in southwest wilderness area in spite of campaign by Lake Pedder Action Committee (LPAC) – beginning of environmental movement.

1972   United Tasmania Group formed at LPAC meeting to contest 1972 election – first Green party in the world; lasted five years.

1972   **Brenda Hean** (1910–1972) of LPAC and pilot disappeared on lobbying flight to Canberra; mystery remains.

1973   Aboriginal legal service established as part of Tasmanian Information Centre in Hobart and Launceston.

1976   To mark the centenary of Trukanini's death, her remains, after a campaign, were removed from the vaults of the Tasmanian Museum and Art Gallery, cremated and scattered in the d'Entrecasteaux Channel.

1976   Formation of Tasmanian Wilderness Society which, with other groups, campaigned between 1978 and 1983 against the proposed hydro-electric scheme on the Franklin River, changing the face of politics.

1977   Formalisation of the Tasmanian Aboriginal Centre (TAC); Ida West (p121) active in Aboriginal politics in 1970s and President of TAC; **Ros Langford,** Secretary.

1980   **Gillian James** (Gill) (elected House of Assembly 1976) appointed first woman minister (Labor).

1986   **Doon Kennedy**, first woman Lord Mayor of Hobart (until 1996).

1989–95   Members of Tasmanian Green party elected, including **Christine Milne** (1953–), a 'housewife' who campaigned against proposed Wesley Vale Pulp Mill, and **Di Hollister** (Dianne, 1947–). Greens held the balance of power (see *The Rest of the World is Watching Us: Tasmania and the Greens* (edited by Cassandra Pybus and Richard Flanagan, 1990).

1991	Jury Amendment of 1990 received Royal Assent creating equality for women with men after a long campaign which included Lynda Heaven and her granddaughter **Robyn Hagen.**
1993	Christine Milne became leader of Green Party, first woman to lead a political party in Tasmania. **Peg Putt** (Margaret, 1953–), spokesperson for Huon Protection Group, elected. When, in 1998, seats were reduced, she was the only Green elected.
1994	Sex Discrimination Act.
1995	Aboriginal Lands Act which acknowledged the dispossession of Tasmanian Aborigines and recognised certain rights. Twelve parcels of land, including Oyster Cove, Risdon Cove, Wybalenna and parts of Cape Barren Island, to be returned and governed by an elected Aboriginal Land Council.
1996	**Lara Giddings** (Larissa) aged 23, youngest woman elected to an Australian Parliament.
1997	'Bringing Them Home' report on Australia's 'Stolen Children'. 1998, the report made accessible in book form: *The Stolen Children: Their Stories* by Carmel Bird.
1997	**Annette Peardon** (1949–), 'stolen' aged nine, addressed House of Assembly (first member of the public) when parliament apologised to the Stolen Generations.
1999	Certain Aboriginal lands, such as Oyster Cove and Risdon Cove, declared indigenous protected areas.
1999	Establishment of not-for-profit Female Factory Historic Site Ltd.
1999	**Sue Napier** (Suzanne) became first woman to lead the Liberal party.
2002	**Kathryn Hay** (1975–), Western Australian Aborigine, elected to Tasmanian House of Assembly (first woman of Aboriginal descent).
2002	Start of campaign to preserve the French Garden at Recherche Bay from logging.
2003	Centenary of Tasmanian women's suffrage celebrated.
2003	**Janie Dickenson,** youngest woman in Australian history to be a city Mayor (Launceston).
2004	Christine Milne elected to represent Tasmania in Federal Senate.
2006	Stolen Generation of Aboriginal Children Act.
2008	106 Aborigines to share $5 million scheme to compensate state's Stolen Generations.
2008	**Cassy O'Connor** of Save Ralph's Bay campaign elected as Green on retirement of Peg Putt.
2009	Female Factory Historic Site handed over to people of Tasmania.
2009	Australian government apology to British migrant children.
2010	Following House of Assembly elections, Green Party Cassy O'Connor is Cabinet Secretary in Labor administration and Lara Giddings, deputy premier since 2008, is Attorney General.
2010	Population of Tasmania 500,000.
2010	**Julia Gillard** becomes first woman Prime Minister of Australia.

Women's Places
(Itineraries)

14 – Around and About Macquarie Street (Hobart)

This itinerary should start at the Cascades Female Factory ruins at the western end of Macquarie Street if historical significance were the criterion, but it is quite a way from the centre of town – all right for the keen walker, but more comfortable by transport. For convenience I am, therefore, beginning at the more central east end of Macquarie Street, or just to the north of it, at the Theatre Royal – an extraordinary contrast to the former women's prison, though their starting dates, 1828 and 1834, are not so far apart. Let the theatre be an overture to the itinerary, and the Female Factory its climax.

The itinerary includes only those women's sites connected with my historical overview; for reasons of length, I have had to leave out some places I had planned to include. Different but rewarding 'places' books are Lindy Scripps' *Women's Sites and Lives in Hobart* (2000) and the allied *In Her Stride: Women's History Walk* (1997), for which Miranda Morris drew on Lindy's research. I bought them from the City Council customer counter (corner of Elizabeth and Davey Streets).

Theatre Royal – 29 Campbell Street

From Macquarie Street, the bijou theatre, easily identified not only by its boldly painted name but by its columns, is on your right, a short walk up Campbell Street. What prompted its creation, the spectacular ceremony when its foundation stone was laid in 1834, its opening in 1837, and the varied nature of its early audience, are featured in Chapter 9 (p135). In a not-too-salubrious neighbourhood, it then resembled a two-storey Georgian house. It has had several expansions since, a major one in the early 1900s, but still manages to convey intimacy; and it has been threatened with destruction more than once. In 1948 those threats were brought to an end by a campaign to save it by Vivien Leigh and Laurence Oliver, then touring with the Old Vic, but it was damaged by fire in 1984; restored to its 1911 designs, it was reopened in 1987.

That there should be women actors, singers and playwrights associated with the theatre is not surprising; what is more unusual was the influence of **Anne Clarke** (née Remans, bc1806) as manager; indeed, it is largely to her credit that women played the part they did in the theatre's success.

Anne Remans arrived in Hobart from England as an assisted immigrant in 1834 and was successful as a singer/actor, often in 'pants' parts; for example, Captain Macheath in *The Beggar's Opera*. Later that year she married widower Michael Clarke and, between 1837 and 1839, she performed in Sydney. Back in Hobart in 1840, she took over the management of what was then called the Royal Victoria Theatre – the first woman in Australia to manage a theatre for a significant period – and also played most of the female parts. It was the shortage of women actors that, it is assumed, took her to England in 1841 to recruit. She returned with several actors, singers and dancers, including **Theodosia Stirling** (née Yates, 1815–1904) and **Emma Howson** (née Richardson) and her husband Frank.

Emma's daughter, also called **Emma Howson** (1844–1928) had great success as a singer abroad, but Nicole Anae shows in '"The New Prima Donnas": "Homegrown" Tasmania "Stars" of the 1860s, Emma and Clelia Howson' (2005), how important to Tasmanian identity were Tasmanian-born young Emma and her actor sister **Clelia Howson** (bc1845).

23.   Amy Sherwin, from Bowler, *Amy Sherwin*

Nicole Anae also wrote: 'Were it not for the enterprise of Anne Clarke, Tasmania might never have produced such a vital collection of theatre women.' Under Anne's management, too, the first Australian production of Mozart's *The Marriage of Figaro* was performed in 1845. In spite of her efforts, however, houses were generally poor and, after estrangement from her husband, named as the lessee of the theatre in about 1847, Anne Clarke disappeared from view.

Opera has had many successful manifestations in the theatre. **Marie Carandini** (née Burgess, 1826–1894), 'the Australian Jenny Lind', arrived with her parents, as assisted immigrants, in 1833, married at 17 one of Anne Clarke's recruits, Jerome Carandini, Italian revolutionary exile and tenth Marquis of Sarzano, and made her professional debut there in 1842. As a girl, as Marie Burgess, she had sung before Jane Franklin and the Governor and, later, her five daughters toured with her and had successful singing careers – particularly the eldest, **Rosina Carandini** (1844–1932, later Palmer); the actor Christopher Lee is Marie's great grandson.

Amy Sherwin (1855–1935), 'The Tasmanian Nightingale', made her professional debut at the theatre in *Don Pasquale* in 1878 (p242). **Lucy Benson** (née Westbrook, 1860–1943; m1881), child prodigy, all-round musician, theatre entrepreneur and mother of six singers, was Amy's voice coach and was, perhaps, the first woman conductor of opera in Australia. Clara Butt sang, as did Victoria de Los Angeles and Leontyne Price. Other international theatrical performers have included Marie Tempest, Jessie Matthews, Lillian Gish, Sybil Thorndike and Margaret Rutherford.

In 1908, then aged 13, the actor later renamed Louise Lovely by Hollywood, played Lady Isobel Vane in *East Lynne*, a stage adaptation of Mrs Henry (Ellen) Wood's novel. Louise's last film was premiered there 17 years later. She is better remembered at 87 Macquarie Street (p239). **Olive Wilton** (c1883–1971), founder of the Hobart Repertory Theatre Society in 1926, promoted women playwrights. Her first production at the theatre, in 1927, was Madeleine Lucette Ryley's romantic comedy *Mice and Men* (1903) and she produced the convict play *Daybreak* by **Catherine Shepherd** (1902–1976) in 1938, and *Jane, My Love*, about Jane Franklin, in 1951 (pp69, 149, 155).

Royal Hobart Hospital

Across from the Theatre Royal, facing onto Liverpool Street, is the Royal Hobart Hospital. There is nothing there, except the site, to remind you of days gone by; you need to use your imagination. In 1805, it was the site of the Sullivans Cove Hospital – a tent (p237). The most evocative descriptions of what went on there in the 1840s come in Oliné Keese' (Caroline Leakey's) *The Broad Arrow*. Our heroine, Maida Gwynnham, is taken for a second time to the hospital and 'consigned to the good kind Mrs Cott'. Knowing how Caroline worked, this is probably **Eleanor Scott** (1809–1846) who arrived in Tasmania from Ireland with her parents in 1833 and who, in 1837, married James Fitzgerald. When he became superintendent of the Colonial Hospital, Eleanor was appointed matron – what training she had is not clear. The convict artist Thomas Wainewright who worked as a hospital orderly and was helped by the Fitzgeralds, painted portraits of most of the Scott family, but only that of Eleanor's sister, **Jane Scott** (1826–1909), seems to have survived, in the Australian National Gallery, Canberra (and on the internet). Eleanor died aged only 37 and was buried in St David's Cemetery (p247).

But it is not Matron Cott/Scott who looks after Maida: she is put in the hands of the drunken, vicious, corrupt convict nurse whom she has come across before and whom she calls 'the Excrescence'. Their relationship does not improve, and the care Maida receives does not do credit to the hospital. Trained nurses were not employed until 1876.

It was here that convict Margaret Morgan, who ended up in the Macquarie Harbour penal settlement, failed to do her duty in 1821 and was punished by six hours in the stocks (p60).

In July 1871, 52-year-old Mary Ann Cochrane Arthur (pp119, 182, 187) had an 'apoplectic fit' at Oyster Cove where only she and Trukanini of the Aborigines remained, looked after by Matilda and John Dandridge (p192). Paralysis set in and she was transferred at once to the Colonial Hospital. The *Mercury* reported on the 25th:

> The day was wet but not stormy and Mr & Mrs Dandridge left the cove with her in an open boat about half past nine o'clock; the voyage, therefore, occupied about twelve hours. It rained all the while; but as soon as the boat reached the wharf a cab was procured, the sick woman placed in it with her two guardians and friends. Being a heavy woman she was got into the hospital with some difficulty, and stimulants were at once administered.

The following day, the *Mercury*, announcing Mary Ann's death, ended its report:

> Mrs Dandridge had sat with her by her bedside the greater part of the previous night and throughout the day. She was at the side of the poor creature to the last, when the vital spark was extinguished, and her presence was evidently grateful and soothing to the dying woman.

Catherine Kearney's Dairy

In Collins Street, behind the hospital and parallel to Liverpool Street, abutting Market Place, is the site of Catherine Kearney's dairy. Stop there, in front of the russet Agricultural Bank building, if it is still standing; when I saw it, guided by Irene Schaffer's careful historical digging, it was in a bad way, with broken and boarded up windows. It was from here, from 1808, that Catherine supplied milk from 7am each morning at 6 pence per quart (p39), and where she had her legendary meeting with Elizabeth Macquarie in 1811 or 1821 (pp49–50).

Irene Schaffer's research paper *Catherine Kearney: Dairy Farmer, Hobart Rivulet 1808–1830* (2007; available from Irene) has illustrations of the area at the time – rather different from today. The Hobart Rivulet, from which Catherine's livestock drank, became Collins Street. Catherine, much respected, died at her home there, aged 61, leaving not only her various properties but also her cattle and sheep, her mare Polly, her horse Erin, and a foal to her two sons and grandson (p276).

Louise Lovely

Return now to Macquarie Street. On the corner of Argyle Street is Montgomery's Hotel; in front of it, on Macquarie Street, at your feet, is a 2004 Women's History Walk plaque which reads:

> 87 Macquarie Street. LOUISE LOVELY'S SWEET SHOP. A star of many Hollywood silent movies, Louise was the star and producer of the movie *Jewelled Nights* written by Marie Bjelke-Petersen and filmed in Tasmania.

Louise Lovely (née Nellie Louise Carabasse, 1895–1890) was the first Australian-born actress to succeed in Hollywood, following her marriage in 1912 aged 16. Dropped by the studio in 1918, over a contract dispute after making 24 films, she moved to another and made many more, totalling about 50. Louise and her husband Wilton Welch returned to Australia and, in 1925, she made (raised the finance, wrote the screenplay, co-produced, casted, acted in, co-directed, and edited) the film *Jewelled Nights*.

Alison Alexander tells the story of the making of the film in her biography *Mortal Flame: Marie Bjelke Petersen, Australian Romance Writer 1874–1969* (1994). Tasmanian-born **Marie Bjelke Petersen** (1874–1969) approached Louise with the idea, and much of the film was shot in the mining area of western Tasmania (Waratah and Savage River) where the story of a woman trying to pass as a young man is set. It was Louise's last film and only a few outtakes and stills – several of them in the biography – survive. *Jewelled Nights* is another of those novels one is embarrassed to have rather enjoyed; the same goes for Marie's other Tasmanian novels, very successful in their day and not difficult to find second hand. Don't read them all at once! More digestible is the biography.

Louise remarried in 1930 and she and her husband, theatre manager Bert Cowen, settled in Tasmania. He managed the Prince of Wales Theatre, Hobart, next door to Montgomery's and, until her death, she ran the theatre sweetshop behind where the plaque is placed. The Australian Film Institute awards are unofficially known as 'the Lovelys'.

Ingle Hall

Across Argyle Street from Louise Lovely's plaque is Ingle Hall, probably not known as that in its early days but even today not that different from when Maria Lord held court there from about 1814 to 1823 (pp33, 80), except that it is now the offices of the *Mercury*. The house may have been built by Rebecca Hobbs' husband John Ingle (p16) and he sold it to Edward Lord; or it may have been built by Edward Lord and sold in 1831 to John Ingle. In any case, it is a classified building and a distinct and very visible touch of old Hobart.

Maria seems to have done business from the house, and had and raised several children there, as well as entertaining. But we should imagine her not only as mother of a large brood, entrepreneur, chatelaine and hostess of glittering parties, but also see her leaving in 1823 – her marriage, her business and the highlife apparently over. It was not quite so bad, for Maria Lord was a woman of some character. Behind Ingle Hall is the site of Mary Hayes Stocker's Derwent Hotel (p39).

Tasmanian Museum and Art Gallery

Cross over Macquarie Street to the Museum and Art Gallery, the first part of which was built in 1863, and it abuts older buildings. Before you go upstairs, walk to the back of the lobby and, outside, tucked away to the right, you will see the cottage of the governor's private secretary, built c1813–14 and almost the only survivor of the old government complex, including Government House, in the area now covered by Franklin Square and the Town Hall. It can also be seen less well from Davey Street to the south, between the old Customs House and the museum.

Where the museum is was a low rise covered by tall gums, with a low bluff towards the water's edge. The only remains of that is the bank on which the cottage stands. The beach curved round to what is now Salamanca Place.

The cottage was originally an outbuilding for the Commissariat Store but, in 1828–29, it was converted for William Parramore, private secretary to Governor Arthur. It was he who, in December 1824, wrote unpleasantly about Maria Lord (p81).

His letter was to his fiancée **Thirza Cropper** (1798–1852), a school mistress at Caen, Normandy, whom he had met before his arrival in Tasmania in 1823 and corresponded with until she arrived in Hobart in 1827, at about the time he was appointed to the governor's office. They married at St David's Church. One source suggests that she became governess to the Arthurs' children.

By 1828, the Parramores had a son and, the following year, I am assuming when they had moved into the cottage, little William died, so the cottage got off to a bad start. Looking at it, somewhat altered and restored since Thirza's day, through glass, and almost craning your neck, allows you to imagine her misery. And her husband was not to escape the odium of having worked closely with Governor Arthur, but he held a number of government appointments until she died in 1852, aged 54.

Governor Eardley-Wilmot died in the cottage in 1847 – broken, it is said, by his dismissal and the rumours behind it of his licentious behaviour. Since he was himself such an inveterate gossip, it is not surprising that he should have been its victim. And it seems that the cottage was one of the places where he housed guests about whom gossip was spread. The diarist Boyes wrote of a conversation with the Colonial Secretary in which he described the Governor's

> Great courtesy and fondness for the younger part of the fair sex. Barrow and his wife and one or two of her sisters were staying at the Govt. Cottage. Sir E. had succeeded in establishing a friendly understanding with girls – sat on

the sofa with them and occasionally condescended to pass his arm around their necks, they seemed to enjoy these little innocent familiarities amazingly.

There was damaging gossip in 1845 concerning **Julia Sorell** (1826–1888), she of the notorious mother Elizabeth Kemp Sorell. Although he was said to have taken her to the government lodge at New Norfolk, there is no evidence that there was anything improper between the 18-year-old and the aging grass widower, but that was not the point – reputations rose and fell on indiscretion and loose tongues. In 1846, Julia was engaged to an Eardley-Wilmot son, but that fell through, as did a couple of other prospective engagements. Her later marriage appears in the 'New Town' itinerary (p266). There is a portrait of Julia in the Art Gallery.

After the Governor's death, many proclaimed his innocence, among them Louise Anne Meredith who had received most courteous hospitality at Government House. Governors' private secretaries lived in the cottage until the new Government House, in its current position, was occupied in 1858.

Having seen one of the oldest surviving buildings of British settlement, the rest of what the museum/gallery offers awaits you.

Aboriginal Gallery:

- The contemporary copy of the portrait of Mathinna by Bock painted for Jane Franklin
- Traditional reed baskets woven by women
- Examples of food collection, for which women were responsible (p7)
- Shell necklaces, including those continuing to be strung by women Aborigines, particularly on Cape Barren Island
- Photographs of the recording session of traditional songs by Fanny Cochrane Smith (p119), and the facility to listen to the recording
- Feature 'Heroes of Resistance' including Walyer (pp32, 112)

Convict Art Gallery:

- The Female Factories – cases and details

Hobart Colonial Art Gallery:

- Portraits of colonial women such as Emma, daughter of Maria and Edward Lord
- 1829 or 1834 Portrait of Truggernana (Trukanini) by Duterreau
- 1836 bust of Trukanini
- Portrait of Tanlebonyer (pp112–13)

Of Tasmanian women artists, the work most easily found is that of **Edith Holmes** (1893–1973) whose 'Sunset', when I visited, hung outside the women's lavatory. In the 1930s she shared a studio at 76 Collins Street with **Mildred Lovett** (1880–1955) (one of her teachers), **Florence Rodway** (1881–1971),

Dorothy Stoner (1904–1992), Ethel Nicholls (1866–1956) and Violet Vimpany (1886–1979). A portrait of Edith by Florence Rodway is also apparently in the gallery, though I have only seen a reprint.

Town Hall

Across Argyle Street, the colonnaded Town Hall is the next venue along the south side of Macquarie Street. It should not be confused with the City Hall (1911) beyond Montgomery's Hotel on the other side of Macquarie Street, where Nellie Melba gave a recital during her 1924 farewell tour of Tasmania (pp301–2).

Lieutenant Governor David Collins pitched his tent about here in 1804; that of his mistress Hannah Power and her husband was just behind (p13). Huts soon replaced tents along what was to become Macquarie Street. This is also part of the site of the Government House complex until 1858. The Town Hall was completed in 1866 and thereafter held many public and musical events.

Here the Women's Sanitary Association held their well-attended public meeting in 1891 (p203). It can, therefore, be said to have witnessed the beginning of women's political activities in Tasmania.

The celebrated soprano Amy Sherwin gave her farewell concert here in 1898/89. In 1920, Tasmanian composer Katherine Parker (Kitty, 1886–1971), who had earlier gone to London to further her career, performed here with her husband Hubert Eisdell during a concert tour of Australia. Her best-known piano piece, 'Down Longford Way' (1928), inspired by her home-place south of Launceston, is included in a CD of her songs and piano music quite easily available on the internet.

In 1924, the potters and cousins Maude Poynter and Violet Mace (p330) held an exhibition here.

Franklin Square

Cross over Elizabeth Street and you are in Franklin Square. Governors' wives, and non-wives, lived, brought up families, and entertained in Government House here. Because of its name, the statue of her husband, and her boundless activities between 1837 and 1843, Jane Franklin is the most obvious to imagine (Chapters 10, 11, 12). Mathinna lived here too (pp119, 176). Guests included Anna Maria Nixon, and the Bishop and their family when they first arrived in 1843 (p148). Elizabeth Gould (née Coxen, 1804–1841), wife of the naturalist and a considerable artist in her own right, gave birth to a son there in 1838; he was named Franklin. Many of her drawings, some of them made at Government House, illustrate her husband's books though the published lithographs of them obscure her name.

Years earlier, in 1808, the intruding Governor Bligh's daughter, Mary Bligh Putland, stayed here until he removed her to save her from the moral turpitude of Collins' mistress Margaret Eddington (pp36–7). From the start of his visit it was too ramshackle for Bligh himself to stay there. Bligh was not the only one too fastidious to stay at Government House, as Macquarie Hotel will suggest (p245).

24. Old Government House (sketched from the sea),
by Mary Morton Allport, courtesy of the Allport Library and
Museum of Fine Arts, Tasmanian Archive and Heritage Office

The last Governor's wife to live there, between 1847 and 1855, was Caroline Denison (p161). She did not mind the house; going for a drive to what she called the Government Garden, now the Botanical Gardens, she wrote in her journal on 27 January 1847: 'We passed the spot where they had begun to build a new Government house which never was finished; and, pleased as I am with the old house, I am afraid I half covet this, from the exceeding beauty of its situation and views ...' She followed that up with an account of a temporary transformation of the existing house on 19 May:

The lower part of our house is undergoing a strange metamorphosis; every Government House certainly ought to be provided with a ball-room; the one at Launceston has one. Not so this, unfortunately, and the consequence is, that there is a regular framework of boards, kept for the purpose, and put up every year on this occasion, to form a temporary room, joining on to the dining-room; and another, enclosing the front verandah, to make a supper room; and the result of this arrangement is that all our lower rooms, except the drawing-room and little ante-room, will be deprived of the light of day till Monday, by this sad framework of boards coming in front of their windows. This process is now going on; the dining-room is already darkened, and the library, school-room, and the housekeeper's room, I suppose, will be in the course of to-morrow.

Hobart Gaol and Gallows

Beyond Franklin Square, you reach Murray Street. On the far side, opposite the Treasury, is the Savings Bank (nos 24–26), established in 1845. This is the site of the former gallows where Mary McLauchlan was hanged in 1830 (p66). In the adjacent few women's rooms of the gaol, Eliza Callaghan in 1822 (p58) and Ann Solomon in 1828 (p63) spent time before women prisoners were transferred to the Female Factory at Cascades in 1828.

St David's Cathedral

Cross over Macquarie Street, bearing in mind that it is a fast and busy through-road. The first St David's church was a small wooden one erected where Collins was buried and where St David's Park is today, but it blew down in a storm. The second St David's was on the site of today's and later demolished. Today's cathedral was consecrated in 1874.

In the earlier church, families who sought to enhance their status had their own pews; typical were Martha Hayes Whitehead and Mary Hayes Stocker (p40). Anyone who was anyone got married in the church, and then the cathedral. Thirza Cropper and William Parramore, the first occupants of the renovated Governor's Cottage, did in 1827 and Julia Sorell in 1850 (p268). Anna Maria Nixon played the organ there (p148).

Allport Library and Museum of Fine Arts/State Library – 91 Murray Street

The professional artist Mary Morton Allport, who painted the 1842 picture of the regatta (pp142–3) and bemoaned being a domestic drudge (p174), was the matriarch of the family that arrived in 1831; her husband Joseph was a solicitor, and the legal practice, long associated with Emily Dobson's in-laws, still thrives (p247). The Allports' great-grandson, Henry, bequeathed the Allport Library and Museum of Fine Arts to the people of Tasmania in 1965.

Situated on the ground floor of the State Library, beyond the pleasant coffee shop, it contains the books, paintings, furniture and *objets* collected by members of the family over more than a century, including Mary's paintings and those of her granddaughter **Curzona Allport** (Lily, 1860–1949). Tutored by her grandmother, Curzona then spent many years abroad, studying in England at the height of the art nouveau period and having works hung in the Royal Academy. In Tasmania between 1922 and 1927, she produced watercolour landscapes, such as that on this book's cover, and, at the age of 72 (or 75), she settled in Hobart and set up a print studio.

Some 400 of Curzona's works are kept here, several of them displayed, and 228 available on the website www.statelibrary.tas.gov.au/collections – a satisfying armchair browse. Look out for special exhibitions of Tasmanian women artists.

Macquarie Hotel

151 Macquarie Street, between Murray and Victoria Street, a walk along from the Cathedral, is today, or was when I clocked it, the Sunflower News Agency and takeaway. On the site was once the grandest mansion in Hobart – Birch Castle, or Birch House.

Sarah Birch (née Guest, 1792–1868) was the daughter of convicts – of a First Fleet father, and a Second Fleet mother. Like Betty King (p9), **Mary Bateman** was one of the few women convicts sent to Norfolk Island where she married George Guest. When Norfolk Islanders were to be relocated to Tasmania, the Guests, with six children and 300 ewes, pre-empted the move and arrived in 1805. Sixteen-year-old Sarah, who has been described as 'a pretty minx', married the merchant and shipowner Thomas Birch, nearly 20 years her senior, in 1808. In 1815, the captain of one of his vessels discovered Macquarie Harbour, where the notorious penal settlement was to be established, and named Sarah Island and Birch Inlet after his employer's wife. By that same year, increasingly prosperous Thomas had built Birch House.

Birch House vied with Ingle Hall as the first brick building in Hobart. It was, at least, the grandest, being three storeys of unpainted, convict-made, red brick with a flat roof and battlements. It was said there were two cannon on the roof so that Birch could fend off the French, should they attack. So grand was the house, and so unsatisfactory Government House that, in 1817, when Lieutenant Governor William Sorell arrived with Louisa Kent to take up his appointment, they preferred to stay at Birch House, and the same when Governor Macquarie and his wife Elizabeth visited in 1821.

But that year Thomas Birch died suddenly, aged 47, leaving 29-year-old Sarah a widow with six children; the eldest, their twelve-year-old son and heir with learning difficulties ('of imbecile mind'). Sarah married Edmund Hodgson in 1823 and, during the years when her late husband's complicated estate was being sorted out and fought over, the status of Birch House changed. By 1823 it was the Macquarie Hotel. Whether or not Sarah and her family lived there is uncertain, so it is difficult to know if the woman described by those who stayed there was her. Certainly, Dr John Hudspeth of Bowsden (p90) refers to arriving at 'Mrs Birch's establishment' that year to find his goods stored there ransacked.

In August 1829 Elizabeth Fenton arrived at the hotel (p76) where 'commodious rooms' with a little balcony overlooking the water had been reserved for her. Later, she moved to a house further up Macquarie Street, to where it gave way to 'the jungle' and, eventually, to what became the family home in New Norfolk (p310).

Jane Roberts, arriving in Hobart in May 1830 (p78) wrote that the 'Macquarie Hotel is not expensive as an hotel, but becomes so by any length of stay.' She added:

> ... the mistress of [the hotel] was a clever, active, and exceedingly well-behaved woman. All cannot thrive, even in Van Dieman's land, for her husband was absent on account of pecuniary difficulties; so that the whole arrangement of the house, a family of small children, and the charge of convict servants, fell entirely on her.

By this time, while Sarah was still the owner, the licensee was James Cox – who did have financial difficulties – and Jane was undoubtedly describing Mary Ann Cox who, with her husband, ran the hotel after 1828 though one source erroneously suggests that Sarah Birch married James Cox. The Coxes later moved to Launceston where Mary Ann appears in more detail (p369).

Although Birch House is no longer there, remnants of it can still be seen behind the modern building that has replaced it. And it continues to be the subject of controversial development proposals.

Eventually, in 1849, Sarah Birch Hodgson was released from the financial tangle of Thomas's estate, and came into her own property, including the regency house she had built in 1847, now the luxurious Islington Hotel at 321 Davey Street. One of the owners is the great grandson of Louisa Anne Meredith (p313), so her presence is felt, particularly in the library.

167 Macquarie Street (Lalla Rookh)

Continue along the north side of Macquarie Street and cross over Harrington Street. On the corner is the Hobart Macquarie Motor Inn incorporating 167 Macquarie Street which, according to Lindy Scripps who has extensively researched this area, would have been the site next along from the corner. This was the house into which Matilda and John Dandridge moved from Oyster Cove in 1873, taking with them the last of the Aborigines in their care, Trukanini, also known as Lalla Rookh, the name given to the house (pp108, 117). The two adjoining houses were demolished in the late 1960s to make way for the slab of the Motor Inn.

Trukanini had been rather unwell in the winter of 1873 with bronchial trouble and the Dandridges felt she would fare better away from the damp of Oyster Cove. Dandridge himself died in 1874 and Matilda was left as Trukanini's sole carer, though for the next couple of years Trukanini revived and became rather social, appearing in Society and the object of admiration as much as curiosity. She was seen, erroneously, as the last of her race, and was even known as 'Queen Trukanini'.

In May 1876, 64-year-old Trukanini began to foresee her death and on the 8th she seems to have had a stroke. Remembering the fate of William Lanney who died in 1869, and whose corpse had not been treated with respect, she called out, when she regained consciousness, 'Don't let them cut me, but bury me behind the mountains.' Her last words, recorded by Matilda Dandridge, took her back to the beliefs of her people. While crowds lined the streets to watch her cortege, she was buried secretly, to protect her remains, in a vault of the Protestant chapel of the Cascades Female Factory. But two years later she was exhumed and, in 1904, her skeleton put on display in the Tasmanian Museum and Art Gallery where, shockingly, it remained until 1947; thereafter it was stored in the vaults there until the year before the ceremony of 1976 (Chronology, Chapter 13).

Amy Sherwin

Cross over Macquarie Street and head down to the bottom of Harrington Street; on the left is the law firm Dobson, Mitchell and Allport. A plaque on the wall by the front door, unveiled in a ceremony in August 2005, reads:

> To Honour Madame Amy Sherwin 1855–1935
> The Prima Donna known as 'The Tasmanian Nightingale'
> Who made her debut in this building, formerly Del Sarte's Rooms

Madame Sherwin was a Tasmanian soprano who received international acclaim throughout her career.

The plaque links Amy's career with the Theatre Royal and the Town Hall earlier in this itinerary, and her background in Franklin (p295). Her life story is best told in Judith Bowler's *Amy Sherwin: The Tasmanian Nightingale* (1982).

St David's Park

In front of you, facing south, is St David's Park. This is a pleasing green space, once the earliest burial ground of those who lived and died here after 1804. The first was little Elizabeth Edwards and then the new-born son of Mary Kearley (p17).

Cascades Female Factory

The last site in this itinerary is a fair stretch along the north side of Macquarie Street to where it bends right to Degraves Street – alongside the Hobart Rivulet. This is certainly the most significant women's site in Tasmania and, in March 2009, the Female Factory Historic Site Ltd, a not-for-profit organisation set up in 1999 to retrieve the site, handed over yards 3 and 4 South (the Matron's Cottage) to the people of Tasmania.

Years of research and much thought by many have gone into reclaiming this monument to women convicts' experience and suffering; as the inscription says, 'Lest We Forget'. I have gratefully drawn on the work of others for the convict chapters in the history section so, on the assumption that you have read them, I do not need to elaborate here on the women's lives.

Before a visit it is worth going to www.femalefactory.com.au. This will give you an idea of forthcoming and past events and continuing work and publications. Typical of past events are the Rajah Quilt exhibition of 2005; 'Treading the Steps' – a re-enactment in 2006 of the 1829 walk of the *Harmony* convicts and their children from Sullivans Cove to the Factory – the first shipload; and 'Roses from the Heart', a display organised by Christina Henri of women's bonnets recreated by participants worldwide, some convict descendants, of the 25,566 women transported from Britain and Ireland to Australia. There are also regular lectures by researchers.

There are organised tours of the site; and Judith and Chris Cornish also take visitors on Louisa's Walk – a guided journey via a theatre performance into the life of convict Louisa Reagan (livehistory@hotmail.com). Attached to the site is a shop selling souvenirs, some of them edible, which allow you to contribute financially to the project.

In spite of so much activity, this is not an obvious tourist site – you may be the only visitor there, and simply standing among the remains or sitting in the garden overlooking them allows you to use your imagination.

15 – Around Hobart

This is a disparate Hobart itinerary including sites away from Macquarie Street near where it starts, but excluding New Town. You would probably not want to visit them all in one go.

Battery Point

Finding yourself at St David's Park just south of Macquarie Street, skip through it down to Salamanca Place where you will find Astrolabe and the Hobart Bookshop and where you should have a cup of coffee and perhaps read Amanda Lohrey's *The Morality of Gentlemen* (1984), a *roman-à-clef* based on a real-life waterside dispute, and then up the hill, perhaps via Montpelier Retreat, to Battery Point.

Narryna Heritage Museum – 103 Hampden Road (closed Mondays)

Turn left into Hampden Road and soon on your left, unmissable, is a solid Georgian house built in 1834, Narryna. Although I see Sarah Benson Walker (p174) there between 1852 and 1854 most vividly, and, indeed, she seems

25.   Anne Coverdale, by Knut Bull, courtesy of
the Narryna Heritage Museum

to have been the first to call the house Narryna, it evokes generations of women inhabitants. The little book, available there, *Narryna: The History of a Colonial Gentleman's Residence* (2002, Peter Mercer), sketches their story, ending with its use in the 1950s as an after-care hostel for female tuberculosis patients. The contents of the museum – which include a room devoted to costumes – are not from any one family; many have contributed to it, but somehow they seem right. An example is a portrait of Anne Harbroe Coverdale (p274).

Most credit for its existence as a historic house opened to the public in 1957 goes to **Amy Rowntree** (1885–1962), a teacher appointed the first woman Inspector of Schools in 1919, and her sister, teacher and artist Fearn (**Frances Fearnley Rowntree**, 1892–1966). On retirement, both became historical researchers and, as lifelong inhabitants of Battery Point, Narryna was an obvious focus. Amy is known for several historical publications, in particular *Battery Point: Today and Yesterday* (1951), and Fearn's most relevant is *Battery Point Sketchbook* (1953?). Their sister **Millicent Rowntree** (Milli, b1883), also involved, was Secretary of the Battery Point Progress Association.

Arthur's Circus

Further along Hampden Road, on your left, is the turning into Arthur's Circus. The only connection, very tenuous, I can find with women is that Eliza Arthur's husband, the Governor, bought the plot in 1829 and, in 1837, registered it in the name of Thirza Parramore's husband, his private secretary, for reasons that Amy Rowntree could not fathom. But so obviously feminine is this enchanting circle of cottages, built in 1843 for pensioners and no two alike, and so surprised would you be if you came upon it without a prompt, that it cannot be left out.

Sandy Bay

From Battery Point – a select residential area – we move to another; and Sandy Bay is well worth a drive around for the privileged aura it exudes. When people say that Hobart reminds them of England, this is the only area I have found that qualifies. There are two private houses once inhabited by literary women. The playwright Catherine Shepherd (p237) lived at 109 York Street after 1960, until she moved into a nursing home to die. Isabel Dick (p309) lived, after 1915 when she was widowed, at 9 Red Chapel Road (now Avenue), quite a bit further along past the University. Here she wrote her novels, including *Wild Orchard* (p97). For many literary women (and men) *Tasmanian Literary Landmarks* (1984) by Margaret Giordano and Don Norman is invaluable.

On the corner of Red Chapel Avenue and Sandy Bay Road was the house Derwent Water where Anne Battersby was assigned to work for Agnes Power in 1847 (p161). Sandy Bay has rather changed since then.

Mount Nelson (Trukanini Conservation Area)

Finally, or first, depending on time in Sandy Bay and preference, just before the University, drive up Nelson Road and follow the winding road up and up to the top of Mount Nelson. You get a marvellous view from up there but the signal station and lookout are not the primary destination; follow, instead, a sign that directs you to 'Truganini Conservation Area: dedicated to the Tasmanian Aboriginal People and their Descendants'. Walk along the path until you come to a rocky clearing in the trees with a plaque set into a rock that reads: 'Trucanini died 8 May 1876; Trucanini Park 8 May 1976; dedicated to the Tasmanian Aboriginal people and their descendants'.

In May 1976, those descendants may have appreciated the gesture; indeed, Ida West wrote in her reminiscences *Pride Against Prejudice*:

> I like to get up to Truganini Park when the weather is warm. It's nice to go up there and say a prayer and look down the Derwent River. There I feel something on the spiritual side, and I always feel better when I come back home again. Sometimes I wonder why that park is not used more often – it's not far out of Hobart. I went up there one day and met a couple sitting around a seat. I went over and spoke to them. They were from Canada and they reckoned they couldn't understand why it wasn't used more. It's a lovely view when you get on the other side, and look down the Derwent River and remembering the past.

Some of today's Aborigines seem to prefer their own initiatives with regard to their past, rather than those of the state government or, indeed, anyone else. But the visitor without such constraints can appreciate this secluded place as Ida West did. There is another site dedicated to the memory of Trukanini on Bruny Island (p288).

Mount Wellington

The two mountains are rather different. Mount Wellington, named Table Mountain by colonists until 1832, is altogether grander and more dominant of the landscape. From the summit, 1,270 metres above sea level, you feel you can see almost the whole of Tasmania; and you can, at least as far as Ben Lomond. You need to choose your day, though: on a clear day it is a perfect experience, but often the mist comes down low, and in winter it is snow-capped. Even on a good day the air is fresh – a jacket is not a bad idea.

To get to the base of the mountain, drive west along Davey Street, past lovely old houses, and follow the signs. Then up the winding road, built as a relief scheme for the unemployed and opened only in 1937, past, at first, tall thick trees which give way to stunted trees and rocks. As you near the summit, it becomes increasingly bare until, at the top, it is a lunar landscape. The change in vegetation owes something to logging but more to the all consuming fires of 1897, 1914, 1834, 1945 and, the most awful and memorable to today's

Tasmanians, 1967, Black Friday, when 62 people died in the Hobart environs. Emily Bowring's sketch 'Mount Wellington, Tasmania', suggests, however, that, even in 1856, it was not luxuriantly covered.

26.   Mount Wellington by Emily Stuart Bowring, 1856, courtesy of the Allport Library and Museum of Fine Arts, Tasmanian Archive and Heritage Office

Of course, if you are a keen walker, that's how you will want to climb Mount Wellington, just as the artist and traveller **Marianne North** (1830–1890) did in 1881. She wrote in *Recollections of a Happy Life* (1893), when she and the head gardener at Government House, where she was staying, had walked to St Crispin's Well:

Four miles of walking took us to the lovely spot where the clear water bubbles out amongst the fern-trees and all kinds of greenery. After a rest we plunged right into the thick of it, climbing under and over the stems and trunks of fallen trees, slippery with moss, in search for good specimens of the celery-tipped pine, of which we found some sixty feet high. It was not in the least like a pine, excepting in its drooping lower branches and its straight stem: the leaves were all manner of strange shapes. We also saw fine specimens of sassafras ... and the dark myrtle or beech of Tasmania. Quantities of the pretty pandanus-looking plant they call grass-trees or richea, really a sort of heath. The whole bunch looks like a cob of Indian corn, each corn like a grain of white boiled rice, which, again, when shed or pulled off, sets free the real flowers – a bunch of tiny yellow stamens, with the outer bracts scarlet. There is also an exquisite laurel, with large waxy white flowers. There were many gum-trees, some of them very big, but mostly peppermint or 'stringy-bark'. The famous blue gum (Eucalyptus globulus) was rare even there ...

One of Marianne's paintings that illustrate that word portrait is included, in colour, in *A Vision of Eden: The Life and Work of Marianne North* (1980). Over 800 of her paintings – a record of the tropical and exotic plants from around the world – fill the Marianne North Gallery at Kew Gardens, London. *Forests and Flowers of Mount Wellington, Tasmania* (nd) by the botanist Winifred Curtis (after whom the Winifred Curtis Scamander Reserve on the east coast is named (p323)), is not readily available.

Some sources suggest that Jane Franklin's Mount Wellington expedition of 1837 (p146) was the first by a white woman, but we know that Salome Pitt had been some way up with her Aboriginal companion in 1810 – the area was well trodden from time immemorial by Miss Story's ancestors, assuming she belonged to the South East nation; and the mountain has several Aboriginal names: Unghanyahletta, Poorantere, and, apparently the most favoured, Kunanyi.

And, two weeks before Jane Franklin's essay, on 8 December, Sarah Poynter (p318), Louisa Anne Meredith's sister-in-law, wrote to her stepmother Mary Meredith at Cambria (p317), how her friend Miss Wandl(e)y had climbed to the top in the hopes of seeing from there where her fiancé, Lieutenant Thomas Burnett, had drowned when his boat capsized during a survey of the River Derwent. A monument to him implying their love was erected in St David's Park (p247).

Jane Franklin's climb or at least the gourmet picnic and the mountain spectacle were described (by her?) in the *Hobart Town Courier* of 22 December 1837:

As you sat hesitating which first should be attacked, you might observe 5 large ships between the legs of the roast fowl, a cold tongue overlapping the whole of Maria Island, a bottle of claret eclipsing Wyld's Crag, Mount Olympus shut out of sight by a loaf of bread, and the whole of that important, that political, that liberal and sensible city, Hobarton, included within the embrace of the teapot's handle.

In 1843, Jane Franklin commissioned the building of two huts – one at the summit and one at the Springs (half-way up) – to encourage more women to climb the mountain; they were burnt in the fire of 1967 but modern chalets have replaced them. Until the 1890s, ice for refrigeration came from an icehouse built at the Springs.

It is not clear how most women ascended the mountain. Anna Maria Nixon, the Bishop's wife (p148) was lent a pony for a week or two in January 1845 and visited the Springs 'which is', she wrote, 'a terrace walk along the side of the hill.' Along the terrace 'is a watercourse for the Springs which supply the

254 Women's Places (Itineraries)

town with water'. It was the 'fresh sweet woodland smell' which appealed to her most strongly.

Writing of the mountain soon after her arrival in 1840, Louisa Anne Meredith noted in *My Home in Tasmania* that 'Several unfortunate persons who at various times have imprudently attempted the ascent without a guide, have never returned, nor has any vestige of them ever been discovered.' The irony is that in 1924 her husband's niece, **Clara Sabina Meredith** (1857–1924) fell to her death, as the *Mercury* of 2 and 3 September reported, from the area known as the Organ Pipes.

You don't have to climb Mount Wellington to be influenced by it; indeed, Emily Bowring's sketch shows how it dominates the landscape (the Organ Pipes are on the left; Timsbury, the house in the foreground, has been demolished). Tasma, whose house in its lee features later in this itinerary, gives us a very purple, but illuminating, passage in her 1885 autobiographical novel *Not Counting the Cost* concerning the children who lived there:

> They had been born under the shadow of Mount Wellington, and consulted him now more as a kind of huge weather-glass than from any aesthetic appreciation of his venerable beauties. According to the aspect he wore in the morning, they built their hopes upon the day before them. When he appeared arrayed, like a monarch, in royal purple, with his giant crown well out-lined against the shining expanse of blue that canopied him, they felt that the heavens would smile upon them. When, on the other hand, he sulked behind the cloud-wreaths, or showed himself grudgingly under rags and tags of wet mist, they got out their umbrellas and waterproofs. For what other motive should the Tasmanians to-day question him? He has no legends of mediaeval days to recount, though, for all we know to the contrary, he may have a thousand tales as wonderful and dramatic as any of these locked up in his gloomy fastnesses. He has seen a primitive race swept from the face of the earth, goaded convicts hiding like rats in the holes and caves, and runaway prisoners hunted to their doom.

I'm not sure that I think of Mount Wellington as male. Nor does Cassandra Pybus who lived for a while on its slopes, and in her autobiographical essays *Till Apples Grow on an Orange Tree* (1998) wrote:

> Beyond the overgrown European façade of garden was the pipeline, a track which followed the water pipe the whole length of the mountain through the dripping forest of giant manferns, where tendrils of water seeped from every crevice in the rock-face and the ground squelched beneath my feet. It was full of secluded hideaways; dank, magical, musty. It belonged in fairytales with goblins, and when snow-covered, it becomes the remote empire of Hans Christian Anderson's fierce Snow Queen.

Mabel Hookey (1871–1953), journalist, artist, author and traveller, climbed the mountain in 1907 with family and friends and took a series of photographs which can be seen in the viewing pod on the summit.

I bought *The Butterfly Man* (2005) by Heather Rose because it was by a Tasmanian woman, even though the apparent subject did not appeal. It is the imaginary story of what happened to Lord Lucan after the murder of the family nanny in London in 1974 and his disappearance. But it is set most sensitively and evocatively in his house on Mount Wellington, which Heather Rose obviously knows well, and worth reading.

Jane Franklin Hall – Elboden Street

Back on Davey Street, returning towards the centre of town, and on your right, just before Davey Street begins to run parallel to Macquarie Street, turn into Elboden Street, to red-brick Jane Franklin Hall. On this site, from 1839, was Aldridge Lodge, home of Mary Morton Allport and family ('Around and About Macquarie Street', p244). Mary died there in 1895.

Since 1950, Jane Franklin Hall, which took over the site of the house in the 1980s, has been a residential college of the University of Tasmania; (it is about 15 minutes' walk from the University to the West and the centre of town to the east). Think of Jane Franklin as an intellectual in her drawing room at Government House, or as a physical adventurer ascending Mount Wellington.

The poet (Marguerite) **Helen Power** (1870–1957) lived at 3 Elboden Street from 1902, with her sister **Lillian Power** (b1862), after their father's death in Campbell Town where they were born and brought up. The house in Campbell Town was called Mount Joy, now renamed Balvaird and can be easily seen just up from the Information Centre, on the right at the top of Queen Street (no. 14). Helen provided von Stieglitz with some evocative childhood memories for *A Short History of Campbell Town* (1948, 1965).

In Elboden Street the sisters ran a guest house and taught, Helen contemporary literature. Her grandfather, with his wife Agnes Power, were the employers of the convict Anne Battersby at Derwent Water (pp161, 250). And Helen was christened Marguerite after his sister Lady Blessington, whom she was said increasingly to resemble, and whose portrait hung on her sitting room wall.

In 1926, Helen helped the impresario Olive Wilton and playwright Catherine Shepherd (p237) found the Hobart Repertory Theatre Society. Helen became appreciated as a poet only later in life, in the 1950s; earlier, her poetry was not considered 'sufficiently Australian in tone'. Some of her poems – but excluding, unfortunately, those written during the First World War – are available in *A Lute with Three Strings* (1964). She was influenced by the French poets she translated and it is startling to read the lines,

> The bourdon of the steady summer rain
> Falls on my heart like music, full of peace

and hear there the rhythm of the Verlaine Second World War broadcast code, and then to find that poem followed by one called 'After Verlaine'. Like Catherine Shepherd, Helen died in St Anne's Rest Home, 142 Davey Street, which is still there. The Elboden Street property is privately owned and surrounded by a wall. The owner when I intruded was extraordinarily civil, but she has since moved.

Salvator Road (Tasma)

Wiggle your way due north now, via Molle Street to Salvator Road, an extension of Goulburn Road which was once a red-light district and where respectable but poor mothers were much visited by Dorcas members (p133). Right at the very end, when you think you can go no further, is no. 41, a private house, Barton Vale; in Tasma's day, it was called Highfield in Salvator Rosa Glen. You don't need to intrude on the owners to get an impression of what inspired Tasma to write about her childhood home.

Tasma (Jessie Couvreur, 1848–1897) was born Jessie Catherine Huybers in England, the eldest of seven children, to parents of mixed European heritage. The family arrived in Hobart in 1852, and her father set up as a general merchant and wine and spirit seller. He prospered and, in 1866, the family moved to Highfield. Jessie married Charles Forbes Fraser at St David's Church in 1867 but the marriage soon faltered and eventually ended. Her husband had accompanied his parents to various penal postings, including the Cascades Female Factory, which Tasma's biographer suggests may have caused him to view women 'as people without rights'. Tasma was to use that background in her writing (pp68, 284).

Settled in Europe, Tasma married the Belgian politician and London *Times* correspondent Auguste Couvreur and began to concentrate more seriously on her writing. Patricia Clarke tells the full story in *Tasma: The Life of Jessie Couvreur* (1994), and her work is discussed by Margaret Harris in 'The Writing of Tasma: The Work of Jessie Couvreur' in *A Bright and Fiery Troop* (edited by Debra Adelaide, 1988). (It includes chapters on Caroline Leakey and Marie Pitt.)

Tasma wrote about Highfield from memory years later and her heroine, Eila, and the rest of the Clare family in *Not Counting the Cost* emigrate to Europe, as she did. In doing so, Eila leaves behind a husband who has made her life a misery and is confined to the New Norfolk Mental Asylum (p305). The unsatisfactory husbands in Tasma's writing tended to be based on her ex. Though the novel is only partly set in Tasmania, the first 150 pages convey an intense nostalgia for her childhood home. We are, happily, acquainted with the current owners of Barton Vale, and so can say that today's house and garden are not exactly as they were in Tasma's day – rather more up-to-date and kempt – and the setting has been modified by development, but Tasma is still there. Writing of visitors arriving in search of the Clare family, she continues:

They came upon them in the flower-garden – a mere longitudinal strip taken from the hill that sloped upwards from the house. The flower-garden it was called by courtesy, for in the tangle of blooms and weeds that encumbered the soil, there was nothing to recall the trim parterres we have learned to associate with the name. Such as it was, thanks to the Tasmanian air and soil, wherein flowers seem to grow, ... for no assignable cause, there was always to be found in the wherewithal to provide a bouquet of fuchsias and geraniums, bordered by springs of fragrant lemon-thyme ... The hardy shrubs and gaily-painted weeds and flowers wove a garland of colour and perfume round the assembled party, and across the city, lying at their feet, the sea glittered and sparkled beneath the afternoon sun.

27.   Tasma (Jessie Couvreur), from Clarke, *Tasma*

Behind them rose Mount Wellington, described by Tasma earlier in this itinerary. *Not Counting the Cost* is available on the internet, but at a price; one which I felt was worth paying; it may be your only way of reading it. *Uncle Piper of Piper's Hill* (1889; 1987), perhaps a better-known novel, and more easily obtainable in paperback, is set in Australia but has nothing to do with Tasmania.

Government House and Royal Hobart Botanical Gardens

Right over the other side of Hobart, to the east, you can hardly fail to notice the neo-gothic Government House up to your right overlooking the Derwent, not long past the bridge on your way from the airport. Tasmania's Governors have lived there since 1858. Before the move, **Eliza Marsh** (née Merewether), a visitor to Tasmania from the Australian mainland in September 1851, set the scene, while staying with Caroline Denison and her husband in the old Government House:

> The view from the new house will be beautiful, looking up and down the harbour, which I think, is very little less beautiful than Sydney, which is considered for scenery and good harbourage surpassing anything in the world. This Harbour is better. The Botanical Gardens are well kept, and very pretty to my eye, being full of English spring flowers. The domain and gardens are about 1½ miles distant from the present Gov. House and when more fully laid out from the mountainous scenery and beautiful views will be delightful.

The first wife to live in the new house, until 1861, was **Augusta Fox-Young** (née Marryat, m1848, d1913). She had previously been with her husband, Henry, when he governed South Australia, and Port Augusta there is named after her, as is Augusta Road in New Town, Hobart (p269). Augusta's husband, governing Tasmania from the time of its 1856 Constitution (p175), did not have a happy time and resigned. Harriet Gore Brown (p200) followed her. And Lady Hamilton's Literary Society and its rows took place here 30 years later (pp206–10). The artist Emily Bowring made at least two sketches in 1858 of the new Government House. Held in the Allport Library and Museum of Fine Arts, they are exhibited from time to time with works by other colonial women artists.

The house is not open to the public, but further along are the Royal Hobart Botanical Gardens, established in 1818, that are well worth a visit. Caroline Denison (p161), last wife to live in the Franklin Square Government House, certainly thought so, as she wrote in January 1847, soon after her arrival and in more detail than her later guest Eliza Marsh:

> At length we arrived at the Government garden, and what a sight was there! The profusion of fruit exceeded anything I ever saw before; plums, of various sorts, dropping and lying about almost in heaps, under every tree; in fact, in greater abundance that we can ever make use of. Pears, apples &c. in proportion; figs, vegetables of all sorts, some English flowers, and some very beautiful native shrubs. The principal of these were, a kind of Mimosa growing quite up into a tree, and bearing little clusters of lilac flowers with a very sweet smell; the *wattle*, a kind of acacia, with a bright yellow flower; the Norfolk Island pine, a very beautiful tree, more like a cedar than a pine, and which, I believe, in its own country grows to an

immense height and size; ... amongst all, there appeared the bright green of an English walnut tree, loaded, like every thing else, with fruit, and some very healthy-looking young oaks. Altogether, it would be thought a delightful garden anywhere; and to us, just come off a long sea voyage, it seemed little short of Paradise!

28. (New) Government House, by Emily Stuart Bowring, 1858, courtesy of the Allport Library and Museum of Fine Arts, Tasmanian Archive and Heritage Office

Some of these plants and trees date from 1838 when Jane Franklin, with Elizabeth Gould's naturalist husband, John, and the colony's leading botanist took shelter in Recherche Bay (p298). They also brought back plants for the Royal Society in London and Jane's gardens at Ancanthe (p270).

The Botanical Gardens are much the same now as when Caroline Denison described them, and they are another place, like so many in Tasmania, where you can roam in quietude. Here you can cast your mind back much further than 1818. Long before 1804, Aborigines established regular camps where English spring flowers now grow, for there were abundant supplies of shellfish from the nearby river.

16 – New Town (Hobart)

Runnymede (open 10am–4.30pm weekdays; 12 noon–4.30pm weekends)

Should you find yourself at the Botanical Gardens and decide to start the New Town itinerary from there, get onto the Domain Highway, taking you north (instead of east to the bridge), and then join Brooker Avenue (which becomes Brooker Highway). Not long afterwards, on your left, is a sign for Runnymede. An alternative for visiting the sites in New Town is to turn off Macquarie Street (one-way east) and left up Elizabeth Street, which starts the journey north for this itinerary.

Three main families are connected, over 125 years, with this elegant sandstone Regency villa at 61 Bay Road, open to the public and available for special events, such as weddings. Like many sites connected with women in Tasmania, historical research is well under way and, at Runnymede, the spur to the manager, Gemma Webberley, was that histories of the house tend to refer to the inhabitants as the Lawyer, the Bishop and the Whaler – the women excluded. The Runnymede Women's Research Group has made headway, starting with the first, **Dorothea Pitcairn** (née Dumas, 1810–1861).

Dorothea's father, an army officer in charge of the guard on a convict transport, arrived in Hobart in 1829 with his wife and seven children. Dorothea, then aged 19, married the reformist lawyer John Pitcairn at St David's Church, Hobart (p244), the following year. They lived at what they called Cairn Lodge from sometime between 1836 and 1840 until 1850. Earlier research by Kathryn Evans for the National Trust resulted in the publication *Robert Pitcairn 1802–1861* (nd) – available at Runnymede. Unfortunately, the letters from Dorothea unearthed by Colette McAlpine date from a later period than Runnymede and are still being assessed. Dorothea had two daughters, born 20 years apart, and three sons, only one of whom survived infancy; the first to die was born and died the year they may have moved into Cairn Lodge. She will also have seen her husband through his anti-transportation battles and she is known to have been constantly worried about his health.

In 1850, Francis Nixon, Tasmania's first Bishop, and his second wife Anna Maria Nixon, bought Cairn Lodge which they renamed Bishopstowe. They moved there from Boa Vista, which features later in this itinerary, with their large family and remained until 1862. Much more is known about Anna Maria than the other women who lived in the house, though the letters to her family contained in their granddaughter Norah Nixon's *The Pioneer Bishop in VDL 1843–1863* (c1953) were written pre-Bishopstowe (p148).

Anna Maria moved in the top echelons of Society, staying at Government House with the Franklins when she first arrived in 1843 and socialising and advising Caroline Denison, and she wrote about those she met and matters of moment, as well as those affecting her combative husband. In addition to playing the organ in his cathedral and being his hostess, she acted as his secretary – without, of course, a typewriter. She also had eleven children to look after; three of them her predecessor's.

It was Anna Maria, according to Patsy Adam-Smith's text for *Hobart Sketchbook* (1968) who created the garden at Runnymede, although the Bishop is credited, in *Tasmanian Historic Gardens* (P. Frazer Simons, 1987), with planting the two lemon verbena and the heliotrope by the front door. I suspect it was Anna Maria. It was she, according to *Bishop Nixon – Drawings* (R. Wilson 2002, also available at Runnymede) who obtained the large Norfolk pine and a number of trees and shrubs from what are now the Botanical Gardens (p258).

29.   Anna Maria Nixon, from Nixon,
The Pioneer Bishop in VDL

Nixon's watercolours are well-known, but Anna Maria also sketched, mostly to illustrate the letters sent home to her family. The most accessible is of their drawing room pre-Bishopstowe and Boa Vista, probably in his official residence in Upper Davey Street. The original is in the Tasmanian Museum and Art Gallery (p240), a facsimile is at Runnymede, and a copy illustrates Alison Alexander's *Obliged to Submit*. Anna Maria's competence is clear. A small, but winning, portrait of her is in the music room (not the one here). It was the Nixons who added the music room where they installed Anna Maria's pipe organ. She died at their home in Italy following his retirement, and he married again.

Eliza Bayley (née Inglis, 1817–1874) and her whaler husband Charles bought the house in 1864 and named it after his favourite ship, the *Runnymede*; the property was to remain in the family's hands for a century. Widowed Eliza

Randolph had married Bayley in 1840 and they had already lost two daughters while living in Battery Point (p249), one in infancy, the second of tuberculosis in 1861 aged 17. Settled at Runnymede, Charles retired from whaling and the couple concentrated on making it productive in fruit and vegetables, much of which provisioned his ships. But Eliza died ten years later, and Charles six weeks after her.

Charles' brother James inherited Runnymede on his brother's death in 1875. James had remarried the year before. With his first wife **Emma Bayley** (née Butchard, c1839–1866) whom he married in 1856, he had three children, but two sons died, leaving only a daughter, **Harriet Bayley** (b1861). Emma often accompanied her husband on the whaler, even when pregnant, and Harriet was born on the *Runnymede* off the coast of New Zealand. But Emma died, aged only 27, when Harriet was five. With his cousin Elizabeth Bayley, James had a daughter who also died, so, when he died in 1895, only Harriet was left to inherit Runnymede. To cause confusion, in 1885, she had married a civil servant with almost the same name as hers, Henry Bayly (instead of Bayley). They had five daughters and two sons.

In 1963, the sisters **Hally Bayly** (1886–1971) and **Emma Bayly** (c1890–1993) sold Runnymede to the state for preservation, and the National Trust has leased it since 1965. Emma lived to be 103, and even in her later years continued to visit the property, helping in the garden and advising. Much of the contents belong to the Bayley/Bayly past, including photographic portraits of Eliza and Emma Bayley. The Japanese vases in niches in the hall were a wedding present to Harriet and Henry Bayly, and there is a photographic portrait of Harriet.

Pitt Farm

Leaving Runnymede, get onto Risdon Road running north east parallel to it. You may have noticed that I am intrigued by Salome Pitt's ascent of Mount Wellington accompanied by the mysterious Miss Story (pp41–2). However high they climbed, Salome seems to have been years ahead of any other white woman to attempt it. The house by the Hobart Rivulet where she, her father, and her two brothers lived is still there, and said to be the second-oldest farmhouse in Australia, though the original, built between 1806 and 1810, was damaged by fire in 2007 and the 100 acres of their farm was reduced by development in the twentieth century. It is now privately owned but you can see it, I'm told, just 100 metres or so up Albert Road East from its junction with Risdon Road.

Queen's Orphan Schools – St John's Avenue

When you've had a view of Pitt farm, drive back westwards along Albert Road until you hit Main Road and drive south until it becomes New Town Road (which is Elizabeth Street nearer the city). Now, on your right, between two sports grounds, is St John's Avenue, at the end of the which is St John's

Church, flanked by the two wings – girls and boys – of what was, when it opened in 1828 (or 1833) the King's Orphan Schools and then, after 1837, the Queen's. No words can better describe how the complex looked in 1858 than Emily's Bowring's drawing 'Queen's Orphan School' (with Mount Wellington in the background). But in the drawing and today you see only its outside, pale stone, so innocuous. In reality it was not a happy or even a well-run place.

30. Orphan School, by Emily Stuart Bowring, courtesy of the Allport Library and Museum of Fine Arts, Tasmanian Archive and Heritage Office

An article in the *Colonial Times* of 23 April 1839 described the interior: 'The majority of the apartments, allotted to the use of children, are cold, comfortless, and ill arranged, upon a most mistaken system of parsimonious economy.' And it continues in that vein.

In the early days, the orphans, under the auspices of the Convict Department, were the children of convicts. When the need for such an institution was first mooted in 1823, there were 394 destitute children; they were either parentless or neglected, perhaps born in the Female Factory (p62). In the early 1840s several Aboriginal children were placed there, including Mathinna and Fanny (pp179–80), and again in 1847; then Caroline Denison visited them (p189). After 1858, the system was expanded to include the orphans of free parents.

Life inside can only be described as wretched and brutalising. In 1859, evidence was received by a royal commission of a little girl who died after being whipped, of **Ann McKenna** who did not know her own age, and of 24-year-old **Amelia Jones** who was illiterate and worked as a housemaid – both had spent their lives there. Usually girls brought up there were sent as domestics to the countryside. There were 70 children to a class, ranging in age from seven to 14. Alison Alexander reports evidence that 20 years later, 29 girls from the Orphan School were found to have become prostitutes.

Then there is the 1841 allegation of adultery with one of the senior girls committed by the Reverend Thomas Ewing. Evidence for the 'serious misconduct' was given by 13-year-old Edward Lord Fry who, Kay Daniels assumes, was the child of **Ann Fry**, assigned servant, and Maria Lord's husband whom Ann was nursing in 1828 (p82). By coincidence, Ewing crops up in the next site to visit.

Boa Vista – The Friends' Junior School

Further down New Town Road (coming from the north) turn left into Upper Argyle Street. All that is left of Boa Vista is the porticoed gatehouse or lodge of The Friends Junior School. But it is here that many of our women lived.

The first was **Lucy Davey Scott** (1797–c1847), daughter of the Lieutenant Governor, recipient of Governor Macquarie's wedding present of land in 1821 (p52), and wife of the colonial surgeon. The Scotts built the house in Italianate style in 1828. Lucy's mother Margaret, abandoned by Davey when he left Tasmania, probably did not live there as she died in 1827.

The most useful information comes from 'Women's Words: Boa Vista' in Miranda Morris' study *Placing Women*. She traces, for example, 17 women convicts working for the Scotts between 1824 and 1835. The best-known is Norah Corbett (p61); in 1828, she was twice found intoxicated during her time at Boa Vista, once at the Union Tavern run by **Agnes Flemming** where her predecessor **Elizabeth Smith** had been caught before being discharged. It may well be from the Scotts that Norah absconded, for it was that same year that she was captured with a bushranger by her future husband. Lucy was left a widow, with the youngest of her six children aged only five in 1837 and died herself ten years later.

Anna Maria Nixon and the Bishop owned Boa Vista between 1846 and 1849 before they bought Runnymede. Caroline Leakey, author of the convict novel *The Broad Arrow* (pp165–70), who arrived in Tasmania in 1848, stayed with the Nixons when she became ill within a year of her arrival. It was there that Caroline wrote some of the poetry contained in *Lyra Australis or Attempts to Sing in a Strange Land* (1854). In the preface she writes:

'Boa Vista: or Songs on the Balcony' my kind friends in Tasmania will at once recognise as the selection that I dedicate immediately to them ... The chapter is named after a house where I resided for a short time, and in the balcony of which many an hour of suffering was soothed into cheerfulness and song by the pleasant voice of nature heard and seen in the lovely landscape stretching for miles before and around me.

A further chapter declares: 'To Lady Denison, this chapter of poems is, with much respect, dedicated by her obliged Caroline Leakey.'

There is an irony about Caroline's voyage out to Tasmania, for she was in the care of **Louisa Ewing** (née Were, m1837) and her husband the Reverend Thomas Ewing who was returning in the hopes of clearing his name after the

1841 scandal concerning his adultery with a girl in his care at the Queen's Orphan School. He was, however, only allowed to remain chaplain of St John's and the Orphan School (not head master). Caroline must have discovered the saga on arrival in the gossip bed of Hobart, and been appalled.

Miranda Morris catalogues subsequent inhabitants of Boa Vista. **Louisa Travers** (bc1834) leaves the most marked impression because there is a typescript of her life in Hobart and at Boa Vista in the University of Tasmania Archives which Miranda Morris has drawn on at some length.

In 1870, Louisa, aged 36, arrived with her husband, nine children, their governess **Miss Gisell**, their nursemaids **Martha Cresswell** and **Grace Roberts,** maid **Mary Roberts,** two cows, a cock, hens and 163 boxes of possessions. At first they rented Derwent Water (p161) which Louisa found dirty and uncared for, and the plumbing basic. She proceeded to have a tenth child. Eventually they moved into Boa Vista and stayed there until at least 1876 when Louisa's diary – which gives a useful view of life in her milieu – ends. Of her first impression of the house she wrote:

> We are to pay 120 pounds for a house twice as large as our Epsom House & 13 acres of land. It is a large house with ten bedrooms, a large garden and beautiful views from the front, is on the rise of a hill and looking out to the river ... The garden is a delight. A hedge of the old cabbage rose scenting the whole drive up.

In 1906, Boa Vista was bought by the Quakers Samuel and **Margaret Clemes** (née Hall, c1849–1923) who had arrived in Hobart in 1886, two years after their marriage, for him to take up his appointment as head master of the proposed The Friends' School. Margaret played an acknowledged part in creating a family atmosphere in the boarding house. The Clemes opened their own school, Leslie House, with its advanced methods, following a mis-understanding with The Friends' School committee. In 1907 it moved to Boa Vista where in 1915 the Clemes' elder son William took over as head master. When Samuel died in 1922, the school was renamed Clemes College; Margaret died a year later. The Clemes' methods had included progressive thinking on education for girls, and employment of women. In 1946, the college amalgamated with The Friends' School, of which the junior part was at Boa Vista, and remains in what were the grounds.

You must imagine Boa Vista as Caroline Leakey and Louisa Travers described it as you look at the lonely gatehouse where I deduce Louisa's housekeeper and family lived.

Brickfields – North Hobart Oval

It is interesting that Caroline Leakey and Louisa Travers should say that the view from Boa Vista was beautiful because GTW Boyes suggested in his diary on 3 April 1850 that the view from Boa Vista was 'not so fresh and fine as it was, for the Brickfields Factory with the most worthless women has been erected in front of it'. Brickfields, established in 1842, was hardly a happy place when it housed women convicts who had spent months on probation and were then waiting for assignment as domestic servants (pp159–60). Caroline Leakey's heroine Maida Gwynnham spent time there (p166).

In later years, the buildings were used as an immigration depot and finally as an invalid depot for men which closed in 1882. The area later became a rubbish tip.

Julia Sorell (Stoke Road)

From the gatehouse of Boa Vista, walk a few steps northwards to the corner of New Town Road and Stoke Street, to where a white painted bungalow is very obvious. This is where the novelist known as Mrs Humphrey Ward was born. In *A Writer's Recollections* (1918) **Mary Augusta Sorell Ward** (1851–1920) wrote: 'I see dimly another house in wide fields, where dwarf lilies grow, and I know that it was a house in Tasmania.'

Mary Ward is known in England for her literary output and her relatives; in Tasmania, it is her mother and grandmother who are of historical note. Her grandmother was the notorious Elizabeth Kemp Sorell who, visiting Europe from Tasmania, abandoned her daughter Julia and siblings in Belgium with her father-in-law, former Lieutenant Governor of Tasmania William Sorell, to run off with an army officer (p55). Julia Sorell became almost as notorious as her mother for, so the gossips alleged, having an affair with Lieutenant Governor Eardley-Wilmot and precipitating his recall (p241).

The gossips, indeed, could not get enough of Julia Sorell, as is clearly shown in Lucy Frost's most usefully edited *A Face in the Glass: The Journals of Annie Baxter Dawbin* (1992). **Annie Baxter** (née Hadden, 1816–1905) was an army wife who, newly married and still only 18, accompanied her husband on duty to Tasmania from 1835–38. Her diary – mainly of her later years on the Mainland, though she often visited Tasmania – suggests a woman of some *esprit* but whose behaviour was not always *comme il faut*. (She liked sprinkling her diary with French phrases.) She obviously had it in for Julia Sorell, probably because Annie, though married, was sweet on Richard Dry (later Premier of Tasmania) – a *tendresse* which lasted many years – and was jealous of his attentions to Julia. (In 1853, he was to marry **Clara Meredith**, daughter of Mary and George Meredith of Cambria (p317).)

What is more, on Annie's return to Hobart in 1844 to visit her brother William who had recently arrived there with his wife **Bessie Hadden** (Elizabeth, née Jacquier, c1816–1848) after a separation of brother and sister of ten years, he stopped on the way to the Regatta with her to pick up Julia and her younger sister Augusta. Annie remarked, 'Neither of them are pretty, altho' both are good looking! Their eyes are small & the eldest have the Vixen depicted in them.' A few days later, invited to a party at Government House, she called Eardley-Wilmot 'a fine, gentlemanly old man, but not as much of the "*Prince*", as I was given to understand'. She noted that Julia Sorell was there too, and added: 'she looked vulgar almost, and springs about in such style!' At a country party in February given by Eardley-Wilmot, Annie described Julia: 'with her bonnet off, to show her good hair'.

Among the guests at a ball in Hobart in 1846 was Julia who, Annie wrote, 'is fallen off exceedingly in her appearance, her two front teeth being decayed alters her very much'. In 1848, Bessie had just died and Annie tastelessly suggested to her brother that she had heard a rumour that Julia Sorell had set her cap at him. 'He began to assure me with much gravity', she observed, '... that she was the last person he would ever think of marrying – but as to her being very fascinating & attractive, he allowed she was all this, and more.'

31. Julia Sorell, by Thomas Griffiths Wainewright, c1846,
courtesy of the Tasmanian Museum and Art Gallery

Whatever Julia's past, within weeks of his arrival in Hobart in 1850 as Inspector of Schools, Thomas Arnold, son of the founder of Rugby School and nephew of Matthew Arnold, had fallen for her. Fifty years later, a dozen years after her death, he was to write in *Passages in a Wandering Life* (1900):

I was at a small party ... On a sofa sat a beautiful girl in a black silk dress, with a white lace *berthe* [large round collar] and red bows in the skirt of the dress. My friend Clarke presently introduced me to her. I remember that as we talked a strange feeling came over me of having met her before – of having always known her.

The couple married in St David's Cathedral (p244) in June that year. Annie Baxter wrote: 'The Bride and her sisters were dressed in white muslin, Chip & straw bonnets – but looked very cold, having no shawls, or any kind of outdoor covering... The awful ceremony took place; & they are now "one flesh". May they be happy.' Two weeks later: 'Yesterday William drove me out to call on Mrs Arnold, who received me with a kiss! To my most thorough amazement. She looks very well; and seems snug in her new domicile.'

The Arnolds were settled in Stoke Street for the next three years. Mary was the first of four daughters and four sons who survived. Unfortunately for the well-being of the marriage, Thomas Arnold decided to convert to Catholicism, which he did in 1856. The scientist Sir Julian Huxley, Mary Ward's nephew and Julia's grandson, wrote in *Memories* (1970):

> During the ceremony Julia, a staunch Protestant and very angry about his conversion, collected a basket of stones from her yard, walked across to the nearby Chapel where he was being formally received into the ranks of Catholicism, and smashed the windows with this protesting ammunition. Even this failed to change his heart, though his conversion changed his prospects.

It is too simplistic to say that, as a result, the Arnolds were forced to leave Tasmania, but the adverse gossip about his conversion played a major part in his decision.

Julia Sorell Arnold left an ambiguous mark in Tasmania, but it was not altogether her fault. The Sorell 'taint' went back further, to her grandfather Governor Sorell and Mrs Kent (pp53–5). The mother of (Jessie) **Madge Edwards** (née Archer, 1889–1930), **Amy Archer** (née Sorell, 1868–1909) was Julia Sorell's niece. Madge left a manuscript of her life and family which her daughter, Rosemary Brown, incorporated into *Madge's People: In the Island of Tasmania and Beyond* (2004). In it, Madge wrote that her paternal grandmother, **Anne Hortle Archer** (1825–1899), never called on her maternal grandmother, **Dora Coverdale Sorell** (c1840–1932). 'You see, she did not think us good enough', was the explanation. And the reason: 'It was all owing to a – peccadillo of Governor Sorell's. He is supposed to have done something not quite – it just put the family a little below the salt, with *some* people.'

In spite of that – and the Tasmanian stories were certainly talked about in the English families – Julia became the matriarch of distinguished dynasties in Britain: Mary Ward's daughter, author Janet Penrose, married historian GM Trevelyan, and Mary's sister, Julia Arnold Huxley, was the mother of both Julian and Aldous Huxley. Although the Arnolds' marriage continued tempestuous, and they often lived apart, he, at least, remained devoted to her. She was crippled for the last eleven years of her life, dying in 1888, the year Mrs Humphrey Ward became rich and famous for her novel *Robert Elsmere* – an exploration of religious conflict. Although Mary helped found the Oxford women's college Somerville, she was also, in 1908, the first president of the Anti-Suffrage League. Julian Huxley, named after his grandmother, donated the portrait of her by the convict artist Thomas Wainewright to the Tasmanian Museum and Art Gallery.

Newlands

Just before New Town Road becomes Elizabeth Street, and almost opposite The Friends' School/Boa Vista, turn right (from the north) into Augusta Road. This is the road named after Augusta Fox-Young (p258). There is a drawing in the State Library of 'Tollgate House Augusta Road 1865' by an unidentifiable Miss Shoobridge, member of the extended New Norfolk family (p309).

Along the road, opposite the Calvary Hospital where many Hobart babies are born, is Toorak Avenue. Turn into it and almost immediately on your left is Newlands, another historic house, built sometime between 1826 and 1833, open to the public and catering for weddings and other receptions. The first inhabitant of the house connected with my sketch of Tasmania's history is John Montagu, the Colonial Secretary who made the Franklins' life such a misery and engineered Governor Franklin's recall. He leased the house in 1842, I presume at the time of his dismissal by Franklin and thus at the height of the imbroglio (pp147–8).

Montagu was the chief of the Arthurite clique, so called partly because two of its civil service members had married nieces of Governor Arthur and were thus preferred during his tenure and felt able to continue exercising undue power. But I have so far failed to find the family connection between **Jessy Montagu**, daughter of Major General Vaughan Worsley, whom Montagu married in 1824, and Arthur. Jessy seems to have moved into Newlands with six children, the youngest barely a year old. So much is known about Jane Franklin's reaction to Montagu's activities; nothing, that I can find, about Jessy's. It cannot have been an easy time for her either.

(Sarah) **Elizabeth Grey** (Lysbeth, c1821–1897) was a recent pupil of Ellinthorp Hall (p138) when, aged 17, she married Frederick Maitland Innes in 1838. Three years later, on a visit to London, this is how she was described in a letter contained in descendant Kate Hamilton Dougharty's *A Story of a Pioneering Family in Van Diemen's Land* (1953):

> Of middle size, light hair, approaching almost to sandy, smart, pretty figure, intelligent countenance, very pleasing, affectionate, in short, Irish manner coupled with an agreeable, lively, but shrewd method of expressing herself, which is taking in the extreme.

Lysbeth was of the Grey family of Avoca who had settled there from Ireland in 1828 (p342). Innes had arrived the year before their marriage and started work on the *Hobart Town Courier*, soon moving to the *Tasmanian*; one of his main concerns was prison reform, influenced by Governor Franklin's private secretary Alexander Maconchie. By the time the Innes family moved to Newlands in 1860, Frederick was a member of the House of Assembly and all-powerful Colonial Treasurer. Lysbeth, meanwhile, had five daughters and seven sons.

Kate Hamilton Dougharty describes Lysbeth's married life, including at Newlands, which then had 32 acres of lawn, shrubbery and orchard, and room for archery, croquet, stables and 'other amusements'. The house also had a fine library. The family lived there until 1881, the year before Frederick's death, by which time he had been Colonial Secretary, Premier and twice President of the Legislative Council. The property started to be divided up and sold in the 1920s.

Ancanthe – Jane Franklin Museum, Lenah Valley (open Saturday and Sunday 1.30pm–5pm, summer; 1pm–4pm, winter)

Continue along Augusta Road, enter Lenah Valley and follow Lenah Valley Road. You cannot then miss Jane Franklin's Greek temple, Ancanthe, based on the Temple of Athene in Athens. (You can also take the no. 6 bus from the GPO, Elizabeth Street).

Several of Jane Franklin's projects were linked. The Natural History Society (p145) created a forum for discussion which led to the collection of natural history and scientific objects, specimens and books which began to fill Government House. In 1839, Jane bought 130 acres of land in Kangaroo Valley (since 1922 Lenah Valley) to create a botanical garden for the plants she had brought back from Recherche Bay in 1838 (p259) and in which was to be a museum to house the accumulating treasures. The property was to benefit Christ College which the Franklins were planning to set up in New Norfolk (p303).

Jane's stepdaughter Eleanor wrote of the land, 'We are told by several people who have visited [it], that it is the most beautiful spot they have ever seen. It is a valley clothed with myrtle, fern, sassafras and mimosa trees, and through which runs a clear mountain stream.' Then Jane, at one of the Society's meetings, got those attending to help her find a name; 'Ancanthe' – which was thought to mean 'Vale of Flowers' – was determined upon.

In September 1841, Jane took a party of experts to choose the right site for the museum and, in April 1842, Eleanor wrote: 'Papa laid the foundation stone of the Tasmanian Museum at Ancanthe.' After a picnic there she noted: 'We returned to the stone where a deputation from the boys [of Queen's Grammar School] waited on Papa to petition for a holiday, which we granted, as well as an annual holiday on that day, which they are to spend at Ancanthe, all of which is to be given to the College.'

Finally, by October 1843, just before the Franklins left, the museum was completed and the specimens and books placed in it. One of them was John Gould's *The Birds of Australia* (1840–48), which includes his wife Elizabeth's drawings. Before her death in 1841, she no doubt made sure the early volumes were sent to her friend (p242).

With Jane gone, the museum did not prosper. In 1846, Christ College was founded but, in due course, frittered its funds and neglected its property. The museum's contents deteriorated and were dispersed in 1853. Ancanthe was still a place to visit, however. In 1874, Louisa Travers (p265) organised a picnic there. Servants set out early to arrange the tables, followed by the food. Then, 40 guests assembled at Boa Vista and walked the mile to Ancanthe, returning in the evening for tea and croquet.

But Madge Edwards (p268) visited it at the turn of the century and wrote: 'We went to Lady Franklin's little Greek Museum at the other side of Hobart and I used to imagine it flanked with cypresses, instead of being piled with cases and rotten apples as it was then.' The watercolour 'Ancanthe, Lady Franklin Museum Lenah Valley' by Curzona Allport on the front cover is likely to date from the period 1922–27 when she produced watercolour landscapes. A sepia wash and drawing by Loetitia Casey (p312) is in the Queen Victoria Museum and Art Gallery, Launceston (p373).

Ancanthe's future was much debated over the years. On several occasions, the National Council of Women offered to take over the building for use as a women's museum at a peppercorn rent. Owned since 1936 by the Hobart City Corporation, 'on the condition that it be used according to the wishes of Lady Franklin', the building looks externally much as it did. Inside, the the Art Society of Tasmania, founded in 1884 by landscape painter (then a student) **Louisa Swan** (1860–1955), has had its headquarters since 1948 and holds occasional exhibitions there.

The most appealing flavour of this incarnation comes from Helene Chung in her memoir *Ching Chong China Girl: From Fruitshop to Foreign Correspondent* (2008). She had more problems than being an Australian-born Chinese growing up in 1950s Tasmania: not only were her parents divorced, but her mother, who insisted on using her maiden name, Miss Henry, lived in sin with a 'foreign devil' and drove a red MG. But there was more:

> Even members of artistic families were scandalised by nude modelling. When Mama posed for the artists at Lady Franklin Museum, rumour had it the wife of the group president kept him at home to protect him from the sight of a naked woman.

Even closed, Ancanthe is certainly a place to visit. Like the town of Franklin (p293), it is a monument to Jane Franklin and her wishes for Tasmania.

17 – Risdon Cove to Port Arthur

Risdon Cove

You have two options to start this itinerary: one is to go north from the New Town itinerary, wiggle east to the Brooker Highway, and cross the Derwent by the Bowen Bridge and so to Risdon Cove. (Before the bridge, on your right, is Prince of Wales Bay; somewhere towards the river, in today's Glenorchy, were the 50 acres Martha Hayes was given to farm in 1804 (p21).)

The alternative is to cross the Tamar Bridge and follow the road northwards on the east bank of the river. If you go this way, driving through Lindisfarne turn into Derwent Avenue. No. 18, with its Chinese moon gate, is Marie Bjelke Petersen's house (p239). She wrote in a sunny room hung with her own paintings and died there aged 94.

Although Risdon Cove is the beginning of this itinerary, because of its controversial history it is not an easy place to visit. On the one hand, since time immemorial, it was the land of the Moomairremener people, and it was there, on 3 May 1804, that the Risdon Massacre took place (p18). Looked at from the point of view of the British who settled in Tasmania, it is the place where Martha Hayes, John Bowen and the rest of the first party came ashore in September 1803 and started to build homes (p10).

In 'Risdon Cove and the Massacre of 3 May 1804' (2004), Lyndall Ryan draws on the archaeological work of Angela McGowan to note that her report 'not only found traces of the original buildings, erected by the settlers at Risdon Cove in 1803–4, but also evidence of Aboriginal occupation of 8000 years, including an Aboriginal tool-making site'.

Since the early 1970s, and the resurgence of Aboriginal consciousness, the site has been a bone of contention and in 1995 it was handed over to Aborigines represented by an elected Aboriginal Land Council. In 1999, the cove and other Aboriginal sites were declared indigenous protected areas (p232). For today's Aboriginal community, Risdon Cove is a place of cultural renewal and celebration where the Tasmanian Aboriginal Centre conducts cultural, educational and environmental restoration programmes.

When I first visited Tasmania in 1980, with my husband who lived there between 1968 and 1978, I was taken to see this historic site. There was little there, and no other visitors; we wandered at will. Now, the easiest way is to drive slowly by. Should you want to enter the site itself, I suggest you contact the Tasmanian Aboriginal Centre (hobart@tacinc.com.au) and ask their advice about the current position; perhaps best, even, ask for permission. My attempts to clarify several points for this book have had a chequered history.

I cannot improve on the suggestion of Phillip Tardif in *John Bowen's Hobart* (2003): 'At some places the burden of history proves too great to bear. For the present, Risdon Cove is one of those places.'

There is some discussion about the exact mooring of the *Anson*, the probation hulk for women convicts between 1844 and 1849, but here is the best place to look out onto the Derwent and see Philippa Bowden, her assistants, and those unhappy women they looked after (pp157–66). Typical is Caroline Leaky's Maida Gwynnham in *Broad Arrow*.

Richmond

I'm taking you now to Richmond, but be warned: it is quite a distance from Risdon Cove, the road winding steeply up and down a hill before you reach the most physically historic town in Tasmania. I have usually approached it from Sorell, an easier and pleasing vineyard strewn drive. Louisa Anne Meredith wrote of the journey from Hobart some time after her arrival in 1840:

> Moving over Grass Tree Hill from Risdon we came to the valley of the Coal River with the little town of Richmond in its bosom hemmed in by ranges of hills, not lofty, but infinitely varied in outline. It breaks upon the sight, gaining beauty at each new turn in the winding road until near the foot of the mountain, where a spot is often pointed out to strangers as the scene of an adventure with bushrangers …

It is worth a visit, for the longevity of its buildings and its charm, but others have the same idea! In spite of its history since 1824 and, indeed, several links with women, for reasons of space and lack of links to my history text I have to omit several of them. I hope, however, to put them under 'updates' on the website www.holobooks.co.uk. I am including here Richmond Gaol, the Old Rectory, St Luke's Anglican Church, St Luke's Cemetery and St John's Roman Catholic Church. In the environs are the properties Carrington and Campania.

Richmond Gaol

The gaol, easily found in the middle of the main street, was established in 1825 as a halfway house for male convicts not deemed hard-core enough to be sent to Macquarie Harbour (p59) and later Port Arthur (p280). Although the inmates were mostly male, some women were incarcerated there, mainly after 1835 when solitary cells and a women's room were commenced.

Between 1837 and 1840, 261 women were jailed, for whom 211 records exist, mainly on their way to the Cascades Female Factory (pp62, 247). Of the 211, only 25 women had long records, three were described as 'common prostitutes', and 62 'on the town'. Prior to conviction, 51 were mothers. Others gave birth in the gaol. On 11 March 1838, **Jane Skinner**, attended by **Mary Watson**, released from solitary to help her, had a boy who was baptised on the 18th. He died a week later. **Mary Haigh**, confined there on her way to Cascades, told Governor Franklin's 1841 inquiry (p155) that she was encouraged by the other women in the party to have 'connection with' the constable in charge. **Anne Gough**, assigned to ex-magistrate James Gordon and his wife Elizabeth (p115), was sentenced to solitary between 1837 and 1838 ranging from seven to ten to 25 days for being absent without leave –

that is, disorderly conduct and disobedience. Elizabeth Gordon appears in the Old Rectory next. Ann ended with three months at Cascades. Ann Solomon's husband Ikey spent time there between 1831 and 1834 (pp63–6).

The Old Rectory

On Edward Street, one along from the gaol, is the Old Rectory, what Jane Franklin, visiting it in 1837, called Headlong Hall. Built in 1831 by magistrate James Gordon and his wife Elizabeth (p115), it is a fine example of colonial Georgian architecture. Now privately owned, it was restored to the original design kept in the State Archives. It can be seen from the road.

In 1838, 20-year-old Anne Harbroe travelled out from Surrey to Tasmania with her brother to marry Dr John Coverdale who had arrived the previous year. The wedding took place at St David's Church (p244) six days after her arrival. In due course, having had six children and numerous grandchildren, **Anne Coverdale** (1818–1875) was to be the great-grandmother of Madge Edwards (p268). In 1840, Coverdale was appointed district surgeon for Richmond. The following year, he was accused of not having properly attended an injured man who later died. It was this accusation and the handling of it that finally destroyed relations between Governor Franklin and Colonial Secretary Montagu and led to the latter's dismissal (and eventually to the Governor's recall). Jane Franklin was implicated by Montagu in defending Coverdale on whose behalf the citizens of Richmond had organised a petition. Coverdale was reinstated.

In 1853, the Coverdales moved to the Old Rectory, or Wykeham House as it was then, and in 1860 their daughter Dora (p268) walked from the house to marry Percy Sorell in nearby St Luke's Church; a red carpet was laid door to door so that her feet would not get dirty. In 1865, Coverdale was appointed Superintendent of the Queen's Orphan School (p262) and, in 1874, he was transferred as Civil Commandant of the penal settlement at Port Arthur, where we briefly meet him and Anne again (p282). In 1908, the house was bought by the Church of England and used as the rectory until 1972.

St Luke's Church

Dora Coverdale did not have far to walk in 1860, the church, completed in 1838, is easy to see beyond the Old Rectory. Throughout the years it has been popular for weddings.

St Luke's Cemetery

You look round for the Anglican cemetery and could mistake the nearby Congregational cemetery for it. St Luke's is over by the historic bridge (Australia's oldest) leading into Richmond from Sorell and spread over a sun-bleached slope (Butchers Hill) where the original church was to have been built. It is not at all like an English country churchyard. Here you will find the graves – often in family vaults, of women who lived in houses yet to visit:

- Ann Jane Hobbs Harris Gunning of Campania (p16)
- Eliza Harris Burn of Campania and Roslyn (p35)
- Susan(nah) Ross Stewart of Carrington (p276)

St John's Church

Opposite St Luke's Cemetery, the other side of the river, and in a crescent leading off the main road just before the bridge, is the oldest Roman Catholic Church in Australia (founded 1835). On the left, facing the main porch, is a little grave. Henry Meagher's father, Thomas Francis Meagher, one of the Irish political prisoners (p164), married **Catherine Bennett** (Bennie, c1831–1854) of New Norfolk in 1851 (p338). Little Henry was born after his father had escaped, and died of influenza in June 1852 aged four months. Catherine travelled to Ireland and then joined Meagher in New York, but their relationship had changed and she returned to his family in Ireland, again pregnant. Soon after giving birth she died, aged 22. **Jeanie Reagan** (Jane Anne O'Regan) married another Irish rebel, Patrick Smyth, at St John's in February 1855.

Carrington

Go back now to the main street and take the road leading to Campania; **it also takes you to the Midland Highway, and thus to the north** and those itineraries. Half-way along, between Richmond and Campania, is Carrington which is of some historical significance, but is one of those properties privately owned that cannot be seen from the road. Its history is for the armchair traveller or for those fortunate enough to be invited to visit it by the owners, in 2008, Robert Bowen and his mother Elizabeth Bowen. I can vouch that it is worth a visit. It is always an idea to ask at an information centre if the status of a historic private house has changed.

The original Carrington house dates from 1815, built by Governor Davey and his wife Margaret after Macquarie awarded him 3,000 acres – the largest granted to anyone – in compensation for possessions lost at sea. Neglected by Davey, Margaret and her daughter Lucy (later of Boa Vista, p264) found solace there. When Davey left in 1817, he sold Carrington to his successor William Sorell, so it can be imagined as a love-nest away from the gossip of Hobart for him and Louisa Kent and their growing family (pp53–5). Sorell, in turn, sold it to his successor in 1825, Governor Arthur, making it a country retreat for Eliza Arthur and their even more numerous children.

It was Arthur, so ungenerous with grants to women, who extended his own property to 4,700 acres and had built for his convenience the so-called Carrington Cut, the road that joined Richmond and Carrington to Risdon and its ferry. When Arthur left in 1836, the property was divided into four and the house bought by James Ross, editor of newspapers that supported Arthur and, at one time, tutor to the Arthur children. Ross substantially rebuilt the house, but he died of apoplexy two years later, leaving his wife **Susannah Ross** (Susan, née Smith, 1796–1871) a widow with 13 children. She therefore opened a boarding school at Carrington, but she sold the house in 1842, moved the school elsewhere and married a Hobart solicitor, Robert Stewart. Although she died at Battery Point, she is buried with her first husband in St Luke's Cemetery (p328).

The new owners of Carrington were Esh Lovell and his second wife **Sophia Lovell** (née Adkins). His first wife, the milliner and matron at Cascades Female Factory, Anne Lovell, had died leaving six children (p124). By Sophia, he had another twelve children – eleven of whom survived – all absorbed into Carrington. Two of his daughters by Anne married two sons of the Lovells' neighbours at Laburnum Park, grandsons of dairy farmer Catherine Kearney (p39). Catherine's sons were granted the land at Coal River and built Laburnum Park – further along the Campania road – before her death

The story of **Anne Lovell Kearney** (1827–1898) and **Margaret Lovell Kearney** (1829–1875) is told in the highly-regarded *Letters to Anne* (John Rowland Skemp, 1956). Moving though this account is, beware of facts being overtaken by later research, particularly regarding Catherine Kearney. What I

32. Anne Lovell Kearney, from Skemp, *Letters to Anne*

tell of her in the history section owes most to Irene Schaffer's recent diligence, and the Kearley family's research concerning confusion between two women. The same problem applies to those facts in Mary Kinloch Whishaw's *History of Richmond and Recollections from 1898–1920* (nd).

William Kearney was stabbed to death in 1853, leaving his widow, then aged 24, with three children and pregnant. Margaret later spent many years in the New Norfolk Asylum, and died there (p306). Several of the letters in the book are from her to her sister, and sad reading they make. Anne's marriage was not a success, but she was a survivor.

There were many owners after the Lovells. The most recent, the Bowens, added a two-storey wing to Carrington in keeping with the original. In her younger days Elizabeth Bowen was an active member of the National Trust. The property is also a working farm.

Campania House

The township of Campania is beyond Carrington and a third of the way (7 kilometres) between Richmond and the Midland Highway. When we visited Campania House, a little way out of Campania itself, one of its virtues was that it offered colonial accommodation run by Paddy Pearl – a chance to stay in a historic house, constructed in sandstone and cedar, and to eat local produce and drink local wines. But, as I prepare to send Paddy what I have written for her to check, the internet tells me that she has just, within the last week as I rewrite, sold the property and donated the proceeds to Walter and Eliza Hall Institute of Medical Research. I do not know what Campania House's future status will be.

Anne Jane Gunning, who is buried in the family vault in St Luke's Cemetery, arrived in Tasmania in 1904 with her mother and siblings and soon married George Prideaux Harris (p16) but she was widowed in 1810 when pregnant with her daughter **Melvina Harris** (Malvina, b1811). As the widow of a respected officer, however troublesome Harris had been (p35), her daughters were granted 100 acres each at Coal River in 1813. By 1815, Anne Jane seems to have been living with George Weston Gunning, former soldier and local magistrate; by 1818 they were developing a farm on their combined lands at Coal River and they married in 1820. Maria Lord, who had featured in Harris's troubles, was a witness. Weston House (now Campania House) started in 1813 was completed at about this time. Anne Jane's daughter Eliza married George Burn, nephew of solicitor Robert Pitcairn of Runnymede (p260) at Campania in January 1827. The Burns then lived at Roslyn, built on the grant to the Harris daughters at Coal River, which can be seen from Campania House, though many of the outbuildings were destroyed in the disastrous fires of 1967. Eliza, mother of ten children, lived there for 65 years, managing the property after her husband's death in 1869 and not dying herself until 1892, in her 84th year. She, too, is buried in the Gunning/Burn vault in St Luke's Cemetery.

Sorell (Hilda Bridges)

Back in Richmond, cross the bridge and head towards Sorell. Before you get there, as you join the major road, **note that to turn left takes you up the east coast (and that itinerary)**. Turning right, you reach Sorell and, some way beyond, the Tasman Peninsula and Port Arthur.

Sorell and the area just past it harbour memories of the writer **Hilda Bridges** (1881–1971) and her ancestors. Hilda's great great grandmother, Anne Hannaway Nash (d1829) was transported to Australia with her three children in the Second Fleet of 1790. Removed to Norfolk Island, she married fellow convict Robert Nash; they prospered, were pardoned, had four daughters, and were transferred to Tasmania with the other Norfolk Islanders (such as Catherine Kearney) in 1808 (p39). Once again, Nash prospered; on land at Hobart Rivulet he became Hobart's miller and on 200 acres granted at Pittwater (later Sorell) he grew wheat which he supplied to the Commissariat.

The Nashs' daughter, Sally, was the friend of Salome Pitt described in *That Yesterday Was Home* by Hilda Bridges' brother Roy when she was about to marry John Wood (p43). (Sally was also the sister of Susan who married Catherine Kearney's son William, and of the first wife of George Weston Gunning of Campania.) Hilda and Roy's mother, Sally's granddaughter, was **Laura Wood Bridges** (1860–1825). Roy's biography of his family, and description of his and Hilda's life is much admired, and it enhanced his reputation as a writer. But it seems clear to me that Hilda, described in biographical details as his 'lifelong companion, housekeeper and amanuensis', researched, retrieved from memory, and wrote parts of it. She copied out his books by hand before typewriters were common; she would also walk the 5 kilometres across the creek – the Sorell rivulet – at the bottom of the garden to Sorell to post his or her manuscript.

Of her 13 novels Hilda is best known for *Men Must Live* (1938) in which she shows deep concern for the denuding of land by firewood carters who are the baddies of the story. Her hero, Derek Carrell, arrives from England to inherit his godfather's property, Windbrakes, near Sorell (which Hilda calls Storby). Since his godfather's illness and death, the baddies have set to work and Hilda writes of Carrell's perception: 'It seemed incredible to him that in the few short years, since the advent of the timber mills and their attendant juggernaut cars – the timber, and firewood lorries – could have wrought such havoc.' And later he explains: 'I told you to look at those hills, stripped of timber, to learn the reason [for either droughts or floods].' And the retort from the carter which gives the book its title: 'us men must make a living somehow'.

It's not the greatest literature; it's the sentiment underpinning it that counts. Hilda was ahead of her time environmentally, just as Jane Franklin and Louisa Anne Meredith were in the nineteenth century and Isabel Dick in *Huon Belle* (1930) (p292): it was the 1970s before Tasmanians started to campaign against the despoiling of their environment (p231). *Men Must Live* is almost impossible to get hold of, even to read, at least in the United Kingdom – the British Library has a copy.

33. Laura Wood Bridges, from Bridges,
That Yesterday Was Home

Hilda and several of her ancestors are buried in the cemetery in Sorell. Turn down Henry Street, and beyond the Scots Uniting Church is a second graveyard, on the left. Her grave is rather less ostentatious than that of her more famous brother.

Driving through and past Sorell, a turning on the left is signed East Orielton. Along Pawleena Road, at 20 Bridges Road is 'Woods Farm' where Hilda and Roy lived. I'm not sure that I found the abandoned cottage, but the extended family over the generations moved home in this area and it is the landscape that is Hilda's.

Forcett–Lewisham (Dodges Ferry)

The *Princess Royal* ran aground off Dodges Ferry in 1832 and passengers Catherine and Charles Price spent a week with Elizabeth and James Gordon (pp115, 128). I suspect the Gordons were not yet living in Richmond – though the house was built in 1831 (p274) – but on Gordon's grant at Pittwater (Sorell) which he named Forcett after his birthplace in England. Elizabeth Gordon inherited her husband's Forcett estate when he died there in 1842. It is included in Alice Bennett and Georgia Warner's splendidly illustrated *Country Houses of Tasmania: Behind the Closed Doors of our Finest Colonial Estates* (2009).

Forcett today, a few miles along from Sorell, straddling the main highway, is hardly more than a postal address. The drive between the two has sparkling views of the sea, and on the drive direct from Hobart to Sorell (rather than going by Richmond), you cross water three times – a delight.

Turn right at the sign to Lewisham and Dodges Ferry and you find evidence of not only the *Princess Royal*'s fate, but also that of Sergeant Samuel Thorne and his wife Ann, the baptism of whose child is one of those confusing the first born in Tasmania (p15); he was, in fact, the first born in what was to become the colony of Victoria.

Drive along that turning, and then turn right along Scenic Drive towards the Lewisham Tavern which overlooks the sea and where an ordinary but convenient meal is to be had with a marvellous view. Half-way along towards the tavern on the left is a recreation ground and a bollard with a plaque naming it the Samuel Thorne Reserve. Unfortunately, by the time Samuel was appointed district constable at Sorell in 1829, which is presumably why he is thus honoured, Ann was dead, but the child born at Port Phillip survived and Ann had another three children, some of whose descendants are those of **Harriet Thorne** (b1805). One of them has written *Sergeant Samuel Thorne* (Malcolm Ward, 2007), a copy of which I have not been able to see. There is some suggestion on a website that the remains of the Thornes' house exists near the Lewisham Tavern, but that, too, has escaped me.

Back on the main road, you are soon at Dodges Ferry and there at the jetty is a plaque commemorating the grounding of the *Princess Royal* and the kerfuffle surrounding its women immigrant passengers. There are some fine beaches round here, but best not to let anyone else know!

Port Arthur

The old penal settlement of Port Arthur at the foot of the Tasman Peninsula is 60 kilometres from Hobart, less distance obviously if you are following this itinerary and just leaving the Sorell area, though I doubt if you would want to do the whole itinerary in one day.

Because of its history of brutality between 1830 and 1877 and the massacre of 35 people, mainly tourists, in 1996, Port Arthur is another place to visit with sensitivity towards the past. And, because it was for male convicts, the history of non-convict women who lived there is a strange one. There is also relevant writing by several women.

In spite of the burden of its past, Port Arthur has been called Australia's prime historic site, and oldest continuous tourist attraction, tourists arriving in droves within ten years of its closure. In the 1880s and 1890s, the coach journey from Hobart took eight hours; most took a daily excursion by steamboat. In 1881, Marianne North (p252) was one of those who did the trip – most got seasick. The journey by car today takes about an hour and a half.

Begun in 1830 as a punishment timber station, it soon replaced Macquarie Harbour (p59) and Maria Island as the main location for secondary punishment – for male convicts committing crimes or infringements after transportation. The system was one of hard labour, corporal punishment, and solitary confinement. Reform of convicts was intended, so there was also religious and educational instruction. The convict labour of many kinds helped defray the expense of its maintenance. Its location ensured that it was virtually impossible to escape from, though several were desperate enough to try.

The women there were, to a large extent, divorced from what went on, and yet they were surrounded by it, and their husbands were involved, in one way or another, in its operation. Margaret Glover provides a useful introduction to them in 'Women and Children at Port Arthur' (1985). She believes that **Elizabeth Brownell** (née Freeman, d1875), wife of Dr Thomas Brownell, religious instructor, was the first when she came in 1832. The Brownells married in Yorkshire in 1825, arrived in Tasmania with two children in 1830, and were posted first to Maria Island. They were at Port Arthur then for only six months, leaving either because of Elizabeth's ill-health, or because, according to another source, Brownell felt he was failing to reform the convicts in his charge. He judged the methods of discipline as 'bordering on cruelty' but 'just'. While Elizabeth worked as a school teacher, he tried medical practice and farming, but, by 1840, they were back at Port Arthur, where he was medical officer in charge, for 15 months, and back for nearly five years in 1853. Meanwhile Elizabeth, whatever her ill-health, had completed her family of eleven children, not all of whom appear to have survived.

Charlotte Lempriere arrived with her husband Thomas, storekeeper for the commissariat, in 1834, and they stayed for 15 years. We have already met them at Macquarie Harbour (p60), and they had also spent time at Maria Island. With these inhospitable postings, their marriage and Charlotte's strength – she had twelve children over 20 years – were much tested, and not found wanting. Their relationship had started propitiously. Charlotte's father was in the army in the West Indies with his family; Thomas, an army adjutant seven years older than Charlotte, was acquainted with them. Her father died and the family returned to England, but the couple met again, by coincidence, on the ship out to Tasmania in 1822, and romance blossomed.

One of their daughters was the very active Emily Dobson (p206). From Thomas's diary (held in the Mitchell Library, Sydney), which Margaret Glover draws on, it seems likely that Emily was born at Port Arthur; Charlotte certainly attended another woman during her confinement. The accommodation at the settlement, in spite of the fine buildings around them, was basic. Whatever the drawbacks, Charlotte led a full social, artistic and intellectual life. She was physically active, musically gifted – she played the piano and sang – and her husband enjoyed her company and sought her opinion. He taught the children French, but Charlotte spoke it as well, and it is no wonder that the adult Emily Dobson was linguistically adept in her international work. Charlotte also collected ferns and seaweed.

A French mariner visiting the Lemprieres at Macquarie Harbour in 1831, and Port Arthur in 1839, declared that the mistress of the house 'looked quite as well and as young as she had in 1831, demonstrating that the best possible cosmetics for a woman's charms are tranquillity of mind, self-respect, the affection of those around her and the knowledge that she had fulfilled her duty'. There is something bizarre about such sentiments, and even her tranquillity, under the circumstances. But what else could she do but try and achieve that?

To add to that bizarreness, and indeed that of some aspects of Tasmania and its reconstruction, Lindsay Simpson, in her novel *The Curer of Souls* (2006), portrays Jane Franklin as having an unrequited love affair with Thomas Lempriere. Jane certainly visited Port Arthur (p146) during the Lemprieres' time there, but I'm afraid that's a step too far for me, and on a par with Richard Flanagan's novel *Wanting* (2009) about Mathinna and the Franklins. Jane Franklin and her husband seem to have become a punchbag for modern Australian writers and these fantasy slurs on the reputation of real people call into question a particular type of historical fiction. Having said that, Lindsay Simpson's first fiction work is well crafted, though she did not need, as she does, to acknowledge the influence of AS Byatt's *Possession* (about imaginary historical characters); it is obvious.

Catherine Mitchell (née Keast, 1812–1899) did not lead so apparently tranquil a life at Port Arthur as Charlotte Lempriere. She arrived in Tasmania in 1839 to marry John Mitchell, Superintendent of Point Puer, the boys' section of the penitentiary, and they lived there until 1849. All we know about Catherine's time there is the haunting pencil sketch, the title of which says it all and is ironic considering her husband's position: 'Isle de Morts, Port Arthur, Tasmania. My first two darlings lie here. Francis Keast Mitchell and Henry John Mitchell – first 8 months, second 10 months.' Her babies died in 1841 and 1843; in all, she had three daughters and seven sons.

34.   'Isle de Morts', by Catherine Mitchell, from www.john-daly.com/deadisle/sketch

The Isle of the Dead is just off Port Arthur and it is possible to access on the internet the names on the graves in the cemetery, though most convict graves are unmarked. Anne Coverdale of Richmond (p274) died at Port Arthur in

1875 when her husband was its last Commandant, but she seems to have been buried elsewhere. The Isle of the Dead, like Point Puer and everything else, has organised tours. In a horrible twist, Anne's brother, Dr Edward Harbroe, found guilty of attempting to solicit a boy near Fingal, was sentenced to Port Arthur – but he had already been transferred to the New Norfolk Asylum when the Coverdales arrived there.

Jacobina Burn's (p74) granddaughter, Jemima Burn Irvine, accompanied her husband when he was appointed senior Assistant Superintendent of 1,300 prisoners in 1846, and they were there until 1850. In her older age she not only told KR von Stieglitz about a childhood attack by Aborigines (p102), but also about Port Arthur. Her memory of it needs to be quoted nearly in full, and I leave it to you to decide what to make of it in conjunction with other accounts (I have left out only her dropping plugs of tobacco for a prisoner to pick up):

> There has been a great deal of exaggeration about Port Arthur and the way the prisoners were treated there, but you have only to look at the numbers of them who came on and did well for themselves to realise that it was not so bad after all. Some of them were flogged, of course, but this did not happen very often. I don't remember a single case of misconduct all the time we were there, so orderly were the prisoners ...
>
> We used to have them as servants and some of them had worked in the best houses in England. You can have no idea what good work they used to do and how much we came to like some of them. They were not the depraved nearly maniac creatures you may have read about, at all. Some of them had been sent out for trifles, and never broke the law again.
>
> In those days there was a charming society at Port Arthur. We had the Commandant and his clerks, the Superintendent and his clerks, Mr Lempriere, the deputy-commissary-general and his clerks, two military officers and a detachment of soldiers, two clergymen – Church of England and Roman Catholic, and two doctors. There were no lawyers – we were a peaceful settlement! Most of these men had families; all were intelligent, musical and altogether delightful people.
>
> There were beautiful gardens, all kept in perfect order and all kinds of flowers and vegetables grew well there.

Caroline Leakey (p165) arrived at Port Arthur to try and regain her health in 1851 and spent a year there staying with the Reverend Thomas Garlick and his wife, **Anne Garlick** (née Miles) and their three children, one of whom had been born that year. In *The Broad Arrow*, the Garlicks become the Harelicks, and the Reverend Herbert Evelyn, father of the sickly Emmeline (who must represent the author herself) is temporarily to replace Harelick as the minister.

In comparing Caroline Leakey's novel with Marcus Clarke's *For the Term of His Natural Life*, the contrast could not be more striking between the control and subtlety of the writing in *The Broad Arrow* and the uncontrolled, unbearable brutality of the treatment of Rufus Dawes.

Caroline describes the ordinary life of the women there but then Emmeline's cousin Bridget – who had earlier visited the women's convict hulk the *Anson* (p166) – stands in front of the lovely English church at Port Arthur and extols its beauty. Her interlocutor replies: 'Beautiful as it is, it was sown in blood, Miss D'Urban, as indeed we may say of the whole civilized structure of this island.' Mrs Evelyn plays the Mrs Bennet role, making the shadows around her darker by careless talk and odd behaviour.

The assigned servant Maida Gwynnham follows the family to Port Arthur and sees the place and its context more clearly than the others as she nurses Emmeline and accompanies her coffin to the Isle of the Dead.

Tasma's short story 'What an Artist Discovered in Tasmania' (1878), from where I took the quotation that starts the preface, is rather idiosyncratic. A London artist arrives at Port Arthur to paint 'the most hardened criminal face on the earth'. That is not how it turns out. The punishment of convicts is over when Tasma (pp68, 256) sees it as the place where Cain would have killed his brother Abel. Setting the scene, she writes:

> Whether from the association that has gathered round it, or from a natural exclusiveness breathed in its rocky boundary, it seems to scowl in its solitude like an outcast from the mainland ... The salt breezes may blow across Port Arthur at the present time, untainted by convict breath, yet I question whether the echo of the clanking chain, and the reprobate's curse, will not sound above the 'swish' of the tide and the rustling of the fruit trees for many a generation to come.

Following the closure of the penal settlement in 1877, Port Arthur was to have a chequered career of selling off of properties and attempts to retrieve them, of decay and attempts at preservation, of fossicking from its structure of materials by inhabitants of the township, named Carnarvan, that had sprung up, and attempts to retrieve them. In any case, the convict bricks had been under-fired and so were of little use. Bushfires in 1895 and 1897 further ravaged it.

In 1888, a pottery was set up at Port Arthur producing artefacts of that name. Well known for their artistic and literary talents were the sisters **Heather Mason** and **Anne Mason**. Heather hand-painted pottery at or from Port Arthur and entered samples of it in the 1894–95 Tasmanian International Exhibition of Industry, Science and Art. The sisters also painted two of the six murals in the Commandant's residence which became a hotel after 1877, one of which shows a boating scene, possibly in Venice, the other the Parthenon. The sisters left Tasmania in 1897. Heather appears to have exhibited at the Royal Academy, London, in 1907. In 1971, the potter **Alice Mylie Peppin** (1907–1992) set up a pottery at Port Arthur in memory of the potter Maude Poynter (who appears in the 'Midland Highway' itinerary (Bothwell, p329)).

Mary Grant Bruce (Minnie, 1878–1958), journalist and children's author, visited from Melbourne in 1913 and published 'Port Arthur Today' in which she described the severe cracking in the edifice of the church and the fire damage to many buildings, destroying woodwork and weakening masonry.

Melbourne lawyer **Anna Teresa Brennan** (1879–1962) (not to be confused, as has been done, with Anna Helen Brennan) was the first Australian-born woman admitted to practice. After a visit in November 1918, she starts 'Peace at Port Arthur' (1918): 'Today Port Arthur is a tourist resort built upon a memory…' The ruins make her think of 'some ancient monastic house'. In spite of the decay and destruction of the buildings, avenues of old trees remain and at the end of one of these, 'stands a willow tree planted by Lady Franklin … She had brought the slip of willow from Napoleon's grave.' Jane Franklin was in the habit of planting trees hither and yon. The two willows she planted at the New Norfolk Asylum (p305) and one at Turriff Lodge (p302) were said to come from the same source. Then there was the pear tree at the Bush Inn at New Norfolk (p301), and a Cypress and a pear tree just outside Franklin (p294). The peace the title refers to is not that of a deserted ruin but, as Anna ends:

> The little township is taking its evening rest, when suddenly a shot is heard, then another. We know what it means. Here, as elsewhere, throughout the Allied nations, the great news has come. The still spring night breaks into pandemonium. There is no sleep till late that night … Next day the little village is astir. It is the children's day. I watch them as, each carrying a flag, they march in procession down the convicts' avenue. The taint of slavery is gone, a new generation hails its ransomed freedom. At night there is a glare across the water. A bonfire is burning upon the Island of the Dead.

Chloe Hooper's novel *A Child's Book of True Crime* (2002), called 'an erotic thriller', is set before 1996 in a small town near Port Arthur and tells of a young school teacher, Kate Byrne, having an affair with the father of one of her pupils. His wife has just published a novel about a wife stabbing her husband's mistress to death. Kate takes her class to the visit the ruins of the old penal settlement and, in the first-person narrative, gives a lyrical description of what she sees.

You might wonder why I now go backwards to 1953; it will become apparent. On Tasmanian-born Carmel Bird's website (www.carmelbird.com) you will find 'Summer at Port Arthur 1953' about a two-week camping holiday her extended family spent there on the 'grassy piece of flat open land that went from the sea to the ruins of the old convict settlement'. While their fathers went fishing, she and her cousin clambered all over the ruined and unstable buildings, in retrospect oblivious of health and safety. The 'golden church' that Bridget D'Urban had admired and that described by Kate Bryne without its steeple, resembled for Carmel 'a romantic little Norman castle'. It was an idyllic childhood holiday.

But in 1996 Carmel's 'Fresh Blood, Old Wounds: Tasmania and Guns' was published following the Port Arthur massacre that year (it can also be found on her website). She wrote: '… people spoke of "Tasmania's loss of innocence". If Tasmania was ever innocent, it was innocent a long, long time ago.' And she wrote of 'many old, old wounds which have been suppurating beneath the surface of Tasmania for years, concealed but active'.

Margaret Scott (1934–2005), poet, teacher and environmentalist, migrated to Tasmania in 1959. Retired from teaching in 1991, she settled on the Tasman peninsula to write and restore a federation homestead which burnt down, together with all her papers, in 2003. By the time she died, there was a growing arts community on the peninsula of which she was an important part. The massacre of 1996 therefore hit her hard, but she was determined to send out a positive message about it in *Port Arthur: A Story of Strength and Courage* (1997), and an account in *Changing Countries: On Moving from One Island to Another* (2000) – a mixture of fiction, essays, autobiography and poetry. She wrote:

> Five people ended up jammed together by the locked door in the gift shop, but the panicky stampede for safety, the screaming and clawing and thrusting away of the helpless, simply did not happen. Perhaps things went on so fast that there was no time for panic to set in, and yet that explanation won't quite do. People did react to danger. A number of people pushed someone else out of the way, but never, it seems, to try and save themselves; it was always in an attempt to save another's life ... They were generous, loving and brave and although many of them died, they demonstrated that, when put to the ultimate test, altruism is alive and well in late twentieth century Australia. For that, in a time when it often seems that selflessness is an outdated virtue, we owe them an immeasurable debt.

I suspect those two reactions by contemporary women writers and thinkers are not contradictory, but compatible, and both necessary.

18 – Oyster Cove to Recherche Bay

Oyster Cove

Take the A6 south out of Hobart in the direction of Kingston, and pass Snug. That is where Cassandra Pybus bought her uncle's house and, for the whole history of this area – Snug, Oyster Cove, Kettering and Bruny Island where the Pybus family arrived in 1829 – you cannot do better than her *Community of Thieves*.

Richard Pybus was granted 2,560 acres on North Bruny where he took his second wife **Hannah Pybus** and their two children, but the extended family of Pybus descendants gradually had property on the shore opposite. *Community of Thieves* tells the story of the family, the area, those they displaced and those who were briefly their neighbours. Cassandra Pybus constantly returns to the past of her family in her writing and the implications for the Aborigines:

> What was done is done ... Those early settlers, my ancestors, were simply creatures of their time, which is to say they were men like other men; no better, nor worse. The past is a foreign country: they do things differently there. Ah, but that is not how it seems to me on this morning ... We have been very happy here in the territory of the Nuenone people. Has any one of us paused to do a reckoning?

Of her home, she writes:

> So it is that I now inhabit the landscape of my dreams. I live in the house that was built by my father's brother beside a narrow unsealed road which winds along the very edge of North West Bay and over the hill to descend somewhat precariously into Oyster Cove – Old Station Road, the original road to the Aboriginal station ... I am the last Pybus in the channel country.

The 'Aboriginal station' is what you have come to see; it is what is left of the place where most of the Aborigines transferred from Flinders Island to Oyster Cove in 1847 spent their last days. Chapter 12 of my historical section tells that story.

Oyster Cove is now Aboriginal sovereign territory (Chronology, Chapter 13), so to visit it the same suggestions I make for Risdon Cove apply (p272). Nevertheless, you can stop outside the gate, which may well be locked and look – though there is nothing left of the 1847 buildings – and think. The smell of eucalypt is strong. If you are fortunate enough to be allowed in, or to be taken in, your thoughts may be more profound.

For today's Aboriginal community Oyster Cove is one of the most sacred of their cultural places, where they hold ceremonies associated with the repatriation of human remains and an annual festival. Cassandra Pybus movingly describes attending one, crossing Mathinna Creek – named for the place where Mathina drowned, drunk and abused (p188) – to do so. A conversation Cassandra had with Carol, a cousin's wife, on that occasion when she proposed writing a book sums up the problem of writing about Tasmanian Aborigines, even for her, let alone an outsider like me; Carol replied sharply:

> 'First we steal the blackfellas' land, then we deny them an identity and now you want to steal their story for your own intellectual purposes. Don't you think that's just another kind of colonialism?' Carol is enrolled in an Aboriginal Studies degree, by correspondence, in Adelaide. She has a point.

Cassandra wrote the book!

The turning first left after the Old Station is Manuka Road and, on the left, is 'Manuka' on the site of the old Crowther house of that name. It burnt down, like so much of the area, in the terrible fires of 1967. The original was built by the brother of Elizabeth Crowther who married William Blyth and went to live at Bushy Park in New Norfolk (p308). The rebuilt cottage is lived in by Mary Cree and her sister, Crowther descendants. Mary Cree's *Edith May 1895–1974: Life in Early Tasmania* (nd) is the story of her mother, **Edith May Crowther Chapman** (Molly), and the Crowther family. Molly was at his side when her brother William donated his collection of books and other historical materials to the State Library in 1964. In her later years, she lived at 11 Cumberland Terrace, Battery Point, Hobart, and there is a commemorative plaque on the wall outside.

Mary Cree records Molly's first view of the destruction of Manuka in 1967: 'When I got down in the Red Cross car a few days later it was like Siberia – white ash and black stumps.' Old pear trees had survived, however, and blossom appeared the following spring.

Bruny Island

Go now to Kettering. You can either continue along Manuka road, round the headland, or go back to the main road and direct. All the land between Oyster Cove and Kettering used to be Crowther or Pybus land. It is from Kettering that you get the ferry to Bruny Island (15 minutes). There is a pleasant café at the Kettering terminal. The ferry takes you to the north half of an island which is, in many ways, two islands joined by a very slender isthmus.

In *Community of Thieves*, Cassandra Pybus – whose family lands were in the northern part – dates Aboriginal occupation of Bruny Island by the Nuenone band, determined by as yet incomplete archaeological exploration, to 6,000 years. The last of the Nuenone, including the most famous, Trukanini, left with Robinson in 1829 (p108).

Several European expeditions landed on Bruny Island before the beginning of white settlement on the Tasmanian mainland in 1803. François Péron of the Baudin expedition who met Ouray-Ouray at today's Cygnet in 1802 (pp6–8), met another interesting and named woman, **Arra Maïda**, a few days later on

Bruny, though his impression of Bruny Islanders was rather different from that he had of Ouray-Ouray and her family.

35.   Arra Maïda, by Nicolas Petit, from
Bonwick, *The Last of the Tasmanians*

Péron and his companion came upon a group of 20 women, naked save the odd kangaroo skin round the shoulders, laden with rush baskets of the shellfish they had been collecting. At first scared, the women were persuaded to engage and, indeed, became lively and mocking. Péron proceeds to describe them in unflattering, mostly crude, terms. In 'François Péron and the Tasmanians: An Unrequited Romance' (2007), Shino Konishi writes: 'It was what he said about indigenous people and how he perceived women that offended me.'

At this meeting, the Frenchmen did not take the lead, that was very much Arra Maïda's role, bossing not only them but the other women when they got nervous. She sang and danced (in a way which Péron found too suggestive for a romantic Frenchman) and covered the visitors' faces with crushed charcoal, as Ouray-Ouray had done with her own face.

Péron noted of the women that they were 'almost all covered with scars – miserable evidence of their fierce husbands' mistreatment of them', without realising that the scarring may have been created as decoration of cultural significance. This mistreatment was the conclusion he drew when he finally saw the women with their men. The attitude of the Nuenone men may have stemmed from earlier meetings with Europeans, particularly sealers lacking French gallantry and friendliness, or from a colleague of Péron's who had earlier bested them in bouts of physical combat intended to be friendly.

Whatever the cause, Péron noted of the women that 'their fierce husbands shot looks of rage and fury at them'. The men also shared out the food placed by the women at their feet among themselves, without offering any to their women. The women no longer spoke or smiled and kept their eyes lowered.

Péron was to meet Arra Maïda again, this time with a small child on her back, and she was sketched by his companion – a portrait showing 'that proud, confident nature which eminently distinguished her from all her companions'.

Trukanini was only able to return to Bruny Island after 1847 and then just for short visits from Oyster Cove (p191). But her ashes are scattered in the channel in between (p231). When you reach the isthmus, driving south from the ferry, you will see a natural mound called the Hummock. At the top of the steps is Truganini Lookout with spectacular views. Well worth the climb. And at dusk on the shore below, you can watch fairy penguins returning, often in phalanxes, to their burrows.

If you decide to stay at a guesthouse on Bruny (as we did many years ago at the Mavista Cottages) you will want a good book to read for lazing on idyllic beaches where once Aboriginal women roamed collecting shellfish or from where they dived into the depths for them. Your best bet is beautifully-conceived and written *The Alphabet of Light and Dark* (2002) by Hobart-based Danielle Wood. It was inspired by the adventures of her grandfather, the lighthouse-keeper at Cape Bruny, on the southernmost tip of the western part of South Bruny.

Twenty-nine-year-old Essie, the novel's main character, returns to the lighthouse when her grandfather dies, and describes the beginning of that journey:

> Bruny Island follows Tasmania like a comma, a space for pause. The ferry chugs towards it, along the dotted line that is drawn on maps across the channel at one of its narrowest points, leaving behind the town of Kettering and its harbour cross-hatched with jetties and the masts of yachts.

What follows is full of history, yearning, romance and tension.

Nicholls Rivulet

If, instead of driving on to Kettering to take the ferry to Bruny Island, you had taken the right-hand turning opposite Oyster Cove, you would have driven inland taking a short cut to Cygnet and come upon Nicholls Rivulet. This is Fanny Cochrane Smith territory (p119), and her descendants still live in the area. She had eleven children with her British husband and taught them traditional Aboriginal skills and respect for their ancestors. From Oyster Cove, Trukanini and other Aborigines living there would visit Fanny and be culturally refreshed.

Fanny gave half an acre of her land for a wooden Methodist chapel and raised money for its construction in 1901 by holding picnics, concerts and parties; she saw it as a bridge between the Aboriginal and colonist communities. It still stands and has been restored by the South Eastern Tasmanian Aboriginal

Corporation as the Living History Museum of Aboriginal Cultural Heritage to celebrate the ways in which Fanny maintained the culture and tradition of her people. The museum is open from 10.30am to 14.30pm seven days a week, excluding public holidays.

36. Fanny Cochrane Smith wearing a shell necklace, courtesy of the Allport Library and Museum of Fine Arts, Tasmanian Archive and Heritage Office (ch18p4)

Cygnet

Nicholls Rivulet is not far from Cygnet at the head of the Port Cygnet inlet. Before the township was a gleam in anyone's eye, this is where in 1802 François Péron and his comrade met Ouray-Ouray of the Melukerdee band (pp6–8).

Lymington

Drive from Cygnet down the west shore of Port Cygnet and, two thirds of the way along, just before the bend into the mouth of the Huon River is Lymington. This is where Isabel Dick (p309) was brought in 1908 by her new husband Ronald, son of a former tea planter in Ceylon. He had trained to be an orchardist, but fruit growing at Lymington was a constant struggle and, in 1913, he took Isabel and their two children back to England to farm; but, in 1915, he died suddenly. Isabel returned to Tasmania and lived in Sandy

Bay, Hobart (p250); and there, to earn her living, she started to write more seriously than previously.

She set the early novel *Huon Belle* (1930, 2008), published under the name Charlotte I Dick, around Lymington. From the Huon Valley, that is, from the south, part of the Wellington Range of mountains is known as the Sleeping Beauty or the Huon Belle – the profile of a giant woman lying on her back. Marie Bjelke Petersen's version gives a fair impression. Seen from the Derwent Valley to the north west, the image shifts and the same part of the range is named by its constituent peaks.

37. 'Sleeping Beauty' (Huon Belle), by Marie Bjelke Petersen, from Alexander,
A Mortal Flame

CA Cranston has described this novel by Isabel Dick, a member of the hop-growing Shoobridge family introduced in the next itinerary, as offering 'an eco-feminist perspective on intrinsic and economic values of land'. But for Virginia (Ginny) Lee, child of nature, who has wangled a job within sight of the Huon Belle, it is less intellectual:

> There was something utterly tranquil in the attitude [of the Huon Belle]; and something infinitely peaceful, tolerant, beautiful in those guarding mountains had affected the little bush girl so deeply that it was just as she had said, she had *got* to live within sight of it; of that maternal dignity, brooding, as the massive figure did, above the lives of those who worked out their days in its shadow. She was too ignorant to express even to herself

the reason she was so affected by the mountains; she had never heard the words lure, enchantment, infatuation; wouldn't have understood them if she had, for she was only a country-bred girl, parented (it was rumoured) by a hardworking timber hand and an immigrant Scotswoman who had found her way to Tasmania, and there ... lived and died.

Having obtained her heart's desire to gain employment on an orchard within sight of the Huon Belle, Ginny has to fight to retain it. 'The patriarchal order', as CA Cranston has it, 'is replaced by the primacy of feminized and productive nature.' Again, less intellectually, the ending is a bit soppy!

Franklin

From Lymington, you can take the long way round, up the west bank of the Huon River, or go back to Cygnet and take the cross-country main road to Huonville. Then drive down the west bank to Franklin. You can also drive direct from Hobart, 47 kilometres on the Huon Highway.

Coming into Franklin on the left is a boat yard. There in 1992 former academic John Young and his wife Ruth Young established a boat-building school which was bought in 2000 by a not-for-profit local community organisation and renamed the Wooden Boat Centre. The Youngs then ran the Living Boat Trust for children with special educational needs. The first boat built at the school in 1992 was the *Lady Jane Franklin*.

In the forecourt of the Boat Centre on a freestanding notice board is the following text, or was when I jotted it down in 2006:

> Not content to sip tea in government house, Lady Jane Franklin pursued her interests in science, education, exploration and agriculture during her husband's term as Governor. She was one of this districts first landowners, taking 644 acres near here in 1837. Lady Jane Franklin made frequent visits to her property sailing in her ketch the *Huon Pine*. Before leaving the colony in 1843, she also encouraged improvements to the rough track to Hobart although it was not passable by carts and carriages until the 1860s.

Jane bought the land for £700 from John Price who, a year later, in 1838, married her niece Mary Franklin (p145). In 1839 she started distributing it to poor and honest settlers, interviewing every applicant before handing over the 100- or 50-acre allotments, and keeping one for herself.

The settlement was not an immediate success, the settlers were so poor, but Jane was determined and paid £300 for the construction of the *Huon Pine* for 'the service of my new settlement', which she called Huon Fernlands. She also had a chapel built in 1839; today's 1864 St John's is on the site of the earlier St Mary's.

When Jane bought her acreage, widower John Clark had just settled on the riverside, one of only three settlers in the area, at what was to be called Woodside. He was also to manage the neighbouring allotment Jane kept for herself and he and his family were to play a major part in her last visit to what became Franklin. In *Woodside Descendants* (1991), Douglas Clark describes relations between Jane Franklin and the Clarks. He also charts who took which Franklin allotment and when they moved in.

The relationship started early. On 19 September 1838, 14-year-old Eleanor Franklin noted in her diary of a trip up the Huon:

> A heavy hail shower drove us in at Clarke's property. He is so industrious that with the help of another man ... he has built a hut, cleared a great deal of land and sown some potatoes etc in 12 months. It is impossible to get through some of this scrub without a hatchet.

As early as the spring of 1838, Clark had planted fruit trees obtained from Government House. When I visited Woodside in 2007, I was taken to see a pear survivor (Black Aachen) – another of Jane Franklin's many Tasmanian trees. It still blossoms and fruits every year. Naomie Clark also showed me the exquisite tea set bought by John Clark in China for his first wife and handed down over the generations to Naomie, though too fine a porcelain and precious to be used. In 1841, Clark began to build a proper house on the site of today's homestead.

On 20 April 1843, in the Huon chapel, he married **Sarah Kellaway** (b1825), whose family had arrived in Hobart in 1834 and settled on the other side of the Huon. The couple had been earlier recognised as man and wife until someone arrived to marry a waiting group. Their first child (of ten) was born on 21 June that year and, on 5 November, she was christened in the Huon chapel by Bishop Nixon with Jane and John Franklin in attendance. They had already left Hobart after John Franklin's recall and were at the beginning of their journey back to England; they met their ship at the mouth of the Huon. Jane's diary records the christening:

> The Bishop on saying, 'Name this child.' Received the answer:
> 'Jane Franklin Louisa' – 'What?' said the Bishop. It was repeated, the Bishop's eyes twinkled and the sweet little baby which had one of the finest pair of eyes I ever saw received its names. Mrs Clark assured me it was not she who desired it, meaning she had not the presumption to ask it, but her husband who would like it so called. I had myself told him that if it would give him any pleasure to give it my name, I would be glad if he did so.

The sleeping arrangements for that night still cause amusement in the Clark family. Jane wrote: '[Clark's] wife and the baby had gone to her father to make more room for us. Clark slept by the kitchen fire and the remainder of the accommodation was given up to us.' That was the women in the party; John Franklin slept on the *Huon Pine*. As well as her name, Jane also gave the baby a Bible and prayer book suitably inscribed, and she had brought a joint of meat for the family. Jane Franklin's sleeping quarters that night were demolished in 1912, but today's house is on the site of the original. It was lucky not to have been burnt down in 1967 when the raging bushfires approached very close.

At the time of the Second World War there were 2000 fruit growers in the Huon Valley; there are now only about 150, the Clarks – father, daughter and granddaughter - being one of the families. Their property is raised up above the road that runs along the river half-way between Franklin and Huonville, with 'Woodside' writ large on a blue corrugated roof. You don't need to disturb the family should you stop at the wayside shelter and buy bags of Woodside apples and pears. Who knows, some may be ancient Black Aachen. You can see the house at the top of a short drive.

As for Jane Franklin, it would be nice to think that the idea for a memorial on the Glebe in front of what was the Huon chapel will soon be given substance. Marianne North gives an impression of Franklin in 1881:

Franklin was a damp feverish swamp. The winters were very long, and strangers seldom came to cheer them. It had been an old convict-settlement, and the place and people had a bad name; wrongly, for they were a most sober, peaceable community. I asked if the people were better off than at home, and was told that out of a hundred cottages I should not find one without a piano! though the master was a mere labourer, and no instrument could be had for less than £30. Wages were very high, and the fruit-shops so abundant that a large profit could be made every year by the sale of the surplus fruit.

The piano is significant, for it is from this background and this area that Amy Sherwin, 'the Tasmanian Nightingale', sprang (pp237, 247); indeed, in the 1860s, Amy, still a child, helped rescue the family's piano from a forest fire that burnt down their homestead.

The town of Franklin fell into the doldrums after 1929, when local government moved to Huonville and road transport replaced river, but has recently recovered owing to a real community spirit initially prompted by a conservation campaign. Activity, much of it led by women, takes place at the Palais Theatre, formerly the Town Hall. The town's decline and beginnings of rejuvenation are neatly covered in John Young's 'Back to the Future: Choosing a Meaning from Regional History' (1995). There are at least two good restaurants: Petty Sessions (the old court house) and Aqua Vita. They may have changed hands.

Dover

Further down the Huon Highway from Franklin is what used to be called Port Espérance, the name of one of the ships of the d'Entrecasteaux expedition that took Louise Girardin to Recherche Bay (p3), next and last stop on this itinerary, in 1792 and 1793.

In the centre of Dover is a cenotaph topped by an Australian soldier and engraved with the names of the fallen but, on the plinth beneath, is a metal plaque which reads, touchingly misspelling her name:

> To commemorate Giradrin first white woman who arrived disguised as an officer of the d'Entrecasteaux expedition 1792–93 unveiled by Minister Industrial Development Hon SCH Frost 3.1.76 donated by APH Ltd.

This unveiling took place before Paddy Prosser of Dover became a Louise Girardin activist (p4). I met her in 2006 and kept in touch. In 2008 she wrote to me of Louise:

> She now has a lane named after her on the hill just behind the cenotaph in Dover. Some friends of mine are developing the land and they fought the local council tooth and nail for the right to give her name to a little street. She also lives on in other ways, I am continuing my work with students teaching them the d'Entrecasteaux story. Louise's tale always seems to engage them and we have had some wonderful discussions about the times, her character, motivation and tragic end. When I have an all girls group I dress up one of them in 18th century female garb including wig, hoop skirt and corset and challenge them to various tasks. I use Louise's life to illustrate the difference between the role of women in the 18th century and today. We have lots of fun and the point is made with laughter, music and story.

Louise started life as Marie Louise Girardin, one of nine children of a former gardener at Versailles who became a wine merchant. In 1776, aged 22, she married a café proprietor at Versailles; their baby died in 1778 and she was widowed in 1881. At the beginning of the Revolution she fled home in disgrace after giving birth to an illegitimate child and arrived in Brest as a youth with a letter of introduction that enabled her to gain employment as steward in the expedition about to set out. As a steward, Louise was exempt from medical examination and had a cabin of her own. Paddy Prosser's play (p4) tells this story, and that of the rest of her life.

Louise's tragic end occurred after the expedition had left Recherche Bay and headed towards Batavia. During that journey she is believed to have formed an attachment, as a woman, with a young ensign on the *Recherche* but, following news of the King's execution, the expedition broke up. They both died of dysentery in December 1794. The ship's surgeon revealed her true gender.

Recherche Bay (pronounced '*Research*')

Driving from Dover to Recherche Bay we played the CD bought at the bakery in Dover, 'Song, Satire and a Big Dose of History', composed and sung by the Recherche Baybes: Paddy Prosser, Deborah Wace and cellist Anna Spinaze. Tracks include, 'Girardin Jive' and 'Louise's Song' – all clever and great fun.

Six days after I met Paddy and bought the disc, the Huon Valley Australia Day Awards recognised the trio for their community work.

The road beyond Southport, south of Dover, is quite hard going, though it may have improved, and you wonder if you have gone wrong somewhere. But persevere. Suddenly you come out of the miles of dark trees and into a wide open bay flooded with light. No one had warned us how beautiful it is. There are some houses here; ignore them and continue round the first bay and part of the way round Rocky Bay. Park at a sign saying 'Whale Walk 10 minutes return' and 'Fishers Point 2 hours return'. The huge whale sculpture looking out to sea is worth a diversion, but then return to the track you passed on your right.

Follow the track through an enchanted wood until you come to a cove where surely Louise Girardin set foot. That, anyway, is what Louise activists believe for it is here that the photograph of the Recherche Baybes on the cover of the disc was taken, and where Louise's duel with the beastly chief pilot was re-enacted – a scene from Paddy Prosser's play 'The Strange Journey of Louise Girardin' – during the Art on the Beach Festival in 2005, part of the anti-logging campaign (p4). A photograph of the duel – with the French actor Annick Thomas playing Louise – is to be found in Bruce Poulson's *Recherche Bay: A Short History* (2005).

If you are lucky, though, you will be alone on that beach and you may feel that you have found paradise.

Of course, long, long before Louise Girardin and her compatriots set foot at Recherche Bay, the Lyluequonny people roamed free there. Trukanini was born at Recherche Bay in about 1812 (p108). Following the murder of her mother during her childhood, her stepmother was kidnapped, it is said from Recherche Bay in 1829. Robinson reported that it was by those who mutinied on board the *Cyprus* taking shelter in the Bay. But his report is the only evidence for this. Trukanini's father told him that 'soldiers' had taken her and that they had gone to England in a ship. But, as Robinson explained, soldiers could also mean armed seamen. However she disappeared, she did so at that time.

The captain of the *Cyprus* was Lieutenant William Carew, newly arrived in Tasmania and in charge of the 63rd Regiment taking 31 hardened convicts to Macquarie Harbour (p59). The mutineers forced 43 passengers ashore, including Mrs Carew, her two children (one of them a babe in arms), two servants (a woman and her husband) and some of the convicts before sailing off. The castaways, particularly Mrs Carew and her maid, were treated courteously by the 'pirates' and no one was manhandled, which may suggest that Trukanini's stepmother was kidnapped by other white men, perhaps on Bruny Island.

Mrs Carew helped build the coracle that allowed a party to set out for help. She was a clever needlewoman and knew how to cut out and fit material. She also had a pair of scissors with her. They were all eventually rescued, Carew to be court-martialled, but exonerated. The full story, as far as the facts are available, is told in *The Pirates of the Brig Cyprus* (Frank Clune and PR Stephensen, 1962).

Jane Franklin and her party also took shelter in Recherche Bay in 1838 on their way to Port Davey where she wanted to see the progress made on the ketch *Huon Pine* she had commissioned (p145). She wrote of the site of the *Cyprus* castaways: 'I believe the landing place in question was the W point of the most western of the coves which I have called Lucas Cove.' Lucas was their pilot and she also named a rivulet after him because he had been shipwrecked with her husband in Australian waters in 1803.

Jane's description of the environs of Recherche Bay ties in well with the successful twenty-first-century campaign to prevent logging and otherwise preserve the environment of the area, including the 1792 French Garden which she had sighted and which was rediscovered in 2003 by environmental activists Helen Gee and Bob Graham. Jane wrote:

I was struck as we moved along with the dense gloom and blackness of the woods as they rose immediately from the shore upon the outer base of dark-hued rocks. Over these the mountains behind Research Bay presented a noble and singular outline. I thought the French writers who expatiate so much on the terrible and severe aspect of nature in these Austral regions were not so much in the wrong.

19 – New Norfolk

From Hobart there are two ways of getting to New Norfolk - which refers to the township and the district north west of the capital through which the River Derwent flows: the road along the north bank of the Derwent (Boyer Road), or the one along the south (the Lyell Highway). Both allow glorious views of a wide river, much of the countryside unspoilt. It is worth it for the drive alone. In 1881, Marianne North (p252) went up the Derwent by steamer and wrote:

> The river spread itself out like a series of lakes, with rocks closing it in where it narrowed, all arranged in horizontal strata like walls of gigantic masonry. It ran through a rich bit of country full of hops, and orchards loaded with fruit. The wheat harvest was going on much in the usual English way, with carts and stacks.

Once there, she was taken by carriage to visit someone and wrote: 'Hedges of hawthorn loaded with red berries, sweet-briar, and blackberries – all was too English – it might have been a bit of Somersetshire, as I drove along the beautiful river-side for four miles.'

Jane Franklin, writing from the old Government House to her sister on 7 September 1840 about their plans to establish a new college in New Norfolk, wrote of the position for it and, thus, of the environs of the township itself:

> New Norfolk about 22 miles from [here is] the sweetest spot imaginable, forming a high peninsula on the Derwent which washes its cliffs and flat garden ground on 2 sides, while the Lachlan a tributary trout stream flows under it on another. It has the loveliest views possible of the winding river its woods and rocks and hills, and opening vales in all directions.

The Lachlan was named after Elizabeth Macquarie's son in 1821. She and her husband, Governor of New South Wales, and so of Tasmania, had also travelled to the area in 1811 and he named the place he thought suitable for a new habitation Elizabeth Town for her (pp49–50). This changed to New Norfolk after 1827, formalising the centre that was growing up to accommodate the families arriving from Norfolk Island between 1806 and 1808 (pp34, 38). In 1826, Governor Arthur had even determined to make Elizabeth Town the capital of Tasmania, rather than Hobart which was too far south and water-bound – yet its water was not palatable. This was not surprising since Catherine Kearney's cows wallowed in the Hobart Rivulet, among other nasty Hobart habits. The merchants dependent on the port ensured that the project was unsuccessful.

The Bush Inn

If you arrive by Boyer Road, cross over the bridge and turn left, the first site you come to is the Bush Inn, but I suggest you go first to the Information Centre and get a map – information centres in Tasmanian townships always reveal themselves. This one is in the centre of the circular street slightly southeast of the bridge and the eastern end of the High Street. Then go back to the Bush Inn on Montagu Street, which might well be marked on the map, and in any case is well signboarded.

Fifty-four-year-old widow **Ann Bridger** (c1777–1857) arrived in Hobart in 1823 with two daughters, a son, £500 in cash and £200 in 'various merchandise for investing in agricultural pursuits'. Whatever her previous life, after her arrival she stayed with Maria Lord just as the entrepreneur's life was taking a nosedive (pp33, 80). Within a year, Ann was running the Black Snake Inn of previous low repute at Granton, on the river half-way between Hobart and Elizabeth Town; under her, it became a respectable staging post.

By 1825, she was the licensee of the Bush Inn, what may have been an unlicensed drinking place from 1815. To cross the river in the years that followed you used Mrs Bridger's ferry, so much so that a rival took her to court over ferry provision. From 1825, everyone who was anyone stayed at the Bush Inn; indeed, it now claims to be the longest continuously licensed pub in Australia. A 1975 plaque outside commemorates 150 years.

Elizabeth Prinsep and her husband stayed there in January 1830 (p77). The book by him, which undoubtedly includes her experiences and possibly some of her writing (and at least one New Norfolk illustration by her, p303) reveals the place and the inn:

> ... the road ended at the church, not very inviting termination to hungry, cold, wet travellers ... I looked in vain for houses ... when a charitable man conducted us over the turf to the inn, which really looked very comfortable, and its accommodation within did not belie its external experience ...
>
> The Inn window faced a splendid rock, clothed in every fissure with luxuriant verdure, which hung over the river. Still I could see nothing of a town, or even a village, and no wonder, for, upon enquiring, I found that besides the magistrate's and the Governors Turriff Lodge which are at some distance, there are but two houses and a half, the third not being completed! Making seven in all, including the church and the inn. I forgot to mention the school house ... which is well attended by children who collect from miles around.

Elizabeth Fenton (p76) spent many months in Hobart waiting for her husband to build them a house at what became Fenton Forest well beyond the New Norfolk township in the area now known as Glenora. Eventually, in July 1831, she started her journey; she later discreetly lets slip that she was pregnant. She passed farms and was not impressed:

I must confess these habitations looked dreary and slovenly in the extreme, – no attempt at neatness, no tidy inclosure for office houses, no little gardens;- but piles of wood for burning, sheepskins, pigs, rude farming implements lay to the very threshold in unsightly mingling.

Approaching New Norfolk it began to snow. She was very glad to arrive at 'its single inn kept by a portly old lady, a female Boniface, who showed us every attention, and had a most excellent dinner on the table ...' The following morning, however, 'Mrs Bridger came up to me with an important face to caution me with respect to my nurse, whom she believed to be one of the worst women in the Colony.' (Why 'female Boniface'? Google refers you to George Farquhar's *The Beaux Stratagem* (1707) in which Boniface is the name of the innkeeper, thereafter used as a name for a host.)

On 25 January 1831, Nora Corbett and her husband Jorgen Jorgenson held their wedding feast at the inn and, true to form, became drunk and disorderly (pp61–2, 338). Jane Franklin's part in the history was also in character: in 1837 she planted a pear tree in the garden (p285). It was showing signs of aging in 1986 and was burnt down by vandals soon thereafter. In 1840, Ann Bridger sold the Bush Inn and then, or later, moved to Melbourne where she died aged 80.

One of my favourite Bush Inn scenes, which took place after Ann's time, comes from the pen of Caroline Denison (p161) and was what she saw from the window when she and the Governor were staying there (for reasons that are unclear) in May 1847:

We were amused this morning by seeing the departure from this inn, of a couple who had come down from Bothwell, or Hamilton, or some of those distant places, to our ball on Monday, and who slept here last night on their way home. This morning we saw them set out, both on horseback; the lady with a sort of bundle, containing, I suppose, her ball finery, hanging at the pommel of her saddle, the gentleman with a little knapsack, strapped in front of his. This is the way, I suppose, that everyone must travel in winter, to and from these out of the way places, as all, except the few great roads, are impassable in winter for carriages.

The most internationally famous Bush Inn guest was undoubtedly **Nellie Melba** (1861–1931) who went there for rest during her 1924 farewell visit to Tasmania (p242). There is a charming account contained in Kym Roberts' 'The Bush Inn' (nd) (which you can download from the internet), recorded by Joe Cowburn, son of the house and later a New Norfolk historian. He came home from school and there was the Diva sitting in his mother's chair, a glass of wine in her hand. Putting him at his ease, she invited him to her recital at the City Hall and, standing in the wings, he watched her pass him onto the stage and the handkerchiefs in the hands of the audience when she sang 'Home Sweet Home'.

He had told her that William Vincent Wallace composed the opera *Maritana* on the inn's verandah in 1838, and she resolved to sing 'Scenes that are Brightest' before she left. So on her last evening, she sang it for 40 guests sitting on the stairs to her private suite, and Joe watched her inscribe, 'with a somewhat shaky hand', the photograph she gave him as a memento of her stay. The dining room is named the Nellie Melba and a portrait of her hangs on the wall.

Turriff Lodge

A recommended route to Turriff Lodge is the walk from the Esplanade in front of the Bush Inn and along the cliff path. But if you are driving, follow Montagu Street north east from the Bush Inn until it becomes the Lyell Highway; then, on the left, is Turriff Lodge Road/Drive. Park where there is space and walk along the path, past the housing development Lady Franklin Court. Ahead of you is the Domain, a couple of old oasthouses, a well-kept garden and, down to the Derwent and up the other side, a stunning view, much as Caroline Denison described it in 1847 a few months before her Christmas party there for the Aborigines (p186):

> The Government cottage stands on the most beautiful spot of all; cottage and farm occupying a sort of spit of land at the junction of the Derwent and a little river called the Lachlan; and the grounds of the cottage, and the banks of the river just opposite to it, comprising every beauty that a mixture of rock, wood, and water can give them ... One of the prettiest views is from the front of the cottage, though this is not quite so bold as the rest; it is a view up the river, with scattered houses on its banks, a bridge across it, and a range of wooded hills in the distance.

Elizabeth Prinsep's sketch, from which the illustration for 'their' book was made, gives a complimentary impression of the scene.

The Government Farm was already there when Elizabeth Macquarie visited what became the town named after her in 1811. The cottage was completed as a summer retreat by 1816 under Thomas Davey and the Macquarie family stayed there in 1821. The cottage, also known as Turriff Lodge, was later extended but demolished (or burnt down) in the 1950s.

Governor Sorell, Mrs Kent and their large family retreated to the cottage between 1817 and 1824 and, indeed, for a month before sailing when his successor turned up unexpectedly (pp53–4). Government House in Hobart was then in such a state of disrepair that Arthur decamped with his numerous children – and Eliza Arthur (p55) pregnant again – to the cottage in Elizabeth Town.

When the Franklins arrived in Tasmania in 1837, there was no higher education available, so they resolved to establish a college and New Norfolk was considered ideal; 82 acres were set aside at the Government Farm. Jane Franklin explained to her sister on 7 September 1840, that the 'tumble down cottage will be pulled down, it is now scarcely habitable, which is one reason why we seldom go there'. Jane was ready, too, to donate a large sum of her own to the project.

38.   New Norfolk, from a sketch by Elizabeth Prinsep, courtesy of the Allport Library and Museum of Fine Arts, Tasmanian Archive and Heritage Office

The Franklins consulted widely in England and brought out the Rugby and Cambridge clergyman John Gell for the purpose; (he was later to marry Jane Franklin's stepdaughter Eleanor). The foundation stone was laid on 7 November 1840 and a celebration held at Turriff Lodge. That night vandals tore up the stone and stole the coins and document beneath. It was only the start. That was as far as the scheme went in New Norfolk, for there were far too many vested political and religious interests to allow it.

Anna Maria Nixon (p148) described on 22 January 1844 how Franklin's successor, Eardley-Wilmot, 'Won't hear of a college and has filled up the foundation which was dug on the Domain at New Norfolk.' The foundation stone, with its Latin inscription, was hurled over the cliff into the Derwent. (Christ's College was eventually established at Bishopsbourne in the north of the State in 1847).

It was Eardley-Wilmot who introduced hops onto the Government Farm, which accounts for the oasthouses that remain. But Turriff Lodge was to come back to haunt the governor, for he is said to have spent a night there with Julia Sorell without a chaperone, an action which, though he tried to bluster his way out of the accusation, added to the list of the indiscretions that led to his recall (pp161, 240).

Round the Domain today is a 'Scenic Walk' which I surmise Jane Franklin would have much enjoyed. I recommend you to take it.

There is some evidence that on the opposite bank to the Domain was the house where Mary Ann McCarty was attacked by bushrangers in 1814 (p91). She and her husband Dennis – leading light from the beginning of New Norfolk and builder, in 1818, of the first, rather rough road to Hobart – had several properties in the area. The Macquaries stayed with them in 1811. McCarty was drowned in the Derwent under suspicious circumstances in 1820 and, four months later, Mary Ann married Thomas Lascelles who had harassed her late husband and who proceeded to run through her money. She ran a school in Hobart until the mid 1850s.

St Matthew's Church

Make your way now up Pioneer Avenue to Arthur Square. On the north east side is said to be the oldest church in Tasmania, given that the original St David's in Hobart (p244) was replaced and St John's in Launceston is four months less venerable (p376). It was begun in 1823 and opened for services in 1825. Mrs Bridger's younger daughter, also **Ann Bridger**, married George Woodward there on 12 February 1829, and she was to have seven children. Norah Corbett married Jorgen Jorgenson on 25 January 1831 before their over-merry wedding feast at the Bush Inn. On 4 February 1832, American Eliza Romney Fisher married editor Henry Melville (p131). On 6 November that year, playwright David Burn, son of Jacobina Burn (p74), and father of Jemima Irvine (p102), married for the second time, having gone home to Edinburgh to divorce Jemima's mother. His new bride was **Catherine Fenton**, Elizabeth Fenton's sister-in-law. Elizabeth's daughter Flora, a baby in her published diary, married there in 1848.

In the east of the Sanctuary is a stained-glass window of the manger scene. The child holding a Bible behind the angel at the crib is **Nancy Hope Shoobridge** (1890–98), who died at sea aged eight on her way to England to see her grandparents. In 1910, her parents (p306) donated a cottage hospital to the town in her memory and continued to contribute much to the social welfare of the community.

Stephen Street Cemetery

You will look in vain for this beside the church; instead, go clockwise round the square and down Stephen Street; there on the right is a gate through which you can see, plumb in the middle, the imposing Lord family vault. On one side is the plaque,

> Sacred to the memory of Maria Lord, wife of E. Lord Esq of Lawrenny Hamilton who died at Bothwell the 22nd July 1859 in her 78th year. A friend to the needy.

So ended the life of one of Tasmania's earliest and most colourful characters (p33). Her eldest son, who drowned at Lawrenny, is also buried there. Her estranged husband died in England two months after her. The Bothwell itinerary will introduce Maria's last home and trading place (p334).

Another grave of note is that of **Mary Mills** (née Collin, c1812–1836), murdered on the New Norfolk Road in October 1836, aged only 24. Joan Goodrick tells the story in more detail, based on the trial of her murderer – it is less accessible in *By George* (nd; produced privately for the family by Peter Mills). Mary's husband of only a few months, former convict and pioneer coach-owner George Mills, remarried in 1837. When he died in 1849, his wife, **Mahala Mills** (née Champion, 1819–1884), took over running the coach service and the licence of the Brunswick Wine Vault in Hobart, and even expanded, though she remarried, had three children with butcher John Maddock, to add to the four with Mills and, in 1854, gave the business up.

The cemetery was established in 1823 – which perhaps suggests there were services in St Matthew's from its very beginnings – and closed in 1875. I understand at one time it was rather untended, but not now.

Willow Court (New Norfolk Asylum; Royal Derwent Hospital)

Stephen Street turns right at the end and George Street leads into the Avenue. On the right there is Willow Court. Its status when you read this is difficult to predict. It could be transformed into a big new development, or a patchy development, or be mostly deserted and full of ghosts of the past, as when I last saw it. Something of the past will by law be retained, whatever its future.

It is known as Willow Court because Jane Franklin planted at least one of her St Helena willow twigs there (p285). The tree that grew was cut down in 1961 but there is now a well-established tree in the main courtyard that at least has the shape of a willow and so gives an impression of Jane's touching environmental gesture.

Some of the buildings date from 1827 when it was a convict depot for invalids guarded by the military with barracks that still stand. When Port Arthur was established in 1830 (p280), the New Norfolk establishment was expanded and became a mental asylum for the free as well as convicts. By 1848, it was exclusively so, though those with learning difficulties mingled indiscriminately with the mentally ill. It was divided into female and male sections. Susan Piddock's *A Space of Their Own: The Archaeology of Nineteenth Century Lunatic Asylums in Britain, South Australia and Tasmania* (2007) provides a detailed, scholarly history. The Royal Derwent Hospital, its last manifestation, was closed in 2001.

Different sources deal with particular aspects. Alison Alexander's unpublished thesis, for example, gives an impression of what it was like for the women staff – at first convict nurses – in this isolated spot. It was 'dark and overcrowded, patients were often rough and dirty, and nurses slept in the ward, so were on duty almost 24 hours a day'. One surgeon admitted in his diary to striking a nurse. At first they were not even paid.

The upper echelons, head nurses, sub-matrons and matrons, had higher status and were paid. Matrons were managers, until the 1840s married to the

Superintendent. Widowed **Jane Fosbrook**, who had taken the job of matron to provide for her children and was considered 'respectable', resigned because of the inmates' obscene language and violent conduct. **Gertrude Kenny**, former matron of the Girls' Industrial School, appointed in 1877, was kicked by a patient, resulting in a tumour. Treated by the Superintendent, she charged him with indecent assault. **Martha Leland,** having worked in six asylums in Britain, was appointed in 1879 but was dismissed, according to a Commissioner, because 'She dared to have an opinion of her own.'

Her place was taken by **Selina Alexander** (bc1855), a qualified nurse with a reference from Florence Nightingale. She was responsible for raising the pay and conditions of her staff. In 1890, aged 35, Selina married, as his second wife, Robert Shoobridge of apple-producing Valleyfield who was a government visitor of the asylum. They were to become parents of Nancy Hope, the girl in the St Matthew's stained-glass window (p304).

Jane Power, promoted from head nurse in 1895, would not be dictated to by any man, and ran the place smoothly.

Kay Daniels gives a glimpse of one convict inmate in her chapter on prostitution (p37). An 1850 letter from **Elizabeth** (surname illegible) to the Quaker humanitarian George Washington Walker survives. She started as a prostitute, or a woman who had been seduced and abandoned, and came to the notice of the Society for the Suppression of Vice and admitted to the Van Diemen's Land Asylum for Unfortunate Women (which may have also been known as the Magdalen) set up under the patronage of Caroline Denison (p198), but ended up in New Norfolk. Her main concern was her son: 'Sir, if you will be kind enough to inform me how my dear litel boy is and wether he is at school or what school he is sent to for I left him at the Magdalen. I am truly sorry for my conduct whilst theire.' She longed more than anything to see her son.

But it was by no means only an asylum for convicts. Margaret Lovell Kearney of Carrington (p277) had a mental breakdown following her husband's death and was sent to New Norfolk where her religious mania deepened. Eventually her doctors were prepared to discharge her. But, 'As regards returning to Richmond,' she wrote in September 1861, 'I would not go back there voluntarily if you were to proffer me a mine of gold.' Those from the upper echelons of society were not housed with the lower, and separate accommodation in the grounds was much discussed over the years; in 1868, 'Ladies' Cottages' were constructed for fee-paying patients.

Madge Edwards' mother, Amy Sorell Archer (p268) was in indifferent health for some years but in 1905 was desperately ill. Although she recovered physically, she was mentally affected and, aged 36, was admitted to the asylum. Rosemary Brown prints her first hospital report, ending: 'She neglects herself in almost every way.' Finally, Amy was diagnosed with dementia.

The stigma attached to having a relative in New Norfolk is hinted at in Tasma's *Not Counting the Cost* (p256). Eila's husband has been admitted and 'At the first word of admiration that her appearance excited, a hundred informants were ready to whisper "She has a husband in the asylum, and they are *such* a peculiar family."' Tasma also introduces the asylum into 'What an Artist Discovered in Tasmania' (p284):

> ... on a knoll girt in by native trees, interspersed with alien elms and willows, stood a building that would have given a Turk the horrors. From its clean, bare corridor and windows, the oldest of old women, in every stage of decrepit, pathetic, grotesque old age, look forth. They appear to mouth at a world that is perpetually renewed, while they cannot make good the loss of a tooth, or a failing sense. Such as have any sensation left are snappish. The oldest of all are the merriest, mumbling with idiotic satisfaction, when they warm themselves like vegetables in the sunshine.

Ghosts, indeed, stalk the extensive buildings and grounds.

Magra (Back River)

Go back over the bridge and now follow the signs north for Magra, what used to be called Back River. After the turnoff to the golf club, turn left along Lawitta Road to the Back River Methodist Chapel, built in 1837. In the graveyard is the burial place of Betty King who lived with the claim of the first white woman to arrive in Australia (p9). The headstone later erected attests to that.

Also, there are 29 Triffitt family graves. One of them is that of **Charlotte Triffitt** (née Young, b1844), born, brought up and married, in 1876, in Back River. In 1935, aged 91, she reminisced to a *Mercury* journalist about the funeral of Betty King in 1856. That's quite some hands across history!

Charlotte, the eldest daughter of a family of eleven, also remembered having to look after her siblings while her mother worked on their small farm. When she was a girl, 'The main water supply for residents of New Norfolk ran down the main street in an open drain and at each house it was stored in wooden casks built into the ground.'

Two Shone headstones lead to the second site in Magra.

Stanton

Less than a mile from the chapel, at 504 Back River Road, is Stanton Bed and Breakfast, run since 2003 by Helen and Mark McDiarmid. The two-storeyed Georgian house, built by Thomas Shone in 1817, was not always the peaceful haven it is today. This is where in 1843 the Shone family was attacked by the bushranger Martin Cash and his crew (p96).

Thomas' wife Susannah had been born on Norfolk Island, the free-born daughter – one of seven children – of convicts. Like most of the Norfolk Islanders, the family, by then free settlers, were transferred to Tasmania in 1808 and, aged 21, Susannah married Thomas in Hobart in 1820. Life at Back River then would not have been easy, and they lost much of material value that night; the family was threatened afterwards by Cash and had their assigned servants removed for giving in to him.

When I contacted Helen McDiarmid, she wrote back to me not only about the Shones but also about Betty King:

> When we first moved here and I heard her story, I wondered whether anyone remembered her passing, so jumped in my car late one afternoon with paper and pen to record the date of her death. There, in that atmospheric graveyard, I read that she had died on my birthday!! Well, since that's easy to remember, I visit her grave every year on my birthday and leave some flowers from Stanton, since she would have been familiar with the people who built the house. It's a small universe!

When I wanted Helen's permission to quote from her email, I received no response, which surprised me because we had become good email friends in 2008. Eventually, I rang and discovered from Mark that Helen died on 30 December 2009. He plans to continue the venture they shared at Stanton – www.stantonbandb.com.

Bushy Park and Hawthorn Lodge

Leave New Norfolk township westward via Glenora Road; indeed, Glenora, some miles further north west, is the furthest port of call in this itinerary. Pass Plenty; it's more relevant to stop there on the way back.

Bushy Park, twelve miles from New Norfolk, was originally the property of Adolarius Humphrey who arrived with David Collins in 1804 and, although he and Edward Lord built the house known as the first in Hobart (from the pen and ink drawing that survives), he did not settle, roaming first in Tasmania as a mineralogist and then on the mainland. He met Harriett Sutton, daughter of a convict storekeeper, in Sydney and took her to Tasmania. Macquarie insisted that he return her to her father (for reasons that sources do not spell out), but Humphrey demurred and they were married in Hobart in 1812.

It was about this time that Humphrey was granted the acres in the Derwent Valley, what came to be known as Humphreyville. By 1814, he had been appointed a magistrate, and later Superintendent of police. This left him little time to manage his land so, as the Land Commissioners described in 1826, it was Harriett who did so, impeccably (p72).

When Humphrey died in 1829, Harriett inherited the property. To save her financial embarrassment, the government bought grain from her. In 1831, she married John Kerr. Other sources say that Humphrey's nephew inherited his property and leased it to John Kerr.

Beatrice Kitty Blyth (1849–1948) aged 92 and living in Melbourne recorded her memories of Bushy Park in 1941; they were drawn upon by KR von Stieglitz. Beatrice's mother, **Elizabeth Crowther Blyth** (1815–1897), arrived in Tasmania with her parents in 1825 and was educated at Ellinthorp Hall (pp138, 336). At that time she amassed a folio of sketches, watercolours and poems by herself and friends; her six Crowther sisters were also artistic. She married William Blyth in 1835, six weeks after their first meeting following his arrival in Tasmania with a letter of introduction to her father, and between 1837 and 1849 they had 14 children, eight daughters and six sons whom Eliza educated herself, but had no more time for her artistic endeavours. The Blyths moved into Humphreyville in 1850, changing its name to Bushy Park and, when they had built another house next door in 1859, their son, Beatrice's brother, lived at Bushy Park.

Ebenezer Shoobridge bought the property in 1867, moving there from Valleyfield, and introduced to the area the hops which his father had brought over from Kent in 1822. Bushy Park was to become the largest hop-producer in Australia. Among the texts, mostly biblical, inscribed on the blocks of the hop kiln, known locally as the Text Kiln, is one that reads: 'Erected by Ebenezer Shoobridge in 1867 assisted by his wife and three sons and five daughters, union is strength. God is love.' Ebenezer's wife was **Charlotte Giblin Shoobridge** (1813–1870) who had married him in 1841; one of the sons was Robert, eventually of Valleyfield (p306). The Shoobridge family were to farm Bushy Park for the next seven decades, 65 of those years continuously growing hops, until the bottom fell out of the hop market.

In the early days, many pickers were women who tended to work in family groups, and it was one job where pay was equal because it depended on the quantity picked during the twelve-hour day, 6am to 6pm. Conditions for pickers were seen as less favourable in the early twentieth century. The annual Bushy Park show and Strawberry Feast was held in the lee of the hop kiln.

Matilda Swynys visited Tasmania from the mainland in the late 1860s and wrote of a trip up the Derwent on a steamer 'decorated with lilies and yellow broom and filled with holiday makers enlivened by a good German band'. In 'A Lady's Trip to Tasmania' (preserved in the family's archives and available on the internet), she added: 'A gentleman at New Norfolk gave a strawberry feast to five hundred visitors.' The hop kiln is still there, but on private property; you can glimpse it from the road.

But my objective in travelling to the area was to visit Hawthorn Lodge, easily found on the corner as you leave Bushy Park and before you turn left to take the road to Glenora. It was Hawthorn Lodge – originally built in 1869 for Robert Shoobridge – and the surrounds that inspired *Wild Orchard*, the best-regarded novel of **Isabel Dick** (1881–1959) (p97). Isabel, or Daisy, was the daughter of **Kate Shoobridge** (b1850), one of Charlotte Shoobridge's hard-working daughters, and Quaker accountant Charles Atkins. In 1887, when Daisy Atkins was six, several died during a typhoid epidemic in Hobart; Daisy caught it from her father and was, for a time, deaf, blind and speechless; her life was despaired of. She recovered, but wore thick-lensed glasses thereafter. To convalesce, she was invited to stay at Hawthorn Lodge which her uncle William Shoobridge and his wife **Ann Benson Mather Shoobridge** (1845–1920, m1869) had taken over from her uncle Robert in 1878.

In *Wild Orchard*, the 1840 property Parklands which Harriat (Harry) and Jan Halifax develop from a burnt-out cottage he had inherited is quite obviously set around here, with New Norfolk their nearest town. Arriving at the property on bullock carts of possessions, they discover the skeleton of the house they were hoping to live in. Harry takes it in her stride:

> 'What does it matter? We can surely sleep in tents until another house is built. This is where we must have the house, Jan, on this bank where we can watch the sunset across the river. Look, just here, not back there with it hidden among the trees.'
>
> 'Why, Harry, you're right. This is the spot; and down there, acre after acre, my hop fields shall stand, easily irrigated from the river; the orchards shall be planted farther up where they have good drainage on the slopes ...

One of the properties in Isabel Dick's turn of the twentieth-century novel *Country Heart* (1947) is Parklands, in the grounds of which grew 'an immense chestnut, planted by Great-grandfather and Granny Halifax'. The typhoid epidemic is also made use of. But this is not such an engaging novel, though the love of the Tasmanian countryside still shines through.

When we visited it, Hawthorn Lodge was a guest house which remained much as it was for Isabel Dick, though framed by a 100-year-old magnolia and a huge cherry tree. But I understand that it has recently been sold, so that its status as I write is unknown.

Fenton Forest

Turn left outside the gate of Hawthorn Lodge and almost immediately left again. A few yards on, on the left, is a petrol station which might prove useful; it also sells take-away fried food. If you have come from Hobart and were expecting a nice little café round here, you will be disappointed; bring a picnic. Not far from there, on the right, by an old railway crossing, is a turning marked 'Fenton Forest'.

You are not really intruding to drive up a poplar avenue, at least to where it asks for cherrypickers, where a herd of cows may block your way, and where an avenue of oak leads up to today's house owned by the Shoobridge family who bought the property in 1878. Elizabeth Fenton's original house was burnt down in 1848, and its successor demolished. So what you are looking at are the surroundings in which she lived for 45 years: hilly, sere in summer, splashes of dark green from fruit trees and eucalypts, and the glory of the Derwent all along the 20 kilometres from New Norfolk which she travelled when she first arrived and no doubt many times in the years that followed.

When Elizabeth left the Bush Inn in the winter of 1831 (p301), she was wearing black satin boots. 'I had to sit down to ease the pain of my bruised feet,' she wrote, 'for the boots were in fragments with the rough ground I had to walk through.' And the first view of her new home was not auspicious:

> It was a long, shapeless, naked brick cottage outside, but oh! within, there was confusion worse confounded. Every article of baggage that had been sent up, furniture, packing cases, had all been piled up, promiscuously, as

39. Old Fenton Forest House, by Elizabeth Fenton, from von Stieglitz, *A History of New Norfolk and the Derwent Valley*

they presented themselves. The vile servants we had sent out had profited by the opportunity to pillage everything they could abstract. All the farm servants had collected in the house, and the nurse – my right-hand woman, as I took her to be – had opened a keg of rum for their refreshment; rum, tobacco, noise and dirt assailed every sense with horror and dismay.

And she had baby Flora in her arms, as well as being pregnant! Elizabeth's sketch of the house dates from 1832 and perhaps shows some improvement. The published volume of her diary is abridged and ends in December that year. Tasmanian historian Margaret Mason-Cox has transcribed the unpublished diaries (1857–67) in preparation for a biographical study of Elizabeth. In the meantime, there are glimpses of the family elsewhere. It is known that Michael's two cousins – like him, army captains – and their families joined them in New Norfolk, and that he brought over 18 Irish families to work and live on the estate; by the time of his death they had grown to nearly 30. He was nominated to the Legislative Council in 1855, made Speaker and, in 1856, elected to the new House of Assembly of which he was, in due course, also appointed Speaker. It is not surprising, therefore, that Beatrice Blyth should write of Elizabeth's arrival at church:

Captain Michael Fenton's wife was the great lady of the district and more often than not was late for the service. But on arrival she would proceed to the pulpit, bow, and apologise for being late. Then the Rector, not to be outdone, would bow too, and begin the service again.

One of Elizabeth's friends was **Loetitia Casey** (née Gardiner, 1819–1863), sketcher and pianist. Her sketch of Fenton Forest in 1838, showing the house from a distance, in its grounds, makes it look nothing short of gracious. Loetitia's widowed father emigrated to Tasmania with his children in 1835 and settled in New Norfolk; there, in 1839, she married surgeon Cornelius Casey. Many of her drawings date from, and reflect, their life there and then. Loetitia's sepia wash and drawing of Jane Franklin's Ancanthe (p271) resulted from their friendship, perhaps forged at New Norfolk.

St John's Church (Plenty)

Retrace your steps towards New Norfolk and stop half-way between there and Bushy Park, at St John's Church, Plenty, now on the left. The reason you should leave this until last is that Elizabeth Fenton died in 1876, two years after her husband, and both are buried in the graveyard. St John's was consecrated in 1852 and replaced a schoolroom between Fenton Forest and Bushy Park, or the drawing room of the latter. It was attended by the Fentons and the Blyths. Beatrice Blyth noted:

> There being no church nearer than St John's at Plenty, the whole Blyth family used to be driven the five miles to attend services in a large two-horse wagonette, especially built by the farm wheel-wright, and fitted out with crimson cushions. The roads were rough, and it took an hour or more each way. Captain Fenton, when driving to Hobart to attend Parliament, used bullocks in the winter to draw his carriage as far as Plenty; the journey to Hobart taking the whole day.

During Michael's absences there was probably an overseer to carry out his instructions; later their son did so. But Elizabeth certainly ran the house and garden, and Margaret Mason-Cox has found evidence that she designed and oversaw the implementation of a small domestic irrigation scheme which watered the home garden.

20 – East Coast (Writers' Coast)

The most direct route to the east coast is via the Tasman Highway (across the Bridge) to Sorell and turn left (instead of right to Port Arthur). Tasmanians and visitors go to the east coast for the reasons one goes to any coast and this one, for Tasmania, and unlike the west coast, is particularly mild and sunny.

Louisa Anne Meredith

I went to the east coast and, therefore, this itinerary goes, because the writer Louisa Anne Meredith lived in five different houses there over a period of 40 years – her husband Charles was not good with money. And, while Louisa was not very 'good' on Aborigines (pp106, 186) or convicts (p158), or even her fellow colonials (p144) she is now recognised as 'the most significant Tasmanian advocate of environmental concerns' during her long and active life in the colony; indeed, Tim Bonyhady devotes a detailed and convincing chapter to her in *The Colonial Earth* (2000).

Because the order of Louisa's homes in this itinerary is determined by geography, it is out of step with the chronology of her life; she therefore needs an introduction, and the string of houses needs to be mentally shuffled to form a satisfactory pattern. The dates set against each house heading should help. (At least six other women writers also feature in this itinerary.)

Louisa Anne Meredith (née Twamley, 1812–1895) was already an established writer in England when she married her cousin Charles in 1839. Her first book of poems was published in 1835 when she was twenty three. She went on to produce several illustrated nature books. Leigh Hunt wrote of her in his mocking 'Blue Stocking Revels', showing that she had surely arrived:

> Then came young Twamley
> Nice, sensitive thing
> Whose pen and whose pencil
> Give promise like spring.

Charles was visiting Birmingham from Tasmania where his family had emigrated in 1821 and settled on the east coast. Living first in New South Wales about which Louisa published her first Antipodean book, the couple arrived in Tasmania in 1840. In *Louisa Anne Meredith: A Tigress in Exile* (1979; 1990), Vivienne Rae-Ellis charts her life and writing; in a 1974 article, she, too, drew attention to Louisa's environmental credentials. Louisa's early years in Tasmania are best captured, though, in *My Home in Tasmania: During a Residence of Nine Years* (1852; 2003). Her biographer writes of it that 'it has a unique place in the history of Tasmania as the first description of life in the colony by a female resident'. It was also successful in London and New York. While the original is rare and expensive, happily it has been reissued in paperback. The first stops on this itinerary, however, postdate that account.

40.   Louisa Anne Meredith, by Mary Morton Allport, 1856,
courtesy of the Allport Library and Museum of Fine Arts,
Tasmanian Archive and Heritage Office

Twamley (Buckland) (1858–67)

The small township of Buckland, 63 kilometres from Hobart, used to be
called Prosser's Plain for the river that runs just to the north. And, when
the Merediths moved to 'Villeneuve' in 1858, they renamed the property
Twamley, Louisa's maiden name. They were to stay there nine years. The house
is privately owned, but you can get a real impression of Louisa's environs
without intruding by looking out for Twamley Road on the right ten miles
from Buckland on the way to Orford and doubling back along a track parallel
to the main road. The very tranquillity of the landscape makes it feel as
isolated as it was in 1858. Louisa was not happy here.

In 1860, Louisa published *Some of My Bush Friends in Tasmania: Native
Flowers, Berries and Insects Drawn from Life, Illustrated and Briefly
Described*, and the following year, *Over the Straits* which, although about a

visit to Victoria, contains a chapter attacking cruelty to animals, a perennial preoccupation about which she was to do more than write.

During the Twamley years, time was also spent in Hobart where she staged theatricals at the Government House of Harriet Gore Browne (p200). Among the participants was the future writer Tasma (p256) and her mother **Charlotte Huyber** (1817–1908). Tasma, or Jessie Huyber as she was then, so appealed to Louisa that she was invited to stay at Twamley. Tasma's biographer wrote: '[I]t is impossible to over-estimate the importance of this friendship between the fifty-year-old woman personifying the successful woman author and the fifteen-year-old girl already possessed of an overflowing imagination.' During the 1860s and 1870s, Louisa's name was being recognised in Tasmania as a writer and painter.

Orford (Malunnah) (1868–79)

The drive from Buckland to Orford along the banks of the Prosser is particularly wild and lovely and the house to which the Merediths moved in 1868 (on leaving Twamley) overlooks the mouth of the river. Malunnah, an Aboriginal word meaning nest, was built of local stone and the porch supported by Oyster Bay Pines. Now in a row, the house is 100 yards before the general store opposite the bridge (so park outside the store and walk back).

Between the house and the river is the main road along which rumble huge log-carrying lorries which would have much upset Louisa who abhorred large-scale clearing. In the Huon Valley section of *Walch's Tasmanian Guide Book* (1871), which Louisa edited, she contrasts the 'natural beauty' with the tree-destroying incursions of 'man' – the 'pitiless exterminator'. Although she painted flowers and plants, they were not her main concern in nature, but she loved ferns and railed against their destruction, particularly on Mount Wellington. After a sketching picnic at Fern Tree in 1846, she complained of 'the empty champagne bottles which bristled beside the rocks, the corks and greasy sandwich papers lurking among the moss'.

Animals were Louisa's main concern – she was particularly opposed to the pursuit and killing of them for sport – and it was while living here, in 1878, that, together with **Mary Selina Gellibrand** (1837–1903), she founded the Tasmanian Society for the Protection of Animals; Louisa was the first Honorary Secretary. Mary took over from her and was Secretary at the time of her death.

From Malunnah, the Merediths moved to a cottage in Hobart in 1879, and Charles was to die the following year, but that is jumping too far ahead.

Swansea (Plas Newydd) (1855–58)

All along this coast, in estuaries and lagoons, you will see black swans, sometimes in large numbers – hence the names Swansea and Little Swanport. To visitors from lands where swans are white, this can be startling. Remember these swans; they are precious to Louisa Anne Meredith.

In 1855, the Merediths, having had a fearful, financially-provoked, long-lasting split with Charles' family at Cambria, moved to a small 1834 cottage – Plas Newydd – in Wellington Street, Swansea. It was for sale when I visited it, so I was able to sticky-beak better than might now be possible, but it can be seen from the road. The Glamorgan Spring Bay Historical Society, just round the corner in Noyes Street, is a good place to drop in. There you can get prints of Louisa's book illustrations and confirmation that Louisa is not buried in Swansea, as a biographical entry has it.

The Merediths lived here for the next three years and it was during that time that their situation changed for the better. By 1856, Charles, prompted by Louisa, had successfully entered parliament. Although her views, other than on animals and the environment, do not appear progressive, she had supported the Chartists campaigning for the reform of the political system in her Birmingham days by writing letters and articles. She expressed herself ambivalently about her political involvement. On 18 May 1833, she wrote to her future father-in-law: 'Don't fancy me a politician in petticoats, but I hear so much that I cannot help now and then talking myself.' And Margaret Swann, in 'Mrs Meredith and Miss Atkinson, Writers and Naturalists' (1929), credited Louisa with using 'her strong powers of organisation' in connection with Charles' election campaigns, though 'this was done as unobtrusively as possible' because of the 'prevailing prejudice against women taking part in politics'. Although being a member of the House of Assembly was unpaid, politics, in which he remained engaged for over 20 years, was to give Charles an aim and a status hitherto lacking. He served four terms as Treasurer and one as Minister for Lands.

They had already left Plas Newydd and moved to Twamley when, in 1860, Charles introduced a Bill to protect black swans' eggs, resulting in the Black Swans Act of 1861, Tasmania's first legislation to protect endangered species. Writing to James Calder, Louisa described how, when 'Charles introduced his bill … he was jeered and ridiculed but he passed it – to my great joy.' In her children's book *Tasmanian Friends and Foes* (1880), she writes of a 'wretched huckster' who carried out the 'greedy, sordid cruel trade' in eggs of black swans. Then, more specifically, and in a way that her contemporaries would recognise: 'This gallant, noble officer had a boat and crew allowed him for public service, and these he employed in a systematic raid upon the swans' nests, far and near, round the bays and lagoons.'

In the same book, she has a male character declare: 'I should advocate and insist on total abstinence in the matter of feather ornaments … happy lives are sacrificed every year to gratify the depraved fancies of vain idle women.'

In his later parliamentary career, Charles called for a select committee to look into the conservation of Huon Pines. A Bill to prevent cruelty to animals had been introduced by another member in 1877; in 1879, Charles successfully introduced one to strengthen the earlier legislation and to recognise Louisa's Society. Ill-health forced him to resign that year.

Aged 80, in 1893, Louisa was still writing to the *Mercury* – two letters in four days – condemning the 'inhuman process' by which sheep and cattle were shipped from New South Wales to Tasmania.

Opposite Swansea is the Freycinet Peninsula with its untamed National Park, forming Oyster Bay (not to be confused with Oyster Cove, p176). (Rose de Freycinet accompanied her husband Louis on a later expedition but not to Tasmania where he met Ouray-Ouray.)

Cambria (Riversdale) (1841–42, 1848–55)

North of Swansea, over the Meredith River and on a bad corner, opposite, in 2003, some colonial accommodation, and off the main road, is Cambria. This is one of the few places where even I, with my cheeky English research methods, was made to feel I had intruded. Riversdale, originally on the same Meredith property, is beyond Cambria but on the other side of the road. If you keep your eyes peeled you can glimpse it. Take note in passing, for both houses are very much part of the Louisa Anne Meredith story, and status of properties can always change or you could be a guest. In any case, you can now appreciate Cambria from the photographs in Alice Bennett and Georgia Warner's *Country Houses of Tasmania*.

Before Louisa appeared on the scene, her future husband's stepmother, **Mary Meredith** (née Evans, c1795–1842), already lived at Cambria. For the lowdown on Mary Meredith within the settler context of that area Lois Nyman's *East Coasters* (1990) is useful, particularly as she also tells the story of families who travelled out with the Merediths, and other east coast denizens such as the Cottons of Kelvedon (p157), just south of Swansea.

Not long before the Merediths were to leave for Tasmania, his first wife died. His plans still determinedly intact, George Meredith needed someone to look after five children, so he married the family's senior servant Mary Evans, who had been with them since 1813 and by whom he already had a child. Emigration went ahead and they arrived in Tasmania in 1821.

Mary and her midwife mother had attended the dying mother in childbirth so, whether for that reason or her lower class, she was never accepted by her new family, to which were then added five more children. Nor it seems could George Meredith forget his new wife's origins, as Sharon Morgan shows in 'George and Mary Meredith: The Role of Colonial Wife' (1989), mainly through their exchange of letters. Meredith spent much of his time in Hobart, doing business and having rows, mainly with the authorities about his land allocation. He wrote to his wife to tell her how to run the estate, how much he longed for her body and how she should be behaving, including her letter-writing to him. She not only had her hostile, inherited family to look after, and her continuing pregnancies, but bushrangers (p6) and the Oyster Bay band of Aborigines to contend with.

As for her most demanding occupation, as Sharon Morgan sums up, 'Since the farm was one of mixed livestock and crops, she must have been kept very busy just seeing things ran smoothly. She was, in effect, an unpaid farm manager, without even the prospect of a holiday in Hobart Town since her husband would not allow it.' The main house, Cambria, much as it is today, was not completed until 1836; the family lived in other accommodation on the property until then.

At a certain stage, Meredith wrote asking his niece Louisa Anne Twamley to come out and be governess to her new cousins (her mother had also married beneath her and the family had fallen on hard times). Louisa replied: 'Where would my literature be in Van Diemen's Land? Writing sonnets to whales and porpoises, canzonets to kangaroos, madrigals to "prime merinos" and dirges to black swans, illustrated by portraits of the engaging and lovely natives?' Then her cousin Charles came a-wooing from Tasmania. And, as for the 'dirges to black swans', she wrote in *My Home in Tasmania* of her arrival at Cambria in 1840:

> The most interesting ornaments of Cambria belonging to the animal kingdom were ... a pair of beautiful tame black swans, the first of these birds that I had seen in their native land. They seem to live very happily in the creek below the house, and always came at a call to be fed with bread or corn.

There follows, as is usual in this book and is part of its appeal, particularly to nature lovers, a long disquisition on black swans, detailing, too, the cruelties inflicted upon them that were leading to their extermination. 'In proof of this,' she wrote, 'I had been above two years at *Swan* Port before ... my desire to see a *wild* black swan was gratified, though, formerly, thousands frequented every lagoon.'

After a few weeks at Cambria, Louisa and Charles lived at Riversdale while their house at Spring Vale was being built, and returned to Riversdale following their years of semi-exile to Port Sorell in the north when, as usual the money had run out (p384).

But the greatest blow was the row with, at its core, Louisa's perceived unfriendly behaviour towards the inmates of Cambria, her uncle and his second family – Mary had died in 1842. This resulted in George Meredith selling Cambria to the eldest son of his second family, instead of the inheritance being shared among both families with Charles, as the eldest son of the first family, receiving the 'lion's share'. Riversdale was also sold. That is when, in 1855, Louisa and Charles moved to Plas Newydd in Swansea, and intimations of a new life. George was to die the following year and the family rift was to last for many years.

Other women Merediths of Cambria worth noting were **Sarah Westall Poynter** (née Merdith, 1807–1869) (of the first family) painter and sketcher; **Frances Meredith** (Fanny, 1831–1910) (second marriage), sketcher whom Louisa encouraged but who later turned against her; and Violet Mace, potter, last Meredith descendant to live there but more usefully met at Ratho (p329).

41. Cambria, by Louisa Anne Meredith, from Meredith, *My Home in Tasmania*,
courtesy of the Glamorgan Spring Bay Historical Society

Spring Vale (1842–44)

The last Meredith home in this itinerary is seven miles north of Cambria,
where the Swan and Cygnet Rivers meet at its southern boundary. If you have
turned the bend to the right and reached Cranbrook, you have gone too far;
but there should be a sign up on the right: 'Spring Vale Vineyards Tasmania'.
Although the house is not part of the commercial set-up, the cellar where you
can buy wine by the bottle or case has been constructed within the original
stables at the back. There shouldn't be a problem if you ask to walk to the
front and retrieve Louisa.

Her biographer suggests that she 'spent the happiest time in her life
in Tasmania in this house.' It was their first proper home, built to their
specification, and the garden just as they wanted it. She wrote of her life there,
in *My Home in Tasmania*:

Roses of various kinds, geraniums, and a host of other good old flowers,
were soon planted, and another pleasant source of interest and occupation
opened to me. Of the latter I had, indeed, no lack, between the care of my
household and our dear children; and besides these there were chickens,

and ducks, and turkeys to rear; butter, cream, cheeses, and other country comforts to make; calves to pet; mushrooms to seek, and convert into Ketchup (these being frequently very abundant and fine); and a whole catalogue of pleasant busy little idlenesses to indulge in, that carried one week after another with reproachful celerity.

Other 'idlenesses' included piano playing in their little library and newspaper reading. There was more to her duties, though: she had to distribute rations, clothing and supplies that arrived by boat to their farmhands: sawyers, stonemasons, carpenters, drainers and fencers, and to keep the accounts. She also finished the manuscript of *Notes and Sketches of New South Wales* (1844), and filled her folio with watercolours – collecting indigenous flowers and berries, and gratefully receiving many little bush creatures brought to her. Several trees she planted still stand.

But Tasmania was descending into economic depression, Charles was no farmer, and he had overspent on building Spring Vale, against family advice. In 1844 he was forced to accept the post of Assistant Police Magistrate at Port Sorell in the north. Louisa was devastated but at least the journey across Tasmania and their homes there were material for her book. They were to stay there until 1848.

After Charles' death in 1880, Louisa lived permanently in Hobart for the remaining 15 years of her life, but so short of money that she was awarded a British government pension in recognition of her work in literature, art and science. She travelled to England for the last time in 1889 to see *Bush Friends in Tasmania: Last Series* (1891) through publication. She died at the home of Melbourne friends.

While Louisa's environmental credentials have been the main focus here, Patricia Grimshaw and Ann Standish draw attention, in 'Making Tasmania Home: Louisa Meredith's Colonizing prose' (2007), to another facet of her writings: '[They] must also be considered as part of an imperial discourse that legitimised white invasion and settlement of Aboriginal lands.'

Half-way between Swansea and Cranbrook is a main road west joining the east coast to the Midland Highway at Campbell Town. This is the road I deduce must have been taken by Kate Webster, heroine of Rachael Treasure's *The Dare* (2007). As a roving government agricultural adviser, she attends the Campbell Show to meet clients. But the sheep farm – a family bone of contention – is more important to her and seems to be just south of Swansea; this is the only defining clue: 'The morning sun rose over the bay, bringing life to the soft silhouette of Schouten Island. The sun lit up a brown tinge in the cows' black coats.' Not much of the novel is as peaceful as that scene.

Kate Webster has a similar background to her creator who went to agricultural college, began her working life as a jillaroo (trainee farmhand) and now lives with her husband and children on a sheep farm in Tasmania breeding and training kelpies, border collies and waler (from New South Wales) stockhorses. Not all Rachael Treasure's novels are set in Tasmania because her experience is Australia-wide. What I like about this holiday-read book is that Kate and her life are so different from me and mine – it gave me access to a whole new world and style. And, because so modern, Kate is rather different from the settler women from whom she is descended. She attends an annual gathering with

Girls who didn't give a damn. Stuff the fact they had a bit of a beer belly, tonight they would walk proud in their not-so-stylish dresses, with their not-so-flash hair. The rougher their ute, the sleeker their dogs, the tougher their hands, the more gorgeous they felt. Strong country girls, flexing muscles and flashing pretty smiles.

And yet, Kate acknowledges her ancestors; in the house she is about to lose, 'She could feel the room filled with the energies of the past ... that gentle tenacious strength of the Webster women who had been there before.'

We didn't take that direct route to Campbell Town, but on one occasion, we did take the rough road just beyond Cranbrook that comes out at Avoca ('Midland Highway' itinerary). This is much the route the Merediths started out on towards Port Sorell. Louisa Anne – who could have been a Webster ancestor – rode most of the way, though sometimes she walked, and the children and nursemaid travelled in a custom-built carriage. The luggage went by sea. If you're in exploration mode, this is an interesting drive via Royal George, with fine landscapes – forest reserve giving way to a wide plain – but tedious in a hire car.

Bicheno

But if you choose to miss those temptations, and that of the Freycinet Peninsula (good for a quiet or strenuous walking weekend) this time, Bicheno is a short drive from Spring Vale. Of the harbour, known as the Gulch, Louisa Anne Meredith, who visited it in 1842, wrote:

Skeletons of huts and skeletons of whales stood side by side and with greasy barrels in long and black array, and remains of putrid carcasses steaming in the sunshine, formed a scene of dirt, desolation and disgust, contrasting powerfully with the clean bright crags, snow-white beach and the pure brilliant character of the surrounding scenery.

Ten years earlier, Wauber Debar, the Aborigine who saved the life of two sealers (p112), was buried on the other side of the headland, easily walkable from the Gulch. Her gravestone, in a little railed plot overhung by trees and within sight of the bay named after her, reads:

Here lies Wauba Debar a Female Aborigine of Van Diemen's Land died June 1832 aged 40 years. This stone is erected by a few of her white friends.

Another Bicheno heroine was **Mary Harvey** (née Blackmore, c1836–1911). She was the Buckland-born daughter of a sexton who married a Bicheno policeman in about 1856. With a babe in arms, she rescued her husband from an attacker; then, when he and his comrades were out searching with a warrant for some renegade whalers, she received a tip off, saddled up, found the poor bedraggled bunch, and inveigled them into eating a hearty meal she made for them which left them easy to lock up. Then there was the bushfire when all were at the regatta. Mary and her on-duty husband put the fire out and saved everyone's homes. Finally, there was the time when two lads were clinging to an upturned boat out at sea. Alerted by their brother, and in her husband's boat, Mary made sure that at least one boy was rescued, jumping into the water to hold the boat steady while he was dragged on to it and nursing him back on shore. She is commemorated by Mary Harvey's Restaurant. It may well do her credit; I only took photographs.

Today's Bicheno is one of those places attractive to sea-changers – that phenomenon of young Australians who can't afford big-city mortgages, or older ones who've had enough of the unrelenting pace, and writers. One of those is English-born, Sydney-based Arabella Edge who, house-sitting in Hobart, visited Bicheno (two and a half hours from the capital) and fell under its spell. She bought a plot and, sitting in a caravan while her husband built them a house, wrote her second novel, *The Raft* (inspired by the French painter Géricault). Then, when it became available, they could not resist buying the Hideaway chalet operation next door.

For five years the couple has run four self-contained chalets, with ocean views from their private verandahs, and the Boathouse which sleeps three couples, together with the herb and kitchen gardens and orchard they have created. Bennett wallabies, possums and echidnas range freely. By happy chance, the Boathouse is in Harveys Farm Road, named after farmland owned by Mary Harvey and her husband.

As I write, Arabella is working on a novel to be called *Fields of Ice*, based on John Franklin's ill-fated 1845 voyage to find the North West Passage (p150). Taxed with what line she is taking on Jane Franklin, she reassured me: 'I realised that Jane Franklin had to be restored to life and shed the cliché persona of repressed colonial monster.' I have not stayed at Arabella's place – I discovered her as a writer on the internet – but I shall, I hope (www. bichenohideaway.com).

The setting of Helen Hodgman's *Blue Skies* (1976) is, perhaps deliberately, impossible to determine, except that it is within striking distance by local bus of Hobart. So it cannot be Bicheno, which means Bicheno people won't be insulted by my suggesting you read it lounging around here. The housewife narrator lives in a weatherboard house by a beach and spends her life trying to escape the loneliness and pointlessness of her existence. All come to a sticky end.

Aged 13, Helen Hodgman arrived with her family as part of a 'Bring Out a Briton' campaign in 1958. She finished her education and started her working life in Tasmania but then did odd jobs in London before publishing this novella. I believe she now lives in Canada. As far as I can see, this is her only fiction set in Tasmania.

Falmouth

From the east coast towards the west, there are two roads, spaced apart like an estuary, that meet up at St Mary's and lead, via Avoca, to the Midland Highway. We took the southernmost, stopping for pancakes, as prescribed, at Elephant Pass. The northernmost runs from the coastal town of Falmouth and just above that is the Winifred Curtis Scamander Reserve (p253).

It was Arabella Edge who alerted me to the fact that not only had Amanda Lohrey, the Tasmanian-born novelist who spent some years enjoying acclaim on the mainland, relocated to Falmouth, but also that she had fairly recently published a novella, *Vertigo* (2008), about a young couple, Anna and Luke, who 'sea-changed' from the big city to a very quiet coastal place.

The story is not overtly set in Tasmania – they have moved from Sydney to a house they found by driving out from the city. But the author obviously drew on her 2006 experience of the bushfires that threatened the east coast of Tasmania following her move to a house she and her husband had built in his childhood place 23 years earlier. Her controversial novel *The Reading Group* (1988) was written there. That fire forms the climax to *Vertigo*. Amanda Lohrey, whom I have failed over the years to contact, told an interviewer about *Vertigo*, 'I'm sick of dark books. When you get to my age, I want to give a sense of hope. There is a sense of endless renewal.' Some of Anna's newly planted saplings survive the fire.

This itinerary has already turned west but many visitors will want to continue north along the coast, or even turn inland further north. Elizabeth Dean's contribution 'The Language Map' in *A Writer's Tasmania* (2000, edited by Carol Patterson and Edith Speers) is helpful. She touches on the Chinese miners of Weldborough and the only wife, that of Ma Mon Chin, as well as the myth that Hollywood's Merle Oberon was born in St Helens. But Helene Chung in *Ching Chong China Girl* goes into more detail about both, as she describes the search for her own roots. She records the impact of **Mrs Chin** after her arrival in the 1880s, as later recalled by Mrs Bill Grose:

> Mrs Chin lived in a nice house overlooking the joss house and was a very gracious lady. Her home and children were kept very clean and smart. It was a pleasure to see her serve her friends and visitors afternoon tea in fine tiny Chinese cups, using Hang Mee tea, often wearing her Chinese robes and tiny, pretty slippers on her tiny feet. Having been born within the walls of China, her feet were bound so that her feet would be becoming to a Chinese lady. Her children attended the Weldborough school and we spent many happy evenings in her home.

Cassandra Pybus also explores the Merle Oberon myth, as well as the north east coast, in the chapter 'Lottie's Little Girl' in *Till Apples Grow on an Orange Tree* (1998).

Mathinna

Not far along the main road west, at the township of Fingal, is a more minor road 26 kilometres north to Mathinna. Please put down the inclusion of Buckland and Mathinna in this east coast itinerary to poetic licence – they are either end of my writers' arc, for Mathinna is part of Marie Pitt's story.

I cannot come to grips with how this township came to be called Mathinna – the name of the Aboriginal girl taken to live in Government House by Jane Franklin. Before it had that name, it was known as Black Boy (diggings) and was not created as a township until 1872 when Mathinna was long dead and the Franklins long departed. Mathinna was not even from any east coast Aboriginal band; indeed, both parents came from the west coast. Township literature simply says it was named after her without explanation.

Mathinna was to grow in the 1890s, but it must have enjoyed some prosperity in the 1870s because Thomas and **Catherine Beswick** (née Clarke/ Pever, 1844–1908; m1862) – of the extended family establishing itself in the north east – moved there and three of the eight beautiful Beswick daughters were born there, while the older ones went to school. Thomas is recorded as a miner but ran a general business, probably finding he could make more money selling goods to the miners. They left in 1877, and they and their descendants were to thrive.

Alice Christina Irvine (1879–1940), daughter of a mine manager, and famous both for pioneering domestic science teaching in Tasmania and for *The Central Cookery Book* (1930), was not only born there but started her teaching career at Mathinna School. Her book is still valued.

Gold was discovered at Mathinna in the 1890s and the Golden Gate Mine became one of the state's highest-yielding gold mines. By the end of the decade, it was the third-largest town in Tasmania. Among its 5,000 population was Marie Pitt, poet and political activist. Her experiences and writing about Mathinna, the mining township, are detailed in the history section (pp218–20). So much prosperity led to considerable exploitation and ill-health for the miners, and drudgery and tragedy for their wives.

Though Patsy Crawford's novel *God Bless Little Sister: A Story of the 1912 Queenstown Mining Disaster* (2004) is about a mining community in the west of the island, it admirably conveys the life of miners' families, trade unionism and tragedy more generally.

In 1994, there was an attempt to re-establish the Golden Gate Mine, and in 2006, 70,000 ounces of gold were expected. That was the year we visited this strange, almost non-place in a lunar landscape caused by logging and mining, a place lost in time. To think of Marie Pitt living there and working as a poet and unionist leaves a lesser wordsmith than her lost for words. Park beside the little wooden chapel with its eccentric bell tower on the road leading to the mining area and read 'The Keening'.

21 – Midland Highway

The Midland Highway linking Hobart and Launceston is reached from either side of the Derwent – the two north roads out of Hobart (the Brooker Highway and the East Derwent Highway) meeting at Bridgewater. In tourist literature it may be known as the Heritage Highway. You would not want to include all the sites in this itinerary in one visit, and some – for example, Chauncy Vale, Bothwell, Ross – could be separate day-trips from Hobart, and the northern places from Launceston. We visited most of them on different trips north and south.

Chauncy Vale (Bagdad)

As you approach Bagdad, about 40 kilometres from Hobart, look out on the right for Chauncy Vale Road which leads to the Chauncy Vale Wildlife Sanctuary. There is a little graveyard just before the turnoff and, if you pass a petrol station on the left, you have gone too far.

Nan Chauncy (Nancen Beryl, née Masterman, 1900–1970) was famous in her day as a children's writer, and her books survive well. She writes sensitively and engagingly about Aborigines and the environment wrapped up in childhood adventures. I quoted from *Mathinna's People* in the history section (pp118–19), but *Tangara* (1960), about a settler girl Lexie, who slips into the past to relive a friendship that her great-great-aunt had with Merrina, an Aborigine girl, also works as an introduction to children of controversial issues – Aborigines frequented Chauncy Vale for millennia before white settlement there. That is not to say that such stories have the imprimatur of today's Aboriginal descendants. Second-hand copies are not difficult to find.

The Masterman family – parents and six children – arrived in Tasmania in 1912. Nan's father was an engineer who had experienced financial bad luck in England. After two years' work as a council engineer on the Hobart Rivulet, he moved his family to Bagdad. There all eight of them worked at clearing the land for an apple orchard. The small stone and concrete cottage where Nan wrote her twelve children's novels was built between 1916 and 1918.

Nan's cultured mother **Lilla Masterman** (née Osmond, m1895), daughter of a prosperous London merchant, had attended the progressive school run by Frances Buss. How she coped with her new and unexpected life is suggested in Berenice Eastman's 'A Biography of Tasmanian Nan Chauncy' (1978) and the later *Nan Chauncy: A Writer's Life* (2000). Ida McAulay, later to make her mark campaigning for women's rights (pp215–16), whose family befriended the Mastermans, wrote:

> Mrs Masterman, who was one of those people who could not have a garden without a lychgate, a sun-dial, a lavender hedge and a rockery, was steeped in knowledge of all the more attractive customs and habits of the Mother Country. Her conversation was sprinkled with allusions to such things,

and quotations from a wide background of reading. She always recognised possibilities for the picturesque in her surroundings and quickly set about achieving what she visualised from what was already there.

Leaving school at 16, Nan later spent some years working in Europe, and on the return journey to Tasmania in 1938, met a German refugee, Helmut Anton Rosenfeld. They married and moved into the Bagdad cottage given to them as a wedding present. During the war, to avoid anti-German prejudice, Nan's husband took the name Chauncy, the name of her maternal grandmother; they became Nan and Anton Chauncy.

Nan's first success came with *They Found a Cave* (1948), a children's adventure story set in the wild hills above Chauncy Vale where a bushranger was said, in earlier years, to have holed up in the caves. This became a film, the making of which is described in *Down Home: Revisiting Tasmania* (1988) by Peter Conrad who, as a 13-year-old boy, took part. Visiting Chauncy Vale today, and reading his account of the on-set construction of the cave, would make one view the film with new eyes! His first hand description of Nan, though not entirely flattering, gives the sort of impression that English women, particularly those retaining their English accent and habits, tend to leave on Tasmanians:

> Nan Chauncy was a tweedy lady who lived in a house without electricity on a nature preserve where a few dejected marsupials sought refuge, near Bagdad in the midlands. To my parents with their electrical appliances she seemed slightly loony, unplugged from the modern world, and my father referred to her as Nancy Chancy; to me, she was the sole available model of literary activity, scribbling beside an oil-lamp in a dilapidated cabin.

Chauncy Vale was gazetted in 1946 as a private wildlife sanctuary under the Animals and Birds Protection Act 1928, following an application made by Nan and Anton Chauncy. In 1988, some years after Nan's death, her widower and their daughter bequeathed the sanctuary to the local council. Today it is visited by bushwalkers, bird watchers, field naturalist groups, picnicking family groups and school parties. Nan Chauncy's cottage, Day Dawn – still without electricity – is open between 2pm and 4pm on the first Saturday of the month, but you can see well enough through the windows. The 380-hectare sanctuary itself is open from 9am to sunset. You might find yourself the only visitors, and it is as wild and unspoilt as no doubt it was in Nan's day. Berenice Eastman writes of Nan's girlhood working on Chauncy Vale:

> From this experience her identity as a Tasmanian grew. Love of bushland and creek soon extended to knowledge of mountain, rainforest and wilderness river. Nan became an experienced bushwalker with strong conservationist beliefs – convictions that gave her an inner strength which was to inspire her best writing.

Kempton

North of Bagdad, and just west of the Midland Highway, is what used to be called Green Ponds. Kempton – named after the husband of Elizabeth Kemp (p26) – is one of those towns on the Highway that deceives the unwary traveller, for you go in one way and come out of the other. The inn run by Mrs Ransom in the late 1820s, early 1830s, the Royal Oak, is now a white, two-storeyed private house set back on the left just before you rejoin the Highway, having entered Kempton and driven the length of Main Road. It was built in 1827 by Thomas Ransom in a township just beginning to develop as a coaching stop on the Highway. The Royal Oak was the main drop-off point for mail for Hobart.

Mrs Ransom is an enigma; she also seems to have been **Catherine Christiana McNally** (d1857). How she met up with Thomas Ransom, a convict sent to Norfolk Island, a freeman by the time he arrived in Tasmania in 1814, is still open to speculation (as an exhausting trawl through the roots exchanges on the internet shows). He retired as a boat builder in Hobart in 1817 and built the Carpenters' Arms (or Joiners' Arms) in Murray Street and was a respected publican. In spite of that, his licence was revoked in 1825 because, as his Australian biographical entry explains, quoting from another source,

> It was discovered that the faithful and valuable female, who had for years borne his name ... was unhappily unable to enter into a legal state of matrimony, in consequence of circumstances ... which she could neither alter nor recur to, and which, under the prying eye of some persecuting hypocrite ferreted out, were before generally unknown.

The Ransoms moved, therefore, to Green Ponds where he had been granted 400 acres by Governor Macquarie in 1817. As the Land Commissioners reported of the Royal Oak, 'Nothing can exceed the civility and attention the Traveller meets with here, an excellent larder, good beds, capital stabling.'

When Thomas died in 1829, he bequeathed his Green Ponds property (grown by another 600 acres granted by Governor Arthur) to 'his friend', Catherine Christiana McNally. She continued to be known as Mrs Thomas Ransom – in that name she attended a community meeting in April 1830 to discuss the need for a church in the general area of Green Ponds, Oatlands and Jericho (p95).

The Royal Oak was a staging post on the way to Bothwell, and Catherine was very much a feature. Henry Savery, convict and author, wrote in his 1829 column for the *Colonial Times*, entitled 'The Hermit in Van Diemen's Land':

> Upon finishing my ride from Bothwell, I found a comfortable resting place at a large and commodious brick residence, standing a little way off the main road. Justice to the excellent entertainment the good landlady's management afforded demands that I give a few particulars of the hostess herself, and of the manner in which I spent two or three days in her truly comfortable

home. As I really feel much to be her due I will say that although she is not all she has been, she has still not yet so far o'erstepped the meridian of her days as to have lost possession of much for which doubtless she has heretofore been greatly admired.

In 1830, James Ross, quite likely travelling with his wife Susannah (p276) set the Royal Oak in its broader context when he wrote:

> After leaving Mrs Ransom's Royal Oak Inn, a comfortable two-storey brick building with good accommodation, the road extends for some miles over a level tract of country. Close to the inn is the Cross-marsh market-place on the left hand side of the road, conveniently and substantially fenced in for the reception of cattle and sheep.

Breakfast at the inn consisted of mutton chops, and home-made bread and butter, washed down with tea. There was also a nearby orchard growing apples, Kentish cherries, pears, apricots and strawberries.

It was Mrs Ransom for whom the bushranger Matthew Brady had worked as an assigned servant and to whose health, therefore, he drank when he turned up at the Royal Oak after a spree in the area (p95).

What is strange about the bar on the marriage of Catherine and Thomas is that, in 1830, the year after his death, in the name of Catherine Christiana McNally, she married Frederick Lewis von Stieglitz, one of several siblings who had arrived from Ireland the previous year. They all obtained property in the Fingal Valley, Frederick, after his marriage, building Killymoon at Fingal (p344). One record suggests that in 1831 he was the owner of the Royal Oak at Green Ponds.

One can only assume that a previous marriage of Catherine's was the impediment to her marriage to Thomas Ransom and that her earlier husband had, in the meantime, died. Alternatively, it was he who was married, his wife having been left in England when he was transported. Catherine had no children with Thomas but she was the mother of two children. Her son, known as Thomas Ransom, was to inherit (or buy) Killymoon when, after his mother's death, his stepfather left Tasmania. The property, though divided, remained in the Ransom family until the early 1990s. In 1840, Catherine's daughter, **Anne Ransom** (1817–1892), married Francis Walter von Stieglitz, her mother's brother-in-law. They lived at Lewis Hill, between Avoca and Fingal, and had six sons and two daughters.

Bothwell

Turn off the Midland Highway at Melton Mowbray and take the Highland Lakes Road (A5); Bothwell on the Clyde River is a third of the way along to the Great Lake. The drive there is special. You pass rolling hills sucked as sere by January sun as the plain through which the Midland Highway passes, relieved by green eucalypts and the Jordan River marshes. Then the road climbs upwards and round until you think Bothwell must be on top of a hill. But it winds imperceptibly down until you reach a wide, dry plain. The journey direct from Hobart to Bothwell takes about an hour; from Launceston, two hours.

Ratho

If you are visiting Bothwell out of genuine interest in its history, you cannot do better than contact its generous historian Mary Ramsay in advance. Her email address is on the internet. She not only knows the area and its history better than anyone, but she also lives in the historic house Ratho, the nineteenth-century home of Mary Reid and her daughter Jane Reid Williams (p76).

Jane was later to write of that first journey in 1822, when they were accommodated at Dennistoun by Captain Wood until their own 'turf cottage' was erected at Ratho:

> The third day brought us to Dennistoun, and often my dear mother expressed her wonder that without any track, and having ridden to that part of the country only once, my father should have been able to drive us direct through the bush and over the formidable Den Hill, one of the most difficult barriers to cross in the colony. Those who drive over the road now made there, after more than forty years of improving it and so many thousands expended on it, can form only a faint idea of what it was then.

The first settlers had only arrived the previous year and it was not until 1823 that town planning began. Even before they were settled at Ratho, but with all their tempting possessions around them, there were bushrangers to contend with (pp92–3), but Mary Reid somehow managed.

Ratho is through the township of Bothwell itself, its drive a turning off the A5. But you would need Mary Ramsay's permission to see it – an intrusion up the drive would be unwelcome.

Just opposite the drive to the Ratho Golf Club are the remains of what was, until it burnt down, a potters' studio – but a stock-crossing road makes it a dangerous place to stop. It was here, from 1918, that **Maude Poynter** (1869–1945), recognised as Tasmania's first studio potter, built herself a cottage and wood-fired kiln on a parcel of land given to her by her brother-in-law Alexander Reid (Mary Reid's grandson who had married a Miss Poynter, a Meredith descendant (p317)).

Maude's pieces, in strong bright colours, often featuring Australian animals and plants, are inscribed 'Ratho'. Her work is described and illustrated in 'Pioneer Craftswomen from the Bothwell Area' (1994, Catherine Ackland and Colin Campbell).

In 1920, Maude's cousin **Violet Mace** (1890–1968), who had become almost unbalanced by the sale of the Meredith family home Cambria (p318), arrived to stay for a couple of weeks – a stay which extended to 20 years. Maude taught her the art of pottery and, in 1924, the two held their own exhibition at the Hobart Town Hall (p242). Although Maude left Ratho in 1925, Violet continued there until 1940 and is said to have produced her best work as an independent craftswoman; her subdued colours and underglaze decoration became more stylised, and include geometric designs influenced by Aboriginal art.

Cluny

Further along the A5 and easy to see on the left from the road is Cluny, built by Captain William Clark and his wife in 1826. One of their daughters, **Jane Clark,** was governess to the children of Governor Arthur and his wife Eliza, which is probably why Arthur lent the colonial chaplain a carriage in 1826 to take him to Cluny to marry Jane's sister **Ann Clark** (d1868) to William Pritchard Weston (later anti-transportationist and, 1857, Premier). Eleven-year-old Jane Reid describes being a bridesmaid (in spite of the two fathers, Reid and Clark, being constantly at loggerheads) and arriving at Cluny in a bullock cart.

In 1849, the Clarks' son John fought a duel over **Mathilde Adelaide King,** daughter of the officer in charge of the military guard, and described by the Irish political prisoner John Mitchel to Jane Reid Williams as 'one of the most beautiful girls I have ever seen'. Their seconds filled the pistols with raspberry jam. Mathilde married neither of them, but Robert Adams in 1857.

On 1 May 1858, recently married **Mary Jane Brown** (née Meikle, b before 1841) and her husband John were at home at Cluny. He had their baby in his arms. Years later, when Mary had been widowed and had married John Edward Nicholas of Nant, she told the story of what happened when three bushrangers arrived, tied up her husband – knocking the baby to the ground – and ransacked the house. Her account is recorded in detail in both KR von Stieglitz's *The History of Bothwell* (1958?) and John Seymour Weeding's *A History of Bothwell Tasmania* (nd) – though both are mistaken in the date of the raid and which husband Mary was then married to.

Mary wrote of the leading bushranger Sydney Jim who had escaped from Port Arthur, 'The moment I looked at him I thought of the description I had read of a brigand of the old days.' He was, however, no ruffian. 'Flowers strode across the room,' she later remembered,

> and caught hold of me so roughly that I thought my last hour had come. And I believe it would have come if it had not been for Sydney Jim. When he saw the man trying to force his hand down my dress, he called out,
>   'Take your hands of her. She will give you all the money and jewellery she has if you leave her alone.'

He also put her baby gently into her arms. 'In the end,' Mary wrote, 'they were betrayed by **Mrs Bradley**, a shepherd's wife at the Great Lake.'

The Browns went on to have four children. The 1866 list of Bothwell residents shows Mary Jane Brown as landowner of Cluny, so she obviously managed the property following her husband's death and until her marriage to Nicholas in 1873. Mary had two more children.

Since 1912, Cluny has been in the hands of the Bothwell pioneer Bowden family. Kate Bowden is the sister of Jane Shoobridge of Fenton Forest (p310).

Nant

Come a little way back along the A5 and on the left (east) is the turnoff to Nant – a road which links to Dennistoun Road, running north parallel to the A5. Nant was the property of John Edward Nicholas' grandfather, Edward Nicholas, who arrived in 1821, either with, or followed by, his wife **Susannah Nicholas** (c1767–1850) and four children. They were the first settlers in the area and built Nant cottage.

Sources do not agree on whether or not this cottage was on the site of the 1857 Nant homestead, which can be seen from the road, or if it is another cottage, with four chimneys and surrounded by barbed wire on the left before you reach the homestead. This, in any case, is where John Mitchel lived in exile after his wife Jenny and children joined him in June 1851 until his escape in June 1853. The cottage is privately owned, although there are dreams that it should be a historic site open to the public.

Jenny Mitchel (Jane, née Verner, 1821–1899) has been rather overshadowed by her famous husband, his Irish Nationalist activities and his *Jail Journal* (1913), the Tasmanian section of which is in *The Gardens of Hell: John Mitchel in Van Diemen's Land 1850–1853* (edited by Peter O'Shaughnessy). Although Jenny was brought up in the Verner household in Ireland, her mother may have been Mary Ward, the unmarried daughter of the estate's coachman, and her father a Verner brother. Whatever her parentage, she was sent to the Misses Brydens' School for young ladies.

Law student John Mitchel spotted her when she was 16, but both families disapproved of their marrying. They had to elope twice before succeeding in 1837. John started his political activities in 1843 and Jenny, too, under the pseudonym Mary, contributed articles to the Nationalist newspaper *The Nation*. In 1848, when Mitchel was arrested and charged with sedition, Jenny organised his defence campaign. Nevertheless, he and several confreres were sentenced to 14 years' penal servitude in Tasmania.

Jenny made a home of Nant Cottage and, in 1852, added another daughter to their five children. Mitchel farmed the 200 acres opposite the cottage and the family were well received by Bothwell's settlers, particularly the Reids at Ratho. Mitchel wrote of Mary Reid and Jane Reid Williams before Jenny's arrival:

> It gave me a sort of home-feeling, when I found myself, for the first time in two years, seated in the pleasant parlour of Ratho, the home of a most amiable and accomplished Edinburgh family; the social tea-table presided over by one of the most graceful and elegant of old ladies, the books, music, flowers and the gentle converse of high-bred women, could not fail to soothe and soften an exasperated soul in any but its darkest hour ...

Mitchel used to hunt with Mary's husband and he and Jenny dined with the Reids. Following his escape, he corresponded with Jane and sent her a copy of his *Jail Journal*. Von Stieglitz also suggests that Mitchel turned to **Margaret Nicholas** (née Espie, 1818–1893; m1838) of Nant homestead for 'understanding and good-humoured advice during his term at Nant Cottage'. Another woman Mitchel admired was long-established Irish settler Margaret Connell (pp94, 104).

Mitchel's fellow exile, John Martin – who had been involved in the couple's elopement – lived with him before Jenny's arrival and until the family further expanded, when he felt de trop. He also kept a diary which shows that he, too, was persona grata at Ratho. On one visit he took translations of German poets to Elizabeth Hudspeth of Bowsden (p334) who was spending the night there; her sister Alice was married to William Patterson of Bothwell.

Mitchel set out to escape from Bothwell in June 1853, but it took him a good month of toing and froing to board a ship, coincidentally the one caught by Jenny and the family. Mitchel wrote to Jane Reid Williams from Sydney on 24 July 1853:

> My poor Jenny tells me you have been very kind to her since I left but that does not surprise me either. She is almost sorry to quit Bothwell. Those three years of my life seem to me now like a detached bit of a landscape, or a cabinet picture framed and finished and to be hung up on the walls of my house forever.

Jenny herself wrote to a childhood friend from Nant Cottage, 'I am now perhaps happier than I would have been had I never known trouble.' The Mitchels' life after Tasmania continued turbulent.

Dennistoun

This is private property; the original 1820s house was replaced after a fire in 1912, though perhaps not on the same site. If you have good reason to visit the family cemetery, Mary Ramsay could perhaps arrange it with the owners. Jacobina Burn (p74) is one of those buried under the pines and eucalypts not far from the house. To get there, continue from the Mitchel Cottage, on the Nant turnoff, past Nant homestead on the right and turn left onto the road to Interlaken; and so to Dennistoun

On the *Castle Forbes* which arrived in Hobart in 1822 were the Reid family (Ratho), Captain Patrick Wood and Myles Patterson and his family. In 1828, Wood, established at Dennistoun, married **Jane Patterson** (d1837). Her mother, **Katharina Patterson** (née Hunter, c1773–1852) was Jacobina's sister. Jacobina had arrived a year earlier with Katharina's son. She often visited her family in Bothwell and was not happy with relations in the township. Her solution is best glimpsed in a letter of 24 June 1834 from Alexander Reid to his daughter Jane's husband in India:

Old Square Toes [Captain Clark of Cluny] took me by a Coup de Main in the Police Office. With one of his *winning smiles* & an unexpected hold out of his paw, which I had not time to think of resisting – so far so well, you will say: and yet more – old Mrs Burn(s) on a visit at Ratho actually lugged me over to call on Garratt [Garrett, resident church minister], to whom I had not spoken for 18 mos; she said she was *determined to see every one on speaking terms*, & I yielded of course to the old Lady.

Bankrupt in 1844, Jacobina left her estate Ellangowan and came to Bothwell to live with Katharina, eventually moving to Clyde Villa, later demolished. The house now on the nearby site is 'Bendeveron'; privately owned, it is just off Logan Road in the centre of Bothwell and can be seen from the road. John Martin visited Jacobina at Clyde Villa and wrote on 22 September 1850:

[Mrs Burn] was up and at her knitting or crochet as usual, but looking pale and sick. She had been suffering from pain last night. Miss Patterson showed me pencilled drawings of herself and by Mrs Blackwood, and other members of the Officer family – all very respectable.

Jemima Officer (1804–1881) was Jacobina's niece and, since 1823, wife of colonial surgeon Robert Officer with properties in New Norfolk and on the Clyde.

Jacobina died the year after that visit, aged 88. Her granddaughter, Jemima Frances Irvine (p102) says that she was buried 'beside her faithful aboriginal maid' but Mary Ramsay has not been able to confirm that. Nearby in the cemetery is the grave of Jane Patterson Wood, who died giving birth to twin daughters, and that of **Mary Daniells** and her two children, murdered by Aborigines on the Woods' property, the Den, in 1831.

St Luke's Uniting Church

Leaving Dennistoun, heading back into town, and turning left, the first site you come to is St Luke's, completed in 1831. Then it was for the joint use of Protestant denominations, the predominant Scottish Presbyterian community and Anglicans, until the Anglican St Michael and all Angels was built in 1891. The sculptures over the doorway are attributed to Mary Herbert's husband, Daniel, famous for the bridge at Ross (p337). The female head is either a Celtic goddess or Queen Adelaide. Inside is a Reid family memorial plaque; it particularly extols the virtues of Mary Reid. Margaret Espie Nicholas of Nant is buried in the graveyard. And it is here that the duel held on account of Mathilde King took place.

The Castle Inn

Before settlement, the Clyde River area was home to the Big River nation, the remnants of which Robinson rounded up in 1831, accompanied by Trukanini and other Aborigines of his team (p114). The plaque beside the entrance to the hotel tells how, before being taken to Hobart, 'George Augustus Robinson brought the few remaining members of the Big River and Oyster Bay people through Bothwell and they performed a corroboree here on January 5, 1832.' The famous Duterrau painting, 'The Conciliation' (in the Tasmanian Museum and Art Gallery), depicts the scene. Contrary to supposition, Trukanini is not next to Robinson but on the far left.

Sarah Jane Duterreau (mBogle 1838; d1885), the artist's daughter, arrived with him in 1832, hoping to teach music at Ellinthorp (p336). When that fell through, she became governess to the Arthurs' children.

Beth Roberts (1924–2001), a fifth-generation Tasmanian who lived in Birch Cottage, Elizabeth Street, writes of the Big River people in her children's novel *Manganinnie: A Story of Old Tasmania* (1977), about an old Aboriginal woman who has lost her people, without realising why, and kidnaps a toddler from a Bothwell settler property to pass on the 'Common Knowledge' and keep her company. It was made into a film in 1980.

The Priory

Back on the A5, as if going to Ratho, turn left into Wentworth Street and right into Frances Street. The Priory is now a luxury hotel, the Priory Country Lodge. When we visited it, it was an empty two-storey Tudor gothic house built in 1847–48. Its significance is that in her later years Maria Lord lived there and, indeed, died there (pp33, 80–3). After the tribulations of a failed marriage, and her glory years in trade in Hobart, she ran a general store in Bothwell.

She acquired the Priory by default. Alexander Reid of Ratho had it as a town allotment; then in 1847, the Reverend Robert Wilson started building. Bishop Nixon had not approved; nor would the government provide funds. Since Wilson owed Maria £1,000, she took the Priory instead. She kept three rooms herself and leased the rest of the house. I'm not sure how easy it is to sense the ghost of Maria there; the rather sad, empty house was a better bet. At least you can appreciate the fine view, as she must have done, from the terrace.

Return now, the way you came, to the Midland Highway.

Oatlands

In 1811, on their first visit to Tasmania (pp49–53), Governor Macquarie and his wife Elizabeth travelled through the area that he did not name Oatlands until their second visit to the island in 1821. And until 1827 it was just a site with a name board. Many buildings erected soon thereafter still stand.

I have a soft spot for Oatlands, though it is another of those places where you have to keep your wits about you because of two ways in and out. One day we turned off the Campania road onto the Midland Highway after visiting Bowsden, formerly the home of the Hudspeths, Mary (p90) and her seven surviving children, including the artist **Elizabeth Hudspeth** (1820–1858), and, from 1928, owned by the Burburys. It was the family home of Mary Ramsay, Bothwell's historian, and her brother Charles Burbury, now that of him and his wife Stephanie. The research visit had left us in good spirits but then we felt and heard something wrong with our hire car. We had an itinerary-laden drive north ahead and disaster loomed. We limped into Oatlands and found a garage where, immediately, without fuss or requiring payment, the branch that was fouling a wheel was removed.

But we already used Oatlands – half-way between Hobart and Launceston – as a pit stop because at 44 High Street is Casaveen, a cafe with cakes worth getting fat for. In addition, it is the work-and-showroom of the knitwear designed and made using locally produced wool by Clare McShane whose husband and business partner is the great nephew of women's activist Alicia O'Shea Petersen (p216).

Oatlands, as much as any other place in Tasmania, shows that there is no evading family history and that it is often circles within circles. This is where the historian Alison Alexander – who has been so generous to me at both the research and writing stage of this book – spent some childhood years after her father became the local vet. In 'Childhood in Paradise' in *A Writer's Tasmania* (2000), she writes of revisiting Oatlands and finding much changed, including 'My old House of Horrors, the preschool, now sells beautiful locally-made jumpers'.

The circle was even wider for Alison: a branch of her convict ancestors – on both sides – not only settled in the area but became respectable, something her parents only discovered when, arriving from New South Wales, they mentioned their family name. One of those ancestors was **Sophia Peters** (1814–1892) who, with her sister Anne, was speared during an attack by Aborigines on their home in Bagdad (p24). Anne died but Sophia's stout stays deflected the spear and she lived to marry James Pillinger in 1836. Their son became warden of Oatlands and the local MP, rising to minister. Although James amassed a considerable landholding to the north of Oatlands, as Alison records, 'By the end of the century the property was sold – clogs to clogs in three generations ...'

In 1864 James Pillinger's brother George married Mary, daughter of convict **Jane Hadden** (née Baird, 1797–1867). Jane left a husband and two children behind in Scotland when she was transported but was eventually pardoned and set up as a laundress in Kempton (p327). 'There', as Alison recounts, 'she had an affair with a local ex-convict landowner, whose wife was found one morning dead, with her head in the fireplace. There appeared to be no inquest; 13 days later the widower married Jane and they lived in some style ...' Jane sent for her children, but not her first husband. **Mary Hadden** (1839–1932) and George Pillinger were Alison's great grandparents.

In Dulverton Lake, the nearby wildlife sanctuary, is Mary Isle, granted by Governor Arthur to Mary Anstey (pp73, 90) who lived with her family at Anstey Barton which once existed by what is now the Dulverton Rivulet, a tributary of the Jordan River.

Midland Highway

This two-lane highway dissects Tasmania like a zip from north to south. When we travel on it in January or February, the landscape is dun-coloured, as are the sheep sprinkled either side, and the sparse, skeleton shrubs. There is usually little traffic. It was different in the nineteenth century. GB Lancaster writes in *Pageant*, as one of her characters speeds south in a tandem changing horses from time to time: '[They were] swinging along the Main Road that was swarming still with beggars, with farmers driving flocks of sheep, with carts of hay and wool; swinging across bridges, clattering through small townships in the twilight.'

In *Exile*, Kathleen Graves (p346) describes a voyage north at much the same date:

> They made good time from Hobart Town. Thirty miles the first day up through passes out of the Derwent valley, then over forty the second day across the plains. There were culverts all the way now and bridges over the creeks and rivers, but the track was still rutted – the rains had laid the dust, but in another month it would be a quagmire.

Ellenthorpe (Ellinthorp) Hall

Just after the southernmost entrance to Ross on the right is Auburn road on the left, easy to miss. Several miles along – through an empty plain with the Western Tiers in the distance – is a drive on the left to Ellenthorpe Hall (as it is now spelt). The two-storey Georgian house built in 1826/27 was once Hannah Clark's school for girls (pp136–9).

Today, Ellenthorpe is private property – comfortably viewed in *Country Houses in Tasmania* – but if you want to get an impression of the environs, it is worth a drive along Auburn Road. It is easy to imagine what it must have been like when, in 1838, bushrangers came out of the plain onto this isolated establishment for young ladies 18 kilometres from the nearest township.

In the barracks, which still stand near the house, were marines who had guarded the 20 convicts building the house and remained to protect the school from bushrangers and Aborigines. One account says that they had been lured away. In any case, there was enough time for the girls and women teachers to block up the windows with mattresses, pillows and cushions, leaving only apertures for the gun barrels; and to pile heavy furniture against the doors. There were also enough men around and enough luck to ensure that the raid was unsuccessful. The most accurate account is in GT Stillwell's 'Mr and Mrs George Carr Clark of "Ellinthorp Hall"'.

Hannah Clark had four surviving children (two had died) at the time, and her health had begun to deteriorate, leading to the school suffering a similar fate. She closed it in 1840 and, ironically, took her own children home to England to complete their education. There she died in 1847. Her husband remained in Tasmania which suggests that their marriage, too, was unsteady; it appears he regretted leaving his life in Hobart as a merchant to become a grazier.

Ross

The Bridge

Ross – 120 kilometres from Hobart and 80 from Launceston – is one of the oldest of Tasmania's townships, proclaimed by Macquarie during his visit with Elizabeth of 1821, though it was first settled in 1812. From the south, you come to Australia's third-oldest bridge; completed in 1836, its 186 carvings by convict mason Daniel Herbert are, not surprisingly, renowned. They are riots of animals, birds, insects, plants, Celtic goddesses and gods and the heads of friends and foes. The most significant for us are those of Herbert's convict wife, **Mary Herbert** (née Witherington), and rambunctious convict Norah Corbett (pp61, 304). In *Ross Bridge and the Sculptures of Daniel Herbert* (1971), Leslie Greener writes of Mary Herbert,

> A photograph taken somewhat later in life – in her middle thirties I should think – strikingly resembles the female mask on [the bridge]. It shows a strong face with high cheek bones, large luminous eyes, firm full lips and a decisive jaw-line. It is not the face of a conventional beauty, but rather handsome, vital and attractive. There is still one more reason for believing that this icon cannot be anyone other than Herbert's wife. It is the only human personification on the bridge which is perfectly serene and untouched by pain or mockery.

The couple are said to have married at the low-slung Barracks just beyond the bridge in 1835. My notes say, 'Don't peer through the window; too many do it.' That suggestion must, I think, have originated from a helpful staff member at the Tasmanian Wool Centre (which doubles as an information centre) on the western side of Church Street. The Herberts were said to have lived at the Macquarie River end of Badajos Street, their white-washed cottage marked on the map available at the Wool Centre. He was promised a pardon for his ornamentation of the bridge and they continued to live in Ross and have three children.

The mask of Norah Corbett, who moved to Ross with her husband Jorgen Jorgenson, is popularly known as 'the Queen', and his 'the King'. He had been sent to Ross by Arthur in 1833 to find out why the bridge was not yet built. Greener writes of Norah,

> Herbert was entirely successful in capturing the sickness of this woman, and I cannot help thinking that the sculptor was profoundly moved by the utter sadness of her human condition. In his own way, he struck fiercely into the stone the symbols that might free her from the troubles that were her demons.

Norah and Jorgenson stayed at the Man O'Ross Inn on the eastern corner of Bridge and Church Streets, and made the place infamous by their drunken brawls.

42.   Mary Herbert, courtesy of the Tasmanian Wool Centre, Ross

Catherine Bennett Meagher

The cottage of Catherine and Thomas Meagher, also marked on the map, is over the road, on the eastern corner of High and Bond Streets. Meagher met Catherine Bennett when she worked as governess to the six children of **Mary Hall** (née Latham, 1807–1887) and the progressive Dr Edward Hall who, a couple of years later, was to campaign against the heavy infant mortality at the Cascades female factory (p62). In *A Short History of Ross* (c1949), KR von Stieglitz tells the charming story of their accidental meeting – as the wheel came off the family carriage, landing her in the mud almost at his feet. For a while, they were happy but the cottage they moved to on Lake Sorell was very isolated and he chose to escape his Tasmanian exile when she was three months pregnant (p275).

In *The Life and Times of Thomas Francis Meagher* (2001), Reg Watson, through Meagher and John Mitchel's accounts, evokes his Ross landlady, **Mrs Henry Anderson,** 'of stupendous proportions and commensurate loquacity'.

43.   Catherine Bennett Meagher, c1851,
from an unnamed internet site

The Female Factory

The Ross Female Factory site is on the 'Heritage Walkway' which runs from the bridge to the original burial ground, and can also be approached from Bond Street. The factory, one of four in Tasmania, dates from 1847 when what had been a male probation station was expanded to include a chapel, dining room, hospital, nursery, twelve solitary cells, dormitories and outer courtyard. The women, to be reformed under the new probation system (pp157–61), were trained for domestic service. But it is clear from the archaeological dig that started under Eleanor Casella in 1995 that not all the women were biddable. Excavations have revealed that, against regulations, the women imported tobacco, alcohol and increased food rations. There is evidence of arson in 1851 – a not uncommon form of rebellion. And they were said to indulge in 'unnatural practices'. **Mary Ann Elliot,** for example, there in 1850, was described as a 'pseudo male individual'.

Eleanor Casella's findings are published in *Archaeology of the Ross Female Factory: Female Incarceration in Van Diemen's Land, Australia* (2002). But the scholarly book is more than that: it includes what is called 'The Historic Landscape', sketching the history of female incarceration in Tasmania and the Australian mainland. The overseer's cottage, the only substantial remains of any of the female factories, is a museum.

Eliza Forlong (Kenilworth)

It was at the Tasmanian Wool Centre in Ross that I first heard of **Eliza Forlong** (Forlonge, Betty, née Jack, 1784–1859) (p72) – not surprising given her contribution to the colony's wool industry, one that continues today.

In 1804 Eliza married John Forlong, a Scottish wine merchant with a French émigré forebear – a man with big ideas but not much earning capacity. Happily for them, John's indulgent sister, **Janet Templeton** (1785–1857), was married to a Scottish banker who financed the Forlongs' scheme to purchase a particularly fine breed of Spanish merino sheep from Saxony and take them to New South Wales. They hoped by the move to save the lives of their two remaining children after four had died from tuberculosis.

To advance the project, Eliza set off on foot in 1827 on an inspection and learning tour of the merinos in Saxony with her sons, leaving the younger one at school in Leipzig and the elder, William, attached to a wool sorting house to learn the trade. She returned the following two summers and, with a pouch of gold sovereigns sewn into her stays, walked with the boys through the countryside purchasing the best sheep she could find, sealing them with a lockable tag bearing the initial 'F' and finally, long staff in hand, driving them before her down the Elbe to Hamburg – a journey full of incident.

William was sent off to New South Wales first but in transit in Hobart in 1829 was, he claimed, persuaded by Governor Arthur to stay in Tasmania. He was given a land grant near Campbell Town, between the Macquarie and South Esk Rivers. The rest of the family left for Australia in a vessel chartered by recently-widowed Janet Templeton; the party included Janet's nine children, more sheep from Saxony and experienced shepherds. The Forlongs were committed to Tasmania, arriving there in 1831 when John was granted land next to William's; it became Kenilworth. Janet proceeded to New South Wales.

The novel *Saxon Sheep: How a Famous Merino Flock came to Victoria* (1961) tells the story from the beginning in Glasgow to the end of everyone's life. Unfortunately for Eliza's reputation, it is written by a descendant of Janet's, Nancy Adams, and, as the two families apparently fell out, Eliza does not come out of it well; she was a strong, and determined woman, perhaps sometimes overbearing, and with a tendency to flout convention. As Mary Ramsay explains in the rather more scholarly 'Eliza Forlong and the Saxon Merino Industry' (2004): 'Unfortunately this novel is often perceived to be factual and caused immense hurt to some members of the Forlonge family.'

Eliza often managed Kenilworth alone, while John went about his schemes. In 1844, however, widowed since 1835, she decided that the Kenilworth property was too unsatisfactory – there was no river access – and moved to Victoria. Kenilworth and half its sheep were sold to David Taylor of the Taylor family who had farmed Valleyfield since 1823 (p96). He had moved to Winton in 1832 and the Saxon merinos he bought from the Forlongs became the basis of the pure-bred Winton Merino stud flock continuing to produce wool clips of superfine quality. Vera Taylor tells the Taylor story in *Winton Merino Stud, 1835–1985* (1985).

Kenilworth today is owned by another David Taylor and his wife Tina Taylor. In the garden is a sundial, erected by the Dilston Country Women's Association and unveiled in 1940 by the governor's wife, Lady Clark, celebrating Eliza's contribution to the wool industry of Australia. Although the Wool Industry Eliza Forlonge Medal, established in 1991, was short-lived, Eliza's contribution continues to be appreciated.

If you have a serious interest in Eliza Forlong, the Taylors are likely to grant you access to the sundial; it has been visited by least one history group. Tina drove me to the remains of Eliza's original house. According to the records drawn on by Mary Ramsay, 'There once stood a farmhouse, buildings designed in the same style as sheep houses in Saxony, wells and the usual outbuildings required in those days such as stabling.' All that remains are a few piles of bricks almost lost in the long grass, but with a splendid view, and something about the air – Eliza Forlong's scent? We had approached Kenilworth from the north, got lost and were rescued by a knight errant in a Land Rover (who is in the acknowledgements); if invited, you will need direction.

44. Eliza Forlong, (assumed to be) from
'Eliza Forlong: The Unsung Woman
Behind Our Wool' (*40° South*)

Avoca

We drove to Avoca off the main roads from the east coast (p321) but an easier and quicker way from the Midland Highway is to take the Esk Highway (A4) towards St Helen's, St Mary's and Bicheno from just north of Campbell Town – Elizabeth Macquarie's maiden name; through it flows the Elizabeth

River, also a remnant of the Macquaries' 1821 visit. It is where, too, the poet Helen Power was brought up (p255).

In the mid nineteenth century, Avoca must have been a vibrant centre, with several families of lively and artistic daughters. It wasn't really on the day we visited, though Shirley Freeman at the post office was an invaluable informant. She is in a fine tradition: **Charlotte Adams**, wife of a sheep farmer, and mother of six children, was post mistress and telegraphist there from 1876 to 1912. She was 'justly esteemed by all' and her work was 'not only rapid but exceedingly accurate'.

By 1900, Avoca seems to have changed. Marie Bjelke Petersen and her long-term companion **Sylvia Mills** (1869–1927, younger sister of Caroline Morton (p214)) went there for a holiday. It started badly: Marie described the Midlands as 'burned up, brown ... most uninteresting to say the least'. Then, as Alison Alexander puts it in her biography of Marie, 'Avoca turned out to be dreadful. They wanted to stay in a quiet country retreat where they could rest, but the boarding house where they had booked a room was nothing but a third-rate cottage, smelling of stale beer and ancient dinners.' Marie describes their room in detail, starting, 'How am I to begin to describe it!'

Should you decide not to make a special visit to Avoca – 'meeting of the waters' – if you are driving through, stop at St Thomas's Church on a hill overlooking where the South Esk and St Paul's Rivers meet. Standing there is to begin to recapture something of those original families who lived on their extensive sheep-rearing estates and created a community around the church which they had built (completed 1842). Trying to marry the boundaries of today's properties with those of the past is enough to make you light headed.

Catherine Grey and her husband, Humphrey, arrived in 1828 and two of their daughters, Henrietta and Elizabeth, went to Ellinthorp Hall, school for young ladies (p138). **Henrietta Grey** (Henny) went first, in 1831, and was there for about seven years. Kate Hamilton Dougharty describes how Maria Clark's advertisement added that 'On a certain date, two bullock drays would attend Avoca for intending pupils from the surrounding districts.' They had an armed escort to protect the girls from bushrangers and Aborigines. Because of transport difficulties, Henny only came home twice a year. Lysbeth, who followed her three years later, then married well and at one stage lived at Newlands in Hobart (p269). The eldest daughter, **Margaret Grey**, married in 1830 and later died from the sting of a poisonous spider. Her brother, Humphrey, was thrown from his horse in 1834 and killed instantly. In 1837, the family attended a ball at Launceston to welcome the Franklins and later a dinner party at the Cornwall Hotel (p368) for their successors, the Denisons. The Greys were a large Irish family with several sons, so they had several properties, a couple of which are incorporated in today's Benham which stretches for miles along the road south to Royal George.

Sarah Birch (1814–1892), daughter of Sarah and Thomas Birch of Birch Castle, later the Macquarie Hotel (p245) married, in 1831, Simeon Lord, son of a convict of the same name who made good in New South Wales and the woman who eventually became his wife, proto-feminist Mary Hyde. The young couple settled on the Avoca property given him by his father; there they built Bona Vista, started in 1831, completed in 1848 when it had 43 residents, 25 of them free. Martin Cash was said to have worked there as a groom and, indeed, surprised young **Catherine Grey** and a friend in his later manifestation as a bushranger when they were out walking unescorted. But he merely asked them their names and destination; the Greys were reputed to treat their assigned servants well, and Cash was renowned as a gentleman (p96).

In 1853, however, absconding Lords' servants who had become bushrangers did attack Bona Vista, murdered Constable Buckmaster, called to assist, and robbed the house. The story is told of how Miss Isobel had to hand over the jewellery she had been wearing but had quickly sat upon. Unfortunately, the Lords do not appear to have had a daughter of that name (of their ten children); perhaps it was **Louisa Lord** (b1833).

Bona Vista is along Story's Creek Road, running north past St Thomas's, alongside St Paul's River and crossing the South Esk just beyond where the two rivers meet – a picturesque route. Soon on the left is a walled estate containing a single-storey old Colonial Regency house with walled courtyards, barns, paddocks for young stock and gardens. Under the ballroom in the east wing are dungeons where convict servants were confined at night. Although it is privately owned, you might be able to arrange, at least, to drive around the internal road which allows you a good view of the house. Another Grey property is now part of Bona Vista.

Pulling the Greys, Bona Vista, Benham and, indeed, Avoca, together is **Maria Raake** (née Lambert, 1832–1932). She was born on one of the Grey estates and baptised with a Grey granddaughter, and then confirmed with her 18 years later. In 1852, she married the music master to the Lords' children. Maria remembered the end of transportation in 1853 and took part in the celebrations (p172). She was witness to the murder of the constable at Bona Vista. As a maternity nurse she attended, often on horseback, the births of 1,000 or so babies over 50 years – the last in her 90th year was at Bona Vista; meanwhile, she had six daughters of her own. She saw five generations of the O'Connor family at Benham where she lived for 73 years. Not only did she watch St Thomas's being built, her father was one of the carpenters; the sandstone came from Bona Vista. To celebrate her 100th birthday she donated a splendid Bible to it.

In 1839 **Emma von Stieglitz** (1807–1880) sketched Brookstead, reproduced in *Early Van Diemen's Land 1835–1860: Sketches by Emma von Stieglitz* (1963, edited by KR von Stieglitz). The house is dwarfed by Ben Lomond rising behind it. Brookstead, ten miles southeast of Avoca on the Royal George road, was Emma's home before her marriage. Her brother, Robert Cowie, arrived in 1828 and was granted the land. Their mother, **Rachel Cowie** (née Buxton, c1770–1846) and the rest of the family arrived to join him in 1834. (The father, left behind, died the year of their arrival.) Georgiana, who tells the nice story about Salome Pitt Bateman in 1834 (p44), was Emma's sister.

Two years later, Emma married John Lewis von Stieglitz of a neighbouring estate, and thus became the sister-in-law of both Catherine McNally Ransom and her daughter Ann (p328). (And Emma's brother, John, married **Charlotte Christina von Stieglitz**).

Robert had, in 1832, married **Julia Luthman**, the Irish-Swedish governess of a Longford family, and two of their daughters are known as Tasmanian artists; indeed, **Emily Bowring** (née Cowie, 1835–c1912; m1854) produced the sketches of Mount Wellington, the new Government House and Queen's Orphanage. Julia Cowie is known for an 1855 sketch of Brookstead, and watercolours and sketches of buildings and plants. It is fair to assume that Aunts Emma and Georgiana (who also sketched) influenced them. Julia was an early proponent of the Methodist Ladies' College, Launceston (p380).

The story of some of these extraordinarily linked Fingal Valley families is told in *An Early Tasmanian Story: With Oakdens, Cowies, Parramores, Tullochs and Hoggs* (2004) by Anne and Robin Bailey. It contains extracts from Georgiana's diary, though it began to peter out after arrival at Brookstead. Not surprisingly, some pages were torn out; writing of her sister **Mary Cowie** (1800–1874), she noted that '[She] has just returned from a visit to the "Goths"' – to Mr and Mrs Henry von Stieglitz. The extended 'Goth' family had gone from Pomerania to Bohemia (in the fourteenth century), then to Saxony, and finally to Ireland, in 1802, before emigrating to Tasmania, in the charge of widowed baroness **Charlotte von Stieglitz** (née Atkinson), starting in 1829.

The Cowie family letters continued, within Tasmania as well as home. Emma, writing to Georgiana about the latter's wish to become a governess because she was unhappy at Brookstead, then captures poor **Mrs Henry von Stieglitz** (to whom Emma was soon to become a sister-in-law), and Avoca more generally. **Jane Cowie** (1802–1884) is another sister of the older generation; several of the Grey male cousins, as well as Humphrey, held army rank, so it is not possible to identify their wives in what follows:

> Jane and I agree to saying we never enjoyed society so much before as we did at the Greys. We felt that we really formed part of it and both Captain and Mrs G are so polite and agreeable. Mrs Major Grey called when we were there and said the visit was expressly for us. She is a very pleasant lady like woman and reminded me strongly of Lady Mordaunt, though she is not quite so pretty ... You will hear, we shall have a new neighbour, Mrs H. Stieglitz in a few months. She is very lovely, friendly but not very polished, nor in the least accomplished, still she is a lady and will be a very kind and pleasant neighbour. We have scarcely been a day quite alone for the last fortnight.

Lady Mordaunt must have been a relative or close family friend because Georgiana, married to Phillip Oakden in 1839, named her last child Mordaunt Oakden.

Nile

Kingston and Ben Lomond – Eliza Callaghan, John Batman and the Camerons

Back on the Midland Highway, you are almost immediately at the old railway junction Conara. Just past it, on the right, is the turnoff to Nile, a minor road running parallel to the Highway which leads eventually to the 'Historic Clarendon Homestead'. But this road has more than that to offer: Kingston, where Eliza Callaghan, absconder (p58) lived with John Batman. Cross the beautiful South Esk River and, in January, there should be poppy fields shimmering pale green in the distance. Just before the turnoff to Kingston is a house on the road providing lovely fresh eggs and information. Thereafter, there is a sign for Nile and Evandale that turns left, but instead go straight on. Kingston Road does not advertise itself obviously and, although it is a public road, it is not tarmacked. The final 150 yards to Kingston homestead is private; please do not venture there unless you have made arrangements with the owner, Simon Cameron, to do so. A branch of the extended Cameron family has owned Kingston since 1905, and 'The Rise and Fall of Eliza Batman' (1985), a scholarly chapter by Max Cameron, shows their continuing interest in its past.

Kingston's original cottage, reconstructed, is there; 2 kilometres walk away are rubble remains of the house where Eliza and Batman lived with their growing family – what Simon Cameron calls 'a pleasant walk to a pile of bricks'. A 1920s photograph shows a roofless and tumbling but substantial two-storey house. When it was abandoned, and why, remain uncertain. Caressa Crouch explores the history of the various buildings on the property, as well as Eliza's place there in 'Kingston – The Residence of John Batman, Van Diemen's Land' (1995).

You really don't need to go beyond the gate into the Cameron property to get the full impact of where Eliza lived for more than ten years. It is an enchanting setting along the Ben Lomond Rivulet, with the frilly, pleated mountain range dominating the horizon. Emily Bowring's 1859 sketch 'Ben Lomond' gives a fine impression, though lacks the refreshing green that marks the rocky passage of the rivulet. Elizabeth Hudspeth's 1855 western face version from a more watery angle can now be seen as a coloured lithograph, while Louisa Anne Meredith's 1852 view from St Paul's Plains is a wood engraving. They are in the Allport Library and Museum of Fine Arts and can be seen on line. A water colour and pencil sketch by Eliza Cox (p355), viewed from near Ross, is in the Queen Victoria Museum and Art Gallery.

It is not known how Eliza Callaghan, or Thompson as she also called herself, and John Batman met. Close's fictional stab – a chance meeting on the road – is as good as any. Batman was the son of a convict transported to New South Wales, and a mother who paid her fare. He arrived in Tasmania from there in 1821, the same year that Eliza was transported directly to Tasmania. By 1824, he had the land grant at Kingston and the following year Eliza gave birth to their first child, **Maria Batman**; they were to have seven daughters and, in 1837, a last child, John.

Tales are told of how, when rumours of Eliza's presence brought the authorities to the house in 1825 in search of the absconder while Batman was absent, she hid in the cellar while their staff fended them off. They did, however, note a woman's effects about the place. She was presumably then pregnant; it would have been harder to hide evidence of a baby in the house.

45.   Ben Lomond from Greenhill, by Elizabeth Hudspeth, courtesy of the Allport Library and Museum of Fine Arts, Tasmanian Archive and Heritage Office

Batman, meanwhile, was responsible for the capturing of the bushranger, Matthew Brady (p90), and took part in the 'conciliation' of the Aborigines (p117). It was these activities that led the governor not only to increase Batman's land grant but also to look kindly on his plea to marry absconder Eliza Thompson; they did so in 1828 (p376). Her pardon was gazetted in 1833. CP Billot in *John Batman: The Story of John Batman and the Founding of Melbourne* (1979) suggests that liaisons like theirs 'were not that uncommon, and involved no ostracism'.

Kathleen Graves (née Priest, 1901–1974) takes a different line in *Exile* (1947) in which the irresistible Kinnaird – married to his assigned servant and ostracised – is quite clearly based on Batman, and his property on Kingston. The story starts in 1826 and is ostensibly about Kinnaird's neighbours, Clair and Richard Thursby, drawing on the diaries of Kathleen's grandfather of Devonport. But Kinnaird dominates the story of the problems and society of settlers and the uncertain and harassed lives of convict servants and Aborigines. It is not at all a bad read. (Kathleen Graves made her name with *Tasmanian*

Pastoral (1953), an account of the first year of making something of their property Woodlands at Lemana, to the west of Launceston – a 'year-long battle against weather, soil and disease', but keenly appreciative of the environment, and harking back to the lives of settlers since their arrival. The house still stands and Kathleen is buried in Deloraine Cemetery.)

Views on Batman's relations with Aborigines are mixed. Bonwick devotes a whole chapter to them and includes several quotations of praise for his efforts. Batman's biographical entry by LP Brown provides a useful paraphrase: he notes his 'persevering leadership in the first conciliation campaign amongst the Tasmanian Aboriginals. He wrote of "that much injured and most unfortunate race", and [Governor] Arthur called him "one of the few who supposed that they might be influenced by kindness".'

Alistair H Campbell, in *John Batman and the Aborigines* (1987), has a more hostile view. In reviewing it, Plomley writes: 'It is a pleasure to read an account of Batman's activities that does not find them praiseworthy.' That, of course, includes those on the mainland where Batman 'bought' from the Aborigines the land that became Melbourne.

Bonwick writes that Batman was the first (before Robinson) to use Aboriginal women to help in his task of 'conciliation', that is, finding Aborigines and rounding them up, supposedly for their own good. Several Aborigines lived at Kingston during this time, briefly or for longer periods. On one occasion, the women emissaries to their people, one of them named **Luggenemenener** (1800–1837), persuaded nine men there, causing some alarm to Eliza and her daughters because they were armed, curious about everything around them, and 'hungry as hunters'. Batman himself, finally arriving home, wrote:

> Their appetite is enormous, devouring everything they meet. They are particularly fond of half-roasted eggs of every description, geese, ducks, and hens; it is all one – so much so, that Mrs Batman's poultry yard will cut but a sorry figure after the company.

Luggenemenener ended up at Wybalenna, called Queen Charlotte by Robinson, and there, like so many others, she died (p116).

Batman also wrote of Aboriginal women at Kingston: 'The women here all day. The evening, the young child, belonging to one of the women, that sucked at the breast, died. I put it in a box and buried it at the top of the garden. She seemed much affected at the loss of the child, and cried much.' The following day, he added: 'This morning I found the woman … over the grave, and crying much.' What was intended as sympathy, or simply a record of fact, could also be seen as surprise that Aborigines had feelings. Writing of life in the bush, there are several entries: 'The black women could not walk well.' 'Caught a kangaroo for the women.' 'The women much tired: made them some tea, and gave them bread and mutton.' Now that really was a suggestion of equality, gender, at least! Campbell gives a full context for these entries.

Batman, with the permission of Arthur with whom he got on well – one of the reasons for Robinson's hostility – had brought some male trackers over from the mainland. But the one who, in 1830, married a Tasmanian woman whose European name was **Catherine Kennedy** – brought up by a settler a Christian and 'a good house servant' – was also local (p376). Batman wrote to Arthur asking for land for the couple, as a reward for the tracker's services, and to encourage others, adding: 'the black women who left my place are well aware that he and his wife are their country people. They seemed to be well pleased to see them clothed and comfortable. They are both now living at my farm.' Although Arthur agreed, the land does not seem to have been allocated. And, of course, it traditionally belonged to the man's people anyway – and ochre had been procured from the area for millennia – even if the land had not been farmed in the European way.

Although by 1835 Kingston consisted of more than 7,000 acres, the terrain was too rugged to be satisfactorily productive. Batman had, since 1827, had his eye on the Mainland; now he determinedly set out. What followed, including the creation, with John Fawkner, of Melbourne, is not a story for here, except that by April 1836, he had built a house there and Eliza, their seven daughters and governess **Caroline Newcomb** (1812–1874) joined him. By then, he was already walking with difficulty. Two years later, he was totally disabled, probably from syphilis, affecting their relationship. Eliza left for England early in 1839, perhaps to further their interests, but heard of his death on her return to Australia. His financial affairs were left in disarray.

Eliza married his former clerk, William Willoughby in 1841 but the marriage does not appear to have lasted. Eliza, now called Sarah, took to drink and became a 'somewhat abandoned character'. The drowning of her son John in 1845 cannot have helped; in a letter to one of her daughters about his death – the only piece of her writing that survives – she wrote: 'all my happiness in this world is buried in the grave with him'. She died at Geelong on 29 March 1852 after being violently attacked, probably by three drinking companions. Documents concerning Eliza's life, from her trial to her murder, are contained in *Callaghan and Batman: Van Diemen's Land in 1825* ('EF', 1978).

As Max Cameron points out, 'Eliza held positions in society that were closely linked with her marital status and wealth'; without them, survival of women in her situation was a not always successful struggle. A year after Eliza's death, one of her daughters, for reasons of her own, described her mother as 'Elizabeth Callan, governess'. She might have tried her hand at it, she had become literate and was obviously intelligent; and it provided a better memory of her.

Continuing towards Launceston/Evandale, just before the little village of Nile, you pass the original grant to the first Cameron in the district. Dr Donald Cameron and his wife **Margaret Cameron** (née Still, m1803; d1860) arrived in 1822 and, by 1823, had built Fordon (now known as Old Fordon). Margaret, who favoured country life in spite of the obvious difficulties of the time and place, was largely responsible for the creation of the water race – a hand-dug channel of three or so miles to carry water from the Nile River to Fordon to make it viable.

Of the Cameron's four children, young Donald's wife from 1847 was **Mary Isabella Cameron** (née Morrison, d1913). She introduced Jersey cattle into Tasmania. She is also the Mrs Cameron who travelled with and described the writer Caroline Leakey in 1848 (p167). Before their marriage, her husband was called in to arbitrate when the Taylors acquired Kenilworth from Eliza Forlong (p340).

Of Mary and Donald's four children, two require mention here. **Adeline Stourton** (née Cameron, b1856; m1875) established the Tasmanian Branch of the Victoria League which encouraged patriotism at the time of the Boer War. Her brother, Cyril St Clair Cameron, had taken part in the war as a captain in the Tasmanian Mounted Infantry. He returned home a hero and advanced in military and civil activities and standing. All this is relevant to the account by Meriel Talbot of her 1909/10 tour of the Antipodes, including Tasmania, as secretary of the original Victoria League from its foundation in 1901–16. Julia Bush, in *Edwardian Ladies and Imperial Power* (2000), writes of two Tasmanian functions she attended:

> Meriel ... continued to benefit from the deference which her own social status inspired among many 'colonials'. In Tasmania ... she noted, 'I'm getting quite to take the "first lady" place as a matter of course and to find all doors opening before me!' On the same day she attended a Victoria League reception at the Masonic Hall.
>
> 'I was brought in late by Colonel Cameron, the sort of Kitchener of Tasmania, and led to a carpet where each guest was brought up and introduced – "presented" to me – some of the dear dim little people almost curtsied! It was all very nicely done – the Hall decorated with red, white and blue flowers and hangings and a great Union Jack behind the little dais place.'

Both Adeline Stourton and her mother, Mary Cameron, who was the first President of the League (1904) – established settlers of substance – were undoubtedly there. Any comment from me is probably superfluous!

Although you now come to Clarendon further along Nile Road, that homestead, within easy driving distance of Launceston, is for the next itinerary. This one assumes that you did not turn right at Conara, but continued up the Midland Highway. But, before you leave this area, with Avoca to the south – where Humphrey Grey and Simeon Lord were friends of Batman (I don't know about the women) – Fingal to the east and Mathinna to the north east, you may wish to explore the Ben Lomond National Park. From two points just north and just south of Nile, or from Evandale, you can drive all the way round, on a sometimes rough road, coming out at Fingal; (we started at Fingal).

It was common, and probably still is, to climb Ben Lomond to watch the sunrise. Eliza Batman certainly did. Annie Baxter even went on a camping expedition there in March 1837 with the *jeunesse dorée* among whom she mixed, riding without a saddle (pp266, 358). They dined, danced and sang the evening away before the climb, about which she wrote:

> Had it been possible I would have undergone twice the difficulty to have seen so beautiful a scene – when we reached the foot we had something to eat and drink & we then went up to the summit – Elizabeth & Mr Cox [of Clarendon p?] remained at the foot – what heart, what soul in this party did not feel the presence of one Great immortal being – the very rocks seemed to confess that altho' high – there was yet a more exalted place – We came down faster than most of us had ever intended I'm sure – for to tell the truth we slipped all the way nearly ...

Today, people also go to Ben Lomond to ski.

GB Lancaster (Edith Lyttleton)

Clyne Vale (Epping Forest)

Back on the Midland Highway and coming into Epping Forest, Belle Vue Road is on the right. Some miles along and past Glasslough on the left is Clyne Vale, also on the left. (If you reach Belle Vue at the end of the road, you have gone too far.)

Unfortunately, I don't know who now owns Clyne Vale, only that the latest purchasers sold all but 80 of the 1,345 acres. Down a lovely avenue of trees is an attractive white Georgian house, with its later (1890) verandah on stilts, overlooking the South Esk River.

The land was granted in 1822 to Captain James Crear RN. When he left the sea in 1831, by which time Clyne Vale was built, he and his wife **Joan Crear** (née Clyne) and their four children settled there. His two daughters were artistic. The atmospheric water colours 'South Esk at Clyneville', 'Ben Lomond, near Tullochgorum' and 'Valley of the South Esk', all dated c1855, held in the Rex Nan Kivell Collection, National Library of Australia, and viewable online, are by **Johannah Clyne Crear** (1824–1884). Although an amateur and disabled, she exhibited twice. **Helen Maxwell Crear** (1827–1860) died young, leaving only a small collection of works. A pencil and wash view of Clyne Vale by Johannah's friend **Sarah Ann Fogg** (1829–1922), dated 1868, is in the Queen Victoria Museum and Art Gallery, Launceston.

When James Crear died in 1859, Johannah inherited Clyne Vale. By 1873, her cousin Westcott (Westcote) McNab Lyttleton was managing the property for her, living there with his new wife, **Emily Lyttleton** (b1848), granddaughter of Captain William and Marie Wood of Hawkridge (p88). The Lyttletons stayed at Clyne Vale for six years and it was there in 1873 that their daughter Edith, better known as GB Lancaster, author of *Pageant* (p88), was born. A short biographical entry is one of many of Tasmania's women writers in *Tasmanian Literary Landmarks* (Margaret Giordano). *An Unsettled Spirit: The Life and Frontier Fiction of Edith Lyttleton (GB Lancaster)* (Terry Sturm,

2003) includes her life and writing beyond Tasmania. *Pageant*, her most highly-regarded novel, is the only one about the island. By its inception, she had long left (she lived for 30 years in New Zealand and died in London just before the end of the Second World War) but returned for a year to do research and write, living with cousins in Pakenham Street, Longford.

Hawkridge (Powranna)

If you are particularly interested in GB Lancaster's *Pageant* and its setting, you will want to pursue her to Hawkridge, the home of her great grandparents (p88). The property was the model for *Pageant's* Clent Hall, and her great-grandparents for the Comyns. The Woods had met in Guadaloupe where he was an officer during the Napoleonic Wars and her French ship had been captured and taken there. They married in 1810, after a courtship of ten days, when Marie de Gouges was 16. Marie's aunt had been lady-in-waiting to Marie Antoinette and guillotined the same day. It was not surprising that Tasmania of 1829 presented a change in environs and lifestyle – even though Hawkridge, like Clent Hall, had plenty of assigned servants and convict labourers. A portrait of Marie Wood is on p88.

Hawkridge is not easy to find, and not what you expect when you get there. As Joan Prevost explains in *From the Epping Banks to the Esk* (1988):

> The original house built by Captain Wood had been burnt down long ago. Another house built to replace that one was also burnt down, so that the four roomed weatherboard house with some additions, was the third house to be built at Hawkridge.

We had to be very persistent in finding Powranna; though marked on the map, there is no sign either side of the Midland Highway. This may well be because of what goes on there. If you get as far as the racecourse at Symmons Plain on the right, you have gone too far. Have the courage of your convictions and take the only turning before then to the right. Soon you come across a sign, 'Feedalot'. The Japanese owners of this cattle estate don't want to be obvious. Go past the company's office, past miserable, crowded pens full of thousands of sad, dull, dusty cattle, on a track going back parallel to the Highway, but hidden from it, and towards a clump of pine trees. There you will come to a modern bungalow called Hawkridge. We turned up unannounced and must have looked disappointed – we expected Clent Hall – but the owner was courtesy itself and allowed us to walk around and take photographs, for which I thank her here. The view is as it was in Marie Wood and Mme Comyn's day; as Joan Prevost puts it:

> The house at Hawkridge has a magnificent view of the river flats and low hills crowned by the Ben Lomond range. It stands in a commanding position on a high bank, as all the houses do which lie on the 'Banks' of

the ridge, which extends for many miles from The Corners at Conara to Snake Banks at Powranna.

Back on the Midland Highway, take the road to Evandale and then backtrack down Nile Road to Clarendon, which starts the next itinerary. Or, if you want to leave GB Lancaster for your return journey south, continue on Nile Road after Kingston.

22 – Around Longford

The places that follow can all be visited easily during a stay in Longford or Launceston. At least two of them, Brickendon and Woolmers, also have accommodation on the estate.

Clarendon

This porticoed, three-storey, neo-classical homestead, 9 kilometres south of Evandale on Nile Road, was completed in 1838 to replace an earlier timber house. Outstanding in its day, it was not in good shape in 1962 when it was donated with nine acres to the National Trust, and took ten years to renovate, opening to the public in 1972. Its history is told in *Clarendon and Its People* (MJ Maddock, 1996). And by 'people', the author means not only the owners of the house and its estate: he lists, with all the detail he could find, those involved in their running over the years, and even the names of horses. The 1850 watercolour by Susan Fereday (p172) gives a good impression of its grandeur and setting. And the Coxes entertained appropriately.

46.   Clarendon, by Susan Fereday, courtesy of the Allport Library and Museum of Fine Arts, Tasmanian Archive and Heritage Office

The bigger, finer Clarendon was built by James Cox when he had been married nearly ten years to Eliza Collins, daughter of Tasmania's first Lieutenant Governor and his mistress, Margaret Eddington (p37). By the time she was ten, Eliza owned 900 sheep; in 1824, under the name Eliza Eddington, she was granted 500 acres not far from Clarendon, and she had been educated at Ellinthorp Hall and Hannah Clark's earlier school (p136) so, aged 19, she did not come empty-handed to her marriage in May 1829 at St John's Launceston (p376).

James Cox moved from New South Wales to Tasmania in 1814. He was to become a magistrate, and twice a member of the Legislative Council, as well as a major pastoralist. I suspect that the Spanish merino ram he bought in 1829 was one of Eliza Forlong's originals (p340). By 1864, his family lived on an estate of over 5,000 acres and he owned other properties let to tenants. He formed the village of Nile (called Lymington until 1910) to house Clarendon's farmworkers and, in 1862, he and Eliza donated three acres for St Peter's Church and burial ground there, together with 200 acres of glebe.

By his first marriage in 1812, Cox had eight children. **Mary Cox** (née Connell, 1793–1828) died a few months after the birth of her last child. Perhaps because she was the daughter of a convict mother, James was not constrained by the antecedents of his second wife. There is some evidence, though, that Cox may have discriminated against his first family once his second was established. It comes from Annie Baxter's journal (p266) and editor Lucy Frost's elaboration. Annie's friend **Rebecca Cox** (1814–1870) had married Walter Glas Cheine/Chiene in 1840 and was widowed on the Mainland the year of Annie's 21 June 1849 entry:

Today I went over to Clarendon; it is a beautiful house, & the Grounds very pretty.

Poor Mrs Chiene! When I spoke to Mr Cox of her coming away from where she was, he said very coldly 'Has she no neighbours? She must live in some small town, where she can educate her children'!

When I looked at the fine house, & heard him say 'That is my Overseer's house, this is my Woolshed'; and then brought his unfortunate child to my mind's eye – the beautiful story of the Prodigal son recurred to me ... Oh! How I grieve for her! But then again this is to be said in his favour; that it would never do to risk her polluting his second family!

Lucy Frost adds: 'When Eliza arrived at Clarendon, Mary's children were dispersed elsewhere ...'

I believe Cox met Eliza at Ellinthorp Hall; she was known to be there aged 18. His own daughters were at the school, as is shown in a historically, as well as contemporaneously, useful letter he wrote some months after their marriage to Hannah Clark and which she forwarded to the *Hobart Town Courier* in October 1829:

Dear Madam, – I can scarcely find words to express my surprise at a report which I understand has been circulated in Hobart town, stating that I had removed my daughters, also Misses Watts and Connelly [Eliza's half sisters] from your establishment. How such a report could have originated I am at a loss to account, it being well known to all my friends and acquaintance, that their visit to Clarendon was a short holyday given them on account of your approaching accouchement, and that from long experience (5 years) of the kind attention you invariably give your pupils, and the excellent management of your establishment in general, I never could entertain the slightest intention of removing the ladies in question, and I trust you will publicly contradict so false a report.

A mystery remains: little Julia, Mary Cox's last child, died at Ellinthorp Hall on 17 April 1829, not quite a year old. One has to assume that she had been with a family party visiting the girls there and been taken ill. But it may have had something to do with the girls' temporary removal. Two weeks after Julia's death, her father and Eliza Collins were married.

With Eliza, James Cox had eleven more children. Four of their daughters are of particular interest. **Eliza Cox** (1830–1897), their eldest child, was a recognised water-colourist. Her 1860 painting of Clarendon shows a different view from Susan Fereday's, one from across a sweep of the South Esk River that ran past the end of the stable block and coach house. Both paintings are in the Allport Library and Museum of Fine Arts. As well as producing a large collection of flower paintings, young Eliza also painted at Marion Villa, the family's 1828 summer home at Low Head on the north coast near George Town; 'Low Head Light House Entrance Tamar River Tasmania' dates from about 1860 and is in the Queen Victoria Museum and Art Gallery, Launceston. Since Susan and her husband lived in George Town, they probably met the Coxes there; Eliza and Susan may even have painted together. Susan's undated watercolour 'Lighthouse at Low Head' is in the Allport. Marion Villa is at 1067 Low Head Road; I have been unable to ascertain its status.

After the death of her widowed mother in 1869, Eliza went to live at Marion Villa and applied for a licence to grow oysters there; traces of her oyster beds remain. In 1877, aged 47, she married the Reverend John Cowpland Dixon, who was also artistic and taught Sarah Ann Fogg (p350). Following her husband's death in England, where they had gone to retire, Eliza Cox Dixon returned to Tasmania and lived at Euroka in Evandale – a house on the High Street and marked on the 'Evandale Heritage Walk' map. She (as Eliza Dixon) and her mother (Eliza Cox) are buried in the Cox family vault in St Andrew's cemetery, Evandale.

Life at Clarendon: The Reminiscences of Cornelia and Rosa Cox (1988) is a slender booklet containing some slight writing by the youngest daughters of Eliza and James Cox. The recollections of **Cornelia Cox** (b1844), who was, in 1873, to marry John Innes, son of Lysbeth Grey Innes and her husband (p269), cover three pages. She writes of one of the most important events in Tasmania's history (p172) when she was nine:

Another of my recollections is when a number of children were given a silver medal to commemorate Cessation of Transportation, which meant that no more convicts would be sent from England to Tasmania or van

Diemen's Land, as it was called, this was a great event and celebrated with enthusiasm.

The reminiscences of **Rosa Cox** (later Woltmann, b1846) are a little longer. She writes of Eliza at Clarendon:

> My mother was devoted to her garden and superintended the grounds and arrangements and that was often very hard work owing to the difficulty of obtaining competent workmen. After the house was built and the grounds were being laid out, my mother had a number of English trees planted which flourished surprisingly well, much to her delight, as many people thought such trees would not do well in our climate.

The trees included elms, which have survived. Eliza, according to Rosa, was also an authority on mushrooms. Of the trip up the river to Launceston (from George Town?) and her sister Eliza, Rosa wrote:

> I have not mentioned the pretty seaweeds which grew in the waters and for which we dredged from a boat. My oldest sister pressed them beautifully and sent her collection to a museum in London, the South Kensington, I think it was. It was a lot of work as the seaweeds had to be floated in a dish of seawater, then cartridge paper was carefully slipped under them they were lifted out the fronds arranged with a thin, pointed stick, dry cloths put over them and then pressed under a weight on flat boards and left for some days to dry. The seaweeds contain some gelatinous substance which caused them to adhere to the paper.

The editor explains that the seaweed specimens are in the Science Museum, labelled 'Miss Cox XII/64'. Her sister, Rosa tells us, was also 'an excellent archeress and joined a Club in Town and won prizes at some of the tournaments there'. Eliza Marsh (p258) visited Clarendon on 11 October 1851 and wrote:

> After lunch we all walked over to Mr Cox at Clarendon, an excellent mansion with a park in which English deer and kangaroos are kept. Miss Cox walked with us. Saw an Emu with four young ones. The male bird was on the nest 8 weeks without tasting a bite of food or once moving. The grounds are not laid out tastefully, there is no good drive up to the house, but the house itself is handsome and well furnished. A very nice family of grown up and little daughters.

In *Placing Women*, Miranda Morris is rather scathing about Clarendon, 'which offers itself as a catalogue of unrelated objects ... one room is called a nursery, but the objects are displayed antique shop-style, rendering them meaningless. Nor is there anything that suggests the life of Eliza Collins ...' While sympathising with Miranda's thesis concerning women, history and places in Tasmania, it could be argued that those who owned the house after the Cox family would not be likely to maintain any trace of previous owners' possessions; indeed, we know that in January 1882 Clarendon was entailed and the latest Cox owner was deeply in debt. A huge clearance sale was held – everything was put up for sale. And in 1917 Mr and Mrs Boyes had the house renovated by Beau Turner of Nile.

The fourth Cox daughter to be noted is Margaret, but she fits better into the story of Entally (p363).

Brickendon, Woolmers, Panshanger and the Archers

If ever there were intricately entwined Tasmanian families, they are those who lived in the three Archer homesteads just south of Launceston and to the west of the Midland Highway. You can approach them from Evandale, or from Longford.

Thomas Archer of Woolmers, William of Brickendon and Joseph of Panshanger were brothers each developing estates near each other in the 1820s; another brother, Edward, and their father also emigrated and established other Tasmanian estates (p365).

Of the three properties today, approaching from Wellington Street, Longford, where it is signposted, you come first to Brickendon. It is a place to spend a night or two pleasantly in a cottage, either one of two built for workers in 1820–30 and renovated, within the extensive gardens of the main homestead, or three new ones constructed from recycled timber adjacent to the farm, across the road from the homestead.

The farm village, dating back to the 1820s, with its old, carefully preserved buildings, including William Archer's original cottage, contributes to the pleasure of the stay. It is a working farm with over 1,000 sheep, cattle, and a variety of crops harvested between December and late autumn, and there are 3 kilometres of river frontage. The beautiful gardens surrounding the homestead are open to the public. The Georgian house itself, started in 1828 just before William Archer married, is still occupied by the family and, therefore, private, though Louise Archer is hospitable to a genuine researcher. Brickendon is the only one of the three houses lived in by descendants of the original Archer.

Woolmers, a colonial-style bungalow completed in 1819 with an 1843 Italianate façade, has been without an Archer in residence since 1994. It is now run by a historical foundation (the Woolmers Foundation Inc.), and open to the public. It is a homestead deserving a visit, with a well-conducted tour of the house and gardens overlooking the Macquarie River and including the National Rose Garden. You get a real impression of Archer family life throughout the generations – they never threw anything out – as well as of other settler families of their ilk. There is cottage accommodation (built in 1840) within the grounds, and a shop and restaurant.

Panshanger, the property furthest from Longford, is a bit of an oddity. The internet suggests that it offers high class accommodation and facilities, and it is extolled there by those who have enjoyed it. But any attempt to enter the grounds along a very long drive just to see a fine house depicted several times by Emily Bowring (p344) whose husband managed the property from 1853–55, is thwarted by a large and insistent keep out sign. Woe betide the adventurous researcher who ignores the sign or, indeed, attempts to mend fences by making an appointment directly on the telephone with the lady of the house; my arrangement went unheeded by her husband and I was once again thrown out.

Two of Emily's drawings 'Panshanger from the North East' and 'Panshanger from the South East' are included in *Sketches in Early Tasmania and Victoria by Emily Bowring* (edited by KR von Stieglitz, 1965). Another, with a wider vista, is in the Allport Library and Museum of Fine Arts.

Elinor Binfield, Hannah Clark's friend who opened a school in Hobart with her in 1823, married Joseph Archer of Panshanger the following year but had no children (p136). On her husband's death, Elinor returned to England and remarried. The paternal grandmother of Madge Edwards was Ann Hortle Archer who was a snob about the antecedents of Madge's maternal grandmother Dora Coverdale Sorell (p268). Ann and her husband lived first at Woolmers. Ann's mother-in-law was also her aunt – **Susanna(h) Archer** (née Hortle 1801–1875) who married Thomas Archer of Woolmers in 1816; six of their 14 children survived. GB Lancaster (p88) was descended from Susanna's elder sister, **Anne Hortle Lyttleton** (1797–1874). One of Susanna Archer's sons, Joseph, succeeded his childless uncle Joseph at Panshanger. But the property passed out of the Archer family in the early twentieth century. Madge wrote of Panshanger in the days of the younger Joseph:

> Farther away still [from Woolmers] was Panshanger where Great-uncle Joseph lived. I thought that one of the loveliest of all the Archer homes.
>
> In the Panshanger grounds I saw what is often called Archer's Folly, a tower evidently at one time used for fowls and pigeons. It was built originally for a sort of fortress in which the family could shut themselves up if raided by blacks or bushrangers.

The area had been Aboriginal hunting grounds, but the tower was never needed. It features in Emily Bowring's sketches.

Of Woolmers, Jane Reid Williams wrote in her journal in November 1836, 'The house is beautifully filled up, but is like a bungala rather than the residence of a man worth £15,000 a year.'

Glimpses of Susanna Archer of Woolmers a year later come from Annie Baxter's journal (p266). She was a bit of a stickler, as Annie found out after her escapade to Ben Lomond without her husband (pp349–50). She records in French in December 1837 (translated by her editor, Lucy Frost):

> On m'appelle *Coquette* – Mais je ne le suis pas – tant qu'on me *dame*, qui doit savoir bien mieux! [I have been called coquette – but I am not – although I have been damned by one who should know better] – My good spirit says – 'Annie don't be scandalous' ...

47. Susanna Archer c1868, from Brown, *Madge's People*

The following July, Annie was again at Woolmers from Wednesday 18, and her behaviour had obviously not improved; Susanna had cause to lecture again: 'We had a long debate today on the propriety (or rather the impropriety) of waltzing – I have found this dance delightful …' And on Friday 20th: 'This evening Mrs Archer & I had a long debate on different subjects – one was that I set a bad example to young persons in this Colony – I cannot understand it – but it's too much trouble to enquire into the matter further –.'

In 1845, though, when Annie visited again, the family had suffered a double blow. Their son and heir, Thomas William, had died the previous year and the family financial house, Archers Gilles & Co, was in trouble. Susanna Archer kept to her room, and her husband, Thomas, to the estate. Annie was entertained by their daughter **Susan Archer** (b1825). Woolmers itself had not changed:

They have beautiful paintings in the drawing room – and a fine piano. The Jessamine is grown over the Verandah in such immense quantities, and looks excessively pretty. The garden is not in good order, as the building interferes with it. They are adding three large rooms at the back of the house. They have reading every evening out of the Bible – and sing Psalms for some time, and prayers at night.

In 1868, Susanna, aged 73, still living at Woolmers, was hostess when Prince Alfred, first Duke of Edinburgh, visited. She wore an incredible diamond necklace. The dining table at Woolmers is set as it was that evening.

Thomas William's widow, **Mary Archer** (née Abbot, 1818–1874) and Susanna looked after Thomas III when, from the age of ten, he inherited Woolmers on his grandfather's death in 1850. He was educated in England and travelled abroad becoming uninterested in the farming of Woolmers which was let to tenants. His mother, Mary, was killed when she was thrown from her carriage aged 56 and crushed by the stampeding horses. By a horrible coincidence, Susanna's mother, **Ann Hortle** (née Wild, 1766–1814) had been run down and killed by a wild horse.

Thomas IV was also an absentee landlord; he was more interested in golf. **Marjorie Archer** (née Patten, 1894–1969) was the wife of the fifth Thomas Archer of Woolmers. He was more interested in growing apples. She was soon known as 'the Duchess' and led a vice-regal life, waving with a gloved hand from the Wolseley bought for her as a wedding present. Pink was Marjorie's colour, and floral her pattern, as her bedroom – its bed curtains and carpet – and her sitting room show. She doted on her only child, Thomas, wrapping him in cotton wool when he developed a chest complaint, and keeping him there. When he died, a virtual recluse, in 1994, it was the end of the dynasty and of Woolmers as a family home.

Within sight of Woolmers, Brickendon had a different history. William Archer and his descendants were committed farmers. They travelled abroad to study, but came home to settle and work. Three generations still live there and farm; the latest William is the seventh.

As at Woolmers, there was a strong mother, this time **Phyllis Archer** (née Bisdee, 1904–2005; m1926). With an ailing husband, she made sure that Brickendon survived and that her teenage son knew his duty and his farming trade. When her husband died in 1952, Phyllis was left in control of the estate. She and Marjorie did not get on; indeed, while Marjorie was alive, the two families had little to do with each other. After her death, the Brickendon son attempted to help the Woolmers one. Phyllis died aged 101, but missed out on a telegram from the Queen because her birth certificate revealed that she had earlier deducted a year.

Louise Archer has said of Brickendon and its women, 'Each wife or female who has come onto the property has had very different attributes to them, but understand that the future of the farm is the most, or the future of the family is the most, important thing to consider.' It was to that end that they decided to open Brickendon to tourism.

Madge Edwards remembered Brickendon as a child at the turn of the twentieth century and wrote:

Of the whole place, I remember best the bell that hung in the back courtyard and once called convict ticket-of-leavers from their labours, the great cedar of Lebanon in front and masses of crimson roses heavy with rain. I think I remember the roses because I had grown a trifle Tennysonian and that would have been just up his alley, to write of rain-drenched crimson roses.

Across the road near the cottage still looking like a mill cottage, where the first Archers had lived, is one of the earliest of the colony's chapels. Architecturally it is a lovely little building, but when I saw it the bell was gone out of the tiny belfry and the chapel itself was neglected. Sheepskins were hung across the altar place and on the floor piles of them formed the only congregation.

Two of the Brickendon Archers' farm labourers were ticket-of-leave men, Thomas and John Flanagan, transported from Ireland in 1849 for stealing to feed their families during the famine, and ancestors of today's well-known Tasmanian family. Prior to transportation, they spent two years in a Dublin gaol. Thomas's wife **Mary Flanagan** (d1880) and seven children joined him in 1853. Martin Flanagan writes in his memoir *In Sunshine or in Shadow* (2002) that 'A number of the women of Thomas's family worked in [the] Georgian mansion.' Brickendon's records show that Mary worked for Mrs Archer, two of the children worked in the house, and two on the estate. Thomas was eventually a tenant farmer on another Archer property.

John Flanagan was assigned to the Archer estate Green Rises, on the road from Launceston to Cressy. He was joined by his wife **Bridget Flanagan** (1810 or 1820–1881). They were to have three sons in Tasmania and their descendant Lyn Flanagan has stood with her father at the gate of Green Rises and wondered how it would have felt to Bridget and John 'to look at the beautiful Western Tiers (mountain range to the west) each morning when they awoke'. Bridget died of a tumour and is buried in the Longford Catholic Cemetery. Tim Flanagan, a local doctor descended from Mary and Thomas, writes tellingly in an email: 'her headstone is about the first one you see as you walk in, [I] often ride my bike past, just to ponder'. The gothic Brickendon chapel, built in 1836 for the convict labour, is still there but in rather better shape than in Madge's day, and available for weddings.

The Flanagans were at Brickendon and Green Rises in the days of William Archer II and his wife **Caroline Archer** (née Harrison, 1804–1862); it was they who hired Kezia Hayter as governess to the next generation (p153).

The experience of visiting Brickendon is about as different from Woolmers as you can imagine. A gentle rivalry would not be surprising. Both are revealing of the different branches of the Archer ancestors. Madge captured conversation and attitudes of the extended family at Christmas:

We visited and were visited. The older women talked gently about friends and relatives, gardens and church happenings. The younger ones had tennis parties and afternoons, and a garden party or two. The older men when they met together were never bored. The talked of sheep – the buying of sheep, the sale of sheep, the price of sheep and wool. Sheep, sheep, sheep. I found that to be a sheep owner was virtually to be an aristocrat. But the sheep must be kept whole. One could trade in whole sheep and still not be in trade. If it were bought by the sheep but sold in pieces, by the leg, the rump or the loin, the owner was in trade and not of the aristocracy.

As I write, new bonds are being forged. A walkway is being constructed between Brickendon and Woolmers allowing visitors to walk the paddocks and even better appreciate the landscape.

Bowthorpe (Mary Bowater Smith)

If you return to Longford and leave it to the north by Pateena Road, half-way along on the left is Bowthorpe. It can be seen from the road. Approaching it from the north when we visited it in 2006, was a fading sign 500 metres in advance saying that it served cream teas, which seemed ideal. But the tea room and antique shop had closed in 1999 and since then it has been privately owned; we were, however, helpfully received.

The house is not that built by Mary Bowater Smith, one of the first women convicts in Tasmania (p27). This one was built just after her death in 1849 by a Cox family. But the Cochranes, in jest or quite seriously, maintain that her ghost roams the house; indeed, I have had an other-worldly email from her.

Mary was certainly a larger-than-life character. Her husband, Thomas, drowned crossing the Esk in 1823, leaving Mary his land and possessions. Irene Schaffer thinks that, anyway, she was the brains behind the marriage. She went on to accumulate much land and stock, and was renowned for her racing stable. She was known as Moll Smith in the Longford and Epping Forest area, and one of her properties was dubbed Moll Smith's Bottom. When she died, aged 84, her family in England benefited, including the son she had left behind but with whom she had kept in touch.

Entally (Hadspen)

Pateena Road leads you to the main highway west from Launceston; a few miles along it, at Hadspen, is Entally. If there are ghosts about, this one would be that of Mary Reibey. It was she, travelling from Sydney in 1818 with her son Thomas, who secured the initial land grant of 300 acres on which he built Entally. By then, she was a widow running a commercial empire. But the Australian life of **Mary Reibey** (née Haydock, 1777–1855) had not started like that. In 1790, the Lancashire lass, aged 13, and dressed as a boy, was caught horse-stealing, convicted and transported. In Sydney in 1794, she married a young Irishman, Thomas Reibey, in the service of the East India Company. He set up a trading company which she managed when he was travelling. I understand that Catherine Gaskin's *Sara Dane* (1954), which I enjoyed many years ago, drew inspiration from Mary's life. Although she remained in Sydney, some of the seven children she was left to bring up when her husband died in 1811, settled in Tasmania so that she had occasion to visit Entally.

The house today, leased from the State and managed as a heritage site open to the public by a private company, is not quite as it was when Emma von Stieglitz sketched it in 1835. Its two towers constructed to protect against raids by bushrangers and Aborigines were removed in the 1850s.

48.   Entally in 1835, by Emma von Stieglitz, from von Stieglitz, *Early Van Diemen's Land 1835–1860*

Entally is a place for the prurient visitor: you can be shown the French windows which led then from the billiard room to the garden through which, so I was told, Thomas Reibey III was spied in 1868 canoodling with **Margaret Blomfield** (née Cox, 1842–1927; m1864) Eliza and James Cox's married daughter. Reibey, by this time an ordained priest and Archdeacon, and his wife **Catherine McDonal Reibey** (née Kyle, d1896) were friends of the Cox family of Clarendon (p353); he was godfather to the Blomfields' daughter and, on James Cox's death in 1866, Reibey had been adviser to Eliza, trustee of the Clarendon estate, and mediator in the family quarrel about the division of property among the daughters.

Blomfield accused Reibey of intimacy with his wife at their Blomfield/ Cox property and waited in Launceston 'for a week, in order to horsewhip the Archdeacon in a public street'. When nothing happened, Blomfield took matters further: Reibey was accused in a petition of having 'intent to commit rape'. He sued for libel and lost. The scandal rocked Tasmania, and Reibey resigned and disappeared from public life to Entally. By 1874, though, he was an elected member of the House of Assembly, then Premier from 1876 to 1877, continually holding office thereafter.

Catherine's feelings in all this can only be imagined. The daughter of Thomas' tutor in England, she had married him in 1842 and travelled to Tasmania where he had just inherited Entally on the death of his father. The couple had no children and Catherine was often unwell. She survived the scandal, however, not dying until 1896. She was buried in the graveyard of the unfinished church at Hadspen for which she had laid the foundation stone 30 years earlier.

Mary Reibey lived to see her grandson's earlier rise, but not his dramatic fall. She was, however, alive when her daughter Eliza's husband was found to have committed fraud. Eliza has her place in the founding of the Methodist Ladies' College, Launceston (p380).

What makes the jigsaw of history so appealing is that eight years before the Blomfield scandal the Reverend Thomas and Catherine Reibey harboured another of his goddaughters, sent to escape scandal – this time Julia Sorell Arnold's physical objection to her husband's conversion to Catholicism (p268).

Mary Arnold was only four when the sky fell in on her family. Thomas Arnold wrote to his mother that Mary's 'temper it appears is greatly improved since she has been under Mrs Reibey's care'. He would travel up to Entally to teach Mary to read but he confessed to his sister that the girl who would become a famous novelist 'is by no means quick at that though so ready-witted in other things'.

Of all the fine Reibey possessions that adorn the house today, what caught my eye was a sampler of letters of the alphabet and numbers signed 'Mary Allen Reibey, Ellinthorp Hall, 1827' on the wall in a bedroom. The embroiderer was the older sister of the scandalous Reverend Thomas, and daughter of **Richarda Reibey** (née Allen), first mistress of Entally. **Mary Allen Reibey** (1818–1895) was nine when she stitched the sampler and must have been one of the first pupils of Ellinthorp (p138). She was to marry a nephew of Governor Arthur.

Franklin House

Franklin village and Franklin House in it are on the old Midland Highway – Hobart Road – 6 kilometres southeast of central Launceston and 6 kilometres north west of Launceston Airport. The National Trust of Tasmania was founded in 1960 to save Franklin House, built in 1838, from encroaching industrial development.

While the village was named after Governor John Franklin and the house named by the National Trust after the village, Miranda Morris, in roundly criticising its heritage manifestation, writes: 'The closest association this house is likely to have had with the Franklins is as a blur in the landscape when they drove past on vice-regal visits to Launceston.' There are a couple of mementos of John Franklin's governorship in the house, and six of the Regency rosewood chairs in the dining room belonged to Jane Franklin. There is also a floral plate from the Franklins' dinner service.

Miranda does not favour the reinvention of the house with furniture and *objets* from hither and yon, but for me there is something touching about the way Tasmanians rallied round, contributing some of their own family heirlooms. And an aging, undated catalogue of the house's contents itemises the objects and their contributors. Among the pictures are at least one watercolour thought to be by Susan Fereday (p172) and a lithograph of one by Elizabeth Prinsep (p77).

From 1842 the house was a select boys' school run by William Keeler Hawkes and his wife since c1833 **Martha Hawkes** (née Green, 1808–1886) who had just arrived in Tasmania; the school lasted until 1866. Pupils included the sons and a nephew of **Hannah Bartley** (née Pickering, b1805; m1826) and her husband Theodore. Their story is told by Yvonne Phillips in *Bartley of Kerry Lodge* (1987). They were to have 15 children, twelve of whom survived early childhood, so it is not surprising that Hannah was to write variations of her 1845 diary entry 'My life is one continual scene of labour, care and anxiety. I am so weary and worn out – both in mind and body.'

Two years after the Hawkes set up their school, Martha successfully approached a local landowner who donated land and built a cottage for her Sunday School. That same year, William's sisters **Marianne Hawkes** (1803–1846) and **Charlotte Hawkes** (1819–1888) arrived in the hopes that the air would help Marianne's tuberculosis, but she survived only two years. Their sister **Elizabeth Hawkes** (1806–1873), also suffering, joined the family in 1854.

When Charlotte's letters to a nephew came to light, Dawn Dyson drew on them for *The Hawkes Family at Franklin House* (1999). Charlotte was a story book spinster: her caring skills no longer needed following Marianne's death, she took herself off from her brother's house to look after the children and run the house of Edward, the fourth Archer brother (p357), of Northbury, Wellington Street, Longford, and his wife **Susannah Archer** (née Moore, 1834–1890; m1834). The couple were to have three daughters and eight sons.

Charlotte stayed with the Archers for more than 40 years. When her widowed sister-in-law Martha died in 1886, she was permitted to reside at Franklin House. She wrote: 'It is a great treat. I have not been so happy for many a long day, 41 years in a situation enough to tire anyone out.' She had only 19 months to enjoy her newfound freedom.

On Charlotte's death, Susannah Archer looked after the affairs of her 'former companion, cook, manager and child nurse', writing to Charlotte's nephew: 'Indeed your Aunt arranged everything and made me promise that her wishes should be carried out.' The members of the Hawkes family are buried in St James's Church opposite the house.

In 1888, William Lyons Shaw Greer and his second wife **Annie Greer** (née Martin, c1853–1894) bought the property and called it The Hollies because of its beautiful holly trees. The Greers might not demand a mention except that, many years later, in 1986, Germaine Greer went looking for her Tasmanian father and described the painful hunt in *Daddy We Hardly Knew You* (1989).

She landed up at Franklin House and ordered a cup of tea and a salad in the café The Hollies; she continues:

> 'Is there a house called "The Hollies" hereabouts?' I asked, with a face red as fire.
>
> 'You're in it,' said the manageress. 'Franklin House used to be called "The Hollies" so they used the name for the tea-room.'
>
> I didn't want to say that it was my forebear who had called the house by that name, or that it was simply someone with the same surname as mine. And I didn't want to explain my absurd situation, prying as I was into matters that may have been none of my business. But, like most Launcestonians, the manageress was expressing a kindly interest, so I told her of my miserable state of not-knowing.
>
> 'Take a look around,' she said. 'You never know. There might be a clue.'

It was a wild goose chase.

The café today is a pleasant pit-stop. Writ large on its walls are the stories of the Leake family of Rosedale (p68) – a house still standing, but in private hands, on the road from Campbell Town to Cressy; and the Cottons of Kelvedon on the east coast (p157). Joy Spence, a volunteer of the National Trust, whose offices are in the house, was as sympathetic an informant as Germaine Greer's.

23 – Launceston

Launceston City Park

The park is a good place to start because it contained the first seat of authority in Launceston. Elizabeth Paterson, wife of the first Lieutenant Governor of the north, had arrived in the new settlement in 1805 (p26). Launceston dates from the following year and the Government Cottage was built in 1807 and used for the next 40 years. It is not entirely clear where the cottage was, but it seems likely that it was in the southwest corner of today's park, where the Crimea cannon now stands. Elizabeth was a keen botanist, so I think she was responsible for the early days of what has become a pleasing public space. There are trees that look as if they could have been planted in her day.

Paterson was the only northern Lieutenant Governor and, after a series of short-term northern Commandants, all authority moved south in 1812. The Government Cottage was used when the Governor visited Launceston from Hobart. It was also available for others. Among the first of these was the Reverend John Youl (p368) and his wife **Jane Stroud Youl** (née Loder, 1793–1877; m1810) when she first joined him with their children from New South Wales in 1819. Eventually they were to have three daughters and six sons – five children were born after Jane's arrival. She was widowed in 1827 while pregnant with her ninth child. How she coped with eight children (a son had gone to England to be educated) under those circumstances we have to deduce, though the family did have land grants and the sons became successful pastoralists.

Occupancy of the cottage could cause friction. It cannot better be exemplified than by quoting from PA Howell's biographical dictionary entry for Judge Algernon Montagu:

> In April 1840, on arriving in Launceston to hold a session of the Supreme Court, he found Lady Jane Franklin in residence in the government cottage, which had traditionally been available for judges on circuit. Believing that the court was affronted when its privileges were waived in favour of vice-regal amusements, he wrote petulant letters to Sir John Franklin until rebuked by Lord John Russell [British Colonial Secretary] and persuaded to apologize.

You can see Jane Franklin giving Montagu, known as the 'Mad Judge', short shrift.

The Albert Hall

To the right of the main gate of the City Park, on the corner of Tamar and Cimitiere Streets, is the Albert Hall (1891), now a cultural and convention centre. There artists such as Nellie Melba (p301), Amy Sherwin (p237),

Adelina Patti and Clara Butt performed. If the doors are locked, which we found, you can admire the Victorian architecture and imagine you hear sweet music.

The Batman Fawkner Inn (Cornwall Hotel)

Back at the park gate and crossing the road, walk a little way along Cameron Street until you see the easily identifiable salmon-and-maize-painted Batman Fawkner Inn. Built between 1822 and 1824 as the Cornwall Hotel (not to be confused with today's Cornwall Boutique Hotel), it is perhaps the most historic of Launceston's women's places, though it is usually described as where Batman and Fawkner planned their incursion into what became Victoria.

49.   Cornwall Hotel, an early sketch, from Reynolds, *Launceston*

The first woman to put her stamp on the hotel was Eliza Cobb Fawkner (pp58–9). We left her in 1819, a newly arrived convict assigned to John Fawkner and setting off with him for Launceston. They married in 1822. Although their marriage is registered at St John's Church (p376), its foundation stone was not laid until 1824. There was no earlier church building so, crossing over from the hotel to the Holy Trinity Church opposite, walk along 100 yards to what is now an office block. In 1822 it was a blacksmiths, also known as the Church in the Bush; there the Reverend John Youl (p367) performed the Fawkner and other marriages and held services.

The Fawkners had a number of ventures – a bakery, timber merchants, bookshop, newspaper, nursery and orchard. He did not receive the hotel licence until 1825, the year of Eliza's pardon; it was partly her convict status that held it up, though he was regarded as slightly unreliable. It is clear that she was then as much involved in the hotel as he, starting a run of women owning and managing it. Although they had no children of their own, they fostered or adopted a number of them, some related.

In 1835, Eliza Cobb Fawkner accompanied her husband, as Eliza Callaghan Batman (pp58, 345–9) did hers, to explore the land and found the settlement on the Mainland that became the city of Melbourne. While Eliza Batman's life was soon to disintegrate, Eliza Fawkner played a role in the family's new businesses – John was to call her his 'guardian angel and true friend'. They were married for 51 years. She was left a rich widow in 1869 and, 15 months later, aged 70, she remarried. Her husband was a barrister aged 44 and father of one of her adopted daughters. She died nine years later, leaving a fortune of £9,000 to those daughters.

By 1836, John Edward Cox was licensee of the Cornwall Hotel; earlier he was licensee of the Macquarie Hotel, Hobart, which he ran with his wife (p246). When he died the following year, he left his widow, **Mary Ann Cox** (née Hall, m1821; d1858), with nine children to support – the last one born and one dying that same year. In spite of all she was going through, Mary Ann took over both running the hotel and her husband's coach service, Launceston to Hobart, which she expanded.

In 1844, one of her coaches was held up at Epping by the bushrangers Cash & Co. (pp96–7) but, as the story is told in *Highway in Van Diemen's Land* (Hawley Stancombe, 1969), 'They robbed the other passengers but spared Mrs Cox because they knew she was a widow.' Following this, Mary Ann employed two guards at 24 shillings a week to protect her cargo and passengers.

When competition arrived on the Highway (p336), rivals would race, sometimes neck and neck. One of Mary Ann's conveyances was thus upset in 1849 and four passengers seriously hurt, perhaps prompting her to sell the business – seven coaches, 150 horses, and 24 sets of four-horse harnesses - though by then she had been able to educate her children at the best schools.

She must have relinquished the Cornwall Hotel at much the same time – the Anti-Transportation Society of Launceston was formed at a meeting there that year, and she is said to have been involved (p168); indeed, for many years the hotel had been the centre of Launceston activity as well as a hostelry. The Grey family of Avoca stayed there when they first arrived in 1828 (p342). Catherine Grey found it 'palatial' after the confines of the ship. Later, her husband and their daughter Catherine attended a dinner party given by Caroline Denison at the hotel; that may have been the ball for 100 guests Lady Denison gave in 1849. Perhaps because of the Grey acquaintance, in 1850 Mary Ann bought the Avoca property Ormley, both sides of the main road east to Fingal, and retired there with a son and her youngest daughter.

Eliza Marsh (p258) stayed at the hotel when she and her family arrived by boat to visit Tasmania from New South Wales in 1851 just after Mary Ann Cox's retirement. By then, James Butterworth Whitehead, a retired army sergeant and hotelier in nearby Westbury, was licensee. His wife and helpmeet since 1846 was **Bridget Whitehead** (née Cashin). Eliza paints a useful prose picture of Launceston, the hotel and the City Park:

About four o'clock we sighted the town of Launceston, having very much the appearance of a Rhenish town, numbers of boats came alongside the ship to take important passengers on shore. I got Matt [her husband] to go to secure rooms at the only decent Inn here, he did not like going as he says people never understand him. I saw him take a cab and he soon returned. Some difficulty in our landing when the steamer was alongside the Wharf, as the 500 sheep were very obstinate, however Bridget and I scrambled out with the sheep, from which with a little persuasion we were 'drafted out', and drove to the Cornwall Hotel, Matt telling us as we went that as he expected, he was not understood and vile rooms had been shewn him, however when we drove up our numerous boxes, dressing cases etc, must have made an impression on the landlady as she informed Matt she was happy to say she could provide him with better apartments ... our church is opposite the hotel, Puseyite clergyman preached a better sermon than one generally hears in the Antipodes. After luncheon looked into the Horticultural Gardens, which appear small, but well filled with English shrubs and tropical plants, the entrance at the end of the street in which is our hotel, has exactly the appearance of the entrance to the Grand Ducal residence on the Rhine ... the children look rosy, have seen no young women, this community seems to consist of children and old women.

The watercolour by Sarah Ann Fogg (p350) suggests the scene that greeted the Marshes on arrival.

50.   Launceston, Tamar Street Bridge area, by Sarah Ann Fogg, courtesy of the Allport Library and Museum of Fine Arts, Tasmanian Archive and Heritage Office

By 1856, and until 1861, **Mary Anne Lukin** (née Wilkins) who managed her husband's brewery after his death, was licensee. Like Mary Ann Cox, she was left with children to support – eight of them. Women continued to be licensee, or joint manager with their husbands, including the couple who renamed the hotel in 1981. Today's hotel, of which a woman is joint manager and another joint proprietor, and whose women staff were most helpful in providing me with research material, is in the budget range, but no longer appealing more to a younger clientele.

The Brisbane Hotel (Brisbane Arcade)

Past the Batman Fawkner Inn, turn left down George Street, pausing to admire the Roman goddesses ensconced in the facade of the cream building (1882) on the corner (best seen from over the road).

Turn right into Brisbane Street and the Brisbane shopping arcade is halfway along the next block. It uses the ornate façade of what was the Brisbane Hotel (1824, Elphin Arms, 1888–99 enlarged to Brisbane Hotel). Nellie Melba stayed there in 1907. Some years earlier she had been due to sing in Launceston. As she describes in *Melodies and Memories* (1925), she arrived after a ghastly sea voyage with a sore and inflamed throat. The doctor sternly advised her not to sing and she left immediately to rest in New Zealand. The cancellation was botched leaving ugly rumours to swirl and she was hooted as her train left for Hobart.

When she returned to Australia for a rest in 1907, and to Launceston where she wished to make up for the earlier cancellation, she did not realise the impact of what had gone before. But the impresario responsible for the new arrangements, sensing the ugly scenes that could ensue, braved the local club before her arrival and had it out with members. He succeeded in reversing the ill-feeling and she was able to write of her recital at the Albert Hall (p367):

> When I stepped on to the platform at Launceston, in a hall packed to suffocation, without thousands who had not been able to obtain admission standing outside, a roar of cheers broke out which was like the cry of a giant doing penance. At the end of the performance all the flowers of the island seemed to be heaped in front of me. They took the horses out of my carriage and fought to drag me through the streets. And when, eventually, I arrived, tired out, at my hotel, the street was overflowing with a sea of faces, and a universal song of welcome broke from the lips of all who were there.

The Quigleys owned and managed the hotel in the early twentieth century and made it very grand. At some stage, the daughter of the family, **Elvie Quigley** CBE (1886–1962) was, according to Joan Prevost, the 'famous owner and manager'. She was also chair of the Board of the Launceston General Hospital. Elvie was kind to **Vera Cameron** (d1945) of Kingston when she was aging and suffering from dropsy. She was the daughter-in-law of Kingston's owner Cyril St Clair Cameron, and wife of Ewan whose life had been turned upside down by the First World War; he was often absent. She had been a famous horsewoman. Elvie often stayed at Kingston (p345) and, when Vera died, she thanked her with the bequest of a magnificent emerald and diamond cross.

The Princess Theatre

Go back to the George Street corner, cross over and walk a little way eastwards along Brisbane Street. You cannot miss a sugary pink-and-white building; next to that is the art nouveau Princess Theatre, opened in 1911. Behind the main auditorium is a smaller modern one (1993), known as the Earl Arts Centre, where in 2003 Tasdance performed 'Fair Game' based on the narrative of Carmel Bird (p126). Carmel described for me a childhood incident there:

> When I was ten I went to an audition to play Wendy in the production of Peter Pan and was only given a small part as a fairy. Very sad, I stood on the steps of the building, beside a door with panels of bevelled glass, and the director of the play offered to buy me an icecream. Pride forbade me to accept.

But for much of its life, the Princess Theatre was a cinema. Here, for many years, **Amy Corrick** (c1881–1968) played the flute in the silent films orchestra. With her family of mother and father, four sisters and three brothers, she arrived from New Zealand in 1914; her father died that year in Launceston. From 1898, they had toured Australasia and internationally as the Corrick Family of Musicians, also renowned for their stage dresses, some of which were embroidered in silver thread in India and made up and fitted in Paris. They performed in Hobart in 1902, though an older sister, **Alice Corrick** (later, Sadleir 1897–1957), a soprano, had sung at the Town Hall some years earlier. They performed for the last time in 1932. Mother of the family, **Sarah Corrick** (née Calvert 1854–1935; m1876), contralto and cellist, died in Launceston in 1935.

The name Corrick is now best known for films which they had incorporated into their touring performances from 1900, usually opening and closing with one; and they had produced and accumulated a substantial collection of them, presented to the National Film and Sound Archives of Australia in the 1970s.

The west coast mining town of Zeehan's tourist material mentions that Nellie Melba sang there, at some unspecified date, at the Gaiety Theatre built in 1899 with 1,000 seats. She, and other material about her, omit this adventure which led me to question it. But **Ruby Paul** (née Pacey, 1893–1988) was born and spent her early childhood in Zeehan. In her oral account, captured by Christobel Mattingley in *Ruby of Trowutta: Recollections of a Country Postmistress* (2003), Ruby remembers:

> Odd concerts we'd get to, if we were lucky, but not very often. Then there was the Corrick family – mother and father and Edie, Elsie and Ruby. Ruby Corrick had beautiful fair hair and she used to play a solid silver cornet.
>
> When Dame Nellie Melba came to Zeehan, the first train after the railway from Mount Lyell was completed brought the miners through for the concert – down to Strahan and then up to Zeehan. Then it took them back and they had to go straight to work.

The Queen Victoria Museum and Art Gallery

The walk along Cameron Street, though Civil Square, over Charles Street to Wellington Street and so to the Royal Park and the Queen Victoria is very pleasant – past old and well-cared-for houses and buildings. The museum opened in 1891 to celebrate the Queen's Golden Jubilee. You could well find an interesting exhibition. On my first visit the paintings of the Australian naturalist writer and explorer Ellis Rowan were on display. Conversely, its paintings and artefacts may be on loan elsewhere. And just to compound potential problems, the museum is closed for renovation as I write, and will not be reopened until April/May 2011.

In late 2009, the exhibition 'Tayenebe: Tasmanian Aboriginal Women's Fibre Work' was held in the Tasmanian Museum and Art Gallery, Hobart. Among the borrowed artefacts was a basket woven by Trukanini (p118) for Catherine Mitchell's husband (p282). By then the family, formerly of Port Arthur, was living in the north east. Their daughter, **Sarah Mitchell** (1853–1946) wrote in her diary, kept from the age of 13 to 93, 'Truganinni the last Aboriginal who lives with Mrs Dandridge gave papa a basket and piece of rope, her own make ...'

The exhibition notes record that 'From October 1836 to March 1838 an experimental weekly market operated on Flinders Island where more than 30 Tasmanian Aboriginal women regularly traded. Trucannini is included in the list of girls and women at Wybalenna ... making it likely that she sold her baskets at the market.'

In 1909, visiting Launceston, Sarah continued the story: 'Went to the museum it is very nice ... promised to lend Launceston Museum Truganini's last basket she made for father.' In 1946, when Sarah was 92, she wrote to the museum:

Are the things I sent together? Is the basket Truganini made with them? Miss Dandridge who took care of her said it was the last basket she made, and it was done for my father who gave her 2/6 [two shillings and sixpence] for it. My sister and I sent her the lily rush by post therefore it is valuable.

In 2002, the museum held an exhibition, 'Strings Across Time', of shell necklaces made by Aboriginal women, drawing on its own collection. It is one of the few aspects of material Aboriginal culture still practised and handed down the generations. Before colonist settlement, women would, for example, smoke 'maireener' shells over a fire, then rub off the coating to reveal the pearly nacreous surface. The necklaces, of various kinds of shells, were worn, given as gifts or traded for ochre and other materials. One of the most important sources of red ochre was Toolumbunner, now in the Alum Cliffs State Reserve west of Deloraine and north of Mole Creek. Settlement brought new methods to the traditional shell preparation and threading. Lucy Beedon (p193) was typical of those whose necklaces survive from the nineteenth century.

A different sort of shell collection is thanks to women such as Jemima Burn Irvine (p102) and **Mary Lodder** (1852–1911) who arrived with her family in 1875 and who originally curated it. The director of the museum wrote: 'Miss Lodder has done good service to the [Royal] Society [of Tasmania] and has classified the specimens of Tasmanian Shells in the Museum, replacing from her own collection, those which were in bad order.'

In 1907, as Gill Morris relates in 'The "Quiet" Miss Mary Lodder – Conchologist and Philanthropist' (2005), a piece for the Launceston Historical Society, Mary settled at 193 George Street, Launceston, and made her books, instruments and knowledge available for the evening classes held at the museum. On her death, she bequeathed to the museum her cabinet cases and collections of shells and other natural history specimens, her microscopic slides and all her books on natural history and travels.

A Chinese temple, or joss house, reassembled in the museum from Weldborough and holding the remaining contents of the Garibaldi and other joss houses from the east coast tin-mining area (p323), links the various Tasmanian Chinese communities. Helene Chung, searching for her maternal forebears (the Gins, who adopted the name Henry), wrote of the temple:

> As my eyes fixed on the ornate figures robed in red, gold and green, the intricate carving, scrolls and plaques, I thought of my ancestors out in the tin fields paying tribute. I imagined each man prostrate himself in turn, place sticks of joss before the altar, smell the incense as it burnt and see the smoke rise to the heavens.

Carmel Bird wrote to me in 2008 of a Chung family from the same county as Helene Chung's paternal forebears:

> When I was a child the Chung Gon fruit and vegetable shop in Launceston … in Brisbane Street near the Brisbane Hotel … was a magnet for me – it was a location of the exotic (along with the Joss House at the old museum). They had Chinese artefacts for sale as well as vegetables. I used to buy little white china horses, and I bought a satin pin cushion shaped like a pumpkin with little 'chinamen' sitting around it. I still have the pincushion. Such things are commonplace now, but then they were quite rare and strange. The silk of mine is very superior to the fabrics of today's examples.

That was the business started by James Chung Gon who arrived in Launceston in 1878. In 1885 he married **Mei Ying Lee** (Mary, d1919), daughter of a wealthy silkworm-farmer, leaving her in China the following year to return to Launceston. But in 1892 he sent for his family, including twelve-year-old Rose who had been given to the couple as a wedding present and whom they treated as a daughter. They also had twelve children of their own and it was some of them, including **Ann Chung**, **Doris Chung** and **Lily Chung**, who were later involved in the family's ventures. Ann became well known in the late 1930s for her work in support of the Chinese Women's Association. In Launceston, Mary had to make her own shoes for her bound feet.

For Helene Chung, the Chung Gons' Pekin Store in Hobart was a magical window on the faraway land of China, which fascinated her, in spite of her mixed feelings about being Chinese.

Although the art gallery is unlikely to have its delicate sketches and watercolours on display, its holdings include Bock's portrait of Jane Franklin, Loetitia Casey's 'Ancanthe' (p271), Sarah Ann Fogg's 'Clyne Vale' (p350), and Eliza Cox's 'Low Head' and 'Ben Lomond' (p355).

The Inveresk annexe of the museum is on the other side of the North Esk River, over Victoria Bridge, in the Inveresk Cultural Precinct, perhaps best visited from the City Park and Tamar Street. It contains a portrait of Mrs William Wood of Hawkridge (p88), hand-painted pieces by the potter Alice Mylie Peppin (p284), and a cell door from the Launceston Female Factory (p156) which was demolished in the early twentieth century to build what is now Launceston College, at the western end of Paterson Street (nos 197–119).

Prince's Square

Wiggle your way south. In the middle of Prince's Square is a fountain best described in Carmel Bird's novel *Red Shoes* (1998), in which the main character, Petra, remembers her Launceston childhood, as Carmel does, though I believe her own was more stable than the one she has created for Petra:

> Green wooden benches beneath the trees; in the centre of it all a wide and shallow pond, circular, with water lilies and goldfish, and in the very heart a piece of large bronze statuary complete with nymphs, mermen, trumpets, vigorous acanthus leaves and gushing fountains. The semi-nakedness of the figures is both welcomed and ignored, it seems, by adults, whereas alert and knowing children such as Petra are fascinated, entranced by breasts and other suggestive bulges in the group. Larger than life these people, these creatures, recline, entwined, gesturing, waving, smiling, promising loud ecstasies from the middle of the pond.
>
> The fountain is the most elaborate public object in the town, and there is a legend that it was sent here by mistake, that a factory in France muddled its orders, and this little town ended up with a fountain destined for somewhere very grand. The people of the town were so impressed, quite overwhelmed by the sight of such a glorious bronze scene of lust, desire and sexual frolic that they raised the funds to keep it. I don't know how much truth there is in the story.

The truth of the fountain – it was ordered, as is, by catalogue from France – can be found in the learned article 'A Permanent Advantage: The French Fountain in Prince's Square, Launceston' (Eric Ratcliff, 1966). It scotches all myths, including that the pineapple atop the fountain replaced a figure too rude for the 1859 denizens of Launceston. Most of Carmel's novel about a religious cult whose devotees, attracted through Petra's malign magnetism, wear red shoes is set in Melbourne, but there is enough about Petra's early life in Launceston, and its effect on her, and with a climactic ending at Cape Grim (p390), to make it a valid and engrossing read as you sit contemplating the fountain.

51.   Fountain, Prince's Square, courtesy of Carmel Bird

St John's Church

Facing onto the square, on St John's Street, is the church which, in 1824, replaced Youl's Church in the Bush. Here in 1828 Eliza Callaghan (pp58, 345) and John Batman were married; so, four years earlier, were Hannah Pickering and Theodore Bartley (p365), in 1829 Eliza Collins and James Cox (p354), in 1830 the Aborigines Catherine Kennedy and William Ponsonby from Kingston (p348), and in 1842 Eliza Churchill and William Weeks (p155). But not all was happiness in the square: in 1993, a man cold-bloodedly shot dead his former wife during his daughter's wedding.

Churches of other denominations also frame the square. The Presbyterian Church is where Madge Edwards was taken as a child by her grandmother, Ann Hortle Archer (p268). She adds: 'Most afternoons grandmother and I went down to St John's Square, bought two Chelsea buns and ate them on a seat near the fountain.'

Morton House

Having originally written in the present tense what follows, I now have to turn it into the past. Diagonally across Prince's Square from St John's, at 190 Charles Street (Morton House), was Fee and Me, a restaurant which we have often travelled specially to Launceston to dine at. Fee, the chef, was Fiona Hoskin. But the elegant, award-laden restaurant, unbeknown to me until now, closed in August 2009 after 20 years; Morton House is up for sale. Meanwhile, Fiona and her partner live there and she teaches cooking. Who knows what will follow.

In 1841, the house was a girls' school run by **Mrs Hudson**. She employed a former 'governess in Colonel Arthur's family' which could have been Jane Clark of Cluny (p330), Sarah Duterreau (p334) or Thirza Cropper (later Parramore) (p240). Mrs Hudson took the school elsewhere in 1845 and the house became St John's Hospital, run by two humanitarian doctors practising an early version of 'national health service'. It was here in 1847 that ether, as a surgical anaesthetic (introduced in Boston by Dr WTG Morton), was first used on a young woman with an infected jaw.

Cataract Gorge Reserve

The Queen Victoria Museum stands in a wedge of Royal Park facing the North Esk river to the north, where it joins the Tamar from the east, and to the west the South Esk joins the Tamar at the Cataract Gorge. This is the real place to get away from it all, though others have the same idea on highdays and holidays. A path runs along the river from behind the museum to the gorge, but you may prefer to go on wheels. Once there, you will find a restaurant and café, a chairlift and suspension bridge, a swimming pool, and lookouts and walks either side.

On 24 October 1847, Caroline Denison (p161) described the gorge in a way that would not be so out of place today:

Yesterday afternoon we took a walk to a place called 'the Cataract', about a mile and a half from Launceston, where the South Esk seems to have burst through a range of rocky hills, and comes pouring down through a narrow gorge, whose wild beauty exceeds any place I have seen here. Fancy a very narrow valley, so narrow that it has every appearance of a rent made in the hills by some sudden convulsion; and, on the side of these hills, enormous masses of basaltic rock tumbled about in all sorts of forms and positions. These masses look more like a great natural Stonehenge than anything else I can think of; some stand quite upright, some are planted on such narrow bases, that you almost fancy they must topple over and crush you as you pass by. In the clefts of these rocks and between and above them, on both sides of the valley, are the most beautiful wild flowers and flowering shrubs; one is a sort of little wild geranium, sticking in between the rocks, and growing everywhere; another a large shrub covered with bright lilac or purple, looking at a distance more like English lilacs in flower than anything else, though the flower is not the least like them when you are near it. Hanging in festoons amongst these purple shrubs is a white creeper of the clematis kind, though of a brighter and purer white than the common clematis. There are trees, too, clinging apparently to the steep sides of the valley, and overhanging the rocks; and at the bottom of all runs the river, foaming and tumbling over masses of rock, like those on the sides of the hills; in one or two places it seems to have an interval of rest, and there it expands into a little basin, as still as possible, where men fish, and where you can scarcely see a ripple on the water. A few steps lower, and there is a sudden change; it meets the masses of rock, and becomes a cataract again. Oh, it is beautiful! And I longed for the power of making a sketch of it.

Eliza Marsh had a less happy experience in October 1851, having returned to Launceston to leave Tasmania:

After luncheon walked to the cataracts, a deep ravine through which flows, with two falls, the South Esk; I became giddy and frightened, and was very foolish, really in a perilous situation as a consequence, and made a vow never to go to such a place again. Left my parasol on a rock. Matt went back for it, wondering at nothing I did, for I was still confused.

For Ann Archer it was even worse. Madge Edwards describes how her grandmother's son had been rowing in a small boat with a friend and gone too near the rapids. The boat overturned and Hughie was drowned. Madge continues:

Once or twice we walked a long way for a picnic at the Gorge. I have memories of slippery tracks, foaming waters, terrible heights and depths when we looked down through the iron rails before we finally came out onto the mild green lawns fluttering with pigeons. Grandmother never came with us, because it was in these foaming waters that Uncle Hughie had lost his life.

But the gorge has a much longer history: it was a sacred site of Aborigines of the North Midland people from time immemorial. The Fairy Dell on the far side of the gorge is reserved as a peaceful place; is that the same place Mrs WI Thrower calls the 'Mossy Dell' in *Younâh: A Tasmanian Aboriginal Romance of the Cataract Gorge* (1894)?

This is, indeed, a romance – the story of a white three-year-old girl, Keitha St Hill, kidnapped by the Pialumma people whose summer place centres on the Cataract Gorge. Where Beth Roberts' old Aboriginal woman kidnaps a little white girl in *Manganinnie* out of loneliness and bewilderment (p334), here it is for revenge: the white settler family has not only taken their lands in the Ben Lomond area, but they also believe it responsible for 'stealing' the daughter of the chief and his wife.

Makooi, the mother, demands the white child's death; her son, Eumarrah, who has done the kidnapping and formed an attachment to the delicate toddler, persuades her that it is in their interests to teach her their ways and eventually use her as a bargaining chip. This discussion between mother, father and son takes place in the seclusion of the Mossy Dell and there, although Makooi sees the sense of keeping Keitha, or Younâh, as she has been renamed, alive, and gives in, Mrs Thrower suggests her power (p114):

> ... she had now reached that age wherein the women of the tribe ceased to be regarded as mere drudges made to minister to the wants of the superior sex, and were instead looked upon as oracles of wisdom, whose counsel was sought upon all important occasions, and whose decision was invariably final.

The language and tenor of the novella are of its time – purple and ethnocentric, distasteful, even, though it is a taut little story and historically interesting for its faults. It was serialised in the *Tasmanian Mail: A Weekly Journal of Politics, Literature, Science, Agriculture, News and Notes for Tasmania*. For my copy, expensively obtained on the internet, episodes of *Younâh!* have been collated and put between rough boards apparently by the Throwers' daughter in 1912.

Susan Martin analyses the novella and its context in Australian Aboriginal politics at the beginning of the twenty-first century in 'Captivating Fictions: Younâh!: A Tasmanian Aboriginal Romance of the Cataract Gorge' (2001). She suggests that at least some of the Aboriginal culture **Marian Thrower** (Mary Anne, née Kean, b1841; m1868) depicts relates to what was then known by whites about the Panninher people of the North Midlands nation, whose last members had long since died at Wybalenna, as did the real Umarrah who, coincidentally, also features in Kathleen Graves' *Exile* (p346).

Carmel Bird visits the Cataract Gorge in the childhood memories of Virginia in *The Bluebird Café* (1990), memories which are also her own. There she imagines Mathinna whom both Virginia and Carmel knew then only as a sad picture on the wall; later she was to epitomise for Carmel the fate of the Aborigines:

> I would sometimes go up the dry hillside on the other side of the Gorge ... I would take my lunch with me in those days when I was a fat little girl, and a book to read, and I would cross the King's Bridge and go up the steep and dangerous Zig-Zag Path. I liked the name of that path, and the path itself

was so rocky and barren ... when I got to the Giant's Grave, which is a huge jutting boulder, I would sit down and have my lunch and read my book.

Far below me was the troubled water of the Gorge, and the wet hillside on the other side of the water was dark with thick wet trees. It looked, from where I was, like a place of menace and mystery. I imagined that the path snaking along the side of the wet hillside was a primitive track. There in the shadows flitted Mathinna in her red dress and stockings. She danced and ran from cave to cave beneath the feathery fronds of cool, damp ferns ...

In 'This Pretty Prison' (in *A Writer's Tasmania*), Robin Friend, who had, in 2000, lived in Launceston for 20 years, uses the Gorge engagingly to explore her ambivalent feelings about the city.

Scotch Oakburn College (Methodist Ladies' College)

In 1857, **Julia Cowie** (1833–1874) of Brookstead, Avoca (p344) proposed to the district meeting of the Wesleyan Church that a college for girls be established in Launceston, and she offered £500 towards it. When **Eliza Thomson** (née Reibey, 1805–1870) built 'Oakburn' in Elphin Road in 1861, it did not seem that the college Julia dreamed of was much closer to realisation.

Eliza was the daughter of Mary Reibey of Sydney, and sister of the first Thomas Reibey of Entally (p362). In 1821, aged 16, she made the mistake of marrying Thomas Thomson. He had met and courted Eliza in England, where Mary had taken two of her daughters to expand their horizons, and continued on board ship where she agreed to marry him. He ran up enormous debts between 1823 and 1828 and, in 1829, as head of customs and treasury in the north, he was found to have embezzled. His property was seized, and Eliza's with it, and he was thrown into gaol. Her family bailed him out but the couple was left with nothing, and Eliza pregnant with her fifth child; she was to have eight. Fuller details are in Nance Irvine's *Mary Reibey – Molly Incognita: 1777–1855* (2001).

Thomas Thomson died in 1844 and Eliza regained her financial security. She began to accumulate land and, in 1860, received a grant from the Crown on which she built Oakburn. She lived in another property on Elphin Road and may have let Oakburn. Following Eliza's death, as the detailed research provided for me by Scotch Oakburn College shows, Eliza's son, also Thomas Thomson, owned Oakburn, and a Miss Thomson occupied it. In 1884, the Trustees of the Wesleyan College purchased it from a later owner, and the Methodist Ladies' College opened on 8 February 1886 with 45 scholars – too late for Julia Cowie to rejoice.

Today, at 74 Elphin Road in East Launceston, Eliza Thomson's house and the girls' school that took it over, is the Elphin Campus of the Scotch Oakburn College which is a Uniting Church school. This campus includes the Junior School, Early Learning Centre and Boarding House; there are other campuses elsewhere. I don't think there is any objection to you driving in and out to view the rather grand Victorian main building; we did so during the holidays, which must be preferable for the school. The oak trees Eliza planted are still there.

Early scholars at the Methodist Ladies' College included the Sutton sisters: **Cecil Sutton** (1885–1971), **Elsie Sutton** ('Todge', 1888–1904), **Irene Truganini Sutton** (b1890; m1920) and **Marjorie Sutton** (1895–1988). Their house, Fairlawn, now in private hands, is just down the road from the school. Miranda Morris, in *Placing Women* (1997), describes and mourns how in 1989, the year after Marjorie's death, Fairlawn and its contents were sold separately at auction after 90 years of Sutton residence – the contents were dispersed, losing their context. They included Elsie's diary for 1903, the year before she died of consumption aged 16. Miranda Morris' paraphrase describes how

> Elsie would study Euclid before breakfast as well as practising piano, go to school, come back for lunch, return to school, have music lessons, eat, study, sing and go to bed. The largest room in the house was the music room, and guests came for tea and music several times a week. Between them the children played the organ, the cornet, the piano and the violin, and annually entered the Launceston Competitions ... During 1903 we see ... the introduction [at the school] of compulsory drill and physical culture classes.

The year of Todge's diary, **Mary Fox** (1877–1962), aged 26, became head teacher of the college where she herself had been educated until she went to the University of Tasmania. The appointment of this progressive educator of girls is described as the 'beginning of a golden age' for the college, with enrolment numbers growing from 30 to over 300, and the expansion of the school buildings. Mary Fox MBE MA retired in 1941 after 38 years in which she had inspired over 2,000 girls.

Mary Fox is so revered and appears so perfect that a girlhood anecdote, told by Veda Veale in *Women Worth Remembering* (nd), must be repeated: 'Accepting a dare [she] rode her horse up the front steps of the college, and clattered briskly over the shiny brown lino of the corridor and out into the quadrangle!'

24 – North West Coast – Launceston to Cape Grim

Port Dalrymple

The women, such as Elizabeth Paterson, who arrived at Port Dalrymple in 1804–05 (p26), did so at a place rather ambiguously defined today. If you travel up the east bank of the Tamar from Launceston, you come to George Town just inside the mouth of the river, and Low Head further towards the sea. Travelling up the west bank, you reach what was York Town, a few kilometres beyond today's Beaconsfield. If you draw a line just south of York Town and George Town, joining them across the river, this area comprised Port Dalrymple, though it might also include Launceston, named in its very early days Patersonia.

This itinerary does not include George Town, home of artist Susan Fereday (pp172) and site of the first Female Factory (p62), nor Low Head, where Marion Villa was the holiday home of the Cox family of Clarendon, depicted by artist Eliza Cox (p355). It goes, instead from Launceston up the West Tamar Highway, and along the north west coast, stopping first at York Town.

York Town

Today's York Town (Yorktown) is a cluster of small farm holdings and an active community and, in the midst of that and bushland, is the archaeological site of old York Town. An archaeological project there from 2000–07 made some interesting discoveries; spasmodic archaeological and regular maintenance work continue.

Three primary sites emerged: Riley's cottage, where Sophia Riley (p26) lived with her storekeeper husband and children from 1805 to 1808; a soldiers' camp; and Government House, where Elizabeth Paterson lived with her husband, adopted daughter Elizabeth Mackellar, and convict maid Hannah Williams. Among the settlement of about 200 were Elizabeth Kemp, sister of Alexander Riley and wife of Paterson's second in command, and convicts Anne Keating and husband, and Mary Bowater (pp25–7, 362) and partner, later husband, Thomas Smith.

At the Riley site, buttons and Chinese exported porcelain were found, as well as brick walls. Government House, on the highest ground, requires more work but it would have been a significant structure. Thin glass fragments, clay pipes, buttons and other artefacts signifying an appropriate lifestyle have emerged.

It is possible to visit the site which is a mix of defined public and private areas. The public, signposted Yorktown Historic Site, on Bowen's Road beside the main highway, includes a car park and WC and barbecue facilities. From there, a 50-metre walking track winds to a block that was at the centre of the 1804 settlement. Some minor ground disturbances and brick fragments delineate some of the early building sites. The evidence is discrete, helped by some interpretative signage. The only building is a rough representation of an early timber hut used as a maintenance store. Across the highway from the site, you can walk along the foreshore of the Tamar River, which has returned to bushland since the time of settlement.

One of the reasons for Paterson's abandonment of York Town was that the land proved unsuitable for cattle; crops were disappointing – though Elizabeth Paterson made a garden - and food supplies ran short. The move started south to what became Launceston, and York Town was finally left in 1811. Clarence Point, where Elizabeth rode to meet ships, is just beyond York Town.

Badger Head

The Highway turns west (C741) at York Town, but also continues north – Badger Head Road (C742) – to the headland on the edge of the Narawntapu National Park. Badger Head was known as Narawntapu by the Norroundboo people who were displaced by copper, asbestos, iron and gold mining in the early nineteenth century. Some say the colonist name derives from wombats, fancifully said to resemble badgers. I prefer the suggestion that it was named after the notorious Charlotte Badger (p28). She was believed to have taken refuge among the Aborigines here. This doesn't really fit in with other Charlotte accounts which have her sailing off straight after taking over the *Venus*. Badger Beach at the foot of the headland is said by the Parks and Wildlife Service to be safe for swimming.

Trying to return to their new home, Poyston, after a sojourn away from Port Sorell in 1846, travel arrangements for Louisa Anne Meredith and her family went awry. Stranded in George Town after Charles had gone ahead, the family, including a child of six, made its way with a horse-cart and two riding horses on an impossible track and along the five miles of Badger Beach. Then it was up the steep side of Badger Head by now sans cart which was replaced by the arms of constables sent by Charles. Louisa writes in *My Home in Tasmania*:

> The horses were led up, with many a perilous plunge and desperate effort, scrambling like goats to keep a footing; and I clambered and climbed along, brave in resolution of well accomplishing the task I had voluntarily undertaken, and anticipating a succession of such difficulties, if not greater ones. On gaining a tolerably level space, I inquired of our servant, 'How much more of the road is as steep as the last bit?' And I began to think how much good heroism had been needlessly aroused in me, when he replied, 'Oh! Ma'am, that's all except one ugly gully, a few miles further on.'

The view from the top was good, though!

52. Poyston, by Louisa Anne Meredith, from Meredith,
My Home in Tasmania, courtesy of the
Glamorgan Spring Bay Historical Society

Port Sorell (Poyston – Louisa Anne Meredith)

On the other side of the Narawntapu National Park, and across the mouth of the Rubicon River, is Port Sorell. Where the Shearwater Country Club (the Boulevarde, Shearwater) is today, stood Poyston, the specially built house the Merediths moved into in 1846, after a respite away from Port Sorell and the unhappy earlier house they had inhabited. Louisa and the children arrived at Poyston after the gruelling journey via Badger Head just described. She wrote of her first impression:

> The next morning we breakfasted at Poyston, our new home ... Since I had last visited it, the exterior had been completed, and the trees cleared away towards the sea, opening a most lovely view of the port and its fairy islands, the bold bluff of Badger Head, the grand Asbestos range of mountains, and the open sea; the western end of the picture being closed by some wooded rocky points and intervening sandy beaches.

At Poyston, Louisa created a garden, kept bees and collected their honey, got pregnant again, and taught her children to swim; she watched them grow healthy. Barely two years later, the Merediths returned to the east coast.

Walyer (pp32, 112) eluded capture by Robinson in 1830 by making her way with two of her sisters to Port Sorell, their original home. There, however, she was captured by sealers.

Latrobe (Sherwood Hall – Dolly Dalrymple)

Cut down southwest to Latrobe. If you go via Wesley Vale on the Port Sorell Road, you are in the territory of Christine Milne's campaign, as a local housewife, against the establishment of a pulp mill there. This catapulted her into state politics and, in 1993, leadership of the Green party (p231). Since 2004, she has represented Tasmania in the Federal Senate.

At Bell's Parade in Latrobe is Sherwood Hall, the home of Dolly Dalrymple (pp30, 195). Born, it is said, in the Port Dalrymple area, hence her name, to Woretermoeteyenner (p30) and George Briggs, Dolly was fostered in Launceston by Jacob Mountgarrett, colonial surgeon at Port Dalrymple, and his wife **Bridget Mountgarrett** (née Edwards, m1811; d1829) when Robinson made her mother join the other Aborigines at Wybalenna. Dolly was christened in their house in 1814 by Knopwood, adding Mountgarrett to her name. Bridget Mountgarrett taught her to read and write, undertake household duties and fit into white society. Dolly was said to be a most attractive child. Mountgarrett fell foul of the law, and when he died in 1828 Bridget was left destitute and died the following year. By then Dolly had left their care.

In *Dolly Dalrymple*, Diana Wyllie tries to establish the unvarnished facts of her life. In 1826, aged about 16, and living with convict stock-keeper Thomas Johnson, she had her first child, though he was probably not the father. Robinson wrote in 1830: 'This stockkeeper lives with a half-caste female, a stout well made person by whom he has two children.'

In May 1831, a group of Aborigines attacked the Johnson house where Dolly was alone with her daughters. One of the girls was speared in the thigh but Dolly managed to barricade the door and windows and, armed only with a musket loaded with duck shot, for six hours held off the attackers, who also tried to smoke her out. As a result of her bravery, she was awarded a 20-acre land grant. Johnson received his conditional pardon that October and he and Dolly, known officially as Dalrymple Briggs, were given permission to marry. As Diana Wyllie puts it, 'This was the first step in their successful life together and a momentous move from the lowest ranked in society, an ex-convict and a half-caste, to being landowners in town.'

In 1836, Johnson was convicted of receiving. Dolly, with four children now to support, petitioned Governor Arthur asking that he be assigned to her; the petition was rejected. Wherever Johnson was assigned, they had three more children before he was legally free in 1841, though one of their daughters died in 1837 aged nine. The year of Johnson's release, Dolly wrote to an influential acquaintance asking for help to obtain permission for Woretermoeteyenner to come and live with them. The application was approved.

By 1847, the Johnsons had ten children, but that same year Dolly's mother, by then known as Margaret Briggs, died. Her release from Wybalenna and the comfort of spending her last years with her daughter and grandchildren must have been unprecedented.

During these latter years, the Johnsons had been living in the township of Perth where Dolly had taken her land grant. The town of Latrobe was only just finding its feet but in 1848 the family moved there and set up a timber-splitting business, palings being needed for the copper mines of South Australia. They were also acquiring land in the area, including Sherwood where in 1854 Johnson built a hotel and, in 1855, opened a colliery. Another Johnson hotel was called the Dalrymple Inn. Other ventures followed. Some time in the early 1850s, they built Sherwood Hall. Gradually, ten of their 13 surviving children married and had children, several with the second forename Dalrymple. Dolly was to have 70 grandchildren, which is why she has so many descendants, including Diana Wyllie. Two other descendants are the sisters Rosalie Medcraft and Valda Gee whose *The Sausage Tree* (1995) helps them reclaim their Aboriginal heritage. Dolly died in 1864 aged 54 and was buried beside a laurel tree on the banks of the Mersey not far from Sherwood Hall. Her funeral was a Latrobe occasion.

In 1970, Sherwood Hall was flooded and, by 1987, deterioration and vandalism had almost destroyed it. But it was declared a unique house and in 1991 a committee was set up to restore and re-site it to Bell's Parade where it was opened to the public in 1995 (best to check opening times). On the Mersey, approximately where Dolly and Johnson were buried, there is a memorial cairn.

Devonport (Home Hill – 77 Middle Road – Enid Lyons)

Middle Road leads off the Bass Highway in West Devonport. The property started as a hill covered in apple trees, an orchard that was never a success but kept the Lyons family in fruit. When politician Joe Lyons married Enid Burnell (pp226–9) in 1915, he gave it to her as a wedding present, and as the site of their dream home. They chose the design of the house from a newspaper competition and it was built by 1916; they moved in two months before their first child was born.

The house was expanded over the years to accommodate twelve children and remained their home no matter how often politics took them away; indeed, it was the refuge to which they retreated whenever possible. It was a special bolt hole for Enid when Joe died in 1939 and during her political life in Canberra; it was her home until her death in 1981.

Home Hill is now owned by the City of Devonport and the contents of the house by the National Trust (best to check opening times).

Historian Faye Gardam in 'Dame Enid Lyons – a Lady with Style' (1996) tells how she ran a small interior decorating shop in Devonport of which Enid Lyons in her older age became a customer. She details how Enid beautified Home Hill, and ends: 'Some of Dame Enid's original room layouts have been altered to cater for tourists and house a caretaker. But it still remains in essence her creation. A visitor there once told me she felt that Dame Enid had just stepped out for a moment or two.'

In Carmel Bird's short story 'The Woodpecker Toy Fact', the narrator spreads a fantasy haze over Devonport:

This is the fact that the Cabbage White Butterfly arrived in Tasmania on the feast of St Teresa 1940, which was the day that I was born. We both arrived in Devonport, and have been constant observers of each other from the beginning. It is possible that the Cabbage White knows more about me than I know about it. I have a photograph of myself with a cloud of Cabbage Whites. I am three and I am standing among the cabbages in my maternal grandmother's garden, wearing the blue dress with white edges that my grandmother knitted me for Christmas.

Tiagarra Cultural Centre and Museum (Bluff Road, Mersey Bluff)

At the opposite end of West Devonport from Home Hill, at the mouth of the Mersey River, is the Mersey Bluff, a sacred Aboriginal site. In 1929, a teacher came across the petroglyphs, or rock carvings, that the centre, designed to resemble a traditional dwelling of the North West people, was established in 1976 to protect. Ten of the 200 or so petroglyphs can be seen on the walking track that surrounds the building. Inside the Tiagarra – meaning keep or keeping place – are artefacts and displays depicting the traditional way of life.

Emu Bay (Burnie)

Continuing along the Bass Highway, you pass Emu Bay where Walyer (pp32, 112, 384) gathered together fighters following her 1828 escape from the sealers who had abducted her in her youth. In the Civic Centre Plaza outside Burnie Town Hall, there has been a three-panelled art work commemorating her by Deloraine Aboriginal artist Carole Horton – but I have been unable to determine its current status. An installation, 'Warriors and Whalers' (1991) by Jennie Gorringe, inspired by Walyer, is in a private collection. Julie Dowling's portrait is said to be in the National Gallery of Australia, Canberra.

Stanley

Two of the imagined Tasmanian places in Carmel Bird's uncannily real fiction are Copperfield and Woodpecker Point. When I asked her, for the purposes of my factual book, where in reality she imagined them, she replied:

> I do not have exact geographical locations for [them] – they are in the general area of Stanley – Woodpecker Point being coastal and Copperfield being inland. Several people have said to me that they realised when I wrote of Copperfield that I was actually describing a place called Balfour – I have never been to Balfour, and had not actually heard of it before.

Part of the action of *The Bluebird Café* takes place in Copperfield; a train journey takes the narrator westward: 'I was looking out of the window most of the time, and the scenery, especially when we were going along the coast after we left Burnie, was beautiful. The sand is white. I pretended I was on a train in the south of France.'

A scene-setting 'tourist' introduction to the short story 'Woodpecker Point' by a member of the fictional family in *The Bluebird Café* (and later novels), starts straight-faced: 'Named for the legendary Tasmanian Woodpecker, which nests only on the north west coast, the town of Woodpecker Point is the site of the first settlement in this part of the island, and is classified as an historic town.'

Although Carmel's *Red Shoes* (p375) is set mostly in Victoria, the story moves to Tasmania, to the same general area as Woodpecker Point, when a girl is kidnapped and taken there to be killed. The novel is loosely related to the true story of Anne Hamilton-Byrne, leader of a sinister cult just outside Melbourne which collected, detained, and brainwashed children.

In Carmel's 2010 novel *Child of the Twilight*, many of the women characters come from Woodpecker Point, though the action takes place in Melbourne and Europe around two Christian icons, a Baby Jesus statue in Rome and images of a Black Madonna in such towns as Boulogne and Montserrat. I don't think I am giving the end away to say that it takes place in Woodpecker Point and, there, Carmel weaves into the story one of the threads of her pre-occupations and writing – the Aboriginal women of Tasmania's past. In the church in Woodpecker Point the narrator finds,

> ... in a tiny cave-like side chapel there is something unexpected, even amazing. The wall is decorated with a dim and dusty fresco, a primitive picture of a delicate Black Virgin standing among local native landscape and a feathering of ferns, moss and tiny pale yellow orchids. The figure is a portrait of an unknown indigenous girl, a member of the tribe of people who were living in this area when Europeans arrived. It is one of the loveliest and most endearing Black Madonnas I have seen.

Whenever I finish one of Carmel's novels, searching for real Tasmania to put in my book, I chide her for confusing fiction and fact so convincingly that I cannot disentangle them. She justifies herself towards the end of *Child of the Twilight*: '... fiction is the perfect place to put the facts'.

For all Carmel Bird's fantasy around the imaginary Stanley, the real place, on an 8-kilometre-long peninsula extending into the Bass Strait, has its own interest and a history as the first settlement in this part of the island.

The Van Diemen's Land Company (VDL Co.) was granted its charter in 1825 in order to produce fine wool, and the following year its surveyors travelled to the Stanley area to find suitable sheep pasturing. Its chief agent was Edward Curr who had first arrived in Tasmania as a merchant in 1820 with his wife of a year, 22-year-old **Elizabeth Curr** (née Micklethwait, 1798–1866). Their first child was born in Hobart ten months later, their second in 1822, and a third on board ship on the way back to England in 1823. They left again for Tasmania for Curr to take up his VDL Co. appointment in 1825 just after the birth of their fourth child. The family moved north in 1827, following the birth of their fifth child, though Elizabeth seems to have returned to Hobart for the sixth child, born just over a year later.

Augusta Mary Curr (b1830) was the first colonist child to be born at Stanley, and six more little Currs followed (and one at nearby Sheffield). Settlers had begun to arrive in the area in 1826, but it was not until 1842 that a design for the town was introduced. Elizabeth Curr's life, let alone her pregnancies and deliveries, must, therefore, have been somewhat rough and ready. There wasn't a coach service to Burnie until 1880, and then the journey took six to seven hours.

Until 1835, although the family was living on the Highfield property, it was not the house that is open to the public there today the completion of which dates from that year, but a 'small cottage'. Rosalie Hare, though, writes that 'It was equal to a genteel English farmhouse.' It was there that Rosalie, who gives evidence of the killing of Aborigines in Chapter 8 (pp106–7), stayed with Elizabeth for a few weeks from January 1828 while their husbands sailed to Port Dalrymple in the ship of which Robert Hare was captain.

Apart from the Currs' house, Highfield, Stanley's main attraction is Circular Head, sometimes called the Nut, which is just what it sounds like, a curious round, high-cliffed lump – a volcanic plug. Rosalie Hare wrote of it:

> The Head justly called Circular presented a rather desolate sight. Here were plenty of trees, but they were of Stringey-Bark so called from their bark continually falling off and hanging in strings ...
> The height of Circular Head appears about four hundred feet. I ascended it in company of the Surgeon without much difficulty. We found sheep grazing on its summit and kangaroo leaping about in all directions ... The descent from the Bluff we found very unpleasant and rather dangerous.

There is a chair lift today! The Nut can be seen from Highfield which is about a mile from the township; the whole area is also known as Circular Head. The property has been Highfield Historic Site since restoration began in 1987.

Rosalie's Tasmania journal is short; she was only on dry land there between 20 January and 6 March, but it is revealing, particularly about Aboriginal women and attitudes to the people on whose land the VDL Co. had intruded. She writes of life at Highfield and about **Mary**, a woman who visited the family speaking a little English and kissing Elizabeth, Rosalie and the children, to Rosalie's consternation. She continues:

> The next day three other native women, or young girls about fifteen, paid us a visit. These poor creatures had joined the crew of a sealing boat while they were looking for seals along the coast and were brought by them to Circular Head.
> How was my very soul shocked when two of these girls took off their kangaroo-skin coats and showed the inhuman cuts these European monsters had given them when they had not been able to find them food. Mrs Curr's feelings were instantly aroused for the youngest of these poor girls, and she thought it might be possible to teach her to take care of the children.

But on consideration it appeared dangerous – as they have been frequently tried as servants, but universally proved traitorous.

One incident in Elizabeth Curr's life stands out in particularly sharp relief, for there is a monument in the garden at Highfield that reads:

Juliana Teresa Curr was buried here in 1835, aged 2 years, [10] months, 14 days. She rests in peace.'

On 24 June, Juliana was playing in a cart harnessed to a mild old dog when it suddenly rushed to join a dogfight outside the yard of the new house. As it did so, Juliana hit her head on the solid planks of the fence and was killed almost instantly. In 1838, a part of the garden was described as a 'winding bowery walk' to Juliana's tomb in an alcove surrounded by honeysuckle and sweet briar.

The Currs left Stanley, Thomas under a bit of a cloud, in 1841, the year Elizabeth gave birth to their 14th child, and settled in Melbourne where their last child was born. When Thomas died in 1850, he left her and eleven surviving children well provided for. In the 1850s, the Hares also settled in Melbourne. There Rosalie, who had taught when they lived for a spell in Cape Town, was first a head teacher then, in 1864, opened her own school. I think we can assume that she and Elizabeth caught up with each other.

Carmel Bird's Woodpecker Point is not quite Stanley, or Circular Head, for in her 2004 novel *Cape Grimm*, a character visits a quite distinct Highfield: 'There were rose bushes in the gardens at Highfield. When she was a child Rosa Mean believed the roses had been planted in her honour.'

To the south of Stanley is a nest of little settlements, one of which is brought alive in the early twentieth century in *Ruby of Trowutta: Recollections of a Country Postmistress* (p372). The postmistress then, and earlier, had a rather wider brief than today's; it included midwifery, whatever the distance or the weather, or the initial lack of training.

Cape Grim

Here on this furthest north western point of Tasmania the air is the purest in the world, monitored by an air pollution station operated by the Australian Bureau of Meteorology. And yet Carmel Bird writes in *Cape Grimm*:

A stench of mournful abject violence hangs in the air, howls in the waves, moans in the wind, rustles in the heath and stirs among the adamantine rocks. Call them ghosts. Call them the sorrow that inhabits the atmosphere, but they are not shapeless, they have the form of tormented human beings, restlessly returning to the place where their lives were lost or taken from them. Even on a sun-filled summer afternoon the land, the sea and the air in this place are haunted. Some ghosts are white, most are black. The figures and voices of sorrowful men who died in the attempt to protect their own lives, and the lives of their women and children. The mournful cries of the violated, mutilated women who saw their babies dashed against the rocks, saw their family groups scattered and dispossessed.

The novel links the massacre of Aborigines which took place here at Victory Hill in 1828 (p106) and an imaginary white cult massacre over 150 years later. The ghost of the murdered Aboriginal girl Mannaginna appears to the cult character Virginia when she sees in her mind what happened in the past.

Does writing of these events help Carmel Bird come to terms with Tasmania's past which has haunted her since childhood? How far is her character, Virginia, an alter ego when she recounts: 'The images fade, the moans, the cries, the whispers die away. I am a dreamer, but Mannaginna herself is not a dream. I sense in myself a great, great longing to merge with this dark bridge spirit who sits beside me in the cave.' Then she adds: 'I don't believe that Mannaginna will ever find peace, will forever and forever haunt the ocean and the cliffside. She will never find peace; I will never find peace.'

The ghost of Mannaginna is part of Carmel's gallery of Aboriginal ghosts, including that of Mathinna which she places in the Cataract Gorge in Launceston in *The Bluebird Café* (p379). She gave me a couple of insights into her creativity when we were emailing each other about Mathinna, the little girl whom Jane Franklin took into Government House and left behind when she returned to England (p179). Carmel wrote of the painting of the child:

I am so pleased Thomas Bock did that picture of Mathinna – I know it is a tragic picture – but because it exists her spirit has travelled down the years, and seems to be really setting fire to creative imaginations. I first saw it in fact in a blurry black and white photograph in a book that belonged to my great-grandfather.

And a few weeks later she added:

[Today's Aborigines] probably think that as people go on and on about Mathinna they are only compounding the original crime committed by the Franklins. Personally, Mathinna's story always brings tears to my eyes – and I have a strange wish that I could reach her and comfort her and tell her how sorry I am.

Cape Grim, with its indelible memory of massacre, Carmel's treatment of it (symbolic of wider wrongs), and its pure, pure air, I hope end this book in as fitting a way as it was begun by the Louise Girardin magnetometer deep in the D'Entrecasteaux Channel at the other end of the island.

Bibliography

Women's Works (General Reader)

Adams, Nancy, *Saxon Sheep: How a Famous Merino Flock came to Victoria* (Melbourne, Lansdowne, 1961)

Adelaide, Debra, *A Bright and Fiery Troop: Australian Women Writers of the Nineteenth Century* (Ringwood, Victoria, Penguin, 1988)

Alexander, Alison, *A Mortal Flame: Marie Bjelke Petersen: Australian Romance Writer* (Hobart, Blubber Head Press, 1994)

— *Obliged to Submit: Wives and Mistresses of Colonial Governors* (Dynnyrne, Tasmania, Montpelier Press, 1999)

— *Tasmania's Convicts: How Felons Built a New Society* (Crows Nest, NSW, Allen & Unwin, 2010)

Bennett, Alice, and Warner, Georgia, *Country Houses of Tasmania: Behind the Closed Doors of Our Finest Colonial Estates* (Crows Nest, NSW, Allen & Unwin, 2009)

Bird, Carmel, *The Bluebird Café* (Victoria, Penguin, 1990)

— *Woodpecker Point and Other Stories* (London, Virago, 1990)

— 'Fresh Blood, Old Wounds: Tasmania and Guns' in *Meanjin*, vol. 55, no. 3, 1996, 389–94

— *Red Shoes* (Milsons Point, NSW, Vintage, 1998)

— *Cape Grimm* (Sydney, HarperCollins, 2004)

— *Carmel the Essential Bird* (Sydney, HarperCollins, 2005)

— *Child of the Twilight* (Sydney, HarperCollins, 2010)

Bjelke Petersen, Marie, *The Captive Singer* (London, Hodder & Stoughton, 1917)

— *Jewelled Nights* (London, Hutchinson, 1923)

Bowler, Judith, *Amy Sherwin: The Tasmanian Nightingale* (Hobart, 1982)

Bridges, Hilda, *Men Must Live* (London, Wright and Brown, 1938)

Brown, Rosemary, *Madge's People: In the Island of Tasmania and Beyond* (Hobart, Berriedale Trading, 2004)

Burke, Colleen, *Doherty's Corner: The Life and Work of Poet Marie EJ Pitt* (London, Sirius, 1985)

Cato, Nancy, and Rae-Ellis, Vivienne, *Queen Trucanini* (London, Heinemann, 1976)

Chauncy, Nan, *They Found a Cave* (Oxford, Oxford University Press, 1948)

— *Tangara* (Oxford, Oxford University Press, 1960)

— *Mathinna's People* (Oxford, Oxford University Press, 1967)

Chung, Helene, *Ching Chong China Girl: From Fruitshop to Foreign Correspondent* (Sydney, ABC Books, 2008)

Clarke, Patricia, *Tasma: The Life of Jessie Couvreur* (St Leonards, NSW, Allen and Unwin, 1994)

Clarke, Patricia and Spender, Dale, *Lifelines: Australian Women's Letters and Diaries 1788–1840* (St Leonards, NSW, Allen and Unwin, 1992)

Couvreur, Jessie, 'What an Artist Discovered in Tasmania' in *Intercolonial Christmas Annual*, ed. G Walch (Melbourne, 1878)

— 'An Old-time Episode in Tasmania' (1891) in *The Penguin Anthology of Australian Women's Writing*, ed. Dale Spender (Harmondsworth, Penguin, 1988)

— *Not Counting the Cost* (New York, D Appleton, 1895)

Crawford, Patsy, *God Bless Little Sister: A Story of the 1912 Queenstown Mining Disaster* (Tasmania, Red Hill, 2004)

Cree, Mary, *Edith May (1895–1974): Life in Early Tasmania* (Toorak, Victoria, James Street Publications, 1983)

Dick, Isabel, *Huon Belle* (London, 1930; 2008)

— *Wild Orchard* (London, George G Harrap, 1946)

— *Country Heart* (London, George G Harrap, 1947)

Dougharty, Kate Hamilton, *A Story of a Pioneering Family in Van Diemen's Land* (Launceston, Telegraph Printers, 1953)

Eastman, Berenice, *Nan Chauncy: A Writer's Life* (Bagdad, The Friends of Chauncy Vale, 2000)

Edwards, Madge (see Brown)

Eberhard, Adrienne, *Jane, Lady Franklin* (Victoria, Black Pepper, 2004)

Female Factory Research Group, *Convict Lives: Women at the Cascades Female Factory* (Hobart, Research Centre, 2009)

Fenton, Elizabeth, *Mrs Fenton's Journal: A Narrative of her Life in India, ... and Tasmania during the Years 1826–1830* (London, E Arnold, 1901; 1986)

Footsteps and Voices: A Historical Look into the Cascades Female Factory (Hobart, Female Factory History Site, 2004)

Foreman, Amanda, *Georgiana, Duchess of Devonshire* (London, HarperCollins, 1998)

Frost, Lucy, ed., *A Face in the Glass: The Journals of Annie Baxter Dawbin* (Port Melbourne, Victoria, William Heinemann, 1992)

Gaskin, Catherine, *Sara Dane* (London, Collins, 1954)

Graves, Kathleen, *Exile* (Bournemouth, W Earl, 1947)

— *Tasmanian Pastoral* (Carlton, Victoria, Melbourne University Press, 1953)

Greer, Germaine, *Daddy We Hardly Knew You* (London, Penguin 1989)

Grimstone, Mary, *Louise Egerton* (London, 1830)

— *Women's Love* (London, 1832)

— *Character: Or Jew and Gentile* (London, 1935; reprint 2007)

Hare, Rosalie (see Lee)

Lee, Ida, ed., *The Voyage of the Caroline* (London, Longmans, 1927)

Hodgman, Helen, *Blue Skies* (London, Virago reprint, 1989)

Hooper, Chloe, *A Child's Book of True Crime* (London, Jonathan Cape, 2002)

Irvine, Alice, *The Central Cookery Book* (Hobart, Tasmanian Government Printer, 1930)

Keese, Oliné, *The Broad Arrow* (London, Eden, 1988; 1st published 1859)

— *Lyra Australis or Attempts to Sing in a Strange Land* (London, Bickers and Bush, 1854)

Lancaster, GB, *Pageant* (London, George Allen & Unwin, 1933)

Leakey, Caroline (see Keese)

Lohrey, Amanda, *The Morality of Gentlemen* (Sydney, Picador, 1990; 1st published 1984)

— *The Reading Group* (Sydney, Picador, 1988)

— *Vertigo* (Melbourne, Black Inc, 2008)

Lyons, Enid, *So We Take Comfort* (London, Heineman, 1966)

— *Among the Carrion Crows* (Adelaide, Rigby, 1972; 1977)

Lyttleton, Edith (see Lancaster)

Mallett, Molly, *My Past – Their Future: Stories from Cape Barren Island* (2001)

Medcraft, Rosalie, and Gee, Valda, *The Sausage Tree* (St Lucia, University of Queensland Press, 1995)

Melba, Nellie, *Melodies and Memories* (London, Butterworth, 1925)

Meredith, Louisa Anne, *Notes and Sketches of New South Wales* (London, John Murray, 1844)

— *My Home in Tasmania: During a Residence of Nine Years* (London, John Murray, 1852; 2003)

— *Some of My Bush Friends in Tasmania: Native Flowers, Berries and Insects* (London, Day & Son, 1860)

— *Over the Straits* (London, Chapman Hall, 1861)

— *Tasmanian Friends and Foes* (London, Marcus Ward, 1880)

— *Bush Friends in Tasmania: Last Series* (London, Macmillan, 1891)

Martineau, Harriet, 'Homes Abroad' in *Illustrations of Political Economy*, 9 vols (London, 1834) vol. IV

Mattingley, Christobel, ed., *Ruby of Trowutta: Recollections of a Country Postmistress* (Hobart, Montpelier Press, 2003)

North, Marianne, *Recollections of a Happy Life*, 2 vols (London, Macmillan, 1893) vol. II

Nyman, Lois, *The East Coasters* (Launceston, Regal Publications, 1990)

Pitt, Marie J, *Horses of the Hills* (Melbourne, Thomas C Lothian, 1911)

Power, Helen, *A Lute With Three Strings* (London, Robert Hale, 1964)

Pownell, Eve, *Mary of Maranoa: Tales of Australian Pioneer Women* (Melbourne, Melbourne University Press, 1964; 1st published 1959)

Prinsep, Elizabeth, ed., *The Journal of a Voyage from Calcutta to Van Diemen's Land ... From Original Letters* (London, Smith, Elder, 1833)

Pybus, Cassandra, *Community of Thieves* (Port Melbourne, Minerva, 1992)

— *Till Apples Grow on an Orange Tree* (St Lucia, University of Queensland Press, 1998)

Rae-Ellis, Vivienne, *Louisa Anne Meredith: A Tigress in Exile* (Hobart, St David's Park Publishing, 1990; 1st published 1979)

— *Trucanini: Queen or Traitor* (Canberra, Australian Institute of Aboriginal Studies, 1981)

Roberts, Beth, *Manganinnie* (Melbourne, Sun Books, 1980)

Roberts, Jane, *Two Years at Sea: Being the Narrative of a Voyage to the Swan River and Van Diemen's Land during the Years 1829, 30, 31* (London, R Bentley, 1834)

Rose, Heather, *The Butterfly Man* (St Lucia, University of Queensland Press, 2005)

Royal Botanic Gardens Kew, *A Vision of Eden: The Life and Work of Marianne North* (Exeter, Webb & Bower, 1980)

Rubehold, Hallie, *Lady Worsley's Whim: An Eighteenth Century Tale of Sex, Scandal and Divorce* (London, Chatto & Windus, 2008)

Russell, Penny, *This Errant Lady: Jane Franklin's Overland Journey to Port Phillip and Sydney, 1839* (Canberra, National Library of Australia, 2002)

Ryan, Lyndall, *The Aboriginal Tasmanians* (NSW, Allen and Unwin, 1996; 1st edition 1981)

Ryley, Madeleine Lucette, *Mice and Men* (London, Samuel French, 1903)

Scott, Margaret, *A Little More: Celebrating a Life of Letters* (Hobart, Summerhill Publishing, nd)

— *Effects of Light: The Poetry of Tasmania* (Sandy Bay, Tasmania, Twelvetrees, 1985)

— *Port Arthur: A Story of Strength and Courage* (NSW, Random House, 1997)

— *Changing Countries: On Moving from One Island to Another* (Sydney, ABC Books, 2000)

Scripps, Lindy, *Women's Sites and Lives in Hobart* (Hobart, City Council, 2000)

In Her Stride (pamphlet) (Hobart, City Council 2005)

Shepherd, Catherine, *Daybreak: A Play in Three Acts* (Melbourne, Melbourne University Press, 1942)

— *Jane, My Love* (1951) in Susan Pfisterer, *Tremendous Worlds: Australian Women's Drama 1890–1960* (Sydney, Currency, 1999)

Simpson, Lindsay, *Curer of Souls* (Sydney, Vintage, 2006)

Sorell, Jane, *Governor, William and Julia Sorell* (Hobart, Citizen's Advice Bureau, 1986)

Spender, Dale, *Two Centuries of Australian Women Writers* (London, Pandora, 1988)

Statham, Pamela, ed., *The Tanner Letters: A Pioneer Saga of Swan River and Tasmania 1831–45* (Nedlands, University of Western Australia Press, 1981)

Sturm, Terry, *An Unsettled Spirit: The Life and Frontier Fiction of Edith Lyttleton (GB Lancaster)* (Auckland, Auckland University Press, 2003)

Tasma (see Couvreur)

Taylor, Rebe, *Unearthed: The Aboriginal Tasmanians of Kangaroo Island* (Kent Town, S Australia, Wakefield, 2002; 2008)

Thrower, Mrs WI, *Younâh: A Tasmanian Aboriginal Romance of the Cataract Gorge* (Hobart, Tasmanian Mail, 1894; 1912)

Tipping, Marjorie, *Convicts Unbound: The Story of the Calcutta Convicts and their Settlement in Australia* (Ringwood, Australia, Viking O'Neil, 1988)

Treasure, Rachael, *The Dare* (London, Preface Publishing, 2007)

Viveash, Ellen (see Statham)

Ward, Mrs Humphrey, *A Writer's Recollections* (London, Collins, 1918)

Weigall, ASH, *My Little World* (Sydney, Angus and Robertson, 1934)

West, Ida, *Pride Against Prejudice* (Canberra, Australian Institute of Aboriginal Studies, 1984)

Whishaw, Mary Kinloch, *History of Richmond and Recollections from 1898–1929* (nd)

White, Kate, *A Political Love Story: Joe and Enid Lyons* (Ringwood, Australia, Penguin, 1987)

Wood, Danielle, *The Alphabet of Light and Dark* (NSW, Allen & Unwin, 2003)

Wood, Mrs Henry, *East Lynne* (London, Bentley, 1863)

Woodward, Frances, *Portrait of Jane* (London, Hodder & Stoughton, 1951)

Wyllie, Diana, *Dolly Dalrymple* (Tasmania, Sherwood Hall Restoration Committee, 2004)

Women's Specialised Works

Ackerman, Jessie A, *Australia from a Woman's Point of View* (London, Cassell, 1913)

Alexander, Alison, 'Teresa Hamilton in Tasmania: First-Wave Feminism in Action' in *Papers and Proceedings of the Royal Society of Tasmania*, vol. 131, 1997, 1–11

Anae, Nicole, '"The New Prima Donnas": "Homegrown" Tasmanian "Stars" of the 1860s, Emma and Clelia Howson' in *Journal of Australian Studies*, vol. 28, issue 84, 2005, 173–81

Bird, Carmel, *The Stolen Children: Their Stories* (Australia, Random House, 1998)

Casella, Eleanor, *Archaeology of the Ross Female Factory: Female Incarceration in Van Diemen's Land, Australia* (Launceston, Queen Victoria Museum and Art Gallery, 2002)

Cowley, Trudy Mae, *A Drift of Derwent Ducks: Lives of the 200 Female Irish Convicts Transported on the 'Australasia' from Dublin to Hobart in 1849* (Hobart, Research Tasmania, 2005)

Crouch, Caressa, 'Kingston – The Residence of John Batman, Van Diemen's Land' in *Australiana*, vol. 17, no. 2, May 1995, 40–8

Curtis, Winifred, *Forests and Flowers of Mount Wellington, Tasmania* (Hobart, Tasmania Museum and Art Gallery, 1963–79)

Daniels, Kay, 'Prostitution in Tasmania during the Transition from Penal Settlement to "Civilized" Society' in *So Much Hard Work: Women and Prostitution in Australian History* (Sydney, Fontana, 1984)

— *Convict Women* (St Leonards, Allen & Unwin, 1998)

Frost, Lucy, and Maxwell-Steward, Hamish, eds, *Chain Letters: Narrating Convict Lives* (Victoria, Melbourne University Press, 2001)

Grimshaw, Patricia, and Standish, Ann, 'Making Tasmania Home: Louisa Meredith's Colonizing Prose' in *Frontiers*, vol. 28, nos 1 and 2, June 2007, 1–17

Irvine, Nance, *Mary Reibey – Molly Incognita: 1777–1855* (Sydney, Library of Australian History, 2001)

Lake, Marilyn, *Getting Equal: The History of Australian Feminism* (St Leonards, NSW, Allen & Unwin, 1999)

Leakey, Emily, *Clear Shining Light* (London, JE Shaw, 1882)

Life at Clarendon: The Reminiscences of Cornelia and Rose Cox (Tasmania, National Trust, 1987)

Mackaness, George, ed., *Some Private Correspondence of Sir John and Lady Jane Franklin*, vols XVII and XVIII (Sydney, Australian Historical Monographs, 1977)

Mckay, Thelma, *The Princess Royal Girls: The First Free Female Immigration Ship to Van Diemen's Land – 1832* (Kingston, Tasmania, 2007)

McLaughlin, Anne, 'Against the League: Fighting the "Hated Stain"' in *Tasmanian Historical Studies*, vol. 5, no. 1, 1995–96, 76–104

Martin, Susan, 'Captivating Fictions: Younâh!: A Tasmanian Aboriginal Romance of the Cataract Gorge' in *Body Trade: Captivity, Cannibalism and Colonialism in the Pacific*, eds Barbara Creed and Jeanette Hoorn (New York, Routledge, 2001)

Moneypenny, Maria, 'Going out and Coming in: Co-operation between Aborigines and Europeans in Early Tasmania' in *Tasmanian Historical Studies*, vol. 5, no. 1, 1995–96, 64–75

Morgan, Sharon, *Land Settlement in Early Tasmania: Creating an Antipodean England* (Cambridge, Cambridge University Press, 1992)

Morris, Agnes M, *Lady Hamilton's Tasmania* (Hobart, Telegraph Printery, 1966)

Morris, Miranda, *Placing Women* (Hobart, Office of the Status of Women, 1997)

Nixon, Norah, *The Pioneer Bishop in VDL* (Hobart, privately printed, 1953)

O'Brien, Patty, *The Pacific Muse: Exotic Femininity and the Colonial Pacific* (Seattle, University of Washington Press, c2006)

Oldfield, Audrey, *Women's Suffrage in Australia: A Gift or a Struggle* (Cambridge, Cambridge University Press, 1992)

— *Australian Women and the Vote* (Cambridge, Cambridge University Press, 1994)

Pybus, Cassandra, 'Mannalargenna's Daughters' in *Heat*, issue 15, 2000, 93–107

Reid, Kirsty, *Gender, Crime and Empire: Convicts, Settlers and the State in Early Colonial Australia* (Manchester, Manchester University Press, 2008)

Rowntree, Amy, *Battery Point Today and Tomorrow* (Hobart, Adult Education Board, 1951; 1968)

Rowntree, Fearn, *Battery Point Sketchbook* (Hobart, Mercury Press, 1953?)

Russell, Lynette, 'Dirty Domestics and Worse Cooks: Aboriginal Women's Agency and Domestic Frontiers, Southern Australia 1800–1850' in *Frontiers: A Journal of Women's Studies*, vol. 28, nos 1 and 2, 2007, 18–46

Russell, Penny, '"Her Excellency": Lady Franklin, Female Convicts and the Problem of Authority in Van Diemen's Land' in *Journal of Australian Studies*, no. 53, 1997, 40–50

— 'Displaced Loyalties: Vice-Regal Women in Colonial Australia' (Trevor Reese Memorial Lecture, London, 1999)

Ryan, Lyndall, 'From Stridency to Silence: The Policing of Convict Women 1803–1853' in *Sex, Power and Justice: Historical Perspectives of Law in Australia*, ed. Diane Kirby (Melbourne, Melbourne University Press, 1995)

— 'Risdon Cove and the Massacre of 3 May 1804: Their Place in Tasmanian History' in *Family and Gender in Australia and Tasmania, Tasmanian Historical Studies*, vol. 9, 2004, 107–23

Schaffer, Irene, *A Remarkable Woman: Mary Bowater, Convict and Landholder 1765–1849* (Rosetta, Tasmania, privately published, 2005)

— *Catherine Kearney: Dairy Farmer Hobart Rivulet 1808–1830* (Rosetta, Tasmania, privately published, 2007)

Snowden, Dianne, 'Convict Marriage: the best instrument of reform' in *Family and Gender in Australia and Tasmania, Tasmanian Historical Studies*, vol. 9, 2004, 63–71

Swann, Margaret, 'Mrs Meredith and Miss Atkinson, Writers and Naturalists' in *Journal of the Royal Australian Historical Society*, vol. 15, 1929, 1–29

Veale, Veda, *Women to Remember* (Launceston, Smith's Printery, 1981)

— *Women Worth Remembering* (Launceston, Foot & Playsted, nd)

Woods, Christine, *The Last Ladies: Female Convicts on the Duchess of Northumberland, 1853* (Hobart, Woods, 2004)

Tasmanian Historical Research Association Papers and Proceedings

Ackland, Catherine, and Campbell, Colin, 'Pioneer Craftswomen from the Bothwell Area', vol. 41, no. 2, June 1994, 85–7

Alexander, Alison, 'Women Earning a Living in the Arts, 1803–1914', vol. 43, no. 2, June 1996, 116–22

Alexander, Cynthia, 'The Itinerants – A Ladies' Literary Society', vol. 32, no. 4, December 1985, 146–50

Bardenhagen, Marita, 'Bush Nursing in Tasmania: A Glimpse of Nursing Women's Contributions in Rural Health', vol. 41, no. 1, March 1994, 89–95

Bartlett, Anne, 'The Launceston Female Factory', vol. 41, no. 2, June 1994, 115–24

Boyer, PW, ' Leaders and Helpers: Jane Franklin's Plan for Van Diemen's Land', vol. 21, no. 2, June 1974, 47–65

Cameron, Patsy and Vicki Matson-Green, 'Pallawah Women: Their Historical Contribution to Our Survival', vol. 41, no. 2, June 1994, 65–70

Campbell, Hugh, 'A Proper Class of Female Emigrants: The "Boadicea" Women, 1834–36)', vol. 35, no. 2, June 1988, 58–78

Eastman, Berenice, 'Biography of a Tasmanian – Nan Chauncy', vol. 25, no. 4, December 1978, 98–113

Ely, Richard, 'Anna Brennan: Armistice Day at Port Arthur', vol. 39, no. 2, June 1992, 83–7

Evans, Caroline, 'State Girls: Their Lives as Apprentices 1896–1935', vol. 41, no. 2, June 1994, 96–100

Finlay, EM, 'Convict Women of the Amphrite', vol. 38, nos 3 and 4, December 1991, 119–30

Foster, S, ' The Corrick Family and Early Cinema in Tasmania', vol. 45, no.1, June 1998, 51–3

Gardam, Faye, 'Dame Enid Lyons – A Lady With Style', vol. 43, no. 2, June 1996, 123–27
Glover, Margaret, 'Women and Children at Port Arthur', vol. 32, no. 2, June 1985, 62–6
Henry, ER, 'Edward Lord: The John Macarthur of Van Diemen's Land', vol. 20, no. 2, June 1973, 98–107
Horner, JC, 'The Literary Associations of Port Arthur', vol. 32, no. 2, June 1985, 56–61
Horner, JC, 'The Themes of Four Tasmanian Convict Novels', vol. 15, no. 1, June 1997, 18–32
Hutchinson, RC, 'Mrs Hutchinson and the Female Factories of Early Australia', vol. 11, no. 2, December 1963, 51–67
Johnson, Susan E, 'The Irish Convict Women of the Phoebe: A Follow-up to Their Arrival in 1845', vol. 45, no. 1, March 1998, 40–50
Kerr, Joan, 'Mary Morton Allport and the Status of the Colonial "Lady Painter"', vol. 31, no. 2, June 1984, 3–17
Lennox, GR, 'A Private and Confidential Despatch of Eardley-Wilmot', vol. 29, no. 2, June 1982, 80–92
Lennox, G, 'The Van Diemen's Land Company and the Tasmanian Aborigines', vol. 37, no. 4, December 1990, 165–208
Levy, M, 'GA Robinson and the Whaling-Sealing Community', vol. 5, no. 4, June 1957, 73–6
McMahon, Anne, 'Tasmanian Aboriginal Women as Slaves', vol. 23, no. 2, June 1976, 44–9
— 'The Lady in Early Tasmanian Society: A Psychological Portrait', vol. 26, no. 4, March 1979, 5–11
Miller, E Morris, 'Australia's First Two Novels: Origins and Backgrounds', part 1, vol. 6, no. 2, September 1957, 37–35, part II, vol. 6, no. 3, December 1957, 56–65
Morgan, Sharon, 'George and Mary Meredith: The Role of the Colonial Wife', vol. 36, no. 3, September 1989, 125–9
Murray-Smith, Stephen, 'Beyond the Pale: The Islander Community of Bass Strait in the Nineteenth Century', vol. 20, no. 4, December 1973, 167–201
Parrott, Jennifer, 'Elizabeth Fry and Female Transportation', vol. 43, no. 4, December 1996, 169–186
Payne, HS, 'A Statistical Study of Female Convicts in Tasmania, 1843–53', vol. 9, no. 2, June 1961, 56–69
Pearce, Vicki, '"A Few Viragos on a Stump": The Womanhood Suffrage Campaign in Tasmania, 1880–1920', vol. 32, no. 4, December 1985, 151–64
Plomley, NJB, 'George Augustus Robinson and The Tasmanian Aboriginals', vol. 5, no. 2, June 1956, 23–30
— 'Notes on Some of the Tasmanian Aborigines, and on Portraits of Them', vol. 102, part II, 1978, 47–54
Plomley, Brian and Kristen Anne Henley, 'The Sealers of Bass Strait and the Cape Barren Community', vol. 37, nos 2 and 3, June–September 1990, 54–124
Rae-Ellis, Vivienne, 'Trucanini', vol. 333, no. 2, June 1976, 26–43
Ramsay, Mary, 'Eliza Forlong and the Saxon Merino Industry', vol. 51, no. 3, 2004, 121–35
Ratcliff, Eric VR, 'A Permanent Advantage: The French Fountain in Prince's Square, Launceston', vol. 44, no. 2, June 1997, 74–90
Roe, Michael, 'Mary Grimstone (1800–1850?): For Women's Rights and Tasmanian Patriotism', vol. 36, no. 1, March 1989, 8–32
— 'Mary Leman Grimstone and Her Sisters', vol. 42, no. 1, March 1995, 36–8
Ryan, Lyndall, 'The Extinction of the Tasmanian Aborigines: Myth or Reality', vol. 19, no. 2, June 1972, 61–77
— 'The Struggle for Trukanini 1830–1997', vol. 44, no. 3, September 1997, 153–73
Sagona, Claudia, 'Vivienne Rae-Ellis, Black Robinson: Protector of Aborigines', vol. 35, no. 2, June 1988, 87–91
Sharman, Robert C, 'John Pacoe Fawkner in Tasmania', vol. 4, no. 3, December 1955, 57–63
Skira, Irynej, 'Always Afternoon: Aborigines on Cape Barren Island, in the Nineteenth Century', vol. 44, no. 2, June 1997, 121–31
— 'Aboriginals in Tasmania: Living on Cape Barren Island in the Twentieth Century', vol. 44, no. 3, September 1997, 187–201

Sprod, Michael, 'Domestic Training in Tasmanian State Post-Primary Schools', vol. 41, no. 1, March 1994, 101–13

Stancome, GH, 'Diarist of Tasmania in the Nineteenth Century', vol. 21, no. 1, March 1974, 30–41

Stilwell, GT, 'Mr and Mrs George Carr Clark of "Ellinthorpe Hall"', vol. 11, no. 3, April 1963, 72–111

Tipping, Marjorie, 'From the Book to the Box: Convicts Unbound and the Problems of a Television Interpretation', vol. 42, no. 2, March 1995, 53–64

Winter, Gillian, 'A Colonial Experience: The Royal Victoria Theatre 1837–1851', vol. 32, no. 4, December 1985, 121–45

— 'We Speak That We Do Know and Testify That We Have Seen: Caroline Leakey's Tasmania Experience and Her Novel the Broad Arrow', vol. 40, no. 4, December 1993, 133–53

General Reference

Adam-Smith, Patsy, *Moonbird People* (Adelaide, Rigby, 1965)

— *Islands of Bass Strait* (Adelaide, Rigby, 1976)

— *Heart of Exile: Ireland 1848, and the Seven Patriots Banished* (Melbourne, Nelson, 1986)

Alexander, Alison, *Glenorchy 1804–1964* (Glenorchy, Glenorchy City Council, 1986)

Arnold, Thomas, *Passages in a Wandering Life* (London, Edward Arnold, 1900)

Backhouse, James, *A Narrative of a Visit to the Australian Colonies* (London, Adams, 1843)

Bailey, Anne, and Bailey, Robin, *An Early Tasmanian Story: With Oakdens, Cowies, Parramores, Tullochs and Hoggs* (Toorak, Victoria, Blenallen Press, 2004)

Bakewell, Sarah, *The English Dane: A Story of Adventure from Iceland to Tasmania* (London, Chatto and Windus, 2005)

Bate, Frank, *Samuel Bate: A Singular Character, 1776–1849* (Forestville, NSW, Brookvale Press, 1987)

Beswick, John, *Brothers' Home: The Story of Derby Tasmania* (Tasmania, Beswick, 2003)

Bethell, LS, *The Valley of the Derwent* (Hobart, nd)

Billot, CP, *John Batman: The Story of John Batman and the Founding of Melbourne* (Melbourne, Hyland House, 1979)

— *The Life and Times of John Pascoe Fawkner* (Melbourne, Hyland House, 1985)

Bolger, Peter, *Hobart Town* (Canberra, Australian National University Press, 1973)

Bonwick, James, *The Last of the Tasmanians: Or the Black War of Van Diemen's Land* (Uckfield, Sussex, Rediscovery Books, 1979; 1st published 1870)

— *Curious Facts of Old Colonial Days* (London, Sampson, Low, Son & Marston, 1870)

Bonyhady, Tim, *The Colonial Earth* (Melbourne, Melbourne University Press, 2000)

Boyce, James, *Van Diemen's Land* (Melbourne, Black Inc., 2008)

Brand, Ian, *Penal Peninsula: Port Arthur and Its Outstations, 1827–1898* (Launceston, Regal Publications, 1998)

Bridges, Roy, *That Yesterday was Home* (Sydney, Australian Publishing, 1948)

Brown, Bob, *Tasmania Recherche Bay* (Hobart, Green Institute, 2005)

Brown, PL, *The Clyde Company Papers* (Oxford, Oxford University Press, 1941)

Brownrigg, Rev Canon (Marcus), *The Cruise of the Freak: A Narrative of a Visit to the Islands in Bass and Banks Straits* (Launceston, Walch, 1872)

Bush, Julia, *Edwardian Ladies and Imperial Power* (London, Leicester University Press, 2000)

Bussey, Gertrude, *Pioneers for Peace: Women's International League for Peace and Freedom* (London WILPF, 1980)

Cahill, Desmond, 'John Potaski, Australia's First Polish Settler: A Problematic Beginning' in *Australia: Challenges and Possibilities in the New Millennium*, ed. Elizabeth Drozd and Desmond Cahill (Illinois, On Diversity, 2004)

Calder, James, *Some Account of the Wars, Extirpation, Habits etc. of the Native Tribes of Tasmania* (Hobart, Henn, 1984)

Cameron, Max, 'The Rise and Fall of Eliza Batman', in *Double Time: Women in Victoria 150 Years Ago*, eds Marilyn Lake and Farley Kelly (Ringwood, Victoria, Penguin, 1985)

Campbell, Alistair H, *John Batman and the Aborigines* (Malmsbury, Victoria, Kibble Books, 1987)

Chance, Camilla, *Wisdom Man* (Camberwell, Victoria, Viking, 2003)

Chapman, Peter, ed., *The Diaries of GTWB Boyes* (Melbourne, Oxford University Press, 1985)

Chick, Neil, *The Archers of Van Diemen's Land* (Lenah Valley, Pedigree Press, 1991)

Clark, Douglas, *Woodside Descendants* (Queensland, Coastal Printing Service, 1991)

Clarke, Marcus, *For the Term of His Natural Life* (Adelaide, Rigby, 1970)

Close, Robert, *Eliza Callaghan* (London, Pan, 1957)

Clune, Frank, and Stephensen, PR, *The Pirates of the Brig Cyprus* (London, Rupert Hart-Davis, 1962)

Clune, Frank, *Martin Cash: The Lucky Bushranger* (Sydney, Angus & Robertson, 1968)

Cobley, John, *The Crimes of the 'Lady Juliana' Convicts 1790* (Sydney, Library of Australian History, 1989)

Conrad, Peter, *Down Home: Revisiting Tasmania* (London, Chatto and Windus, 1988)

Cotton, Frances, *Kettle on the Hob: A Family in Van Diemen's Land, 1828–1885* (Orford, Joan Roberts, 1986)

Cowburn, Joe, and Cox, Rita, *New Norfolk's History and Achievements* (New Norfolk, New Norfolk Council, 1986)

Cranston, CA, 'Quaker Writers in Tasmania (Australia)' in *The Encyclopaedia of Religion and Nature*, vol. 2, ed. Bron R. Taylor (New York, Thoemmes Continuum, 2005), 1319–21

Cree, Nicholas, *Oyster Cove* (Latrobe Tasmania, Geneva Press, 1979)

Curry, John, *David Collins: A Colonial Life* (Victoria, Melbourne University Press, 2000)

Davidson, Jim, 'Port Arthur: A Tourist History' in *Australian Historical Studies*, vol. 26, issue 105, October 1995, 653–65

Davies, David, *The Last of the Tasmanians* (London, Frederick Muller, 1973)

Davis, Bev, *Guide to Bruny Island History* (Bruny Island Historical Society, 1990)

Davis, Richard, *The Tasmanian Gallows* (Hobart, Cat and Fiddle Press, 1974)

Davis, Richard, and Petrow, Stefan, eds, *Varieties of Vice-Regal Life by Sir William and Lady Denison* (Hobart, The Tasmanian Historical Research Association, 2004)

De Quincey, Elizabeth, *The History of Mount Wellington: A Tasmanian Sketchbook* (Hobart, de Quincey, 1987)

Dunbar, Diane, *Thomas Bock: Convict Engraver, Society Portraitist* (Launceston, Queen Victoria Museum and Art Gallery, 1991)

Duyker, Edward, and Duyker, Maryse, eds & trans, *Voyage to the Pacific 1791–1793/Bruny d'Entrecasteaux* (Carlton, Victoria, Melbourne University Press, 2001)

— *Citizen Labillardière: A Naturalist's Life in Revolution and Exploration* (Carlton, Victoria, Melbourne University Press, 2004)

— *Exploration: A Bulletin Devoted to the Study of Franco-Australian Links* (Melbourne, ISFAR, December 2005)

Dyson, Dawn, *The Hawkes Family at Franklin House* (Franklin, Franklin House, 1999)

EF, *Callaghan and Batman: Van Diemen's Land in 1825* (Adelaide, Sullivan's Cove, 1978)

Elias, Peter and Anne, eds, *A Few From Afar: Jewish Lives in Tasmania from 1804* (Hobart, The Hobart Hebrew Congregation, 2003)

Emmett, ET, *Tasmania By Road and Track* (Melbourne, Melbourne University Press, 1952)

Engels, Friedrich, *The Condition of the Working Class in England in 1844* (London, William Reeves, 1887)

Evans, Kathryn, *Robert Pitcairn 1802–1861* (Runnymede, National Trust of Australia (Tasmania), nd)

Fawkner, John Pascoe, *Reminiscences of Early Hobart Town 1804–1810* (Malvern, Victoria, Melbourne Banks Society, 2007)

Fenton, James, *History of Tasmania* (Hobart, Melanie Publications, 1987; 1st published 1884)

— *The Life and Work of the Reverend Charles Price* (Melbourne, Robertson, 1886)

Fitzpatrick, Kathleen, *Sir John Franklin in Tasmania* (Carlton, Victoria, Melbourne University Press, 1949)

Flanagan, Martin, *In Sunshine or in Shadow* (Sydney, Picador, 2002)

Flanagan, Richard, *Wanting* (London, Atlantic Books, 2009)

Flannery, Tim, *The Future Eaters* (New York, Grove Press, 1994)

Giblin, RW, *The Early History of Tasmania 1642–1804* (London, Methuen, 1928)

Goodrick, Joan, *Life in Old Van Diemens Land* (Adelaide, Rigby, 1977)

Gould, John, *The Birds of Australia* (London, privately published, 1840–48)

Haw, Camilla M, 'John Connolly's Attendants at the Hanwell Asylum 1839–1852' in *History of Nursing Journal*, vol. 3, no. 1, 1990, 20–58

Hawkins Nicholson, Ian, *Shipping Arrivals and Departure, Tasmania 1803–1833* (Canberra, Roebuck Society, 1983)

— *Shipping Arrivals and Departures, Tasmania, 1834–42* (Canberra, Roebuck Society, 1985)

Hamilton-Arnold, Barbara, *Letters of GP Harris 1803–1812* (Sorrento, Arden Press, 1994)

The Hobart Town Magazine (Hobart, H. Melville, 1834)

Hookey, Mabel, *The Chaplain: Being some Further Account of the Days of Bobby Knopwood* (Hobart, Fuller's Bookshop, nd)

Hordern, Lesley, *Children of One Family: The Story of Anthony and Ann Hordern and their Descendants in Australia, 1825–1925* (Sydney, Retford Press, 1985)

Howard, Patrick, *To Hell or Hobart* (Kenthurst, NSW, Kangaroo Press, 1993)

Howell, PA, *Thomas Arnold the Younger in Van Diemen's Land* (Hobart, Tasmanian Historical Research Association, 1964)

Hughes, Robert, *The Fatal Shore: A History of the Transportation of Convicts to Australia 1787–1868* (London, Pan, 1987)

Huxley, Julian, *Memories* (London, George Allen & Unwin, 1970)

Jackman, SW, *Tasmania* (Newton Abbot, David & Charles, 1974)

Keneally, Thomas, *The Great Shame: A Story of the Irish in the Old World and the New* (London, Vintage, 1999)

Knopwood, Robert (see Nicholls)

Lempriere, Thomas, *Penal Settlements in Van Diemen's Land* (London, 1839)

Lennox, Geoff, *Richmond Gaol* (Hobart, Dormaslen Publications, 1997)

Lilley, FEM, et al., 'Seeking a Seafloor Magnetic Signal from the Antarctic Circumpolar Current' in *Geophysical Journal International*, vol. 20, no. 22, 26 March 2004, 175–86

Lilley, FEM (Ted) and Day, Alan A, 'D'Entrecasteaux, 1792: Celebrating a Bicentennial in Geomagnetism' in *Transactions, American Geophysical Union*, vol. 74, no. 9, 2 March 1997, 102–3

Lovelace, George, *The Victims of Whiggery* (London, Effingham Wilson, 1837)

McGoogan, Ken, *Lady Franklin's Revenge* (London, Bantam, 2006)

Maddock, MJ, *Clarendon and its People* (Launceston, Regal Publications, 1996)

Masters, David, *St Pauls Plains Avoca 1834–1984* (Launceston, The Mary Fisher Bookshop, 1984)

Melville, Henry, *The History of Van Diemen's Land: From the Year 1824 to 1835* (Sydney, Horwitz Publications, 1965)

Mercer, Peter, *Narryna: Built for a Merchant* (Hobart, Narryna Heritage Museum, 2002)

— *A Most Dangerous Occupation: Whaling, Whalers and the Bayleys* (Runnymede, National Trust of Australia (Tasmania), 2002)

Miller, Morris, *Pressmen and Governors* (Sydney, Sydney University Press, 1952; 1973)

Mitchel, John, *Jail Diary* (Dublin, MH Gill & Son, 1913) (see also O'Shaunessy)

Moore, James FH, *The Convicts of Van Diemen's Land* (Hobart, VDL Publications, 1995)

Murray-Smith, Stephen, ed., *Mission to the Islands* (see Brownrigg) (Launceston, Foot & Playsted, 1987)

Nicholls, Mary, ed., *The Diary of the Reverend Robert Knopwood 1803–1838* (Hobart, Tasmanian Historical Research Association, 1977)

Nixon, Francis, *The Cruise of the Beacon* (London, Bell & Daldy, 1857)

O'Neil, Judith, *Transported to Van Diemen's Land* (Cambridge, Cambridge University Press, 1977)

O'Shaunessy, Peter, ed., *The Gardens of Hell: John Mitchel in Van Diemen's Land 1850–1853* (Kenthurst, Kangaroo Press, 1988)

Philipps, Yvonne, *Bartley of Kerry Lodge* (Tasmania, Privately Printed, 1987)

Piddock, Susan, *A Space of Their Own: The Archeology of Nineteenth Century Lunatic Asylums in Britain, South Australia and Tasmania* (New York, Springer, 2007)

Plomley, Brian, and Piard-Bernier, Josiane, *The General: The Visits of the Expedition led by Bruny d'Entrecasteaux to Tasmanian Waters in 1792 and 1793* (Launceston, Tasmania, Queen Victoria Museum, 1993)

Plomley, Brian (NJB), *Weep in Silence: A History of the Flinders Island Aboriginal Settlement, with the Flinders Island Journal of George Augustus Robinson, 1835–1839* (Hobart, Blubber Press, 1987)

— 'Notes on Some of the Tasmanian Aborigines and Portraits of Them' in *Papers and Proceedings of the Royal Society of Tasmania*, vol. 102, part II, 1978, 47–54

— 'The Westlake Papers: Records of Interviews in Tasmania by Ernest Westlake, 1908–1919', occasional paper, Queen Victoria Museum and Art Gallery, no. 4, 1991

— *The Tasmanian Aborigines* (Launceston, The Plomley Foundation, 1993)

Poulson, Bruce, *Recherche Bay: A Short History* (Southport, Tasmania, Community Centre, 2004)

Pugh, Sheenagh, *The Beautiful Lie* (Bridgend, Seren, 2002)

Pybus, Cassandra, and Flanagan, Richard, *The Rest of the World is Watching: Tasmania and the Greens* (Sydney, Pan Macmillan, 1990)

Prevost, Joan, *From the Epping Banks to the Esk* (Launceston, Foot & Playsted, 1988)

Rae-Ellis, Vivienne, *Black Robinson, Protector of Aborigines* (Carlton, Victoria, Melbourne University Press, 1988)

Raynor, Tony, *Female Factory, Female Convict* (Dover, Tasmania, Esperance Press, 2005)

Refshauge, WF, 'An Analytical Approach to the Events at Risdon Cove on 3 May 1804' in *Journal of Royal Australian Historical Society*, June 1, 2007

Reynolds, Henry, *Fate of a Free People* (Camberwell, Victoria, Penguin, 2004)

Reynolds, John, *Launceston: History of an Australian City* (Melbourne, Macmillan, 1969)

Robinson, GA (see Plomley)

Robson, Lloyd, *A History of Tasmania – Van Diemen's Land from Earliest Times to 1855* (London, Oxford University Press, 1983)

Robson, Lloyd, and Roe, Michael, *A Short History of Tasmania* (Oxford, Oxford University Press, 1997)

Roe, Michael, *A History of the Theatre Royal, Hobart, from 1834* (Hobart, Law Society, nd)

Rules and Regulations for the Management of the House of Correction for Females (Hobart-town, J Ross, 1829)

Russell, David, 'Hanwell Lunatic Asylum 1831–1844: The Golden Years', in *International History of Nursing Journal*, vol. 4, no.1, autumn 1998, 4–9

Sackville-O'Donnell, Judith, *The First Fagin: The Story of Ikey Solomon* (Melbourne, Acland, 2002)

Shakespeare, Nicholas, *In Tasmania* (London, The Harvill Press, 2004)

Shelton, D & C, eds, *The Parramore Letters: Letters from Thomas Parramore ... to Thirza Cropper* (Epping, NSW, D & C Shelton, 1993)

Skemp, John Rowland, *Letters to Anne* (Carlton, Victoria, Melbourne University Press, 1956)

Stancombe, G Hawley, *Highway in Van Diemen's Land* (National Trust of Australia (Tasmania) 1969)

Sutherland, John, *Mrs Humphrey Ward: Eminent Victorian Pre-eminent Edwardian* (Oxford, Clarendon Press, 1990)

Tardif, Phillip, *John Bowen's Hobart: The Beginning of European Settlement in Tasmania* (Hobart, Tasmanian Historical Research Association, 2003)

Taylor, Vera, *Winton Merino Stud, 1835–1985* (Geelong, Victoria, Neptune Press, 1985)

Thompson, John, 'Hobart History Written in the Blood of Risdon Cove' (Hobart, *Mercury*, 28 November, 1992)

Von Stieglitz, KR, *A Short History of Campbell Town and the Midland Pioneers* (Evandale, 1948; 2nd edition 1965)
— *A Short History of Ross: With Some Tales of Pioneers* (Evandale, 1949)
— *Entally, 1821: Pageant of a Pioneer Family 1792–1912* (Hobart, Scenery Preservation Board, 1950)
— *Richmond* (Evandale, 1953)
— *Pioneers of the East Coast from 1642, Swansea, Bicheno* (Evandale, 1955)
— *Six Pioneer Women of Tasmania* (1956)
— *The History of Bothwell and its Early Settlers at the Clyde in Van Diemen's Land* (Launceston, Telegraph Printery, 1958?)
— *Oatlands and Jericho* (Evandale, 1960)
— *A History of New Norfolk and the Derwent Valley* (1961)
— *A Short History of Circular Head and its Pioneers: Also of the V.D.L Company* (Launceston, Telegraph Printery, 1962)
— *A History of Hamilton, Ouse and Gretna* (Evandale, 1963)
— ed. *Early Van Diemen's Land 1835–1860 by Emma Von Stieglitz* (Hobart, Cox Kay, 1963)
— ed. *Sketches in Early Victoria and Tasmania by Emily Bowring* (1965)
— *A History of Evandale* (Evandale, Evandale History Society, 1967)
Walch's Tasmanian Guide Book (Hobart, 1871)
Walker, Peter Benson, *All that We Inherit ... [including] Reminiscences [of] Sarah Walker* (Hobart, J Walch & Sons, 1968)
Ward, Mrs Humphrey, *Robert Elsmere* (London, Macmillan, 1889)
Ward, Malcolm, *Sergeant Samuel Thorne: A Royal Marine in the Napoleonic Wars and a First settler of Port Phillip and Hobart Town* (South Hobart, 2007)
Watson, Reg, *John Bowen and the Founding of Tasmania* (Lindisfarne, Tasmania, The Anglo-Keltic Society, 2003)
— *The Life and Times of Thomas Francis Meagher, Irish Exile to Van Diemen's Land* (2001)
Weeding, John Seymour, *A History of Bothwell Tasmania* (Hobart, Drinkwater Publishing, nd)
West, John, *The History of Tasmania* (London, Angus & Robertson, 1981; 1st published 1852)
Wilding, Michael, and Myers, David, *Best Stories Under the Sun* (Rockhampton, Queensland University Press, 2004)
Williams, John, *Ordered to the Island: Irish Convicts and Van Diemen's Land* (Darlinghurst, NSW, Crossing Press, 1994)
Wilson, R, *Bishop Nixon – Drawings* (Runnymede, National Trust of Australia (Tasmania) 2002)
Young, John, 'Back to the Future: Choosing a Meaning from Regional History' in *Tasmanian Historical Studies*, vol. 15, no. 1, 1995–96, 114–31

Reference Books, Guides and Sketchbooks

Adam-Smith, Patsy, and Angus, Max, *Tasmania Sketchbook* (Adelaide, Rigby, 1971)
Adam-Smith, Patsy, and Phillips, Arthur, *Launceston Sketchbook* (Adelaide, Rigby, revised edition 1982)
— *Hobart Sketchbook* (Adelaide, Rigby, revised edition 1982)
Alexander, Alison, ed., *The Companion to Tasmania History* (Hobart, Centre for Tasmanian Historical Studies, University of Tasmania, 2005)
Woodberry, Joan, and Alty, John, *Historic Richmond (Tasmania) Sketchbook* (Adelaide, Rigby, 1977)
— *Battery Point (Tasmania) Sketchbook* (Adelaide, Rigby, 1978)
Brace, Matthew, *Tasmania: The Bradt Travel Guide* (Chalfont St Peter, Bradt, 2002)
Giordano, Margaret, and Norman, Don, *Tasmanian Literary Landmarks* (Hobart, Shearwater Press, 1984)
Horton, David, general ed., *Encyclopaedia of Aboriginal Australia* (Canberra, Aboriginal Studies Press, 1994)

Kerr, Joan, *Dictionary of Australian Artists* (Sydney, Power Institute of Fine Arts, University of Sydney, 1984)

Simons, P Frazer, *Historic Tasmanian Gardens* (Canberra, Mulini Press, 1987)

Tardif, Philip, *Notorious Strumpets and Dangerous Girls: Convict Women in Van Diemen's Land* (CD 2004; 1st published 1990)

Tasmania (Insight Guides, Singapore, APA Publication, 1st edition 2006)

Tasmania (Melbourne, Lonely Planet Publications, 2002)

Wooley, Charles, and Tatlow, Michael, *A Walk in Old Hobart* (Tasmania, Walk Guides Australia, 2007)

— *A Walk in Old Launceston* (Tasmania, Walk Guides Australia, 2007)

Unpublished Material

(Where a source is not given, the material was provided by the author, for which I am grateful.)

Alexander, Alison, 'The Public Role of Women in Tasmania 1803–1914', unpublished University of Tasmania PhD thesis (1989)

Calder, James, letter dated 27 March 1870, from Calder papers, Fbox 89/3 pp300, State Library of Victoria

Cockburn, RWP, 'The Family of Robert Pitcairn of Tasmania', provided by Runnymede, National Trust

Frost, Lucy, '"At Home" on a Mission Station and in a Female Factory: Imaging Mary Hutchinson' (awaiting publication)

Marsh, Eliza, Diary of, from 1 March 1851 to 15 April 1851 – a detailed account of their trip to Tasmania, 17pp typescript, MS000892, Box 191/3, Royal Historical Society of Victoria

Mills, Peter, 'By George' (nd)

Prosser, Paddy, Poulson, Bruce, and Hogg, Gregg 'The Strange Story of Louise Girardin' (a play in 14 scenes, 2001)

Prosser, Paddy, 'An Impulse of Curiosity' (radio play, 2005)

Schaffer, Irene, 'The Forgotten Women Convicts, Macquarie Harbour 1821–1826'

Scripps, Lindy, '"Islington" 321 Davey Street, Hobart: A Brief History of the House and its Occupants' (September 2003)

— 'Macquarie House, 151 Macquarie Street, and 3 Victoria Street Hobart: A Brief History' (September 2005)

Internet

I don't always give you websites here since so often I simply put a name into Google, and up pops a website, and that is much easier than following the intricacies of a web domain.

If you put 'Tasmania colonial archives' in, you can then go immediately to the 'portal' and fill in first names and surname and often be given dates and family; watch out for false marriage dates, sometimes given as the date of birth of the first child in Tasmania.

With just a name, assuming they have an entry; *The Australian Dictionary of Biography* comes straight up with the one you want. The same applies to the *Dictionary of New Zealand Biography*. As for the *New Oxford Dictionary of National Biography*, you have either to belong to an institution that has an entrée, or to pay.

Family members are often generous in putting material on the internet; unfortunately, such material does not always easily re-emerge.

Alexander, Alison, 'The Women's International League For Peace and Freedom' (2003) in 'Reflections on Social Justice: Reclaiming our Identity as a Nation with a Heart and Soul' (Anglicare, Tasmania, 2003), www.anglicare-tas.or.au

Balmer, Jayne, and Horton, John, 'The Kearley Family'

www.Bichenohideaway.com (Arabella Edge)

Bird, Carmel, 'Summer at Port Arthur'; 'Mathinna'; 'Fair Game: The Story of the Princess Royal', www.Carmelbird.com

Evans, Caroline, 'Landmarks in Mothering: Tasmanian Child Welfare Legislation 1895–1918' (2006) www.anzlhsejournal.Auckland.ac.nz

www.familysearch.org

www.Female.factory.com.au

Konishi, Shino, 'François Péron and the Tasmanians: An Unrequited Romance' (2007), www.epress.anu.edu.au/aborig_history

Macquarie, Lachlan, 'Journal to and from van Diemen's Land to Sydney in N.S.Wales 1811', www.lib.mq.ed.au/all/journeys

— 'Journal of a voyage and tour of inspection to Van Diemen's Land 1821'

Merry, Kay, 'The Cross-Cultural Relationships Between the Sealers and the Tasmanian Aboriginal Women at Bass Strait and Kangaroo island in the Early 19th Century' (2003), wwwehlt.flinders.edu.au/projects/counterpoints

Mickleborough, Leonie, 'Lieutenant-Governor Colonel William Sorell: Appearances of Respectability' (nd), www.femalefactory.com.au/FFRG

Morris, Gill, 'The "Quiet" Miss Mary Loder – Conchologist and Philanthropist' (2005), www-launcestonhistory.org.au/2008/lodder

Robert, Kim, 'The Bush Inn' (nd)

Ryan, Lindall, 'Abduction and Multiple Killings of Aborigines in Tasmania 1804–1835' (nd), www.yale.edu/gsp/colonial/downloads/aborigines

Seale, Shirley, 'The Life of Mary Putland', www.hawkesburyhistory.org.au/seale/putland

Stanton Bed and Breakfast (Shone/McDiarmid), www.Stantonbandb.com

www.Statelibrary.tas.gov.au/collections

Swynys, Matilda, 'A Lady's Trip to Tasmania'

www.womenaustralia.info

Index

I have had to be ruthless, and sometimes arbitrary, in what could have been a never-ending index. Even some women, if they only appear fleetingly, have unfortunately had to be omitted. Men are only included where they are significant, otherwise their first name is in brackets after the woman they relate to. Several women of the same family are often under 'surname, family'. Some omitted women can be found under headings such as 'theatrical performers'. Most of the modern women in the easily accessible chronology at the end of chapter 13 appear only there. But their campaigns come, where appropriate, under 'Environment', 'Peace' or the extensive Aboriginal sections. To help identify the myriad women who are included in the index, a clue (such as a property, ship or book) is, where practical, in brackets. The cross references in brackets in the text fill in some of the gaps.

Modern authors are included only if drawn on so extensively or significantly that they have become part of the story. Others are, of course, in the bibliography and their contribution may be revealed in the index's several themes.

Individual newspapers mentioned or quoted from are itemised under 'newspapers'. They are not in the bibliography because I drew on them from secondary sources.

Places that appear only once, and are in the table of contents (itineraries), are not included; but places not in an itinerary often are. 'Hobart' and 'Launceston' are, for obvious reasons, omitted. Places with primarily Aboriginal connections, eg Flinders Island (Wybalenna), are under 'Aborigines (general)'.

Hobart's streets are individually entered under 'Streets, Hobart' in case you find yourself in one and wonder what you should see there

Individual Aboriginal groups, rivers, ships and types of trees come under those headings. But *Anson* is under 'Female factories/depots'.

Page numbers in bold where there is more than one entry for a woman indicate main biographical details in the text.

Also from HOLO Books: The Women's History Press

Of Islands and Women 1
Susanna Hoe   MADEIRA: WOMEN, HISTORY, BOOKS AND PLACES
paperback 180pp published 2004 £7.99 1 map and 25 illustrations ISBN 0953773086
Madeira – Travel – History (update www.holobooks.co.uk 2005)

In the 19th century, many people visited Madeira in the hopes that the dry, warm winter might help them recover from illness – usually consumption (tuberculosis). Today, travellers still go for the winter sun and for the magnificent walking, tropical and temperate gardens 100 or more years old, glorious wild flowers and trees and unparalleled mountain views. The history of Madeira's women and the writing of women travellers about the island are less well known than they should be. This livret combines a flavour of all these elements for the visitor or the armchair traveller.

Of Islands and Women 2
Susanna Hoe   CRETE: WOMEN, HISTORY, BOOKS AND PLACES
paperback 408pp published 2005 £9.99 2 maps and 31 illustrations
Crete – Travel – Archaeology – Legend – History ISBN 0953773078
(updates www.holobooks.co.uk 2007)

Once upon a time, Europa emerged from the waves at Matala on the back of a bull – the god Zeus in disguise. There, too, the author broke her ankle as she followed Europa to nearby Gortyn – whose famous law code has much to say about women. Europa was the mother of Minos, of the Minoans, (and of the concept of 'Europe'). Millennia later, Harriet Boyd was the first woman archaeologist to discover and direct her own dig, at Gournia – a perfect Minoan town. This livret links legend and archaeology by writing and place, but does not neglect the island's other women. Over the centuries they were subject to numerous violent changes of overlord – Mycenean, Roman, Byzantine (twice), Saracen, Venetian, Ottoman – but somehow have emerged as Cretans.

Susanna Hoe   AT HOME IN PARADISE: A HOUSE AND GARDEN IN PAPUA NEW GUINEA
paperback 208pp published 2003 1 map 215 × 240mm £10 ISBN 0953773094 – Papua New Guinea – Travel – Autobiography/Biography

How would Margaret have written her story if she had been able to? I tried to help her to learn to read and write but I could never see into her mind – there was too much that divided us, in spite of all that drew us together. But sometimes, and once in particular, I felt that she knew I was recording everything she told me.

This is how the author introduces us to the family's cleaner in her diary of a stay in Papua New Guinea – home of the bird of paradise. Through the gradual accumulation of detail, the reader gets to know Margaret, her extended family, her unreliable husbands and her independent spirit. Then there is Kaman, the outrageous gardener, who has to be prised away from his creation so that his employers can enjoy planting and tending, as well as admiring and eating its produce. There is endless scope for misunderstanding and enlightenment as the tropical seasons come and go and relationships develop.

CHINA

Susanna Hoe   WATCHING THE FLAG COME DOWN: An Englishwoman in Hong Kong 1987–1997
Paperback 224pp published 2007 £12 1 map ISBN 9780954405670
Hong Kong – China – Autobiography – Biography – Travel – Politics – History – Women's Studies (updates www.holobooks.co.uk 2007)

At midnight on 30 June 1997 Hong Kong reverted to Chinese sovereignty after 150 years of British rule. The moment when the British flag came down was dramatic enough but the 10 years leading up to it were full of surprising incident and change. These 'Letters from Hong Kong', written by an Englishwoman who was involved in those events from 1987, are both an unusual historical record and a heartwarming account of women's domestic, intellectual and political activity. An epilogue brings Hong Kong up to date ten years after the Handover.

Susanna Hoe   WOMEN AT THE SIEGE, PEKING 1900
Paperback 430pp published 2000 £15 4 maps 44 illustrations ISBN 095377306X
China – History – Women's Studies

The Boxer uprising; the siege of the legations; 55 days in Peking; foreign troops looting China's capital; these are images from books and films over the past 100 years. Now the story is told from the women's point of view, using their previously neglected writings and giving a new dimension.

HOLO Books is agent in the United Kingdom for:

Susanna Hoe   CHINESE FOOTPRINTS: EXPLORING WOMEN'S HISTORY IN CHINA, HONG KONG AND MACAU
Roundhouse Publications (Asia) 1996 paperback 351pp 41 illustrations £10
ISBN 9627992038
China – Hong Kong – Macau – History – Historiography – Women's Studies – Travel

This book is as much about the author's task of historical re-creation as it is about the lives, loves and struggles of women such as the 1930s civil rights campaigners Shi Liang, Agnes Smedley and Stella Benson; autobiographical writer Xiao Hong; Olympic sportswoman, traveller and writer Ella Maillart; icon of revolutionary China Soong Ching Ling; philanthropist Clara Ho Tung; and Clara Elliot, who lived in Macau at the time of Hong Kong's cession to Britain.

Nan Hodges & Arthur W. Hummel (eds)   LIGHTS AND SHADOWS OF A MACAO LIFE: THE JOURNAL OF HARRIETT LOW, TRAVELLING SPINSTER
Bear Creek Books (USA) published 2002 2 vols paperback 833pp 10 illustrations
£27 (set) ISBN 0938106295
China – History – Historiography – Women's studies

Lights and Shadows of a Macao Life, the title chosen by Harriett Low for her journal, aptly describes the conflicting emotions of the first American woman to live in China. Making a rude transition from the tranquillity of Salem, Massachusetts into a world of sampans and sedan chairs, women with bound feet and men with queues, the lively young American records a detailed portrait of her life in Macao from 1829–1834. In these diaries, published for the first time as a complete edition, Harriett Low displays wit and courage as she metamorphoses from a socially naive girl into a mature, independent woman. This is an important addition to the historiography of the China Coast.